Who are they? A bigamist. A ruthless robber baron. A woman flaunting her lovers and her radical ideas. A philanthropist giving away billions, yet keeping the family wealth intact. An alcoholic. One of the most power-hungry men in modern America. A world-weary cynic. A drifting divorcee. A homeowner spending $600,000 in renovations, while a nearby cousin lives in an abandoned railroad caboose. Owners of huge feudal-like domains in South America. Polluters. Environmentalists. Lovers of art. Manipulators of money. Cold war warriors. Enemies of the existing social order.

Each of them so very different—yet all facing the awesome power and subtly corrupting peril of being part of—

THE ROCKEFELLERS
An American Dynasty

Please turn page for more critical acclaim

MENTOR and SIGNET Titles of Interest

THE
ROCKEFELLERS
An American Dynasty

by Peter Collier
and David Horowitz

Ⓢ
A SIGNET BOOK
NEW AMERICAN LIBRARY

Contents

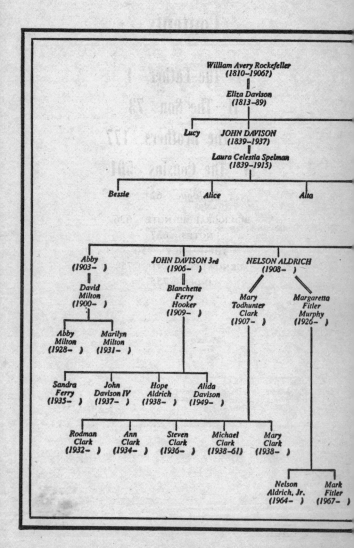

THE ROCKEFELLERS

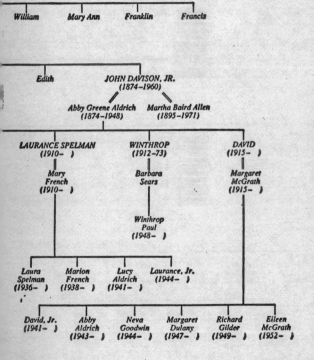

William	Mary Ann	Franklin	Francis

Edith

JOHN DAVISON, JR.
(1874–1960)

Abby Greene Aldrich   Martha Baird Allen
(1874–1948)   (1895–1971)

LAURANCE SPELMAN (1910–)	WINTHROP (1912–73)	DAVID (1915–)
Mary French (1910–)	Barbara Sears	Margaret McGrath (1915–)
	Winthrop Paul (1948–)	

Laura Spelman (1936–)	Marion French (1938–)	Lucy Aldrich (1941–)	Laurance, Jr. (1944–)

David, Jr. (1941–)	Abby Aldrich (1943–)	Neva Goodwin (1944–)	Margaret Dulany (1947–)	Richard Gilder (1949–)	Eileen McGrath (1952–)

PART I

The Father

"Two men have been supreme in creating the modern world: Rockefeller and Bismarck. One in economics, the other in politics, refuted the liberal dream of universal happiness through individual competition, substituting instead monopoly and the corporate state. . ."

—BERTRAND RUSSELL

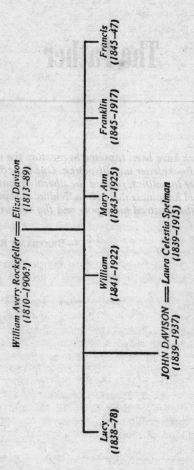

William Avery Rockefeller == Eliza Davison
(1810–1906?)   (1813–89)

Lucy — JOHN DAVISON == Laura Celestia Spelman — William — Mary Ann — Franklin — Francis
(1838–78)   (1839–1937)   (1839–1915)   (1841–1922) (1843–1925) (1845–1917) (1845–47)

1

IN THE EARLY YEARS of the twentieth century, when the Protestant church was united in its crusade to save the heathen world, the Congregationalists worked hard to conscript their share of Christian soldiers for assignment to the dark lands where the climactic battles between good and evil were to be fought. It was an expensive war, and under normal circumstances a group of the church's ministers meeting in Boston in early 1905 might have reacted to the announcement of a $100,000 donation to its Board of Foreign Missions with a prayer of rejoicing and perhaps a spontaneous chorus of the Doxology. But when they found that this great gift was from the purse of John D. Rockefeller, angry murmuring filled the room. One of the ministers rushed to the podium to demand that the Congregationalist elders return the gift of "tainted money" at once.

"Is this clean money? Can any man, can any institution, knowing its origins, touch it without being defiled?" the Reverend Washington Gladden—the most eminent Congregationalist in the land—had asked. On every side, wealth had been accumulated "by methods as heartless, as cynically iniquitous as any that were employed by the Roman plunderers or robber barons of the Dark Ages. In the cool brutality with which properties are wrecked, securities destroyed, and people by the hundreds robbed of their little, all to build up the fortunes of the multi-millionaires, we have an appalling revelation of the kind of monster that a human being may become."

The controversy eventually spread from the small rented hall in downtown Boston to the whole nation. Newspapers were flooded with opinions on the mixed blessings of accepting the offering. The term "tainted money" entered the vocabulary of the common man. ("Sure it's tainted," went a vaudeville routine of the day. " 'Taint yours, and 'taint mine.") Yet few of the many Americans who pleaded with the Congregationlists to reclaim the $100,000 in the service of the Lord went so far as to suggest that the soul of the donor might also be saved. For John D. Rockefeller was the most unrepentant sinner of the day. Senator Robert LaFollette called him "The greatest criminal of the age." He was pilloried in newspaper cartoons as a long-shanked hypocrite giving away coins with one hand while stealing bags of gold with the other, and the laconic Mr. Dooley had said that he was a "kind iv society for the prevention of croolty to money. If he finds a man misusing his money, he takes it away from him an' adopts it." If there had been any lingering doubts about this strange, secret man with impassive eyes and a cruel slash of a mouth, Ida Tarbell's recently published *History of the Standard Oil Company* was enough to convince anyone that the name Rockefeller was a synonym for unbridled ruthlessness and power.

Of all the men Theodore Roosevelt indicted as "malefactors of great wealth," John D. Rockefeller was indeed the wealthiest. At the time of the "tainted money" controversy, his fortune amounted to $200 million; it would coast effortlessly, of its own velocity, to the $1 billion mark within a few years. (The sum staggered the imagination; one astute Christian calculated that it was more than would have been in Adam's bank account if he had deposited $500 every day since his precipitous exit from the Garden.) Yet in other ways Rockefeller was far different from the other great robber barons who had terrorized the land for the previous twenty years. A pillar of the Baptist church since his youth, Rockefeller's tithes already approached $100 million in 1905, and he was even then devoting his attention to creating the widest-ranging system of philanthropy the world had yet known. A loyal husband and devoted father, his courtly manner had disarmed many a government lawyer and made him wonder if this man was indeed not more sinned against than sinning.

He was retired now, but even in his heyday at the helm of the great Standard trust he had lacked the vaulting ambition and sharkish appetites of the Fisks, Goulds, Vanderbilts, and others. They knew no bounds; he was a man of balance. He never engaged in their daring vandalism on the stock market, never bilked the public with their abandon, never took part in their audacious securities swindles. He knew what business was and what it was not; no one would ever say of Rockefeller—as crafty James Stillman of the First National Bank had said of the mighty J. P. Morgan—"He was a poet."

Withal it was Rockefeller—confessed plodder and conservative—whom the public identified as the symbol of a heartless economic system seated firmly in the saddle and riding mankind. Whatever his private personality, the John D. Rockefeller they knew had invented a new form of economic power—the corporate trust—for a nation whose very lifeblood was business. And the menace he had come to exemplify was not that of the pirate operating outside the social norm, but of the unjust and uncontrollable power inherent in the norm itself. He was, in some sense, the system carried to its logical and unchecked extreme—the competitor who utterly destroys the competition. It was no accident that the era Mark Twain had called the Gilded Age chose John D. Rockefeller to be its representative American.

As the trajectory of his business career climbed from triumph to triumph, people had scrutinized newspaper stories about his private life for some sign of unhappiness and failure, as though searching for a lost principle of equity in the world. When a New York journalist reported with satisfaction that Rockefeller's stomach was so disordered he was forced to subsist on milk and bread and would have gladly given part of his bulky fortune for the ability to digest a steak, there was exultation.

Yet there was an inner strength that defied them all—not arrogantly, but with the calm certainty that he was right. Unlike the other robber barons, who had come to accept and even revel in their outlaw status, making no bones about what they were up to and defying society to stop them, Rockefeller remained always convinced that he had been as much the Christian gentleman in business as in his private life. And the strong feeling that he had been unjustly maligned coupled with the equally strong desire for vindication would become important traits in the life of the family he sired.

The 66-year-old Rockefeller would live for another 32 years, becoming in a sense the only survivor of that heroic and lawless age. Long after the Congregationalist hierarchy had admitted with chagrin that they themselves had solicited the tainted contribution their ministers had assumed was the oil man's guilty effort to sneak through the eye of the needle, long after that and other controversies had been forgotten, Rockefeller would live on, surrounded by a newfound respect and power his philanthropy had won for him. Long after the others who had risen in the great industrial wars of the nineteenth century were gone, the Fifth Avenue mansions where they had lived like dissolute Renaissance princes having passed to other hands and their fortunes scattered, Rockefeller's name and power would be carried into the future by a dynasty without peer as an enduring institution of American life.

The making of the great Standard Oil fortune was an accident. It was as if a door had stood open for a brief historical moment and Rockefeller, who just happened to be passing by, managed to squeeze in before it closed. Never before had it been possible for an individual to build the organization he built; it would never be possible again. It was the random collision of a man with an opportunity. To a lesser degree, the same could be said of the other great concentrations of wealth that occurred at this time. Only later would justifying the accidental and investing it with the magnificence of predestination become important, the job of the publicists and "kept" biographers all the robber barons hired.

One man who made myth as well as money was Andrew Carnegie, the Scottish bobbin boy who had come to America and made himself King of Steel. The millionaires who controlled American industry, he wrote later in his career when he had turned to belles lettres, "started as poor boys, and were trained in the sternest but most efficient of schools—poverty." It was Carnegie's comforting version of the gospel of the self-made man, and it would soon become the cohesive myth of the American polity. Those who raised themselves by their bootstraps were not just beneficiaries of chance. They were an elect, and their wealth proved it: they had demonstrated their right to privilege by triumphs in the democratic marketplace.

It was an appealing view for the survivors of a generation of all-out economic war, and it is not surprising that John D. Rockefeller, whom Carnegie once referred to in pique as "Reckafellow" (and later, more affectionately, as "my fellow millionaire"), tended to put more emphasis on the poverty of his origins, the older and wealthier he grew.

"Did anyone have less to start with than I?" he often asked. And later in life, when indulging an old man's prerogative for remaking the past, he referred constantly to his humble beginnings, as if to emphasize the distance he had come in his miraculous journey. Yet as his sister Mary Ann later said with rough grammar: "The stories are ridiculous that we were poor. We were not rich, of course, but we had enough money to eat and wear and every reasonable comfort. We used to save money always."

Rockefeller was born on July 8, 1839, in a modest box-shaped house ringed by apple trees and flanked by two barns, a hard two hours' drive by buggy over the rutted roads leading from the small hamlet of Richford. His father had paid $631 cash for the 160-acre farm. William Avery Rockefeller stood out among the sinewy, taciturn farmers who had been left behind in this part of western New York after the flood of emigration led west along the Erie. Slightly over six feet tall, with broad shoulders and a barrel chest, the elder Rockefeller had a ready laugh and a quick wit. Calculating eyes were set deep in his broad, genial face, and an auburn beard fringed his chin and cheeks. Twenty-nine years old at the time of his first son's birth, he was already one of the most talked-about young men in Tioga County. As famous for pitching horseshoes as for pitching woo, he was said to ride like an Indian and shoot like Hawkeye, owning several rifles and claiming to be able to down a swallow in flight.

William Avery was the sort of man who could tell a tall tale and also take pleasure in the knowledge that others made up exaggerated stories based on his own plentiful exploits. It was this talent for self-dramatization, the ability to see himself as a character in the human comedy, that made him different from the other Rockefellers who had spread in family units across the dense woods of New York and Pennsylvania in the hundred years since 1723, when the first Rockefeller, Johann Peter, had arrived in the new land from Germany. Most of them were like William Rockefeller's own father, Godfrey, who had arrived in Tioga County from unknown parts, married a local girl named Lucy Avery, and now lived a mile and a half up the road from his son's Richford homestead: thrifty, hardworking, and anonymous, blending into the customs and morality of his time and place.

"Big Bill" Rockefeller decidedly did not. Wearing brocaded vests and a diamond stickpin, he drove the rough roads with a fine matched team, and although he did not partake of hard liquor himself, frequently stood a round of drinks for friends in taverns around the county. He distrusted banks, according to family legend, and could always put his hands on large sums of money. David Dennis, one of John D.'s boyhood friends, later confirmed the rumor of a cache of greenbacks at the Rockefeller house: "I've seen it—ones, twos, threes (we had three dollar bills then), fives, tens, twenties, fifties, all corded like wood and the bundles tied up with twine." William Avery was able to make a $1,000 cash down payment for the seven-room white clapboard farmhouse on ninety-two acres near Moravia in Cayuga County, where he moved his growing family in 1843, and was able to pay off the $2,100 mortgage in a few years.

How their father amassed these large sums of money, however, was a subject that was not discussed in front of John; his younger brothers, William and Frank; or his sisters, Lucy and Mary Ann. He was a jack-of-all-trades, they were told, who sold land, traded fur, sold salt, and even distributed herbal medicines. They knew from experience that his "work" took him away for long periods of time, often months, and that during his absence the family could expect to exist on a broad line of credit obtained from the local general store and the generosity of neighbors. But then he would return as suddenly and mysteriously as he had departed, climb down from the buggy and affectionately slap the lathered rumps of his horses, pick his children up one by one as they ran to meet him, and press gold coins into their palms after kissing their cheeks.

John D. Rockefeller would later discover that his father's primary occupation was that of pitchman and con artist. Cut from the same mold as the legendary P. T. Barnum, he was far from chagrined by his secret life. In fact, he seemed to revel in his petty larcenies. When he visited Indian reservations with his buggy full of goods for sale, William Rockefeller pretended to be deaf and dumb, he admitted to a friend, because he believed the Indians took this to be a sign of supernatural power. But there was not that much money to be made flimflamming the Iroquois in upstate New York, and so he found a more promising career in patent medicines. He journeyed for hundreds of miles to camp meetings, passing out handbills that read: "Dr. William A. Rockefeller, the Celebrated Cancer Specialist, Here for One Day Only. All Cases of Cancer Cured unless too far gone and then they can be greatly benefited." He sold bottles of his elixir and gave consultations for the princely sum of twenty-five dollars, a good two months' wages at the time.

"Doc" Rockefeller (as he was known) was also something of a fancy man. In 1849, he was indicted under cloudy circumstances for the rape of Anne Vanderbeak, a hired girl who had worked in the Rockefeller household. From then on, he steered clear of Cayuga County jurisdiction to escape the sheriff, who carried a warrant for his arrest. He appeared rarely and then only late at night, signaling his arrival by throwing pebbles at the windowpanes. Soon he sold the Moravia homestead, moving his family north to the village of Oswego, New York.

If young William came to resemble the father in his robust physique and expansive good nature, John did not. The photographs from his youth show a narrow, almost expressionless face, eyes that were hooded and impassive, and a mouth accustomed to silence. The hair was parted so far to the left that his head seemed almost lopsided. It was the face of his mother Eliza, who had named her firstborn son after her father, a prosperous New York farmer named John Davison. A thin, hatchet-faced woman with flaming red hair and equally stark blue eyes, Eliza Rockefeller was different from her genial, meandering husband in almost every way. (They were opposites with a strong attraction, however, and had married quickly in 1836 after a brief courtship.) As William Avery was roving the countryside, she was doing her best to normalize her children's youth, protecting them from the rumors that swirled constantly around the family, filling in for the peculiar man she had married in an uncharacteristic fit of passion.

The father taught lessons of a negative kind: that impulsiveness was dangerous, deceptive. Some of the pain of these lessons stayed with John D. all his life. In 1905, shortly after the "tainted money" controversy had been touched off, he wrote a letter to a Cleveland acquaintance asking him to straighten out a misunderstanding. Every year, the local Italian Boys' Band came to Rockefeller's suburban home to perform and enjoy a picnic. The previous year they had left with the impression that some young pigs Rockefeller kept on the grounds would be roasted for their lunch the next time they came. In the meantime, however, the pigs had been sold, the master of Standard Oil took pains to explain in a letter that concluded: "I simply want an explanation so that [the boys] will feel happy about it. If they do not, we must see what we can do. . . . I remember to this day that my father promised me a Shetland pony near sixty years ago, and I never got the pony."

His mother's influence was quite the opposite—moral,

strict, severe with harsh Scottish piety. Her Calvinist maxims filled her oldest son's mind, and he would recollect them all through his life. One would be particularly appropriate to his career: "Willful waste makes woeful want." Long after her death, he recalled an instance in which his mother switched him for an offense he had not committed. In the middle of the punishment, after he had finally convinced her of his innocence, she said, "Never mind, we have started in on this whipping, and it will do for next time." Yet she was predictable, rational even in anger. And however much he might have been secretly attracted to his bold and amoral father, his mother's way would be his way. He would always remember her plight: a humiliated, abandoned woman spoken of in backfence gossip, who spent long nights alone in a rocking chair staring into the fire, with a Bible on her lap and a corncob pipe in her mouth.

After piling his family and their possessions into a westbound train and settling them in Cleveland in 1853 so that he could be closer to the "marks" flooding into the West by covered wagon, William Rockefeller appeared less and less often. Eliza received an occasional letter between visits and knew of an address out west where he could be reached in an emergency. But she went to her death in 1889 a grass widow. For years after, though, the elder Rockefeller would drop in unannounced at the elegant Cleveland estate of his now famous son. He would alight from the streetcar as he had from his buggy in the old days, bringing a .22 rifle or some other present for John D. Rockefeller, Jr., and trinkets for his sisters. The grandson had warm memories of the old man. As he recalled years later: "He was a great storyteller. He played the violin too, holding it down on his waist instead of tucking it under his chin." But then, after playing with his grandchildren for a few days and occasionally borrowing money from his wealthy son, he would vanish as suddenly as he had come.

Knowledge of his whereabouts, guarded so jealously by the family, became something of a public mystery. In 1900 Joseph Pulitzer offered a reward of eight thousand dollars for information regarding William Avery's mysterious life. By 1908 one of his reporters had finally pieced together the astonishing story. "Doc" Rockefeller had died two years earlier at the age of ninety-six and was buried in an unmarked grave in Freeport, Illinois; for the previous forty years he had been living in South Dakota under the assumed name of Dr.

William Levingston in a bigamous marriage with a woman some twenty years his junior.

John D. never replied to the story. Indeed, very little of a personal nature ever did escape his thin lips. This was true even when the series of official biographers later hired to chisel the story of his life in massive Romanesque arches attempted to question him. When they asked him about his growing up, they got the bare bones of a life with the marrow sucked out. It was a text that might have been coauthored by George Babbitt and Horatio Alger, each anecdote little more than an epiphany of the businessman-to-come.

Under his mother's thrifty eye (Rockefeller told writers asking about the significant events of his childhood), he had accumulated a flock of turkeys by watching a wild hen nest and then taking her brood as it hatched; he raised them and sold them for a good profit. He was all of seven years old. By this time, he had also begun to save coins in a blue china bowl which his mother placed on a chest in the living room, and in the space of three years had enough money to lend a neighboring farmer $50 at 7 percent interest. When the principal was returned a year later with the $3.50 in interest, he claims to have been indelibly impressed. It was more than he had made in ten days' work at ten hours a day hoeing potatoes. "From that time on," Rockefeller noted in his semiautobiographical *Random Reminiscences* in 1908, "I determined to make money work for me." His older sister, Lucy, phrased the lesson he had learned in a more piquant, if less flattering way: "When it's raining porridge," she once said, "you'll always find John's bowl right side up."

The Cleveland he settled in at the age of fourteen was like a seafaring town. At the lakefront, white-sailed ships headed for harbor with passengers and cargo. There were side-wheelers and even some screw-propeller-driven ships built in local yards. The docks were crowded and dirty, worked by husky stevedores, and ruled from afar by local merchants. Rockefeller often strayed there after school to watch commerce taking place, usually standing alone and observing the bustle. One day he fell into step with a schoolmate who asked, "John, what do you want to be when you grow up?"

Without hesitation young Rockefeller spoke up, "I want to be worth a hundred thousand dollars, and I'm going to be, too."

He had a few friends in Cleveland's Central High School, where his mournful countenance won him the nickname "the

Deacon," although he did form a lasting bond with classmate Mark Hanna, later to be a U.S. senator, presidential king-maker, and political fixer for the Standard Oil Trust. Graduating in 1855, Rockefeller decided to go into business instead of to college. For several weeks he walked the streets of Cleveland looking for work, determined to take not just any job, but *the* job that would prepare him for his great expectations. He had set his sights high. "I went to the railroads, to the banks, to the wholesale merchants," he recalled later. "I did not go to any small establishments. . . . I was after something big."

On September 26 he was hired as a clerk accountant by Hewitt and Tuttle, commission merchants and produce shippers dealing in grain and other commodities. This date became a red-letter day on his personal calendar, and he always celebrated it thereafter as a sort of second birthday. On his Pocantico estate along the Hudson, September 26 was the day that a special flag was run up the pole. Once, well into his sixties, while driving through Cleveland on a *voyage sentimental* he passed the site where he had first reported for work. Suddenly he jumped up in the open carriage and shouted, "Look! Look at that rectangular building. I commenced my career there at four dollars a week." He got the driver to stop so he could take a misty-eyed silent walk around the much changed building.

He was at work by six-thirty every morning, his thin figure hunched into a clerk's stoop, squinting down at the ledgers by the light of the whale oil lamps he would soon help to make a relic of the past. But if business was an almost religious calling for Rockefeller, his religion was distinctly businesslike. In the Sunday school classes he had begun to teach at the Erie Street Baptist Church, a favorite text read: "Seest thou a man diligent in his business? He shall stand before kings." He approached his first job with a dedication that surprised and delighted his employers. They would have been even more impressed had they known that in the privacy of his room each night he rethought the day's activities and counseled himself: "It is an opportunity. But be careful. Pride goeth before a fall. Nothing in haste, nothing ill done. Your future hangs on every day that passes."

Discipline, order, and a close reckoning of debits and credits would be the code of his life. The only surviving relic from his youth is Ledger A, the commonplace book he kept during his first years on his own. In an exact and spidery hand, he wrote down, day by day and to the penny, the income and expenses, the saving and investment, the business and benefactions of his life. Besides the modest $1 for a week's room and board, there might be 75 cents for the Mite Society and 5 cents for Sunday school at the Erie Street Baptist Church, or 10 cents for the poor and 10 cents for foreign missions. The church was his only recreation, almost his only connection with the world outside the commission merchant trade. The total of the gifts he made was almost invariably 10 percent of his $3.50 weekly income. Other than grudging purchases of clothing, there was little else besides this disciplined giving. Ledger A was as close to keeping a diary as Rockefeller ever got; the figures recorded there were his autobiography.

By 1858 he was earning $600 a year. He knew his worth to the company to the exact penny and asked for a raise to $800. When Hewitt and Tuttle equivocated, Rockefeller began to look for a new job. He had previously made the acquaintance of Maurice Clark, an Englishman twelve years his senior, who was a clerk in another commission firm in Cleveland. Together they decided to start their own commission merchant business.

In three years with Hewitt and Tuttle, Rockefeller had managed to save about $800. But he needed another $1,000 for the initial investment in his new venture, and to get it went to his father, who had promised each of his children such a sum when they came of age. John got the money, but had to agree to pay 10 percent interest on it for the year and a half until he turned twenty-one. His father came away from the arrangement vastly amused. For him, the school of hard knocks gave the only education worth having. As he was fond of saying, "I cheat my boys every chance I get. I skin 'em every time I can. I want to make 'em sharp."

He had the opportunity often in those early years. The son returned to his father time and again for loans to pay for the expansion of his fledgling business. The money was always there at 10 percent interest, but William Rockefeller increased the burden on his son by his habit of capriciously calling the loans due at precisely those moments when John needed the money most. The loans were promptly repaid, often at a considerable cost. Yet Rockefeller never allowed himself to complain. Only late in life did he write: "I confess that this little discipline should have done me good, and perhaps did, but while I concealed it from him, the truth is I was not particularly pleased with his application of tests to discover if my financial ability was equal to such shocks."

In its first year, the firm of Clark & Rockefeller netted a tidy $4,000 profit on a gross business of $450,000, and a year later the profits had risen to $17,000. The partners had been fortunate in beginning their enterprise in the upswing of the business cycle. But even greater good fortune was in store for them.

The Civil War, which had begun in April 1861, caused unparalleled grief for millions of Americans, but a chosen few—the Morgans, Armours, and Vanderbilts—made overnight fortunes from it, and a whole new business class made an audacious entrance on the American scene. While Rockefeller's bonanza was not quite as dramatic as some, it was impressive nonetheless. As war orders came pouring in to Clark & Rockefeller, commodity prices rose sharply. The rising price levels made success a matter of methodical planning, attention to detail, and a relentless pressure for the hard bargain—tasks to which Rockefeller was singularly well suited.

With the opening of hostilities, his younger brother Frank, not yet sixteen, tried to enlist in the Union Army. Rejected once because of his age, he tried again. With that punctilious and literal regard for morality all the children had inherited from Eliza, he chalked the number 18 on the soles of both shoes and then went to another recruiting station. When the sergeant asked him how old he was, he stood and said, "I'm over eighteen, sir."

Frank managed to get to the front and suffer two wounds. Back in Cleveland, his prospering brother paid twenty-five dollars for two large maps on which he followed the progress of the war with interest. "I wanted to go in the army and do my part," Rockefeller explained long afterward. "But it was simply out of the question. There was no one to take my place. We were in a new business, and if I had not stayed it must have stopped—and with so many dependent on it." Instead, he contributed money to the Union cause and told associates his contributions had outfitted ten soldiers. "I sent more than twenty men, yes, nearly thirty," he remembered later in life, doubling and then tripling the number he had sent into battle against the rebels.

Outside of Clark & Rockefeller, his only activity was the Erie Street Baptist Church. When he was made a deacon at the age of nineteen, it was less for conspicuous religious passion than because he had become an important resource to the church. Once, when a $2,000 mortgage had been called due, he raised the money by buttonholing members of the congregation after the service and begging for their pennies. He used the Sunday school class he taught as much to preach his own gospel as to tell about the good news of the New Testament: "Be moderate," he lectured the children. "Be very moderate. Don't let good fellowship get the least hold on you."

An event that impressed Cleveland businessmen almost as much as the outbreak of war would, two years later, was the successful drilling of the first oil well by Edwin Drake. Titusville, Pennsylvania, lay beside a wide stream called Oil Creek because of the black film on its surface. For years people had known of the oil on local streams, and though early settlers had condemned it as a nuisance, the Indians had valued it as a medicine. By the time Rockefeller joined Hewitt and Tuttle, oil bottled in small vials was an important part of the pharmacopoeia of his father and other frontier doctors. It had also been established as the cheapest, most efficient, and longest lasting of illuminants, so that in 1859 Colonel Drake's Titusville well set off a stampede into the area, which soon became known as the Oil Regions.

Overnight, as wells were brought in, tiny settlements along the basin grew into thriving cities. It was an invasion like the one John Sutter's discovery had touched off in California a decade earlier: wildcatters, entrepreneurs, and the whole demimonde that their big spending supported. Values skyrocketed: in one celebrated case, a piece of land selling for $25,-000 was resold for $1.5 million three months later. Forests of rickety derricks soon dotted the skyline of this Oil Dorado where a metropolis could become a ghost town overnight as wells went dry. It was a landscape dominated by oil. Wildcat fires burned day and night; smoke billowed up from engines straining to pump out the precious fluid; oil mixed with mud to form a sticky ooze clinging to horses' legs and wagon wheels and making the roads nearly impassable.

With their heavy whips snaking out over their teams, the hard-bargaining teamsters were the masters of the region. They carted the oil out of the fields to be refined, first in Pittsburgh and New York, and then in refineries that sprang up in Cleveland, some of them just blocks away from the prospering firm of Clark & Rockefeller. The junior partner was impressed by the bonanza and, along with other Cleveland businessmen, considered making an investment in oil. But he knew that the *real* money would be made not at the pump but in the middleman stages of haulage and refining. He knew as well that transportation was still too quixotic and refining processes were not yet sufficiently developed. Rockefeller thus decided to stick with consignments of meat and grain for the time being.

Four years after the Titusville oil strike, a momentous event occurred at the Cleveland junction. The Atlantic and Great Western Railroad line ran its first trains into the city to connect with the Erie and give Cleveland a direct communication to New York, also providing a broad-gauge line into the heart of the Oil Regions. One refinery after another sprang up along its tracks in the city. In 1863 the Atlantic and Great Western carried more than 1.5 million barrels of petroleum and at once became the principal oil carrier in the nation. In turn, Cleveland became one of the emerging capitals of oil. A local historian described the city as being "flavored and saturated with oil. The river and lake were smeared with it. Oil wagons rumbled through the streets. Oil fires kept the city firemen eternally vigilant and filled the valley with painful apprehension."

It was also in 1863 that Samuel Andrews, an acquaintance of Maurice Clark, came to the partners with a proposition to go into the refining business. Rockefeller also knew Andrews, whom he had met at the Erie Street Baptist Church, but the 23-year-old John D. was still skeptical. He had enough money saved to hazard a $4,000 speculative investment as the silent partner in the new firm of Andrews, Clark and Company, but he made it clear that for him the oil venture was subsidiary to the grain business, which had proved itself time and again in recent years as a reliable, if not spectacular enterprise.

Sprouting thick reddish-brown mutton chops and dressing in black broadcloth suits that were often shiny with wear, Rockefeller had reached that time of life and level of prosperity where he could think about a family. And in March 1864 he became engaged to Laura Spelman, a pretty young Cleveland woman from a strong political and religious background whom he had known in high school. Her father, Harvey Buel Spelman, was a successful businessman who had served in the Ohio legislature, had been a conductor on the underground railroad, and was now passionately involved in the temperance movement. He and his wife were proud

enough of their two daughters, Laura and Lucy, to have them
frequently photographed in sepia tintypes that show Cettie
(as Laura was known) as a handsome young woman with
broad features and luxuriant dark hair parted in the middle
and worked into a knot behind. After graduating from high
school, the Spelman girls had both gone to Oread Collegiate
Institute in Worcester, Massachusetts, and returned to Cleveland to become teachers, both deeply committed to Christian
living and Negro welfare.

John's sister Lucy gave this somewhat ambivalent description of Cettie: "She was full of mirth and cheer, yet always
gentle and rather inclined to be grave and reserved." Yet
John had abundant respect for her abilities, commenting later
on: "Her judgment was always better than mine. Without her
keen advice I would be a poor man." In piety, she was the
perfect mate for John; in outlook she was able to broaden his
single-minded devotion to making money with a feeling for
art, culture, and society that would become an important element of the Rockefeller dynasty.

John appreciated the enlargement of his life that she
represented, but was hardly thunderstruck by love. He pursued his fiancée with the same dogged determination that had
already made him one of Cleveland's leading businessmen.
By this point in his life he had long since run through the
pages of Ledger A and begun Ledger B. No more were the
items concerned with a few cents here and there for the Mite
Society and other small charities. The figures were in dollars.
Under the heading of "Sundry Expenses" he told the story of
his courtship: 50 cents a week spent for several weeks on
courting bouquets; $1.75 rental one weekend for a hansom
cab to drive the couple and their chaperone down to the
Rocky River. The wedding ring cost $15.75. On September 8,
1864, he found time for the following entry: "Married at 2
o'clock P.M. to Miss L. C. Spelman by Reverend D. Wolcott
assisted by Rev. Paige at the residence of her parents."

Having accomplished marriage, he returned his full attention to business. By 1864, dozens of oil refineries had sprung
up in Cleveland, and more appeared with each passing
month. At first, Rockefeller worried that this was another fad
that would pass and spent his days shaking his head distaste-
fully at the clumsily made barrels leaking sticky crude on to
the floors of his warehouse. Yet he soon realized that the oil
was not going to dry up. He began to transfer his attention
from the commission business to refining, spending more and

more of his time at the Andrews, Clark and Company head-quarters on a three-acre site just outside the city limits.

There was a natural division of labor among the partners. Andrews had a fine competence in the early technology of oil and took care of the mechanics; the genial Clark made deals with the Oil Regions producers for the crude and with the teamsters for shipment; Rockefeller took care of finance and sales. Business procedures in the new industry were still primitive and there was much inefficiency. Always alert to any tendency to willful waste, Rockefeller was in his element and lost no time in asserting himself. Instead of continuing to be dependent on the obstreperous teamsters for deliveries of crude, Andrews, Clark and Company soon had its own force of wagons. Instead of buying barrels of indifferent quality from others, Rockefeller bought up stands of strong white oak and set up his own cooperage. The bright blue barrels it turned out would soon be the hated symbol of Standard Oil's omnipresence, but for now Rockefeller was satisfied with the fact that they cost 96 cents apiece instead of the $2.50 his firm had previously paid.

The training and discipline to which Rockefeller had subjected his life soon began paying business dividends. A reputation as one of the shrewdest dealers in a town filled with sharp operators took hold. His very narrowness was an invaluable asset in driving the hardest bargain possible: he had made himself into a perfect instrument for the conduct of business, and the only pleasure he allowed himself came from success in his transactions. When she was compiling her history of Standard Oil, Ida Tarbell was told by an acquaintance of Rockefeller: "The only time I saw John Rockefeller enthusiastic was when a report came in from the Creek that his buyer had secured a cargo of oil at a figure much below the market price. He bounded from his chair with a shout of joy, danced up and down, hugged me, threw up his hat, acted so like a madman that I have never forgotten it."

Early in 1865 the thriving firm of Andrews, Clark and Company was split by dissension. Rockefeller, the formerly silent but now most enthusiastic partner, had become increasingly annoyed with Clark's timid attitude toward expansion. The firm was $100,000 in debt, but Rockefeller wanted to extend the operation further and take advantage of the booming market. An impasse resulted, and it was mutually agreed to sell the business to the highest bidder.

The auction was held on February 2, 1865, with Rockefeller representing Andrews and himself against Clark. Clark began the bidding at $500, which Rockefeller raised to $1,000. The price went up and up, to $40,000, to $50,000, and then to $60,000. Gradually, with both sides unyielding, it crept up to $70,000. There was a long silence.

"Seventy-two thousand," said Maurice Clark in desperation.

"Seventy-two thousand five hundred," Rockefeller replied without hesitation.

Clark threw up his hands: "The business is yours."

Looking back in a later reminiscence with a friend, Rockefeller said that this day was "one of the most important in my life. It was the day that determined my career. I felt the bigness of it, but I was as calm as I am talking to you now." It was the calm of absolute confidence, of one who had methodically taken the measure of the field and the opponent, and knew what the outcome would be.

Although only twenty-six years old, he already had good enough standing in Cleveland's financial community to be able to borrow the purchase price. He took control of the business—rechristened Rockefeller and Andrews—on the crest of an oil boom that was making Cleveland rich, and at the apex of the great Civil War business bonanza that would introduce the word "millionaire" into the vocabulary of Americans. Rockefeller and Andrews was already the largest refinery in Cleveland, with a capacity of 500 barrels a day, or twice that of its nearest competitor, and annual revenues of $1 million, which grew to $2 million the following year. Rockefeller had been right. For the moment, expansion, not restraint, was the rule of success. A tremendous confidence in the future of the industry and in his own future possessed him. He convinced his brother William to come into the business and sent him to New York to handle the export trade, which accounted for two-thirds of the sales of Cleveland oil. It was about this time that a startled bystander watched one day as Rockefeller, thinking himself alone in his office, jumped up in the air, clicked his heels together, and repeated to himself, "I'm bound to be rich! Bound to be rich! *Bound to be rich!*"

If the other robber barons, with their mistresses, excesses of body and spirit, and artistic booty imported from the Old World, made Rockefeller seem a dull and predictable man, it was simply that he poured his passion and genius into his work, into the creation of Standard Oil, instead of his life. The development of the great trust would in retrospect seem the result of an almost unbelievably cunning plan; it would establish Rockefeller as an industrial Napoleon. Yet, while his amazing single-mindedness did help Rockefeller build the company, a good part of the Standard Oil epic involved his uncanny ability to be in the right place at the right time and always to have his "bowl right side up." He later admitted as much to a would-be biographer who was looking for a more stirring genesis. "None of us," he said, "ever dreamed of the magnitude of what became the later expansion."

Though he had no very clear conception of the industrial giant he would create, Rockefeller did know that the Standard must grow. It was almost a reflex with him, and he spent much of the next few years borrowing from Cleveland banks and individuals, offering for security only the impeccable balance sheet of the company he was building.

He was also looking for new men to become his lieutenants in the firm. In 1867 a new name was added to the enterprise, which then became Rockefeller, Andrews, and Flagler. A distinguished-looking man with dark wavy hair and a walrus moustache hiding his full mouth, Henry M. Flagler had appeared in Cleveland several years earlier, seeking to rent space from Rockefeller as he prepared to set up in business as a grain dealer. He had already made and lost a fortune, profiteering from contracts for food and commodities for the Union Army, and then becoming a bankrupt after a disastrous investment in the fledgling salt industry. Now he got a rare second chance. A good marriage to the daughter of whiskey tycoon Stephen V. Harkness allowed him to bring a $60,000 investment into the firm, and also to bring in another $90,000 of working capital from his new father-in-law.

Flagler, who would one day retire from Standard Oil a multimillionaire and devote his old age to developing Florida's virgin coastline into an American Riviera, became one of Rockefeller's few real friends, in or out of business. Their desks were in the same office. Before long, they would move into homes a few blocks from each other on Euclid Avenue, attend the Erie Street Baptist Church together, and walk into the office each morning in earnest conversation about the day's plans. "It was a friendship," as Rockefeller later wrote, "founded on business, which Mr. Flagler used to say was a good deal better than a business founded on friendship, and my experience leads me to agree with him."

Flagler was just the first of a group of bold and sometimes reckless executives Rockefeller brought into the firm, men who resembled his own father and did not stickle at taking care of those aspects of business from which Rockefeller himself preferred to establish a certain distance. "The ability to deal with people is as purchasable a commodity as sugar or coffee," Rockefeller once remarked, "and I pay more for that ability than for any other under the sun."

The people Flagler was best at dealing with were the railroad men. It was a talent Rockefeller prized because of the significance of the freight problem. In the first days of the oil boom, there had been a natural community of interest between the producers and the men who brought the oil to market. The teamsters may have driven a hard bargain with the well owners, but in the end each shared the other's interest in maximum production. No such common bond, however, linked the producers with the railroads. The railroads preferred a steady, high-level movement of oil; what they faced was a widely fluctuating supply, the result of disorganized production in the highly competitive fields, where rushes of overproduction would come one week and shortages the next. To the railroad interests, this meant costly irregularities in the demand for cars, locomotives, and yard space. In this situation, the key element was the middleman who could organize the flow of oil from the fields and establish a steady and high freight volume to conform to the railroads' needs. The natural candidate for the task was the large refiner. Accordingly, even as Rockefeller was using the large chunks of capital at his command to expand his refining capacity, he also set Flagler to the task of cornering the available tank cars and containers for the shipment of oil. Soon competitors seeking to transport their oil discovered that the railroads on which they had always depended had no tank cars for them because Rockefeller, Andrews, and Flagler had leased every available car.

Sometime late in 1867, Flagler visited General James Devereaux, the new vice-president of the Lake Shore Railroad, and told him that Rockefeller, Andrews, and Flagler would stop shipping by canal and guarantee sixty carloads of oil per day to his railroad in return for a large rebate on freight charges. The official freight rate was 42 cents a barrel on crude from the Oil Regions to Cleveland and $2 on the refined oil from Cleveland to the eastern seaboard. As Devereaux later testified before government investigators, the

Lake Shore gave Flagler secret new rates of 35 cents and $1.30. When other Cleveland refiners heard of the rebate, they protested. The Lake Shore agreed with them that it was indeed an advantage and said that they too could have a rebate if they would also make a comparable freight guarantee.

The word "rebate" quickly became one of the most hated in the oil man's lexicon. Rockefeller's competitors didn't have to recognize that the term came from the French *rabattre* to know its meaning was "to beat down." The rate advantages Rockefeller received were a powerful addition to his already formidable arsenal. It was as the humorist Artemus Ward had said: "Them as has, gits."

Parlaying his freight advantages with loans and new investors, Rockefeller formed a new company on January 10, 1870, with a capitalization of $1 million. Its name was Standard Oil.

Eighteen seventy was a depression year. Total freight-car loadings were falling, and the heads of the mighty but hard-pressed railroads began to seek better solutions to their problems than the free market afforded. Why suffer the ravages of a competitive situation that was costing them money, they asked, when they could pool their resources with the largest refiners and plot out their own prosperity? They conceived a plan. It bore the innocuous name of the South Improvement Company.

The chief architect was Tom Scott, former Assistant Secretary of War to Abraham Lincoln and now president of the Pennsylvania Railroad. One of the items of business that Tom Scott had for the 1870 Pennsylvania legislature (which he and others in Pennsylvania's emerging business elite brazenly manipulated) was the chartering of a new kind of corporation, a holding company, which would allow its owners to control stock in companies both in and outside the state. The charter was so broad and vaguely defined as to permit the company's owners to conduct any business they wanted, in whatever manner they chose.

What they did choose was simplicity itself. The railroads would combine with the largest refiners in each major refining center to plan the flow of oil for their mutual benefit. Freight rates would rise, but the rebate to members of the scheme would more than compensate them. Those who refused to join the cartel would be driven to the wall. Participating refiners would not only receive rebates on their own shipments, but "drawbacks" on the shipments of nonmembers as well.

Throughout the winter of 1871, the scheme went forward in absolute secrecy, with Rockefeller and other large refiners frequently journeying to New York to hold clandestine summit meetings with Scott, William H. Vanderbilt, Jay Gould, and the other railroad bosses. The promoters in each area decided which refineries they wanted in on the scheme and circulated an oath that prospective participants were forced to sign before learning the particulars of the plan. It read in part:

> I, ———, do solemnly promise upon my faith and honor as a gentleman that I will keep secret all transactions I may have with the corporation known as the South Improvement Company; that should I fail to keep any bargains with the said company, all the preliminary conversations shall be kept strictly private. . . .

Among those holding the original 2,000 shares of South Improvement Company stock, Rockefeller, his brother William, and Flagler each had 180 shares, which gave the Standard more than any other single interest.

Rockefeller saw the plan as a way of eliminating the Standard's annoying competitors in Cleveland. They had two alternatives—collapse their businesses into his in return for stock, or go it alone and be bankrupted by the rebate system. Starting with his largest competitors and working downward, he would make an appointment to see a rival and then with his usual civility explain how the plan would work to the benefit of all. The offer could be refused only by those who valued principles more than economic survival. To add leverage to the already crushing advantage of the secret rebates and "drawbacks," Rockefeller had offered the executives of Cleveland's leading banks stock in the Standard; thus independent refiners who held out would have a hard time financing their lonely uphill battles.

Isaac Hewitt, Rockefeller's former employer, who had since become a partner in the large refinery of Alexander, Scofield and Company, was urged to commit himself to the scheme and to take stock in the Standard. When he questioned the plan, Rockefeller shrugged him off cryptically: "I have ways of making money that you know nothing of." Others who were reluctant to join because they were already doing a good business were shown a hint of the iron fist underneath the velvet glove Rockefeller habitually wore. Frank Rockefeller, by then a partner in a firm competing against the Standard, was told by his older brother: "We have a combination with the railroads. We are going to buy out all the refiners in Cleveland. We will give everyone a chance to come in. . . . Those who refuse will be crushed. If you don't sell your property to us, it will be valueless." Frank did not sell and, when his brother's prophecy came true, remained bitter for the rest of his life, testifying publicly against him on several occasions and eventually moving his two children's bodies from the family burial plot in Cleveland lest they be forced to spend their eternity with John D.

The cabal went along smoothly for almost two months. When word accidentally leaked out revealing the nature of the South Improvement Company, there was immediate panic in the Oil Regions: all-night meetings, torchlight parades, angry petitions (one of them ninety-three feet long) carried to legislators, and threatening telegrams to railroad presidents. It was not only the creation of a combination that outraged the producers; they too had tried to form associations in order to keep prices of crude high. It was rather the cold and calculating nature of the plot, the combination of the strong against the weak, and most of all the use of the loathsome "drawback" that aroused them. As Ida Tarbell later wrote: "The rebate system was considered illegal and unjust, but men were more or less accustomed to it. The drawback on other people's shipments was a new device, and it threw the Oil Regions into a frenzy of rage."

Until this time, the name of Rockefeller had been unknown outside a small circle in Cleveland. Almost overnight, it became identified with infamy. For the duration of the conflict, the *Oil City Derrick* printed the names of the conspirators in a black-bordered box on the front page of each edition; notable among them was John D. Rockefeller. It was the first of many public battles Rockefeller would fight, the first time that words like "octopus" and "anaconda" would be used to describe the organization built by his methodical talent.

Yet, at the height of the South Improvement furor, Rockefeller displayed that characteristic inner discipline and iron self-confidence, the unflagging belief in his own rectitude, which he would always possess under fire. As he said later: "It was right. I knew it as a matter of conscience. It was right between me and my God." When Cettie worried that public outcry might endanger his life, he wrote her reassuringly, "We will do right and not be nervous or troubled by what the papers say."

This event was a Rubicon for Rockefeller, and forever afterward when he relived its crossing he would remain utterly convinced that he had not erred. Late in life, he told W. O. Inglis, who had been commissioned to write his life story: "The procedure was without precedent. We find here the strongest and most prosperous concern in the business ... turning to its less fortunate competitors . . . and saying to them, 'We will stand in for the risks and hazards of the refining business. . . . Come with us, and we will do you good. We will undertake to save you from the wrecks of the refining business.' " What other men saw as villainous self-interest, he regarded as Christian charity. The harsh program of the South Improvement Company became for this narrow but effective man an act of religious piety: "The Standard was an angel of mercy," he told Inglis, "reaching down from the sky and saying, 'Get into the ark. Put in your old junk. We will take the risks.' "

Unhappily for Rockefeller, the stiff-necked people in the Oil Regions persisted in their inability to understand his benevolence. Producers and refiners united; they clamored and threatened and agitated until the railroads finally backed down. Even imperious Jay Gould of the Erie was forced to cable his surrender, claiming that he had gone along with the South Improvement Company only because he was forced to by the other promoters. As a gesture of peace, the railroads signed new contracts with the producers to end the South Improvement Company and equalize the shipping rates for all parties. The Pennsylvania legislature rushed through a bill repealing the South Improvement Company's charter, which the governor signed with a great public flourish. The oil men formed a Producers' Protection Association, raised a million dollars to support the refiners in the Regions, and pledged to send no crude to the Standard Oil Company.

It looked as though Rockefeller and his angel of mercy had suffered a major defeat. But as the euphoria dissipated and people in the Regions looked around, they were stunned to realize that the Standard now had Cleveland's refining capacity in its hip pocket. In the three-month blitzkrieg, Rockefeller had managed to buy up all but three of his twenty-five competitors in the city. It was as Mark Twain said of the

Sandwich Islanders: the missionaries had been so successful in their efforts that the natives' vices no longer existed in name—only in fact. So it was with the hateful provisions of the South Improvement Company. Surveying his *fait accompli*, Rockefeller (called "the Mephistopheles of the Cleveland Company" by one rival) passed a chilling judgment on his victims: "They would not hope to compete with us. We left them to the mercy of time."

In the years following this coup, he could easily have relaxed. The Standard was thriving, with one-quarter of the refining capacity of the entire country. He himself was a prosperous citizen of Cleveland, rich even beyond his dreams, and raising a growing family in a rambling 700-acre country estate he had bought in Forest Hill on the outskirts of Cleveland. Yet he pushed ahead, driven by a passion for completeness.

In May 1872, with the smoke from the South Improvement battle hardly cleared, Rockefeller—together with W. G. Warden, head of the Atlantic Refinery, Philadelphia's largest; Charles Lockhart of Lockhart, Frew and Company, the biggest refinery in Pittsburgh; and several other of the large refiners who had been in on the scheme—went on a pilgrimage to the Regions. They came to shake hands with those who, like themselves, had become "prisoners of a misunderstanding" and to get their cooperation in a new association of refiners, called the Pittsburgh Plan, which would be open to anyone who wanted in.

It was hoped that the refiners of the Oil Regions would bury unpleasant memories and agree that the problems of overproduction and cutthroat competition could be solved only through such a central association. Rockefeller did manage to make one important convert in the person of John Archbold, the cunning independent who had led the refiners' opposition to the South Improvement Company and who one day would head the Standard itself. Otherwise there was only antagonism. Although themselves separated by economic interest, the Regions' refiners and producers were united by a common xenophobia concerning Rockefeller and Cleveland that was stronger than economic laws.

During a meeting held to discuss the plan, an independent refiner, finishing a fiery speech against the Standard, glanced over at Rockefeller, who had been sitting impassively in a rocking chair, just as John D.'s hands fell away from shading his eyes. "You never saw such eyes," the man remembered later. "He took me all in, saw just how much fight he could expect from me, and then up went his hands and back and forth went his chair."

Having seen the voluntary association spurned, Rockefeller returned to Cleveland with the calm knowledge that there must be war to bring the Oil Regions to their knees. The producers had never worried him. He had taken their measure and found them self-indulgent and weak. They wanted premium prices for their crude, but could not discipline themselves enough to combine to restrain production. Their repeated attempts to form protective associations invariably fell apart when anyone approached a few of their number with a large enough order. In this way Rockefeller himself had easily beaten the producers' boycott against the Standard in the aftermath of the South Improvement scheme.

Unlike the producers, however, the Oil Creek refiners were a force to be reckoned with. (It was about this time that observers noted the appearance of a map indicating all the Regions' refineries on the wall of Rockefeller's office.) Their output of 10,000 barrels a day was close to his own in Cleveland, equal to the combined capacity of the seaboard refineries, and some 4,000 barrels a day greater than that of Pittsburgh. Furthermore, the refineries in the Regions had pipelines running the crude from the well to their doorstep, while he had to have his shipped by rail to Cleveland, and then, after refinement, on to the seaboard. Rockefeller knew he must begin his campaign by squeezing the railroads to eliminate the advantages of geography that his opponents enjoyed.

The monopoly he had won in Cleveland had given him an even greater hold over the railroads who depended on his freight. By playing them off against each other, he was able to secure freight agreements that would eliminate the Regions' advantage while increasing his own control over the freight market and the shippers. Formerly, the Regions had paid $1.50 a barrel to ship direct to the coast while he paid $2, in addition to a 40-cent-a-barrel charge on crude from the Regions to Cleveland; henceforth all refiners would pay the same amount to the coast, $2 a barrel, and Rockefeller would get a rebate on the charges he paid to bring crude into Cleveland.

But this was only part of his offensive. In something anticipating the Appalachian gatherings of latter-day syndicate chieftains, Rockefeller and Flagler arranged a meeting with their counterparts, W. G. Warden and Charles Lockhart. Sitting in the sun of Saratoga (later called "that Mecca of schemers" by Ida Tarbell), Rockefeller spoke in his thin, reedy voice, assuring the others that the only way to head off constant fighting and uncertainty in the refining business was to come together in one organization. The Standard, because of its size and the advantages it commanded with the railroads, was of course the ideal candidate. The other men were, naturally, skeptical. Rockefeller invited them to come to Cleveland and inspect the books of Standard Oil. They did and came away believers. Both men traded their refineries and equipment for stock in the Standard.

Almost simultaneously, the Charles Pratt Company of New York came into the Standard fold, bringing the considerable daring of Henry H. Rogers, who was later also the friend and patron of Mark Twain. These firms at first did not make public their new status as part of the Standard combine, for Rockefeller wanted them to buy up as much of their own local competition as they could before the outlines of his plan became known. Along with John Archbold's newly formed Acme Refining Company in the Regions, the firms proceeded to act as stalking horses for the Standard, purchasing competitors in their own name. Everything was clandestine; there was a cryptography for telegrams and letters (*Doxy* was the Standard; *doubters* were refiners; *mixer* meant freight drawback; *Druggist* stood for Philadelphia; and so on). Rockefeller himself dealt with his colleagues as if handling state secrets. "You'd better not know," he would often tell someone who had asked about a sensitive matter. "If you don't know anything, you can't tell anything."

When he began his campaign, the Standard was flanked by 15 refineries in New York, 12 in Philadelphia, 22 in Pittsburgh, and 27 in the Oil Regions. When he finished, there was only the Standard. The shape of the emerging monopoly in oil became apparent only after it was almost a *fait accompli*, and Rockefeller had already reached a stage in his plot where neither the public outcry of refiners or producers, nor even the actions of legislatures, could stop him. In the Regions the refiners tried to wrest from the railroads some acknowledgment that as common carriers they had certain public responsibilities, but it was not forthcoming; nor could they secure redress in the form of regulatory laws that would check the Standard's momentum and preserve what was left of the competitive market. For the legislatures also had been

bought by the Standard's largesse. As the socialist scholar
Henry Demarest Lloyd later said in *Wealth Against Commonwealth*, the first great broadside against Rockefeller:
"The Standard had done everything to the Pennsylvania legislature except refine it."

By 1877 the Standard had no competition in the Regions,
Philadelphia, or Pittsburgh. Only in New York was there a
small pocket of resistance left among scattered independent
refiners. In April 1878, Flagler wrote an acquaintance noting
that the total refining capacity in the United States was 36
million barrels a year, and that of this the Standard produced
33 million. By 1880 Rockefeller refined 95 percent of the oil
produced in the nation. Not since the early days of the New
World when the Crown gave out monopolies had an enterprise cornered a market so completely.

2

ON A CHILLY DAY in the winter of 1874, John D. Rockefeller
burst into his office and grabbed Flagler by the sleeve. With
tears rimming his eyes, he told his only close friend the good
news: Cettie had finally given birth to a son. There had been
four girls; now there was a male heir, John D. Rockefeller, Jr.
Mr. Junior (as the boy would be known from the time he was
a teenager) and sisters Bessie, Alta, and Edith (another, Alice,
died in infancy) would have few childhood memories of Standard Oil. Once in a while they visited their father at the huge
plant on the edge of town, but most of their memories of their
increasingly famous father were of more relaxed moments.
They saw him in a way no one else did and would always
remember the simple joy he took in doing things like driving
the fine team of matched horses at breakneck speed over
Cleveland's bridle paths; dog-paddling around a lake in the
summer months, his face held high out of the water and a
straw hat on his head; ice-skating with geometric precision for
a few minutes in high hat and frock coat before leaving for
work in the winter.

Not long before the birth of his son, Rockefeller had celebrated his prosperity by purchasing a large brick townhouse on Cleveland's increasingly fashionable Euclid Avenue. Some people were calling this elm-lined street "Millionaires' Row" because of the stately Victorian mansions being raised by the men who had struck it rich in the city's booming commerce. But while others of the new rich spent their leisure trying to bring culture and status to Cleveland, parading Bret Harte, Mark Twain, Oscar Wilde, and a host of other celebrities through town on weekend lecture tours, the Rockefellers weren't interested. Their time was devoted to weightier things. And on Sundays, when the sleek carriages streamed up Euclid Avenue carrying many of his neighbors to worship at St. Paul's Episcopal Church, John Rockefeller would be getting his three young daughters settled into their own buggy; then, after gently handing Cettie, now expecting their fifth child, into her seat, he would lead his team the opposite way, downtown, to the Erie Street Baptist Church.

It was also shortly before young John's birth that Rockefeller had acquired Forest Hill, 79 heavily wooded acres on the outskirts of town which he added to until it was a 700-acre estate. Originally it was an investment. Thinking to make it into a "water cure and place of public resort," Rockefeller sent contractors in to start remodeling the huge rambling house that came with the property and was to be the sanitorium in his scheme. But soon the problems his Standard Oil company faced were so pressing that he decided to forget the venture and make the Forest Hill mansion his summer house.

He loved it there. But with its dozens of rooms, chaos of turrets, towers, and verandas—all of it adorned with scrollwork and gingerbread—the house seemed wasted on his family. Rockefeller had a hard time abandoning the idea that Forest Hill might somehow turn a profit. Four years after buying it, he installed some Negro waiters and briefly tried to run it both as a hotel for paying guests and as a vacation retreat for his family. (One Cleveland woman remembered years later how her grandfather, a business acquaintance of Rockefeller, had been invited to Forest Hill for what he assumed was a weekend holiday, only to receive a bill for ten dollars a few days after returning home.) But gradually he accepted the estate as a non-profit enterprise, and it soon became the favorite residence for him and his family.

The Rockefeller children grew up unaware they belonged to the richest family in Cleveland. They kept to themselves.

All four did chores to earn spending money; all kept their small replicas of Ledger A; all burned with indignation when they began to understand that the world condemned as a heartless monster the father they worshiped.

The John D. Rockefeller they knew was incapable of the crimes attributed to him. He had developed a sense of whimsy over the years or, at least, had relaxed enough to release some part of the youthful humor it had been necessary to suppress as a child. His children were delighted by what had emerged as a real talent for mimicry, which usually manifested itself at the dinner table. Other people close to Rockefeller also saw it occasionally. George Rogers, his private secretary, later recalled an occasion when they had been strolling down the street in Charlotte, North Carolina, during a business trip. Rockefeller struck up a conversation with a black man sitting on a porch, egging him into a tirade against wealth and privilege, which he later imitated in the richly exaggerated tones of a "darky" at dinner.

Rockefeller shunned the other great industrialists who were beginning to make their appearance. One prominent banker complained to George Rogers: "We never see Mr. Rockefeller. He does not mingle with us in clubs and social gatherings, and so we have come to look upon him as a great spider sitting back in his web seeking whom he may destroy." It was more likely that those moments away from the Standard Oil command post were spent with his family; Rockefeller would be at home, bearing up genially under his father's eccentricities, holding hands fondly with his mother at the dinner table, pecking his wife on the forehead, and playing blindman's bluff and other games with his children. The family was not an encumbrance to be made bearable by a harem of mistresses and other amusements. It was the first and final line of defense. Building the family was as important as building the great corporation. In fact, the corporation was being built *for* the family.

Yet this private Rockefeller was not the same man who commanded the great Standard leviathan that now surfaced after swallowing up or terrorizing the smaller fish. Within the company, he was a benign tyrant, and the corporation bore the imprint of his personality. He was constantly on the prowl around the several Standard units, looking things over, dropping in unannounced on young bookkeepers, running a practiced eye over their ledgers, and perhaps whipping out the notebook he carried in his breast pocket to jot down small economies to be passed on to the workmen. In the midst of some of the most momentous struggles in American industrial history, Rockefeller would find time to dash off memoranda to plant foremen with money-saving ideas and criticisms. "Your March inventory showed 10,750 bungs on hand," he said in one of these notes. "The report for April shows 20,-000 bungs bought, 24,000 used, and 6,000 bungs on hand. What became of the other 750 bungs?"

On one occasion he was inspecting one of the plants where kerosene was placed in cans for shipment abroad. For a moment he watched the five-gallon tins being constructed, and then he found out from one of the workers that forty drops of solder were used on each. After observing a moment longer, Rockefeller said, "Have you ever tried thirty-eight? No? Would you mind having some sealed with thirty-eight and letting me know?" Although some of the cans sealed with thirty-eight drops leaked, none did when thirty-nine drops were used, and in the future this became the specification in the Standard factory. Late in life, when asked about these economies, Rockefeller would smile broadly and say, "A fortune. That's what we saved. A fortune."

He was obsessed with minutiae, it seemed to some who knew him, even more than by the great matters of the Standard. But if they had looked deeper into his character, they would have realized that everything was part of a continuum connecting great things to small. Late in his own life, Rockefeller's son would recall that during a family vacation in France in 1888, his father became convinced their guide was cheating them, fired him, and took over his functions himself. "I can see him now," the son remembered, "going over the long French bills, studying each item, many of them being unintelligible to him. . . . Father was never willing to pay a bill which he did not know to be correct in all its items. Such care in small things might seem penurious . . . yet to him it was the working out of a *life principle*." The tension between thrift in small things and audacity in the larger ones was superficial; Rockefeller's efforts were, in reality, unified toward a single end—pushing his operation ahead to a position of ubiquitous and unchallengeable control.

The Standard's eye was all-seeing. To it the sale of a rival barrel of oil was as the fall of a sparrow. An independent named John Teagle later told a congressional committee of his discovery during these years of expansion that his bookkeeper had been bribed by an agent of Standard Oil: for a down payment and annual salary, the bookkeeper was to make a transcript of the daily activity of Teagle's plant, including where his shipments went and what they cost to produce, and forward the information to Cleveland.

Another independent oil man later told a team of Ohio state investigators: "If I put a man on the road to sell goods for me and he takes orders in the amount of two or three hundred barrels a week, before I am able to ship these goods the Standard Oil Company has gone there and compelled those people to countermand those orders. . . . If they don't countermand them, [Standard] will put the price of oil down to such a price that they won't be able to afford to handle [my] goods."

It was now that the reputation for ruthlessness began to spread like a blight from the Oil Regions and the few major cities where Rockefeller had done business to the nation as a whole. It had been one thing to war against large competitors or unscrupulous railroads; it was quite another matter to go about blithely exterminating small independents and modest wholesaling operations. Yet even after it had secured its monopoly in refining and control over the transportation of oil, the leviathan plunged immediately into the tumultuous seas of marketing. Parceling the country into regions, Standard affiliates began sending their own horse-drawn tank wagons into the small towns of their allotted territories, where they used price cutting to eliminate those who had been selling kerosene before them. Rockefeller became a household word.

Things were done at this time that even Rockefeller would later regret; enemies were made that would haunt him for decades. One was George Rice, a small Ohio refiner who had been selling a modest amount of oil in the South for many years when the Standard's marketing affiliate there, Chess, Carley and Company, was given the word to rub him out. Knowing that he was involved in a dubious battle, Rice decided nonetheless to fight back. He lowered his prices, assuming that the usual rules of a price war obtained. But dealers who had bought his oil for years stopped their orders even though his prices were lower than those of Standard products. One dealer told Rice that he couldn't afford to defy Chess, Carley and Company because he knew the firm had been authorized by the Standard to spend up to $10,000 to break anyone selling Rice's oil. And later, when Chess, Carley and Company found out that a Louisiana retailer named Wilkerson and Company had received Rice's oil by rail, they wrote the friendly freight agent of the Louisville and Nashville Railroad: "Wilkerson and Company received car of oil Monday 13th—70 barrels which we suspect slipped through at the usual fifth class rate—in fact we know it did—paying only $41.50 freight. Charge $57.40. Please turn another screw."

For years afterward, Rice dogged Rockefeller like one of Dickens's pathetic bankrupts. At the turn of the century, Rockefeller was testifying in an Ohio courtroom when he saw George Rice sitting in the back of the audience. He went over after getting off the stand and said, "How are you, Mr. Rice? You and I are getting to be old men, are we not?"

Refusing to shake the millionaire's extended hand, the distracted Rice said loudly enough for the curious crowd to hear: "You said you would ruin my business and you have done so. By the power of your great wealth you have ruined me."

As he elbowed his way toward the door, Rockefeller shook his head and murmured through pursed lips, "Not a word of truth in it, not a word of truth."

Rockefeller was no innovator in petroleum. He subscribed to Carnegie's homey theory, "Pioneering don't pay." This had never been clearer than when, in 1879, the Tidewater Company attempted to break his stranglehold on the railroads and oil distribution by building a 110-mile pipeline from the Oil Regions to the sea. Regarded as a miraculous gamble and compared as an engineering feat to the Brooklyn Bridge, the Tidewater succeeded in building the line despite the fact Rockefeller had his agents buy up rights-of-way to block its path, intimidate workmen, and even sabotage the pipe itself. When this did not work, John Archbold bribed his way into the company and besieged it with stockholder fights and other problems until it finally sold out to the Standard, which was soon copying the Tidewater's engineering knowledge to build giant pipeline systems of its own.

Rockefeller's strength was not in pioneering, but in the organization and deployment of power, which he liked to refer to as "combination and concentration." Marshaling the right clout at the right point in the system, making the appropriate alliance, engaging the vulnerable opponent, and buying up the startling new innovation at the most advantageous moment was his forte. His contributions had far less to do with the technology of oil than with the technology of power. Others discovered ways of getting and moving petroleum; he was at work on different kinds of structures, like the creation of the corporate trust.

Under the existing laws, Standard Oil of Ohio's expansion was menaced because it could not take possession of manufacturing facilities outside the state and operate them. To find a way out of this dilemma and to continue his untiring effort to integrate the national market, Rockefeller turned to Samuel C. T. Dodd, who was not only one of the most gifted attorneys of the time (even though a voice weakened by disease had rendered him ineffective in the courtroom), but also one of the first to devote himself solely to the service of a single corporate client. Like so many others who enlisted in the Standard over the years, Dodd had once been an energetic foe of Rockefeller. In 1872, during the South Improvement scheme, he had denounced the "anaconda" of Standard Oil in a Pennsylvania state constitutional convention, and afterward he had represented the Regions in their legal battles with the company. But Rockefeller did not let this history stand in the way of a valuable acquisition any more than he had with John Archbold or would later in the case of Barton Hepburn, the New York state legislator who launched the first great investigation of the Standard but was later made a trustee of the Rockefeller Foundation. As for Dodd himself, he replied to those who accused him of turning coat in this way: "Well, as the ministers say when they get a call to a higher salary, it seems to be the Lord's will."

The trust agreement Dodd authored was signed early in 1882. It provided for the transfer of all outstanding Standard stock to nine trustees, including John D. and William Rockefeller, Flagler, and Archbold. In return the stockholders received trust certificates in hundred-dollar blocks. The trustees were empowered to dissolve participating corporations and begin setting up others—Standard of New York, Standard of New Jersey, and so on—in each state. The new organization had no name or charter. It was just a trust—the common-law concept describing the relationship between parties when one held property for the benefit of another. But in the emerging world of modern finance the major benefits it provided were to those seeking to build monopolies. One of the first governmental agencies to investigate Dodd's brainchild, a New York senate committee of 1888, would call the Standard trust "the type of a system which has spread like a disease through the commercial system of this country."

As the great storms of public hostility swirled around the "octopus" of Standard Oil, with its tentacles extending across whole continents, it was ironic that its organizational basis should be a "trust," much as "family" later seemed an incongruous term for Mafia syndicates. This semantic problem never troubled Rockefeller, however, who always insisted that the Standard was indeed a benevolent institution in its relationships with competitors, employees, and owners alike. The exchange he had with an interrogator during an investigation by the New York legislature was typical:

> Q: Really your notion is that the Standard Oil trust is a beneficial organization to the public?
> A: I beg with all respect to present the record that shows it is.

In a contemporary account of these hearings, the New York *World* parodied Rockefeller's public testimony with this tongue-in-cheek definition of a trust: "A philanthropic institution created by the benevolent absorption of competitors to save them from ruin, combined with the humane conservation and ingenious utilization of natural resources for the benefit of the people."

The Standard trust encompassed forty corporations, of which fourteen were wholly owned. Its very complexity set up a maze of legal structures that successfully rendered its workings impervious to public investigation and exposure. Under the trust arrangement, it was never clear who owned what or who was responsible for which actions. The problem it presented to the analyst was ontological. As Ida Tarbell later wrote: "You could argue its existence from its effects, but you could never prove it."

The trust took up headquarters in New York, where Rockefeller regretfully moved his family, leaving deep roots in the soil of Forest Hill and in the foundations of the Erie Street Baptist Church. He learned to become a New Yorker, buying a fashionable Fifth Avenue town house and going daily to work at the new corporate offices at 26 Broadway, soon to become the most infamous business address in the world. Yet in some sense Rockefeller never changed from the provincial businessman. He joined another Baptist church, refusing to move up in class to a more respectable denomination. "Most Americans when they accumulate money climb the golden ramparts of the nearest Episcopal Church," H. L.

Mencken was to write. "But the Rockefellers cling to the primeval rain-God of the American hinterland and show no sign of being ashamed of him." John D. arrived at the office as unobtrusively as any clerk. His secretary, George Rogers, later said, "I never knew anyone to enter an office as quietly as Mr. Rockefeller. He seemed almost to have a coat of invisibility." Rogers remembered that his employer often jotted down notes in pencil on his left cuff during the trip downtown.

Every day he sat down to lunch at 26 Broadway with the proconsuls of the great Standard empire. There was William Rockefeller, good-natured and placid, with two sons who would marry two of banker James Stillman's daughters in a dynastic alliance whose descendants, the Stillman Rockefellers, controlled the First National City Bank that one day would contend for supremacy of the financial world with their cousins' Chase Manhattan. There was Henry H. Rogers, called "Hell Hound" by people on Wall Street because of the spectacularly lethal swoops he made into the market as a private investor; Flagler, a proven warrior in the Standard battles; John Archbold, who, after making a pledge to the teetotaling Rockefeller to control his drinking problem, had risen steadily in the Standard hierarchy and was to achieve unwanted notoriety later as its "Great Corruptionist." There was Oliver Payne, treasurer of the Standard, whose father, Henry B. Payne, would become a U.S. senator from Ohio and make common cause with the powerful Mark Hanna. Rockefeller himself sat demurely beside Charles Pratt, to whom he had surrendered the head of the table because he was the oldest of the group. He listened calmly as the others discussed, only occasionally injecting his opinions. His behavior reflected one of his basic ideas—"Find the man who can do the particular thing you want done and then leave him to do it unhampered"—which Rockefeller publicists would later quote as if it were an epigram by Oscar Wilde.

The "Standard Oil Gang" comprised the most potent array of executive talent yet gathered in one organization. They were all millionaires. When they deliberated, it was as if they were a government cabinet. At the Hepburn Committee investigations into railroad rates, even the formidable William Vanderbilt had shaken his head on the witness stand and said to his governmental interrogators: "There is no question about it but these men are smarter than I am a great deal. . . . I never came in contact with any class of men as smart and able as they are in their business. . . . I don't believe that by any legislative enactment or anything else, through any of the states or all of the states, you can keep such men down. You can't do it! They will be on top all the time, you see if they aren't!"

Each executive was a Jonah heading a committee in the belly of the leviathan. Rockefeller never allowed the corporation to be the showcase for the personality of one man; he kept the strong egos in balance and instilled what he called "the Standard Spirit" in the operations, developing a new breed of institutional man whose loyalties never faltered. It was primarily the caliber of its executives that allowed the Standard to take advantage of the fact that the frontier on which it operated was expanding explosively along every front—technological, geographic, and industrial.

The economic revolution that accompanied the Civil War had precipitated a university revolution, sponsored by the masters of the new age. Railroad men and industrialists pioneered the investment in scientific schools and laboratories (it was at the Yale Scientific School that Benjamin Silliman developed the first commercial process for refining petroleum). Here the quest for technical discoveries to fill the economic cornucopia began to replace Cicero and Vergil as the basis of the academic curriculum.

By the end of the century, the new industrial science was developing dozens of derivative items for the by-products of refined oil: paraffin, lubricants, vaseline, and even chewing gum. At the very moment that the light bulb was about to make kerosene obsolete as an illuminant, the internal combustion engine—which would alter the energy basis of modern industry and cause the struggle over petroleum sources and supply to affect the relations between nations—was about to drive Standard Oil to riches and power undreamed of even by Rockefeller. In 1903, Standard agents were at Kitty Hawk offering their gasoline and lubricating oil to the Wright brothers, and in 1904 their salesmen set up a service station for use by contestants in the first international automobile race from New York to Paris.

Rockefeller's unflagging attention to the expansion of the trust—even at a time when the incredible future for oil could not have been predicted—put the Standard in a good position to take advantage of what was to come. He was eternally, almost maniacally, optimistic. Just as Pennsylvania's great Bradford oil fields had begun to dry up, the even more prodigal Lima fields were opening up in Ohio. Standard was there, Rockefeller rushing in over the objections of Pratt and Rogers, who had been told by scientists that the "sour," sulfur-laden Lima oil could never be satisfactorily refined. Even as John Archbold was telling everyone who would listen that he would "undertake to drink all the oil that will be produced there" and selling some of his stock for 85 cents on the dollar, Rockefeller offered to put up $3 million of his own money as a guarantee that some way would be found to treat the oil and make it saleable. He was right: within a few years, Standard scientists had perfected the Frasch process for doing just that.

The Standard's huge reserves of Lima oil put it in an advantageous position for a new struggle that was shaping up in the international market. Oil had from the outset been an international commodity, with exports exceeding domestic consumption by a considerable margin. For twenty-five years following Colonel Edwin Drake's first gusher at Titusville, America had been the sole source of an exportable surplus in oil, and 90 percent of that oil had come from the Standard. Ever since he sent his brother William to New York in the days of Rockefeller, Andrews, and Flagler, John D. had recognized the importance of exports. The Standard fought for overseas markets with the same ferocious intensity as it had for its domestic concessions, with no quarter given or expected, defying foreign governments as routinely as it had state legislatures at home.

The wall of Standard's international oil monopoly had been breached with the opening of Russia's great Baku field on the Caspian Sea. By 1883 a railroad had been built to the Black Sea, and the Czar had invited the Nobel brothers and the Rothschild family to help develop these great oil riches. By 1888 Russia had overtaken America in the production of crude, and Russian kerosene, unheard of a few years earlier, had already cornered 30 percent of the English market and was moving in elsewhere in Europe.

The brain trust at 26 Broadway met on a crisis footing and began to fight back with a price-cutting war. It decided to eliminate the European importing firms it had previously used, substituting a system of foreign affiliates—the Anglo-American Oil Company, Ltd., in England, the Deutsch Amerikanische Gesellschaft, and others. It sent John Archbold abroad for secret conversations with the Rothschilds with an eye toward "rationalizing" the market; it tried to buy out rivals and at the same time bore into them through secret purchases of stock. Its success was impressive, but also incomplete. Though exports of U.S. oil to Europe grew five and a half times between 1884 and 1899, the Standard was at best able to maintain only 60 percent of the market until the Great War of 1914 changed the terms of the struggle altogether.

In its expansion overseas, the Standard enjoyed a better relationship with the federal government than at home. The Standard may have been regarded as a domestic menace, but when it went abroad, it was the American presence personified. Its prosperity was America's prosperity; its manifest destiny was at one with the nation's. In tracking the operations of its competitors not only in Europe but in the Middle East and in Southeast Asia, the Standard drew on the secret reports of the consuls and ambassadors of the United States, many of whom were also on its payroll. It functioned as a shadow government with a foreign policy of its own.

The Standard's success and failure became the subject of letters borne in diplomatic mail pouches. When the trust sent an energetic agent named W. H. Libby to the Orient, the consul general of India wrote back praising his efforts there. John Young, U.S. minister to China, was even more helpful, preparing a circular in Chinese that argued the efficacy of kerosene as an illuminant and then having his consular officers distribute it at the same time Standard agents were handing out tin lamps among the people. When the vast market of China was threatened with closure by European colonialism, Secretary of State John Hay issued the famous "Open Door" notes; the military might of the United States thus placed indirectly secured the rights of Standard Oil and other patriotic corporations to ply their wares in the China trade. "One of our greatest helpers," Rockefeller would acknowledge in his *Random Reminiscences*, "has been the State Department in Washington. Our ambassadors and ministers and consuls have aided to push our way into new markets to the utmost corners of the world."

By the 1890s, American oil was seeping into the unexplored reaches of the globe. As in a Conrad novel, Standard agents were rushing into hearts of darkness everywhere, carrying their products by sampans, camels, oxen, and on the backs of native bearers. They went along the east coast of Sumatra, to Siam, Borneo, and French Indochina. A transoceanic empire lay before them; in Brooks Adams's phrase, the Era of American Economic Supremacy had begun.

It was more than thirty years since he had begun his career, and Rockefeller was the central figure of the most spectacular success story in business history. The Standard was indisputably the most powerful industrial organization in the nation, and the most visible symbol of growing American might abroad. But for Rockefeller personally the price had been heavy: he had become identified with all the excesses the Standard had committed in its rise to power; hatred clung to him like iron filings to a magnet. He tried to dissociate himself from some of the onerous charges against the corporation by insisting that figures like Henry Rogers and John Archbold, the Standard hatchet men, were free agents acting for themselves and beyond his control. Yet this was one case where the country believed, as Emerson had said, that the institution was only the lengthened shadow of the man. Rockefeller had pursued his leviathan with complete dedication. But now he found himself lashed to its back as inextricably as Ahab, and in equal danger of being taken down for good.

Years later, when his image had benefited from the cosmetic surgery provided by the skillful hands of public relations men and three decades of association with philanthropy, Rockefeller would see it as just a problem of communication. He speculated on how different things might have been if the Standard had just "called the reporters in" (as he claimed to have wanted to do) and told its side of things in the aftermath of the South Improvement scheme. But the fact was that Rockefeller, always the fastidious bookkeeper, invariably weighed the debits and credits of any policy with extreme care. From the beginning he had understood the danger of hostile public opinion and spent thousands to influence attitudes in his favor. Although the Standard was gaining a reputation so black that almost anything negative said about it would be believed, when Rockefeller chose silence it was not because the accusations were too base to dignify with a response, but because having to admit the validity of the many accusations that were true overshadowed the opportunity to refute those that were false. His attitude was captured in a comment that he once made to a companion as they were walking down a Cleveland street and talking about the attack on the Standard. "Look at that worm there on the ground," Rockefeller said. "If I step on it, I call attention to it. If I ignore it, it disappears." It was probably the only serious accounting error he ever made. Instead of disappearing, the worm grew into a fire-breathing dragon.

It was not only before the tribunal of public opinion that Rockefeller was tried. By the turn of the century, the trust found itself subjected to one official investigation after another. At first, the Standard executives saw these inquisitions simply as nuisances to be treated with contempt. Archbold, Rogers, and other leading figures in the corporation perjured themselves freely under examination, knowing that the records of the trust were encompassed by a maze of secrecy and legal deception so thick it would not yield to investigation. Rockefeller himself would evade subpoenas when possible and in the last resort would appear before committees, coached and protected by Dodd and a phalanx of other attorneys. Crossing his long legs and smoothing the wrinkles in his pin-striped pants with nervous hands, he would put on his saintly disposition and say things were one way when he knew full well they were another. "No, sir," he once replied to an interrogator during an 1888 New York state senate hearing, "no, we have had no better [railroad] rates than our neighbors, but if I may be allowed, we have found repeated instances where other parties had secured lower rates than we did." On another occasion, when an investigator asked with a slip of the tongue if he had ever participated in the South*ern* (instead of *South*) Improvement Company, Rockefeller pounced on the error and punctiliously answered that he had not.

But usually he found his best defense was an evasiveness that seemed to border on aphasia. Replying to questions about rebates, drawbacks, and the organization and assets of the Standard, he would utter a litany of phrases like "I could not say" and "I cannot recollect about that," and drive investigators to the far side of exasperation. A New York *World* correspondent, after watching one of these performances, wrote: "The art of forgetting is possessed by Mr. Rockefeller in its highest degree."

If it was not quite the "Let the Public Be Damned" attitude of old Commodore Vanderbilt, it was close enough to convince Americans that Rockefeller had crimes to hide. In *Wealth Against Commonwealth* (1894), Henry Demarest Lloyd saw Rockefeller as the prime representative of the malaise of wealth and power infecting the body politic. "If our civilization is destroyed," he wrote,

it will not be by barbarians from below. Our barbarians
come from above. Our great money makers have sprung
up in one generation into seats of power kings do not
know. The forces and the wealth are new, and have
been the opportunity of new men. Without restraint of
culture, experience, the pride or even the inherited caution of class or rank, these men ... claim a power without control, exercised through forms which make it
anonymous and perpetual. ... They are gluttons of luxury and power, rough, unsocialized, believing that mankind must be kept terrorized. Of gods, friends, learnings,
of the uncomprehended civilization they overrun, they
ask but one question: How much?

The hatred that surrounded him was so complete that it
mistakenly blamed Rockefeller for excesses of other members
of the Standard Oil Gang for which he was not responsible
and which he didn't even approve. In 1899, for instance, H.
H. Rogers, William Rockefeller, and James Stillman had
bought the Anaconda Copper Company for $39 million, writ-
ing a check drawn on Stillman's National City Bank with the
understanding that the seller would hold the check in the
bank for a certain time before it was cashed. They then organized the Amalgamated Copper Company and transferred
all the Anaconda mines to it, issuing $75 million worth of
shares in the new corporation. After they borrowed $39 mil-
lion on these shares from the National City Bank to allow the
check to clear, the stock was offered to the public, which
bought it immediately, enabling the triumvirate to liquidate
the $39 million loan and pocket a profit of $36 million on
no investment at all.

Rockefeller himself had not participated in this scheme and
had drawn his personal funds out of the National City Bank
in protest over it. But it didn't matter. When the affair came
to light, it was a "Rockefeller plot." This time the charge
may have been unjust, yet a larger truth was concealed
within it. For it was the great accumulation of wealth Rockefeller had made possible by creating the Standard "money-
making machine" that had financed this maneuver. The issue
was no longer which of the robber barons was specifically responsible for a certain act, but the way in which the sum of
these acts was to place control of the American economy in
the hands of a small circle of men who might war against
each other intermittently but were unified by a philosophy of

power and accumulation. Although himself a celebrant of this new economic order, John Moody captured the threat it posed in *The Truth About the Trusts*, published in 1904:

> Viewed as a whole, we find the dominating influences in the Trusts to be made up of an intricate network of large and small groups of capitalists, many allied to one another by ties of more or less importance, but all being appendages to or parts of the greater groups, which are themselves dependent on and allied with two mammoth or Rockefeller and Morgan groups. These two mammoth groups jointly . . . constitute the heart of the business and commercial life of the nation, the others all being the arteries which permeate in a thousand ways our whole national life, making their influence felt in every home and hamlet, yet all connected with and dependent on this great central source, the influence and policy of which dominates them all.

Especially after 1902, when Ida Tarbell's *History of Standard Oil Company* began its serialization in *McClure's*, the antagonism surrounding Rockefeller spread from his public affairs into his private life. Editorial writers treated him as the archetypal monopolist; he also routinely received threats to his life. By the time he arrived at church each Sunday, hundreds had gathered to gawk, and the pastor was alarmed enough to hire armed Pinkertons to mix with the crowds. During this period of his life, Rockefeller kept a revolver beside his bed.

Publicly he remained calm and imperturbable. Privately, however, the burden began to take its toll. "You know," he later told an acquaintance, "for years I was crucified." By the 1890s, he clearly had reached a crossroad in a life that until then had room for neither doubt nor reflection. He had come a long way from the youthway days when the mere thought of great wealth had made him click his heels in delight. He had accumulated a great fortune—more than a hundred millions. But now, as his days were absorbed in the endless orchestration of his income and expenses, of investments and charities, of corporate strategy and legal defense, it became questionable whether he had mastered the money or the money had mastered him.

He had become, as he once said, "a regular dumping ground" for the stock of those, like his friend Flagler, who had projects they wanted to pursue and needed to dispose of some of their Standard holdings for cash. "Commodore Vanderbilt has all his money in ties and cars which wear out and have to be replaced," he told his secretary, George Rogers. "Others have fortunes in ships or houses which deteriorate; others in goods or purchases that change or decay. I guess Standard Oil will make me my fortune. I'll just stick to that."

Over the years he had steadily increased his share of the corporation, and as the great Standard money machine pumped its way toward the twentieth century, fantastic dividends poured into Rockefeller's hands. He tried to dispose of them in investments but it had become literally impossible for him to keep pace with himself.

Under the accumulating pressures, the body that he had pushed so remorselessly for the past forty years finally rebelled. Letters between Rockfeller and his wife during this period tell of sleepless nights. He began to suffer from serious digestive disorders, and his doctor insisted that he retreat from his cares. The tall figure with the dignified and composed features who had stridden confidently through the wars on America's corporate frontiers in the seventies and eighties underwent a sudden change; almost overnight the people who visited Rockefeller came away shocked by his stooped and careworn demeanor. Bearing whatever look was in vogue—first muttonchops, then a brush moustache and sideburns, and finally a more modest moustache, his face had been somehow nondescript. Now people who had not really noticed his appearance before suddenly found themselves aware of how he looked. His face had become deeply lined; he had put on weight, sagging at the midsection. He was ravaged by a nervous disease—generalized alopecia—which left him without any hair on his body, and in the first noticeable vanity of an otherwise spartan life, he began to worry about his baldness, hiding it first with a grotesque black skullcap and later with a series of ill-fitting white wigs, each of them slightly different in length so that he could imitate a natural growth of hair over a two-week period.

In another man these outward signs might have mirrored an inward turmoil: perhaps a stricken conscience or fear of the sudden realization of the frailty of his mortality in the face of the hatred he had earned. But in Rockefeller, who kept a daily record of his responses to external events in thousands of meticulous letters and diligently scripted notebooks, there is no evidence of any inner reckoning or reflective torment. In him, the physical faltering signified no more than that: the failing of the machine that he had driven so mercilessly. The cure was not spiritual medicine but simply rest.

Slowly, John D. Rockefeller began to relax his grip on the affairs of Standard Oil. In 1896 he stopped going to 26 Broadway every day. The following year, he stopped going at all, making John Archbold his regent in the corporation and staying in daily contact with him by a direct wire to his home.

The legendary attention and energy was now applied to such tasks as landscaping the new estate located in Pocantico Hills on a spectacular range overlooking the Hudson. With that perfectionism that once charted his campaigns across the undiscovered country of corporate America, he plotted the seventy miles of road to be built over his estate, moved in several tons of topsoil so that breathtaking formal gardens could be planted, and arranged the views to his liking by moving trees around as an interior decorator would move chairs. He moved into Kikjuit (Dutch for "the lookout"), a magnificent Georgian mansion his son had persuaded him to build. In all, the Pocantico estate was (as a Broadway wit of later years wisecracked) an example of what God could have done if He'd only had the money. On the sculpted greens of the golf course he built there, Rockefeller's attention more and more drifted from oil rates and competitors' prices to his scores for nine holes, which he whittled down as persistently as he had the drops of solder that sealed up the Standard's tins.

If his life had ended here or if he had spent the rest of his days clipping the coupons he had accumulated, the Rockefellers who followed him would probably have been no different from any of the other descendants of the great robber baron industrialists. But in his leisure, the master of Standard Oil began thinking about the creation of another kind of institution, one that would find a more receptive place in the public heart than had his great trust. He had made his money; now he would put it to work to make sure his heirs did not face the same hatred he had in his life. Almost imperceptibly, he began to change the habit of the monopolist for that of the philanthropist. Slowly, the grand acquisitor began the metamorphosis that would transform him into a benefactor of mankind.

3

As a STUDENT of the scriptures, Rockefeller was aware of the verse from 1 Peter: "Charity shall cover a multitude of sins." Yet unlike Gould, Fisk, and some of the others, he had not conveniently managed to discover charity late in life and then frenetically begun endowing schools and hospitals to salve a guilty conscience and burnish a darkened reputation. For him, the tithe had always been part of his continuing commitment to Eliza Rockefeller's Baptist religion. As Ledger A shows, Rockefeller had given to churches and church-related charities when first beginning as a $3.50-a-week clerk in Cleveland. As his income grew, so did his gifts. In 1882 he was giving away some $65,000 a year; a decade later his annual benefactions had risen to $1.5 million.

Giving was a Christian duty to be taken care of without a flourish. Yet as he grew older, Rockefeller began to have the semimystical feeling that he had been especially selected as the frail vessel for the great fortune. He startled a reporter during a rare interview in 1905 by blurting out: "God gave me my money." As the statement began to raise eyebrows, he elaborated: "I believe the power to make money is a gift from God ... to be developed and used to the best of our ability for the good of mankind. Having been endowed with the gift I possess, I believe it is my duty to make money and still more money and to use the money I make for the good of my fellow man according to the dictates of my conscience."

The English economist J. A. Hobson pointed out the oddity of the partnership: Mammon made the money and then God decided how to spend it. But as this century of industrial accumulation pressed on to its conclusion, the league between godliness and riches came to seem more logical, given the peculiar theology of the Gilded Age. The prophet who set the tone for philanthropy, however, was a man wholly outside the church, an atheist and ardent disciple of Social Darwinism named Andrew Carnegie.

By his own stunning disbursement of one of the greatest fortunes in history, Carnegie made sure the public was interested in the way the princes of industry used their money. He then allowed the self-dramatizer and amateur essayist to take over from the steel magnate. In an article appearing in the *North American Review* of June 1889, Carnegie set forth the "Gospel of Wealth," which would quickly become a standard credo for the new industrial philanthropists. "The problem of our age," he began, "is the proper administration of wealth, so that the ties of brotherhood may still bind together the rich and poor in harmonious relationship." While populists and radicals clamored for a *redistribution* of wealth, Carnegie proposed merely a refinement in its *administration;* the premise of his argument was that the present social order was the best of all possible orders. It might indeed lead to certain inequalities and injustices, but progress in human society was dependent on the ability of the best elements to accumulate wealth and administer it for the general good.

As one liberal theologian remarked after reading the article, Carnegie had indeed given the world a new gospel statement: "The inevitable factor in society is not so certainly the poor as the rich. The rich ye have with you always." John D. Rockefeller, who also read the article, was more pleased. "I would that more men of wealth were doing as you are doing with your money," he wrote Carnegie, "but be assured your example will bear fruit."

A distant cooperation in philanthropy sprang up between the two men, which the newspapers dramatized as a competition in giving, the New York *American* in 1910 printing a box score that showed the impressive totals of the first two decades: Carnegie $179,300,000; Rockefeller $134,271,000.

In Carnegie's charities, there was always a large element of self-advertisement, for which at least one aristocratic acquaintance criticized him. "Never before in the history of plutocratic America had any one man purchased by mere money so much social advertising and flattery," wrote Poultney Bigelow. "He would have given millions to Greece had she labelled the Parthenon 'Carnegopolis.'"

Rockefeller's benefactions followed a less flamboyant course. He had given millions to the Baptists. But this had been in piecemeal donations. By the late 1880s, with all the talk of the rich man's burden in the air, the church elders felt emboldened to ask him to make a large "investment" in a great center of Baptist learning. Some favored a new university on the East Coast, but others urged Rockefeller to rebuild the University of Chicago, which Stephen Douglas had founded in 1856 as the Morgan Park Theological Seminary. This institution, they argued, could be made to rise again as a powerful mother school for the handful of run-down Baptist colleges in the West and could exercise a powerful religious influence over the new states being rapidly carved out of the frontier. In 1887 Rockefeller gave $600,000 to begin this great work.

Rockefeller became absorbed in the university's reconstruction and direction. In some sense it was a vexing tax on his already overburdened time, but he never regretted his involvement. When he came to the 1896 convocation, it was one of the first times his public appearance had been greeted by cheers instead of hostile curiosity. Seeing him, the undergraduates chanted:

> John D. Rockefeller, wonderful man is he
> Gives all his spare change to the U. of C.

Nor could he have been unhappy when a University of Chicago literature professor later published a study arguing that he was superior in creative genius to "Homer, Dante, and Shakespeare." By 1910 the "spare change" he had given the university amounted to $45 million. To the end of his life, Rockefeller said of the university: "It was the best investment I ever made."

Yet the problem remained of how to organize his philanthropy into the "scientific giving" Carnegie had been first to realize was important. The field of philanthropy seemed as much a jungle as the world of industry he had spent forty years trying to tame. Everywhere he went he was deluged with appeals for gifts and help. He received begging letters by the bushel at 26 Broadway. It was as if there were an elemental struggle between two estates of men—those with money and those trying to get it from them. Finding a solution became a matter of survival. As the unique man who would finally solve Rockefeller's problems for him later wrote: "Neither in the privacy of his home, nor at the table, nor in the aisles of his church, nor during business hours, nor anywhere else was he secure from insistent appeal. . . . He was constantly hunted, stalked, and hounded almost like a wild animal."

The author of these words was the Reverend Frederick T.

Gates, who was destined to be a pivotal figure in Rockefeller's future. The son of a New York preacher, Gates had the noble features of a character out of a stage production of *Ben Hur*, the strong facial lines set off by a shock of thick wavy hair. He was ambitious and energetic, his personality an odd blend of worldly concerns and evangelical zeal. As a young man he had worked as a bank clerk and dry goods salesman before attending Rochester Theological Seminary. His first pastorate was in Minneapolis, and there he had met George A. Pillsbury, founder of the flour fortune. Dying of an incurable disease, Pillsbury had asked Gates to help him decide on the benefactions in his will, giving the young clergyman his first experience with philanthropy and making Gates understand that he would not be content to tend a remote flock the rest of his life.

Raymond B. Fosdick, who later worked in the Rockefeller Office and served as president of the Rockefeller Foundation, left an incisive picture of the contrast between the aging Rockefeller and the man who for two decades would sit at his right hand:

> One would have to search over wide areas to find two men who were so completely different in temperament. Mr. Gates was a vivid, outspoken, self-revealing personality who brought an immense gusto to his work; Mr. Rockefeller was quiet, cool, taciturn about his thoughts and purposes, almost stoic in his repression. Mr. Gates had an eloquence which could be passionate when he was aroused; Mr. Rockefeller, when he spoke at all, spoke in a slow measured fashion, lucidly and penetratingly, but without raising his voice and without gestures. Mr. Gates was overwhelming and sometimes overbearing in argument; Mr. Rockefeller was a man of infinite patience who never showed irritation or spoke chidingly about anybody. Mr. Gates summed up his impression of Mr. Rockefeller in this sentence: "If he was very nice and precise in his choice of words, he was also nice and accurate in his choice of silences."

Having first met and been impressed by the dynamic Gates during the often trying negotiations with the Baptist national hierarchy that finally led him to underwrite the University of Chicago, Rockefeller, in March of 1891, asked the 38-year-old minister to call on him at 26 Broadway. As he was led into the spartan office, Rockefeller motioned him to a chair. "I am in trouble, Mr. Gates," he began with uncharacteristic directness. "The pressure of these appeals for gifts has become too great for endurance. I haven't the time or strength, with all my heavy business responsibilites, to deal with these demands properly. I am so constituted as to be unable to give away money with any satisfaction until I have made the most careful inquiry as to the worthiness of the cause. These investigations are now taking more of my time and energy than the Standard Oil itself." He asked the minister to come to work for him.

Three months later, when Frederick T. Gates began doing business as Mr. Rockefeller's chief almoner, it could not have been foreseen that this represented a first step in making the Rockefellers an American institution; that the small office Gates began work in would one day take up three floors in a Rockefeller Center skyscraper and employ over two hundred people whose daily work would consist only of servicing the Rockefeller dynasty; or that the minister himself would be the first in a long line of dedicated and talented people who would be full-time retainers to the Rockefeller family.

Soon, all applications for help came directly to Gates's office. Winnowing away the chaff, he passed on to Rockefeller those appeals he felt had merit, distilling the information and his recommendations into terse, cogent memorandums that would become the trademark of all the Rockefeller family's associates. He cut down on the volume of requests by insisting that all individual churches channel their pleas through a central Baptist agency. He personally visited and investigated all prospective recipients of Rockefeller's philanthropy. Even in those cases where it was decided that help would be given, Gates insisted that other donations besides Rockefeller's be secured. In a sense, he became the first investment banker in the benevolence business. Reflecting on these early days he spent setting the Rockefeller philanthropic house in order, Gates later said: "I found not a few of Mr. Rockefeller's habitual charities to be worthless and practically fraudulent. But on the other hand, I gradually developed and introduced into all his charities the principle of scientific giving and he found himself in no long time laying aside retail giving almost entirely and entering safely and pleasurably into the field of wholesale philanthropy."

Rockefeller soon saw that Gates's business acumen might well be useful in another area where he also sorely needed help, that of his personal finances. These had become chaotic during the past few years, when he had been devoting every waking minute to steering the trust from one crisis to another. He was indeed being victimized by the sheer velocity of his income. In the ten-year period from 1885 to 1896, his share of the dividends of the trust alone totalled some $40 million. (Ironically, his total fortune, which amounted to some $200 million at the time of his "retirement" in 1897, would increase with the advent of the internal combustion engine until it reached the $1 billion mark in 1913, quadrupling during his years of inactivity.) Meanwhile, he had been putting money into a series of schemes and investments, almost as if to get rid of it. By the early 1890s, when Gates was hired, Rockefeller had 67 major investments in other than oil-related industries, valued at nearly $23 million: $13,750,-000 in 16 different railroads; nearly $3 million in 9 mining companies; almost $2 million in several banks; and another $4 million in miscellaneous operations. After making the initial investments, however, Rockefeller, busy elsewhere, would let months go by without checking on them.

Impressed by the keen business sense Gates had exhibited, Rockefeller urged him to take time off when traveling to investigate proposed philanthropies to also check on nearby investments. The minister was startled to find that many of Rockefeller's interests were either losing money or well beyond his control. In the Pacific Northwest, for instance, Rockefeller had been led by land speculators into a variety of dubious investments: steel and paper mills, a nail factory, lumber and smelting properties, and railroads. "Most of these properties," Rockefeller admitted later, "I had not even seen, having relied upon the investigations of others respecting their worth."

In 1893, after receiving a few of Gates's shrewd and observant memorandums on his investigations, Rockefeller asked the minister to take up an office at 26 Broadway and combine management of the philanthropies and personal investments under one hand. Gates was overjoyed. He wrote to his parents of his employer:

> He is shrewd and keen and knows which end of a bargain to take hold of. He does not mean to be cheated, though he sometimes is, in the multiplicity of his business interests. . . . He is chary of praise. Me he never praises to my face. But I hear of good words about me

to others. He is confiding great interests in me, and I am exercising great caution, taking no step until I know where my foot is going down, and whither it leads.

Someone who could make such observations was a man after Rockefeller's own heart, and he threw open all his voluminous personal investment files to Gates. Seeing that there were at least twenty corporations of which Rockefeller was part owner that were in trouble, Gates either bought out enough other stockholders to obtain control or disposed of the stock entirely. In the end, Rockefeller controlled thirteen of these corporations, and Gates was made president of them all.

Gates's greatest coup in his new role was the consolidation of Rockefeller's ownership over the great Mesabi ore deposits of Minnesota. Eventually providing some 60 percent of the nation's iron ore, this rich area had been pioneered by the five Merritt brothers, who had by 1893 a 40 percent interest in mines that contained as much as 50 million tons of high-grade ore. To build a railroad connecting their properties to Duluth, they had issued bonds, and Rockefeller had been persuaded to purchase $400,000 worth.

Starting with this foothold and taking advantage of the Merritts' speculative greed, Gates used the leverage of Rockefeller's enormous capital to gain control over the properties. In the process, he could not avoid a nasty and much publicized lawsuit by the brothers, who claimed that they had been bilked. Paying $525,000 in an out-of-court settlement, Rockefeller enabled Gates to have a free hand assembling more properties. It was not long before he was made master of the richest ore deposits in the world.

By a fortuitous combination of circumstance and Gates's good business sense, Rockefeller had thus slipped in between the steel manufacturers and their raw materials. But while never discouraging rumors that he intended to use the Mesabi property in a war with Carnegie for control of the steel industry, the fact was, Rockefeller really wanted less involvement in business, not more. In 1896 he made an agreement by which the Carnegie Company leased his properties for 25 cents a ton, agreeing to mine not less than 600,000 tons a year, which they would match with an equal amount from their own pits, shipping the total 1.2 million tons over Rockefeller's railroad and the huge fleet of ore-carrying ships Gates had been building up on the Great Lakes. The Carnegie Steel

Company got high-grade ore and control over the competition; Rockefeller got a lease fee and guaranteed freight for his rail and shipping lines.

Still, it was clear that the steel business would have to be consolidated. Carnegie was the largest but not the only steel maker; he had formidable competition from Elbert Gary's Federal Steel Company, among others, and every day new producers were springing up to challenge the large companies. Either Carnegie or Rockefeller could have stepped in to exert control over the competitive maelstrom, but Rockefeller had gotten into iron only by chance, and Carnegie wanted to get out and devote himself to spreading his new gospel.

Only one man in the country could ensure prosperity for the steel industry by eliminating competition without a protracted struggle: J. P. Morgan, who had earned the title of the Jupiter of Wall Street by virtue of the powerful bolts he shot out of his chambers at 23 Wall Street into the financial world, asserting his undisputed supremacy as the greatest centralizer of a centralizing age. And in 1901, Morgan formed the largest business aggregation the world had yet seen, the United States Steel Corporation. It took over all the competition, including Carnegie, to whom Morgan paid $300 million in steel bonds which the philanthropist promptly used to create a battery of foundations. Morgan had never bothered to hide his distaste for the ascetic Rockefeller, and when he went to call at 26 Broadway to see about the Mesabi properties and the completion of his plan, he was served up humble pie. For Rockefeller, who understood Morgan's feelings (and later said of Jupiter, "I have never been able to see why any man should have such a high and mighty feeling about himself"), waited on his caller, but declined to discuss business. When Morgan offered a "proposition," Rockefeller replied with his chilliest courtesy that he himself was retired but his son "would undoubtedly be glad to talk with Mr. Morgan."

Some days later, when Henry Frick went up to Pocantico with an offer from Morgan, Rockefeller allowed himself to be persuaded, after indicating that he didn't like ultimatums. He told Frick in the gentlemanly code he had perfected, "I am not anxious to sell my own properties. But as you surmise, I never wish to stand in the way of a worthy enterprise." Rockefeller accepted $8.5 million for the fleet of ore carriers; and for the Mesabi property itself, he got $80 million, half in common stock and half in preferred stock of the U.S. Steel Corporation.

When the papers were finally completed, Frederick Gates came to Rockefeller's office to review the fine points in the contract. Rockefeller knew that Gates's steady hand had guided the Mesabi investment, building up the Great Lakes fleet from nothing and helping direct the strategy of the dealings with the Merritt brothers, Carnegie, and then Morgan. After they had finished going over the bargain, Rockefeller rose and shook hands with Gates, saying with unusual warmth, "Thank you, Mr. Gates, thank you."

Gates looked back steadily and replied, " 'Thank you' is not enough, Mr. Rockefeller."

Rockefeller may have run the same shrewd appraising glance over Gates's face as he savored this solecism, and the same half-smile may have passed over his immobile features, as on those occasions when he pulled a handful of change out of his pocket and let a porter or waiter take for himself the tip he thought he deserved. There is no record of the amount of the minister's tip for his service in securing the Mesabi properties, but for the time being it was enough.

On the afternoon of September 14, 1901, J. P. Morgan had put on his hat and coat and was heading out of his Wall Street office to go sailing at Great Neck in the famous yacht he had defiantly named *The Corsair*. As he walked out the door, a half-dozen newspapermen rushed up out of breath. One of them yelled, "Mr. Morgan, President McKinley is dead."

Morgan stood stunned for a moment, then turned around, went back into his office, took off his hat and coat, and sat down again at his desk, mumbling, "This is the saddest news I have ever heard."

The McKinley administration, overseen by Rockefeller's old friend Mark Hanna, had been a time of official patronage for the economic combinations that populists and muckrakers denounced as agencies of a new feudalism. It was a time, as Henry Adams acidly observed, of "the final surrender of the country to capitalism." It was also a time when the Standard was able to flaunt its power without fear of reprisal, routinely buying and paying off U.S. senators by the fistful. Two letters from Rockefeller's lieutenant John Archbold to Ohio Senator Joseph B. Foraker, who would contest William Howard Taft for the Republican party's presidential nomination in 1908, give the flavor of the Standard's lobbying techniques:

Feb. 16, 1900

My Dear Senator:

Here is still another very objectionable bill. It is so outrageous as to be ridiculous, but it needs to be looked after and I hope there will be no difficulty in killing it . . .

Very sincerely yours,

John D. Archbold

April 17, 1900

My Dear Senator:

I enclose you a certificate of deposit to your favor for $15,000. . . . I need scarcely again express our great gratification over the favorable outcome of affairs. . . .

Very sincerely yours,

John D. Archbold

During the McKinley years these excesses had become commonplace. When Theodore Roosevelt ascended to the presidency in the same year that Morgan created U.S. Steel, public outcry made the chief question facing him the issue of the trusts. It was a political dilemma. Antitrust legislation, the new President declared, was about as effective as a papal bull against a comet. The trusts were "inevitable" not so much because of their efficiency (as their defenders claimed), but because they were so entrenched, as Roosevelt put it, that the effort to destroy them "would be futile unless accomplished in ways that would work the utmost mischief to the entire body politic."

On the other hand, the trusts could not simply be left to run the country as they had for the last fifteen years. Popular resentment was too great and the economic chaos that their unregulated competition provoked was too dangerous. If a few public examples were necessary to ensure a more responsible sort of conduct, Roosevelt was prepared to make them. There were, he suggested, good trusts and bad ones. "We draw the line against misconduct, not against wealth," he told the country. Yet the precise considerations on which the distinctions were to be made remained his secret.* Morgan's

*Secret also was the fact that he himself had gone to the men he would soon castigate as malefactors of great wealth, seeking contributions for his 1904 reelection campaign, and that they had raised some $300,000. Once he was back in office, he loosed his Bureau of Corporations on them in a gesture that appeared so ungrateful that Henry Frick said, "We bought the son of a bitch, but he didn't stay bought."

steel trust, sprawled over the most basic of modern industries, would be overlooked by Roosevelt's regulators and trust busters, as would his New England railroad monopoly. On the other hand, the railroads of his rival, E. H. Harriman, who had failed to jump on Roosevelt's political bandwagon, would feel the crashing blade of the regulatory axe. But the most obvious sacrifice for which the public clamored was John D. Rockefeller and Standard Oil.

Suits had dogged the Standard since its creation, but in the second Roosevelt administration the pace intensified noticeably. By midsummer of 1907 there were seven federal suits pending against the Standard and its various subsidiaries, and these were supplemented by suits on behalf of the state governments of Texas, Minnesota, Missouri, Tennessee, Ohio, Mississippi, and Indiana. The most spectacular legal fireworks of the year came in the celebrated Landis case, in which action was taken in the state of Indiana against the Standard under the Elkins Act; at issue was recovery of all the rebates the company had extorted in its years of dealing with the railroads. In handing down the decision, which found the company guilty of 1,642 separate counts of price fixing, the flamboyant Judge "Kenesaw Mountain" Landis thundered at the Standard lawyers from his bench: "You wound society more deeply than does he who counterfeits the coin or steals the mail." News of the astronomical fine of $29 million Landis had assessed for the trust's past sins was quickly cabled to New York, where Rockefeller was beginning a round of golf with friends. He paused momentarily to look at the words on the yellow telegram, said, "Judge Landis will be dead a long time before this fine is paid," and continued on to the next hole.

The Landis decision was indeed overturned on appeal. (When it was revealed that Rockefeller's personal benefactions amounted to $15 million in 1908, one wit noted that it was a 50 percent split with the Lord in his savings on the $29 million fine.) But there was little time for rejoicing at the Standard, for even as it was saving $29 million, the U.S. Department of Justice began a suit in federal circuit court in Missouri, petitioning for the dissolution of the trust itself as a conspiracy in restraint of trade. Finally comprising 21 printed volumes with 14,495 printed pages of painstaking testimony, the suit was the first and last time the inner sanctum of Standard Oil was exposed to the gaze of the uninitiated. What had begun forty years earlier as a skeptical $4,000 investment by a young commission merchant now poured out 35,000 barrels of refined oil and gasoline every day. It had more than 100,-000 miles of pipeline and an armada of 100 tankers carrying its products abroad. The trust was worth some $660 million.

The government won the case, and kept winning on the long road to appeal. It was on a chilly March day in 1911 that Chief Justice White of the Supreme Court rose to read the decision that finally dissolved the Standard trust: "No disinterested mind can survey ... the jungle of conflicting testimony relating to innumerable complex and varied business transactions extending over a period of nearly forty years without being irresistibly driven to the conclusion that the very genius for commercial organization soon begot an intent and purpose to exclude others." After hearing the news, Rockefeller sent a humorous obituary to his old partners: "Dearly beloved, we must obey the Supreme Court. Our splendid, happy family must scatter."

In the complex procedure severing Hydra's many heads, the stockholders received shares in the various Standard companies proportionate to their holdings in the Standard trust. (Of 983,383 shares in the holding company, Rockefeller—who had steadily continued to add to his holdings over the years—had 244,385, worth over $160 million.) The octopus was broken down into 39 different and theoretically competitive companies at the time of dissolution, but ownership remained in the hands of the same shareholders who had always been in control, and for years the new firms would continue to respect each other's territorial imperatives.

The trust's life after death proved an ironic epilogue to the suit. For within a week after stockholders received their shares, the Standard companies were traded on Wall Street for the first time. It exploded in the biggest bull market yet known for a single stock, dramatically increasing the value of the former trust. Standard of New Jersey rose in worth from $260 per share to $580; Standard of Indiana from $3,500 to $9,500. Thus, while people were celebrating the breaking of the trust, another $200 million was added to the value of Standard stock in the space of five short months. It seemed to be the exemplification of one of Rockefeller's favorite homilies: "Try to turn every disaster into an opportunity." President Roosevelt himself saw the irony of it all. In a 1912 speech, he pondered the results of trust-busting and remarked: "No wonder that Wall Street's prayer now is: 'Oh Merciful Providence, give us another dissolution.'"

Yet for the time being at least, Rockefeller was as concerned with giving as he was with getting. He knew that the decisions he must make about the great fortune would be as momentous as any he had ever made about the slain trust. He had Frederick Gates to remind him of the dangers of inaction. "Your fortune is rolling up, rolling up like an avalanche! You must distribute it faster than it grows! If you do not, it will crush you, and your children, and your children's children."

Gates had more in mind than simply giving away money, even large amounts, to individuals and organizations requesting help. When he mused about the future of philanthropy, it was with an evangelical fervor. He dreamed of great charitable trusts that would equal in impact the trust Samuel Dodd had created for Rockefeller. They would be corporate philanthropies that would "rationalize" the world of giving the way the Standard had the world of oil.

In his private papers, Gates reflected about Rockefeller and what had come to be known between them as "the difficult art of giving":

> I trembled as I witnessed the unreasoning popular resentment at Mr. Rockefeller's riches, to the mass of people, a national menace. It was not, however, the unreasoning public prejudice of his vast fortune that chiefly troubled me. Was it to be handed on to posterity as other great fortunes have been handed down by their possessors, with scandalous results to their descendants and powerful tendencies to social demoralization? I saw no other course but for Mr. Rockefeller and his son to form a series of great corporate philanthropies for forwarding civilization in all its elements in this land and in all lands; philanthropies, if possible, limitless in time and amount, broad in scope, and self-perpetuating.

These foundations, Gates might have added, would be highly visible, concerning themselves with problems that were part of the lives of every American. Rockefeller would be the screen on which Gates's own dreams were projected.

Gates began by inducing Rockefeller to create the first institution to bear his name, the Rockefeller Institute for Medical Research, which half a century later his grandson David would transform into Rockefeller University. In 1897, inspired by Osler's *Principles and Practice of Medicine,* Gates dictated a memorandum to his principal proposing the creation of a medical research facility modeled on the Pasteur Institute in Paris and the Koch Institute in Berlin. Gates felt that medicine as practiced in the United States at the time was a "failure," and that remedying this situation "would give Mr. Rockefeller an immense opportunity." However, even if the Institute were to fail to discover anything, "the mere fact that he, Mr. Rockefeller, had established such an institute of research ... would result in other institutes of a similar kind, or at least other funds for research being established."

In 1901 the Rockefeller Institute for Medical Research was officially launched, the first of its kind in America, and a year later Rockefeller added $1 million to the original $200,000 endowment to build and equip a major laboratory on the upper east side of New York City. Dr. Simon Flexner of the University of Pennsylvania was chosen to head the Institute and to select a staff of equally brilliant scientists and administrators.

In 1905 Flexner developed a serum for the treatment of epidemic meningitis, the first of several dramatic and highly publicized scientific advances made by the Institute, which eventually included important research in the development of a vaccine for yellow fever and work on infantile paralysis and pneumonia. But even more important, the Institute would provide the expertise for the medical and public health campaigns that the Rockefeller Foundation and other philanthropies would shortly take to the farthest corners of the globe.

When Gates cast his eye over the medical institute that his energy and vision had helped to create, he waxed religious: "In these sacred rooms He is whispering His secrets. To these men He is opening up the mysterious depths of His Being," he wrote. If Rockefeller thought such thoughts, he did not express them. He continued to puzzle people, moreover, by retaining the services of Dr. H. F. Biggar, a homeopath, as his personal physician, maintaining a basic distrust in modern medicine while spending millions to sponsor its advance.*

*This inconsistency bedeviled Gates. At Rockefeller's suggestion, Dr. Biggar prepared a paper touting homeopathy at the time the Institute was being founded. Upon reading it, Gates exploded: "He has not kept up with the progress of medicine and is still living in the twilight of two or three generations ago. His paper represents the current sentiments of about fifty years ago.... A man who can bring himself so easily to believe what he wants to believe ought to be a very happy

Gates might have succeeded ably as one of Rockefeller's lieutenants in Standard Oil if he had come along thirty years earlier. The minister understood those principles of monopoly that had allowed his employer to organize the oil industry, and he proposed to apply them to philanthropy. At Gates's urging, Rockefeller wrote Carnegie inviting him to become a trustee of his next great philanthropy, the General Education Board, incorporated in 1903.

From its inception, the GEB had been an illustration of the principle of monopoly, choosing Negro education in the South as its subject. It started by putting its financial power behind the combination that had already been drawn together in 1901 under the aegis of the Southern Education Board. This combination included the Peabody and Slater funds, which were among the earliest examples of philanthropic foundations in America, and the Tuskegee-Hampton educational complex, which had dominated such "higher education" as had been available to freedmen in the post-Reconstruction era.

Its influence in the South was soon unrivaled, and the General Education Board broadened its focus to include the rest of the country. In 1905 Rockefeller added $10 million to the initial endowment of the GEB, accompanying the gift with a letter specifying that the income had to be used "to promote a comprehensive system of higher education in the United States." The key word, as Gates later emphasized in a memorandum to the trustees, was *system*. The purpose of the $10 million was "to reduce our higher education to something like an orderly and comprehensive system, to discourage unnecessary duplication and waste, and to encourage economy and efficiency. Mr. Rockefeller desires the fund all the time to be working toward this great end."

The GEB next combined the Rockefeller Medical Institute's interest in medicine with its own interest in education in a campaign that was to revolutionize the whole system of professional medical training. The paradigm institution for the new medicine was to be Johns Hopkins; the standards for the reorganization of medical education were set forth in a famous report commissioned by the Carnegie Foundation and

man and I have no doubt Dr. Biggar is." Yet Rockefeller maintained a relationship with Biggar until the doctor's death. Afterward he wrote to his son of Biggar's more contemporary replacement: "The doctor came to see me today. He wouldn't give me the medicine I wanted, and I wouldn't take the medicine he presented, but we had a lovely talk."

written by GEB Trustee Abraham Flexner, whose brother Simon was the head of the Institute. Within five years of the Flexner Report, with the General Education Board supplying the funds to sponsor its recommendations and support those institutions willing to adopt its standards, the number of medical schools in the country had declined from 147 to 95. The less than two dozen beneficiaries of the $45 million made available for medical education included Johns Hopkins, Yale, the University of Chicago, Columbia, and Harvard. They would henceforth be the standard-setting institutions for the field.

Rockefeller was pleased at the good works of Gates's charities, pleased that they seemed to soften the harsh public opinion that had followed him remorselessly since the South Improvement plan and that they offered an area where his delicate and skittish son, John D. Rockefeller, Jr., could take hold. Yet he himself was not particularly interested. He was content for Gates and his son to handle the details of the Institute and GEB while he played golf, toyed with the stock market, and enjoyed his "retirement." They were the entrepreneurs; he was merely the investor. He had a different, more practical view of philanthropy, and rarely was excited by it. When he was galvanized, as in the 1909 meeting of the GEB to create the Rockefeller Sanitary Commission, it was because he suddenly saw a pragmatic application for philanthropy.

Dr. Victor Heiser, involved with the Sanitary Commission and subsequently director of the Rockefeller Foundation's international health programs in the Far East, later recalled being summoned, along with a small group of leaders in the medical profession, to meet with Rockefeller. "I want to ask you gentlemen a question," he said. "Is there a disease affecting large numbers of people of which you can say, 'I know all about this and I can cure it, not in fifty or eighty percent of the cases, but in one hundred percent'?"

"Nobody," as Dr. Heiser later recalled, "had ever presented such a problem to these eminent physicians." It was a practical question from a man used to getting his money's worth. Fortunately, a U.S. Public Health Service physician, Dr. Charles Stiles, had been trying to draw attention to the role of hookworm in causing widespread lethargy among cotton mill workers in the Southern states. It was a disease that affected millions, yet could easily be cured and prevented (for fifty cents a person, as was later shown). The government (in this pre-income-tax era) did not have the means to launch such a campaign, but a Rockefeller Sanitary Commission could. The dramatic success of the hookworm campaign would begin a far-reaching change in attitudes toward the Rockefeller name.

Yet Gates had been thinking of something even bigger than the Institute, the GEB, and the Sanitary Commission, something that would stand as the final philanthropy. Its outlines had been hinted at in a letter he sent Rockefeller soon after the "tainted money" controversy in 1905. "I have lived with this great fortune of yours daily for fifteen years," he began with his customary hyperbole. "To it, and especially its uses, I have given every thought. It has been impossible for me to ignore the great question of what is to be the end of all this wealth." He went on to suggest that the best course open was for Rockefeller to "make final disposition of this great fortune in the form of permanent corporate philanthropies for the good of mankind."

In 1910 the great institution that would embody the world mission of the Rockefeller wealth was created when Rockefeller signed over to three trustees—Gates, Mr. Junior, and Harold McCormick, his son-in-law and heir to the International Harvester fortune—$50 million worth of Standard Oil securities for the initial funding of the $100 million Rockefeller Foundation. The following year, Senator Nelson Aldrich, father-in-law of John D. Rockefeller, Jr., and one of the most powerful men in Congress, introduced a bill to obtain a federal charter for what would be the greatest philanthropic foundation in the world.

Despite Rockefeller's munificence during the previous decade and the exaggerated first announcement of the Foundation, which indicated that it would administer an endowment of some $500 million, there was still suspicion. Skeptics pointed out the peculiar timing of the Rockefeller gifts—that a large $32 million gift had been made to the General Education Board in 1907 at the time of the Landis decision, and now $100 million five days before the Standard's attorneys filed their briefs with the Supreme Court in the dissolution suit against the trust. President Taft opposed the Aldrich measure and said that it was really a "bill to incorporate Mr. Rockefeller." Theodore Roosevelt remarked, "Of course no amount of charities in spending such fortunes can compensate in any way for the misconduct in acquiring them." And AFL President Samuel Gompers snorted, "The one thing that the world could gracefully accept from Mr. Rockefeller now would be the establishment of a great endowment of research and education to help other people see in time how they can keep from being like him."

The idea that John D. Rockefeller meant well was still greeted with skepticism. For a full three years, Aldrich struggled mightily to push the bill through Congress, allowing amendments to dispel suspicions: no more than $100 million in total property would be allotted to the Foundation; new trustees would be confirmed by a majority vote of the President and Vice-President of the United States, the Chief Justice of the Supreme Court, president pro tempore of the Senate, speaker of the House, and other officials. But it still didn't pass.

Rockefeller revoked the initial gift and then tried for a charter from the state of New York, where legislators were not so particular. In 1913 the Foundation was finally chartered, and true to his word, Rockefeller put aside $100 million for this institution whose stated purpose was nothing less than "to promote the well-being of mankind throughout the world."

Within a few years after its establishment, the Foundation had in fact become the international presence Gates had foreseen in his early dreams, involving itself in a variety of relief and educational campaigns at home and abroad and carrying the campaign against hookworm and yellow fever into the same tropical lands of the Pacific where Christian missionaries were laboring and U.S. corporations and military expeditions were establishing outposts. The Foundation became a major factor in the national life even sooner than Gates had dared hope. Not long after its creation, he was writing proudly to an associate that they had been fortunate to be "engaged together in an exacting, stupendous enterprise pregnant with measureless destinies."

The full impact of the institutions he had been so instrumental in creating would become clear only in the life and times of John D. Rockefeller, Jr., and his children. When the 73-year-old Gates stepped down from the leadership of the institution that was his *summa,* he realized that one day it might well be as powerful as Standard Oil itself. "When you die and come to approach the judgment of the Almighty God, what do you think He will demand of you?" he asked his colleagues at his retirement dinner. "Do you for an in-

stant presume to believe that He will inquire into your petty
failures or trivial virtues? No. He will ask just one question,
What did you do as a trustee of the Rockefeller Foundation?"

4

THOREAU ONCE OBSERVED that "philanthropy is almost the
only virtue which is sufficiently appreciated by mankind."
Americans were indeed impressed by the great Rockefeller
charities. Their advent happened to come at a time when the
wave of hatred had crested. The great muckraking attacks by
Lloyd and Tarbell had come and gone; the "tainted money"
controversy had long since been resolved to the embarrassment of the Congregationalists. Rockefeller's benefactions—
which would reach over $500 million by his death—had been
well publicized and well timed.

In the iron law of the pendulum's swing, there began a
slow reversal of the public's reaction to the Rockefeller name,
a reshaping of opinion that seemed spontaneous but in its
own way was an impressive labor. The most crucial step was
the decision to abandon the policy of silence that the Standard had always pursued, a policy nicely summarized in a
maxim of Rockefeller's personal attorney, Starr J. Murphy:
"Uncover no surface unnecessarily." In 1907 the company
hired a former journalist, Joseph I. C. Clarke, to be its publicity agent. This was a bold step. It was not merely the fact
Clarke was only the second public relations man ever retained by American industry (the first and the acknowledged
master of the craft, Ivy Lee, later became a loyal Rockefeller
man but was then working for the Pennsylvania Railroad);
but, more important, it meant that there would now be an offensive on behalf of the trust and its creator.

Given an office staff of three and complete access to the
Standard's files and executives, Clarke went right to work. As
he later said in his autobiography, "I followed my plan of going into the open for the Company. When a paper made an
attack on the Standard Oil I hunted up the facts, stated them

briefly, had the local Standard Oil agent call on the editor and demand that he should print it. It worked wonderfully. Standard Oil emerged from the sub-cellar."

Rockefeller himself benefited as much as the company. Instead of scathing chronicles of his money-making schemes and the human wreckage he had left behind him published by muckraking journals like *McClure's*, Clarke arranged for him to discuss his philosophy of giving in the pages of *Woman's Home Companion* and other magazines willing to entertain a gentler view of an aging millionaire. Two official biographies of Rockefeller were commissioned. The first, by a Baptist minister, was read aloud to the Standard board of directors as each chapter was completed, but was left unfinished at the author's death; the second, by Syracuse University's Chancellor James Roscoe Day, was finished, but was such a whitewash that it was dismissed out of hand even by Rockefeller partisans.* In 1908, with the able assistance of Starr J. Murphy, Rockefeller recollected his past in tranquillity in the pages of *Random Reminiscences*. The autobiography was serialized in *World's Work* by editor Walter Hines Page, one of the trustees of the General Education Board and later ambassador to the Court of St. James's.

Imperceptibly a change began to occur, especially after 1913, when the masterful Ivy Lee took over the job of beautifying Rockefeller's public image. The question of how much emphasis to place on the immense benefactions had been a sticky one since Gates first formed the Institute for Medical Research. Rockefeller himself realized that it should not look like guilt money. In a letter to his son he said, "In some of the papers we notice from time to time the statement that after I had accumulated the great fortune I began to give it away. I think that gradually and carefully, through Mr. Lee ... this should be corrected, and made to appear as it really was, that in the beginning of getting the money back in my childhood, I began to give it away."

Yet Lee didn't have to be schooled in his art. He never announced the large sums with which Rockefeller occasionally increased the endowments of the foundations, fearing it would appear egocentric. Instead he arranged for the recipients of Rockefeller bounty to make grateful announcements.

*The search for the right biographer for Rockefeller would take a good deal of time, energy, and money before historian Allan Nevins was finally selected. An interesting story in its own right, it is discussed in the bibliographic note beginning on p. 626.

Lee planted feature stories of the aging billionaire's trips to church, his relations with neighbors, his golf games. His idea was to promote, in a low-keyed way, a new view of Rockefeller the human being.

The attempt to change the public's view of the family was aided by Rockefeller's unflagging belief that he had indeed been traduced. Late in life, when describing the South Improvement plan, he proposed the unique view that the Standard actually acted in self-defense. "Cleveland was some distance from the oil fields, and under a mistaken idea the producers who drilled for oil in Pennsylvania started a war on us. One said, 'We will wipe Cleveland off the map as with a sponge.' And soon we were fighting for our lives." But most of all he was aided by his amazing longevity. Hale and hearty through his seventies and then his eighties, he outlived all who had worked with him. H. H. Rogers had died in 1909, his funeral being the last occasion that would draw Rockefeller back to 26 Broadway; John Archbold had passed from the scene in 1916, and William Rockefeller in 1922.

The old guard was passing on, and the generation that had come of age thinking Rockefeller a demon was succeeded by one that knew primarily of the international munificence of the Rockefeller Foundation, or of the fact that the father of Standard Oil had bought millions of bonds for the Great War. When the public saw John D. Rockefeller, it was not in top hat, cutaway, and pin-striped pants surrounded by Pinkertons on his way to a Senate hearing, but playing a round of golf in his knickers or posed with his son's five boys on the spacious lawns of Pocantico. He was becoming a legend in his own time. By 1926 the *Saturday Evening Post* was writing, "It can be said with accuracy that John D. has met all the problems that life presents to a man—fatherhood, personal purity, finance, duty to posterity, longevity, religion— and answered every one with brilliant finality." He had become an oracle to be consulted on finance and a variety of homey problems.

For others, old age might be a time when an autumnal spirit of reconciliation replaced the passions of youth, but for Rockefeller, who had never allowed himself such passions, it was just another passage from one stage of a self always under control to another. He was known to cry only twice— once when returning to the breakfast table after learning of his wife's death, and the other time when hearing—incorrectly as it worked out—that the upstate New York farmhouse where he had been born was being raised on jacks for transport to Coney Island. He went to his first stage entertainment—a Weber and Fields musicale—but was not impressed enough to go again. He remained what he had always been—a businessman. Each morning he retired for two hours to a private office at Kikjuit, the manor house at his Pocantico estate, to buy and sell stocks over the telephone. It was business, but also a type of diversion—a form of shadow boxing that reminded him of the great fights of the old days.

After the marriage of his daughter Edith to Harold Fowler McCormick, Rockefeller held up to $30 million worth of International Harvester stock. His agreement with Morgan on the Mesabi property had made him the largest stockholder in U.S. Steel and given him a seat on the board of directors. He had invested heavily in a fledgling enterprise called General Motors and continued to hold controlling interests in Consolidated Coal and Colorado Fuel and Iron. The trust was dead, but Rockefeller continued to hold controlling interest in the constituent companies. As late as 1931, he had some 23 percent of Standard of New Jersey, 18 percent of Standard of Ohio, 15 percent of Standard of California, and 10 percent of Standard of Indiana.*

Rockefeller's old schoolmate and chum Mark Hanna had once said that John D. was "mad about money," and there was nothing in his retirement to dispel that notion. He was never especially ungenerous with his employees, nor was he extravagant. One of the army of groundskeepers at Pocantico would be amused but hardly surprised when he received a five-dollar Christmas bonus, only to be docked five dollars for spending the holiday with his wife and children. The Rockefeller family employees never got Labor Day off, John D. explaining, "Instead of spending money on amusements, my employees will be given an opportunity of adding to their savings. Had they been given a holiday, no doubt their money would have been spent foolishly."

He was the sort of man who had gone around after work turning down the gas jets, who had once admonished George Rogers after Rogers had told Rockefeller he need not return a nickel he had borrowed for a phone call: "No, Rogers,

*World War I greatly increased the value of these companies. In 1918 Standard of New Jersey had a net income of $45 million, Standard of New York $29 million, and Standard of California $31 million. The constituent companies that formerly made up the Standard trust showed an income of $450 million for the year.

don't forget this transaction; this is a whole year's interest on a dollar." Yet he was no miser. His family lived regally, if not in the ostentatious elegance of the Goulds, Fricks, and Morgans. But they were not allowed to waste the money he had consecrated his life to making.

Rockefeller really had no way of understanding value except in dollar terms. He was not interested in books or ideas. Money was the philosophical center of his world throughout his long life. Even when he was supervising the building of his Pocantico estate, his greatest joy would be in keeping accounts that showed the paper profits being made by the nursery that sold seedlings to his other estates. Everything had a price in his orderly universe. In 1915, when his 41-year-old son asked him for permission and money to buy what was held to be Praxiteles' *Aphrodite*, Rockefeller replied: "The price you propose to offer for it is four times as much as the price at which we supposed we had secured it in the beginning. I am wondering if we could realize this on it?" Afterward, he always obscurely referred to the brown-colored statue, with rare sarcasm, as the "Chocolate Venus."

Rockefeller had had one great passion—the Standard—and once he stopped his involvement with this institution that had so consumed his life, he was like a salmon at the end of spawn, content to remain in the shadows, confident that he had fulfilled his destiny. He relaxed. He had always been given to odd moments of excitement. His son, who had been manager of the Brown football team, would always remember coaxing him to come to watch the Carlisle game; the elder Rockefeller began by making the journey out of a sense of family obligation, but by the fourth quarter was striding nervously up and down the sidelines in his top hat urging the Brown team on. Now, as he grew older, he allowed himself the eccentricities befitting one who had weathered the storm of public resentment and become a sort of national resource, a name to be used in jokes and the lyrics of popular songs as a harmless synonym for great wealth.

There was the matter of giving out coins, for example—at first nickels, and then nickels for children and dimes for adults. In part this was a public relations ploy, sprung from the fertile imagination of Ivy Lee. But Rockefeller took to it with enthusiasm. Of the estimated thirty thousand shiny new dimes he gave out in his later years, most were accompanied with the sort of admonition that might well have fallen from his own mother's lips: "A dime for the bank, a penny to spend." Wherever he went, people waited with palms up, clamoring for one of the coins as if in hopes that some of the genius of the giver would rub off on them. Rockefeller kept a few horse chestnuts in his pockets and would occasionally slip one of them into an outstretched hand, saying playfully that it was good for the rheumatism.

His sister-in-law, Lucy Spelman, had once said that Rockefeller was "soberly mirthful," and a certain distant humor did manifest itself as he became increasingly aware of his age and mortality. Often he would rise from the breakfast table and head for his office, saying: "Well, I guess I'll see what I can do to keep the wolf away from the door." Once, when getting a massage and hearing the bones snap, he was heard to mutter under his breath: "All the oil in the country, they say, and not enough to oil my own joints." On another occasion, when the famous sculptor Jo Davidson had come to do his bust, Rockefeller asked if the preliminary work of the sitting could somehow take place while he played golf, since he hated to waste time.

"That would be rather difficult," Davidson told him. "I can hardly carry my clay with me."

Rockefeller thought for a moment and then replied, "No? I have to carry mine with me—all the time."

He had homes in New York, Florida, and Seal Harbor, Maine. He built a retreat in Lakewood, New Jersey, called "Golf House," where he pursued the passion of his old age. But after the old Forest Hill estate in Cleveland burned down in 1917, Pocantico remained his true love. He had come there first in 1893 after his brother William had bought a small piece of property near the Sleepy Hollow area of the Ichabod Crane legend. He came to love this area. His sons and grandsons might have large, international aspirations, but after his retirement, spiritually he never strayed from Pocantico. Whenever he traveled to his other homes, he had the fresh vegetables and fruits grown there trucked after him; the water from its Rock Cut Spring was bottled and sent to him also.

His activity varied so little from day to day that it seemed almost a ritual. In the itinerary handed the press on one of his birthdays was a regimen befitting a man whose earlier life had gone far to illustrate Poor Richard's dictum that Time Is Money: 6:30—gets up; 7:00 to 8:00—reads daily papers; 8:00 to 8:30—breakfasts; 8:30 to 8:45—chats; 8:45 to 10:00—attends to business affairs; 10:00 to 12:00—nine holes of golf; 12:00 to 1:15—takes bath and rests; 1:15 to 3:00—lunches, plays Numerica; 3:00 to 5:00—takes an auto ride: 5:00 to 7:00—rests, is read to; 7:00—dines; 8:00 to 10:00—plays Numerica, listens to music played by valet; 10:00—retires.

He seemed to shrink with the passing years, and by the time he reached his nineties, weighed less than a hundred pounds. His thin face had become the texture of an old brown parchment manuscript, as brittle as the Dead Sea Scrolls and so seamed that the mouth and eyes appeared held in place by a carefully constructed network of tiny scars. He ate like a bird, taking a mouthful of food from each of several dishes set before him. He became a vestige from a former age, given a kind of grace by the sheer number of the years he had accumulated. He became an eccentric figure, "riding" a bicycle by balancing on the seat and having a valet push him with one hand and hold a parasol over him with the other. He played golf every day, even if it meant calling out a small army of servants to shovel several inches of snow off the course, and even when he was in his late eighties could hit a ball over one hundred yards off the tee. Whatever the weather, Rockefeller would ready himself for his daily automobile ride by donning a paper vest, aviatorlike goggles, and a duster cap whose flaps hung down the sides of his face like a hound's ears. Each year he would appear before the whirring newsreel cameras on the day of his birth, tipping his straw hat, smiling, and occasionally delivering a sober message, preserved by Pathe talking newsreels, which captured him murmuring almost inaudibly through an old man's shrunken lips, "God bless Standard Oil, God bless us all."

His birthdays were a major event for the local people, whose children came to see the bands play and to gorge themselves on ice cream and cake. He fell into the role of the "Laird of Kikjuit," watching his family expand and multiply according to the best biblical injunction, outpacing the Stillman Rockefeller line his brother William had sired. Bessie, his oldest daughter, had married Dr. Charles Strong, a professor at Cornell and son of the prominent Baptist clergyman Augustus Strong. She died in 1906 at the age of forty. Her only child, Margaret, married the Marquis George du Cuevas, a Spanish nobleman, in an international romance that John D. found somewhat shocking. The second daughter, Alta, married E. Parmalee Prentice, a young Chicago lawyer who later moved to New York to found the law firm that handled the Rockefeller family business and through mergers eventually became the blue-ribbon firm of Milbank, Tweed. Only Edith, the third daughter, gave him pain.

After her 1895 marriage to Harold Fowler McCormick, heir to the International Harvester fortune, in an event seen more as a merger of two mighty corporations than a wedding, Edith had moved to Chicago and adopted a regal style. One evening she wore a $2 million string of pearls; the next a $1 million emerald necklace with 1,657 small diamonds; her sumptuous dinners were served on gold service that once belonged to the Bonapartes. Her father might have tolerated simple ostentation; it was her extramarital affairs and peculiar intellectual predilections that embarrassed him. She became fanatically involved in psychoanalysis, studying in Switzerland under Jung for several years and then returning to America to claim that this new art would allow her to cure tuberculosis and other diseases. She then gravitated to astrology and reincarnation, claiming once that she was the reappearance of Akn-es-en-pa-Aten, child bride of a pharaoh.

In 1921 Edith divorced her husband, who remarried at the age of fifty and underwent a well-publicized gland transplant.* She went on to squander her millions and have flamboyant affairs with male secretaries, bequeathing one of them, a Swiss named Edward Krenn, one-half of her estate on her death in 1932.

But while Edith, Bessie, Alta, and their children would occasionally show up at Christmas or on the patriarch's birthday, it was clear that Pocantico was one place where primogeniture ruled. The daughters were given liberal inheritances during their lifetimes, but the son, John D. Rockefeller, Jr., got the family name and its burdens, and eventually the vast fortune of some $500 million for himself and his heirs. For the future, he and his line would in effect be the only Rockefellers.

---

*The donor was said to have been a blacksmith, which inspired a rhyme that went around Chicago drawing rooms:
> Underneath the spreading chestnut tree
> the village smithy stands;
> The smith a gloomy man is he,
> McCormick has his glands.

PART II

The Son

"The root of the kingdom is in the state. The root of the state is in the family. The root of the family is in the person of its head."

—MENCIUS

The Son

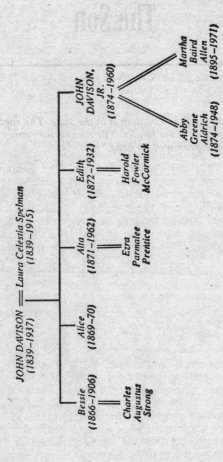

JOHN DAVISON == Laura Celestia Spelman
(1839–1937)   (1839–1915)

Bessie   Alice   Alta   Edith   JOHN DAVISON,
(1866–1906)   (1869–70)   (1871–1962) (1872–1932)   JR.
                                                     (1874–1960)

Charles   Ezra   Harold
Augustus   Parmalee   Fowler
Strong   Prentice   McCormick

Abby   Martha
Greene   Baird
Aldrich   Allen
(1874–1948)   (1895–1971)

IN THE WINTER of 1874, John D. Rockefeller, Sr. was at the midpoint of his career. Twelve years earlier he had begun the firm of Clark & Rockefeller; twelve years ahead lay the creation of the great Standard trust. It was a momentary calm in a career whose velocity was unequaled by any of the other giants of the Gilded Age. He was not yet notorious, but a perceptive few understood that he was a young man who was going places. If he was not yet the richest man in the world or even in Cleveland, he was still able to hold his own among the new class of industrial patricians that had taken over this tough city of iron and oil. Everything he touched seemed to turn to profit. And on January 29, the good fortune that had followed him through his life touched him once again when Cettie was delivered of a son and heir. The boy was fat and healthy. Naturally he was named John D. Rockefeller, Jr.

Years later, Edith Rockefeller would refer to her brother, not without an undertone of jealousy, as the "Crown Prince." Yet the title related more to his position as bearer of the name and fortune than to any special privileges accorded him, for his childhood was far from pampered. A short, somewhat sickly child with a Spelman's square jaw, large mouth, and vulnerable eyes, Mr. Junior (the nickname came from his precocious insistence that there could be only *one* John D. Rockefeller) grew up shy and serious, and usually alone. No playmates came to the Euclid Avenue home; his walks through the woods around the family estate at Forest Hill were solitary except at those times when the gatekeeper's son could be conscripted as a companion. There were long hours at church, but they did little to relieve his loneliness, since the congregation, as he later said in an unguarded moment, "was made up of lower middle class people whom we didn't find particularly congenial."

The family was his only resource, and his growth was inward toward it. He saw his father as the kind of hero out of whom legends are made. The elder Rockefeller was just then at the peak of his manhood, a figure to stay forever in a boy's imagination—tall and purposeful, with blue eyes that looked as if they could freeze steel, and full, reddish whiskers. If others saw the thin mouth as cruel, at home it was often turned up in laughter. Later in life, reminiscing warmly about his father, Junior said, "He was one of us. He taught us to swim, row, skate, and drive horses. . . . At Forest Hill he loved to make footprints through the woods and when we learned to bicycle we used to ride these paths in the moonlight."

Such tantalizing moments of intimacy were memorable mainly because they occurred so infrequently. As Junior grew up, his father was more and more occupied with the wars of conquest he fought as the head of Standard Oil. It was not that he enjoyed time spent away from wife and family; on the contrary, home and family for him were bastions against the world. Once, on a trip that kept him in New York longer than he liked, he wrote back forlornly to Cettie in Cleveland: "I feel more than ever . . . the world is full of Sham, Flattery and Deception; our home is a haven of rest and freedom." Yet the empire he was building demanded his fullest energy and attention.

During these frequent absences, his son's only role was as the harem male in the matriarchy that made up the Rockefeller household. There was Grandmother Eliza, thin and severe and as fond of her successful son as she was sensitive about her own absent husband. ("She always sat next to Father at the table," Junior recalled of her, "and how well I can remember often seeing him hold her hand lovingly.") There was also his mother's sister, Lucy, the aunt he called "Lute," who changed from a frequent visitor to a permanent part of the household when she passed that invisible line separating eligibility for marriage from spinsterhood. There was Grandmother Spelman, who had come to live with her son-in-law after her husband's death. As ardent a supporter of Prohibition as she had been of abolition two decades earlier, she was a leader in the Ohio Temperance Union's crusade against the Demon Rum and convinced her only grandson to become active in children's temperance meetings. Before his tenth birthday, she got Junior to take the pledge to "abstain from tobacco, profanity and drinking intoxicating beverages." When he stood before her and repeated the poem it had taken days to memorize, Grandmother Spelman was moved to tears:

Five cents a glass, does anyone think
That this is really the price of a drink?
The price of a drink, let him decide
Who has lost his courage and his pride
And who lies a drowning heap of clay
Not far removed from a beast today.

There were his sisters: Bessie, Alta, and Edith, eight, three, and two years older than he. They were his playmates and mentors. Apprenticed to them, he became as proficient at sewing and knitting as he was awkward at sports. The four of them spent long hours sitting in the forks of a favorite beech tree at Forest Hill. Bessie read stories, Junior crocheted his fancywork, and Edith and Alta swung their legs and stared off into the distance. In a peculiarly unnecessary economy, Junior wore their cast-off clothing until the age of eight. "I had to wear hand-me-downs from my sister," he confided to a friend late in life. "Their dresses were always being made over for me."

But of all the women who made up his daily life, his mother was by far the most influential. The small, frail woman with a remarkably strong will moved through his days like a divinity, concentrating her intellect and energies (her son later recalled) on "exemplifying the life of Christ." Her gentle discipline was theological—and irresistible. Coercion was unnecessary. As her sister Lute remarked, "There was a persuasion in her touch as she laid her fingers ever so gently on your arm." Late in life, Junior told a friend that he could not recall having heard his mother so much as speak a "sharp or petulant word to her husband, her children, or any of her household." She was as much a paragon of the household as the father was of the business world.

When someone told the elder Rockefeller that his two finest accomplishments were the Institute for Medical Research and his son, he answered, "The boy's mother must be given credit for the last." Indeed, while Cettie Rockefeller devoted most of her waking hours to all of her children's instruction, calling them rather somberly "my precious jewels, loaned to me for a season to be given back when the call comes," she concentrated special care on the serious boy who would carry the family name on to the next generation. She was not unlike her husband's mother, except that duty, not abhorrence of waste, was her watchword—duty to God, to family, and, in a way, to self. Junior learned her lessons well. Thinking back on his early years, he once said that he could not remember having done anything as a child that he really didn't want to do. This, he said, was "due entirely to Mother, who talked to us constantly about *duty*—and displeasing the Lord and pleasing your parents. She instilled a personal consciousness of right and wrong, training our wills and getting us to want to do the things we ought to do." *Want* and *ought*—there was no war between the two in the Euclid Avenue house.

Every morning there were breakfast table prayers, each member of the family reading in turn from the Bible. Friday was prayer meeting night. On Sunday Mrs. Rockefeller held the "Home Talks," for which she made notes as thoughts came to her during the week. At these fireside chats each of the children was asked to concentrate especially on one sin, discuss it with her, pray with her over it, and resolve to conquer it the following week. The children were urged to consider each act. "Am I right?" the mother made them ask in measuring desire against consequences. "Am I doing my duty?"

The women living in the controlled quiet of the Rockefeller household waged a determined struggle against the profane world that had laid its claim upon their men—the infrequently seen William Avery Rockefeller, John D., and Junior. They clung to their Baptist sobriety and to the principle that life was basically a grave business, where (in Samuel Johnson's words) there was much to be endured and little to be enjoyed, and if good were to triumph over evil, temptation had best be avoided altogether. Cards were forbidden in the Rockefeller home; there were no hot meals on Sundays lest the labor of cooking desecrate the Sabbath. Levity was discouraged on weekdays as well; even the family of uncle William Rockefeller was thought to be a little too frivolous, and this led to a gradual chill between the two Rockefeller branches. "Everything centered around the home and the church, and there was nothing else," Junior remarked later. "We had no childhood friends, no school friends." It was not Ida Tarbell or Henry Demarest Lloyd who were the enemies of Junior's boyhood, but the World, the Flesh, and the Devil.

The sisters, especially the spirited Edith, whose later escapades would be a mighty burden to her father and brother, may have entertained furtive thoughts of rebellion, but it is unlikely that Junior ever did. As he grew up and began to practice handwriting in his copybooks, one of the homey maxims he copied hundreds of times in neat Spenserian script seemed to summarize what he had learned from life thus far: "He who conquers self is the greatest victor." The heirs of the other nineteenth-century fortunes might prepare for a lifetime of amusement and pleasure, but John D. Rockefeller, Jr., was meant for larger things. He had been given custody of the family name and therefore of its honor. It was his duty to see that the world knew his father as he did—as a great man.

Try as she might, there was no way for Cettie Rockefeller to maintain her children in their prelapsarian innocence. For one thing, her husband's associates were always coming and going, many of them smoking black cigars, bearing traces of whiskey on their breath, and swearing loudly in the parlor as they sat late into the night charting strategy for Standard Oil's struggles. For another, money was plentiful in the Rockefeller household, so plentiful in fact that Junior remembered, "it was there like air or food or any other element." The hand-me-down clothes or the fact that the children were made to share one bicycle couldn't change that. But the greatest threat lay outside the walls of Forest Hill and Euclid Avenue. By the time Junior was a teenager, the great fortune had been made and the public outcry against it was reaching its height. He didn't believe the muckraking exposés, yet the feelings of guilt his father managed to escape descended to the boy in double measure.

He worked hard to keep the money at bay. His father helped him, insisting that the fortune had been put in their custody by the Lord and was a special trust not to be wasted. He showed Junior how to keep accounts in a ledger book that mimicked his own Ledger A. It was one thing to keep such accounts if you were an eighteen-year-old bookkeeper setting out to make your way in the world, however, and quite another if you were the crown prince to the throne of Standard Oil. Junior must have suspected that his entries were a parody of his father's: "Practicing the violin at $.05 per hour; Drinking hot water at $.05 per glass; Killing flies at $.02 per fly." But the form was more important than the content; he kept his accounts as the sort of chastening experience he would later require of his own children, as if by meticulous, scientific accounting of the money he could exorcise the taint that contaminated its spirit and control the boundless desire that it called forth.

When he was ten years old, Junior got a change of scene. His father, forced to spend increasing periods of time in New

York, had started bringing his family along. During the Standard's protracted eastern negotiations, he installed Cettie and the children in elegant suites at residential hotels like the Windsor and the Buckingham. When this became impractical, he bought the massive, ivy-colored brownstone at 4 West 54th Street that had once belonged to Collis Huntington, the California railroad man.

The bedrooms, with silk-covered walls, parqueted floors, and mother-of-pearl inlays in the wainscoting, would eventually go on permanent display at the Museum of the City of New York, and the site itself would become the outdoor exhibit area of the Museum of Modern Art. But when Junior first lived in this house, the neighborhood was still so sparsely settled as to seem almost pastoral. He always remembered the sound of the hooped wagon wheels rumbling down the cobblestones of Fifth Avenue, and he took long walks over the vacant lots. What homes there were in the area seemed to make it almost a Standard Oil colony: Flagler had built across the street, and the William Rockefellers had a brownstone down the block.

After 1884, New York was the Rockefellers' legal residence although Cleveland, especially Forest Hill, always remained home in a sentimental sense. The family took up membership in the Fifth Avenue Baptist Church, John D. becoming a deacon and trustee and Cettie Rockefeller teaching Sunday school with such meticulous dedication that she marked a "C" in the margins of her rollbook beside the names of the lucky children she thought to be Christians and therefore saved.

Junior's secular education had been in the hands of tutors, but now his mother decided that it was time for him to go to school. He attended the New York School of Languages for a year and then, at the age of sixteen, enrolled in the fashionable Cutler School. He did well academically, but the strangely neurasthenic quality that had always worried his parents now became more pronounced. It was as if something was always bothering the child; he seemed constantly afraid of making a mistake and allowed himself no moments of high spirits. What his parents circumspectly referred to as a "nervous condition" soon put him in a state of near-collapse. He dropped out of school and went to Forest Hill to recuperate, spending his seventeenth year in seclusion there. It was a year devoted to raking leaves, sawing logs, and cutting down trees, as if such furious labor would drive out his undiagnosed demons, keep him from being so weepy, and make him strong enough for the great work that lay ahead. He spent much of the winter among the frostbitten maple trees, bleeding their syrup and boiling it down to sugar. It was pleasant work, but even such innocent pleasure had to be justified, and Junior kept a detailed account of the yield and the money it brought in a tiny ledger carried in his breast pocket.

The next year he was able to return to Cutler. There followed two years at the Browning School, which he attended along with his cousin Percy Rockefeller and Harold McCormick, the International Harvester heir who was soon courting his sister Edith. By 1893 he was ready for college. Although nearly twenty years old, he was, as he admitted later, "shy, ill-adjusted, and not very robust."

Junior toyed with the idea of going to Yale, but became discouraged on hearing that a "fast set" of students established the tone of that school. After consulting with family friend William Rainey Harper, the man his father had installed as president of the University of Chicago, he decided a smaller college would be more in keeping with a person of his own conservative nature and outlook, and selected Brown. When he left the family for the first time in his life, he was wished godspeed by his grandmother and admonished to follow the path of righteousness by his mother. He arrived in Providence very much the naïf. He couldn't dance and didn't want to; he thought the center on a football field was called "the middle." He was 5 feet 6 inches and weighed 127 pounds, and his square-jawed face, habitually pinched in the forehead and serious, made him seem less like a carefree underclassman than a sanctimonious young vicar out of *Middlemarch*.

He set up housekeeping in a suite of rooms at Slater Hall, the newest dormitory on campus, and amused his new roommates by immediately sitting down to hem his own dish towels. But whatever else he was or wasn't, he was not insincere, and for the first time in his life he began to make friends. He wrote home enthusiastically after his first week to tell his family that the freshman class had already had a spirited prayer meeting, which augured well for the four years ahead, and added that Grandmother Spelman, with her racial sympathies, would be "interested to know that there are three colored men in the class."

In his first year at Brown, Junior expanded considerably.

Although he wrote home weekly to get his mother's advice on such matters as the right clubs to join, he was on his own for the first time in his life. Cettie wrote to say that she could only conclude from the tone of his letters that his life was "largely given over to pleasure." He admitted to inviting friends to his room for snacks of graham crackers and chocolate milk late at night. He even screwed up the courage to tell Grandmother Spelman that he had weighed the matter carefully and decided that he could no longer justly prohibit those who visited his quarters from smoking. But the major crisis—whether or not to dance—did not come until his sophomore year. Primarily because of his mother's well-known objections to such amusement, he had declined all invitations as a freshman. But in his second year, he decided that to continue to do so would mark him off as a wallflower for the rest of his college days. Apprehensively, he accepted an invitation. He was afraid he would slip on the glassy ballroom floor. He was afraid he would forget the geometry of the steps (and had one of his roommates waltz with him before the dance started to make sure he remembered them). But returning home that night, he had to admit such entertainment wasn't bad.

In his second year at Brown he turned twenty-one, and the long arm of the family reached from New York to Providence to mark the occasion by reminding him that great things were expected of him. He got notes of congratulation from Grandmother Spelman and Aunt Lute, and from his mother, who told him: "You can celebrate your birthday in no better way . . . than by such earnest work as I know you are giving for God and the saving of the souls of your fellow students." His father sent him a check for twenty-one dollars, in lieu of candles to mark off the years, and a brief note which said in part: "I cannot tell you how much happiness we all have in you, and how much we are looking forward to and relying on you in the future."

College was in some sense a normalizing experience, momentarily blocking out the future that loomed ahead. For the first and probably the only time in his life, he did the things other young men his age did. He dated girls, went to football games, and attended dances; the summer before his senior year, he grew a neat beard and made a bicycle tour of Europe with a friend. Yet he also persevered in the rituals by which he conserved and controlled money, earning a reputation as something of an eccentric. His fellow students were amused to see the heir to one of the greatest fortunes in the country acting like a scholarship student, trimming frayed edges of his cuffs or standing in rapt concentration over a tea-kettle steaming two stuck postage stamps apart. A standing joke at Brown was that by the time young Rockefeller had finished his careful audit of a dinner check, someone else in the party would have already paid the bill. Stories of Junior's stinginess—for that was the way his efforts were inevitably perceived—circulated through the school. Once, when he was managing the football team (and putting it in the black for the first time), he answered a burly lineman's request for new shoestrings by saying, "What did you do with the pair I gave you last week?" All this became part of the character of "Johnny Rock," his college persona. When he was named chairman of the Junior Celebration, it was expected that he would try to make this traditionally drunken bacchanal into a dry outing. And it was taken with good grace when Johnny Rock succeeded—as he wrote home triumphantly to his mother and grandmother the next day—in marching the party back to Providence at two A.M., "every man on his own feet and without aid—a thing which has never been true of the Junior Celebration before."

His last year at Brown, Junior decided to host a dance to pay back all those who had been hospitable to him. He needed a chaperone and wrote his mother about the problem: "It would give me the greatest pleasure to have you receive upon such an occasion, but feeling as you do about such things it would, I suppose, be quite out of the question." Cettie Rockefeller asked her husband about Junior's request, wondering if perhaps they might not make the counter offer of a musicale, and thus "set a standard of enjoyment better than the dance." But her son insisted, and she reluctantly agreed to appear in evening dress to greet some four hundred of his guests at a rented hall. On the night of the event, however, she was suddenly stricken by a headache, the final recourse of the Victorian lady, and did not leave her hotel room. Attired in tails and white gloves, John D. Rockefeller, Sr., stood solemnly in the receiving line by himself.

By graduation, Junior had rid himself of many of the parochial attitudes with which he had entered Brown. He had become a good enough student to win a Phi Beta Kappa key; the rigorous Spelman morality was now tempered somewhat by a philosophy more in keeping with his father's pragmatic cast of mind. As Junior wrote his Grandmother Spelman,

"My ideas and opinions change, I find, in many ways. I would stickle less for the letter of the law now, more for the spirit."

As the interlude at Brown ended, the future began once again to lean heavily on Junior. By this time his father was under such heavy attack that even his iron constitution had broken, and he had seemingly lost his health. As much as Junior liked to hide behind the carefree plebeian quality of "Johnny Rock," he was still the son and heir, and his duty was clear: to stand by his father in the battle against those who vilified him. He had always known that this would be his lifework. Later in his life an associate asked him if he had ever considered going into the ministry, for which he seemed perhaps better suited. Junior answered, "Absolutely not. My one thought from the time I was a boy was to help my father. I knew from the beginning I was going into his office." It was almost a religious calling, evoking Christ's own words: I must be about my father's work.

6

In 1897, thousands of young men of good family took a last, nostalgic look at the ivied walls and Gothic arches where they had spent their college years and went out to take their places in the bustling world of business. It was a heady moment for the forces of finance and industry in America. In the presidential campaign of the previous year, Mark Hanna, John D. Rockefeller's old schoolmate, had engineered the victory of the gold standard and of "class money" over "mass money," opening the door to a vast boom for American business. Huge corporations were born overnight, and watered stock flowed like a Niagara over the frenetic exchanges as fortunes were won and lost and the center of gravity of American industry shifted inexorably to Wall Street, where the captains of finance ruled the securities markets. It was the money men's version of the frontier epic, the Era of Frenzied Finance.

If 26 Broadway was one of the most fabled financial storm centers of the period, for Junior the romance was missing. The son of John D. Rockefeller could not prove himself in the usual ways: his arrival at this famous address was not an achievement, but an inevitability. With no other alternative, he dutifully journeyed to the office, where he found a heavy oak rolltop desk set aside for him in the small, sparsely furnished room on the ninth floor in which the Rockefellers' private affairs were handled. There he joined George Rogers, his father's personal secretary; a clerk named Charles O. Heydt; Mrs. Tuttle, the telegrapher who also had the task of answering the hate mail; and a contingent of bookkeepers. Presiding over the whole operation was the august Reverend Frederick T. Gates.

Gates's energies were too undisciplined and his passions too much on the surface for Junior to be comfortable with him. But Junior respected Gates and understood that he was to be his mentor; he settled down to an apprenticeship in the family business under the former minister's guidance. After learning the office routine, Junior began taking long rail trips with Gates to visit the Rockefeller investments scattered all over the country. He listened to his father's chief adviser discuss his pet theories: how a fortune as large as his could easily curse a family; how money must be made to pay a social dividend. Junior agreed, but he couldn't quite see where he fit into Gates's plans. In fact, what he was supposed to do in the office was never made explicit. Later he would say this had been a clever strategy on his father's part to make him develop his own interests, but in his early days at 26 Broadway he suffered from the fear that he had stepped into a world where everything was given and nothing could be won on one's own. "I never had the satisfaction of earning my way," he once said wistfully when looking over the office. "The secretaries here have an advantage I never had. They can prove to themselves their commercial worth."

These early days were not happy ones for Junior. He had two strong personalities to deal with—Gates and his father— and no way to define himself. "From the day I entered my father's office until the day of his death," he recalled, "my one desire was to help him in every way in my power. I was always as glad to black his shoes, to pack his bags ... as I later was to represent him in various of his interests, business and philanthropic." But even his one romantic indulgence— to see himself as a paladin bent on removing the stain from the family escutcheon—was balked. It was too large a job, and he did not know how to begin it.

Junior took refuge in details, as he would throughout his life in times of crisis. He became the paymaster for the staff at 26 Broadway and the servants in the various Rockefeller households. He picked out wallpaper for his sister Alta's apartment when she married. He took charge of investing the money his father gave all the family members for Christmas and birthday gifts. He became a kind of master bookkeeper of Rockefeller affairs. At one point he was put in command of filling the inkwells at 26 Broadway. It was the sort of work he had done a decade earlier when he kept accounts of family prayer attendance; while he found a certain security in mastering the routine, these menial jobs only emphasized the chasm between his duties and the expectations that were held for him.

At about this time, Henry Cooper, an old college friend who would eventually become a Rockefeller executive, visited Junior in New York and was surprised to see how melancholy "Johnny Rock" had become. He took it upon himself to write a letter of advice to his old friend: "I think it would do you good, for instance, to take up smoking an occasional cigarette or something of that sort. ... Just try being a shade more reckless or careless ... and see if you don't find more happiness." He might as well have counseled Junior to change his name to Tarbell and take up muckraking: such an unbending was impossible. It would be several decades before Junior could bring himself to admit he had been unhappy at this time, and even then he did not blame his state of mind on his peculiar status at the office (for that would have been to hold his father responsible, however belatedly and indirectly); instead he blamed his own inadequacy. "I had no difficulty when I entered my father's office," he said, "except for my own sense of unfitness. I didn't have any confidence in my own ability." Every time an indication of his state of mind during those early years seemed about to slip out, he always caught himself. In 1921, when he had long since resolved his problems, he told an interviewer from the *Saturday Evening Post*: "I had no opportunity to shape my life. There came great responsibilities which had to be met. I was not necessarily the best one to meet them, but I was the only one ... I suppose if I had had a decided bent for some other line of activity I would not have been at this work, but such was not the case." But then he quickly added, "But don't get the impression that I have not been the happiest of men ... I am grateful for and humble in the presence of the great opportunities that have come to me. Then too, the burdens which I carry are not so oppressive to me as if they had come upon me in middle age. I was born with them and have never known anything else."

If Junior had ever secretly dreamed of following his father's giant footsteps, he had a rude awakening when given his first considerable sum of money to invest. Since first coming into the office, he had borrowed money from his father (at 6 percent a year) to invest in a margin account for himself and Alta, with the profits jointly shared. After a few modest successes, Junior met an investor named David Lamar. Lamar managed to persuade him he had secret information concerning certain important developments that would soon dramatically increase the value of the stock of the U.S. Leather Company. With an eagerness that betrayed an anxiety to prove his commercial worth, Junior invested heavily. Once committed, he bought all the U.S. Leather stock he could get. It was only later that he realized he had been gulled. Lamar (who subsequently became known as the "Wolf of Wall Street") himself owned the stock he had touted and had been unloading it on the rising market that Rockefeller's impetuous buying had created.

Junior's losses amounted to more than a million dollars. He went to his father to confess what had happened. Looking back at him with his impassive eyes, the old man (whom the office staff had begun to call "Mr. Senior") said simply, "All right, John. Don't worry. I will see you through." If anything, the lack of criticism made the pill harder to swallow. A few days later, Junior wrote his father in a paroxysm of contrition: "My one thought and purpose since I came into the office has been to relieve you in every way possible of the burdens which you have carried so long. To realize now that instead of doing that I have been ... instrumental in adding to your burdens is bitter and humiliating."

Like Christian in *Pilgrim's Progress* (with whom a minister would later compare him), Junior tried to turn from worldly matters and concentrate on the Celestial City. In 1900 he took over from future Supreme Court Chief Justice Charles Evans Hughes as leader of the men's Bible class at the Fifth Avenue Baptist Church. In doing so, he became a public person for the first time in his life and immediately got a taste of the odium attached to his father's name. The press, which had snickered at news of his baptismal fleecing by the Wolf of Wall Street (some newspaper accounts joyously inflating Junior's losses to as high as $20 million), now seized upon his publicly professed religion as evidence of hypocrisy. One editorial said, "With the hereditary grip on the nation's pocketbook, he talks on spiritual matters are a tax on piety."

Yet he kept going. After he had been teaching the class for a year, the membership had grown from fifty to over two hundred, although he realized that the increase was not necessarily due to the eloquence of his ministry. Noting that many of the young men seemed to be there hoping for jobs, a *New York Times* journalist who had infiltrated the class later reported Junior's explication of a text from the book of Matthew ("The kingdom of heaven is like unto treasure in the field") with barely concealed irony. "You will find," young Rockefeller was reported to lecture the class, most of whom were clearly of modest means, "that worldly pleasures and possessions are not worth having—not worth having at all when they are gained ... at the expense of character and self-respect. You may be sure that if an individual has no personal character, no ideas, no clear conscience to take home with him at the end of the day, he will have found nothing and will have nothing at the end of his life."

Another Sunday, the two men sent by the church's central office to sit inconspicuously in the class as Junior's bodyguards were amused when he exhorted the young men: "Men, we need fifteen dollars each Sabbath to meet the expenses of the class. I have thought out a plan—let seventy-five men give five cents, fifty contribute ten cents, and twenty-five give us fifteen cents each Sunday. That's twelve fifty. I am sure we can raise the additional two fifty."

Despite a hostile press chortling over such solecisms, Junior's confidence grew to the point that he was ready for something more ambitious, and he arranged to give an address at the Brown University YMCA. In it, he set out to show that Christianity and business were not antithetical, as the populists were then claiming, but actually complementary. Going farther, he argued that competition inevitably led to combination and that his elimination of smaller, less efficient units was a beneficial process. Only through pruning, he said in a turn of phrase he would soon regret, could the American Beauty rose have been developed.

This horticultural metaphor occurred at exactly the moment when Ida Tarbell's *History of the Standard Oil Com-*

pany was being serialized in *McClure's* and making a vast reading public aware of the way the elder Rockefeller had, in cultivating his monopoly, wielded the pruning hook against the independent producers and refiners. Seizing on Junior's imprudent image, the press descended wrathfully. One widely circulated cartoon portrayed him as a ticker tape machine preaching stock market quotations to a Sunday school class. Seven years later, a high-ranking Michigan clergyman could still make news by recalling the metaphor and commenting. "A rose by any other name will smell as sweet, but the odor of *that* rose to me smacks strongly of crude petroleum."

Junior now found his daily habits carefully researched. One enterprising journalist reported that the scion of the world's greatest fortune spent thirty cents a day for lunch. Another titillated his readers with an exposé of young Rockefeller's tipping habits: going one better than his father's shrewd technique of holding out a palmful of change for a porter or waiter to take what he dared, Junior didn't tip at all. When, under the barrage of publicity, he did relent and tipped his barber five cents, the coin was framed and hung on the barbershop wall; this too found its way into the papers.

These were hard times. Far from being able to defend his family from attacks, everything he did seemed to bring even more ridicule on it. And if the addition of "Junior" after his name meant he was a different person from the man who had built Standard Oil, the public never comprehended the difference. He was a Rockefeller, and the world was just then finding out how much it hated Rockefellers.

It was as if his career were foreordained to be the antithesis of his father's: one defeat piled upon another. During his first years at 26 Broadway, Junior would often, on finishing work, hurry to the stone stable behind the 54th Street house; there, he would take off his coat, pick up a saw, and spend hours cutting the logs he had had freighted in from the countryside. He would work furiously until sweat drenched his body and his breath came in hard gasps; then, picking up his coat and running to the house, he'd fling himself down on his bed in physical and spiritual exhaustion.

If Junior's early years at 26 Broadway were marked by fits and starts and emotional crises, there were also moments that would later be seen as turning points. One of them occurred in 1901, when his first and only serious love affair reached a climax.

He met Miss Abby Greene Aldrich at that first fateful dance he had attended at Brown seven years earlier. The daughter of Senator Nelson Aldrich of Rhode Island, she was a pleasant-looking young woman with a long nose, prominent chin, and luxuriant hair in love curls. If not as attractive as other young ladies he had met, she nonetheless made the best of her good features and was the sort of woman who would be called handsome when she reached middle age. More important, she was outgoing, graceful, and cultured—all qualities that Junior lacked. By the time they met, in Junior's sophomore year, she had already made the grand tour of Europe with her sister, stopping at the great art capitals of the world.

Although not as wealthy as the Rockefellers, the Aldriches were a powerful family and had an undeniable legitimacy. Nelson Aldrich was descended from a Bay Colony family on his father's side and from Roger Williams on his mother's; his wife could trace her ancestry back to a Brewster who had made his passage to the New World aboard the *Mayflower*. It was a moment in the country's evolution when such things mattered. A truly national upper class with a common need to define and assert itself had emerged for the first time in American history. Recent decades had seen a frenzied flowering of aristocratic institutions and genealogical societies (like the Sons and Daughters of the American Revolution) through which the old-line families of the eastern seaboard could draw together and distinguish themselves from the suddenly wealthy newcomers of Cleveland and other such provincial outposts.

The Rockefellers did not aspire to genealogical eminence. (Later, when some distant relatives who had founded a Rockefeller Family Association informed John D. that their researchers led them to believe the name could be traced back to noble European origins, the billionaire remained unmoved.) Yet Senior was not unmindful of the practical benefits an alliance with "family" could bring to a tainted name. His own social circle had been bounded by the YMCA, the Temperance Society, and the Fifth Avenue Baptist Church, but he expected Junior to extend the family's social and political reach.*

---

*Most of the storybook marriages of the time were between continental nobility and wealthy young American women. Yet the significant marriages occurred at home, serving to unite almost all the wealthy families as distant cousins or even closer. There was the bond of the

Nelson Aldrich was almost as commanding a name in the U.S. Congress as Rockefeller was in industry. Entering the Senate in 1881 as a man whose worth was estimated at $50,-000, he left thirty years later, having ruled the upper chamber under seven presidents and amassed a fortune of $30 million. At a time when the Senate was irreverently known as the "Millionaires' Club," when senators were not yet elected by popular vote and were each said to represent one of the Vested Interests, Nelson Aldrich was reputed to represent them all. The political "boss of the United States," Lincoln Steffens called him in a 1905 muckraking article in *McClure's* that drew attention to his favors to the sugar trust. And when David Graham Phillips came to write *The Treason of the Senate,* a sensational series appearing in William Randolph Hearst's *Cosmopolitan,* the second article was devoted entirely to the senator from Rhode Island. A close friend of Morgan and a bitter enemy first of William Jennings Bryan and then La Follette, he saw his major task (as he once said) to be "bringing politics and business closer together."

Even if the match hadn't been such a natural alliance for both families, an obvious affection between Junior and Abby existed from the first time he had gotten up the courage to ask her to dance with him. Taking pity on his social backwardness, she had helped him conquer an instinctive urge to consort with wallflowers, and during the rest of his college career, his name was penciled frequently on her social calendar. He traveled extensively with her family and became familiar enough with her wants to keep a supply of graham crackers in his jacket pocket for her to snack from when they went on walks in the woods near the Aldrich summer home in Maine.

All the signs of a serious courtship were present. Almost every Sunday he would take her to church in Providence, then off to some amusement like a canoe trip down the Ten-Mile River, and finally back to the Aldrich home at 110 Benevolent Street for a light supper of Welsh rarebit. She, in turn, had come to New York to visit his parents and let them look her over.

William Rockefellers and the Stillmans. One of the girls of this union (Geraldine Stillman Rockefeller) married Marcellus Dodge, scion of the Remington arms fortune. A son, James Stillman Rockefeller, married Carnegie's niece Nancy. Meanwhile, the blood of John D.'s old partners at the Standard, Harkness and Payne, soon mixed with that of the Vanderbilts and Whitneys. "High" society became an increasingly small world.

Throughout his senior year, it was widely assumed that their engagement would soon be announced. But when Junior graduated and went off to work at 26 Broadway, he went as Abby's beau, not her fiancé. From 1897 to 1901 he often commuted to Providence to spend weekends with the Aldriches, and he traveled with the family to Cuba in March 1900 aboard President McKinley's yacht, *The Dolphin*. The knowledge that his ambivalence allowed other suitors to call during the week at the Benevolent Street house and enjoy Welsh rarebits and games of charades with Miss Aldrich hardly helped to lift the sense of dread that began when he boarded the midnight sleeper Sunday night so he could be at 26 Broadway on Monday morning. Still, he could not make up his mind.

A decade afterward, in a talk to his men's Bible class, Junior referred mysteriously to a dilemma he had faced earlier in his life and had overcome only by "years of fervent praying to learn what God wanted." Almost half a century later, he admitted that this crisis was whether or not to marry Abby Aldrich. "I was very fond of her," he explained in a candid conversation with his friend Raymond Fosdick, "but I always had a dread of marrying somebody and finding out I loved somebody else. . . . I prayed about it for four years."

Yet it was his mother, not his Lord, who finally came to the rescue. Junior and Abby knew that their romance was not progressing and had decided to submit it to one of those trials by ordeal so popular in the middlebrow fiction of the day. They would not see or write each other for half a year. But long before the test period had expired the agitated Junior, already miserable in his career, had turned to Cettie for advice about this lingering affair of the heart. "Of course you love Miss Aldrich," his mother bluntly wrote him. "Why don't you go and get her?" Two days later, Junior was on a train heading for Warwick, the Aldrich summer home on an island in Narragansett Bay. He had a formal audience with Senator Aldrich on his yacht moored off Newport, and while he did not beg for Abby's hand on bended knee, he did amuse his future father-in-law (who, according to Aldrich family tradition, always secretly believed young Rockefeller to be something of a prig) by launching seriously into a detailed audit of his financial prospects.

The marriage took place in October 1901 at Warwick. For his guests, the elder Rockefeller reserved several suites of rooms at the Narragansett Hotel. He chartered two steamers to take them across to the island, where streetcars conveyed them to the estate. "For several days past," went the *Times* account of the reception, "every boat and train from New York, Washington, Newport and other cities has brought its quota of guests prominent in social and political circles in the country." Over one thousand guests were present, and to the mild annoyance of the Rockefeller entourage, champagne was served.

The newspaper headlines blazed "Beauty Weds Wealth," and reporters tried to follow the couple on their honeymoon, but Junior managed to escape with his bride to Pocantico, which his parents had vacated to ensure their privacy. It was an interlude of long walks in the white frosts of early morning and the fiery autumn colors of the afternoon. The romance consummated there would, in a true sense, last forever. A few weeks later, Junior wrote his mother a rhapsodic letter thanking her for helping him make up his mind. There had been only one discordant note in their first idyllic days together: when Junior had commanded his bride to keep a close account of daily expenses, in the Rockefeller manner, she had flatly refused. He didn't mention this small insubordination to his mother, although he did note, a little uncertainly, that she had never given an opinion of his new bride. "She seems a wife made to order for you," Cettie had written back, thus resolving the son's last doubts.

Abby was his antithesis in many ways. She was gay and social while he was constrained; she was as impulsive as he was cautious. If not brilliant, she was clever enough to humor one elderly lady who kept calling her "Mrs. Roosevelt" all during a long afternoon visit. In fact, her new father-in-law felt that she was perhaps too frivolous. "Your father is afraid that I shall become intimate with too many people," she wrote Junior when she, leaving him at work in New York, had accompanied his parents on a trip. "So generally we eat in what I call the old people's dining room where he feels I am safer." Yet the Rockefellers soon accommodated themselves to her.*

---

*Junior would always be a one-woman man, but his touching affection for Abby had its humorous side. Washington *Post* reporter Chalmers Roberts was told a story about Rockefeller by onetime Secretary of State Christian Herter, who had heard it from his father, an artist and acquaintance of Junior's. "Pa" Herter, who lived in Paris, was painting a beautiful nude model when Rockefeller called to say he was coming for a visit. "Pa told Yvonne that a rather straitlaced visitor would soon arrive, and so she should sit immobile while he talked with

After their honeymoon, the newlyweds moved in with Junior's parents at 4 West 54th Street until the home they had rented across the street at 13 West 54th was vacant. Soon after moving in, they began to fill it with children. Their firstborn, Abby (1903), was their only daughter: then came the five sons who were destined to play so great a role in the next generation: John D 3rd (1906), Nelson (1908), Laurance (1910), Winthrop (1912), and David (1915). By the time Laurance was born, the family had moved into the town house Junior had built next door to his father's house. Number 10 West 54th, where the children would spend their youth and adolescence, was one of the largest private residences in Manhattan at the time, its nine stories including a nursery, a gymnasium, and spacious quarters for servants and employees.

The growing family alternated between 54th Street and Abeynton Lodge, the old house that had come with the Pocantico property and sat within shouting distance of Kikjuit. And whenever he could take time from 26 Broadway, Junior and Abby traveled. They fell in love with the brooding Maine coast, especially the island of Mount Desert, a beautiful twenty-mile oval of green mountains and lakes. Nelson was born there in a cottage they had rented for the summer. Two years later, in 1910, they found a mansion for sale. Perched above a cove at Seal Harbor and aptly named the Eyrie, it had 104 rooms and was built of Maine granite and had shingles deeply weathered by the moist coastal climate. They remodeled the huge house and landscaped the spacious grounds, adding an Oriental garden and surrounding the property with a fence topped with tiles that had once been part of the Great Wall of China.

Abby Aldrich Rockefeller soon became active in the cultural and social life of New York. She had become a partisan of the modernism pounding at the gates of the tradition-bound art establishment shortly after the celebrated Armory show of 1913. She had collected the Old Masters that appealed to her husband's taste, but began to buy more contemporary works, as she said, to have artifacts her children

---

Rockefeller. He had hardly arrived when he caught sight of the sensuous nude. He could hardly take his eyes off the girl. His not very furtive glances began to annoy Yvonne. Without a word she slowly stood up in all her naked splendor, touched the floor with her fingers, threw herself upside down, and walked on her hands directly up to Rockefeller. With a look of horror, he fled to the door. Before reaching it he turned to Pa and cried out: "Don't ever tell my wife about this!"

would "be interested in and want to live with." In 1929 she
became one of the founders of the Museum of Modern Art,
to which the family ultimately donated all its property on
West 54th Street. But for Junior, she was more than a society
matron enhancing the prestige of the Rockefeller family. She
was the one person with whom he could be himself, indiscriminately revealing weakness and strength, momentarily
relinquishing the awesome control that had governed his public and private existence for the first twenty-five years of his
life. Junior hated to be away from her; when he was, he
wrote back impassioned love letters graphically describing the
ways in which he longed for her. Toward the end of his own
life, when Abby had been dead for many years and he was
going through his private papers for the family archives, he
came across these letters, which Abby had saved. After
rereading them and discussing the matter with an associate
who was helping him sort through the papers, he decided that
some of the correspondence should be burned because of passages that were so intensely private, and so passionately real.

7

AT THE TURN of the century, when many of the great figures
who had reshaped American industry were beginning to pass
on, the attention being paid to the transfer of their fortunes
was as great as if they had been titled nobles. It was expected
that most inheritors would simply waste the money. The famous John W. Gates, whose raids on the stock market and
daring gambles in the steel industry had earned him the sobri-
quet "Bet-a-Million" Gates, left his fortune to a son whose
excesses so delighted the public that the newspapers dubbed
him "Spend-a-Million" Gates. No one thought Junior would
become a prodigal, but there was curiosity about what he
would do with the great Standard Oil fortune. In 1905
Hearst's *Cosmopolitan* published a symposium titled "What
Will He Do With It?" The lead article began:

No little interest is centered upon the world's greatest fortune, that of Mr. John D. Rockefeller. The fortune will in the course of years be inherited by the Son, Mr. John D. Rockefeller Jr. It is needless to say that the power of the money covers so vast a territory that a man inheriting such a fortune has it within his power to revolutionize the world . . . or use it so evilly as to retard civilization for a quarter of a century.

Yet these were questions for others to ask. For the time being at least, Junior would be happy simply to take hold at 26 Broadway and pull his own weight there. Marriage and a family of his own had helped stabilize any doubts he had about his mission. Moreover, there had been signs that he had become more comfortable in his father's office even before he had put the question to Miss Aldrich. He had scored his first unqualified success as a Rockefeller during the latter stages of his father's struggle for control of the Mesabi iron ore properties. Frederick Gates had been the general in the affair, yet Junior had made an effective soldier in the protracted negotiations. The high point came when Henry Rogers, most colorful of the brigands from the Standard Oil Gang, took him to call on J. P. Morgan, then negotiating to obtain the properties for the giant U.S. Steel syndicate he had almost finished assembling.

"Well, what's your price?" Morgan had growled, his thick brows contracting and his huge carbuncular nose flaming angrily.

"I think there must be some mistake," Junior had replied with a self-possession that made this a favorite anecdote for his father to mimic for dinner guests in years to come. "I did not come here to sell. I understand you wished to buy."

After word of the encounter reached his parents at Pocantico, Cettie Rockefeller wrote to congratulate her son, telling him that when his father read the letter describing the meeting with Morgan, he had said aloud, "Great Caesar, but John is a trump!"

After this, Junior became more prominent in the family's affairs, his father entrusting him with more and more responsibility until he had become a vice-regent for the Rockefeller interests. He was put on the boards of the National City Bank, United States Steel, Standard of New Jersey, Colorado Fuel and Iron, several railroads, and the University of Chi-

cago. In all, he became a director of seventeen of the largest
financial and industrial corporations in the country. A sign
that he was doing well was his father's decision to increase
his salary. Like the time he had given Cettie a knitting basket
containing one hundred $5 gold pieces for Christmas, it was
the elder Rockefeller's way of showing affection. The 28-
year-old son wrote his father an effusive note of thanks:

> Dear Father;
> My breath was completely taken away by what you
> told me regarding my salary for the year that has passed
> when I was at the house the other night. I appreciate
> more deeply than I can tell you this added expression of
> your love and confidence. I cannot feel that any services
> I can render are worth to you such a sum as $10,000 a
> year. Of my ability I have always had a very poor opin-
> ion, but I need not assure you that such as it is, it is
> wholly and absolutely devoted to your interests, that
> now and always you can trust me as you always have.
>
> Affectionately,
> John

Junior's upbringing had taught him to do his duty, but it
had also filled him with yearnings that succeeding in business
could not satisfy. Given the sort of person he was, it was only
natural that he should feel more at ease working in the
philanthropic foundations the Reverend Gates was building
than in corporations like Standard Oil. The one represented
virgin territory; the other would always have a certain taint.

The elder Rockefeller was neither interested in the details
of Gates's philanthropic schemes, nor especially informed
about the issues in question. His emotional remoteness from
organized benevolence—prodigious though his financial investment would be—created an opportunity toward which
Junior was inexorably drawn. "Gates was the brilliant
dreamer and creator," he recalled later. "I was the salesman—the go-between with Father at the opportune moment."
By picking a strategic time when the elder Rockefeller was
"in a relaxed mood"—after dinner or out for a drive—Junior
was able to secure his approval of ideas "which others
couldn't have secured because the moment wasn't right." Often the quest for such a moment would involve Cettie as well,
and Junior would send her a report on one of his projects
along with a note asking her to seize a good opportunity to

"read it aloud to Father" and in that way acquaint him with the work and its "possibilities."

Over the next twelve years, the father would invest $446,719,371.22 (a true Rockefeller reckoning) in four vast corporate philanthropies, the Institute for Medical Research, the General Education Board, the Rockefeller Foundation, and the Laura Spelman Rockefeller Memorial Fund. In the process, he would endow Junior with "businesses" in which, rather than merely occupying a family seat on a board, he could take an active role in management—business worthy of the heir of the Rockefeller fortune that could also serve the son's fervent wish to restore honor to his father's name.

If, as Junior maintained, Gates did all the "heavy thinking" in these projects, his own role was far more than his avowed aim of persuading his father and opening the family purse. He helped in the investigative groundwork, which usually involved consultation with eminent figures in the field, and in the search for key personnel to direct it. When Gates conceived the idea of a medical research institute, for instance, it was Junior who sought out Dr. William Welch of Johns Hopkins, one of the foremost medical figures of the time, to become president of the new Institute. It was Junior who helped recruit Simon Flexner as director and also sought out the remaining members of the board of directors, and it was Junior who then became the intermediary with his father on behalf of the Institute and its evolving plans for expansion.

As a result of his involvement with the new Medical Institute, Junior was immediately thrust into the national mainstream of a philanthropic movement and on his way to becoming a significant figure in his own right. In 1901 he had received an invitation from the philanthropist Robert Ogden, long an important figure in the southern education movement, to join fifty other prominent personalities for a historic train tour of Negro schools in the South. Dubbed the "Millionaire's Special," the tour visited such famous institutions as Hampton, Tuskegee, and the Atlanta Female Baptist Seminary, which, in 1884 (after receiving a gift somewhat in excess of $5,000 from John D. Rockefeller, Sr.), had been renamed the Spelman Seminary to honor Junior's abolitionist grandparents.

The climax of the trip came at a conference in Winston-Salem, where a campaign to promote tax-supported public schools in the South was launched. But the implications of the conference extended far beyond education. Its keynote speaker, Charles B. Aycock, fresh from a victorious white supremacy campaign for the governorship of North Carolina, proposed a "tacit bargain" of far-ranging significance. In the words of a standard history of segregation in the South, "The philanthropists acquiesced in disfranchisement and Jim Crow laws and undertook to promote acquiescence in the North, while Aycock pledged publicly that the schools of the disfranchised Negroes would have protection from hostile state legislation through the power and prestige of his high office."

Aycock's campaign was part of a broader movement of southern conservatives to open the region to northern capital, modernize its educational system, and bring about the birth of a new industrial South. The Southern Education Conference in Winston-Salem solidified a national coalition of northern philanthropists in support of this movement organized under the aegis of the newly formed Southern Education Board, behind which Junior and the immense resources of the Rockefeller wealth were to play a unique role.

Upon his return from the Ogden tour, which he later described as "one of the outstanding events in my life," Junior promptly began a series of discussions about the trip with Gates, Senior, and the plump secretary of the Baptist Home Mission Society, Dr. Wallace Buttrick. The result of these meetings was the formation of a small group that met in February 1902 at Junior's house to form the General Education Board. On behalf of his father, young Rockefeller pledged one million dollars to the new foundation to be spent over the next ten years. Most of the trustees for the new General Education Board were drawn from the Southern Education Board, including its chairman, William H. Baldwin.*

Within two weeks of receiving the letters from Junior proposing the creation of the GEB, Senior gave $10 million, and he followed that, a year and a half later, with a gift of $32 million. Over the next decade, these gifts would mount until a grand total of $129,209,167.10 was reached in 1921. It was Rockefeller in magnitude and from it would flow a character-

---

*Vice-president of Morgan's Southern Railway and chairman of the board of trustees of Tuskegee, Baldwin was a pivotal figure among the forces shaping the new industrial South. A benefactor of the Negro, Baldwin's philosophy of race relations and advice to his wards was: "Face the music, avoid social questions; leave politics alone; continue to be patient; live moral lives; live simply; learn to work and to work intelligently . . . learn that it is a mistake to be educated out of your environment."

istic Rockefeller influence. Men of vision would be attracted to this foundation as a practical fulcrum for their social plans and dreams; prospective recipients would shape their programs to the contours of its philosophy in the hopes of receiving their own enabling funds.

Acting as a bank for the programs of the Southern Education Board, the GEB became the centralizing power behind a movement that would affect the course of education and race relations far into the nation's future.

> On the Robert Ogden trips to Hampton and Tuskegee, in the organization of the Southern Education Board, and finally in the founding of the General Education Board [wrote the noted Negro scholar W. E. B. Du Bois] a new racial philosophy for the South was evolved. This philosophy seemed to say that the attempt to over-educate a "child race" by furnishing chiefly college training to its promising young people, must be discouraged; the Negro must be taught to accept what the whites were willing to offer him; in a world ruled by white people and destined so to be ruled, the place of Negroes must be that of a humble, hard-working group of laborers, whose ultimate destiny would be determined by their white employers.

While his father's philanthropic investment in the Institute and the GEB made Junior a central figure in a powerful constellation of social and cultural institutions at home, the missionary fervor of Frederick Gates, which had entered the international programs of the Rockefeller Foundation, was drawing him into a community of men and ideas that would come together after World War I in a select circle of America's overseas empire builders. Gates had begun to understand the possible international implications of Rockefeller philanthropy at the turn of the century, when he had read a comprehensive review of the work of English-speaking missionaries of all denominations and had been struck by how much the philanthropic effort had increased in the last decade in America until the funds and foundations seemed to "overlap and crowd each other." But there was relatively little effort in foreign lands.

Like Rockefeller's own early efforts in the Oil Regions, the missionary enterprise abroad seemed to Gates to be scattered and uncoordinated. For this reason he was favorably disposed in 1905 when the Congregationalist church solicited the donation for their work abroad that would soon erupt into the "tainted money" controversy. After studying the proposal, Gates wrote his employer that "a study of the map of the world discloses a comprehensiveness of organization, a unity of plan, a masterfulness of strategy and tactics, which suggests that the whole is being carried on in accordance with one great, preconceived plan, and that its movements are controlled and directed by one master mind."

The divine inspiration of the missionary movement went hand in hand with its commercial shrewdness:

> The fact is that heathen nations are being everywhere honeycombed with light and with civilization [Gates concluded], with modern industrial life and applications of modern science, through the direct or indirect agencies of the missionaries. Quite apart from the question of persons converted, the mere commercial results of missionary effort to our own land is worth, I had almost said, a thousand-fold every year of what is spent on missions. For illustration: Our commerce today with the Hawaiian Islands ... is, I am told, $17,000,000 per year. Five per cent of that in one year would represent all the money that ever was spent in christianizing and civilizing the natives. ... Missionaries and missionary schools are introducing the application of modern science, steam and electric power, modern agricultural machinery and modern manufacture into foreign lands. The result will be eventually to multiply the productive power of foreign countries many times. This will enrich them as buyers of American products and enrich us as importers of their products. We are only in the very dawn of commerce, and we owe that dawn, with all its promise, to the channels opened up by Christian missionaries.

This vision had been laid out for Junior and the other trustees of the Rockefeller Foundation at its very first meeting. The sense of world mission and the metaphors of conquest and salvation that accompanied them were more than a literary flourish. Gates was an avatar of an age of imperial optimism for the "English-speaking races": the duty to spread light to the dark continents was a common theme of those like him who sought to promote America's Christian and industrial stewardship of the world.

As part of this duty Gates and the Foundation launched a series of ambitious campaigns against the diseases that plagued the tropical regions of the world and made them inhospitable to civilized influences and undertakings. (Soon after the Foundation was chartered, the trustees merged the antihookworm effort of the Rockefeller Sanitary Commission with its own programs, renaming the crusade the International Health Board and resolving to extend its work "to other countries and people.") The public health emphasis was not mere charity; it had grown out of America's military and colonial occupations in the Philippines and the Caribbean, and the key personnel who were to conduct the global effort for the Foundation were recruited from this source.

In 1914, as the Foundation was initiating its Yellow Fever Commission under the direction of General William C. Gorgas and beginning its greatest effort in eradicating disease, Gates got the trustees to create the China Medical Board and to lay plans for the creation of a modern college of medicine in the Imperial City of Peking. Housed in the fifty-nine jade-roofed buildings abutting the old palace of Prince Yu, where Junior's slightly nasal voice would soon echo eerily across the tiled courtyard in dedication ceremonies, the Medical Board's Peking Union Medical College and Hospital would be "the Johns Hopkins of China"—the foremost medical school in Asia.

In an age of expanding empires and rising nationalism, the Medical College was inevitably an ambivalent symbol. Three years before the creation of the China Medical Board, China had begun her modern history as a republic under the leadership of Sun Yat-sen. But the yoke of foreign domination remained, and she was to be torn by civil war for the next forty years. Junior may not have fully understood why it was important to establish this outpost in China, but John R. Mott, whom he and Gates would make first chairman of the trustees of the college, had invoked China's instability and national weakness in a 1914 speech urging that the project be undertaken. "If we wait until China becomes stable," Mott told the China Medical Board, "we lose the greatest opportunity that we shall ever have of dealing with the nation."

Ever since the declaration of China's first republic in 1911, Mott had been obsessed with the "absolutely unique opportunity" presented by the turn of events. "There is only one nation of 400 million people," he had written. "That nation will have only one first generation in its modern era. This first wave of students to receive the modern training will furnish a vastly disproportionate share of the leaders of the New China—they will set the standards and the pace." The task was to win the minds and hearts of these pacesetters for Christianity and the West.

Woodrow Wilson had attempted to persuade Mott to become ambassador to China, but he declined because he considered the role too constricting; the claims of the private world mission he shared with F. T. Gates and a number of other far-seeing men came first. That mission was to shape the future of the international system through education and missionary work. It was a crusade that the Rockefeller Foundation would not only join, but consciously secularize as an "investment in leadership" through the international fellowship and education programs it launched in 1914.

Working behind the scenes of the Foundation, the Institute, and the General Education Board, Junior got to meet some of the most brilliant men in the country. He said little, yet he felt the power of their ideas. His unassuming demeanor, his riveting focus on detail, and his access to the funds that made everything possible allowed him to function in contexts where he was otherwise out of his depth. The architects of the ambitious programs that the corporate philanthropies undertook and that were changing the contours of American medicine, education, and social policy were all dynamic figures, businessmen like Ogden and Baldwin, missionaries like Mott and Gates, or scientists and administrators like Flexner and Wickliffe Rose, a former professor of philosophy at Peabody College who had come to work at the GEB in 1910. Junior's influence on them had been through the power of the purse. Yet there was one philanthropy, the Bureau of Social Hygiene, that elicited his attention in ways that the others did not, and that more than any other bore the stamp of his own character and sensibility.

In 1909, prostitution was a major issue in the New York mayoralty campaign, and in its aftermath, Tammany Hall "arranged" to have a special grand jury investigate the white slave traffic in order to dispel any implications that it had been complicit in the trade. As someone unlikely to rock the boat, Junior was asked to serve as foreman of the grand jury. At first he hedged. "It seemed like an impossible task," he said years afterward. "It was such a grim, depressing subject, and they couldn't have picked anybody who knew less about it." When it was pressed on him as a civic duty, however, he relented because "the training of my parents was to the effect that a duty could not be evaded."

Once committed, he threw himself into the task with a vigor that frightened Tammany. "I never worked harder in my life," he recalled later. "I was on the job morning, noon, and night." Scheduled to sit for only a month, the grand jury sat for six, in the end issuing a detailed report that called for the appointment of a commission to study the laws relating to, and the methods of dealing with, this social evil "in leading cities of this country and of Europe, with a view toward minimizing the evil in this city." When the mayor refused to set up such a commission, Junior decided to go ahead and do it himself.

With typical diligence, he began by interviewing educators, intellectuals, and businessmen about the project. In all, he spoke to more than one hundred individuals, including a dynamic young attorney named Raymond B. Fosdick. A protégé of Woodrow Wilson at Princeton who was then serving as New York's commissioner of accounts, Fosdick was to become one of the most influential men of his generation, as well as Junior's lifelong associate and biographer, a future undersecretary general of the League of Nations, and president of the Rockefeller Foundation.

Having marshaled the best advice available, Junior set up the Bureau of Social Hygiene in 1911. It would spend more than $5 million of Rockefeller money, playing an important if largely unrecognized role in the social life of the nation. The bureau was infused with the New Deweyite optimism regarding the application of scientific methods to the problems of social reform. As one of its earliest acts, the bureau sent Abraham Flexner (brother of Rockefeller Institute head Simon Flexner) abroad to conduct a comprehensive survey of prostitution in Europe and how it differed from the American variety. Carrying letters of introduction from Secretary of State Elihu Root and others, Flexner stopped at major cities all over the continent. Although drawn to the liberal Scandinavian treatment of the prostitute, he concluded that the way to control this vice would be to drive it underground, thereby isolating the evil if not wiping it out.

Another of Flexner's conclusions was that it was impossible to understand prostitution without also understanding the legal environment that allowed it to flourish. The bureau's next major project, accordingly, was to send Fosdick to Europe to conduct the first systematic international survey of police administration. After seeing the professionalism of European police, Fosdick came back to the United States and was appalled by the casual and undisciplined nature of police work. With the publication of Fosdick's studies, Colonel Arthur Woods, former New York City commissioner of police, became associated with the bureau and oversaw the production of more than two dozen studies of police and police systems, all of them arguing for scientific procedures and administration. By 1936, *Fortune* would say of the bureau's efforts in this area: "So much was contributed to the science of crime detection that G-man J. Edgar Hoover traces much of the success of the present federal system to [the bureau's] investigations."

The bureau was also one of the first agencies to look into drugs, developing the complementary lines of criminalization and treatment that would become official federal policy once the opium menace became publicized and drug experts had gone to work for the federal government. In every subject it pursued, the Bureau of Social Hygiene created a group of experts who would concentrate their expertise on social problems with the object of quarantining sin and removing it as a temptation and, in the process, transforming sinners into criminals. For all this modernity, the social science of the bureau bore a striking resemblance to the staid Baptist atmosphere of the Cleveland household where Junior had grown up.

8

IN ONE OF HIS LETTERS trying to sell John D., Sr., on the creation of the philanthropies, the Reverend Gates had stressed that they should be so large "that to become a trustee of one would be to make a man at once a public character." This would be dramatically true later, when men like John Foster Dulles and Dean Rusk graduated from the Rockefeller Foundation to become Secretaries of State. But it was also true of Junior himself in the beginning of the enterprise. Only a few years earlier he had been a nullity in the public mind. ("Young Mr. Rockefeller offers only a spectacle of the passive and innocuous," a magazine writer had asserted in 1905. "Without virtues as without vices, he is the sublimation of the mediocre—the negative in apogee—a climax of the commonplace.") But as he became associated with the foundations and the millions of dollars they dispensed, Junior's image started to change. He became a celebrity.

His new eminence did not pass the notice of the shrewd minds that now guided the Standard—Archbold, Rogers, and A. C. Bedford. At their invitation, Junior had been made a vice-president of the trust. He had gone on tours (a *real* Rockefeller for oil men in the hinterlands of the Southwest to see) and had taken on a broad range of diplomatic duties, including cultivating Nelson Aldrich's Senate colleagues and acquainting them with the Standard's view of legislation affecting the prospects of the oil industry. Yet, in the middle of his service as foreman of the White Slave Grand Jury, which was winning him new acclaim, the Hearst papers made their revelation of the infamous Archbold letters. If Junior hadn't known before, the public fury that surrounded the trust in the wake of these revelations convinced him that he could no longer afford to be identified with the administration of the Standard. To continue as a front man for business would equivocate his efforts as a philanthropist. He knew he had to choose once and for all between business and charity, and there was no doubt in his mind about which of the two endeavors was more promising. After discussions with his father, he resigned as vice-president of Standard Oil and U.S. Steel. The other directorships were soon to follow. One of the few companies he kept an association with was a relatively innocuous coal-mining operation out west. It was called Colorado Fuel and Iron.

The Rockefeller interest in Colorado Fuel and Iron went back to the turn of the century. In the years when Junior was still trying to come to terms with his frustrating apprenticeship at 26 Broadway, the notorious Jay Gould's son, George, a sometime business associate of the elder Rockefeller, managed to persuade the billionaire to look into Colorado Fuel and Iron stock. His huge cash reserves swollen even more than usual by the recent sale of the Mesabi properties to Morgan's U.S. Steel syndicate, Rockefeller had sent F. T. Gates on a secret journey to Colorado to look over the property: Gates's report convinced Rockefeller to risk an initial $6 million investment.

Over the next few years Gates also convinced him that CF&I could become profitable only when its management policies were changed, and accordingly, Rockefeller increased his investment to more than $20 million; with 40 percent of the common and preferred stock, as well as 43 percent of the company's bonds, he now had effective control. Having removed the old CF&I management in 1907, Gates looked for the right man to send to Denver to take over. As it worked out, LaMont Montgomery Bowers, Gates's sixty-year-old uncle, who had proved himself a worthy lieutenant by building the fleet of iron ore carriers that were so crucial to the success of the Mesabi affair, had recently been ordered by doctors to take his consumptive wife to the Colorado area. Agreeing to do what was necessary to make the coal company turn a profit, Bowers was made chairman of the board of directors and told to report regularly to Gates and Junior at 26 Broadway.

The company he now commanded was a prime example of what the liberal press would later call "industrial absolutism." The miners' low wages (about $1.68 a day) were paid in scrip redeemable only at company stores charging extortionate prices. The miners usually lived in small two-room shacks provided by the company at exorbitant rents, and from which they could be evicted on a three-day notice. The churches they attended were the pastorates of company-hired ministers; their children were taught in company-controlled schools; the company libraries carefully censored their collection to make sure that books they deemed subversive (like Darwin's *Origin of the Species*) did not appear. More than $20,000 a year was spent by the company to maintain a force of detectives, mine guards, and spies whose job it was to keep the camps quarantined from the virulence of unionism.

Colorado Fuel and Iron was by far the largest of the producers in the area, the spokesman for all the operators, and a major political power in Colorado. Bowers later boasted that when he arrived in Denver, the company registered and voted every man and woman in its employ, including the 70 percent who were not even naturalized citizens, and that "even their mules . . . were registered if they were fortunate enough to possess names." This political power helped the operators make sure that even the primitive mine safety standards of the time were not enforced; the result was, predictably, an epidemic of accidental deaths and injuries to the workers. The miners had no place to go to complain. County courthouses, it was commonly said, were like branch offices of CF&I, and local sheriffs enjoyed a status similar to mine superintendents.

The United Mine Workers had provided a focus for the dissatisfaction and anger present in the camps. In turn, Bowers blamed union organizers (whom he called "disreputable agitators, socialists and anarchists") for the trouble CF&I began to have with its employees. Rising to the challenge, he accepted the leadership in the coming struggle which the smaller operators pressed on him. "When such men as these," he said in a battle cry directed at the unionists, "together with the cheap college professors and still cheaper writers in muck-raking magazines, supplemented by a lot of milk and water preachers ... are permitted to assault the businessmen who have built up the great industries ... it is time that vigorous measures are taken." Back at 26 Broadway, his nephew agreed. In his usual flamboyant manner, Gates eyed the coming struggle as nothing less than an apocalyptic clash between good and evil. "The officers of the Colorado Fuel and Iron Company," he declared, "are standing between the country and chaos, anarchy, proscription and confiscation, and in so doing are worthy of the support of every man who loves his country."

The operators in Colorado hired the Baldwin-Felts Detective Agency to spearhead their war against the UMW. Made up of drifters and former gunmen left over from the closing of the West, the Baldwin-Felts detectives were more detested than even the strike-breakers that Pinkerton's had sent into the West. Armed with new Winchesters and given the status of deputies by local sheriffs, the detectives began to move through the coal fields like a vigilante army. Their appearance convinced the UMW that the time had come for a decisive test of strength, and its organizers bought up all the rifles and ammunition they could find in the general stores of the small Colorado towns.

On the morning of September 23, 1913, with events now moving forward of their own momentum, some 9,000 miners and their families—close to 70 percent of the working force—walked out of the mining camps. They settled into tent colonies the UMW had set up for them near the small, nearly anonymous mining towns of the area. One of them was named Ludlow.

What previously had been regarded as isolated incidents between the detectives and miners now turned into military skirmishes. One of the most serious occurred on October 17, when the Baldwin-Felts men piled into the armored car the miners called the Death Special and raced through a tent colony near Forbes, raking the area with fire from two mounted machine guns and then speeding off into the dusk.

The miners retaliated as best they could, and two weeks later Colorado's Governor Ammons finally called out the National Guard in an attempt to restore the peace. For a time, the militiamen tried to enforce the Colorado law that forbade bringing scabs into an area where there was a labor dispute. But in the bitter winter months ahead, the state found itself unable to meet the militia's payroll without help from the business interests; the Guard became openly partisan, escorting into the coal fields strikebreakers who had been imported by rail from as far away as Pittsburgh and Toledo. Then, in late February, with the state treasury depleted, Governor Ammons pulled out all but a few strategically stationed units; most of the militiamen who remained were openly antagonistic to the strikers.

On the morning of April 20 the labor war that had thus far cost dozens of lives came to its bloody climax. A company of militia that had repeatedly clashed with strikers took up a position on a rise overlooking the tents of Ludlow. The chill wind whipped at laundry drying stiffly on the clothesline and curled the smoke climbing out of stovepipes poked through the tent tops. The strikers stared suspiciously at the men above them. Just after daybreak, a shot rang out from an unknown source, and the jittery militiamen responded by opening fire from their Hotchkiss guns, beginning a battle that would last all day.

As their tents, punctured with bullets, caught fire, the strikers retreated to positions in cellars dug under the floorboards. By nightfall, the scene was one of complete devastation. There were forty dead and countless wounded. But the worst was to come. For, next morning, as the people of Ludlow emerged from under ground and walked through the smoldering colony counting their losses, they discovered the bodies of two women and eleven children who had suffocated in a cellar when the tent above them had burned. The outrage had found its symbol, and as news of it spread, other

colonies of strikers began an offensive against the mine operators, seizing towns and attacking company outposts within a
250-mile radius of Ludlow. President Woodrow Wilson ordered federal troops into the area to end what threatened to
become an all-out war.

In the early days of the strike, Junior had been busy with
other crises, such as the Wilson administration's apparent intention to push anti-trust legislation through Congress, which
he had discussed with J. P. Morgan and other business leaders on Senator Aldrich's yacht. Gradually, he became nervous
about events in Colorado and began following the dispatches
from Denver with more than usual concern; soon most of his
time at 26 Broadway was consumed by the strike and its violence. Even before the miners had walked out, he faced
pressure from as high as the White House to use his influence
to settle the conflict. His response had always been the same:
he was merely a stockholder of the corporation; the management in Denver had charge of the day-to-day operations of
Colorado Fuel and Iron. When criticized for such an attitude,
as he frequently was in the months between the strikers' ex-
odus and the massacre, he pointed out that 26 Broadway was
two thousand miles from Colorado and that his hands were
tied by his situation.

Yet in truth his mind was far from open on the question.
There was no doubt that he had completely aligned himself
with those he recognized as authorities: Gates and his father.
The elder Rockefeller held unusually strong beliefs on the
matter. He felt that employment was a charity to workers;
faced with unions, captains of industry were justified in taking strict countermeasures. Years earlier, when he heard that
Frick had ordered strikers at Carnegie's Homestead steel-
works shot down, John D. had immediately fired off a telegram of support to the coke magnate. Frick had become a
symbol of employer resistance, not only because of his actions at the Homestead but because of his behavior later,
when a grief-stricken sympathizer of the murdered workers
assaulted him at the office. Shot once and stabbed several
times, Frick fought off the attacker and then insisted on continuing the day's work swathed in bloody bandages. His comment to newsmen at quitting time set a standard for all members of his class: "I do not think I will die, but whether I do
or not the Carnegie Company will pursue the same policies
and it will win."

Correspondence, which was subsequently subpoenaed and made public by the Industrial Relations Commission, showed that Junior subscribed completely to his father's views. As early as September 15, 1913, a week before the miners walked off their jobs, Secretary of Labor William Wilson had sent Ethelbert Stewart, his chief mediator, to 26 Broadway to plead with Rockefeller for help in avoiding the coming conflict. Junior had referred Stewart to family legal adviser Starr J. Murphy, but not before instructing Murphy to direct him in turn to the CF&I offices in Denver. Bowers, at CF&I, reported on his meeting with Steward in a letter to Junior: "[The mediator] was told that he would work such mines as we could protect and close the others, and that the writer, with every official of this company, would stand by this declaration until our bones were bleached white as chalk in those Rocky Mountains." Three weeks later, Junior sent Bowers a letter endorsing his stand: "We feel that what you have done is right and fair and that the position which you have taken in regard to the unionizing of the mines is in the interest of the employees of the Company. Whatever the outcome may be, we will stand by you to the end." Four days afterward he added: "I realize these are trying days for the management of the fuel company. Its actions are watched with great interest by this office, and its strong and just position will not lack backing at this end."

A few months later, Bowers wrote Junior a Christmas note informing him of the pressures that had been applied to change Governor Ammons's position on the crucial question of allowing militiamen to escort strikebreakers to work in the mines. Up to this point, the state administration had refused such escort, and its seeming fairness to the miners had done much to keep the violence sporadic and contained. "You will be interested to know," wrote Bowers, "that we have been able to secure the cooperation of all the bankers of the city, who have had three or four interviews with our little cowboy governor.... There probably has never been such pressure brought upon any governor of this state by the strongest men in it as has been brought upon Governor Ammons."

Junior, who until then had been fretting over the effectiveness of the strike, was pleased with the results and ignored the insult to Governor Ammons in his reply. "I assume this means that conditions have become so nearly normal," he wrote Bowers, "that business can be very generally resumed. It is most gratifying to feel that this struggle is so rapidly becoming a thing of the past. I know that Father had followed the events of the past few months in connection with the fuel company with unusual interest and satisfaction."

Things did not return to "normal." With events careening out of control, President Wilson tried to find some formula acceptable to both sides. When Bowers and the mine operators, who were now confident of victory, refused offers of federal mediation, a subcommittee of the House Committee on Mines and Mining opened hearings on the situation. They began in early February, and in March, just a month before the Ludlow Massacre, Junior was called to testify.

The chairman of the subcommittee, Representative Martin Foster, immediately raised the issue of Junior's philanthropic and business interests. "I believe that you are concerned with sociological and uplift movements and that you were recently the foreman of a Grand Jury which reported upon White Slave Traffic," the chairman observed. "Do you not think you might have paid some attention to these bloody strike conditions out in Colorado, where you have one thousand employees in whose welfare you seem not to have taken any deep personal interest?"

"I have done what I regard as the very best thing in the interest of those employees and the large investment I represent," Junior replied evasively. "We have gotten the best men obtainable and are relying on their judgment."

The chairman, however, continued to press him: "But the killing of people and the shooting of the children—has not that been of enough importance to you for you to communicate with other Directors and see if something might be done to end that sort of thing?"

In answer, Junior invoked the principle his father and Gates held to be so vital. It was, he said, not a local but a national issue that was at stake, as to whether workers would be allowed to work under any conditions that they might choose. "As part owners of the property, our interest in the laboring man in this country is so immense, so deep, so profound, that we stand ready to lose every cent we put in that company rather than see the men we have employed thrown out of work and have imposed on them conditions which are not of their seeking and which neither they nor we can see are in our interests."

"You are willing," the chairman shot back, "to let these killings take place rather than to go there and do something to settle conditions?"

Junior answered, "There is just one thing that can be done to settle this strike and that is to unionize the camp and our interest in labor is so profound and we believe so sincerely that the interest demands that the camps be open camps, that we expect to stand by the officers at any cost."

"And you will do that if it costs all your property and kills all your employees?"

"It is a great principle," Junior replied.

Some criticized him for his uncompromising stand, but Junior's parents were elated. In a telegram sent from Pocantico, his mother said proudly that his testimony "was a bugle note . . . struck for principle," and his father sent word that he was making his son a gift of ten thousand shares of Colorado Fuel and Iron stock, relying as usual on the golden sound of money to express his feelings. Junior felt stronger than ever in his views. The only miscalculation he made, in fact, was in the impact Ludlow would have on public opinion.

Yet this was a crucial mistake, and soon after news of the massacre had flashed around the country, the hatred that stalked him was equal to anything his father had ever faced. Upton Sinclair's pickets followed him everywhere, their black crepe armbands a *memento mori* connecting him with the bodies that had been dragged out of the smoldering tents at Ludlow. There were rallies and demonstrations. Feelings reached such a fever pitch that at one UMW meeting in Colorado, an organizer named Marie Ganz shouted to a group of jeering men: "If you were men of spirit, John D. Rockefeller wouldn't be alive tomorrow." Shortly thereafter, a handful of Wobblies blew themselves up in a Lexington Avenue tenement in New York, and police said that their homemade bomb had been intended for Junior's town house on West 54th Street. The Socialist periodical *Appeal to Reason* printed a poem with uncertain rhythms but unmistakable emotions:

> . . . As long as he has the cash to spend, it's easy the people to fool,
> As long as he builds a cottage or two and teaches Sunday School,
> The toadies fawn, and the lickspittles kneel.
> He's worshipped by all the freaks,
> While the bodies of little children are burned 'neath Colorado peaks.

And this skulking, sanctimonious ass, this breeder of
crime and hate
With the greed of a jackal and a heart of brass
Whines "Nothing to arbitrate."

Criticism came from more than a handful of radicals, however. "Every prayer Rockefeller utters is an insult to the
Christ that died for suffering humanity," a Denver paper
wrote. The opening lines of a lead story in the Cleveland
Leader said: "The charred bodies of two dozen women and
children show that ROCKEFELLER KNOWS HOW TO WIN!" And
the liberal press, including such prominent magazines as *The
Nation, The New Republic, The Survey,* and *Collier's,* were
uniformly sympathetic to the side of labor in the conflict.

Reading the papers was often painful for him, and Junior
learned how to hide from bad news, a lesson he would
remember whenever he became embroiled in controversy
later in his life. When he was busy building Rockefeller Center and the giant development's architecture was being attacked almost daily, one of Junior's associates asked him if
he wasn't bothered by the news and comment. "I never read
the papers when there's apt to be any trouble," Rockefeller
replied. "I learned that in the old days during the strike out
west."

It was clear that Ludlow threatened to become the al-
batross around Junior's neck for the rest of his life. Even if
he could have tolerated the image he saw in the mirror of
public opinion, he realized that his patient work to create
goodwill and respect for the Rockefeller name was now in
jeopardy. The worst of it was that the two men he had always relied on, his father and the Reverend Gates, could no
longer help him. Their ideas were fixed in the amber of the
last century.

Junior began looking for new advisers and new advice. He
found two men who seemed to be in tune with the changing
times and offered a way out of the chaos all around him. Ivy
Lee, a southerner, and Mackenzie King, a Canadian Liberal,
may have seemed strange allies for the son of the world's
richest man. Yet they had one trait in common: each in his
own way was a prophet of the new age; each had proved
himself able to combine a visionary sense of progress and a
practical identification with the existing order of things. Each
in his own way would become a midwife to the Rockefeller
rebirth, not only by making possible Junior's escape from the

guilt for Ludlow, but by providing him with indispensable strategies for building and maintaining an institutional network that would propel the Rockefeller dynasty into the twentieth century.

"Crowds are led by symbols and phrases," Ivy Lee once told a gathering of railroad men to whom he was explaining the principles of his craft. "Success in dealing with crowds ... rests upon the art of getting believed in. We know that Henry the Eighth by his obsequious deference to the forms of the law was able to get the people to believe in him so completely that he was able to do almost anything with them."

If he cannot be credited as the inventor of modern public relations, there is no doubt that Lee was the man who made it an art as well as an indispensable part of the country's corporate life. A tall, slim, almost poetic figure with blue eyes, chestnut hair, and a slight limp that became pronounced when he was tired, Lee stood apart from the other men Junior made into Rockefeller associates. It was not only his drawl and elegant southern manners that set him off from the others who served the Rockefeller family, but the fact that his upbringing had given him a different angle of vision.

The son of a liberal Georgia preacher who claimed descent from the Virginia Lees, Ivy Lee was one of the aristocratic advocates of a new industrial identity for the South, part of the group who would be so receptive to the General Education Board's southern education program. As a child he had spent time with family friend Joel Chandler Harris, listening to the creator of Br'er Rabbit tell nostalgic stories of the vanished plantations and the faithful slaves and kind masters. The Lee household was frequented by many who devoted their public lives to trying to heal the ugly wounds of the Civil War by adjusting southern sensibilities to the domination of northern industry, and by attuning northerners to the quaint prejudices of the suppliant South. It was a mission of conciliation that Ivy Lee would carry into the realm of industrial relations and the conflict between business and the working man.

After graduating in 1898 from Princeton (where he, like Raymond Fosdick, had fallen under the spell of Woodrow Wilson), Lee went to New York to make his way in the world. When no suitable opportunity offered itself on Wall Street, he went to work for the New York *Journal*, the first of a series of newspaper jobs that allowed him to write about business matters. He was fascinated by the way corporations functioned, by their shortcomings as well as their power; but he was no muckraker. On the contrary, it occurred to him that while the muckrakers' publicity was now magnifying the warts on the face of business, the techniques of journalism might also be used to emphasize its nobler features. In 1903 he quit the newspaper to become a publicist, hoping, as he later said, to accomplish for business what Billy Sunday had done for religion.*

When Junior sought out his services in May 1914, Lee was working as executive assistant to Samuel Rea, president of the Pennsylvania Railroad. The two men met at 26 Broadway and Junior lost no time indicating that he wanted to master the art of getting believed in. With typical understatement he told Lee: "I feel that my father and I are much misunderstood by the press and the people of this country. I should like to know what your advice would be on how to make our position clear."

Lee began his work by issuing a series of bulletins on events in Colorado, with the mine operators' cooperation and Junior's approval. Later collected in a booklet titled *The Struggle in Colorado for Industrial Freedom*, the bulletins were sent to the network of "opinion makers" Lee had built up over the years. Made up of selected reprints of newspaper stories, opinions by leading citizens, and a miscellany of other material, the bulletins attempted to put the best face possible on the operators' actions in the strike and to discredit the union.

One of Lee's bulletins contained the statement of a vice-president of Colorado's Law and Order League to the effect that the death of the two women and eleven children had occurred because of their carelessness in overturning a stove in the tent, rather than because of the militia's gunfire. Such enterprising misstatements impressed those at 26 Broadway but earned Lee notoriety in avant-garde literary circles. Upton Sinclair gave him the nickname "Poison Ivy." John Dos Pas-

---

*Eventually he would do just that, becoming in the course of things a millionaire and gaining a niche in the *Social Register* (his listed profession, Public Relations, contrasting oddly with those listed by the great titans of industry). He would count people like Walter Chrysler, Charles Schwab, George Westinghouse, and Henry Guggenheim as clients, as well as such corporations as Standard Oil, American Tobacco, and General Mills. To the last he would make such enduring contributions as the creation of Betty Crocker and the "Breakfast of Champions" slogan that adorns the Wheaties box.

sos caricatured him mercilessly in *The 42nd Parallel*. Carl Sandburg wrote: "He is below the level of the hired gunman and slugger. His sense of right and wrong is a worse force in organized society than that of the murderers who shot women and burned babies at Ludlow."

Yet, if anything, Lee's views were less reactionary than those of his employer. After journeying to Colorado in August 1914, he advised Junior to publicize the entire Rockefeller holdings in Colorado Fuel and Iron and told him that Bowers and the company management had been far too unyielding in their attitude toward the strikers. He advised that placards should be posted throughout the mines informing workers that the companies wanted to treat them fairly and were interested in hearing their complaints. "I believe this publicity policy will be of substantial value *as a start* in getting the complete confidence of the miners and the public of this state," he wrote to Junior. But he added, "It is of the greatest importance that as early as possible some comprehensive plan be devised to provide machinery to redress grievances. Such provision would not only take the wind out of the union's sails, but would appeal, I am confident, to the soundest public opinion."

Lee was not the man to construct such a plan, and he knew it. Yet even as he was completing his work in Denver, the right person had been caught in the Foundation's broadly cast net and brought to Junior's attention.

When he joined the Rockefeller team, Mackenzie King was a former boy wonder of Canadian politics whose once promising career seemed permanently stalled. Fifteen years earlier he had begun work in the Ministry of Labor and so distinguished himself that by the age of thirty-four he was elected to Parliament and chosen to be Secretary of Labor in the government of Liberal Prime Minister Sir Wilfrid Laurier. But in 1911 the Liberal government fell, and King fell with it. For the next few years he jockeyed unsuccessfully for party leadership, and he was defeated when he stood for reelection to Parliament. The responsibility of caring for his aging parents fell to him, further burdening his already meager resources. He looked in vain for a wife, thinking that perhaps marriage would make him a better political prospect. The future, which had looked so bright a few years earlier, now seemed to promise only grinding obligations with no means of discharging them. "How terribly broken down on every side is the house of life around me!" the forty-year-old grandson of Canadian patriot William Lyon Mackenzie mourned in his diary.

But then, on June 1, 1914, King received a telegram from the Rockefeller Foundation asking him to come to New York for a discussion about a major project it was beginning. He did not know it at the time, but the invitation had come because of a speech he had given at Cambridge on labor theory a few years earlier. One of those in attendance, Harvard's august president, Charles W. Eliot, had been much impressed, as had been Jerome Greene, the secretary of the Harvard Corporation. Now Greene was secretary of the Rockefeller Foundation and Eliot was its most distinguished trustee, and it had occurred to both that a man with Mackenzie King's background in industrial relations might be useful in helping their friend, young Rockefeller, find his way though the ugly aftermath of Ludlow.

The invitation, therefore, was actually for a conference with Junior, Starr J. Murphy, and Greene. When King arrived at 10 West 54th Street for a meeting on the morning of June 6, Junior felt an immediate rapport with the shy, oddly mystical Canadian who was his equal in years and shared his sense of personal inadequacy. After their first meeting, Rockefeller felt he had found someone who could help him design a dignified exit from the Colorado conflict and restore peace and honor to his family. "Seldom have I been so impressed by a man at first appearance," he later said of King.

Putting his affairs in order, King prepared to leave his homeland for an indefinite period. Before he finally accepted Junior's offer, there had been some wrangling over salary, with the nearly bankrupt King maintaining that he needed $15,000 a year to meet his obligations, while Junior, in one of those severe economies inherited from his father, said that $10,000 was closer to the figure he had in mind. Finally they compromised on $12,000—which coincidentally was the figure Ivy Lee was being paid.

By late August 1914, much of the criticism caused by the strike had died down: the production of CF&I and the other companies was almost back to normal as a result of scab labor and the gradual return of the starving and terrorized miners to their jobs. What King's task boiled down to was giving flesh to Ivy Lee's plea for a grievance machinery that would show the company's concern for fairness to its defeated and chastened labor force. In the privacy of his diary, King wrote that he knew which text he must preach to Junior: "They made me the keeper of the vineyards, but mine own vineyard have I not kept." The Canadian concluded—prophetically, as it was to work out—that "the greatest thing [Rockefeller] could do in his life [was] to make of that scene of past conflict a garden where men and women could dwell in happiness; and that he could begin now to make it apparent to the public that it was his intention to take that up as a great piece of work."

King wrote a six-page preliminary report that would be the basis of his later Industrial Representatives Plan. The core of the plan was the creation of means whereby representatives of labor and management could meet under company auspices and establish communications and contact without the divisive presence of an independent union. What he had done was to invent the "company union," which, before it was outlawed by the Wagner Act of 1935, was to prove an invaluable instrument for management in blunting the great union drives of the period. When he learned of the proposal, AFL leader Samuel Gompers snorted, "What influence can such a pseudo-union have to insist upon the remedying of a grievous wrong or the attainment of a real right?" Yet when the plan was first unveiled, it seemed to some as if the white flag were being run up at 26 Broadway. Stunned that young Rockefeller should suddenly appear to desert the great struggle to which he had seemed as committed as anyone else, L. M. Bowers fired off a hasty letter saying that even though the King plan didn't explicitly mention recognizing the union, it would be taken by others as an intention to surrender. He was supported by Gates, and even the moderate Starr J. Murphy, whom Junior had sent to Denver to reconnoiter the situation, urged a "fight to the finish" against the weakened miners.

Junior let the matter simmer for a while, but he realized that there had to be some resolution, and in January 1915 he asked Bowers for his resignation. When questioned about it later, he would say that the old man had not been ready "to go forward into the new day." For Bowers the struggle was over, but for Junior it was just beginning. Meanwhile, with King off touring the mine fields, word had been received at 26 Broadway that Junior would be required to appear in January before Frank Walsh and the President's Commission on Industrial Relations.

The Industrial Relations Commission had been created in 1912 in the wake of a wave of industrial violence that had put the country in a state of shock even before the tragedy at Ludlow. Established by Congress with a wide mandate to probe the origins of labor unrest and propose legislative reforms, the commission was headed by lawyer Frank Walsh, a colorful Progressive from Missouri who had once defended the son of Jesse James in a sensational trial over a train robbery. Broad-faced and raw-boned, Walsh had made it clear that the commission would not, as some hoped, quickly review the labor problem and issue a perfunctory report. He intended to conduct the most searching inquiry into American industry ever undertaken.

In the course of the hearings, Walsh subpoenaed Carnegie, J. P. Morgan, Henry Ford, and the other titans of the age, but their days in court were basically comfortable ones. It soon became apparent that Walsh was fascinated more by the Rockefellers than anyone else, and was interested more in the son than the father.

When Junior first appeared before the Industrial Relations Commission, in January 1915, he had been extensively coached by King. His defense was built around the contention that responsibility for what had gone on in Colorado rested solely with the corporate management, and that, as a director and stockholder, he was neither consulted in the formulation of policy nor well informed about conditions. His opening statement contained the ideas of King couched in the felicitous style of Ivy Lee; it marked the unveiling of the new man. "I believe it to be just as proper and advantageous for labor to associate itself into organized groups for the advancement of its legitimate interest as for capital to combine for the same object," Junior told the commissioners, many of whom remembered him flatly opposing unions before the Foster Committee two years earlier. Sometimes, Junior continued, such associations of labor "provide benefit features, sometimes they seek to increase wages, but whatever their specific purpose, so long as it is to promote the well being of the employees, having always due regard for the just interests of the employer and the public . . . I favor them most heartily."

Chairman Walsh was not impressed. For the next three days he probed Junior's relationship to the events in Colorado, always returning to the question of ultimate responsibility. Did Mr. Rockefeller believe that the stockholders of a corporation had any responsibility for labor conditions in the industrial concerns in which they owned stock? Junior certainly did believe that. Did Mr. Rockefeller, as a stockholder and director, know that the average amount of compensation paid for the death of heads of families in the Colorado coal industry prior to the strike was seven hundred dollars? Junior did not know that. Was Mr. Rockefeller aware, Walsh persisted, that twenty-five persons had been killed or maimed in the last year alone in industrial accidents at Colorado Fuel and Iron, and that there had been no verdict rendered by any court in Colorado in the case of an injured person, or the survivors of a dead workman killed in his industry, for the past twenty-three years? Junior had no inkling of that.

Walsh tried to break Junior's calm by bringing up the issue of Ivy Lee. If he was as guiltless as he claimed, why had he stationed a full-time publicist in Colorado? He had dispatched Mr. Lee, Rockefeller replied smoothly, because he felt people had a right to know what was happening at the scene of this tragic strike. Walsh put the UMW's John Lawson on the stand and guided the discussion to the Rockefeller Foundation's Colorado philanthropies. The flamboyant UMW leader, who had kept the strike going and become a legendary figure in the coal fields with his red bandanna around his neck and a .45 strapped to his hip, said sarcastically, "It is not their money that these lords of commercialized virtue are spending, but the withheld wages of the American working class. ... Health for China, a refuge for birds ... pensions for New York widows, and never a thought of a dollar for the thousands who starved in Colorado."

But by the end of the first round of hearings, Junior had won over most of the people in the audience. He had remained the well-intentioned, if somewhat remote, gentleman in the midst of what seemed an unprovoked attack. He seemed far too weak a person to have actually had a hand in making such murderous policy. Writing in *The New Republic,* the youthful Walter Lippmann noted:

> Here was a man who represented an agglomeration of wealth probably without parallel in history, the successor to a father who has with justice been called the high priest of capitalism. Freedom of enterprise, untrammelled incentives of the profiteer culminate in his family. He is the supreme negation of all equality and unquestionably the symbol of the most menacing fact in the life

of the republic. Yet he talked about himself in the commonplace moral assumptions of a small businessman.

As he was leaving the hearings, Junior was informed that
his correspondence pertaining to the strike in the files at 26
Broadway was under subpoena. Over the next few weeks, as
this material came into the commission's hands, Walsh realized that the information would put Rockefeller just where he
wanted him. The chairman announced his dramatic findings
on April 23 in a press conference in his Kansas City office.
The letters and memoranda he read to newsmen showed a far
different man from the serious young heir who had testified
with measured reason and flexibility in January. They revealed a committed anti-unionist who regarded collective bargaining as an issue to be fought with every weapon at hand, a
man who not only did not differ from his Denver employees
who had been the field marshals of the Colorado strike, but
who had backed up their actions every inch of the way.

When Walsh recalled Junior to the stand in Washington,
D.C., on the sweltering afternoon of May 19, 1915, the confidence that had marked his appearance a few months earlier
was gone, as was the sympathy he had evoked in the audience. As young Rockefeller entered the Shoreham Hotel this
morning, one man spat at him and another shouted menacingly, "Murderer!" He waited in an antechamber off the
main ballroom where the hearings were taking place, sitting
bolt upright with folded hands showing white knuckles and
sweat beading at the hairline. It was a sultry day, and as the
audience tried to start wind currents with cardboard fans,
Junior took the stand and began to sweat freely under
Walsh's questioning. In the previous round, his answers had
resonated with confidence; if somewhat unclear about the details of events in Colorado, he had usually been able to seek a
moral ground above the level of the conflict. Now, as Walsh
took that ground from under his feet, he was hesitant and uncertain. For three more days, while Lee and King watched
helplessly from the audience, Junior was examined with a total lack of deference for his station in life. Fosdick would
later describe the interrogation as "merciless."

The commission inquired into the family's wealth and influence in a way that would be unequaled for nearly sixty
years, until Junior's son Nelson opened the family records in
his bid to gain confirmation as Vice-President. Walsh brought
up the fact that one of Ivy Lee's bulletins had been built

around the anti-union views of several of Colorado's educational leaders, among them the president of Colorado College and the dean of liberal arts at the University of Denver, schools which had respectively received grants of $225,000 and $100,000 from the Foundation. He pointed out that after the Ludlow Massacre, Junior had arranged for another $100,000 Foundation grant to the Colorado Committee on Unemployment and a like amount for the southern Colorado YMCA.

But Walsh's special ire was reserved for Junior himself. The farther the proceedings went, the more acute Walsh's desire became to wring an admission of guilt from the shaken witness sitting before him. He explored all the surfaces of Junior's character, probing the Rockefeller motives and outlook in a way that would never be allowed again.

This passage between the two occurred after Walsh read to the commission Junior's December 26, 1913, letter to Bowers mentioning how satisfied his father was with the progress of the strike:

> *Chairman Walsh:* How did he express satisfaction; say that he was glad to see how things were going, or just laugh?
>
> *Mr. Rockefeller Jr.:* It is a little difficult to recall, it being a year and a half ago.
>
> *Chairman Walsh:* You can not tell how he expressed it, but he was unusually satisfied with the trend of events in Colorado?
>
> *Mr. Rockefeller Jr.:* You seem to know.
>
> *Chairman Walsh:* I will read it to you. "I know that father has followed the events of the past few months in connection with the fuel company with unusual interest and satisfaction." The fuel company is Colorado Fuel and Iron Company?
>
> *Mr. Rockefeller Jr.:* Yes, sir.
>
> *Chairman Walsh:* Now, on September twenty-sixth, nine thousand of his faithful employees took to the canyons of Colorado rather than work under the conditions they had been working under . . . ?
>
> *Mr. Rockefeller Jr.:* I would think something like that came out, from the reports that came to me.
>
> *Chairman Walsh:* And a few months prior to the time that you wrote that letter about your father, Jeff Farr [sheriff of Huerfano County] had deputized three

hundred twenty-six gunmen and allowed your company to arm them and turned them loose in the community; that is true, is it?

Mr. Rockefeller Jr.: That is the statement made; I don't know from personal knowledge.

Chairman Walsh: Is it not true that these deputized gunmen, before you wrote about your father's unusual satisfaction, that the gunmen had riddled the Forbes tent colony with machine guns, and had shot a boy of one of the striking miners nine times through one of the legs?

Mr. Rockefeller.: I cannot say as to that.

Chairman Walsh: Prior to the time you wrote that letter about your father's unusual satisfaction is it not a fact that an effort was made to have the officers of this company meet the representatives of the striking miners, and they were brought together at the statehouse for that purpose, and that the representatives of your company refused to go through a door, a thin partition to meet those men? ... I will ask you if prior to the time that you wrote that letter about your father's unusual satisfaction you had not received a letter from Mr. Bowers stating that he had used every weapon at his command to coerce the governor of the state and whip him into line?

Mr. Rockefeller Jr.: I don't recall. If you have such a letter from my office, I have seen it.

Chairman Walsh: Do you mean to say that on such an important matter as that, that an officer of your company boasted that he would whip the governor of the state into line, that you have forgotten it after submitting it to this commission?

Mr. Rockefeller Jr.: There is a mass of letters there.

Chairman Walsh: Then you have forgotten it?

Mr. Rockefeller Jr.: Yes, sir.

It was an ordeal. Under similar questioning, the crusty Bowers had broken down, covering his eyes at the mention of the massacre and fluttering his fingers. "It was a sickening, disgusting, disgraceful piece of work ... I wish I could forget everything about it."

Junior had held fast. Under Walsh's merciless probing he had not been able to sustain the posture of the naïf remote from the goings-on in Colorado; he could only play the reluctant dragon refusing to answer St. George's call to battle. Yet in the long run it was a strategy that worked. For Walsh's interrogation finally ran up against the stone wall of Junior's distance from events at CF&I. However sympathetic Rockefeller may have been with the operators' bloodthirsty attitude toward the strikers, however much he had endorsed their actions, he in fact had not masterminded the response to the strike.

The second round of hearings produced nothing to add to what had been known since the triumphant April 23 news conference. When Walsh was finally forced to let Junior off the stand, the wind went out of the sails of the investigation. The Walsh Commission issued its final report, calling Ludlow "anarchism stripped of every pretense of even the chimerical idealism that fires the unbalanced mind of the bomb thrower. ... [It was] anarchism for profits and revenge." Yet Walsh was hamstrung by internal divisions in the commission, by criticism from the New York *World* and other influential newspapers, and by the fact that the mandate of the Industrial Relations Commission had expired. He tried to raise private funds to continue the commission's work, as Junior himself had done following the termination of the White Slave Grand Jury. But pursuing a governmental function on a private basis was the prerogative of wealth, not conscience, and it was Junior, not the Missouri crusader, who had the final word.

Shortly after the harrowing hearings were over, Junior received a letter of advice from King. "It seems to me you will have to lead ..." the Canadian wrote, "whether you will or no. Your modesty and your humility does not permit you to see this, but those who have your interests and your life most at heart see it, and it is in the field of industry primarily that this leadership must be conspicuous." It was an audacious plan. Less than two months after being grilled by the Industrial Relations Commission, young Rockefeller would become a pioneer in industrial relations. The metamorphosis was to begin with a pilgrimage to Ludlow and other points of interest in the Colorado coal fields.

The Rockefeller party finally got under way in September, the trip having been put off once because of the death of Cettie Rockefeller. (Public feeling against the family was running so high that the elder Rockefeller, who had been unable to transport his wife's remains to the family plot in Cleveland because he feared he would be served with a subpoena in a tax suit by the state of Ohio, had to station guards at the entrance of the Archbold family's mausoleum, where Cettie's body was temporarily housed.) Junior showed unusual insistence in vetoing his father's order to Charles O. Heydt to carry a pistol on the trip in case there was an attempt on his life.

Because he had already visited the Colorado sites, King acted as guide. The first stop their small caravan of automobiles made was the barren, windswept spot where the Ludlow tent colony had once stood. The Rockefeller group got out of their cars and stood for a moment in silence, the dust settling on their dark suits as they walked to the place where two charred railroad ties formed a cross above the pit in which the thirteen had died. After standing awkwardly for a minute or two, they got back into the cars and continued to wind along the road leading them to the small southern Colorado mining camps.

During the next fortnight, Junior was as approachable as any Smith or Jones who might have been touring the camps. The miners with whom he mingled were surprised at first to have a Rockefeller walking in their midst. He talked their problems over with them, shared their lunches of beans and mashed potatoes on tin plates, and like them, sopped up the gravy with pieces of bread. He went to their homes and chatted by the dirty yellow light of kerosene lamps while sitting on beds with springs sticking up through the mattresses. With King, he put on overalls and a miner's cap with headlight and descended into deep shafts to explore the safety features of the CF&I mines.

The climax of the two-week visit came when Junior was a guest of honor at an evening social in the camp at Cameron. After standing up in the schoolhouse and giving a short talk to the workers and their families, he surprised everyone by suggesting that the floor be cleared for a dance. The orchestra struck up a fox-trot, and Junior, asking the superintendent's wife to do him the honor, began to circle the floor with the stiff formality left over from his college days when he had worried that he would slip on debutantes' glassy floors.

As the first strains of the orchestra filled the air, the newspapermen traveling with the Rockefeller entourage headed for the one available telephone. "That incident, and the publicity that was given to it throughout the State," said F. A. McGregor, King's aide, "was more effective in fostering good will than a dozen speeches or conferences." In the course of the evening, Rockefeller danced with all of the twenty or so women present. When the dance was over, he announced that he was ordering a bandstand for Cameron at his personal expense and that he would throw in a dance pavilion for good measure.

On October 2, Rockefeller and King met in the small town of Pueblo with some two hundred representatives of the employees of Colorado Fuel and Iron and the officers of the company to discuss the Industrial Representation Plan. Junior spoke first: "I went into your washhouses, and talked with the men before and after bathing. As you know we have pretty nearly slept together—it has been reported that I slept in one of your nightshirts—I would have been proud had this report been true." When a man in the audience yelled out, "I think we are getting somewhere," Rockefeller, with a toastmaster's poise, told the audience that this comment reminded him of the story of the man in a theater who sat on his neighbor's hat, then rose quickly and said, "'I think I have sat on your hat,' whereupon the hat's owner said, 'You think you did? You know damn well you did!'" Then he looked at the man who had made the comment and said, "You think we are getting somewhere? You know damn well we are!"

Next came a lesson in economics. Junior referred to a square table that had been placed nearby. In the parable he proceeded to create, the four sides represented the stockholders, the directors, the officers, and the employees. "This little table illustrates my conception of a corporation," he began. "First you see that it would not be complete unless it had all four sides. Each side is necessary: each side has its own part to play." Junior then placed a pile of coins on the table and reminded the workers of "those Rockefeller men in New York, the biggest scoundrels that ever lived, who have taken millions of dollars out of this company." While carrying on this patter, he suddenly swept more than half the coins off the table, saying that this represented the wage earners' share of the CF&I revenues, paid punctually each two weeks. As the audience watched spellbound, he next removed a smaller part of the pile, which he said was the wages of the managers. Then he took away the few remaining coins, the directors' fees. "And hello! there is nothing left! This must be the CF&I company! For never since my father and I became interested in this company as stockholders, some fourteen years ago, has there been one cent for the common stock. I just want you to put that in your pipes and smoke it and see if it tallies with what you have heard about the stockholders oppressing you and trying to get the better of you."*

The lesson in economics imperceptibly transformed itself into a lesson in morality. Anyone not satisfied with his fair portion upset the harmony of the corporation and jeopardized the earnings of all. The coins were placed on the table again, and one of the legs raised to show what would happen to the earnings if one of the parties tried to get more than its fair share. The implication was that this was the objective of the United Mine Workers. There were men going around the country from one end to the other, Junior observed, telling employees that they should try to get the shortest possible working day and do the least possible work they could get away with. "Any man who preaches that doctrine, instead of being your friend, is your deadliest enemy." If labor were to take that attitude, there would be nothing left for anyone.

Junior stepped down and turned the rostrum over to King. The Canadian proceeded to present his plan. The company's employees were to elect their own representatives by secret ballot, one representative for every 150 men; these representatives would serve with those of management on joint committees to decide on working and living conditions, safety, sanitation, housing, and education. District conferences were to be held at least every four months, and there were elaborate provisions for dealing with grievances. Balloting took place on October 4. Although some 2,000 miners failed to vote, 2,404 of the 2,846 ballots cast favored the program that would soon become known to the world as the Rockefeller Plan.

Returning from Colorado, Junior knew that the agony was finally over. He took Mackenzie King home to visit his father, who, after an evening's conversation, said to the Canadian, "I wish I had had you in the thirty or forty years I was in business to advise me on politics."

His son rejoined, "I'm glad you didn't because I would be prevented then from having Mr. King the next thirty or forty."

*Those watching Junior's performance were probably not aware that this issue had come up in the first round of the Industrial Relations Commission hearings, when Junior had claimed in his defense that his family had gotten only $371,000 in dividends on their investment from 1902 to 1914. Yet Walsh had established that CF&I stock had appreciated some $19 million in value during that time, and that the bulk of the Rockefeller equity was in interest-bearing bonds (not stock), whose payment had never been in default. This computation meant that the Rockefeller return on the CF&I investment was actually over $9 million.

Although King was to serve Junior for a relatively brief interlude,* the impression he made was immense. "I was merely King's mouthpiece," Junior said of this seminal period in his life. "I needed education. No other man did so much for me. He had vast experience in industrial relations and I had none. I needed guidance. He had an intuitive sense of the right thing to do—whether it was a man who ought to be talked with or a situation that ought to be met." Raymond Fosdick, Junior's lifelong associate and biographer, concurred. Mackenzie King, he thought, "had influenced the thinking of the younger Rockefeller perhaps more than any man except his father."

Ludlow was both a terrifying experience for Junior and an exhilarating one. Long after the massacre had slipped into the vast forgetfulness of American history, Junior, reminiscing with Raymond Fosdick, called it "one of the most important things that ever happened to the family," a statement he would later repeat to his grandchildren. It marked that moment when the Rockefeller family entered the twentieth century, and even more, it marked Junior's personal liberation from the past. By handling the crisis, he won his spurs; family leadership passed to him and his associates, Gates having left 26 Broadway to concentrate on the administration of the Foundation. Now he was on the course that would make him a national figure in his own right and would ensure that his voice was taken seriously when he made pronouncements on such widely diverse phenomena as Prohibition and the ecumenical movement.

Ironically, he was also established as an industrial statesman. In 1919 President Wilson invited him to attend an industrial conference in Washington to discuss cooperation in

*He was always available to Rockefeller, yet he declined offers to become a permanent employee. "I doubt if I could be happy continuing indefinitely with Mr. Rockefeller and doing work for large corporations," King wrote in his diary. "I never regarded the connection as more than a 'stepping stone,' a means to lay aside enough [money] to 'get into the fight.'" Association with Junior helped him do this. In 1919, King returned to his homeland and picked up the pieces of what had seemed a ruined political career. He was elected leader of the Liberal party, and in 1921 became Prime Minister of Canada, a position he would hold for all but five of the years until his retirement in 1948. As a token of his affection for King, Junior sent him a gift of $100,000 when he left the government and had the Rockefeller Foundation provide another $100,000 to help King prepare his private papers and diaries for publication.

industry. The forty-five conference participants were divided
into three groups, representing the general public, organized
labor, and business. It was a sign of how successful King's
campaign had been that Junior was chosen to head the conference group representing the general public. Moreover, he
seemed to fulfill these expectations when he sided with the labor and public groups against the business representatives by
supporting recognition of the union principle (although actually it was a hard, behind-the-scenes struggle for King to get
him to admit the validity of collective bargaining). It was
gratifying to see himself referred to in newspapers as "a distinguished labor relations statesman," and to have his name
coupled with such phrases as "moral courage" and "high convictions."

The public attitude toward the Rockefellers was slowly
changing. It was in part due to the new mood of patriotic
unity that had followed America's entry into World War I.
At the outset, Junior made sure to connect the family name
to this movement, getting the Foundation to embark on a
massive effort for war relief. In 1917, with Ludlow now behind him, Junior threw himself into the task of mobilizing the
philanthropic community for the war effort. Even as Ivy Lee
was planting stories in the newspapers that the Rockefeller
heir spent his free time knitting scarves for the doughboys
overseas, he embarked on a speaking tour of the military
camps, making as many as thirty-five speeches on one ten-day
trip, in a program conducted by the YMCA for the War Department. He also enlisted his father's help, bringing the old
man along on several of the swings, and getting him to make
heavy—and well-publicized—contributions to the Red Cross,
the YMCA, and other war-work organizations.

But his most notable achievement was to compel the seven
service organizations, including the YMCA, and YWCA, the
National Catholic War Council (Knights of Columbus), the
Jewish Welfare Board, and the Salvation Army, to come together in a single campaign. The director of the campaign
fund was his old friend John R. Mott; Ivy Lee handled publicity. The Rockefeller Foundation gave $11 million to the
campaign, which eventually raised more than $200 million. It
was kicked off with a gala meeting at Madison Square
Garden, and Junior, as chairman of the Greater New York
region, introduced the permanent chairman of the national
campaign, Charles Evans Hughes, with the words, "This
gathering represents the united American people."

The war's end would usher in the "Era of Normalcy," and with it a new conservative acceptance of business and wealth. But even before the cessation of hostilities, there was the beginning of a subtle change in the public's attitude toward the oil industry and families like the Rockefellers who had been its pioneers. The "Age of Illumination" had passed over into the "Age of Energy," as the advent of the internal combustion engine made oil a vital element in the machinery of modern transportation. "He who owns oil will own the world," warned France's wartime oil commissioner, reflecting the new appreciation of its importance. The Allies, Lord Curzon had declared in his famous postwar statement, "had floated to victory on a wave of oil."

In 1916, five years after the government's successful suit against the Standard trust, A. C. Bedford, who had succeeded John Archbold as president of the Jersey Company, was invited by the White House to become chairman of a Committee on Mobilization to organize the entire industry for the defense effort. In a gesture charged with symbolism, the committee, which included the heads of some of the old pillars of the Standard trust and the new majors—Gulf, Texaco, and Sinclair—met at the famous headquarters at 26 Broadway, under the portrait of John D. Rockefeller himself. The national organization of the oil industry, which John D. Rockefeller had devoted his life to building and which public outrage and the Supreme Court had thwarted in 1911, was now being achieved under government auspices in the name of the national interest.

After the war, Bedford was invited to become president of the U.S. Chamber of Commerce. He declined the position, but the significance of the offer was appreciated by Ivy Lee, who watched these events with a glow of satisfaction. "Now realize what it means for the president of the Standard Oil of New Jersey, the lineal business descendant of John D. Rockefeller, to be asked to become the head of the association speaking for the united businessmen of the whole United States!" he exclaimed. At the instigation of Lee, the American Petroleum Institute was founded by the same men and companies that had been represented on the Bedford committee, carrying into peacetime the cooperative working arrangements between petroleum companies that had been forged during the war. Bedford accepted leadership of the institute, and Ivy Lee agreed to handle its public relations.

So zealous had Washington's support of the oil industry become under the leadership of Harding's Secretary of State, Charles Evans Hughes (Junior's former mentor at the Fifth Avenue Bible class), that critics called him the "Secretary of Oil." A member of the British Foreign Office complained that "Washington officials begin to think, talk, and write like Standard Oil officials."

Oil was now a crucial factor in national power, and rivalry for its sources was so intense that Washington formally identified the national interest with the efforts of U.S. companies, led by the Standard, to control foreign reserves.*

Meanwhile, the new international presence of American power and the increasingly complex articulation of foreign policy had created the need for new organizations to shape policy at the highest levels. In 1921 the Council on Foreign Relations was formed by the leaders of finance and industry, men like Thomas W. Lamont, Wilson's financial adviser and senior partner in the House of Morgan, and John W. Davis, a Morgan lawyer, standard-bearer for the Democratic party in 1924, and a trustee of the Rockefeller Foundation. Junior and the Rockefeller philanthropies were also drawn into the early funding of the council, whose charter members included not only Rockefeller's business and social friends but Fosdick and Jerome Greene from his inner circle of advisers.

It was as if the laws of political and social gravity had changed, and Junior found himself drawn to the center of things. The times had passed when he and Abby would be invited to tea at the White House, as they had been by President Taft, only to be asked at the last minute to enter by a rear door for fear knowledge of their presence would cause a scandal. Soon he would be breakfasting in the Oval Office with President Coolidge—not as a crony, campaign contribu-

*The government would so orchestrate the pursuit of foreign oil that it would effectively establish a syndicate of the major U.S. oil companies abroad. Jersey Standard President Walter Teagle had understood this would be so by the late twenties, when he received a memorandum from a top executive regarding new Mideastern discoveries. "The Standard Oil Company cannot hope to get serious backing from the State Department if it attempts to enter the Mesopotamian field alone. I believe it will be necessary to take some other interests with us and a part of whom, at least, should be outside of the subsidiaries.... Personally, my suggestion would be Standard Oil Company of New York, Sinclair, Doheny, Texas, and it seems to me necessarily the Gulf. I think the effect of any success in Mesopotamia would result in bringing all these people into competition with us in the Mediterranean and that the association is highly undesirable except to gain the support of the State Department."

tor, or even a representative of business as usual, but as the head of a blue-ribbon citizens' group on national law enforcement.

Ludlow was the crisis in the fever that had afflicted the Rockefellers would make policy, not be the object of it.

9

JUNIOR WAS now in control of a constellation of cultural and economic institutions whose reach was international and whose power was unrivaled in American life. He breakfasted with Presidents and was accepted in circles where his father's name had been anathema. He had a plan for the future. If he could be said to lack anything, it was, ironically, financial independence. After he concluded his testimony before the Walsh Commission, his father had sent him another forty thousand shares of Colorado Fuel and Iron stock. It was a gratifying sign of approval, yet it symbolized his problem. Over forty years old, he was still dependent on the old man's periodic generosity.

The question of finances might ultimately have created problems between him and his father if it were not for a law passed in 1916 whereby the federal government dramatically increased its inheritance taxes to 10 percent on estates of more than $5 million; the following year, it increased the rate to 25 percent on estates of $10 million or more. It was then, without ever formally indicating exactly what he was doing or why, that the elder Rockefeller started making his fortune over to his son. First came a huge block of Jersey Standard, Socony Mobil (Standard of New York), Standard of Indiana, and the other splintered companies of the great trust. Then came the industrial properties he and Gates had worked for thirty years to assemble. In all, the transfer took more than four years; but by 1921 it was complete. The amount placed in Junior's hands was close to $500 million. It was about the same amount his father had already given away, leaving the old man only some $20 million to amuse himself with in the stock market.

Although the transfer of the huge fortune was legally complete and final, in another sense it was an optical illusion. Junior had the money, yet in a larger sense it would always belong to the man who had accumulated it; the power it brought in the financial marketplace would remain his, as would the glory in the philanthropies it built. Junior had gained nothing for himself. His father had said that the money was a gift from God; Junior had no choice but to believe it was so. He himself was only the trustee, dispensing the money in ways he assumed his father—if the old man had been interested in such things—would have approved.

Twelve years after the transfer was complete, when Junior was on his way to becoming one of the most admired men in the world because of his wide-ranging philanthropies, he wrote a letter to his father in which he indicated that this feeling of stewardship had not changed:

> In all these years of effort and striving, your own life and example have ever been to me the most powerful and stimulating influence. What you have done for humanity and business on a vast scale had impressed me profoundly. To have been a silent partner with you in carrying out these great constructive purposes and benefactions has been the supreme delight of my life.

The conception entailed a curious reversal. If either of them was a "silent partner" in the thirty-odd years of their collaboration, it was the elder Rockefeller, who had never attended a meeting of the foundations, who had expressed only a passing interest in his son's impressive achievements, and who had played a subsidiary role in family affairs from the time he "retired" from 26 Broadway. In describing himself with this phrase, Junior was unconsciously passing a poignant judgment on his own life. It was as close as his finely controlled character could come to recognizing the awesome suppression of self that his life of service had entailed.

The unconditional reverence in which he held his father had the inevitable effect of establishing a distance between them. "Neither Father nor I," Junior later recalled, "had the temperament which gives itself freely. We talked about whatever he had to talk over—never discursively." It is difficult to imagine what the older man, wise in the world's ways and suspicious of the flattering phrase, made of the stream of effusive letters that regularly flowed to him from the pen of his middle-aged son, who though financially independent still thanked him for the most trivial convenience or gesture.

In 1920, for example, when the 46-year-old Junior was receiving the last pieces of his great legacy, he wrote:

> For your Christmas check of $1,000 I send you most cordial thanks. Not only for this further and beautiful gift would I express my appreciation, but for all the wonderful gifts you have made me this past year, and for those recurring gifts which add so much to the comfort and convenience of our family life and are nonetheless gratefully received by reason of their being so continuous. I refer to the use of electricity in the city, the horses and carriage in the country, and the participation with you in the enjoyment of the farm produce, the flowers and plants from the greenhouse, the occupancy of Abeynton Lodge, and the many services rendered to our family.

Junior's attitude toward his father was all the more striking given the fact that the old man became capable of bewildering eccentricity as he entered his nineties. Controlling every conversation he could and ignoring those he didn't control, he held forth in the ornate dining room at Kikjuit as the host of large dinner parties at which he himself hardly ate at all. In these years, as Raymond Fosdick later admitted in a private letter, he often "greatly embarrassed his children, particularly John Junior." Yet this was something Junior himself was never able to admit. The father was always seen through a child's eyes: a figure too powerful to criticize, too revered to suspect of succumbing to senility.

In 1932, when Senior was in his ninety-second year and Junior was fifty-eight, the son could still be wounded by a gesture that might have been better dismissed as an old man's momentary humor. Senior had complained one evening to Thomas M. Debevoise, Junior's personal attorney and close adviser, that he felt his son owed him something in the neighborhood of $3,500,000 to make "an equitable adjustment" between them in the matter of expenses for maintaining the family office during the previous ten years. Told of the claim, a stunned and heartsick Junior wrote Debevoise the following morning:

In all the years of my business association with Father, I have sought in matters both small and large to be scrupulously conscientious and just. . . . I cannot concede that anything has been done on my part which is inequitable and which now makes appropriate a readjustment for the past. For my own self respect, for the sake of my standing with my wife and children, I cannot for a moment recognize or seem to recognize any such claim or the existence upon which such a claim can justly be made.

Having drawn his line of defense, Junior turned to the "other side of the picture" and came as close to baring his soul as he ever would:

Never once in my life that I can recall have I asked Father for a single cent. He has been generous to me beyond anything that has ever been known. The vast sums he has given me, I have sought to use in ways which he would approve, having in mind his own broad philanthropies. . . . I did not seek nor choose to be the recipient of great wealth, with the staggering responsibilities inevitably coupled with its marvellous opportunities. It has not meant the greatest happiness. From my earliest years I have had but one thought and desire, namely to be helpful to Father in every way in my power. This I have striven all my life to be. I have ever been proud to lay the credit for things accomplished at his feet, where alone it belonged. I have gloried in the greatness of his unparalleled achievements in industry and his worldwide services to humanity. I have never sought anything for myself. I have striven always to serve his interests. Perhaps you can understand, then, how deeply wounded I have been by the criticism which Father's request implies. Nothing in my life has hurt me as much.

The old man, however, had forgotten about the matter long before his son set signature to this letter. It is not known if Debevoise told John D. how deeply wounded Junior had been. The issue disappeared as suddenly as it had come, never again entering the almost daily exchange of letters between the two men that continued until Senior's death. John D. went on playing golf; Junior went on building the Rockefeller myth that sprang from his father but somehow did not include him.

In 1923, as if to objectify the passing of the torch from one Rockefeller to another, Junior took a major step in institutionalizing the Rockefeller mission: he decided to redecorate the office, now *his* office, in the Standard Oil Building at 26 Broadway. Never more than functional during the decades when it had served Gates and his father, it had become somewhat shabby, the drapes bleached from the sunlight, the wallpaper discolored, and the furniture frayed and ready for reupholstering.

For the elder Rockefeller, an office had been a place merely to transact business. ("Anything to do with convenience or utility interested him," Junior once remarked of his father, "but he had no eye for beauty.") In the next generation, however, the office would become less a place where business took place than a Cabinet where high policy was conceived; it required a majesty appropriate to this task. Junior called in the celebrated Charles of London, paying him seventy thousand dollars to renovate the place from top to bottom. Oak paneling was shipped over from an English Tudor mansion; there was a hand-carved Elizabethan mantelpiece over the fireplace; there were Jacobean chairs and refectory tables, and chandeliers. The elaborate bookcase on one wall was not filled with calfskin volumes of Victorian classics, as one might perhaps have expected, but with books on the work of the General Education Board, the Foundation, the Bureau of Social Hygiene, and the Rockefeller family itself. The whole character of the place changed. It was no longer an office, but *the* Office. It was the symbol of the interconnectedness of all future Rockefeller endeavors—charitable, financial, and dynastic.

When Junior first came to work for his father, the office had been a one-man show presided over by the venerable figure the clerks called "Pop" behind his back. But Frederick Gates had long since ceased to be influential in the Rockefellers' personal affairs (although he remained, until his death in 1923, a powerful presence in the corporate philanthropies his genius had inspired). Gates, whose eclipse had begun with Ludlow, had deeply mistrusted experts, feeling that they inevitably put their own bureaucratic interests ahead of their principal's welfare. Time and again he had warned Junior against them, once going so far as to predict that in the future, the

Rockefellers might well find themselves in Lemuel Gulliver's predicament: tied down and controlled by scores of Lilliputian advisers.

But Junior was comforted by bureaucratic structure. Ludlow had taught him the value of informed advice, and of a staff that (as Fosdick once urged) could multiply his eyes and ears and reflect his viewpoint abroad. It was a nice solution to the problem of insulating oneself while at the same time retaining the ability to intervene.

Thus a new classification was born in the Rockefeller Office: the Associate. Junior had already accumulated lieutenants; he now gave them a kind of official status and began to forge them into the nucleus of an organization that would be a major force in his own life and would continue to serve his children and grandchildren as well. His habit was to lunch daily with these advisers, when he was in town, to discuss the Rockefeller family's diverse affairs. It was reminiscent of his father's meetings with his Standard executives; and in their own way, the individuals Junior collected would have a power transcending even that of the Standard Oil Gang of the past. Rockefeller Associates would move with ease between service to the family and service in local and national government. Their network would extend across the whole range of Rockefeller interests, from oil and banking, through foreign policy and education, religion and medicine, politics and art. They would worry about succession within the Office, and be constantly on the lookout for other well-connected people who could be brought into the organization to augment its power. They would be the thread out of which the dynasty would be spun. Junior's Associates would institutionalize the Rockefellers as an enduring feature of American life in the way that Senior's aides had institutionalized Standard Oil.

The full development of the Office to a staff of several hundred took decades. It began modestly with aides Junior had inherited from the Gates regime. One was Charles O. Heydt, who had been hired in 1897, the same year Junior came down from Brown, and whose interest was in real estate development. Another was Bertram Cutler, who entered the service of the Rockefellers in 1901 as a bookkeeper and developed such expertise as a financial adviser that, after Gates's departure, he was able to take over management of all the family's investments. In the fifty-one years he served the Rockefellers, Cutler would come to be known on Wall Street as "the man who votes the Rockefeller stock."

Junior was soon filling pivotal roles in the Office with people his own age who owed their allegiance only to him. When Starr J. Murphy died in 1921, the crucial post of family legal adviser was left open for three years until Junior finally decided on Thomas M. Debevoise, an old fraternity brother. Debevoise was different from the cultured, conservative Murphy in that he had no ideology and never confused his interests with the Rockefellers'. He was fond of illustrating his points with didactic stories such as the one about the man who was hanging a picture on the wall and after discovering that he had been hammering the nail on its point instead of its head, concluded that he had been attempting to hang the picture on the wrong wall. Some found these moral tales tiresome, but no one ever mistook the extent of Debevoise's power. In the twenty-five years he served Junior, he attained an influence over the Rockefellers' development that no one else, with the exception of Gates, was ever to exercise.

Most of Junior's Associates were not full-time employees, but rather, forming an inner circle, functioned as consultants. It began with those who had advised him before and during Ludlow. Mackenzie King could no longer be called on for anything except general advice. Ivy Lee, however, continued to represent the Rockefellers on a retainer of $10,000 a year. Taking charge of the public relations of the family and handling it the same way he did his corporate accounts, Lee would be on the scene to promote great philanthropies like Colonial Williamsburg and great dramas like Junior's later fight to oust the chairman of Standard of Indiana. It was Lee who helped persuade Junior to withdraw support from the Eighteenth Amendment, paving the way for the repeal of Prohibition. It was he who got the Associated Press to rewrite the obituary it had on file for John D., Sr., replacing data taken from Tarbell and the muckrakers with more favorable material collected by W. O. Inglis, a journalist he had hired to do hundreds of hours of interviews with the elder Rockefeller as the first step in an authoritative biography.

There were Associates who had been around Junior from the days of the Bureau of Social Hygiene. Colonel Arthur Woods was one, a former Groton schoolmaster who had married a Morgan (and named one of his sons John Pierpont). Woods had been New York's police commissioner from 1914 to 1916 and had done much to reform those halcyon days of crime when the head of the New York detectives had permitted pickpockets and confidence men to operate on the condition that they stay off Wall Street and Fifth Avenue, and report all outside crooks coming into the city. Although Woods took leaves of absence from his service with Junior to serve the government as director of the Committee on Public Information during World War I and later as head of the Commission for Employment during the Hoover administration, he would, during his service, be the detail man in the Office and Junior's man Friday.

Unlike Woods, however, most of the men Junior was attracted to were innovators, not administrators. Although they came under the gravitional influence of the great Rockefeller wealth, their operational orbits were outside the Office itself. They were drawn to the fortune in the first place because they were, to one degree or another, missionaries who saw in its power a great potential for the realization of their hopes.

Gates would be only the first of a succession of talented men who were to guide the Rockefeller social investment: Wickliffe Rose, the Flexner brothers, John R. Mott, and others. In Junior's own generation, the outstanding example was Raymond Fosdick. The long-faced, ambitious Fosdick was a Democrat and a Wilsonian progressive. He entered Junior's orbit through the Bureau of Social Hygiene. Fosdick, who had been among the early proponents of a private organization to promote efficiency in government, obtained Rockefeller's backing for the Institute of Government Research, which shortly was transformed into the influential Brookings Institution. In 1916 he was called to Washington by Secretary of War Newton Baker as chairman of a Commission on Training Camp Activities, and utilizing his experience with the Bureau of Social Hygiene, he worked to close every red light district in the United States and thus make soldiers "fit to fight" when war came in 1917. Following the war, President Wilson appointed Fosdick an under secretary-general of the League of Nations; after the United States failed to join the League, he became a moving force in the creation of the Foreign Policy Association and an organizer of the Council on Foreign Relations. It was Fosdick who got Rockefeller involved and interested in the question of the realignment of global power that would begin to take place in the decade after World War I.

Fosdick also assisted and encouraged Junior in investments in the field of social relations. Along with Mackenzie King, he convinced Rockefeller to put up the money to begin Industrial Relations Counselors, Inc., an organization based on the assumption that labor relations was a field to bear watching, and the best opportunity for influencing its development was in the realm of management counseling. In its sales pitch, it stressed that a satisfied labor force meant more profits and that any increased costs from accommodating the human weakness of laborers would be more than counterbalanced by increased efficiency and contentment. Fosdick's next step was to encourage the development of the emerging science of industrial relations and industrial management in American universities. Beginning with the creation of an Industrial Relations section at Princeton in 1922, he went on to develop similar programs at other major schools. The first five years of the Princeton program were funded by Junior, as was every other institute of industrial relations set up at a major university in the interwar years.

The inner circle of Associates was constantly expanding. Fosdick had first brought Arthur Woods to Junior's attention, and in 1921 he hired another young man with formidable talents, Beardsley Ruml. It was to Ruml that he entrusted the task of making a survey of the Metropolitan Museum of Art, the American Museum of Natural History, and the New York Public Library, to which Junior proposed to give a sum of one million dollars each. A psychology Ph.D. from the University of Chicago, Beardsley Ruml was a huge, florid-faced man of Czech parentage who had already established himself in business and philanthropy when Fosdick brought him to Junior's attention. Formerly employed as an adviser to the Armour and Swift companies, and assistant to the president of the Carnegie Corporation, Ruml was one of the new breed of intellectual entrepreneurs able to move smoothly between the worlds of universities, business, and government, creating agencies, assembling networks of influence, and in general helping to blueprint the emergence of the new administrative state.

Upon completion of his museum survey, Ruml was invited to become director of the Laura Spelman Rockefeller Memorial Fund. Least sharply defined and with the smallest endowment of any of the Rockefeller foundations, its goals had been "to promote the welfare of women and children," but until Ruml took over, it had been largely inactive. He promptly reoriented the Fund to make a concentrated effort to reform the social sciences and make them more applicable to the problems of social management and control as encountered by the expanding government and corporate bureaucracies. Throwing the full weight of the Fund behind the efforts of Charles E. Merriam, head of the Political Science Department at Chicago, Ruml helped underwrite the conquest of the academic world by Merriam and his "behaviorist" school.*

As the first years of Junior's leadership passed, the Office came to function more and more like a business. Decisions that had once been made according to Gates's and Senior's individual quirks and interests were now made through established channels. The foundations had their own administrators; in making his personal charitable gifts, Junior came to rely heavily on what became known in the office as the "philanthropic unit." It was headed by Arthur Packard, a former field secretary to the World Peace Foundation. Packard hired a team whose sole duty would be investigating possible recipients for Rockefeller charity. Organizations from developing fields as diverse as civil rights and birth control would pass under Packard's glance, as he decided whether they were responsible and potentially significant enough for Rockefeller support. Under his leadership, giving was soon integrated into the smooth operation of the Office and its routines, allowing Junior to master the art of spending money as well as his father had mastered the art of making it.

His checkbook seemed to hang suspended above every new development in American life, and he himself seemed to be involved in everything from helping rebuild war-ravaged Versailles to supporting Egyptologists on missions into the Middle East. As his wife, Abby, once commented when asked where Junior was, "I never know where John is anymore, but I'm sure he is out saving the world somewhere."

There was much that his Associates did in his name, especially in the more innovative fields. The philanthropic projects that had the most appeal for him personally were the traditional ones, like the building of museums and the resto-

*Together, Ruml and Merriam created the Social Sciences Research Council, which Fosdick would later say "became the most important instrumentality in America for furthering intercommunication between students and social problems and sponsoring cooperative research among the several disciplines." In seven years, Ruml spent over $40 million creating a network of personnel and institutions dedicated to the administrative outlook, which was to have wide applications in the future expansion of the American state and greatly to extend Rockefeller influence in the academic world.

ration of palaces and cathedrals. It was the sort of thing wealthy families had been doing for years on a "Lady Bountiful" basis. Yet Junior's means were so great and his ambition so large, that even here he did things nobody else had dreamed of.

In 1923, for example, the Reverend Dr. William Goodwin, professor of sacred literature at William and Mary College and sometime chairman of the school's endowment fund, met Rockefeller at a Phi Beta Kappa meeting he was attending in his capacity as chairman of the fund-raising committee. For years, Goodwin had cherished a private dream of restoring the slightly shabby, worn-out little town of Williamsburg, three centuries earlier the cultural and political epicenter of the Virginia Dynasty, which had played a major role in the creation of the Republic. That evening, Goodwin broached the subject to Junior, astutely sensing that a Rockefeller might have more than a passing interest in being associated with a project to create a national shrine connected with the birth of American democracy.

Junior was politely encouraging, yet declined to get involved at that time. Then in 1926 Goodwin received word that Junior and Abby were to motor through Williamsburg on their way back from a trip south, and he decided to try again. He arranged to give them a guided tour of "old" Williamsburg with special emphasis on the buildings still standing from the colonial period. At this time Goodwin gave the Rockefellers sketches he had made showing what a restored city might look like. He was heartened when Junior agreed to take the sketches back to New York with him.

When one of the few remaining old brick buildings in the town—a public house immortalized by a reference in Boswell's *Life of Johnson*—came on the market, Junior agreed to buy it. He signed his telegram telling Goodwin the good news, "David's Father" (after his last-born son), later adopting the pseudonym "Mr. David" to use in land purchases, for fear knowledge of Rockefeller involvement would send prices skyrocketing. Working under the strict secrecy Junior demanded, Goodwin began to buy up a large portion of the old town. It was only after a year of secret purchases that Junior told Goodwin he was now prepared to go ahead with the plans as originally presented and to restore the entire city. It was another year before Goodwin was able to announce the name of the patron and the intention of the project to a crowded hall of expectant Williamsburg citizens, who greeted the announcement with a spontaneous ovation.

At first it was assumed that Williamsburg would be an antiquity that would draw modest numbers of people: the old inns and ordinaries were rebuilt to accommodate the visitors. But they were always booked. Soon Williamsburg was on the verge of financial success; Junior set up Colonial Williamsburg, Inc., first under Arthur Woods and later under Woods's assistant, Kenneth Chorley. It became his favorite philanthropy. He brought his family there for at least two months a year for the rest of his life, staying at Basset Hall, the most elegant manor house in the city, which he had reserved for his private use. From his front yard, he could look out onto eighteenth-century America and see how his $50 million investment was progressing.

Junior felt comfortable when surrounded with re-created antiquity. The same was true of art. He had never allowed himself to become a compulsive collector like Frick and some of his father's other contemporaries. Yet he did have personal weaknesses, especially for Chinese porcelains.* Just as he kept himself abreast of even the most mundane details of the Williamsburg purchases, going over floor plans and old maps of the city with great care, so he spent countless hours minutely inspecting each new porcelain before and after its acquisition, having it photographed and then cataloguing it himself. Later, as Abby began to improve the walls of their town house with Italian primitives and Goyas, Junior struggled to keep up. He educated himself to the point that

---

*In 1915 the famous procelains of J. P. Morgan had come on the market after the great man's death. Junior had an opportunity to buy one-third of the collection, but it was before the fortune had passed into his hands and he had to ask his father for the million-dollar purchase price. Art collection was something the elder Rockefeller simply could not understand. A few years before Junior's request, he had written his son: "I am convinced that we want to study more and more not to enslave ourselves to *things* and get down more nearly to the Benjamin Franklin idea of living, and take our bowl of porridge on a table without any tablecloth." Now he told Junior that he had considered the request for the Morgan collection but thought "that it would be wiser not to make this investment now." Junior wrote back in rare petulance, obliquely reminding his father of his sacrifice: "I have never squandered money on horses, yachts, automobiles or other foolish extravagances. A fondness for these porcelains is my only hobby. . . . I have found their study a great recreation and diversion, and I have become very fond of them." He added what was undeniably true—that he had never asked his father for anything—and the money was advanced.

he felt comfortable with paintings of the Mannerist school, but even as he did so, there was a certain kind of art entering the top-floor museum (formerly the children's playroom) of his 54th Street house that he did not like at all. These were the modern works which Abby ordered and paid for with her own Aldrich inheritance—the O'Keeffes and Bellowses along with the Braques and Picassos.

These canvases presented a challenge to Junior's sensibility which he never quite managed to handle. "I am interested in beauty," he once said, "and by and large I do not find beauty in modern art. I find instead a desire for self-expression." It was the sort of indulgence he had never allowed himself, and it upset him enough so that late in life, when his son Nelson (by then the foremost Rockefeller in the art world) asked Junior to sit for the Italian sculptor Marini and showed him photos of his work, Junior wrote back: "As much as I hate not to do anything one of you children ask me to do, I would not be happy to go down in posterity or to be represented in the manner shown by the photographs."

Yet uncomfortable as he was with the uncontrolled individuality in the paintings Abby collected, Junior deferred graciously to her on this matter, suffering through dinners with Matisse and other artists who barely concealed their contempt for him, and finally donating $5 million to help his wife become a co-founder of the Museum of Modern Art in 1927. After his children had grown and left home and he and Abby had moved to a smaller apartment on Fifth Avenue, he even made the property on West 54th Street available for the outdoor gardens of what was always referred to in the family as "Mother's Museum."

A project far closer to Junior's own heart was the Cloisters, a museum of Romanesque arches, Gothic sculpture, and medieval tapestries. As in Williamsburg, Junior was here an investor in another man's vision—this time an eccentric artist named George Grey Barnard, who would later be described as "one of the most romantic and rugged collectors of our time," and whose lack of funds had compelled him to comb the ruined abbeys and churches of Europe personally to discover his treasures. Junior bought the Barnard Cloisters for the Metropolitan Museum of Art and arranged for their transfer from the small museum Barnard had opened on 190th Street to Fort Tryon Park, on the upper west side of Manhattan, which he had purchased earlier. In 1935 he began the construction of a monasterylike building to house

Barnard's dazzling collection. Completed in impeccable taste by 1938, it was surrounded by lovely gardens that gave it the atmosphere of a refuge. As a perfect finishing touch, Junior donated the famous Unicorn Tapestries that had adorned the walls of his town house.

The impulse to build enclaves of quiet harmony was a deep-seated one in Junior, and the interest in cultural conservation led naturally to the conservation of nature. The 3,500-acre estate at Pocantico, which Junior had been primarily responsible for building, itself had been an experiment in conservation. And when Junior bought his vacation home at Seal Harbor, he found that former Harvard President Charles W. Eliot, Edsel Ford, and his other affluent neighbors there were concerned that Mount Desert Island would be altered by tourists and traffic brought by the automobile. Junior took on the major role in their attempt to preserve the area. By 1916 he had helped assemble some five thousand acres, which was given the federal government for the first national park in the eastern states.

Had his activities gone no further than this, it might have been said that the creation of Acadia National Park was merely a way of isolating and protecting his retreat at Seal Harbor (Junior continued to buy up Mount Desert land and give it to the park, including a long narrow strip running to the ocean, which, in effect, completed the barrier around the Eyrie). In fact, it was only the beginning of a major Rockefeller involvement in the growing field of conservation.

In 1924 Junior journeyed west for an extensive sightseeing trip wih Abby and the three older boys of his growing family, John III, Nelson, and Laurence. They went first through New Mexico and Colorado, and then made plans to stop at Yellowstone, the jewel of the fledgling National Park Service that had been created in 1916. The superintendent of Yellowstone, Horace Albright, was cabled from Washington to expect a visit from Mr. Rockefeller, Jr., who would be traveling under the alias of Mr. Davidson. When Albright met the Rockefellers at the railhead, he found that Junior had already arranged to have a chauffeured limousine on hand and had a timeable drawn up for their visit. Albright was further surprised when Rockefeller ordered his boys to run over and help the depot's one black porter unload all the passengers' baggage. Then he and Abby and the doctor traveling with them drove off to the lodge with Albright, leaving his sons to catch the bus.

For the next three days, Junior traveled through Yellowstone and then headed north for his next stop at Glacier National Park, where he and the boys went on a two-week pack trip up into the mountains. Returning to New York, he wrote Albright to say that he had had a good time, but was distressed by the amount of debris that had gathered at the side of the rough roads through Yellowstone. He asked Albright how much it would take to clean it up, and after receiving a figure in Albright's letter of reply, sent him a check.

Two years later, Junior returned to Yellowstone, bringing Laurance and the two younger boys, Winthrop and David. This time, Junior allowed Albright to give them a tour, and the superintendent arranged an itinerary that took them to the magnificent Jackson Hole area in the Grand Tetons. He purposely led the Rockefeller party past a number of dilapidated ranches and cabins cluttering the landscape, and told the curious Junior that he feared the scenic drive might further degenerate under the impact of roadside stands and billboards about to move into the area. Albright concluded the tour by taking the party up to a rim high in the Tetons. It was a breathtaking view looking down at the Snake River winding through the Jackson Hole valley. Albright remarked, seemingly in passing, that the piecemeal speculation and commercialization then taking place was a sad fate for such a beautiful area, and that it had always been his dream to find a way to save it.

That winter Junior asked Albright to come to New York to present plans for preserving the area. The superintendent thought he meant the area along the drive, and he armed himself with maps and visual aids to make the presentation, intent on telling Rockefeller that it would cost $250,000 to buy up these lands. However, when he got to New York, he found that Junior had it in mind to buy up all of the Jackson Hole valley Albright had shown him from the top of the rim. Rockefeller said, "I'm only interested in *ideal* projects. You showed me an ideal. That's the only project I'm interested in." Then he told the stunned Albright to go to Colonel Woods's office to begin working out the details.

On the second trip west, Junior had also stopped in northern California, where he was met by members of the Save-the-Redwoods League, who took him on a motorcade through the redwood forest to Eureka and then Crescent City. Newton Drury, president of the league, recalls stopping so that Junior could call in a telegram to wish his father a happy birthday. There was trouble with the phone, and Junior was shouting, "This is Mr. Rockefeller! This is Mr. Rockefeller!" Suddenly he listened for a moment, then turned around and made a face and said, "The man on the other end keeps saying, 'Yes, and this is Mr. Carnegie!'" The lighthearted mood persisted through the trip, and at the end, Junior agreed to make the first of contributions that would eventually amount to over $2 million in the cause that culminated in Redwood National Park.

Later Junior would give money to such conservation projects as the Big Trees in the Sierra Nevada and the Great Smoky Mountains National Park in Tennessee. Men he worked with in building these monuments soon found their careers accelerated into the high reaches of the Interior Department. Albright and Drury, who remained part of the Rockefellers' so-called "outer circle," would become heads of the fledgling National Park Service and would do much to solidify the Rockefellers' identification with the conservation movement.

Whether the field was conservation or education, foreign policy formulation or medical research, public administration or the collection of fine art, Junior was coming to occupy a unique place in the most prestigious and influential of the nation's institutions. Other wealthy families were setting up foundations and making bequests—it was an activity that would intensify with the advent of New Deal tax laws—but most of the large gifts went to museums or hospitals, or to a remembered alma mater, while the smaller ones were based on fleeting personal whim or an irrecoverable impulse of *noblesse oblige*. With Junior it was different. Such impulsive generosity as had managed to sneak through the cracks of the bleak Baptist ethos of his upbringing was banned as inefficient and potentially dangerous. Giving for him was a profession, a vocation, a *métier*. Always on the lookout for new fields in which to make charitable investments, he pursued the spending of the prodigious sum he had been given with the same solemn industry his father had marshaled while in command of his great trust. Junior too seeded the growth of subsidiary enterprises, and soon the philanthropic empire he had assembled was in its own way as impressive a creation as Standard Oil.

He also had inherited his grandmother Eliza Rockefeller's tendency to consolidate and trim wastefulness. The philanthropic field where this was most needed was in Protestant theology and theological education. The older he got, the less involved Junior became in the Baptist church where he had spent his youth, and his parents their life * He saw that by a stubborn adherence to fundamentalist beliefs and by intramural strife, the church was likely to lose its influence (much as his father had seen that unrestrained competition of oil refiners would keep prices down). As early as 1910, under the influence of Gates and Mott, he had been struck by how much effort the competing Protestant denominations spent in sectarian squabbles, and how this weakened the missionary effort abroad. After World War I, he became deeply involved in the Interchurch World Movement, which was based both on the optimism engendered by the victory in Europe (if a united effort could defeat the Kaiser, why not heathenism?) and on a practical feeling that another crusade was needed to bring the warring factions of Christianity together. The formation of the Federal Council of Churches in 1908 had given the ecumenical movement a preliminary organizational form, and Junior was among those who thought the hour had come to launch the movement in the rest of the world.

Becoming swept up into the mission, he took his first and last plunge into the public arena as something more than a ceremonial figure. In an address delivered at the Baptist Social Union in December 1917, he had spoken with uncharacteristic passion of the church and its future:

> Would that I had the power to bring to your minds the vision as it unfolds before me! I see all denominational emphasis set aside. I see co-operation, not competition. In the large cities I see great religious centers. . . . In small places, instead of half a dozen dying churches, competing with each other, I see one or two strong churches, uniting the Christian life of the town. I see the church molding the thought of the world as it has never done before, leading in all great movements as it should. I see it literally establishing the Kingdom of God on earth.

Junior gave himself to the Interchurch World Movement, both financially and administratively, contributing more than

---

*Oddly, though, the emotional experience of evangelism retained a kind of hold on him. He became a major (although unpublicized) supporter of Billy Sunday in 1917 and contributed $75,000 to Billy Graham's New York Crusade forty years later.

$1 million to the movement's initial operating budget of $40 million, and exhausting himself in a national speaking tour. He had not reckoned on the cynicism of the various denominations, which used the movement as a fund-raising pitch to bring in nearly $200 million for their own coffers although they contributed less than $2 million of it to the crusade itself. Soon the organization was bankrupt, and Junior was raising money not to send legions of Christian soldiers around the world, but simply to discharge the movement's debts.

After this, Junior took a more cautious approach to ecumenism, although he continued to fund on a more modest scale agencies such as the Federal Council of Churches and the Institute of Social and Religious Research, which conducted many religious surveys using the new social science methods. Inspired by his friend and mentor John R. Mott, he also sponsored an ambitious inquiry into the effectiveness of missionary work. After almost a year of intensive survey of the Orient (principally India, China, and Japan), the study group issued its report, *Re-Thinking Missions*. It was as pragmatic as the Interchurch World Movement had been quixotic, criticizing foreign missions in the underdeveloped world, recommending less preaching and doctrinalism, a more sympathetic attitude toward the indigenous cultures, greater emphasis on education, medicine, and agriculture, and a gradual transfer of responsibility for the missions into the hands of foreign nationals.

When the report first appeared in 1932, it caused considerable controversy. But Junior was satisfied that it was an important piece of work. He read several sections before publication. ("I have done so with a lump in my throat," he wrote the commission that had compiled the study, "and with a fervent song of praise in my heart.") The conclusions of *Re-Thinking Missions* complemented the new view of global alignment he had obtained from involvement in the Institute for Pacific Relations, the Foreign Policy Association, the Council on Foreign Relations, and the rest of the new "internationalist" organizations in which Mott, Fosdick, and other advisers had involved him.

All of these strands came together in the early thirties to make Junior the most important financier of liberal and ecumenical Protestantism and a rallying point in the demands for change inside the church. In this cause he was as usual greatly influenced by friends and Associates, including Charles Evans Hughes, a leading layman of the Fifth Avenue (now Park Avenue) Baptist Church, the Reverends Buttrick and Gates from the charitable trusts, John Mott, and even Ivy Lee. All were partisans of modernism in the church, endorsing the "progressive" trends that were transforming the life of the country: the centralization of administrative units, the growth of scientific ideas and technology, the internationalization of American influence and power. They wanted the church to relate to these tendencies in a positive way, and thereby retain its effectiveness as a cohesive social force in American life. Arrayed against them were the fundamentalists, responsive to the small-town conservatism of rural America and clinging to the old doctrines and the old ways.

These conflicts had broken in a storm about the head of one of the rising young clerics of the time, the Reverend Harry Emerson Fosdick, brother of Raymond and pastor of the Old First Presbyterian Church at 11th Street and Fifth Avenue. Fosdick had begun as a conciliator, not a warrior, and when he rose in the pulpit one May morning to deliver his sermon "Shall the Fundamentalists Win?" it was little more than a plea for tolerance for the liberals under assault.

"There might have been no unusual result" of the sermon, Fosdick later observed, "if it had not been for Ivy Lee." Taken by Fosdick's pragmatic liberalism, Lee promptly printed the Sermon in pamphlet form, changing its title and adding subheadings and a flattering introduction. He then began distributing it to a nationwide clientele. The attack that followed made headline news and called forth "an explosion of ill-will [in Fosdick's words] that went the limit of truculence." When the smoke cleared, Fosdick had resigned from the First Presbyterian.*

As Fosdick was about to leave his pastorate, he received an invitation to lunch with Junior. The two men already knew each other, and after the young clergyman arrived at the new Rockefeller town house on Park Avenue, Junior wasted no time in offering him the ministry of his own Park Avenue Church, whose pastor was scheduled to retire soon. The only surprise was Fosdick's refusal. When Junior asked him why, he replied bluntly: "Because you are too wealthy, and I do

*The confrontation was continued in the Protestant General Assembly. The fundamentalists, led by William Jennings Bryan, tried to excommunicate Fosdick, charging that he was guilty of heresy in casting doubt on the virgin birth. Fosdick was aided in his parliamentary victory over the Bryan forces by a young attorney who had become a leading layman in the church and who felt strongly about this question. His name was John Foster Dulles.

not want to be known as the pastor of the richest man in the country."

There was a long silence, and then Junior drawled: "I like your frankness, but do you think that more people will criticize you on account of my wealth, than will criticize me on account of your theology?"

In the end, the Park Avenue congregation removed the two final obstacles that had stood in the way of Fosdick's taking the job when it relaxed its insistence on baptism by immersion and agreed to move to a less swank area. After Junior provided $26 million toward the construction of a new interdenominational church on Riverside Drive in Morningside Heights, Fosdick agreed to accept the calling, which was not the most influential pastorate in the country and the one that would be largely responsible for the victory of the Protestant liberals.

Fosdick continued to be attacked on the question of modernism, and Junior continued to support him, even though they often had disagreements. In December 1927, for instance, Rockefeller wrote to his new pastor to complain about the previous week's sermon. The subject had been the conflict between capital and labor, and Fosdick had been somewhat critical of the former. "As you know," Junior noted in broaching an issue that was especially sensitive to him, "all my life I have sought to stand between labor and capital, trying to sympathize with and understand the point of view of each, and seeking to modify the extreme attitude of each and bring them into cooperation. . . . The middle ground of sympathy with both," he repeated, emphasizing the peculiar ground he had assumed for himself in the controversy, "recognizing the shortcomings of each, encouraging their improvement and helping to bring them together, has been the position which I have sought to occupy."

Fosdick responded with a somewhat unyielding answer and drew yet another note in which Junior pressed his argument more strongly. "The introduction of standards [for workers' safety and welfare] into industry where they do not already exist is a slow process of education. . . . I have been years in making such progress as has been attained. But progress is being made, and I am everlastingly taking in the slack and pressing forward." Finally understanding how upset his patron was, Fosdick answered quickly: "Of course, I took it for granted that you were a liberal, and if I had been sure of your devotion to progressive policies in industry, I never would have dreamed of taking the pastorate of a church in which you were a prominent and powerful member. Be sure, therefore, if ever in the pulpit I shoot off a gun on the industrial question, I am thinking of you as behind the gun and not in front of it."

On October 5, 1930, six thousand people gathered for the opening service in the massive Gothic edifice of the Riverside Church, whose effort to bridge the gap between traditional and modern architecture was derisively styled "neo-eclectic" by its critics. To symbolize the interdenominational spirit and its further reconciliation of religion and science, the tympanum arching the main portal contained the figures of non-Christian religious leaders and outstanding heroes of secular history, Confucius and Moses, Hegel and Dante, Mohammed and even the dread Darwin. .

The building itself was located a block away from the northern boundary of New York's leading university, Columbia (an institution that had been the recipient of numerous large gifts from the Rockefeller Foundation, the General Education Board, and the Laura Spelman Rockefeller Memorial Fund) and adjacent to Barnard College (to which Senior had given money half a century earlier, and in recognition of which Cettie had been put on the first board of trustees). Across Claremont Avenue, which bounded Riverside Church on the east, was the Union Theological Seminary, whose site Junior had helped to choose and whose 1922 endowment drive he had launched with a $1,083,333 gift, amounting to a quarter of its goal. Already one of the foremost divinity schools in the land, whose faculty would boast such formidable voices of modern Protestantism as Reinhold Niebuhr, Henry Pitney Van Dusen, and John C. Bennett, the Seminary's influence was to be greatly enhanced by its proximity to Riverside Drive and the other institutions the Rockefellers had helped to locate there.

By the time of his death, Junior had contributed nearly $75 million to these developments, including $23 million to the Sealantic Fund (the foundation he had established for his religious charities) "to strengthen and develop Protestant theological education" for a little more mortar in the edifice of the Protestant establishment he, more than any other individual, had made possible.*

---

*To some degree, Junior's dream of a united and streamlined church came true. In 1950 the Federal Council of Churches merged with twelve Protestant missionary agencies to form the National Council of

10

BY THE EARLY 1930s Junior's success was undeniable, yet it had been purchased at a high price. His letters from the previous decade show a man terrified of sickness and often exhausted almost beyond his endurance. In 1922 he had excruciating headaches that none of the doctors he visited could cure. He spent three weeks at a Michigan sanatorium, where he took a battery of tests and was finally told that his problem was "auto-intoxication" brought on by strain.

It was inevitable, given who he was. His father had learned how to unbend, relaxing in the methodical exertion of the golf course and the whimsy of dinner table conversation. Junior did not have the old man's rejuvenating wit and irony. He was always looking to the next project, searching for new ways to push the dynasty he was building one step farther, hoping to accumulate yet a greater degree of public regard and personal influence and honor for the Rockefeller name. His quest centered on his father, yet in the last analysis he was his mother's son and unconsciously condemned unearned joy as a sign of unworthiness. Abby knew this tendency well and struggled against it most of their life together. Once, having taken her reluctant husband to see *Harvey*, she wrote to one of her sons that, after the performance, Junior "asked if it proved anything. I told him it proved the importance of having pleasant people in the world. Though the principal character was a drunkard, he was so very delightful that you had the feeling all the time that perhaps to be pleasant and amusing might be more important than to be sober and disagreeable."

Churches, with Rockefeller providing the initial capital to fund a wide-ranging study of organizational structures for the new group and donating a large parcel of land near Riverside Church for its headquarters. Soon the fifteen-story Interchurch Center would rise on this plot as the headquarters of the principal Protestant denominations in America, their Home and Foreign Missions, and their National Council.

Junior managed to transcend many of his limitations, but he was never able to become pleasant and amusing. The sanctimony he had adopted as a proper child of Spelman heritage never quite rubbed off. Harold Ickes, Roosevelt's Interior Secretary, wrote in his private diary after a visit to the Junior Rockefellers at Pocantico: "At this large dinner, neither cocktails nor wine was served, and he said grace. He had to rap for order for this and Mrs. Rockefeller remarked to me that he always insisted on saying grace himself even if a clergyman was present." There was also an unyielding formality. He called even close associates like Mackenzie King and Raymond Fosdick "Mr. King" and "Mr. Fosdick" during the decades of their working together. He was capable of rewarding loyalty with money ($100,000 to King, $50,000 to Kenneth Chorley, and other generous gifts to loyal aides), but not with emotion. There seemed to be a constant war in him between the magnanimity he admired and the penuriousness that was closer to his true self. When Winthrop Aldrich's three-year-old son died suddenly, Junior tried to help by immediately arranging to charter a private railroad car to carry the mourners to the funeral, but afterward he fretted about the cost until he finally billed his brother-in-law the $229 he was out of pocket for expenses.

He was an odd little man, filled with contradictions. If he had been asked what exactly he thought he had accomplished with the millions he dispensed, he might have said that he had tried to bring men and nations closer together, consolidate important but disorganized social fields, and build the sort of landmarks that great numbers of people could enjoy and learn from. In some of these ambitions he had succeeded. But underneath the altruism, his philanthropy had a shrewdly practical side in which good works interfaced smoothly with power and a sense of the control that could come from intimate involvement in the social movements his growing band of Associates forecast would be important in coming years. His approach to giving was businesslike. This was only fitting, for while he had found it convenient to sever his public ties with business after Ludlow, he never lost sight of the importance of the business process. Publicly he tried to convey the impression that making money was no concern of his. As he once said to a reporter from the New York *Tribune*, "What do I want with more money, or what does Father want with more? Nearly all my time and nearly all the time that my father gives to financial affairs is devoted to studying how best and wisely to distribute the money accumulated." But privately he never relinquished his obligation to manage and preserve the family fortune. In fact, his life was like the parable of the loaves and fishes, for even while he was giving away vast amounts of money, he was taking steps to make sure that his five sons would have something like the sum his father had put in his custody.

Even before he controlled the fortune himself, Junior had tried to convince his father to streamline it for the new age. As early as 1911 he had strongly urged the old man to invest part of the money in lending and trust companies. Senior was like Henry Ford in his aversion to bankers and their institutions. He had seen too many securities schemes in his day to feel comfortable having his money tied up in a bank. But his son pressed the suit strongly. He wrote his father, quoting approvingly from a memorandum he had solicited from Gates:

> This estate is going to require at all times in the future a number of qualified men if it is to be handled properly. Large interests in several trust companies will give the estate the right to put its agents on the boards of such companies. The associations on such boards and the information got at such meetings cannot fail to be of great value to the agents and cannot fail to bring the important facts necessary to be known at all times in the commercial world to your father's attention.

Others in the Rockefeller circle strengthened his view that finance was the business hub of the era. His own father-in-law, Nelson Aldrich, was the voice of the financial bloc in Congress, and a major force behind legislation creating the Federal Reserve System in 1913 and establishing a partnership between the bankers and the government in managing the nation's money. With the help of this circle, Junior finally persuaded John D. to buy a controlling interest in the Equitable Trust Company, formerly a subsidiary of the Equitable Life Assurance Society that the 1911 reform law had forced them to sell.

The latent power of the Rockefeller fortune made the Equitable Trust Company's expansion rapid. By 1920 it had more than $254 million in deposits and had become the nation's eighth-largest bank. By 1929 it had eaten up fourteen smaller banks and trust companies in a series of astute mergers and was not only one of the nation's strongest banks, but had opened a number of foreign branches as well. It had become an important part of the family's increasingly complex financial planning, and when Equitable President Chellis Austin died suddenly in December 1929, Junior was concerned about the institution's future. With his trusted counsel, Thomas Debevoise, he went to his brother-in-law Winthrop Aldrich to convince him to take on its leadership.

Abby's younger brother was an ideal candidate for the position. Handsome and distinguished-looking with a full brush moustache and green eyes, he had graduated from Harvard Law in 1907, married a granddaughter of Charles Crocker, who brought a portion of the California railroad baron's fortune with her as a dowry, and started work in the firm of Byrne, Cutcheon and Taylor. But like many other Aldriches, his career was to be made in the service of the Rockefellers. In 1918 Junior wrote Charles Evans Hughes to ask him to find a suitable place for his brother-in-law. "[Winthrop] had inherited many of the fine qualities and abilities of his father, Senator Aldrich. He is well educated, cultured, widely acquainted socially and most popular. . . . I believe he is one of the most able young men in the city today." After the future Secretary of State wrote back that he didn't at the moment have a place for Aldrich in his firm, Junior found him a spot in the firm of Murray, Prentice and Howland, which for years had been counsel to the family.*

The leading client of the Murray firm was the Equitable Trust, and its legal affairs—especially the negotiations for the series of mergers making it one of the largest banks in the nation—became young Aldrich's primary responsibility. He was then the natural man for the vacant Equitable presidency, and soon after he had settled into his new post, it was decided that the trust company's position in the troubled economy would be best served by a merger with an even larger institution. Junior and his associates narrowed the pos-

---

*George Welwood Murray, senior partner in the firm, had begun his career with the Rockefellers in connection with litigation over the Mesabi iron ore range. E. Parmalee Prentice was the husband of Junior's sister Alta. He had been groomed to oversee the Rockefellers' legal interests, but instead devoted most of his time to projects like translating *Treasure Island* and other classics into Latin for the education of his children. Aldrich brought some of his old law school friends into the firm, including Harrison Tweed, grandson of Rutherford Hayes's Secretary of State. In 1921 the firm became Murray, Prentice and Aldrich.

sibilities to the Chase National Bank and in 1930 made its management an offer.

Headed by Albert H. Wiggin, who over a twenty-year period had masterminded its impressive growth and had won a reputation as one of the leading bankers in the country, the Chase had assets of more than $2 billion. Much of its success was due to Wiggin's personal connections. He had put together an illustrious board of directors including Charles Schwab of Bethlehem Steel, GM's Alfred Sloan, and Kuhn, Loeb's Otto Kahn, and he himself sat on the boards of fifty other companies as well as the Chase, making it a condition of his service that each should maintain its account at his bank. Following the paths of "dollar diplomacy" like its rival, the National City Bank, Wiggin had made the Chase a power in several Latin American countries, particularly Cuba.

After the merger was formally agreed on, the officers and board of the new institution were selected. Wiggin was made chairman of the board and Aldrich was appointed president, the only major executive position that went to the Equitable. The Chase was now the world's largest bank in assets, with 50 domestic and 10 foreign branches, not including the 34 domestic and 66 overseas offices of its subsidiary, the American Express Company.

In 1932, when Wiggin reached the age of sixty-five and retired, the executive committee of the Chase board voted him a $100,000 annuity and expressed its gratitude in a resolution that said, "The Chase National Bank is in no small measure a monument to his energy, wisdom, vision, and character." But even as these words of praise were being written, events taking place in Washington were to give them a bitter twist.

It was a bad time for banks, and soon to be a bad time for bankers. Monetary gold stock fell by $173 million within two months of Wiggin's retirement. Financial institutions failed with such frequency that one state after another declared bank holidays to head off the panic of the small depositors afraid their life savings would vanish without a trace. From the White House, Roosevelt denounced the bankers and other "economic royalists" who ruled the country's financial destiny with a self-serving and arbitrary will.

Baited by the President and attacked by the public, the lions of Wall Street raged back, denouncing Roosevelt in private as a "traitor to his class," and in public as a new Caesar leading the country to collectivism. But even the most hidebound Wall Streeter could not disagree with the statement in

Roosevelt's message to the Seventy-third Congress: "Our first task is to reopen all sound banks." With encouragement from the Rockefellers, Winthrop Aldrich went a step farther. On Wiggin's retirement, he had become the spokesman for the Chase, and he spent the first part of 1933 in a series of hectic trips back and forth to Washington, speaking before one congressional committee after another and clearly aligning himself and his bank with the spirit of the President's approach to the crisis. Whatever his private feelings, Aldrich became a public champion of banking reform, acting with the pragmatism and sensitivity to public opinion that Ludlow had branded into the Rockefeller consciousness. Aldrich may have seemed a turncoat to his colleagues in the banking fraternity, but the Rockefellers had seen that the system was in jeopardy and could be saved only by reform.

He became the one prominent Wall Streeter to offer public support for the divorce of investment from commercial banking functions, the long-term funding of companies from their short-term financing. The unity of these functions, of course, had been the source of Morgan's great power. It was the way he put together U.S. Steel, General Electric, and other giant combinations and then controlled them. In the rumors that swirled through Wall Street there was talk that Aldrich was a stalking horse in the Rockefellers' attempt to break the hold of the House of Morgan over the financial affairs of the country. Actually, it was more a case in which the Rockefellers and the Chase would not be hurt significantly by the reform, since the Chase's strength was in its commercial business, while their support for progressive change would enhance their public prestige and influence.

In 1933 counsel Ferdinand Pecora and the Senate Banking and Currency Committee met to investigate the financial community. The hearings opened on a bizarre note as a female midget leaped into the younger J. P. Morgan's lap to pose for photographers. But a more serious drama had begun to develop in the background. Knowing that the wolves were looking for an offering, the Rockefellers decided to throw them Albert Wiggin. Like his counterpart Charles Mitchell, who headed the National City Bank, Wiggin had been a market operator in the grand manner during the days of the golden boom. None of his colleagues up to the time of the investigations had thought his activities irregular, although they had included such practices as speculating in the Chase's own stock using funds borrowed from the Chase Securities Company (the investment banking affiliate), of which he was also president. These practices now came under grueling review.

Wiggin appeared before the committee and tried to defend himself. But it was impossible: he had been cut adrift. In his own testimony, Aldrich dissociated himself from the man whom he had once praised as the country's leading banker. Albert Milbank and the Chase's legal counsel provided assistance to Aldrich and others who testified at the hearings, but not to Wiggin, although he was still a major stockholder in the bank. Ivy Lee was there making sure that newspapers put the best possible face on Aldrich's testimony, but he did not advise Wiggin. By the time the hearings had concluded, Wiggin was a broken old man, his reputation tarnished, and his influence inside the bank he had brought to greatness destroyed.

Wiggin's successor as chairman of the Chase board, Charles McCain, followed him to the witness stand and was forced to admit under oath that he also had profited personally by accepting loans and other favors from the bank. He was compromised, and as President Roosevelt told Aldrich in a personal interview at the White House shortly after McCain's appearance, such people couldn't be allowed to remain in power. It was not unexpected, therefore, when McCain abruptly left his position shortly after appearing in Washington; nor was it a surprise when Winthrop Aldrich replaced him as the new chairman on the Chase board.

In one move, the family had gotten control over the largest bank in the world, also publicly aligning itself with the cause of banking reform and making a national figure out of Aldrich. It was now up to Aldrich to parlay his position into one of general influence. Thomas Debevoise wrote him after the Pecora hearings had concluded, "I think now it should be recognized that the leadership you want . . . cannot come because we seek it for you, but only as the result of your rendering a service of the highest and most enduring character to the bank itself, to the community and the country."

While he was making the Chase Bank the cornerstone of Rockefeller financial power for the years to come, Junior was also reinvesting some of his Standard stock in IBM, General Motors, General Electric, and other new corporations. Yet he did not forget the origins of the great fortune. Although he had renounced the high position in the administration of Standard Oil that was his by right of birth, he maintained his influence inside the companies. Despite his huge philanthropies, he still owned the largest individual blocs of stock in the Standard companies, and indirectly controlled other large blocs through the endowments of the foundations. He was a personal friend of Jersey Standard's A. C. Bedford, Standard of California's Walter Teagle, and the other presidents of the companies created by the splintering of the trust. Yet he realized that Standard Oil would always be a sore spot as far as the public view of his family was concerned, and with the able assistance of Ivy Lee he tried to keep his proprietary relationship out of sight. There was one occasion, however, when his identification with the Standard was turned to his advantage—in 1929, when he became locked in a celebrated battle with Colonel Robert W. Stewart, the dynamic president of Standard of Indiana.

Stewart was unlike most of the executives who took positions of leadership in the thirty-three companies created when the trust was dissolved. He had not worked his way up through the ranks of the trust, but had been brought in as a promising young attorney from South Dakota to help in the legal problems of the Indiana division. During the Supreme Court proceedings, Stewart had impressed the Rockefeller office, and in 1918 he was appointed as chief counsel to the Indiana company and elected to its board of directors with Junior's personal endorsement. Three years later, after the death of W. P. Cowan, longtime Rockefeller associate and president of Standard of Indiana since the Supreme Court decision, Stewart became the chief executive officer and chairman of the board.

It would have been hard to imagine a person more different from Junior. "Colonel Bob," as Indiana's workers called Stewart, was a former Rough Rider with boundless energy, a dominating personality, and other of Teddy Roosevelt's own rawhide qualities. Over 6 feet tall and weighing 250 pounds, with what one journalist once called "a handsome roll of fat at the back of his neck," he commanded the fierce loyalty of his colleagues and subordinates. Profoundly dedicated to the oil business, Stewart became a familiar figure on the luncheon and speech-making circuit connecting the small towns of the Midwest. He barnstormed through the states served by his company, defending the Standard and big business generally against the assaults of La Follette and the populists. He often closed his speeches by singing in a fine bass voice a ditty he himself had composed:

Standard Oil, Standard Oil,
Turns the darkness into light;
Makes the customers feel all right.
Standard Oil, Standard Oil,
Curse it, damn it,
You can't do without it,
Standard Oil!

But if he was a consummate showman, Stewart had also made himself one of the commanding figures in American business. He had aggressively gone out to obtain a supply of crude to match Indiana's extensive refining and marketing capacities. He was a pioneer in the development of the service station as a marketing outlet, and while competitors were still dispensing their gas from tank wagons, he managed to win a territory for his company's chain of stations. Under his hard-driving leadership, Indiana was in a good position to take advantage of the revolution in mass production that had begun when Henry Ford announced his determination to make "a motor car for the multitude." By 1928, Standard of Indiana had control over an area containing 50 percent of all registered automobiles, not to speak of tractors and farm vehicles. Under Stewart's leadership, the Indiana had seen its net assets more than triple, so that *The New York Times* wrote of him: "If petroleum is to have another Rockefeller, or more modestly, another Jim Hill or Harriman, Stewart may play the role." Like many another Icarus of oil in this era, however, Stewart was headed for a fall.

After the dissolution decree, the Standard Oil empire had been separated as with a jeweler's eye. The trust had been broken up to foster competition, yet the divisions were drawn in such a way that they were complementary rather than competitive, and the men who headed them retained a basic loyalty to the old central regime. The allegiances were buttressed by financial considerations. W. P. Cowan, for instance, Stewart's predecessor at Indiana, had been a stock-holding executive with the Standard trust who received 303 shares (worth $165,135) in his own company after the dissolution. But in accord with the terms of the Supreme Court decree, he also got 420 shares (worth $228,000) in Jersey Standard, 320 (worth $172,000) in Standard of New York, and so on. Even if there had not been this community of self-interest to nourish, the proconsuls of the old empire knew without being told (it *was* the motif of the Standard's history, after all) that competition could be mutually harmful.

By the 1920s, some of the old Standard guard had either retired or died, and been replaced by a second generation with less personal loyalty to the Rockefeller family and less allegiance to the old trust. Stewart was one example, chafing under the constraints of the old order and threatening to break the unwritten rules by which the trust had kept together as a ghostly monopoly. He had refused to do business with the Union Tank Car Company, the fleet of railroad cars that the elder Rockefeller had built up years earlier to break his competitors. Instead of employing these cars as a matter of course, as did the other Standard companies, Stewart had commissioned the building of Indiana's own fleet. More important, he had balked at the limits imposed on his company in the aftermath of the dissolution, especially the provision that it was to concentrate on refining and be dependent on other elements of the old trust for its crude. Shortly after taking over, Stewart had begun the search for mergers that would improve the Indiana's position and widen its territory. In 1921 he almost pulled off a merger with the Standard's giant rival, the Mellons' Gulf Oil Company. A year later, he stunned the oil world by acquiring partial ownership and control of E. L. Doheny's Pan American Petroleum and Transportation Company, one of the largest crude producers in the world, with huge reserves in Mexico and Venezuela (where its subsidiary, the Lago Petroleum Company, pumped out some 45,000 barrels a day) and a tanker fleet worth $10 million. With this new supply of crude, Stewart began to drive the Indiana company along a road that had no visible limit, daring even to enter territory of the mighty Standards of New Jersey and New York.

Stewart was an interloper, throwing things out of balance. An ugly battle to oust him from the company was unthinkable, yet there must have been many anxious discussions on the East Coast about how to deal with the Indiana upstart. But then fate was kind enough to provide the Continental Trading Company scandal, a way of dealing with him from a strong ethical position.

If there were a law of politics condemning every administration to get the scandal it deserves, Teapot Dome would have to be a case of perfect justice. Harding himself was a product of Mark Hanna's political machine and had pushed John Archbold's protégé, Senator Joseph Foraker, for the presidency in 1908. His official Cabinet, dubbed by its critics the "Oil Administration," included a Standard Oil attorney (Charles Evans Hughes) as Secretary of State, Gulf Oil's owner (Andrew Mellon) as Secretary of the Treasury, a Sinclair Oil attorney (Will Hays) as Postmaster General, and a protégé of Doheny, Harry Sinclair, and Cleveland Dodge (Albert Fall) as Secretary of the Interior and custodian of the public lands. It was Fall's acceptance of a bribe from Sinclair in exchange for a lease on the navy's oil reserves in Teapot Dome, Wyoming, that triggered the scandal.

Stewart's own involvement began on November 17, 1921, when a small group gathered at the Hotel Vanderbilt in New York. Present along with Sinclair, Stewart, and the presidents of the Midwest Oil Company (a subsidiary of Indiana Standard) and Prairie Oil and Gas (a unit of the old trust), was A. E. Humphreys, a wildcatter who had just struck it rich in the fabulous Mexia oil fields of Texas. Humphreys agreed to sell the group 33,333,333⅓ barrels of his crude at $1.50 a barrel. The oil was to be bought, however, not for the companies they represented, but for the oil men themselves, who had formed the Continental Trading Company for the purpose. Continental was to resell the oil at $1.75 a barrel to the Sinclair and Prairie Oil and Gas companies, making what would have been an $8 million profit for the consortium. But Teapot Dome erupted in the meantime, and the group was forced to terminate their corporation and destroy their books. They had been able to consummate only $3 million of their deal, $750,000 for each of them.

As it was, Continental Trading might never have come to public attention had not Harry Sinclair used part of his $750,000 cut for the payoff to Secretary Fall. But the slip was made, and Colonel Bob Stewart was sucked into the vortex of the national scandal. In March 1925, Sinclair's trial began in Cheyenne, Wyoming, and Stewart was expected to be the star witness. But when the trial got under way, the court was informed by a Standard executive that Stewart had left on business for an "unknown destination" in Latin America and could not be reached.

A furor ensued, and Junior, who had tried to stay out of the early stages of the investigations (pleading, as always when Standard Oil came up as an issue, that the family was no longer actively involved in its operation), now began to feel the heat. People knew that he was by far the largest stockholder and criticized him for allowing Stewart to flaunt

Congress's attempts to get to the bottom of a scandal whose continuing reverberations were destroying confidence in the government to a degree unmatched until Watergate exploded half a century later.

Junior was particularly stung by a New York *World* editorial appearing on March 23, 1925:

> Where are the men who act and speak for the rich and respectable interests controlling these companies? What have they done and what are they doing for the protection of their own reputations and their personal honor? John D. Rockefeller, Jr. is a large stockholder in the Prairie Oil and Gas Co., so is the Rockefeller Foundation. The General Education Board is a large stockholder in Prairie Oil and Standard Oil of Indiana. Both are supported from Rockefeller endowments. Mr. Rockefeller breakfasts at the White House and discusses law enforcement with the President. But how much has he contributed toward the enforcement of the law as it affects the oil companies in which he is already interested? When does he propose to begin and what does he intend to do in the case of his own company where officers and directors have failed in their duty toward the government?

That same day, further worried by Fosdick's warnings that the affair was affecting the various foundations (themselves large Standard stockholders) and that it might escalate into another Ludlow if not checked quickly, Junior fired off a telegram to the offices of the Indiana Company, demanding that the officials there forward it to Stewart wherever he was. In angry tones it warned the executive that his behavior was bringing criticism on "yourself, your company and your larger stockholders, specifically named including myself, the General Education Board and the Foundation." Junior urged Stewart to take immediate action "to remove any just ground for criticism."

On March 27, Stewart returned to New York and saw Junior. Resentful at the implication that he had been absent from the country for any but legitimate purposes, Stewart told Junior in no uncertain terms that as far as he and his company were concerned, nothing improper had taken place in the Continental Trading Company transaction, and furthermore, it had been beneficial to the company. The colonel was in no mood to be chastised, and Junior did not press the matter further.

But the uncertainty persisted, as did the public criticism of Rockefeller. Indeed, the attacks in the *World* and the St. Louis *Post-Dispatch* got so bad that Junior and Debevoise went to see Ralph Pulitzer to explain the delicacy of the Rockefeller position. The press was now saying that Rockefeller should oust Stewart, a move he did not want to take because it would give the lie to the fiction he had been promoting concerning the family's remoteness from Standard Oil. Then, in January 1928, Senator Thomas Walsh, the chairman of a Senate committee investigating the Continental Trading Company, wrote to Junior to ask him to compel Stewart and other Standard employees to testify and to tell the truth. Junior said he would do what he could and publicly called for his testimony. Stewart then finally consented to appear.* But he denied any irregular actions and refused to answer some crucial questions that were put to him. Then Junior himself took the stand to express his disappointment at Stewart's failure to answer the questions put to him. "I have personally," he said, ". . . a large investment in the oil industry. More than that, my father was one of the pioneers in the development of the industry. . . . The present situation affected not only certain individuals, but the whole industry." After testifying, he went on national radio hookup to condemn dishonesty in business.

On April 24, 1928, Stewart was again on the stand. His $750,000 had been discovered by investigators, and this time, in a striking reversal of his previous testimony, he admitted to having received the money, although he still claimed that

---

*Cleveland Rodgers, editor of the Brooklyn *Eagle*, later recalled suggesting to his managing editor that they do a follow-up story on Junior's criticism of Stewart. They called Ivy Lee and asked him what Rockefeller would do next. The publicist said that there was nothing more he could do. Rodgers then wrote an editorial accusing Junior of trying to satisfy a moral responsibility with what amounted to no more than a "pious gesture." A few days later Rodgers was surprised when Winthrop Aldrich and Junior himself were ushered into his office. "Mr. Rockefeller told us that while Mr. Lee undoubtedly wanted to be helpful," Rodgers later wrote, "he didn't know what he was talking about." Junior assured the *Eagle's* editors that he intended to pursue the matter vigorously. After he left, Rodgers sat down with the other editors and talked about the visit. They agreed that it probably meant a proxy fight for the control of Standard of Indiana, which would drive up the price of the stock. They called a broker and bought several shares. Later, they were able to sell it at enough of a profit to go to Cuba for a vacation.

he had intended from the beginning to give it to his company and had placed it in trust with this in mind. Already under indictment for contempt from his previous appearance, Stewart was now charged with perjury.

This forced Junior's hand. He had vacillated for three years, but now he would have to act and could only hope that what followed would be seen as a crusade, not a battle for economic control. He called Stewart to 26 Broadway and asked for his resignation. Colonel Bob refused. The next day Rockefeller issued a statement telling what had happened and saying that he had lost confidence in Stewart. He was now committed to what would become one of the most publicized proxy fights in American corporate history.

The annual stockholders' meeting was scheduled for March 7, 1929. By January, Junior had set up a committee which met on a wartime footing and which would ultimately spend $100,000 to unseat the defiant colonel. Winthrop Aldrich was the field marshal for the operation; Thomas Debevoise did the detail work and Ivy Lee the publicity. Bertram Cutler, Fosdick, and Colonel Woods also commanded posts in the fray, and Charles Evans Hughes served as the proxy committee's legal counsel. Directing their efforts as stockholders living in twenty-four major cities, the Rockefeller committee met every morning at ten A.M. for the next two months to discuss how the battle was going. They communicated with each other by coded telegrams because of Junior's almost obsessive fear that Stewart would find out they had the contest locked up in advance and "knowledge of this sure defeat [would] prompt our opponent to mud-slinging."

Stewart was enough of a realist to know that Junior was the sort of man who wouldn't begin a battle unless he was sure of winning, yet he carried the fight to the Rockefellers. It was as a grass-roots politician campaigning for electoral office in the "world's greatest democracy" that he waged his struggle. To cheering audiences at mass meetings of the Standard's employees, he invoked his record as one who had launched an ambitious employee stock purchase plan and other reforms. He now marshaled the grateful employees as proxy hunters to conduct a virtual house-to-house canvass of potential "voters." Advertisements bought and paid for by the Standard's employees appeared in newspapers with a picture of Stewart and a caption: "He's For Us—We're For Him." And at every turn the campaign was based on the impressive performance of the Indiana Standard under Stewart's leadership and administration. On January 29 he announced that earnings for the year were double those of the preceding one and would pay stockholders nine dollars a share. A week later, taking full advantage of his incumbent status and the prosperity of the company, he and his board voted the greatest stock and cash dividend ever declared in the company's history, creating an overnight boom in Standard issues on the exchanges.

It would have been an overwhelming and unbeatable combination if the Standard had indeed been the "democracy" Stewart had claimed it was. But it was no democracy at all. As early as January 25, two weeks after their campaign had begun, the Rockefeller proxy committee already had in hand 43.5 percent of the shares, and two weeks later, on February 7, Aldrich announced publicly that they had 51 percent. Of this, about 15 percent belonged directly to Junior, his family, and foundations. A good portion of the rest belonged to Flagler, Harkness, Rogers, and other of the old Standard Oil families who had quickly heeded the call.

About ten-twenty A.M. on the morning of March 7, a squad of motorcycle police pulled up in front of the Whiting Community House, where the annual stockholders' meeting of the Standard Oil Company of Indiana was to be held. They were followed by a cluster of limousines bearing the twenty-five members of the Rockefeller party led by Winthrop Aldrich. Junior was not among them. Two months earlier, on January 9, when the struggle was barely under way, Junior had sailed to Egypt, determined to put himself out of reach when the conflict erupted. He was in Palestine that raw and chill March morning, and was informed by cable of the results.

Few in the packed hall yet knew the result for certain, but Stewart did. He had come to preside over his own defeat and make of it a last triumph. He called the meeting to order and read out the record of the last year. It had been the most spectacular year in the company's history, and Stewart hammered home its achievements. Net earnings had doubled, cash reserves were the largest ever, and the profit on invested capital was 17 percent.

When the time for nominating the new board of directors came around, Stewart's personal attorney presented the incumbent slate, and then Winthrop Aldrich rose from the area in the front of the room that had been reserved for the Rockefeller group, introduced himself, and nominated the same slate except for Stewart and L. L. Stephens, a director whom the Rockefeller committee decided had shown unwarranted personal loyalty to Stewart in the proxy struggle. The proxy vote got under way. But it was anticlimactic. Results showed that 31,000 stockholders had voted for Stewart and only 15,000 for Rockefeller, but Rockefeller stockholders controlled 60 percent of the shares and Stewart's only 32 percent. The new board was in, and though its numbers, except for Stewart and Stephens, were identical with the old, it was a very different board indeed. Not only had it lost its leader, but—since the Rockefeller proxies were good for a year and could be used to dismiss all or any of the board's members at any time—it had gained a master.

All through the struggle, Rockefeller's main outside asset had been the press. During January and February, Ivy Lee collected 428 editorials on the fight from 45 states, the overwhelming majority of which supported Rockefeller. "In all the discouraging mess which has been spread before the people of the United States in the story of oil and its corrupt political dealings," commented the Chicago *Evening Post*, "the attitude of John D. Rockefeller Jr. stands out as a conspicuous and cheering example of conscience and courage." And a widely quoted editorial phrase declared "Rockefeller never served his country better than he is serving it now in his fight with Colonel Stewart."

Many in the Midwest, and not a few who had voted against the Rockefeller proxy, regarded the struggle against Stewart as an effort by the eastern Standard Oil companies to curb the independent growth and expansion of the Indiana. This interpretation received an air of plausibility when, in 1932, Indiana's new directors decided to sell the rich foreign properties of Pan American Petroleum and Transport to Standard of New Jersey, at the latter's request.* These for-

---

*The suspicion was considerably strengthened by the fact that less than three weks after the Rockefeller victory an investigation was begun of the Pan American Petroleum and Transport Company (which was headed by Stewart's son) and its Venezuelan properties. On April 5, Debevoise, who now spoke for the proxies, wrote to the president of Indiana: "The more I hear of Pan American and Lago, the more clear it seems that a thorough investigation of their affairs (not simply the books) should be made, and the more likely it seems to me that such an investigation will result in a thorough house-cleaning. I doubt that you will wish to retain either of the Stewarts. On general principles it would be better not to have any of the father's family affiliated with the company, but you will probably find ample ground to make a change for the purpose of securing better management."

eign properties included the Mexican and Venezuelan sources of crude which it had been Stewart's master stroke to acquire. The Venezuelan property was soon to become the basis of the fabulous Creole Petroleum Company, whose incredible profits as a Jersey subsidiary caused *Fortune* to describe the entire deal as "the steal of the Century."

The purchase was made with Jersey stock, and in the process, Indiana became a major stockholder (7 percent of the shares) in the Jersey company, creating a formal community of interest between the companies that Stewart's leadership had challenged. The bond was further enhanced by the invitation to the executives of the both the Indiana and Jersey companies to take seats on the board of the Chase National Bank. By a further twist, six years after the proxy fight Junior's son Nelson invested in Creole Petroleum and was put on its board of directors, thus beginning the involvement in Latin American affairs that would ultimately lead him to a career of public service and politics.

The Stewart fight had reinforced Junior's position as the leading spokesman for the nation's responsible business interests. Yet on the Black Thursday of October 24, 1929, when the first precipitous plunge of the Great Crash sent stock prices tumbling downward, the future of these interests seemed seriously jeopardized. At the offices of J. P. Morgan & Company at 23 Wall Street, the heads of the nation's leading banks gathered in a well-publicized effort to restore confidence, recalling the drama twenty-two years earlier when the senior Morgan had stopped the Panic of 1907. Nearby, at 15 Broad, Ivy Lee was on the phone, urging Junior to consider the benefits of a public utterance from the ninety-year-old Rockefeller patriarch at this momentous historical juncture.

Senior was drawn with reluctance into the turmoil that younger and less prudent generations had wrought. But to please his son, he finally agreed to read a press release prepared by Ivy Lee. In it, the figure that had once been the scrouge of the American economy took the posture of its Ecclesiastes. "These are days when many are discouraged," he said in the quavering voice that had not been heard in public for a decade. "In the ninety years of my life, depressions have come and gone. Prosperity has always returned, and will again." He added: "Believing that the fundamental conditions of the country are sound, my son and I have been purchasing sound common stocks for some days." (Many must have appreciated Eddie Cantor's rejoinder: "Sure, who else had any money left?") Two weeks later, the market plummeted another 82 points, or a quarter of its remaining values, and the papers reported that the Rockefeller family had entered a million-share buying order to peg Standard Oil of New Jersey at $50.

Senior's pronouncement on the nation's soundness had never been intended as considered economic analysis, but only to show once again that the Rockefellers were bullish on America. The role of Winthrop Aldrich and the Chase in banking reform and Junior's struggle against Stewart would go far to place them on the side of Right in those trying times. But the symbolism of the decision to erect Rockefeller Center in the wake of the stock market disaster seemed unmistakable. It was an epic sign of faith in the American future despite the darkness of the present moment.

In time, Ivy Lee would succeed in making the project seem almost a privately funded public works program. Yet it didn't begin that way. In fact, it had been initiated in 1928, at a time when the economy was spiraling upward in what seemed like a never-ending boom. The Metropolitan Opera Company, deciding on the need to move from its old quarters, had opened negotiations with Columbia to lease the area the university owned between 49th and 50th Streets and bordered by Fifth and Sixth Avenues. Junior had been introduced to the project by Otto Kahn, and after consultation with "five real estate experts," all of whom pronounced the project "good business," committed himself to a $3.3 million 24-year lease.

Then came the crash. The opera company pulled out, and Junior was faced with the collapse of his scheme and the loss of $3 million a year until the economic indicators turned upward. His decision at this point reflected the same practical sense shown earlier when, complimented by Fosdick on his courage, he replied: "Often a man gets into a situation where there's just one thing to do. There is no alternative. He wants to run, but there is no place to run to. So he goes ahead on the only course that's open and people call it courage." With no place to run to, he would use his immense resources to build his own commercial development.

The economic situation made the financing difficult, even for a Rockefeller. The buildings alone would cost an estimated $120 million, $45 million of which came from a loan by the Metropolitan Life Insurance Company on Junior's personal guarantee, and the rest of which he raised himself despite the staggering losses it involved. One day Junior came into the offices of Wallace Harrison, Chief architect for the Center and the man who got RCA as a prime tenant. Noting that Rockefeller looked downcast, Harrison asked him what was wrong. Junior replied that he had just been forced to sell some Standard of New York stock at $2 a share. Yet bit by bit the project began to rise. In 1933 the RCA Building was opened and Junior celebrated by moving the Rockefeller Family Office from the Standard Oil Building at 26 Broadway to the 56th floor of 30 Rockefeller Plaza. The Office was now Room 5600.

Three architectural firms worked on the project, and this provided Junior with the opportunity to fill the role of mediator, a role he knew so well. He threw himself into the plans and details of the construction with the zeal and delight he had shown in Williamsburg and other building projects. He spent time with the architects and contractors, periodically whipping out of his back pocket the four-foot folding ruler that came as close as anything ever did to being a characteristic trademark. (Years later, Nelson's children Steven and Ann accidentally broke their grandfather's ruler and went in vain to dozens of stores in New York seeking a replacement.)

While it was widely felt that Junior's decision to go ahead with the development showed spunk, some thought it seemed odd a philanthropist should devote such resources to construction. Yet Junior had always been obsessed with building. Williamsburg, the Cloisters, Versailles—his favorite works had all involved construction, a kind of progress he could see and measure as it occurred day by day. It was a way of leaving his mark on the world. Each new structure he raised bespoke his worth in concrete and steel, and he was never so happy as when going over blueprints and talking to workers on one of his construction sites. (A prominent New York real estate developer who was once seated next to Junior at a banquet was startled when Rockefeller suddenly leaned over to him and whispered, "You know, I envy you. Yes, I envy you. You have built great monuments to leave behind you.")

Behind the great city within the city lay several less successful experiments to hybridize a financial investment with a project that could be seen to have redeeming social merit. (*Fortune* called it "philanthropy at 6 percent.") Least successful of all had been Junior's attempt to develop the old Cleveland estate at Forest Hill. After the mansion burned in

1917, the Rockefellers had not bothered to rebuild; in 1928 Junior got his father's permission to turn Forest Hill into a fine residential development for successful young Cleveland businessmen. Dividing the land into homesites with some common land set aside for parks and a golf course, Junior decided to have built 1,000 homes in the $25,000 to $40,000 range. They would be Norman chateaux with careful landscaping and all the modern appointments. It was a $75 million venture.

While there might have been an executive class in New York able to afford to move to such a bedroom community, Cleveland had not yet reached that point. Despite his offer of full financing at attractive terms, Junior could sell only three hundred of the homes, and he stopped construction on the rest of the development. He eventually donated the remainder of the land to the city.

He later became involved in enterprises to build modern housing for Jersey Standard employees at Bayonne and for trade union members in the Bronx, both developments failing because the apartments were too expensive. He had also purchased the entire block between 149th and 150th Streets and bordered by Seventh and Eighth Avenues for a housing development for Negroes. Called the Paul Laurance Dunbar apartments after the famous Negro poet, it was, as Rockefeller aide Charles O. Heydt said, "erected to show what could be done along the lines of a cooperative apartment for colored people with the definite purpose of encouraging others to do the same." It was opened in late 1929, but failed to thrive despite such illustrious tenants as W. E. B. Du Bois and Bill "Bojangles" Robinson. By 1932, Junior had been forced to revise the original cooperative notion and began renting the Dunbar apartments; later he sold the entire complex.

Rockefeller Center, however, was destined to be different. If the philanthropist in him saw this as an opportunity to do something for the city, the real estate promoter in him realized that it had a good chance for success. From the beginning of negotiations he had insisted on a commercial quotient for the project. After Ivy Lee first told him about the opera company's negotiations with Columbia University and sold him on the project, Junior had gotten the plans changed so that the part of the property not used for the opera house could be developed for commercial purposes. He had consulted several experts to find out what could be realized if the development were subleased to companies that would then raise their own buildings. The estimates went as high as $5.8 million, which had been one of the reasons for his original enthusiasm.

When the Depression deepened and the opera company was forced out of the project, Junior decided to go it alone on a grand scale; from that point on, there was no longer any ambiguity about the purpose of the development. As its board of directors resolved. "From now on the Square should be based upon a commercial center as beautiful as possible consistent with the maximum income that can be developed."

The sense in which it was a personal monument for Junior was at once more complex and more complete than the sense in which it was an investment. It was an homage to the greatest name in business and philanthropic history. Some architecture critics like Lewis Mumford might carp, but midway through completion the papers were already calling it the Eighth Wonder of the World. In fact, as the superlatives rolled off the public relations presses in a seemingly endless stream, Debevoise became alarmed. "Through all the publicity about Rockefeller Center,' he wrote Ivy Lee in January 1933,

> there has been the most rampant boasting about size. If that kind of publicity ever did any good, the good must have been accomplished long since. Surely it can do no good to carry on longer propaganda based on the fact that the Center is the largest single development ever produced with private capital; that the RCA building has the largest floor space of any building in the world; that the Music Hall is the largest theatre in the world, etc., etc., ad infinitum and ad nauseam. If it is not stopped, the only conclusion the public can possibly reach is that Mr. Rockefeller and his people have the biggest heads in the world.

Yet sensitivity to public opinion was built into the project in the same way that it was built into the rest of the family's endeavors. Noting that large numbers of people stopped each day to watch the huge excavation, Lee and Junior collaborated in setting up what they called a Sidewalk Superintendent's Club to facilitate the vigil; they handed out membership cards in the club to the more persistent rubberneckers. There were no strikes on the project; the Building and Construction Trades Council was happy for the windfall of several millions of working hours for its members. It took young Nelson Rockefeller, fresh out of Dartmouth and looking to work his way into the family business, however, to persuade his father (who had claimed he "didn't want the family name plastered all over a real estate development") to change the name of the project. What had been "Radio City" on the drawing boards would be Rockefeller Center in fact.

It was in 1937, when the great monument was nearing completion, that John D. Rockefeller, Sr., finally passed from the scene. His spirit never failed him, but as he entered the middle of his ninth decade he became aware of just how frail his body was. "I'm like your bike when you're coasting down-hill," he once told his grandson Laurance. "I can coast just so far and nothing much can be done about it." Living to be one hundred was the goal he had set for himself, but there were laws that even a Rockefeller had to obey. Early on the morning of Sunday, May 23, Junior was sent for by his fa-ther's physician. His agitated arrival woke the servants, who huddled in the kitchen wondering what was going on upstairs. At four A.M. the old man lapsed into a coma; an hour later he was gone.

The next day Abby wrote her sister:

> I think you might say he died in his sleep. So really it
> was a wonderful ending. At times both John and I
> rather feared that he might become bedridden and might
> be uncomfortable, but as it was he motored 40 miles on
> the Friday before he died and sat in the garden comfort-
> ably for four hours on Saturday, and missed his morning
> prayers only on Sunday morning. So it was a remarkable
> record.

On May 25, funeral services were conducted at Pocantico by the Reverend Harry Emerson Fosdick. Two of Junior's sons, Nelson and Winthrop, had been in Latin America when the news reached them, and they traveled for forty-eight hours straight to be home when their grandfather was laid to rest. The descendants of William Rockefeller were present, along with the families of John D.'s original partners in the trust, and a few old friends he had made in his years of re-tirement. After the service, the workers of Pocantico filed through the big house, hats in hand, for a last look at the Laird of Kikjuit. At six-thirty that evening Junior and his five young sons boarded the two private railway cars that were part of a funeral carrying the body home. On May 27 John D. Rockefeller was back in Cleveland, where he had begun the great adventure three-quarters of a century earlier. As he was lowered into place between his mother and his wife in the plot he had purchased decades earlier, the offices and shops of Standard Oil and its affiliates across the country and all over the world ceased work for five minutes, as the employees paused to honor the man who had once been loathed but was now admired as a benefactor of mankind.

Two years later, with his father dead but far from forgotten, John D. Rockefeller, Jr., put on a hard hat and heavy workmen's gloves, and with the strain of concentration showing in his forehead, drove the last rivet into Rockefeller Center. He was sixty-five years old. He had many years of life left to him, yet in some sense what he had set out to achieve was done. The voice of the people speaking through Ida Tarbell, Frank Walsh, and all the others had once indicted his father's fortune; Junior had tried to show that the wealth was only entrusted to his family to invest in the well-being of mankind. They had said that the name Rockefeller was synonymous with irresponsible power and privilege; Junior had tried to prove that it was the embodiment of responsibility and obligation. As he stepped back from the girder and handed over the rivet gun amid a burst of applause, he was not only a personal success in a way that had somehow not seemed possible forty years earlier; he was also the author of a myth regarding the Rockefeller family that strained upward in the same way as the structures rising in awesome spires above him. Rockefeller Center was the capstone of a life, Junior's *summa*. Yet his real achievement would prove to be the children waiting in the wings.

PART III

The Brothers

"The family today, in no slighter degree than two or three centuries ago in imperial Rome, is supreme in the governance of wealth—amassing it, standing watch over it, and keeping it intact from generation to generation. Because it is (unlike that relatively new device, the corporation) a private entity which in the strictest legality may resist public scrutiny, the family lends itself admirably to alliances of a formal character and serves as an instrument for confidential financial transaction. By definition, the family is a sacrosanct institution, and no agency of government may pry into it without offending inculcated prejudice. . . . The family alone provides a safe retreat from democratic processes, not outside the law, but above the law."

—FERDINAND LUNDBERG

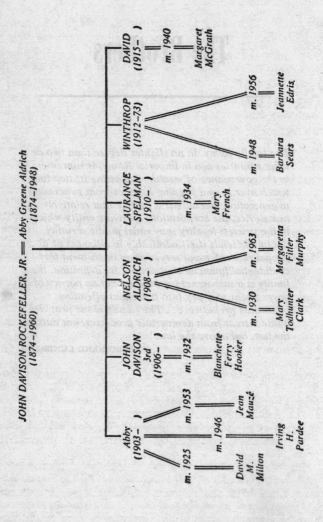

JOHN DAVISON ROCKEFELLER, JR. = Abby Greene Aldrich
(1874–1960)   (1874–1948)

Abby (1903–)

m. 1925 — David M. Milton

m. 1946 — Irving H. Purdee

m. 1953 — Jean Mauzé

JOHN DAVISON 3rd (1906–)

m. 1932 — Blanchette Ferry Hooker

NELSON ALDRICH (1908–)

m. 1930 — Mary Todhunter Clark

m. 1963 — Margaretta Fitler Murphy

LAURANCE SPELMAN (1910–)

m. 1934 — Mary French

WINTHROP (1912–73)

m. 1948 — Barbara Sears

m. 1956 — Jeannette Edris

DAVID (1915–)

m. 1940 — Margaret McGrath

11

FROM THE BEGINNING, things were easier for Junior's children than they had been for Junior himself. When Mrs. David Gardiner, matron of a socially prominent New York family, forbade her son to play with the five Rockefeller boys, commenting, "No child of mine will play with the grandchildren of a gangster," it was looked upon as a tasteless, even comic faux pas. The Rockefellers had long since been accepted into the exclusive ranks of American Society. They were not only received by the Right People, they were themselves people to know. Mrs. Rockefeller, Jr., was one of the few ladies in town who could go to a party at the William Vanderbilts one night and attend Mrs. Cornelius Vanderbilt's soiree the next, and still manage to maintain neutrality in the bitter social war between the branches of the family.

While he understood that it was necessary for his children to grow up with the "proper" connections, Junior also knew that they must not be too conspicuously identified with the upper classes. Such people were not as adaptable to the changing conditions in American society as he wanted his boys to be. Moreover, he worried about the effect moving exclusively in "high" society would have on their characters. All around were examples of other inheritors of the great fortunes floundering in a sea of options, caricatures of the idle rich without purpose or motive who squandered their fortunes on what H. L. Mencken called the two principal occupations of the wealthy—polo and polygamy—and in the end became little more than stock figures in the melodramas of the tabloid press.

While the world may not have known what exactly went on behind the walls of the estates where the Du Ponts, Astors, Vanderbilts, and others lived, lurid details of divorce and debauchery nonetheless somehow managed to filter out into the morning papers. Junior intended to keep the Rockefellers' private lives private. And he succeeded. People knew only what he wanted them to: that John D. was now retired and somewhat eccentric, shuffling from one magnificent home to another with the alternation of the seasons, and appearing publicly only for a round of golf or to give out an endless supply of dimes; that his son was involved in the most ambitious philanthropies ever conceived; that there were six children in the third generation. The first, a daughter named Abby (but called "Babs" to distinguish her from her mother), had come in 1903, followed by John 3rd in 1906, Nelson in 1908, Laurance in 1910, Winthrop in 1912, and David in 1915. Their names and birth dates were all that appeared in the newspapers until 1922, when it was recorded that Nelson had accidentally shot himself in the leg with an air rifle.

It was not that people didn't try to penetrate the genteel curtain Junior had drawn around the family. Scarcely a week went by that the guards at Pocantico didn't catch some reporter or photographer trying to scale the fences or burrow underneath them to find out the inside story. None ever succeeded; if they had, they would probably have been surprised to find that while Junior and his children made frequent trips to the estate, they did not live there.

Junior realized that he had suffered from growing up in a sheltered, almost hermetically sealed atmosphere and did not want to repeat the mistake. At any rate, his affairs placed him in New York City, and there the family lived in the huge nine-story town house at 10 West 54th. It was just a short walk to Central Park, where the six children went unrecognized to play every day after school in the company of French governesses (inevitably called "Mademoiselle"), nurses, or male companions hired from the Union Theological Seminary.

Many motifs of their father's upbringing were repeated in their own, but the austerity of the boyhood at the old Forest Hill estate in Cleveland, where he shared one bicycle with his sisters and wore their hand-me-downs, was not one of them. Although not surfeited with possessions, Junior's children had what they wanted. Yet, like their father, they earned their spending money—by killing flies for pennies, shining shoes, hoeing the garden. Like Junior, they kept accounts, having been shown grandfather's Ledger A and allowed to study its yellowing, brittle pages and faded ink entries as if it were a church incunabulum. "I was always so afraid that money would spoil my children," Junior later said, "and I wanted them to know its values and not waste it or throw it away on things that weren't worthwhile." Any child with an unaccounted-for item in his ledger at the end of the week was fined five cents; those keeping accurate accounts received a five-cent bonus. Junior was interested that John 3rd was most often rewarded and Winthrop almost always in the red. He liked to think that this means of coming to terms with their great financial expectations was a success, and was delighted by one story (admittedly apocryphal) told about his boys: one of their friends, having seen the boys' comparatively small sailboat, asked, as they passed an elaborate yacht tied up nearby, "How come you guys don't have one like that?" only to be answered scornfully, "Who do you think we are, Vanderbilts?"

It took a while for the fact that they were Rockefellers to make an impression on them. They lived in their own world, playing with each other on the top floor of the 54th Street house. Sometimes, before being taken up to bed, they were allowed to meet the important dinner guests their mother and father entertained, and heard snatches of the conversation. They experienced all great events through the medium of the family. The Great War, for instance, would be recalled as the time their mother conscripted them to work in the Red Cross bandage unit she had organized in the basement. Even Winthrop, only five years old, was issued a white uniform and allowed to help carry the bandages from the area where they were wrapped to the place where they were packed for shipment. They assumed that all children did these things, that all children had a patio from which they could look out at the veterans' parades going down Fifth Avenue, the large gaps in the ranks maintained to indicate comrades fallen in battle.

They spent their summers at Seal Harbor and played with the children of the Edsel Fords, the Eliots, and other prominent families who had, with their father, gotten Mount Desert Island designated a national park to protect its misty beauty and their own secluded refuges. Surrounded by lush gardens of annuals that were changed several times a year, Oriental statuary, and carefully manicured lawns, their father's house looked like a huge inn and was a stone's throw from the shoreline where they learned to sail, venturing out into the Atlantic in their small boat. On these family vacations in Maine, each of the children had his own personal governess; occasionally, Junior and Abby would escape to go for walks alone, stopping at Rest House, the spacious "cabin" deep in the woods behind the Eyrie, where they ate blueberries and bread and butter and, after finishing their snacks, happily went about the unfamiliar task of doing their own dishes.

The children were fond of Seal Harbor, but it was nothing like Pocantico, the rambling 3,500-acre estate where they spent weekends and short vacations. The house they grew up in, Abeynton Lodge, was within hailing distance of the Big House, Kikjuit. Standing on a rise that commanded the hillside and looked down to the woods and the flowing Hudson tide, the stately Georgian mansion dwarfed the wrinkled old man they formally addressed as Grandfather. Yet they understood that it was more his monument than his home, the centerpiece of the estate that was richly landscaped with eighteenth-century tiered gardens of ornamental shrubs and immense flowerbeds, with orange trees from the estate of the Marquis d'Aux in Le Mans, larch from Scotland, yew from England, with stone fountains feeding the sunken brook paved with colored stones, and a nine-hole golf course encircling the whole.

Junior had a playhouse built for Babs—four furnished rooms the size of a small apartment—so that she would have a place to go when the girls from the town of Pocantico Hills came to play with her. But when people spoke of *the* Playhouse, they meant the two-story gymnasium with its indoor swimming pool, indoor and outdoor tennis courts, indoor basketball and squash courts, and billiard room and bowling alleys, which he had built for his boys. It was here they played as children and entertained as teenagers, often having up to fifty of their friends in for parties, the music produced by bands that Junior brought up from New York and the chaperones provided by Abby. (Later, when Nelson was governor, the dances would lack this decorous quality. After watching the tipsy couples trailing back from an intermission with rumpled and grass-stained evening clothes, a watchman left over from the old days commented acidly, "It was never like this in Mr. Junior's day.")

Pocantico was ten times larger than Monaco, five times the size of Central Park. It cost $50,000 a year just to maintain the Big House, $500,000 for the entire property. The boys could go to the stone stables and have the riding master take them out on the trails; they could check out one of the fleet of electric cars that sailed silently around the grounds of the 250-acre "park" that lay at the core of the estate. The place had an intentional magnificence, the other side of the coin from the austerity of keeping accounts and doing chores. It was as if their father were showing them the rewards that hard work and bearing up under the pressures of being a Rockefeller could earn them. It was a way of teaching them, without ever needing to say it directly, that if they learned to control their wealth, they could discreetly enjoy it.

If the estate was in part a teaching device, Junior's children would always remember the simple joys more than the lessons: playing cards with Abby and eating hand-turned ice cream on humid July afternoons; going with the grounds-keepers every spring to hunt for newborn animals in the forest surrounding their home; killing copperheads and turning them in to their grandfather's steward for the 25-cent bounty. When they got to be ten or twelve, all the boys got "red bugs"—four-seated buckboards with red wooden-slat sides that were powered by Smith motors. They drove "to town" to see friends in the tiny hamlet of Pocantico Hills. In wintertime, a mechanic from Tarrytown came to the estate and replaced the wheels with spiked runners so they could negotiate the icy roads. When they were teenagers, the groundsmen regularly rescued and then shooed away young women who had become entangled climbing the six-foot fence around the estate in hopes of getting inside where some young Rockefeller would see, fall in love with, and marry them.

Pocantico was the spiritual center of the family's existence, as much involved with being a Rockefeller as Blenheim was with being a Churchill. They grew up with a proprietary attitude toward it. One of the groundsmen later recalled the time he had seen young David Rockefeller walking along the bridle paths with his fiancée, Peggy McGrath, who had casually peeled an orange as they sauntered along, dropping peels behind her. When David saw what she had done, he went back to pick up the peels; putting them in his pocket, he admonished her, "We never leave any litter on the grounds."

But the most special thing about the estate was the fact that Grandfather lived there. They knew that they were not his favorites. In his impenetrable way, he seemed to prefer Fowler McCormick, the only son of his renegade daughter Edith. Yet he liked them well enough and saw far more of them than any of his other grandchildren. Living with his housekeeper and valet in the mansion that was far too large for him, he constantly amazed them by how different he was from their father. Each one of the boys remembered playing tag with the surprisingly spry old man, and each had some favorite anecdote. For Winthrop, it was the time he accompanied his father on a visit to Kikjuit. His grandfather had been sick and was still in bed. He awoke when they entered his bedroom, and smiled, but said nothing to them until he had asked his valet to bring the afternoon newspaper. Only after the paper had been brought and he had scanned the late stock market quotations did he begin talking to them.

Sunday afternoons were state occasions. The brothers were required to dress in their Eton collars, dark coats, and pin-striped pants for dinner at Grandfather's house. They would remember him best at the head of the table, his white wig slightly askew with the cloth backing visible at the part, his lashless eyes darting from one face to another as he picked at his food and mimicked people they all knew, in his slow, ironic drawl. He occasionally seemed to embarrass their father, but Junior's reverence toward this parchment-faced old man told them he was no fool. If they were different, they learned early in life, it was not because they were rich, but because they were of Grandfather's blood.

Junior's children had been born during the hardest period of his life, punctuating the moments of the family's greatest crises. Babs had come as Ida Tarbell's book was being serialized, Laurance in the year the Standard was ruled an illegal monopoly, Winthrop in the year before Ludlow, and David at the time of the Walsh investigations. When they were infants, the family received threats so regularly that Junior feared for their lives and assigned 24-hour guards to watch over them. "Father wouldn't even permit us to have our pictures taken," David later recalled. "He thought it would be an invitation to criminals."

By the time they were teenagers, the conflict had begun to subside, leaving their father more time to spend with them, more time to prepare them for what he liked to call "the large affairs that have fallen to us." As he commented in a later Princeton commencement address: "Even in the machine age there are certain things so important that they demand personal attention. The business of being a father is surely one." The children were a duty, and he strove to be equal to all duties.

He enjoyed the role of teacher. He tried to make sure to see them at least during breakfast, which occurred precisely at seven forty-five, leading them in prayer and examining them about their schoolwork and opinions. He catechized them on their accounts and insisted that they avoid the crime of waste by turning out lights and eating all the food on their plates. When they were at Pocantico, they went on long walks in which he taught them the names and growth patterns of the native trees; the boys knew he carried chunks of maple sugar in his pocket and that he would hand them out only as a reward for reaching their final destination.

He insisted that they sit respectfully at church on Sundays and occasionally lectured them on the special trust being a Rockefeller entailed. Wednesday nights were given over to "domestic education," with the children in charge of the kitchen, each one preparing a different course in the evening meal. This was to chasten them out of any high opinions they might have of themselves. When they went west in 1924 for a camping trip in Yellowstone, Junior made them help the porter unload the baggage car and then had them ride to the lodge with the other tourists while he and Abby were chauffeured in a special car. After Babs was married, he decided to invite onlookers who had gathered outside the 54th Street house to come in, assigning his sons to usher groups through the bottom floor of the home and show off the mountainous wedding cake. "I think this experience did a lot for my sons," Junior later told his friend Fosdick. "They must learn neither to scorn nor fear the common man."

Junior also introduced his boys to those who had become his associates and advisers over the years. They grew up knowing that Mr. Debevoise, Mr. Cutler, and the other men in the office at 26 Broadway were there to serve them as well as their father. When they went to Yellowstone, park superintendent Horace Albright personally guided their tour. When they went on a cruise up the Nile, Dr. Charles Breasted, America's foremost Egyptologist (whose expeditions Junior had underwritten), accompanied them and gave a slide show on the deck of the launch every evening to preview the sites they would see the next day. Even when they were at home and decided to stroll up to the Museum of Natural History on a Saturday afternoon, Director Henry Fairfield Osborn himself often came out of his office to show them the new items in the collection.

Yet while Junior could be a conscientious father, it was hard for him to be an affectionate one. His was a character that rationed emotion carefully. Even after Ludlow was safely behind him, he was often under great pressure and his children grew used to seeing him sick in bed with colds or blinding headaches. He was easily annoyed by their boisterousness and somewhat at a loss as to how to deal with them. He left that to his wife. Abby was the center of the real intimacy in the Rockefeller household, and she recognized that they were all a strain on her husband. "Your father is so wonderfully thoughtful himself," she once wrote in a letter to one of her sons, "and so considerate to all the people with whom he comes in contact that I am sure he must occasionally find the rest of us somewhat difficult. Perhaps there is too much Aldrich in us and not enough Rockefeller."

The Aldrich quality Abby had brought to the family was new and vigorous, as Laura Spelman's contribution had been before her. Yet in this case, it was not a sense of humanitarian duty, but rather a spontaneity and exuberance lacking in her husband and his forebears. Abby's "zest for life" was something people would always comment on, along with her taste for floppy hats. It was part of her family heritage.

Their Aldrich grandparents died while the Rockefeller children were still young, leaving only a slight memory. Yet there were always other members of their mother's family around—their uncles Richard Aldrich, later a congressman from Rhode Island, and Winthrop, first a legal adviser to their father and then head of the Chase. There were Aldrich cousins to play with, and time spent with their adventuresome (and deaf) maiden aunt, Lucy Aldrich, who was always traveling in some remote corner of the world and, on a 1923 trip to the Orient, made newspaper headlines when she was kidnapped by Chinese bandits for several days and managed to save her chastity by cantankerousness and her valuable jewels by stuffing them into the toes of her shoes.

Noting that the family prayers her husband prescribed for the children to learn were an ordeal, Abby copied out Bible verses on cardboard flash cards so they would be easier to memorize. When interviewed about his philosophy of child rearing, Junior might make pronouncements such as this: "For the rich, as for families of modest means, family rearing presents the same problems with the same solutions— insistence on set studies . . . and the basic necessity of moral example through inculcation of religious habit." Yet largely through Abby's intercessions, the ban against tennis and other entertainments on Sunday was lifted, and a reign of domestic liberality unknown in either of the two previous Rockefeller generations was established.

Indeed, there often seemed to be a kind of conspiracy between Abby and her children, who were all impatient with certain of Junior's habits, such as gathering them all together on Sunday afternoons for impromptu band concerts (they each studied a different musical instrument) or spending an evening singing hymns. Once, when she was absent from one of these occasions, young Nelson wrote his mother a note that summarized their lack of enthusiasm. "We sang hymns tonight but luckily Pa had to go to church so we stopped at a quarter of eight." The Baptist authoritarianism of Junior's youth so deteriorated in this permissive atmosphere that when he tried to secure pledges of abstinence from cigarettes and spirits from his sons until they reached twenty-one, he had to rely on bribes of $2,500, and even then only Nelson and David managed to persevere long enough to collect.

Junior often tended to see the children, especially the five boys, as a unit. In his mind, they represented the next Rockefeller generation, which would inherit not only what was left of the great fortune, but also the complex financial and philanthropic apparatus he was building to deal with it. But to Abby, they were individuals growing up with problems and quirks that would last a lifetime. Babs was out of place in this man's world. It was not that she wasn't valued; on the contrary, Junior's tender feelings for her are clear in a letter she wrote him during her early teens when away from home: "I certainly miss you very much, specially in the morning when you used to come and sit on the tub and rub my hands and say nice things to me." But Babs's gender was against her: in the due course of things she would marry and have children. This was the logic of her role, but it meant she would no longer be a Rockefeller.

John 3rd, or "Johnny," seemed somewhat stunned by the name he bore, his long face always frowning in puzzlement and his lean frame given to sudden jerky and self-deprecatory movements; he took after his father, and Abby often hurt his feelings by jokingly calling him "demiJohn." There was Nelson, with Abby's own square jaw and Aldrich energy. He was always interested in outdoing his other brothers and only rarely failed. Tom Pyle, a longtime bodyguard and handyman at the Pocantico estate, who occasionally supervised the boys' marksmanship on the firing range, recalled Nelson coming only once. He shot for a while and then asked, "Can I beat my brothers?"

Pyle answered, "No, not yet. They're all good. You'll have

to practice to catch up to them." The boy left and never returned.

Laurance was frail and often ill, but he was the only one of the children with a sense of irony. He became Nelson's accomplice in all things; his sharp features and self-deprecating laugh reminded some of the first John D. In contrast, Winthrop, pudgy and moon-faced, was good-natured, awkward, and easily goaded; his brothers sensed he was the weak link in the family and picked on him constantly. David was still in velvet knee pants and brocaded shirts when the others seemed grown-up. He had a kind of serenity and self-confidence they lacked; secure in the role of the baby of the family, he didn't need to struggle so hard for advantage. Pocantico employees remembered him wandering solitarily around the estate with a butterfly net or a straw basket filled with roses he'd picked for his mother.

They made shifting alliances, the strong bond between Nelson and Laurance and a treaty for mutual defense between Winthrop and David the only ones that would ripen into permanent relationships. The family situation was filled with ambiguities, and they wrestled for precedence and power. Babs, John 3rd, and Laurance were clearly Rockefellers, colder than the others in temperament and taking most seriously their father's strictures about responsibility. Nelson, Winthrop, and David were Aldriches, both in body type and character, hardier, warmer, and more experimental than the others, and favored by their mother.

Despite the fact that Nelson was always annoying his father and calling down punishment on his head as he set off epidemics of giggles with his antics at the dinner table, Abby felt that the Aldrich toughness would always see him through. But about Winthrop she was not so sure. She knew that Nelson and Laurance teased and ridiculed him to make him lose his temper so they would have an excuse for ganging up on him. When Winthrop was sick with a kidney disease that had shortly before killed his cousin, Winthrop Aldrich, Jr., Nelson terrified him with a litany that promised him a similar fate: "Two cousins, both the same name, same disease; killed him, how are you feeling today?"

Abby's tendency was to try to soothe the conflicts. She once wrote Nelson: "I hope when you boys come home, you will do nothing to disturb David's present friendly feelings with Winthrop. It seems cruel to me that you big boys should make Winthrop the goat all the time. I realize he is often trying, but you know very well that the only way to help him is by being kind to him. Abuse only makes him angry, and much worse, while for love and kind treatment he will do anything." Junior, on the other hand, was driven to administer rare spankings by such outbreaks of disunity. One well-remembered punishment occurred when Nelson got Winthrop on a seesaw, took his end to the ground, and then hopped off. After crashing down, Winthrop retaliated by stabbing his older brother in the knee with a pitchfork. Both boys were spanked.

Babs, who had been sent to the conservative Miss Chapin's School for Girls, was the most rebellious of the children. Despite the affection between her and Junior, she carried on a running struggle for many years with her father, which intensified after her graduation in 1921, when she became the first Rockefeller in three generations (excepting Eliza, with her corncob pipe) to smoke openly and take an occasional drink. Once she fell asleep with a cigarette in her hand and set a mattress afire. Growing into an extremely attractive young woman, she adopted the flapper dresses, cloche hats, and feverish hedonism of the Jazz Age, spending the year after her coming-out going to parties and dinners, coming in late and sleeping until noon so that she could begin again the next night. She was courted by a young attorney named David Milton. He was tall, blond, athletic, and came from a good family with a summer home in the Pocantico area. He had a red Stutz roadster and shared Babs's passion for fast driving. (She made news by getting a series of speeding tickets; her parents' anger, according to one of her nephews, "sent her into a cerebral nunnery.") They would roar over the paths of Pocantico, parking to carry out their romance beyond their parents' view, but ignoring nearby workers (as one commented later) "as so many sticks of furniture." They married in 1922, much to the dismay of local scandalmongers, in whose diet they had become a staple item.

John 3rd, Junior's oldest son, followed his father's footsteps to Browning School and finished at Loomis, a boarding school in Connecticut. It was while there that he received a letter from his mother, who was worried he would inherit his father's saturnine disposition along with his name, entreating him to go to dances. "I got your very discouraging letter on Monday," he answered. "I can't say that I feel very enthusiastic at present about going to that dance. . . . It seems to be your one ambition to get me to go to dances. I suppose I *will* go if you want me to." In his schooling, as in other things, John 3rd was marked off from his younger brothers, who were able to participate in one of the interesting educational experiments of the time.

Lincoln School was the brainchild of Abraham Flexner, longtime family Associate whose brother, Simon, was head of the Rockefeller Institute for Medical Research. For years Flexner had operated a successful private school in his hometown of Louisville, running it without examinations or report cards and with a curriculum stripped of the old classics and in tune with twentieth-century progressivism. Many of Flexner's students would end up at Harvard, and there come to impress President Charles W. Eliot. In 1914, when both Eliot and Flexner were trustees of the General Education Board, which had become concerned that American high schools were both "slow and ineffective," they decided to resurrect aspects of the Louisville experiment in a demonstration high school that would provide a laboratory for the kind of education that was, in Flexner's words, "adapted to the needs of modern living."

In 1917, the GEB established Lincoln School in collaboration with Columbia Teachers College. Located in a large building at 123rd Street and Amsterdam Avenue, it was, from the beginning, a model of Deweyite pragmatism. Latin and Greek were banished and rote memory in the study of history was deemphasized; units of study about modern culture were instituted, drawing from the new initiatives of social science. Lincoln School took a flexible attitude toward the students, allowing them to learn at their own speed and without conventional forms of coercion. For the sake of the educational experiment and because of the philosophy of the Rockefellers and other wealthy patrons, it brought in a sprinkling of poor and minority students through scholarships. When Lincoln opened its doors in 1917, there were 23 of the best graduates of Teachers College ready to instruct the 116 students.

The Rockefeller boys would set out early in the morning for school. During the first few years, they walked or roller-skated up Fifth Avenue until they tired, at which point they would get into the back seat of the limousine Junior had ordered to crawl along beside them. Their mother would call for them at three o'clock in an electric car called a "hatbox" because of its high square shape. When they got older, they all drove in Nelson's hiccuping old Ford roadster. A classmate, Mrs. Linda Storrow, recalls: "Everybody in the school knew they were Rockefellers, but after a while forgot about it. They just became part of the total atmosphere. Nelson, especially, was always clasping people and laughing with them. He was terribly popular, always running for class chairman and winning. All the girls thought he was terribly handsome and had crushes on him."

The Rockefellers brought a lot to the school in addition to the money that helped set up the experiment. Admiral Byrd, whose polar expedition Junior helped to finance, was one of many who spoke to the Lincoln student body because of the Rockefeller invitation. Yet the Rockefellers received a great deal as well. It was less from the experimental curriculum (at which Laurance and David excelled, although Nelson did so poorly that it was feared for a time that he would not have the grades for college and Winthrop failed so completely that he had to be taken out of Lincoln and sent to Loomis), than from the fact that Lincoln played an important role in the continuing lesson of the brothers' youth: how to mix socially without being debilitated by an awareness of the unbridgeable distance separating them from others. In a perhaps extreme formulation of the kind of bonhomie Lincoln and other "normalizing" experiences were supposed to instill, Nelson later said, "I never in my life felt any conscious embarrassment or concern about the family name or the family's money. . . . The only times I ever felt shy or uncomfortable was at certain society affairs when I didn't know the boys who were from the better prep schools. I didn't fit into their group."

In 1929 the press was allowed to meet one of Mr. Junior's sons for the first time. It was the oldest boy, John D. 3rd, recently graduated from college and ready to carry on a family tradition by going to work for his father. Tall, thin, slightly gangling, he blushed easily and had that square-jawed innocence Charles Lindbergh and Gary Cooper would soon popularize as the face of the archetypal American hero. After watching him go through his first question-and-answer session, the reporter for *Outlook* magazine wrote: "Here, if there ever was one, is plutocratic America's opportunity to have a Prince of Wales. The young Rockefeller is no mere rich man's son; he is the sign and symbol of a vast fortune carried into the third generation. His is a proud dynasty which he must administer wisely and hand on intact. . . . He will have more money than anyone can visualize. Whether he will have much fun is another matter."

This was exactly the problem. "Mr. John," as he would be called around his father's office, had consented to go to dances to please his mother, but he had never allowed himself to enjoy them. Princeton's Class of '29, in an act of supreme whimsy had voted him Most Likely to Succeed, but he had never really felt at ease in the school Scott Fitzgerald, "Bunny" Wilson, and their friends had made into an academy of the Jazz Age. Despite his family's wealth and connections, he had felt provincial, hampered by his name the way another might have been by hands that were too large. Acquaintances delighted in telling of the time he had tried to cash a check at a store near campus, only to have the proprietor glance at the signature, sigh in disgust, and then tack it up with the J. P. Morgans, Abe Lincolns, and other forgeries decorating the wall above his cash register, leaving John 3rd beet red with embarrassment. This was one of the few times he would have to convince people of his identity. Much more often he was having to fend off their curiosity about the Rockefellers. He not only inherited the name and temperament of his father, but bore the same burden of self-doubt Junior had had as a young man: his lifelong search would be for space in which to define himself while coming to terms with the ceremonial role forced on him as the first male of his generation.

For a time at Princeton, he sold advertising for the school newspaper. He tried to win the spot his father had held at Brown, manager of the football team, but failed. JDR3 (the abbreviation he picked out for himself) spent his spare time tutoring immigrant children and doing volunteer work for the YMCA as a way of "making a contribution." Everyone noted how he agonized for long periods over apparently easy decisions. A comment Junior later made to a reporter told more than he possibly intended about his eldest son and about the relationship between them:

> "I don't think any [of the Brothers] drank before he went to college and I don't know how much any drinks now. John was the only one who ever asked my advice about it. At some initiation at Princeton, it was the custom to pass around a loving cup. John asked me whether he should refuse it, or pretend to drink it, or take a sip so as not to appear prudish. I suggested he raise the cup before him and pass it on to the next man.

What he did I don't know; but I'm inclined to think he did not drink.

JDR3 was also afflicted with an almost painful naïvete. A few years after his graduation, he married Blanchette Ferry Hooker (whose mother was heiress to the Ferry seed fortune and whose father was a distinguished engineer who became president of the Hooker Electrochemical Company). "Hookie," as she had been known at Miss Chapin's School for Girls and then Vassar, was an immensely attractive woman ("a cool, pale beauty with a regally poised head that gives her the look of a Despiau sculpture," one writer later said); when she stepped off the boat from their Bermuda honeymoon with her husband, reporters asked them what the high point of the trip had been, and the blushing young Rockefeller blurted out, "Well, there was the honeymoon part."

The summer before his senior year in college JDR3 had spent working as an intern in the information center of the League of Nations. After graduation, he went to Kyoto as his father's representative to a conference of the Institute for Pacific Relations (the preview of a lifelong interest in the Orient), and then continued around the world on an international tour. When he came home, he immediately entered his father's office, looking for an area where his strengths—a starchy morality and a capacity for dogged concentration—could be an advantage. He became involved in a New York study on juvenile delinquency and spent long hours talking to youth and penal authorities. He might have ventured into other areas that particularly interested him but his father had plans.

The great difference between Junior and his sons was that he had grown up with a single overriding purpose in mind—to help his father. He had succeeded well enough so that his own boys had no comparable quest to undertake. But the family's affairs had grown to vast proportions in the last thirty years. Although he had no master plan for fitting them into these affairs, Junior did expect his sons to become involved with him. He decided that his eldest and most compliant son had the temperament to take on the family philanthropies. By 1931, JDR3 had become a trustee for the Foundation, the General Education Board, the Institute, the China Medical Board, and others—in all, thirty-three different boards or committees.

Forty-three years later, sitting under a Charles Eastman portrait of the first John D. in his oak-paneled office on the 56th floor of the RCA Building in Rockefeller Center, JDR3 recalled these early days with an irony that masks a lingering (but unadmitted) bitterness. "My father had the idea that his sons would follow the same pattern he had. My brothers and I would do what was useful for him. I got involved in a considerable number of his activities. I came in young into all these established institutions where I worked among older and more capable people. It was all intensely interesting and worthwhile, but I was in a position where it was all done for me, where I couldn't make a mistake of my own. I was chairman of a personnel search committee here, and chairman of a finance committee there. I was on everything with father, boards and committees, I think, which ranged from the Rockefeller Foundation to the Seal Harbor Tennis Club. I was chairman of the Seal Harbor Tennis Committee for him, and my job was to find the pro each year. That shows you the range of my opportunity."

The lessons in JDR3's experience were not lost on his younger borthers. They saw the same fate awaiting them—to have their lives parceled out in bits and pieces as they submitted their ambitions to the requirements of an institutional role. Yet to rebel, at least for JDR3, was unthinkable. If you were the Prince of Wales, you simply did not recoil from ceremony or worry about a career to fit your interests. You just waited to be put on the throne.

Most people assumed that the major drama of the third generation, therefore, would be how well JDR3 would do with the power his father had doled out to him and how far he would advance the family's affairs. But those who were close to the Rockefellers realized that the first son did not have a unique vision of the family's role and destiny to support his hereditary claim to leadership. The drama of the third generation would be the overthrow of primogeniture and JDR3's relegation to a position of secondary importance in the generation of brothers.

There was no overt struggle for power: everything had been decided by the order of birth and the caprice of the genetic code. As Howard Knowles, a longtime family employee, recalled: "John was removed and aloof. You felt he was always trying to draw back. He was very shy and he'd slide right by you without saying a word if he could. Now Nelson, on the other hand—he would come into the room and slap you on the back and ask how you were doing. He was different. And he muscled John out by the sheer force of his personality, without even trying. I remember once when all the boys—actually they were young men then—were sitting for a photograph. More or less naturally, Nelson was sitting in the middle, the center of attention, wisecracking and making everybody laugh. John was off to the side, quiet and serious. The photographers got ready to start and suddenly Nelson realized what was happening. He went over and put his arm around John and said, 'Come on, Johnny, you're the oldest, you ought to be in the middle.' John came, but it didn't matter. Wherever he sat, Nelson would always be the center of things."

When he was a boy, Nelson seemed to have unlimited energy. It delighted his mother, but was often difficult for his father to cope with. If he secretly admired his son's high spirits and envied him the regard he kindled in his mother, Junior's tendency was still to try to curb the boy and make him conform more closely to his own more stringent notions of responsibility. It was a deep, almost irresolvable conflict, affecting a wide area of behavior. One especially telling crisis had come over Nelson's left-handedness, which Junior had seen as a bad habit that needed changing. At mealtimes, he put a rubber band around the boy's hand and attached a string to it, which he held, jerking it each time his son backslid and failed to reach for something with the right hand. Some saw this strong pulling as a metaphor for what Junior sought to do with all his boys, but the real lesson was that, in the struggle between him and his expansive second son which simmered over the years, the boy did not give in.

From the beginning, Nelson felt he was marked for something special. He had been given the name of his maternal grandfather, Nelson Aldrich, whom he didn't remember except in the stories of the senator's political prowess his mother told. He regarded it as even more of a portent that he had been born on the birthday of John D. Rockefeller, Sr. (It was the year the old man had mounted the witness stand in the dissolution suit to tell the court the Standard trust had been formed by the "benevolent assimilation" of its competitors.) He was always aware of this dual tradition. Later he said: "The example of my grandfathers made me feel a terrific challenge. . . . Grandfather Rockefeller was a leader of men. Grandfather Aldrich was completely different, a great man with the people." Unlike John III, Nelson didn't try to understand the tradition that had produced him; he simply embraced it, joyously and without doubt.

Originally Nelson had hoped to follow JDR3 to Princeton, but his grades were so poor that for a time it was not clear if he would be able to get into any of the "good" schools. Although he had to do remedial work with tutors, his self-confidence was never shaken. (He once admitted to a friend, "You know, I don't have a very high I.Q." The friend asked why he thought so and Nelson replied cheerfully, "Because I took one of those tests and found out.") He "buckled down" in his final year at Lincoln School and managed to get into Dartmouth, where he worked hard enough to overcome what he later understood was an undiagnosed case of dyslexia (he transposed words and phrases when reading) to become Phi Beta Kappa. He was interested in facts rather than ideas, and showed a tendency to subject every concept to a pragmatic test, almost as if he wanted to be sure it had a market value before accepting it.

Classmates would remember him as a student who dressed casually in baggy sweaters and corduroy pants, with curly hair and a quick grin that narrowed his eyes and convulsed the lower part of his square face. Several inches shorter than JDR3, he was powerfully built and in his first year managed to take an active enough role in the annual freshman-sophomore brawl to get a black eye. He was the kind of young man who might have been called "Rocky" even if his name hadn't been Rockefeller. As it was, the nickname was inevitable. Some of his Dartmouth classmates mistrusted him, claiming they discerned beneath his familiarity what Dr. Johnson had called the easy arrogance of wealth. But most were drawn to his carefree manner and crumpled good looks and elected him vice-president of the junior class, although he was twice unsuccessful in campaigns for the school presidency.

Nelson was a paradox: of all the brothers, he was most in touch with his impulses and desires and least affected by the guilt that seemed as much a part of being a Rockefeller as the money. But this freedom did not lead him to strike off on his own. On the contrary, he was quick to defend the family. When it came time to select a topic for his senior thesis in economics, he chose to write a defense of his grandfather's creation of Standard Oil. The old man was amused to hear about the project, but declined Nelson's request for a formal interview. All that was past history to him, and he had never really agreed with Junior's attempt to make a heroic enterprise out of something that had been, in its own way, just a business. But Junior was pleased by Nelson's interest, regarding it as a vindication of his own attempts to foster loyalty toward the family. When Nelson had reported his American history teacher's position on the founding of the Standard, Junior had called it "a warped and erroneous view" and arranged for W. O. Inglis to appear before the class with "the truth." In the matter of the thesis, he sent Nelson the unpublished manuscript about Senior that Ivy Lee had commissioned Inglis to distill from a series of conversations with the old man. Nelson was not curious about the critiques written by Tarbell and the other muckrakers, but he avidly devoured the Inglis manuscript and wrote home after finishing it: "I don't know when anything has interested me more. . . . For the first time I felt that I really knew Grandfather a little—got a glimpse of the power and grandeur of his life."

It was a curious moment in the Rockefeller legacy. The vision of power that had burdened Junior's soul whetted this son's appetite. Rather than something to live down, it was something to live up to. As the years passed, the coincidence of his birthday's falling on the same day as his grandfather's gained more and more meaning for Nelson. "It seems funny to think that today is Grandfather's 90th birthday and my 21st birthday," he wrote to his parents at the end of his junior year at Dartmouth. "The 90 makes my 21 seem mighty small and insignificant, just like a little sapling standing by a mighty fir. But the sapling still has time to grow and develop and someday it might itself turn into a tree of some merit. Who knows?"

It sounded good, but Nelson (as his parents well knew) was not one to be content with slow or uncertain growth. When he saw his older brother given duties in their father's office that made him little more than a glorified clerk, he began to wonder about his own future there. As he neared graduation, the question of exactly where he would fit into the family's affairs became increasingly bothersome. He declared himself indirectly in a letter written to his parents just before graduation: "Just to work my way up in a business that another man has built, stepping from the shoes of one to those of another, making a few minor changes here and there and then, finally, perhaps at the age of sixty, getting to the top where I would have real control for a few years. No, that isn't my idea of living a real life."

But this decision was put off for the time being by one that loomed even larger. In between his junior and senior years, Nelson, along with his brother Laurance, had gone on Sir Wilfred Grenfell's expedition to Antarctica. On the way home, worries about his future were entwined with thoughts about Mary Todhunter Clark, a girl he had met at Seal Harbor years earlier and dated ever since. For his first three years at Dartmouth, "Tod" was only one of many girl friends. But now, with graduation approaching, he decided to "get serious." He wrote his mother, "You know, I'm beginning to think that I really am in love with Tod, whatever being in love means. She is the only girl I know who measures up anywhere nearly to you. . . ." By early fall in his senior year, despite his father's urgent advice to wait, he had gotten himself engaged.

Junior was irate at what he saw as yet another sign of impetuousness in Nelson. As for the girl herself, however, he and Abby both liked her. A tall brunette with a long aristocratic face, Mary Clark had grown up on a Philadelphia estate given to her ancestors by King George III. After attending the exclusive Foxcroft School in Virginia, she had gone to Paris for a year to be "finished." An intelligent woman with a good sense of humor, she looked equally at ease in a riding habit or a formal evening gown. She had impeccable manners and an icy sense of dignity that would, in time, grow almost regal as she stoically suffered the scandal of her husband's extramarital affairs and the decision to seek a divorce.

Abby eventually soothed Junior into accepting the engagement; the match itself was not unlike their own marriage in that it brought the family a socially elevating contact. (Tod's maternal grandfather, George B. Roberts, had been president of the Pennsylvania Railroad; her cousin, Joseph Clark, would serve as a liberal Democratic senator from Pennsylvania.) In the winter of 1929, Junior sent the couple to see Senior at his winter home in Florida, and the old man indicated his approval of his future granddaughter-in-law by playing a ritual round of golf with her. When Nelson married Tod in an elegant Philadelphia wedding after his graduation in 1930, Junior informed Senior that twenty thousand dollars, the same amount he had given Babs when she married, would be sufficient as a wedding gift. ("I am confident they would lay the sum away in some safe investment as a nest egg," he wrote.) Junior's own present to them was a trip around the world.

It was the sort of grand tour only a U.S. Ambassador at Large or a Rockefeller could have taken. The ports of call were exotic—Honolulu, Tokyo, Seoul, Peking, Java, Sumatra, and Bali among them. Yet this was far from being a journey into the heart of darkness; Standard Oil had been spreading its civilizing light in these regions for half a century, and at each stop the newlyweds were met by a company representative who treated them to elephant rides through the jungle and other exotic diversions, while also escorting them to state dinners with princes, kings, and local dignitaries. Junior had obtained letters of introduction for them from Prime Minister Ramsay MacDonald, which allowed them entrée in areas of the British Empire even beyond the Standard's reach. In Delhi they saw the poet Tagore, and then went to the home of Gandhi, who was having one of his silent days but passed them a note saying he would welcome them the next morning.

When, after an absence of nearly nine months, they returned to New York and moved into an apartment on Fifth Avenue, Junior hoped that Nelson would be ready to settle down and apply himself to family tasks as his older brother was doing. But if anything, the people he had met and the sights he had seen only inflamed Nelson's ambition to begin some great task of his own.

A few months later, in the summer of 1931, when he did go to work at 26 Broadway, he found his worst fears confirmed. Things proceeded there according to the slow, steady rhythms his father had perfected over forty years. Everywhere Nelson turned, he found his ambitions blocked by the monolithic caution practiced by Cutler, Debevoise, and Junior's other advisers.

In 1932, Nelson's first child, Rodman Clark Rockefeller, was born and the four Rockefeller generations posed for a historic photograph. (Babs had already had two girls, "Mitzi" and Marilyn, but the appearance of heiresses did not call for a dynastic photo.) Despite his pride at fathering the first male heir of the next age, however, Nelson continued to chafe under the regimen at 26 Broadway. Finally, he began to spin out of his father's orbit. Defying Junior's expressed wish that he conserve and focus his energies on projects whose importance they agreed upon, Nelson accepted an invitation to become a trustee of the Metropolitan Museum of Art. (He already had taken on an active role in the Museum of Modern Art.) "My justification for spending the time which I do in this work," he wrote his father, "is that I feel . . . that the aesthetic side of a person's life is almost as important as his spiritual development or his physical will-being. And finally, as I said before I feel that the contacts which such a position offers are not to be disregarded. I am sorry to go against your feelings in the matter, but I hope you can see my point of view."

Nelson never really quit working at his father's office. He just gravitated to other projects. In 1932 he and a couple of friends formed a firm they called Turck and Company, which was an odd combination of brokerage and the rental of office space. Nelson showed a sharp entrepreneurial eye and a willingness to trade on the family connections that did not please Junior. (It worked this way: if Turck and Company found a certain cement firm that wanted to expand its operations, for instance, it would arrange a loan from the Chase Bank and a contract for some part of the work at Rockefeller Center; in return, the cement company would agree to rent office space at the Center; Turck and Company would receive a brokerage commission for its efforts.) Soon Nelson bought out his partners, changed the name of the company to Special Work, Inc., and limited the operations to renting space in the Rockefeller Center development.

Finally, however, he was forced to admit that the family alone possessed the institutions that could give him the kind of power he wanted. The turning point came late in 1933, after he had just returned from Mexico City on a trip to acquire paintings for the Museum of Modern Art. On his return, he wrote his father a letter admitting he had been "in a state of flux as far as my ideas and theories are concerned," and promising he had "just emerged into a new period." It was a letter that showed he was willing to adopt the long view to attain his objectives:

> Special Work gave me a chance to do things on a smaller scale—where I made mistakes it didn't make so much difference as the responsibility rested squarely on my shoulders. There is no question but that this work has been of the greatest possible value to me and I have confidence where before I was groping fearfully in the dark. However, I have come to see things more nearly in their true proportions and now realize that the activities of

Special Work, Inc., are not all-important. Furthermore, I am beginning to see more clearly the importance, and even the international significance, of some of the things that take place in this office. One thing that has been particularly helpful to me in gaining a perspective on these matters is the study I have been making of the office's activities. Until I stopped to think, I did not grasp the significance of what is going on here. . . .

The purpose of this letter is to tell you that . . . I hope that I will be able to be of distinctly more assistance to you. I don't think the time spent outside the office has been wasted, for I am much richer in experience now than I was two years ago and therefore should be able to make myself correspondingly more useful. For the immediate future, my plan is to become more familiar with all phases of your real estate interests and to avail myself of every opportunity to get acquainted with your oil, coal, and banking interests. Of course, if there are special problems which I can handle or help you with, I will be only too glad to do what I can.

To summarize, I might say that I simply want you to know by this letter that I am back in the fold as far as my interests are concerned and that from now on my desire will be to be of as much help to you as I possibly can with my limited experience. . . .

One element of his rapprochement with his father was selfish: the recognition that by helping develop the family's influence, he would also enhance his own importance. But it went deeper than that. Although different from his father in other things, he was similar in feeling that the family was on the threshold of accumulating the sort of power no other group had ever wielded in American life. Like Junior, he felt the Rockefellers had a manifest destiny and that it was his duty to further it.

Back in the fold at the Family Office in Rockefeller Center, Nelson questioned his father's Associates on the way the third generation should conduct itself. If most of the advice was mundane, a note from attorney Thomas Debevoise on the kinds of charitable donations the brothers should make rose to a philosophical level:

For many years it has been generally recognized that Rockefeller gifts to charity are made only after careful investigation and consideration. The result has been that the presence of the Rockefeller name in a list of contributors had been all the endorsement needed to satisfy the public of the worthiness of the cause. . . . there can be no question as to the desirability of a continuance by Mr. Rockefeller Sr. and Mr. Rockefeller Jr. of the policy outlined. Should this policy be followed by the family of Mr. Rockefeller Jr.? It is, of course, quite true that in one respect the five boys do not need to be as careful as their father has been. No one of them will be subjected to the pressures from the outside that have caused him so much trouble—no one of them will have the burden of anything like the same fortune with its almost unlimited responsibilities. But the name handed down by the father will be used by five instead of one, and unless the five have some common policy of the same general character as their father's, the name their own children take will be nothing like it is today. It has been made by one in each of the two generations, and it can easily be destroyed by five in one generation. It will be five times as hard for five to protect the name as for one unless the five follow the same general policy.

Debevoise's advice was the conservative wisdom expected of a man who functioned almost as a family solicitor. But its logic was arresting. If the hostility that once surrounded the fortune had diminished, so had the fortune itself. This was partly because of new tax structures and partly because large amounts had been invested in the philanthropies as well as in the dynasty itself (the Office and the estates). But most dramatically it was diminished because five male heirs stood to inherit in the present generation, instead of one. On the other hand, just as the fortune had diminished, the name had grown. This was a capital that could be preserved and expanded.*

A strange cooperation sprang up between Junior and the son who in most ways was least like him. Nelson became his father's surrogate in the third generation, anxiously watching his brothers' progress and cheering them along. As he gravi-

---

*Years later, one of the Brothers told a writer: "What we really have is our name. That is our big asset. It opens doors and, as our money is dispersed, it is of far greater value than anything else as long as it remains a good name. Seeing that it does must be our first consideration."

tated back into his father's Office, he was conscious of the others' development and anxious to work out a scheme in which their future efforts would be complementary. He reveled in the image, already in the process of creation, of five remarkable young men: selfless, unspoiled by wealth, and dedicated to the common good, a conspicuous national resource.

In December 1934, Junior wrote each of his sons a letter to inform them that he was settling most of what was left of his fortune on them in the form of trusts composed primarily of Standard Oil stock and amounting to about $40 million dollars each. "I have today set up a trust for your benefit and also trusts for each of the other children," the letter to Laurance ran.

> I have already spoken to you about these trusts and my reasons for establishing them. They have been created in accordance with the policy which your Grandfather Rockefeller adopted with his children and which I hope your children will ultimately follow. . . . As you know, Grandfather and I have always been keenly alive to the responsibilities inherent in the possession of wealth. He believes, as I do, that these responsibilities and the opportunities which they bring for useful living and unselfish service to mankind should be shared with those of the next generation when and as soon as they have reached such an age and attained such a maturity as justifies their being entrusted with them.

In parceling out the fortune, Junior had acted more hurriedly than he would otherwise have liked because of the New Deal's new inheritance tax, which would have laid claim to more than 70 percent of his estate if he were to die without having so disposed of it. The year 1934 was also the year that the new Securities and Exchange Act required individuals owning 10 percent or more of a corporation's stock to report the extent of their holdings. With the setting up of the " '34 Trusts" (as they would be called), Junior had disposed of enough of his Standard of New Jersey and Standard of California stock so that he did not have to report under the act.

If the timing had been dictated by external circumstances, the transmission of the fortune from one generation to the next would have come in any case. It marked a fateful moment for the Rockefeller dynasty, and the brothers knew it as well as Junior. It seemed to spur Nelson in particular to even greater efforts. He had been a director of Rockefeller Center since first coming to work, when headquarters was still 26 Broadway, but now he threw himself furiously into the campaign to rent its space in the Depression market.

It was a bad time to be trying to attract tenants. Even the Empire State Building, which had Al Smith as president and an express elevator to take tourists up to see the roof where King Kong had swatted down fighter planes, was only two-thirds full. Nelson was, nonetheless, spectacularly successful—so much so, in fact, that real estate rival August Heckscher filed a $10 million suit against him, charging that he had paid money to lure tenants away and had offered deals on space that added up to less income than the taxes, interest, and operating costs on the Rockefeller Center buildings. But Nelson understood how important it was that his father's gamble pay off, and he forged ahead, using his considerable skills to fill empty space and form friendships—like the one with young George Meany, then business agent for plumbers in the Bronx. Nelson told the Building Trades Unions of Greater New York that he wanted to deal with one person. Meany was appointed to sign the master agreement. Rockefeller Center did not lose a single day to strikes, and by the end of the project Nelson had a firm hold on Meany's admiration. He even managed to slip by the crisis over the Diego Rivera mural, which stood as the only contretemps of Rockefeller Center's construction.*

He became the Center's public relations man and seemed to enjoy giving what a *New Yorker* writer described as

*The famous Mexican artist had been commissioned to do the central murals by Nelson in the first place. Nelson owned several of his canvases, and Rivera was a great favorite of Abby, having done a prized portrait of Babs as a young woman. Nelson was upset at what soon became an allegory of capitalism: degenerate cardsharks, pathetic girls with tertiary syphilis, rapacious capitalists. The final straw, given the anti-Communism that had become a strong part of Nelson's youthful politics, was Rivera's insertion of a heroic portrait of Lenin into the work. He tried to get the offending image changed. When Rivera refused, Rockefeller tried to arrange for the work to be removed and reassembled at the Museum of Modern Art. When this failed and Rivera's work was effaced from the Center, Nelson had managed to persuade New Yorkers that he had been more than reasonable and preserved enough goodwill with Rivera that they became friends again after a decent interval.

"graceful little speeches in the manner of a particularly successful high school basketball coach" to commemorate the openings of its buildings and plazas. The fact that by 1938 the Center could see its way through the dismal economy to a time when it would not only break even but make money was due largely to Nelson's efforts. As a reward, Junior made him Rockefeller Center's president.

It was the same with whatever institution he entered. Drawing on seemingly inexhaustible energy, he was able to apply himself to several different enterprises at once, and manage to make them intersect, however contradictory they might seem. At the same time he was becoming deeply involved in the family's affairs at Rockefeller Center, he was also moving into the avant-garde of the modern art movement. The latter was a natural development, for, by the time he was a college freshman, he fully shared his mother's obsession with modern art. On his honeymoon trip around the world, he collected the first object (a Sumatran knife handle in the shape of a shrunken head) in what would become the best primitive art collection in the country. Shortly after his return to New York, his mother had arranged for him to go on the Museum of Modern Art's Junior Advisory Committee. In the period when he was trying to make it outside the Family Office (and perhaps in reaction to his father's well-known aversion to modernism), he had become deeply involved in MOMA, mastering the infighting that took place there and getting himself elected to the board of trustees in 1932. (He would later say, "I learned my politics at the Museum of Modern Art.") With Abby looking after his art career from her position as one of MOMA's founding mothers, Nelson became treasurer in 1935 and was elected president four years later.

If some of the trustees distrusted his aesthetics, winced when he referred to the permanent collection as "the stuff downstairs," and were annoyed when he brought in time-and-motion specialists to study the museum's operation, they had to admire the way he raised memberships and broadened MOMA's base of support. In 1939, when the museum moved into its permanent home on 54th Street (the very building site another example of Rockefeller largesse), the grand opening was marked by a nationally broadcast radio speech by Franklin D. Roosevelt. There followed a speech by Nelson A. Rockefeller, whose words rather pointedly failed to make clear that MOMA had been in existence for a decade and had had previous presidents.*

The business of art and the art of business would often merge into a single act as Nelson traveled to international conferences and came home laden with treasures. In 1937, when he went on his first trip to Peru, his chartered twin-engine plane was so bloated with artifacts on his return that it was barely able to negotiate the steep mountain passes of the Andes. Three years later, when he visited Mexico's President Cardenas to talk of expropriated Standard Oil properties, he presented himself not as "El Principe de Gasolina" (as some members of the Mexican press were calling him) but as the president of the Museum of Modern Art, on a trip to arrange a show in New York that would portray the early cultural history of Mexico.

Nelson's was a uniquely integrated life. It was inevitable that he would sooner or later be attracted to the powerful oil companies with which the family maintained discreet ties. In 1934, upon reentering the family fold, he had taken the advice of Debevoise and gone to work for the Chase Bank as a way of getting acquainted with its operations and understanding how it fit into his father's other interests. But the only part of the Chase that really interested Nelson was the foreign department and its relations with international politics and the oil companies. His father had refused to answer correspondence dealing with the Standard and had done everything in his power to foster the illusion that, except in times of extraordinary moral crisis like the Stewart affair, the Rockefellers were simply stockholders with no special influence.† Yet Nelson remembered how the presidents of the

*In his history of MOMA art critic Russell Lynes writes: "There is no question that the Rockefellers were the reigning family of the Museum and that the dynasty persisted from the inception of the Museum . . . and still continues today." After Nelson, David was the next Rockefeller to take over the presidency of the museum, followed by JDR3's wife, Blanchette. The family would be in an excellent position to shape the development of modern art in America, helping make the careers of artists they patronized and collected, while also establishing aesthetic trends.

† In one of the letters he periodically sent to all his sons, Junior later wrote: "From time to time my father received, as I do, requests of many kinds from stockholders and past employees of one or more of the Standard companies and also from people who have felt they in one way or another have been injured by the actions of the officers or representatives of those companies. Father never attempted, nor have I, to answer these inquiries directly. . . . This policy protects us both from

various Standard companies had stopped by the 54th Street house for long talks with Junior. His father had been anything but ambiguous in the opinions he expressed during these private meetings, and he himself had no qualms at all about using the family's connections and its leverage.

While doing his apprenticeship in the Chase, he became close to Joseph Rovensky, who, as head of the bank's foreign department, knew the leading figures in the international cartels controlling raw materials markets. Rovensky was also well acquainted with the important personalities in the world of oil. When Nelson went to London as a Chase representative in 1935, Rovensky helped him make contacts and watched with satisfaction as his young protégé began to maneuver between the institutions in the family's sphere of influence in a way his father wouldn't have dreamed of doing, at least not directly. When Fred Gehle, a vice-president of the Chase, urged him to get the accounts of the Standard Oil companies transferred to the bank, Nelson replied: "I have talked with him [the treasurer of Standard of New Jersey] at some length yesterday and he is arranging to transfer, gradually, some twenty accounts of their subsidiaries to the Chase National Bank. . . . Upon my return from Europe I will take up with Socony-Vacuum [Standard of New York] the question of a closer relationship."

The talk of the international oil set attending the parties Nelson hosted in London and Paris was the fabulous oil fields of Lake Maracaibo, which almost overnight had made Venezuela the biggest producer of oil in the world after the United States. Over a hundred companies had vied with each other for Venezuelan crude, but in the end only three controlled 99 percent of it: Standard of New Jersey, which had acquired the properties of Indiana Standard in the wake of the Stewart fight and owned a 49 percent share; Shell, which owned 36 percent; and Gulf's Mene Grande subsidiary, which owned 14 percent. The biggest Venezuelan producer by far was the Creole Petroleum Company, the crown jewel in the Jersey system. It was to this company that Nelson was drawn. Asking his father to exchange some of the Standard shares that had

the embarrassment of investigating personal grievances, answering personal requests, and from the danger of taking any position which suggested control in the slightest degree of the activities in which a large stock interest might imply a more direct connection. It has proven such a wise policy that I urge all you boys to adopt it for the protection of the family."

been put in his trust fund for enough Creole shares to make him a significant stockholder, he arranged to have himself put on the board of directors.

The year was 1935, a turning point not only for Nelson Rockefeller, but also for Creole and the other companies that controlled Venezuela's oil wealth, for in mid-December Juan Vicente Gómez, dictator since 1908, died. The Gómez regime had been one of the cruelest and most corrupt in Latin American history. While the Venezuelans suffered, however, the foreign oil companies had grown rich. During the oil boom of the twenties, when the rights to the Maracaibo Basin were opened up, Gómez had given foreign companies everything they asked and was paid handsomely for his service. At his death, oil amounted to 99 percent of Venezula's exports. Yet some 70 percent of the country was illiterate, 60 percent lived in houses of straw and sticks with dirt floors, and only 32 percent of the entire Venezuelan population was employed.

After the dictator's death, the oil men in whose circles Nelson was now moving were alarmed at the tough petroleum reform laws the new government passed to mollify the forces of nationalist outrage and social unrest that had been bottled up during the Gómez decades. But they were far more worried about the fact that the entire hemisphere seemed increasingly inflamed by the politics they associated with Communism. In 1937 the rebel Bolivian regime nationalized the Standard Oil properties there; the following year, Mexico's Cárdenas government, acting on the program of the Marxist labor leaders, announced the expropriation of foreign oil interests.

Young Rockefeller was in the middle of this ferment, intrigued by the oil business and understanding intuitively the role it was destined to play in international power politics. In the spring of 1937 he embarked on a twenty-nation tour of Latin America climaxed by a journey up Venezuela's Orinoco River in a Standard Oil company yacht. His party included Rovensky, Standard executive Jay Crane, his wife Tod, and his brother Winthrop (who was also becoming interested in oil). After touring the Creole Company properties and visiting Caracas—where at two parties he met Gómez's successor, General Lopez Contreras, his entire cabinet, and the governors of four Venezuelan states—an exhilarated Nelson reported home to his parents that "unless something unforeseen happens, it looks as if this would turn out to be one of the soundest ... countries in the world—and there's certainly plenty of oil here."

The trip was a turning point in his life. It marked the moment when Nelson found that "something big" he had been looking for. Returning from Caracas, he began a crash course in Spanish at Berlitz, and only those who didn't know him well suspected that this was another of his momentary enthusiasms. He was serious about Latin America. He tried to convey his sense of crisis and opportunity to a meeting of executives of the Jersey company. He urged upon them a more active policy of social responsibility, pointing out that the corporation held property only by the will of the people and the laws of its governments. If the corporation didn't recognize its social responsibilities, he said, "they will take away our ownership."

No oil man could afford to ignore a Rockefeller, even if he had only just turned thirty, but the Jersey board was a power in its own right and was not compelled to take his advice. They had complied with the Venezuelan government's new regulations and saw no reason to undertake the campaign Nelson seemed to be advocating. But Nelson was not discouraged. He simply packed up and went to Venezuela, using his status as one of Creole's directors to demand an increased sensitivity to local conditions. He forged ahead with even more than his usual zeal, pressing for an end to the more blatant manifestations of cultural chauvinism that characterized the behavior of U.S. business abroad.

Seasoned veterans in the oil game suddenly found themselves under assault by this Rockefeller heir who spent weeks on end touring their operations and trying to explain that the changes he had in mind had less to do with fuzzy idealism than making sure they did not create an opening for the Communists and thus lose everything, as in Mexico. ("He wasn't much of a reader," Nelson's Venezuelan associate Carl Spaeth recalls. "But he had read a book about Esso's misadventures in Mexico that had a great effect on him. He made sure that all of us read it too and had the Mexican precedent in mind.")

Nelson found reluctant allies in Arthur Proudfit, the general manager of Creole, and Eugene Holman, chairman of its board. (Holman later became president of the Jersey Company, and Proudfit moved up to the presidency of Creole.) They too sensed the intensity of the revolt simmering in Latin America. The problem for the oil companies, as Proudfit later expressed it, was to prove to Venezuelans "that we are an asset to the culture, education, and general welfare of the country."

Those in the Creole organization who opposed young Rockefeller's ideas or mistook his glad-handing for weakness quickly found themselves transferred, retired, or kicked upstairs to a stateside desk. Soon the barbed wire around Creole's compounds in the Maracaibo Basin came down. Twelve Berlitz instructors were hired to help the company's American executives and staff brush up on their Spanish and learn the rudiments of Venezuelan culture. A public health program, like those pioneered by the Rockefeller Foundation, was introduced, funded in part by government aid to combat hookworm, malaria, and other tropical diseases that plagued workers in the oil-producing regions.

One of the chief cries heard against the oil companies in the years following Gómez's death was that the oil boom had made Venezuela a one-product economy, wrecking agriculture and inflating prices and thus ruining domestic industry. All factions in the country agreed that economic diversification was necessary to lessen the dependence on oil production. To demonstrate the path such diversification might take became Nelson's next crusade.

Gathering together a group of friends and business associates in 1940, he formed the *Compania de Fomento Venezolano* (Venezuelan Development Company). He raised $3 million in initial capital, a third coming from his family, a third from Venezuelan partners, and a third from the oil companies. (Nelson had gone to Jersey Standard with this idea of developing the Venezuelan economy, and they had agreed to an investment of $300,000 if he could secure equal commitments from Gulf and Shell, which he surprised them by doing.)

The first effort was a huge resort hotel, the Avila. As the *Compania's* pilot project, it took much of Nelson's time. He made quick trips to Venezuela himself and shuttled as many as five aides back and forth between New York and Caracas to oversee its progress. In the summer of 1940, Robert Bottome, whom Nelson had recruited from the Rockefeller Center rental department, wrote back suggesting that they consider other investments to go along with the hotel.* But

---

*Shortly after it was formed, the *Compania* had been approached by Henry Linam of Standard Oil with the suggestion that it get into a water-drilling service. Standard would provide the drilling equipment in

with war approaching, Nelson wanted to know if such investments would be safe, whatever the possible outcome. He sent Carl Spaeth to Caracas to evaluate the situation. "To postpone such programs as ours until after the war," Spaeth wrote back, "is to lose an excellent opportunity to get in a substantial position in advance of German commercial interests, which will certainly come here in great numbers, supported by substantial subsidies in the event that Germany wins the war."

It was the sort of *Realpolitik* that appealed to someone who was in many ways more fearful of the Communists' inflaming nationalist passions in Latin America than the hemispheric consequences of a possible German victory in Europe. Yet the approaching war had clearly created a new set of circumstances in the hemisphere, and Nelson's ambitions pointed him in the direction of Washington. About the same time that he was founding the *Compania*, he brought together a number of people, most of them his own age with similar views, whom he had met since making his first South American tour. The regular briefings they held about the state of things in Latin America, and plans to cope with them, resembled a war council.

Twenty years older than anyone else, "Uncle Joe" Rovensky was the *éminence grise* of the group. Rovensky, who had had a brush with the New Deal during the investigation of the Chase in the Pecora hearings, sneered at Roosevelt's brain trusters as "the sort of men who won't be satisfied until they've levelled the whole country off at the height of three feet." But he was an insider's insider when it came to the economic affairs of nations, and when Nelson later went to Washington to join the Roosevelt administration, Rovensky went along with him. Jay Crane of Jersey Standard was also in the Rockefeller study group, as was Wallace Harrison, the tall laconic New Englander who had gained attention while still a young man by becoming the leading architect of Rockefeller Center. Others of his contemporaries would be more in-

exchange for the geological rights to anything other than water that might be discovered. "The idea rather appeals to me," Bottome wrote Nelson. "... Such a company would give us the perfect excuse to get around the country, to get to know the local political and business people in the rest of Venezuela, and, as always, to keep our eyes open for other possibilities for ourselves." In August 1940, some five months later, Bottome wrote again suggesting that they consider investments in pharmaceuticals, asbestos, and food distribution.

fluential aesthetically, but "Wally" would go on to design over a billion dollars' worth of real estate, as he became designer laureate for the Rockefeller family and someone on whose loyalty Nelson could always rely.

Finally, there was Beardsley Ruml, the large florid-faced Czech economist who had been brought into the family's orbit by Raymond Fosdick years earlier and who now was the main intellectual resource among "the Group" (as they were called by outsiders, although they preferred Ruml's name, "the *Junta*"). Robert Moses said of Ruml, "He was a big, round, rumbling man, full of fun and wit, a natural-born, provocative teacher, unorthodox and at times outrageous in his expressions." The Group met first at his place in Greenwich Village and later at Nelson's Fifth Avenue apartment. As the world crisis deepened, their discussions began to focus on the outlines for a hemispheric policy consistent with Nelson's ideas. By late spring 1940, Ruml had distilled their thinking into a sort of white paper called "Hemisphere Economic Policy," outlining ways of increasing U.S. investments in Latin America and preventing the Nazis from winning a diplomatic war there with the same lightning speed their armies were displaying as they raced across Europe.

On the evening of June 14, 1940, Nelson appeared at the White House with the three-page memorandum and delivered it to Roosevelt's right-hand man, Harry Hopkins. At Hopkins's request, Rockefeller read out loud what began more like a manifesto than a mere policy recommendation: "Regardless of whether the outcome of the war is a German or Allied victory, the United States must protect its international position through the use of economic measures that are competitively effective against totalitarian techniques."

Less than a month later, on July 8, Nelson was celebrating his thirty-second birthday with his family and close friends when the telephone rang with a long-distance call from Washington. It was James Forrestal, special assistant to President Roosevelt. An intense, suspicious, man, Forrestal had already made a name for himself as the "boy wonder" of Wall Street by pulling off the merger of Chrysler Automobiles and the Dodge Corporation. Years earlier, under subpoena by the Pecora Committee, he had admitted to self-dealing in millions' worth of foreign securities during the boom days of the twenties, but like many whom the President had denounced as "economic royalists," Forrestal had since done penance by grudgingly supporting Roosevelt's reforms and had thus become eligible for national duty in the country's hour of need.

Now he was on the phone to Nelson asking about a job: Could Nelson come to Washington to talk further? The following evening Nelson dined with Forrestal in the garden of the F Street Club. When offered the newly created post of Coordinator of Inter-American Affairs, Rockefeller asked for a few days to think it over. Then he immediately boarded a plane for Salt Lake City to ask permission from the Republican presidential standard-bearer, Wendell Willkie, who was on the campaign trail in a candidacy Nelson's Uncle Winthrop had helped create and whose effort the Rockefeller family was heavily backing. But he knew before he hung up what his answer would be—not only because (as Willkie would tell him) accepting the post was his patriotic duty, but because he himself had proposed the idea of creating such a position in his talk with Harry Hopkins barely a month earlier.

12

LAURANCE SPELMAN ROCKEFELLER had been Nelson's buddy as a child and would continue to be as a man. Yet by the time Forrestal called from Washington, Laurance had begun to grow out of his brother's shadow, a tall and dignified young man with a promising career of his own. Features which were impish when he was younger had now sharpened to a fine point. There was something in the long face with the straight nose and knowing eyes that recalled the first John D., something in the turned-down, mocking quality of the mouth that made people assume a degree of cynicism that was not always there. He had become the sort of man who looked good in a dinner jacket and Art Deco surroundings. Hair parted precisely as if by calipers and flawlessly combed, he seemed most at ease at a cocktail party, drawing on a cigarette while furtively studying the faces in the crowd. As a boy he had tinkered with machines to see how they worked; as a man he professed to have the same interest in people.

If he was socially adept, it was not because he shared Nelson's easy familiarity. He was incapable of that kind of self-promotion. For him, being with people was a pleasurable game of give-and-take in which he enjoyed parrying attempts to penetrate his defenses. He would be the brother most sensitive to the conflict between the role of Rockefeller and the private person it menaced. His quiet agnosticism in regard to the family was similar to that which had manifested itself when he was a teenager and felt constrained to confess to doubts about God while the other brothers simply accepted the form of their father's religious views, even though its content was beyond them. More than the rest of them, Laurance was a freethinker.

He followed John 3rd to Princeton, where he too was named Most Likely to Succeed. He majored in philosophy, taking every course available in the department. His bachelor's thesis was entitled "The Concept of Value and Its Relation to Ethics." Later in his life, however, when his career was swinging him into the public light, Laurance's interest in Immanuel Kant gave way to Norman Vincent Peale (*The Power of Positive Thinking* became a favored guide) as he—the brother most sensitive to the moral problems inherent in his position—tried to make difficulties disappear by an act of will.

By the time Laurance was graduated from college, his two older brothers had already become young men of affairs. (In 1932, for instance, while he was working on his senior thesis, they had been part of the dramatic meeting with Thomas Debevoise, the Fosdick brothers, and George Wickersham—a former Attorney General heading a national committee investigating Prohibition—at which Junior had made his historic decision to withdraw his support from the Eighteenth Amendment.) Laurance's task was to find some distinctive path for his life that would allow him to succeed on his own and not have to be content with leftovers from JDR3 and Nelson.

Of all the brothers, he was most interested in the outdoors, having fallen under the spell of Horace Albright on the 1924 trip to Yellowstone. A memorable camping trip through the western states the summer after his junior year heightened his interest. But while the budding field of conservation may have been an acceptable philanthropy, it was not something strong enough to support a Rockefeller career, at least not then.

Partly because his mother thought it would be nice to have a lawyer in the family, he enrolled at Harvard Law School. But he never really got going. In the middle of his first semester, he fell ill. Abby had worried over his frailty as a child, and in his last year at Princeton he had been so sick from German measles that she had taken him home for a time. To save his eyes, they would sit in a darkened room while she read aloud to him from his texts to help prepare for his final exams. But this time he had pneumonia, and she took him out of law school and sent him to Florida to spend the winter months with his grandfather.

He returned to Harvard in 1934 and finished the year. The difficulty he had passing his finals convinced him that he was no longer interested in the law. That same year, he decided to marry Mary French, sister of Nelson's roommate at Dartmouth and a descendant of Vermont's Billings family, founders of the Northern Pacific Railroad. Gossip columnist Cholly Knickerbocker noted the occasion by observing that "the Frenches are among our most conservative families. Mary, with her simple and charming manners and rather retiring nature, follows a tradition the Rockefellers have always tried to maintain in their children." Now that there were two Marys in the family, Abby took to referring to them as "Mary Nelson" and "Mary Laurance."

Setting up housekeeping in New York (later they would acquire the mansion in Mary's family seat at Woodstock, Vermont), Laurance began working in Room 5600. He did a few months' apprenticeship in the Chase and then went on the board of Rockefeller Center. But as he later said, he was looking for something that was "non-competitive with the family interests, and thus with no built-in anti-climax." It was a sign of how far Junior had moved the family from its origins that the activity that fit this description most closely was business.

Laurance had become interested in the contemporary Scandinavian furniture that had become *de rigueur* in the mid-1930s, and as his first enterprise, he joined with architects Wallace Harrison and Harmon Goldstone in 1937 to form an import and sales company called New Furniture, Inc. But for Laurance, business was less a way of making money—although this too was important as an indication of success—than a place to define himself by "taking certain kinds of risks." Within weeks of Senior's death, Laurance had purchased his grandfather's seat on the stock exchange. The established companies he saw traded there interested him less than the fledgling enterprises he could help by applying some of the force available in the family name and connections. Intrigued by the chic existential implications of the term, Laurance began to call himself a "venture capitalist."

The first of the new technologies he backed was aeronautics. Neither his grandfather nor his father had ever set foot inside an airplane, but Laurance was as much a child of his age as they had been of theirs. In 1938 he was invited to participate in a syndicate that was being formed by Kuhn, Loeb to back one of Laurance's boyhood heroes, Captain Eddie Rickenbacker. The World War I flying ace wanted to buy Eastern Airlines (a company he had run and made successful) from General Motors and needed $3.5 million to do it. The Kuhn, Loeb syndicate raised the capital, including a modest $10,000 from Laurance. Hard-driving and energetic, Rickenbacker intrigued Laurance, who increased his investment in Eastern over the next few years, availing himself of stock splits and options until he was the largest individual stockholder and a primary influence on the board of directors.

Meanwhile, in 1939, another ambitious, self-confident young entrepreneur contacted him. A slender, energetic Scot from Arkansas, James S. McDonnell, had been working for years as chief engineer for the Glenn L. Martin Corporation. But with war on the horizon, he had decided to form his own company and build airplanes of his own design. Renting an office above the American Airlines hangar at the St. Louis municipal airport, he hired fifteen engineers and turned them loose designing a new pursuit plane while he went off looking for backers for the company and buyers for the product.

Laurance first listened to McDonnell as a courtesy to a fellow Princeton man. But he became interested in McDonnell's proposition—not only because he was tooling up for production at a time when fighter planes would obviously be needed, but even more because of McDonnell's interest in aircraft powered by jet propulsion. Laurance made an investment of $10,000 and cast about for ways of helping the enterprise get off the ground by securing government contracts for it.

By 1940, Laurance was so deeply involved in these and other ventures that he petitioned his father to be allowed to dip into the principal of his '34 Trust. "As you know, according to the Trust which you so generously set up for my benefit," he wrote,

> I am eligible to receive the entire income plus additional principal at the end of the year I become thirty years of age. As this moment has arrived, I should very much like to formally request ... additional capital. ... In asking for this principal, I have in mind the following: the diversification of the oil stocks into investments in the air transport industry, primarily through Eastern Airlines. I am already committed to invest an additional $50,000 in our South American Development Company and may feel justified in going further in the future. I have already invested almost $100,000 in various small companies in the aircraft industry and as a result of which the Assistant Secretary of the Navy, Mr. James Forrestal, had asked me to organize a company to aid his department in managing and financing certain companies.

It was during his navy service in the war that these tentative beginnings would develop into a profession important enough for Laurance to commit himself.

Aside from Nelson's eagerness to get into the action in Washington, the coming war seemed far away from the Rockefellers. This unique family looks almost idyllic in the formal photographs from the period in which six smiling children surround proud parents. But beneath this surface were the categories that make up all families—victors, survivors, and victims. Later, some of John 3rd's children would claim that their father's growth as an individual had been stunted by the hold Junior had on him; and Babs's daughters would feel a shadow had been cast over her life by Abby's open preference for the boys. But these wounds were minor in comparison with Winthrop's. Abby had realized his vulnerability but had been too removed from the daily events of his childhood to be able to do anything about it. As a boy, his good nature and naïveté, as well as his fits of crying and petulance, had been viewed by the other brothers as signs of weakness. They took advantage of him and punished him for being different. It often seemed that only by hurting him were they able to establish the powerful unity of purpose that was to stay with them for the next half-century.

In some sense, the problems he faced were those of any

middle child. Bullied by Nelson and Laurance from above and outshone from below by the precocious David, he was squeezed out of any psychological space in the family he might have claimed as his own. The problem, once begun, seemed to feed itself: the more he was abused, the more difficult he became; the more difficult he became, the more justified the abuse seemed. Soon he began to see himself as an outsider, someone who did not fit into the family. One childhood impression that was branded into his memory, he later confided to an aide, was that of going to bed every night looking up at the shadows cast on his bedroom wall by moonlight streaming in through the railings his father had workmen place over the windows. The bars were meant to keep trespassers out, but Winthrop assumed that they were intended to keep him in.

He became the "black sheep" of the family. He wanted desperately (almost pathetically, some family friends felt) to succeed on his father's terms. But by the time he was a teenager, his brothers already occupied the range of alternatives, from gamely struggling to live up to the awesome Rockefeller tradition to eagerly embracing it. It appeared that the only way Winthrop could distinguish himself was by failure.

At Lincoln School he was affable and got along well with the children who were not his brothers, but his academic performance was abysmal. Junior assumed it was because he needed a more authoritarian environment and shipped him off to boarding school at Loomis. When Winthrop managed to finish his final year there, Abby wrote her sister Lucy in relief, "Thank fortune, he is really graduated!" After a summer's hard work with a tutor and his father's intercession, he also managed to get into Yale. But outside his father's field of vision, he began to slip. He let his account book go untended for weeks at a time, panicking in the middle of his freshman year when it came time to show Junior his ledger in order to get the following semester's allowance. Once, the situation became so bad that he thought of stealing money from another student in order to balance his books; to avoid a major crisis with his father, he begged a large loan from Babs. It took him three years to repay her.

He entered in the Class of '35. After a couple of disastrous semesters, he had succeeded only in being pushed back to the Class of '36. About the only thing he felt he learned, when he surveyed his college career several years afterward, was to smoke and drink. The latter had taken some work. At first he couldn't take more than three drinks without getting violently ill. But as he reminisced sadly, "Unfortunately, I later got over that." He told his mother and father it was pointless for him to continue. They agreed. As he left New Haven for the last time, he was troubled but not unhappy. "Easygoing" and "good-natured" were the terms most often used by contemporaries to describe him, although such virtues did not seem to recommend him to his family.

With his smooth, regular features and vulnerable eyes, Winthrop had grown into the best-looking of all the Rockefeller boys. (When he sprouted a military moustache in the army, some women would say he looked like a baby-faced Clark Gable.) He was also the biggest: 6 feet 3 inches and 225 pounds. He seemed almost embarrassed by his size, by the unmobilized mass he represented, and he agreed with his father that it would be well not to try to squeeze his bulk into an office just yet. Instead, Junior arranged for him to go to work for the Humble Refining Company, Standard's giant crude subsidiary in Texas.

Winthrop spent most of 1936 in the Texas oil fields, working as a "boll weevil," an apprentice roughneck. He was the first of the brothers to mingle with the public. After he received the first threat against his life, his father tried to hire bodyguards; but Winthrop refused to have any around him, although he did go so far as to spend one dollar on a deputy sheriff's commission which allowed him to carry a revolver. A more serious problem was the suspicion of his fellow workers, who at first sullenly assumed he was a spy set on them by the management. They finally agreed with him that it was unlikely an oil company would pick a spy with the last name of Rockefeller, but they continued to play practical jokes on him and figure out tests for his endurance and patience. He always acquitted himself well, and by the end of his year in the fields he had worked at every phase of oil production (geophysics crews, roustabouts, refining, pipe laying). His coworkers liked and respected him, calling him "Rock." Winthrop had been attracted to this world where a man, whatever his name, was measured by how quickly and how well he dug postholes. He always regarded this year as the best of his life.

Yet succeeding as a laborer did not offer a permanent solution for him. However much he liked the work, he knew it was only a prelude to the job awaiting him in New York; however close he got to ordinary people, he felt himself irresistibly drawn back into the vortex of the family. After his year with Humble was over, Junior recalled him and installed him as a trainee in the Chase Bank, while keeping an eye open for a position in one of the oil companies in which he had influence. In 1937, after returning from Nelson's trip up the Orinoco and the tour of Venezuelan oil fields, Winthrop took a job in the foreign trade department of Socony-Vacuum and assumed a share of the family's philanthropic obligations by becoming vice-chairman of the Greater New York Fund. He was trying to be part of the family team, but it was hard to win their respect. At twenty-five, most of them still called him "Winny," and Nelson, who knew how much he loathed the childhood nickname, still introduced him as "my little brother, Wissy-Wissy."

The United States was poised on the terrible expectancy of world war, and many young men, waiting to know what would happen, stalled in planning their future. But Winthrop's sea of opportunity was vaster than most, and he seemed especially adrift. His father was so bothered by rumors of his drinking and by the frequency with which Jimmy Fidler and other gossip columnists placed him at the El Morocco and other nightspots, that he was almost relieved when his most troublesome son enlisted as a private in the infantry in 1941.

During their get-togethers, the brothers occasionally joked about the global power some social critics ascribed to them. Once, in Winthrop's absence, they got into the game of dividing the world according to their special interests. Nelson was "given" Latin America, John got Asia, David Europe, and so on. One of their associates recalls someone asking the question, "Well, what about Winny?" It was Laurance who had a drollery equal to the occasion. "Winny? Oh, let's give him the army."

If Winthrop was the most unaffected of the Rockefeller boys, his younger brother, David, was the most serious, the one who was conscious of the birthright from the beginning. (Years later, his daughter Peggy would say, "Uncle John doesn't seem comfortable in the role. My father is *very* comfortable. If he has any conflicts about it at all, they don't show.") In his caution and formality, he greatly resembled his father. Yet with David, reserve was not a manifestation of insecurity, but of insularity. He was the last child of the family, the baby. The solipsisms of his childhood would become part of an unshakable self-confidence as he grew older.

He grew up sure of himself, intelligent, and unquestioning, fortunate in having four older brothers who had won battles whose victories he could enjoy without taking the risks of fighting them. Horace Albright recalls him as a chubby little boy scurrying around the forests of Yellowstone turning up rocks in search of fossil leaves and beetle specimens. It was the first stage of a lifetime hobby that had begun when a fifth-grade teacher at Lincoln School interested him in entomology. By the time David entered Harvard, his fixation with beetles was so complete that he was able to get the instructor's permission to take a graduate entomology course, although still a freshman. (His only undergraduate "A" came in this course.) Later in life, even after he was head of the august Chase Manhattan Bank, he would surprise colleagues and acquaintances, most of whom had an even more exalted idea of how a Rockefeller should behave than he did, by appearing to go into a trance in the middle of a conversation; slowly, he would put his hand into his breast pocket while staring fixedly at the ground, whip out a small vial, pounce on a specimen, and then cork and pocket it, resuming the conversation as if nothing had happened. His private collection of beetles, one of the best in the world, would be catalogued by the Museum of Natural History, and in return, he subsidized a research station in Arizona that made collecting trips throughout the Southwest. Two of the species they isolated were named for him: *armaeodera Rockefelleri* (a small brown beetle with yellow spots) and *cincindela Rockefelleri* (a type of tiger beetle).*

As a boy, David was fat and ungainly. One of the gardeners who served the family at Pocantico later reminisced about the time he happened to look up from his work and see David sitting under a tree, being examined by his tutor while he languidly shot his bow and arrow. Nelson and Winthrop, in a rare alliance, sneaked up and turned the hose on him, making him scream with rage. When the gardener asked why they had done it, Nelson replied saucily, "Because he's fat and lazy, and we want to keep him moving." According to another family story, when David accompanied his parents to

---

*Once David became a leading executive of the Chase, foreign dignitaries and businessmen who knew of his odd passion often would send specimens for his collection. According to Edna Bruderle, one of his secretaries, the beetles weren't always pinned to a specimen board. "The rule," she said of all oddly shaped packages, "is to cut the string and then stand back."

Egypt in 1926 and decided to climb one of the pyramids, they had to hire two Arab porters, one pulling and the other pushing, to get him to the top.

At Lincoln he was not particularly popular. A classmate of the Rockefeller boys, Mrs. Louise Marr, recalled that everyone liked Nelson, Laurance, and Winthrop. "David was younger, and he was always boasting about his money, and boasting about where he had been, about having gone to Europe and how much money his family had. So, from a high school girl's angle, he was a pain in the neck."

By the time he graduated from Harvard in 1936, David was a large young man but no longer fat. "Fleshy" was the word that came to mind. He had a long vulpine nose sticking out of a pleasant face. His father sent him up to Canada to visit Mackenzie King and get the benefit of the Prime Minister's advice. Junior wrote to his old friend from Ludlow days about his youngest son: "He has a fine mind and a wide interest both in world affairs and in cultural subjects. Whether he will enter some form of business, whether he will ultimately be attracted to a political life or to the diplomatic service, only time will tell." King agreed that the sky was the limit as far as this Rockefeller son was concerned, but his feeling was that the decision should be delayed. With the world situation so unpredictable, the best thing David could do was go to graduate school.

David went to London that fall to enroll in the London School of Economics and found himself invited to the kind of cocktail parties usually reserved for diplomats and high-ranking civil servants. He met the family of Ambassador Joseph Kennedy and dated his daughter Kathleen. He spent several hours a week working in the London branch of the Chase.

As he was finishing his second year at the LSE, David received a letter from Nelson, who was just then beginning to take his new role as leader of the third generation seriously. It was filled with avuncular advice about living abroad and optimistic news about the family:

Winny is coming along in fine style and developing a much broader outlook, and Larry, as usual, is his own inimitable self. The chances of our family being of real service and playing an important part in the life of the country seems to grow brighter with the passage of time. The background which you are developing is going to be invaluable to the group and I am certainly looking forward to the day when you will have completed your studies and can bring us a point of view which is sadly lacking at the present.

The "point of view" was a specialized knowledge of economics. Finishing his studies in London, David returned to the University of Chicago to take a Ph.D. in 1938. In yet another reprise of Eliza Rockefeller's solemn maxim "Willful waste makes woeful want," he wrote a thesis titled "Unused Resources and Economic Waste." In it, he charged monopolies with being counterproductive, but family training and the old Baptist background asserted itself in his critique of idleness as "the most abhorrent form of waste."

He returned to New York in 1940 and soon thereafter married Margaret McGrath. At this point—just before Nelson got the telephone call from Forrestal—it was David of all the brothers who was thought to have the potential for a political career. He was steady and analytical and had spoken out publicly on the issues of the day when at college, even though he knew that in doing so he would inevitably have to defend his family. In 1939, Interior Secretary Harold Ickes wrote in his diary: "David Rockefeller was in. He looks very much like his mother and is a nice boy. He made up his mind to go into politics and wanted to ask my advice. He has had an offer of some sort to start under Mayor La Guardia and his mind is undecided between accepting that offer or possibly coming to Washington."

David did become a troubleshooting aide to La Guardia in 1940. He enjoyed working for the city, although the mayor had to put an end to his habit of picking up the phone and answering, "City Hall, Rockefeller speaking." But after this internship, he decided he really wasn't interested in politics, at least not in electoral politics. It wasn't that he didn't share Nelson's ambition, but rather that he didn't have the stomach for conflict. He too was interested in power, but unlike Nelson, he wanted it to be of a more dependable variety than the fickle electorate could give. "The danger in that field [politics]," he noted later, "is that you spend all of your time running for office."

For David and his brothers, World War II was, as Virginia Woolf had said of a prior conflict, a step over the past. Yet a scandal at its onset showed how far the family had come from the days when Standard Oil and Rockefeller were synonymous, and proved again the wisdom of Junior's decision to minimize public identification with the company. For as America was beginning to mobilize, Standard Oil was once again the subject of shocking revelations. In the 1920s the Jersey Company had entered into a cartel with the German petrochemical monopoly, I. G. Farben. The business relationship had continued even after Hitler's rise to power. In 1941, on the eve of Pearl Harbor, during hearings of the U.S. Senate Committee to Investigate the National Defense, Assistant Attorney General Thurman Arnold read a letter from Standard Vice-President Frank A. Howard noting that the company had renewed the cartel agreement with the Nazis in Holland in 1939. The terms had seemed so distinctly lacking in patriotic concern ("We did our best to work out plans for a complete modus vivendi," the letter stated, "whether or not the U.S. enters the war") that committee Chairman Harry S. Truman had left the hearings snorting, "I think this approaches treason."

Ivy Lee had already been tarred with a similar brush. In 1934 the Jersey Company had sent him to Germany to consult with Farben on ways to improve its image, as well as that of the Third Reich, to which it had deep political and economic ties. He came home to face a severe inquisition by a Special House Committee on Un-American Activities. The committee testimony was released in early July, a week and a half after the "night of the long knives." The close coincidence between Lee's appearance before investigators and Hitler's blood purge of the SA resulted in headline news: "Lee Exposed as Hitler Press Agent."

Ivy Lee was already dying of brain cancer, and the storm of adverse publicity broke his spirit and what was left of his health. When he died later that year, it was in disgrace. In Berlin, Washington's ambassador noted in his diary: "It is only another of the thousands of cases where love of money ruins men's lives.... I cannot say a commendatory word about him to the State Department." And in Ormond Beach, Florida, where reporters gathered that evening at the door of the first John D. to hear his reaction to the passing of the man who had helped win him back his good name, they were told that Mr. Rockefeller could not under any circumstances be disturbed after six. Young Nelson Rockefeller, however, quickly telegraphed Lee's widow, "The country has lost a great leader." Junior waited nearly nine months to send his elegant letter of condolence.

With memories of the Lee scandal in mind, Junior grew greatly concerned as the Truman Committee probed the intricacies of the Standard-Farben cartel. (By 1942, Farben was known to be operating with slave labor from the Nazi concentration camps.) He privately requested a memorandum from Standard executives explaining their dealings with the Axis powers which he could use in his defense if it should come to that. But it never did; he had become a citizen above suspicion. Ludlow was truly a thing of the past.

13

By 1942 THE ROCKEFELLERS were mobilized. John 3rd had characteristically faced up to the coming of war by going on more boards: the Child Refugee Committee, the USO, the American Red Cross, and a host of others. By late 1942 he had joined the navy and moved to Washington. Laurance was also stationed there as a naval lieutenant, having parlayed both his acquaintance with Forrestal and his connections with the burgeoning aircraft industry into a job overseeing fighter production and development. David, who enlisted just after Pearl Harbor, emerged from Officer Candidate School, served in intelligence in North Africa for two years, and then went to Paris as assistant military attaché. Winthrop was the only brother to make his way up to officer by progressing through the ranks. He enjoyed the democratic spirit of the infantry, as he had of the oil fields, saw action in the Pacific, and was slightly wounded in the Okinawa invasion.

Meanwhile, Junior was as active on the home front as he had been in World War I, becoming the moving force behind the USO and related efforts to help the troops by concentrating on morals and morale. With her sizable Aldrich inheritance (the "mad money" she used to purchase most of the modern art her husband detested), Abby was somewhat more whimsical in her war work, perceiving types of problems that were outside her husband's range of vision. On a vacation trip to Colonial Williamsburg she noticed that furloughed soldiers were fond of watching the coeds at William and Mary, but always had to stand, squat on the grass, or lean against something. To alleviate their plight, she paid for a series of benches placed at strategic locations so that they could do their ogling while sitting comfortably.

Abby fretted about her sons who were in the service and often stayed up late into the night listening to the war news. She had to sit, ear cupped, on the edge of the bathtub, where she had taken the radio to avoid disturbing her husband's righteously kept bedtime. Winthrop and David were the only boys in battle zones, and while she worried about them especially, she also feared that John and Laurance might somehow be conscripted into combat. But the son whose doings she followed most closely was not a soldier at all. It was Nelson, her favorite, who was in fact much closer to the war than the others, although he spent it as a civilian.

When he went to Washington in 1940 to take over as coordinator of the Office of Inter-American Affairs (OIAA), Nelson was (as future AEC Chairman David Lillienthal said) "the Eager Beaver to end all EBs." Senior officials of the State Department, already concerned about the cross-jurisdictional lines of the new office (indeed, annoyed that the President should have consented to its formation in the first place), were not reassured when the brash 32-year-old brought a staff of experts with him. "Bee" Ruml would not take a full-time job but agreed to come to Washington regularly as a consultant for Nelson. Key positions in the office were given to Joe Rovensky and Wally Harrison from the Group; John Hay Whitney, family friend, producer of Gone With the Wind, and future ambassador to the Court of St. James's; Carl Spaeth from the Compania; and John Lockwood, a mild-mannered yet incisive young attorney from Milbank, Tweed whom JDR3 had recommended to Nelson. With the exception of Spaeth, who would later earn Nelson's displeasure by agreeing to work for a rival agency within the State Department, all of these men had in common their absolute loyalty to their boss. "Nelson doesn't expect you to be a yes-man," as one aide said, "but he does expect you to be a Rockefeller man—first, last, and always."

By this time, Nelson and Tod had five children. In addition to Rodman, there were Ann and Steven and the twins,

Michael and Mary. They had moved into a large Washington residence on Foxhall Road, where almost all the OIAA aides would board at one time or another, some (like the Spaeths) staying on a semipermanent basis. Although the Rockefeller home bustled with Nelson's crushing charm, it never became quite the salon for Latin American culture he had wanted it to be. Despite roving mariachi bands and plates piled with tortillas, the parties he gave tended to be stiff and didactic. One woman, present frequently during the war years, remembers Nelson greeting guests at the door and handing them a mimeographed sheet of songs in Spanish, which they were called upon to sing at some point in the evening.

He was clearly out of place in the rarefied atmosphere of the New Deal, uncomfortable with the intellectual fashions of Roosevelt's brain trusters and suspicious of some of their more idealistic schemes. Yet he plunged ahead energetically, knowing better than they how power worked and having no reluctance to put his knowledge to practical uses. He had assembled a formidable staff of experts, and obviously intended to make the "Rockefeller shop" (as it was known) the center of hemispheric diplomacy. Washington was a brave new world for him, a world whose elders did not have the hold on him that his father had. He was galvanized by the prospects that stretched out before him.

Starting work as early as six A.M., he listened to news broadcasts under the sunlamp, wrote out memos while breakfasting, and often managed to get in a doubles match with tennis partner Henry Wallace (then Agriculture Secretary) before arriving at his office at eight-thirty. He worked through the lunch hour and carried unfinished work home with him along with a car full of his aides. ("Nelson was addicted to having people around him," an associate from this period recalls. "It was as though he had to see his reflection in their faces.") He would dine with Latin American diplomats or American bureaucrats, and not infrequently he would keep going until he fell asleep at midnight in a living room chair in the middle of a conversation.

If his home took on the aspect of an office and dormitory, his office soon started to look like a war room. Regular army-type briefings, complete with maps, charts, mechanical layouts, projectors, and other paraphernalia, were part of the routine there. The military style was part of Nelson's idea of how to get things done efficiently. Moreover, it was justified by his presence on the Advisory Committee of the National

Defense Council. Latin America was unlikely to become a theater of war, but as a raw materials supplier, it would be an important part in the military struggle with the Axis powers.

No one in Washington embraced the campaign to "delouse" the continent of "Axis pests" with more enthusiasm than Rockefeller. Even as he had read Ruml's memo aloud to Harry Hopkins, proposing ways of strengthening hemispheric ties, he knew that the European war was creating new opportunities. As a result of the British blockade, one-third of Latin America's markets were cut off, and the situation was ripe for a major reorientation of trade in the direction of the United States. "A major objective of the long-range program of the [Coordinator's] Office," Rockefeller explained in an official memorandum, "is to lessen the dependency of Latin America upon Europe as a market for raw materials and a source of manufactured articles." This, he added, was important as "a hemisphere defense measure."

As the struggle with the Axis intensified (though the United States was still technically neutral), Rockefeller's office moved to the front line with a propaganda and pressure campaign to force U.S. firms in Latin America to purge themselves of German and Italian nationals, an effort that occasionally included a visit by the coordinator himself to the chief executive of an offending company to secure compliance with the blacklist. Not even the British were exempted from the crusade to purify the hemisphere of alien commercial influence. Joe Rovensky, whom Nelson had made assistant coordinator, came up with a complex plan to compel the British allies to put up some of the most valuable holdings in Chile and Argentina as collateral for food supplies in their war effort.*

As the war progressed, it became increasingly clear that Britain would pay for her survival with what had once been the tribute of her empire. Even lend-lease aid was a trade-off against her valuable bases in the Caribbean. ("Just as the last century in Latin America was a 'British Century,'" the president of the U.S. Chamber of Commerce was declaring as these developments were taking place, "the next will be an

---

*An OIAA memo in connection with the Rovensky plan could not resist the stock-market analogy. It noted that there were "good properties in the British portfolio" and then recommended that "we might as well pick them up now," adding that here was "a lot of trash which Britain should be allowed to keep."

American Century.") Yet Nelson would have been the last to admit that his efforts were in any way part of the conquest of a continental market. He thought of Latin America in a deeply personal way, with a collector's passion for its culture and art. He liked the people, and when on some fact-finding tour would often find an excuse to plunge shirt-sleeved into a *mercado*, speaking to the sellers and buying some of their wares, or he would disappear into the adobe shack of some peasant craftsman to bargain for folk art to take home. He had bought a splendid mountain estate in Venezuela, at the very site where the liberator Simón Bolívar had lived when he made his famous comment, "The United States seems destined by Providence to plague the Americas with miseries in the name of liberty."

Nelson was aware of the charges that U.S. policy toward Latin America was based on principles that were something less than idealistic, but he was prepared to deal with them. "Totalitarian propaganda is already attacking this government's hemisphere solidarity policies on the ground that they are insincere expedients to use these countries for our selfish purposes during the emergency," he warned in an official statement. "To combat such plausible untruths and to establish the sincerity and permanency of our policies," he continued, it was necessary to "develop closer cultural and spiritual ties" to supplement the commercial ones.

Under his direction, the OIAA organized an array of tours and exchanges that included art shows, ballet troupes, athletic competitions, technical experts, and political dignitaries. It was a far more ambitious program than anyone had envisaged, causing costs to skyrocket. When Forrestal first offered him the coordinator's position, he had told Nelson that OIAA's budget would be $3.5 million a year and whatever else he could wheedle from Congress. By the end of his fourth year on the job, however, Rockefeller had gotten and spent $140 million and had hired hundreds of employees.

For this, he would draw the fire of conservative critics in Congress. It was the beginning of a reputation as a "big spender" that would dog him throughout his political career. One State Department official criticized his selling of the United States below the border as an example of "flamboyant national boasting," and a Republican congressman once interrupted hearings to accuse Rockefeller of being "just another New Deal bureaucrat." But Nelson was able to outmaneuver the critics he wasn't able to charm into acquiescence and thus continue his tightrope act. As Henry Wallace noted in his diary, "I told the President today that Nelson Rockefeller's definition of a coordinator is a man who can keep all the balls in the air without losing his own."

The Office of Inter-American Affairs had become one of the most glamorous agencies in Washington. Its most visible operation was the Publications and Information Division, and the principal figure in this division was a thin, prematurely graying former AP journalist named Francis Jamieson. Jamieson had not only won a Pulitzer Prize for his inside stories of the Lindbergh kidnapping, but had also proved himself as a first-rate political strategist by managing Charles Edison's campaign for governor of New Jersey against the Hague machine. Later he had met Winthrop Rockefeller when both were involved in efforts on behalf of the Greater New York Fund. Winthrop, in turn, had recommended him to Nelson. Attracted by Jamieson's hard-bitten candor, Nelson offered him jobs as head of public relations for Creole Petroleum and as publicity chief for the Willkie campaign, both of which he turned down. But when the job in Washington came up, he accepted.

Colleagues from the OIAA days would remember Jamieson sitting in meetings with a cigarette dangling from his lips—he was a former alcoholic who had become a chainsmoker—apparently absorbed in digging at his fingernails with the flap of a match book. But his incisive comments showed how intently he was listening, and his colleagues came to rely on him for summary and analysis of detailed discussions. Along with attorney John Lockwood and Wally Harrison, Jamieson became part of Nelson's innermost circle. He was known as the devil's advocate in the coordinator's office, arguing the "no" position as a way of testing the depth and resilience of Rockefeller's sudden enthusiasms. It was the politically savvy Jamieson who saw that the OIAA was the perfect vehicle for a career in national politics and promoted Nelson as much as the OIAA programs.* Soon he was "Frankie," the closest friend and adviser Nelson would ever have.

*"Incidental to his job of selling the United States to Latin America," *The New Republic* commented toward the end of the war, "Jamieson has also built Nelson Rockefeller into an international personality, doing a job that Ivy Lee himself would have to admire—and at the United States government's expense.... Frank Jamieson is more interested in seeing Nelson Rockefeller follow in the political footsteps of his grandfather Aldrich than anyone but Nelson himself."

Under Jamieson, the Publications and Information Division became the central thrust of the OIAA program and also the first functioning propaganda agency in government, predating Archibald MacLeish's Office of Facts and Figures. Its efforts included *En Guardia*, a lavish and innovative monthly (in Spanish and resembling *Life*) circulated throughout Latin America and ultimately reaching an audience of more than half a million people. The division printed a weekly edition of *The New York Times* in Chile and distributed it everywhere except Argentina, where censors banned it. Jamieson's operation was also in charge of radio broadcasts beamed throughout Latin America, the forerunner of the Voice of America.

The other, more ambitious parts of the coordinator's program, such as fostering long-term economic development in Latin America, proved far more difficult than selling a good image of the "good neighbor" below the border. Much of the resistance to an attack against feudal living conditions, in fact, had come from the coordinating committees that Nelson set up in each of the Latin American countries. They were "composed of the biggest businessmen" (as one senior American diplomat complained in a letter to the Undersecretary of State), including executives of Standard Oil, Guggenheim, General Electric, and United Fruit. "They have very definite ideas as to what our general policy should be, and in general their ideas have been the most reactionary."* Large arms shipments to Latin American dictators and the built-in conflict between what Joseph Rovensky called "emergency action" and "long-term planning" put democratic reforms and economic development far down on the OIAA agenda.

There was strong criticism from Latin American intellectuals. "In Latin America," wrote Peruvian educator Luis Alberto Sanchez in the magazine *Inter American*, "the war has further impoverished the poor and enriched the wealthy. It has increased the army's power, both politically and militarily. . . . The large exporting concerns of Latin America . . . are making fat profits. Meanwhile . . . our average man has yet to see material or moral benefits from this war on which

---

*In 1942, Rovensky was forced to resign from the coordinator's office. Following the Catavi massacre of Bolivian tin miners and the revelations that the U.S. ambassador in Bolivia had triggered the conflict by intervening on behalf of the tin magnates, it was revealed that Rovensky was a vice-president of Patino Mines, the country's biggest tin producer.

he staked his hopes long before his government took a stand."

Yet among those who counted, this was a minority view. Long before it was clear that the outcome of the war would favor the Allies, Latin America was securely in orbit around the United States, a fact that was in no small part due to the efforts of young Nelson Rockefeller. On May 17, 1944, the Pan American Society awarded him its gold medal for his wartime work. The following morning his father wrote him a letter of congratulation which concluded: ". . . and so with a full heart of pride and gratitude, I say—Well, done, my son, you have wrought a good work, you have maintained the family's high standards of public service, you have brought added credit to the family name."

It was the following November, when Nelson was touring Haiti, that he was informed of a change in command at the State Department that would usher in a new phase of his Washington career. Cordell Hull had just resigned as Secretary of State and his successor, former U.S. Steel executive Edward Stettinius, Jr., informed Nelson that the President wanted him to be his new Assistant Secretary of State for Latin American Affairs. Nelson, whose relentless drive for influence had already earned him many enemies at the State Department, understood the significance of Stettinius's formulation: It was the *President* who wanted him for the job, not the Secretary of State. He was hesitant to accept, and only after an audience with Harry Hopkins, who assured him that FDR was fully committed to his ideas concerning hemispheric unity, did he turn the coordinator's office over to his friend Wally Harrison and accept the new job.

The career on which Nelson now embarked was destined to be brief; but its ramifications were far-reaching, setting off the kind of shock waves only possible when the whole framework of international affairs is undergoing a period of upheaval and transformation. Nelson would be Assistant Secretary for a scant nine months, but during this period the Big Three's fateful meeting would take place at Yalta, the founding conference of the United Nations would be held in San Francisco, and the atomic bomb would be dropped on Hiroshima—shortly after Potsdam. At an even more profound level of change, the old colonial empires of Europe and Japan were passing from the international scene, while a new power, the Soviet Union, was making its presence felt in unsettling ways. An old order was dying with the end of the war, and a new one was being born and baptized in a new kind of war, a cold war.

In 1944, Nelson had attended a meeting of the Inter-American Defense Board to hear a grim assessment of the postwar world by its chairman, General Embick, who was also Chief of War Plans. The meeting made a powerful impression on him. In the future, General Embick told the Defense Board members, war could only be waged with raw materials, industrial capacity, manpower, and land mass; only two areas in the world would have those things: the Western Hemisphere and the Soviet Union. China, he added, would hold the balance of power between them.

With a few chosen others involved in the events that followed, Nelson felt that he was, in Dean Acheson's memorable and revealing phrase, present at the creation. The principal cold war scenes would be set first in Europe and then Asia, but for one brief, charged moment in the spring of 1945, a significant prologue to the unfolding drama was played out on his own Latin American stage.

The Latin American republics had taken a backseat position in the struggle against the Axis powers. Only two of the twenty republics had sent even token forces to the war zone. Seven others, led by Argentina, had failed to declare war at all. As the conflict drew to a close, Rockefeller and the State Department pressed for a tighter anti-Axis front in the hemisphere. The Latin American nations that had not yet declared war on Germany and Japan were put on notice to do so before February 1 in order to qualify for admission to the new United Nations organization. At the same time, plans were set in motion for an Inter-American Conference to formalize the emerging inter-American system and hammer out a formal defense pact.

The conference was held at Mexico City's famed Chapultepec Castle, and from the beginning it was a Rockefeller show. In a grand gesture of paternal diplomacy, Nelson chartered a special plane to fly the Latin ambassadors in Washington personally to the conference. Secretary of State Stettinius was there, but he was, in the words of the U.S. ambassador to Mexico, "completely beyond his depth." It was not long before a schism developed within the American delegation that would have implications for the U.N. Conference in San Francisco two months later.

The dispute arose over the mutual defense agreement,

which became known as the Act of Chapultepec and was the most lasting achievement of the Mexico City conference (as well as a prototype for the later NATO and SEATO alliances). The agreement guaranteed existing borders and provided that an attack against any American state would be considered an attack against all. It was the regional concept in the pact that brought down the wrath of the State Department's International Division, led by Special Assistant to the Secretary of State Leo Pasvolsky. Such an agreement, Pasvolsky and his allies pointed out, contradicted the commitment the United States had just made at Dumbarton Oaks to refer all international disputes to the new world organization. It invited the Soviet Union and other great powers to create similar regional security pacts with clusters of smaller states whom they could easily dominate. In the heated controversy within the U.S. delegation in Mexico City, however, the day was carried by Rockefeller, A. A. Berle, Jr. (who had recently been moved from the State Department to the ambassadorship in Brazil), and Senator Warren Austin, senior Republican on the Foreign Relations Committee; they were backed by the army and navy brass, who exploded at the idea of sacrificing a military security arrangement for what they saw as an idealistic concept.

With the war almost over, Nelson was reorienting himself to the struggle against Communism, jettisoning the ideological baggage of the antifascist crusade and taking the sort of stance that would characterize Washington's cold war policy in the coming years. Shortly before the conference, Nicolo Tucci, then head of the Bureau of Latin American Research in the State Department, resigned and asked Secretary Hull to abolish his bureau because—as he later put it—"my bureau was supposed to undo the Nazi and fascist propaganda in South America and Rockefeller was inviting the worst fascists and Nazis to Washington." When Tucci took his complaints to Nelson, he was told: " 'Everybody is useful and we're going to convert these people to friendliness to the United States.' And then Rockefeller's lawyer Larry Levy said to me, 'Don't worry, we'll buy those people.' "

One purchase that caused outrage in the liberal press involved Argentina (only recently denounced by former Secretary of State Hull as "the refuge and headquarters in this hemisphere of the fascist movement"). At the Chapultepec conference, Nelson introduced a resolution Berle had drafted specifying the internal reforms necessary for Buenos Aires's reentry into the inter-American system and the community of democratic nations. It was part of a larger strategy: aside from the fact that he was committed to a hemisphere united under U.S. leadership, Nelson knew that the Latin American regimes that would be most pleased by the gesture toward Argentina—*caudillos* like Stroessner, Somoza, and Trujillo—could be relied on to be staunchly anti-Communist in the up-coming struggles.

Few believed that the Argentine government would change, but Nelson was only looking for gestures. When Perón finally declared war on the Axis a little less than two weeks before V-E Day, Nelson dispatched his deputy, Avra Warren, to make a *pro forma* assessment of political conditions there. The choice of Warren was calculated. A former ambassador to the Dominican Republic and an intimate friend of the dictator Trujillo (he had enrolled his own son at the "Benefactor's" military academy), Warren spent two days in Argentina before returning to assure Nelson that the military regime was no longer fascist in sympathy or fact.

The day after receiving Warren's report, Rockefeller boarded a specially chartered plane filled with Latin American diplomats and headed for the founding conference of the United Nations in San Francisco, determined to defeat attempts by Pasvolsky and other opponents in the State Department both to subordinate the Chapultepec agreement to the new world body and to deny Argentina admission.

Originally he had not been invited to the U.N. Conference. When FDR died, Nelson no longer had a patron in Washington. Yet when Stettinius reached San Francisco and realized that bloc voting would be useful, he gave Rockefeller the green light to attend as a sort of parliamentary whip for the Latin American nations. Once on the scene, Rockefeller plunged into conference politics with characteristic gusto. ("He jumped energetically from one thing to another," said Alger Hiss, who was also at the conference. "He was the perennial adolescent.") Conferring constantly with hemisphere representatives and caucusing with members of the U.S. delegation sympathetic to his position (especially the powerful Republican Senator Arthur Vandenberg), Rockefeller worked hard to swing the official U.S. position into line with his views. Announcing that he was convinced that unless the United States "operated with a solid group in this hemisphere, we could not do what we wanted on the world front," he was like a ward politician garnering votes and maneuvering with an almost reckless disregard for consequences. As one State Department official complained, "Sometimes nobody seemed to know what he was doing. He acted as if he were a separate delegation."

Although concentrating his energies on parliamentary maneuvers, Rockefeller did not neglect the politics of the social circuit, including dinners at the exclusive Bohemian Club and Trader Vic's, and a special affair at the St. Francis Yacht Club to which he personally imported a group of Hollywood entertainers, with Carmen Miranda's Chiquita Banana act providing the Latin touch.

One incident among many during those days indicates Rockefeller's meticulous attention to the most mundane detail that might influence the course of events, as well as his continuing sense of the symbolic gesture. Soon after arriving in San Francisco, Rockefeller paid a visit to the naval adviser to the U.S. delegation, Rear Admiral Harold C. Train, who had also been at Chapultepec and taken part in the struggle against Pasvolsky and the internationalists of State. A career navy man who had risen through the ranks to become head of Naval Intelligence, Train was an old hand on the Latin American scene, a veteran of the days of gunboat diplomacy who had been decorated with an Oak Leaf Cluster for his part in the intervention in Nicaragua in 1912.

A native of Missouri, Train bore an isolationist distrust for any world council in which the United States could not be sure of controlling the votes. He was therefore more than willing to listen when Assistant Secretary Rockefeller came to explain the importance of the Latin bloc, which represented nineteen votes to Europe's nine in the new U.N. Assembly. Could the rear admiral help, Rockefeller wanted to know, in getting the laundry done for the Latin American delegations? The answer was prompt: from that day forward, the Latin delegates' laundry was done at the Treasure Island Naval Station in San Francisco Bay. "A small matter," as Train later observed, "but it helped." And Nelson, attentive to the last detail, later sent the admiral a note thanking him for his service. "Your collaboration at Mexico City and San Francisco," he wrote, "are memories I shall never forget."

Resistance to Rockefeller's viewpoint within the U.S. delegation was strong, however, and feelings ran high. Three other Assistant Secretaries of State (Dean Acheson, James Dunn, and Archibald MacLeish) shared the fears of Pasvolsky and others in the International Division about Rockefeller's support for the Perón regime. Roosevelt had promised Stalin twice at Yalta that the United States, because of Argentina's fascist record, would not support that nation's bid to enter the world organization. Yet such considerations did not restrain Rockefeller in his determination to ram the admission of Argentina through, no matter what opposition he encountered.

He had even—or so his State Department critics would claim—taken advantage of the ailing President's feeble state in getting his assent, only a month before his death, to the Argentine maneuver. Years later, Charles E. Bohlen, the senior diplomat who had been at Yalta and the big wartime conferences with Roosevelt, would write with measurable bitterness:

> I was continually worried by Roosevelt's appearance, and it was now obvious to many that he was a sick man. His hands shook so that he had difficulty in holding a telegram. . . . Because President Roosevelt's powers of concentration were slipping, and his general energy was lessening, he was forced to rely more than he would have normally on the good faith and judgment of his advisors. Some persons took advantage of his condition, I am sorry to say. For example, an officer of the American government—I was told it was Nelson A. Rockefeller, then Assistant Secretary of State—put before Roosevelt a memorandum authorizing an invitation to Argentina to be a founding member of the United Nations. This is a nearly forgotten matter now, but it was a direct breach of our agreement at Yalta that only those nations that declared war on Germany could be initial members. Argentina did not qualify. Roosevelt signed the memo without fully realizing its intent.

When the showdown with the Russians took place in the General Assembly, the steamroller Rockefeller had built behind the scenes was irresistible. The preliminary verbal skirmishes had provided a field day for Molotov, the Soviet Foreign Minister, who embarrassed the American delegation by quoting choice denunciations of Perón and Argentine fascism that Roosevelt, Hull, and Rockefeller had issued in the recent past. But when the chips were down, the United States had the votes: the final count showed thirty-two for Argentina's admission and only the four Soviet bloc votes (Russia, the Ukraine, Belorussia, and Yugoslavia) against.

The Act of Chapultepec was the next item on the agenda at San Francisco. It came up at a time when Nelson had flown back to Washington to confer with President Truman in the wake of adverse criticism caused by the vote on Argentina.* When he returned to the U.N. Conference on May 5, he found that Stettinius had acceded to pressure from within his own delegation and tentatively agreed on an amendment to the U.N. Charter stipulating that, except for "measures against enemy states in this war," no enforcement action should be taken "under regional arrangements or by regional agencies without the authorization of the Security Council."

This amendment would have formalized the "one-world" concept of international order, which the United States itself had proposed at Dumbarton Oaks as a replacement for the system of imperial blocs and military alliances that had produced two disastrous wars in a generation. But Nelson saw it as a threat to the hemispheric bloc he had put together. He immediately sought a private audience with Stettinius on his return to San Francisco but was told that the Secretary of State was "exhausted" and he should instead see Pasvolsky or Assistant Secretary James Dunn, both of whom represented the opposition. Instead of retreating, Nelson launched a counteroffensive, setting up a dinner with Senator Vandenberg, not only a formidable member of the delegation in his own right but also the key to Senate approval and thus avoidance of a repetition of the League of Nations fiasco.

In conversations that took place in the Rockefeller suite in the Saint Francis Hotel, Nelson played on Vandenberg's well-known fears of the Soviets. He said that the proposed

---

*The press was taken aback by the aggressive behavior of Rockefeller and Stettinius on this issue. Citing a recently published news dispatch on the police-state atmosphere in Buenos Aires, the Washington *Post* printed a scathing editorial indicting the vote on Argentina's admission: "The regime which is described . . . as having done things 'recently that exceed anything this correspondent can remember in his seventeen years' experience in Fascist Italy'—this regime was railroaded into the company of 'peace-loving states' in San Francisco by Secretary Stettinius and Assistant Secretary Rockefeller. . . . We don't know whether the heroes of the San Francisco exploit think themselves smart or merely cynical." And in a series of articles referring to the action as "riding roughshod through a world conference with a bloc of twenty votes," Walter Lippmann warned that the United States had "adopted a line of conduct which, if it becomes our regular line, will have the most disastrous consequences."

charter amendment seemed to invalidate the Monroe Doctrine and claimed that the British and French were hoping for the passage of the amendment because it would weaken the inter-American system that blocked their political expansion into the hemisphere. By the end of the evening, Vandenberg announced he would write a letter to Stettinius demanding a specific exemption for the Act of Chapultepec as a regional alliance that was "the expression of a continuous inter-American policy for more than a century and which is without possibility of current parallel anywhere on earth."

When Stettinius received the letter the following morning, "Hell broke loose" in his penthouse headquarters (as Vandenberg later wrote in his diary). The bulk of the U.S. delegation opposed the Rockefeller-Vandenberg position. Some who objected, like Pasvolsky, had been skirmishing with the abrasive young Rockefeller for months and had hoped to recoup in San Francisco what they had lost in Mexico City. But the opposition was not limited to idealists or those who mistrusted Rockefeller for political or personal reasons. In fact, one of his sharpest critics was John Foster Dulles, a Republican foreign policy adviser and a leading international lawyer. As senior partner in the law firm of Sullivan & Cromwell, legal counsel to Standard Oil, and longtime trustee of the Rockefeller Foundation, Dulles was an important figure in the Rockefeller social galaxy, but in this instance he was so outraged by Nelson's connivance with Vandenberg that he accused him of pushing a "dangerous and damaging" course that "might wreck the conference."

It was the view of Dulles and others versed in international diplomacy that under the *de facto* right of self-defense recognized in the U.N. Charter, the United States retained enough flexibility for regional defense, including the power to intervene in troublesome Latin American countries if that should become necessary in the future. Explicit recognition of such rights, they feared, might invite a Russian demand for similar prerogatives in Eastern Europe and other contiguous areas. The argument was subtle and seemingly persuasive, but Rockefeller and Vandenberg were adamant. "I served notice on the Delegation," Vandenberg later noted in his diary, "that if this question is not specifically cleared up in the Charter, I shall expect to see a reservation on the subject in the Senate and that I shall support it."

Following the meeting, Assistant Secretary of War John J. McCloy put through a call to Henry Stimson, his superior in the War Department, for advice. Stimson was then recognized as the dean of American diplomacy, having served as Secretary of War or State in four Cabinets going back to the Taft administration; he was the guiding eminence of the Council on Foreign Relations, and his office had become a kind of academy for young men like McCloy, Robert Lovett, and others who would shape American policy in the postwar era, the best and brightest of their time and place, but who, outside their own elite world, were virtually anonymous.*

"I've been taking the position," McCloy told Stimson in the emergency telephone call from San Francisco, "that we ought to have our cake and eat it too; that we ought to be free to operate under this regional arrangement in South America, at the same time intervene promptly in Europe." The proponents of the Dumbarton Oaks draft within the delegation, McCloy reported, felt that a broadening of the regional concept (such as Rockefeller was advocating) would undermine the very basis of a world organization. "They will say that the Security Council and the World Organization has been defeated. And I'm not at all sure that it wouldn't be."

Stimson agreed. However, he thought it might be possible to argue that the desire of the United States to retain a right to intervene in Latin America was unique. He further suggested that the U.S. delegation could argue against any Russian claim to similar prerogatives in Europe because Russian interventions would not be "moderate"; she would tend to compensate for her relative weakness in Europe by overkill. By contrast, "our fussing around among those little fellows [in Latin America] doesn't upset any balance in Europe at all."

That afternoon, McCloy reported to the U.S. delegation that the Secretary of War favored a frank exception for the inter-American alliance, even at "the expense of the immediate non-concurrence of the Soviet Union." Stimson hoped, according to McCloy, that there would be no further requests for such exceptions. The formula then drawn up by Harold Stassen, at Rockefeller's request, explicitly recognized the Act

---

*McCloy, for instance, a Cravath, Swaine lawyer who later became a partner in Milbank, Tweed, would have a career including such posts as High Commissioner in postwar Germany, the coordinator of U.S. arms control activities, the chairman of the Chase Manhattan Bank and the Ford Foundation. Lovett was a Brown Brothers Harriman banker who would be Secretary of Defense in the Truman administration.

of Chapultepec and the Monroe Doctrine as exempt from the caveat against regional alliances. The British, whose interest in Latin America was affected, called it "regionalism of the worst kind," but a compromise among the Allies was finally reached. Reference to Chapultepec was dropped and the regional concept was formally recognized in a self-defense clause, which because known as Article 51 of the U.N. Charter, and which would serve as the "legal" basis for all the postwar military alliances.*

Nelson had won again, yet he had spent himself in this battle. His popularity, which had never been high at the White House after Harry Truman took occupancy, fell dramatically when the San Francisco conference ended and James Byrnes replaced the hapless Stettinius as Secretary of State. Appropriately, it was a reprise on the Argentina question that precipitated Nelson's departure from Washington. With liberal and labor groups continuing to attack the alliance with Peronism, Rockefeller's removal from office was the gesture needed to save the policy. On August 23, he met with Secretary Byrnes to talk about postwar Latin America. But Byrnes brusquely interrupted Rockefeller's opening statement: "Frankly, there's no use talking. The President is going to accept your resignation." Nelson went to the White House for an audience with the President. "I told him I didn't want to resign," Rockefeller later said. "I said South America was too important." Truman agreed politely, but said that he would have to back Byrnes. When telling the story of this White House meeting to friends later, Nelson would end by saying, as if still incredulous, "He fired me!"

---

*Under Article 51, the United States would put together the Rio Pact in 1947. The North Atlantic Treaty Organization (NATO) would follow two years later (the Soviets countering with the Warsaw Pact), and the Southeast Asia Treaty Organization (SEATO) in 1954. Under the aegis of SEATO, U.S. troops would enter Vietnam. John Foster Dulles—architect of this last and most ill-starred of America's alliances—soon apologized to young Rockefeller for opposing him at San Francisco, acknowledging his important contribution in laying the groundwork for the foreign policy he himself would pursue as Secretary of State under Eisenhower.

14

FOR THE ROCKEFELLER BROTHERS, the war years provided a release from the discipline of their father and a time for midcourse steering corrections in the trajectory of their lives. Nelson, the only one who might have retraced his grandfather's path to a career in oil, discovered that for better or worse his quest would be for political power in Washington. John 3rd, out of his father's grasp for the first time in his life, was now ready, as he said, "to find my real interests." Laurance had discovered ways to blend his talent for making money with an interest in the new technologies that had become so important in armaments and defense. David had seen that the best of his many alternatives was to join the Chase Bank. Only Winthrop was still uncommitted. His future mistakes, however, would not be the peccadilloes of a young man, but the errors of an adult. He, like the rest of them, had definitely come of age. When the war began, they were still Mr. Rockefeller's boys; when it was over, they were the Rockefeller Brothers.

They came home filled with confidence—in their generation's ability to manage the world and in their own ability to take control of the family from their father. In 1940, just before America entered the war, they had united to form the Rockefeller Brothers Fund to handle their personal philanthropy. In its articles of incorporation, they had inserted a statement of purpose that sounded more like the preamble of a constitutional document:

> We, the undersigned, being brothers and having interests and objectives in common, have joined together in our desire to continue the tradition of public service and fearless leadership established by our grandfather and carried forward and extended by our parents. In uniting our efforts and coordinating our activities, we hope to be more effective in aiding in the preservation and develop-

242

ment of the republic form of government and the private enterprise system which in our opinion have been fundamental factors in making the United States a powerful nation of free people. . . . In line with those convictions, we are prepared to subordinate personal or individual interests as and when necessary for the sake of accomplishing our broader objectives. We propose to use our individual abilities and those material resources which are at our disposal to further these objectives. By acting together with a common purpose, we will be in a stronger position not only to promote our common interests, but also to foster and effectuate our individual interests. We will be free to pursue independent and varied careers, at the same time taking full advantage of our diverse interests in the attainment of common objectives. Accordingly, we hereby form a partnership, the objective of which shall be to carry out the foregoing objectives.

Pearl Harbor had partially forestalled them from this enterprise, but now, six years later, they came back to the offices on the 56th floor of the RCA Building in Rockefeller Center to take up where they had left off. Their father had designed space for them at the time when the family office was moved there from the historic address at 26 Broadway, even though Winthrop was working in the oil fields then and David was still in college. In the central space of Room 5600 (as the family headquarters was known) stood the heavy furniture of Junior's own office for the last several decades, reflecting his own staid personality just as the modern paintings that appeared like splashes of color on the walls of the Brothers' offices reflected theirs. It took no particular eye for design to see that these two styles clashed.

"This was a fresh period," John 3rd later said. "We all came together and decided there should be a reallocation of assignments." Nelson was allotted responsibility for Rockefeller Center; John, for the Foundation; Laurance took over Jackson Hole Preserve, Inc., and the other conservation interests; Winthrop became involved in the Urban League and Colonial Williamsburg; and David went onto the board of the Institute for Medical Research (soon to be renamed Rockefeller University) and took on responsibility for Riverside Church.

There was some confusion, but that was to be expected, and on the whole things seemed to be working out much as

Junior had always hoped they would. He was seventy years old, but still in good health and enjoying his high prestige; far from considering retirement, he was looking forward to working with his sons in this hour of great national opportunity and need. John Lockwood, the attorney from Milbank, Tweed who had gone to Washington with Nelson and now returned with him, recalls thinking that the Office ideally resembled a solar system: "Mr. Rockefeller, Jr., was like a sun and the boys like the planets. If one of them got too close, he got burned; if he got too far away, he spun off into space. The situation was supposed to make each of the boys find his own perfect orbit around the father."

Yet it was something less than a Platonic harmony of the spheres. Underneath the surface of cooperative unity and absolute propriety that the Rockefellers would manage to preserve even at times when tensions were high between them, there was conflict and a struggle for precedence among the sons, and a chafing desire to be free of their father's authority. As usual, Nelson was the center of it. He was used to Washington, where one could get as far as his capacity for political manuvering would take him. He was not pleased to return to a situation dominated by a more restrictive order, particularly one that didn't adapt to the changes he had gone through in the past five years. Almost immediately he was acting with an abandon and disregard for proprieties that caused some of the old antagonisms between him and his father to flare up.

Nelson had been appointed by Mayor O'Dwyer to a committee attempting to persuade the United Nations Organization to locate permanently in New York. Initial hopes of getting delegates to accept the old World's Fair grounds in Flushing Meadow had collapsed. Now it seemed that Philadelphia and even San Francisco had better chances of becoming the new world organization's permanent home. Nelson had impulsively offered the Rockefeller Center Theater as a meeting place for the General Assembly, a gesture that had been picked up by the press. But his father, annoyed at not being consulted and unwilling to break a lease with the Center's tenants, vetoed the idea, forcing his annoyed and embarrassed son to retract the offer.

The U.N. delegates had set December 11, 1946, as the deadline for the decision. Nelson had been in Mexico with Frank Jamieson attending the inauguration of President Aleman. When New York Times editor James Reston told Jamieson that he felt the delegates still preferred New York if the proper site could be found, Nelson decided to fly home to make one last attempt. On the morning of December 10, he was in Room 5600 brainstorming with his close aides Jamieson, Harrison, and Lockwood and his brother Laurance. Pocantico came up as a possible site. Nelson quickly ordered maps and got on the phone to begin cajoling his absent brothers into agreeing with the plan to give up all or part of the family lands in Tarrytown. One by one they did, John 3rd with great reluctance and David only after asking plaintively, "Couldn't I just give money instead?" He even got an anguished OK from Junior, but then the site selection committee indicated that delegates felt Westchester County was too far away.

It was that evening, just hours before the U.N. decision was to be made, that Wally Harrison suggested a seventeen-acre tract that the flamboyant real estate man William Zeckendorf was developing along the East River between 42nd and 49th Streets, called "X City." Harrison (who was to be the principal architect) figured that Zeckendorf would be willing to sell for $8.5 million. If the deal could be concluded, it would also have the added advantage of wiping out a potentially serious rival to Rockefeller Center, which even then was only 60 percent occupied, and of upgrading the whole midtown area.

With spirits raised considerably, Nelson put through a call to his father, who offered personally to donate the entire amount. "Why Pa, that's most generous!" Nelson exclaimed. Even before he hung up the phone, he had dispatched Harrison to find Zeckendorf, whom he located at the Monte Carlo nightclub, where the deal was concluded.

Two mornings later, after the East River site had been formally accepted by the U.N. delegates, Junior breakfasted with Nelson and signed the papers. As Nelson was about to dash off to deliver them to Senator Warren Austin, chief of the U.S. delegation to the U.N., his father reached up, grabbed his coat, and said rather gently, "Will this make up for the Center Theater?" Observing the scene, Frank Jamieson wasn't sure until afterward that Nelson had realized what his father meant, so excited was he about finalizing the deal. He embraced his father around the shoulders and then left for the meeting with Austin. It ended well, but the episode had helped convince him that he would be cramped until the centers and symbols of family power had passed over to him and his brothers. It was not something to be done overnight. But it was something that had to be done.

This was not Nelson's feeling alone, but was shared by all the Brothers. As Lindsley Kimball, an aide Junior had brought into the Office in 1940, recalls, "The brothers felt that they *had* to get out from under the shadow of their father. It was a necessity. I remember once when Winthrop came to me with tears streaming down his face and said, 'Oh, how I wish I could do *something* on my own.' The father was a tough man. A couple of brothers had what amounted to awe for him—they wouldn't go near him if they could help it."

As the nerve center controlling the family's financial and philanthropic investments, the Office was a logical place to start the assault. As early as 1933, on the occasion of his decision to devote himself to the family, Nelson had commissioned a consulting firm to do a study of its functions and to survey and tabulate its activities, because (as he had written his father) "The Rockefeller family is entering upon the third stage of its development, a period which will afford further great opportunities for serving society, but during which the unity of the family is going to be seriously tried."

Junior was not wholly at ease with Nelson's precocious interest in planning the family's affairs. Remembering his own early days in his father's office at 26 Broadway, he was perhaps taken aback by Nelson's proposal to divide the patrimony; probably he was amused by his 25-year-old son's intention to solve possible conflicts by flow-charts and thus bypass the flexibility that was the peculiar genius of his Office. There was a sense in which the Office was departmentalized, Arthur Packard taking responsibility for the philanthropies, Bertram Cutler for the investments, and Tom Debevoise for legal problems, but they were all generalists really: they pulled together. And above all, they were Junior's Associates. When he was in town, they all lunched together informally and conducted business in gentlemanly ease.*

This calm was shattered now, as the Brothers returned from the war and Nelson in particular took up the old

---

*By allowing their associates to share a small measure of their magnificence and become almost-Rockefellers themselves, the Rockefeller family got loyalty. Commenting on this later, one family Associate noted how Robert Kennedy had commanded fealty by thrusting out his shirt sleeves for some aide to put on the cuff links. "No one in *this* family would ever do something like *that*," the aide commented.

scheme to divide authority. The Brothers brought new ideas with them, along with an impatience with their elders they wouldn't have dared show before the war. Not having a close emotional relationship with his sons, Junior was somewhat bewildered by it all. His old-guard Associates were more than bewildered; they saw the Brothers as a threat to the whole way of performing this complex and unique service that they had perfected over the years, and thus anathema to the interests of the man and the mission they had always served. In their view, the Brothers generally and Nelson in particular would make the Office a circus and a business all at once, cheapening the stately quality of its operations.

The conflict revolved around Debevoise. He had become old and set in his ways. He saw the boys as chaos; they saw him as an old fogy. Called "the Prime Minister," he was determined that there would be no departures from the standard operating procedures established over the years. The boys felt that the Office had to be bent into a more contemporary posture to accommodate the postwar world and their own individual preferences. Nelson knew that by controlling the allegiance of the family *consiglieri*, he would control the family, and he began to campaign to replace Debevoise.

For a time the conflict simmered, but by 1947 it had broken into the open. Nelson wanted to hire John Lockwood (who had become in effect his personal lawyer) as the official legal counsel for the entire family. Knowing that his time had come but feeling a responsibility to the rest of the old guard, Debevoise tried to have Vanderbilt Webb, who had been involved in the Office since 1939, named as his replacement. The resulting struggle for power was carried out at an almost elegant level, the discussions couched in so genteel a code that some lower-level employees never knew what was happening. It was the sort of thing Nelson had mastered during his years in Washington. By the time the smoke had cleared, Lockwood was appointed the principal attorney for the family, Webb was out except for special assignments, and Debevoise's status had been limited to that of an emeritus advising Junior personally.

"Nelson got me in in a squeeze play," Lockwood recalled years later, after having reached the mandatory retirement age of sixty-five established by the Brothers and returned to his old desk at Milbank, Tweed. "He sensed that the time was right to move, and he moved. It all happened because Junior really didn't know what was going on—he was isolated from his sons. When the *coup* was complete and I was officially hired, he called me into his office and said, 'Mr. Lockwood, you are the family adviser now, and one of the things I want you to do is explain my boys to me.' "

Once Debevoise had been replaced, resistance to the Brothers collapsed. Packard, Cutler, and the others in the old regime were more willing to divide their loyalty between father and sons and acquiesce in the inevitable dynastic process. In return, the Brothers made it clear that they had no intention of purging Room 5600, but would be content to let the old guard stay on until they reached retirement age. Although technically still their father's guests (he never charged them rent or asked them to share in the Office's considerable expenses), the Brothers began to create mini-offices of their own, bringing in personal associates with whom they replaced Junior's staff as they died or retired. The stencil on the door of Room 5600 now read, "Rockefeller: Office of the Messrs." There were so many principals to serve that the staff took to calling them "Mr. John," "Mr. Nelson," "Mr. Laurance," and so on.

Next came Rockefeller Center. After lengthy negotiations, Nelson convinced his father that the time had come to transfer the stock in the Center to him and his brothers. A multimillion-dollar gamble in the thirties, the Center had now turned the corner and was New York's most imposing and valuable real estate, its market value rising with each surge of the postwar construction boom that had overtaken midtown Manhattan in the wake of the U.N. project. Not only did controlling it give them a significant voice in the affairs of the city, but it also provided dozens of high-paid jobs in which they could (and did) place people whom they wanted to keep in a holding pattern around them. Nelson knew it would be his generation's most significant asset and persuaded his father to "sell" the Center to the '34 Trusts he had set up for the Brothers.

For a man considered by his sons to be aloof and authoritarian, Junior capitulated to the demands of their manhood more easily than they expected. The only time he really bridled at their takeover was when it came to Pocantico itself. New houses had been raised on the estate and there was already a new and growing generation—the fourth—of Rockefeller children playing in its woods, but it was still as quiet and remote as it had been when Junior first helped talk his father into buying it half a century earlier.

Since then, he had expanded the estate's borders by buying up any piece of nearby land that happened to come on the market. He had moved into the Big House after Senior's death, assuming the role of the Laird of Kikjuit. His children moved into homes that seemed to mirror the character and interrelationships of the third generation. After their marriage, Babs and David Milton had moved into the Saportas place (so named for an eccentric old man who had originally built it and later sold it to Junior). It was a large house of native stone with an 1812 sundial set into the rose gardens. It was tucked romantically into the thick woods, but Babs had felt too far away from her parents living in the "park" area of the estate, and had commissioned a house to be built nearer her father. The Miltons moved there in 1939.

JDR3 built a slate-roofed French chateau two miles from Kikjuit on a long, rolling stretch of pastureland near the town of Mt. Pleasant in 1940. But if this seemed a desire to escape the pressures of the role by living apart from the patriarch who embodied it, two of his younger brothers reacted quite the reverse, moving into the spiritual center of the estate. After his marriage, Nelson claimed Hawes House, an old Dutch colonial with deep gashes on the door that according to local legend, had been made by the sabers of Hessian soldiers during the Revolution. Laurance built a contemporary building in white brick, which he called Kent House, a stone's throw from Nelson. David, however, with the thrift that might be expected of one whose Ph.D. thesis was about waste, bought Babs's newly built house after her divorce in 1943 and began calling it Hudson Pines. Winthrop never got around to building a permanent home at Pocantico, but periodically lived in Breuer House, an ultramodern structure in wood and glass designed by Marcel Breuer, which, after being displayed at the Museum of Modern Art, had been cut into sections, loaded onto trailers, and trucked to Pocantico for reassembly. It was always called "the guest house."

Whatever other residences the Brothers had (and most of them eventually had three or four), they were encouraged to settle at Pocantico. It was as expected of them as taking careers in public service. Yet, while they all had the prerogatives of princes, it was still very much Junior's kingdom. As the other areas he had always controlled were taken away one by one, Junior retreated to his fief for a final stand. Even in the postwar period, horses and carriages from the stable and the electric cars were checked out only at his pleasure.

His stewards apportioned the abundant produce and dairy goods of Pocantico. One hot day when Nelson's wife, Tod, brought her children to wade in the Japanese brook, Junior caused a scene by commanding her to take them out.

Now Nelson was proposing that the Brothers take legal title to Pocantico, as they had to Rockefeller Center, and it didn't sit well. Perhaps the bruised feelings and the necessity for protracted negotiations could have been avoided if Abby had been there to smooth things over in her old role of mediator between her husband and children. But she had begun suffering from heart trouble in the middle of the war; by 1946 it was serious enough to require spending the harsh winter months in Tucson, where she and Junior found a small inn that delighted them. She spent the days sitting in the sunshine underneath a giant pepper tree, writing letters to her children and grandchildren. Junior read aloud to her from *Jane Eyre*, although he refused to finish *Wuthering Heights*, claiming that its Gothic excesses disturbed him. Early on the morning of April 5, 1948, Abby suffered a stroke and died, leaving an unbridgeable gap in her sons' lives and in their relations with their father. (Nelson had been particularly upset by his mother's passing. As his son Steven later said, "I don't think I have ever seen him disturbed in any way comparable to when Grandmother died." He commissioned Matisse to do a stained-glass window in the little church in Pocantico Hills in her memory.)

After lengthy discussions, in 1950 Nelson finally convinced Junior to form Hills Realty, a holding company for the family lands, including Pocantico. In the beginning, Junior was the only stockholder. But by 1952, Nelson was pushing him to sell his interest in Hills Realty to the Brothers. He sent a memo to his father pointing out that "the sale of the stock to the brothers would in no way change Father's relation to his or their use of the property during his life. However, it would be understood that if he wanted to raise or discuss any problems about the property, the President of the corporation (by agreement among the Brothers to be Nelson) would have complete authority to deal with him."

Junior balked at the idea, although he accepted Nelson's arguments about the tax advantages of having the property in a holding company and understood his concern about the confusion of the estate in the event of his death. Still, it was hard for him to agree. As he noted in a letter to his friend Debevoise in the spring of 1952, "I presume I should make this sale for every reason and that there is really no reason why I should not go forward with it. On the other hand, I still have the foolish feeling that it is pleasant to own the house in which I live. Perhaps by fall I shall have realized the folly of maintaining this position in view of the many advantages a sale would bring about."

Later in the year, Junior finally gave in, agreeing to sell his stock in the Hills company to his sons, subject to his life tenure. The shares were allotted in percentages indicating the Brothers' respective interests in and use of the "park" area: Nelson and Laurance, whose homes were there, each got 30¾ percent; David, who lived close to the park, got 23 percent; John 3rd and Winthrop each received 7¾ percent. The price they paid for the 245 acres and buildings would have shocked real estate specialists: $311,000 for an area worth ten or twenty times that.

Although somewhat disconcerted by the haste with which his sons had taken over the family institutions, Junior realized that it was what he had been training them for since they were children. It was not only inevitable, but fitting. If he worried about anything, it was that Nelson's ambition and competence seemed so much greater than the other Brothers', and also that none of his sons with the possible exception of JDR3 seemed as interested in giving as he had hoped they would be.

The family still had influence in the Rockefeller Foundation, but no longer had the absolute control it had maintained in the first two decades of its existence. The turning point had come as early as 1936, when Raymond Fosdick made it clear that independence from the family was necessary if he were to take on the presidency of the Foundation. Yet even before this—perhaps since the Walsh Commission had revealed the way the Foundation had been conscripted to a partisan role in the Ludlow struggle—Junior realized that if the greatest of the family philanthropies were to play a central role in the life of the country, it could not risk being attacked as a plaything of the people who had endowed it. He himself had inherited such a great sum of money to give away that he did not need the Foundation in his charitable work, which had at any rate taken on an extremely personal character. His sons, however, would not have nearly as much to spend. He realized that they would need an institution to magnify the impact of their giving and allow them to control and channel their philanthropy into fields central to the careers on which they were about to embark. That was why the Rockefeller Brothers Fund had been created in the first place. That was why Junior gave it $58 million in 1951, overnight catapulting it into national prominence as the fourth-largest foundation in the country.

With a major philanthropy and all the centers of family power in their possession, the Brothers were now ready to strike out on their own.

15

BOTH AS INDIVIDUALS and as a group, the Rockefeller Brothers seemed to embody the best in the tradition of America's great and powerful families. Presenting a front that was wholesome and enthusiastic, yet dedicated and involved, they were an argument on behalf of noblesse oblige. They were responsible wealth and power; the group portraits taken of them in the early 1950s show five knights in three-piece suits ready to sally forth to act for the "well-being of mankind" in the manner established by their father.

Yet there were certain things the photographs didn't show. One of them, quite literally, was Babs. As a woman, she was not expected to achieve much more than a happy marriage, which was the one thing that seemed completely out of her grasp. By 1942 the workmen and servants at Pocantico, always the first to know what was going on, had noticed that her husband, David Milton, was absent from their home for increasingly long periods of time. By the next year, he had stopped coming altogether, and the couple made their separation official. After the divorce, Babs sold the Pocantico house to her brother David and moved to Long Island, marrying Irving Pardee, the next of her three husbands. When asked why she came to the estate so seldom, she would answer that its bittersweet memories overwhelmed her.

Junior was upset by Babs's troubles, but he had already seen the difficulties of a strong-willed yet aimless woman in his sister Edith. In some sense, he was prepared to be disappointed in his daughter. Winthrop's falling off was a far more serious problem.

Aside from the fact that his hair was beginning to thin and he was still scarred from burn wounds suffered when a kamikaze plane struck the ship he was on during the Okinawa invasion, Winthrop had come back from the war much the same as when he had left. In certain ways, he was very much like the rest of them—conservative, well-mannered, Republican. It showed in a letter he had written to his father after the 1944 election returned FDR to the White House once again: "They say that 67% of the soldier vote went to Roosevelt. It is hard to believe that those of us who are fighting to make our country free for opportunity are willing at the same time to turn right around and vote for a fourth term."

Yet in other ways he was different. He could not take hold of an event or opportunity and bend it to his purpose the way his brothers could. After coming home from active duty, he had proposed to Secretary of War Robert Patterson* that he should do a study of veterans' problems. Patterson OK'd the project, and for the first half of 1946, Winthrop toured the United States by automobile studying how men who had given the best years of their lives were welcomed back to their hometowns. In the report he forwarded to the Pentagon at the end of the year, he concluded that the GI bill was just "an effort to buy veterans off with cash" and suggested that what was needed was for each community to have citizens' committees to work out the veterans' problems on an individual basis. He offered to put up the first million dollars for such a project out of his own pocket. But President Truman, who had just gotten rid of one Rockefeller, was not anxious to appoint another to an important policy post and turned thumbs down on it.

Nelson might have found a way to bull the project through on his own, but Winthrop just gave up. He went back to New York and took up his old job at Socony-Vacuum. Even after they gave up on other hopes for him, his parents believed he could succeed in business, specifically in the oil business, and had tried to groom him for such a career. Before the war, he had been in the Foreign Department. As liaison officer for the Near East, he had toured Iran as a con-

---

*A Wall Street attorney, Patterson had enlisted at the same time as Winthrop and been with him in basic training. The two men had been on KP duty together at the moment word came that Patterson had been elevated to the Cabinet.

sultant for the Anglo-Iranian Oil Company and had been in Egypt looking over oil properties when Hitler invaded Poland. But on his return, Socony gave him a less glamorous position in the Production Department. It was a desk job and he embraced it with scant enthusiasm. He was on the outer edge of the upheavals remaking the family, although he accepted the obligations thrust on him by his father. Yet there was a sleepwalking quality to his work; it was as if he were being fitted for clothes he could never wear. His aging mother had seen what was happening and was alarmed by it. In 1947 she wrote her sister Lucy, "I think Winthrop is still going through a stage that is the aftermath of the war in which he is a little bit afraid the family will try to manage him."

He picked up his nightlife where he had left off before the war. He dated actress Mary Martin frequently enough for gossip columnists to speculate that they would marry. Seeing the family name bandied about in such a way annoyed Junior and increased the distance between him and his only wayward son. Winthrop often felt humiliated by his father's impatience and condescension. One of his close friends recalls an incident in 1947 that seemed to sum up the gulf separating the two men. Winthrop, who had been looking for a permanent home in New York, had gotten his sister, Babs, to agree to sell him an apartment she owned. He was anxious to move in immediately, but his father had vetoed the transaction. Thomas Debevoise was currently renting the apartment, and Junior didn't want his old friend and associate inconvenienced by an eviction. Winthrop made a phone call to Junior to discuss the matter, but his father cut his protest short. Winthrop slammed the receiver down, saying angrily, "By God, if I ever have children, I'm going to *talk* to them, not just make an appointment to see them and then get up after five minutes to go get a haircut."

Winthrop began to drink heavily and acquired hangers-on in New York's cafe society. ("He was an awfully nice guy," a close family friend recalls, "but you'd have to say that he was pretty much a confirmed alcoholic by the time he was thirty-five.") Then, in 1948, he married a buxom blonde named Barbara ("Bobo") Sears at fourteen minutes after midnight on Valentine's Day morning. The marriage took place at the Florida home of Mrs. Winston Guest. The previous afternoon, the toast of Palm Beach's winter society, including the Duke and Duchess of Windsor, had given a champagne reception for the couple. Laurance was the family's representative at the wedding. Junior and Abby were conspicuous in their absence.

When news of the "playboy" Rockefeller's marriage flashed over the wire services, the papers scrambled to find out just who this Bobo Sears was. Cholly Knickerbocker haughtily informed his readers that she was Mrs. Barbara Paul Sears of the Philadelphia Main Line Sears. But she was in fact Jievute Paulekiute, who had been born to Lithuanian immigrant parents in a coal patch near Noblestown, Pennsylvania. Starstruck as a young woman, she had taken the more glamorous first name of Eva, shortened her last name to Paul, and begun angling for a screen career. She had been named Miss Lithuania in a Chicago beauty contest when she was seventeen and had gotten bit parts on the stage, managing to win the lead role in a road company production of *Tobacco Road*. In 1945 she married Richard Sears, a proper Bostonian who became third secretary at the American Embassy in Paris. Even after divorcing him, she clung to some of his social prejudices. "Actually I was surprised to find the Rockefellers included in the *Social Register*," she had replied to a reporter's question about how it felt to have made a "Cinderella" marriage. "The Sears family considered them merchants."

In September, when the couple had their first and only child, Winthrop Paul, *The New York Times* marked the birth without noting also that the marriage was barely seven months old. Yet even before the child came, the Cinderella marriage was nearing its midnight hour. Within a year, the couple separated. Bobo took their young son and moved in with her mother in the Midwest. She decided on divorce, and her attorney held out for a huge $6 million settlement.

The Rockefeller brothers rallied around Winthrop, lending him money for the divorce settlement and temporarily taking title to his share of Pocantico and other holdings so that Bobo could not claim them as community property. Yet they were all aware that he had made a fool of himself and disgraced the whole family. Nobody had to say it; there was no other conclusion to draw. For Winthrop himself, it was the climactic incident in his life, showing once and for all that there was no way for him to succeed in the fast-paced milieu of his father and brothers. He quit his job at Socony and gradually began cutting ties with the world he had grown up in. He drank heavily, his eyes showing yellow and his large

frame buoyed by a look of bloat. Early in 1953 he went to
Arkansas, partly because of the state's ninety-day residency
requirement for divorce but also to visit Frank Newell, an
old army buddy who lived there. Newell took him around the
state and introduced him to some of the leading people of
Little Rock. He found the area pleasantly provincial, and it
occurred to him that while he had been one of five in New
York, he could easily be one in a million in Arkansas. After
several trips back and forth between Little Rock and Manhattan, he decided to move to Arkansas for good, not realizing
that once he had left the family his father would stand like
the archangel barring his return with a flaming sword.

He had gone south in defeat, but he did not take up a
monastic life. One of his first acts was to buy some 927 acres
of prime land on top of heavily wooded, craggy Petit Jean
Mountain near the backwoods Arkansas town of Morrilton.
He hired an army of workmen to clear the trees and literally
shear off the mountain top to make room for the massive
farm he called Winrock and which some would see as an attempt to re-create Pocantico. Winthrop invested $2 million in
the estate, creating long, rolling lawns and carving an airfield
into the wooded valley from which he would be able to take
off in his Falcon Jet and be in Little Rock in five minutes. He
built two lakes, which he named Lake Abby and Lake Lucy,
after his mother and aunt. He brought in breeding stock of
the celebrated Santa Gertrudis cattle that would soon make
his ranch famous among cattle buyers.

Within a few years, Winrock Farm was the first wonder of
Arkansas. It attracted over 50,000 visitors a year, most of
them citizens of the second poorest state in the nation who
came to gawk at all the marvels of the place, including a
$31,000 stud bull named Rock. Winthrop began to play a
role in the civic life of the state, donating several million dollars to establish a demonstration school that would show what
might be done with the state's abysmal educational system,
and to build a medical clinic. As he told a reporter, he liked
the state because "what you do here shows up in a hurry.
You can see the results."

In 1956, after he had been appointed head of the Arkansas
Industrial Development Commission, observers speculated
that he might have a good political future if he were to rereg-
ister as a Democrat. The same year he married a pretty
divorcée named Jeannette Edris, daughter of a theater-chain
operator. He seemed happy: it was as if he had found his

métier as the "hillbilly Rockefeller." Once, when taking a group of Eastern newspapermen on a tour of Winrock, he stopped to gesture down at the broad valley visible from the height of Petit Jean Mountain and said, "This is my show. It doesn't have anything to do with any Rockefeller family project."

While Winthrop was declaring himself an odd man out, the other Brothers were trying to remain faithful to the pledge they had made "to subordinate personal or individual interests as and when necessary for the sake of accomplishing our broader objectives." Yet there were strains. Nelson had not led the struggle against the father merely to submit family policy to a collective. They were all equals, yet one was more equal than the others. Whenever there was an opening at Room 5600, Nelson filled it with one of *his* associates. He dominated the Office and made it reflect his personality. He had argued in family councils, for instance, that since the third generation was "going public," in a way that no Rockefeller had before, they needed someone at a high policy level to give coherence to the family's public relations. The natural candidate for this post was Frank Jamieson. When Nelson proposed him for the position, nobody could object: Jamieson had, over the years of his work with Nelson, become friends with the other brothers. Yet this was as much a *coup* as replacing Debevoise with John Lockwood had been. As Lockwood himself later commented, "The public relations position was crucial because whoever controlled him was effectively the leader of the family. And it was always clear that Frank worked for Nelson first and the rest of the brothers second. He was interested mainly in Nelson's career. There were moments of terrific competition and jockeying for position among the brothers in those early days."

The others never rebelled against Nelson. He exuded a kind of warmth none of them was capable of and which, after Abby's death, had become the emotional matrix within which all family bonds were revitalized. Moreover, his ambition itself was ambiguous. If there had ever been a moment when it seemed too flagrant, there might have been a movement to block what he was doing. But all the Brothers had profited from his willingness to lead the oedipal battle against Junior. And after it was won, he, as the new dynast of the family, urged them on to accomplishments as much as he drove himself.

Ironically, the potentially explosive situation in Room 5600 was finally stabilized by exactly the element that threatened it: Nelson's ambition. As John Lockwood observed, "Nelson was always a 'chart man.' He liked to know where everybody was and what their authority was. That way he could have a hand in things. His attitude toward the Office was too rigid. I don't doubt that if he had stayed around Room 5600, in time the operation would have collapsed. The fact that it survived as well as it did was due mainly to his absence." He had taken the family by storm, but his imagination still rotated on an axis stretching from Washington to Latin America.

The day after he "resigned" as Assistant Secretary of State on August 26, 1945, Nelson had returned to New York and called a meeting of the Group—his prewar brain trust on Latin America, which had been enlarged by the addition of Lockwood, Frank Jamieson, and Berent Friele, a Norwegian whose family had been in the coffee business for five generations and who had resigned the presidency of the American Coffee Corporation and a directorship in the A&P Company to become Nelson's Associate. The announced goal of this and subsequent postwar meetings of the Group was to find a vehicle for the ideas Nelson felt were vital to the future of inter-American "cooperation." It was understood that this would also speed Rockefeller's own triumphant return to Washington.

The result of their deliberations was a nonprofit foundation called the American International Association for Economic and Social Development (AIA), organized "for the purpose of promoting self-development, and better standards of living, together with understanding and cooperation among peoples throughout the world." This grand rhetoric was continued in a letter Nelson wrote his father asking him to become chairman of the board of the new organization:

> You more than anyone have become a symbol to people throughout the world that democracy and the capitalistic system are interested in their well-being. The people must increasingly have reason to feel that their best interests and opportunity for the future are identified with our country and our way of life. Now more than ever before it is important that we as a family carry on with the courage and vision that led you and Grandfather to pioneer new fields and blaze new trails.

AIA's programs were designed principally as a training effort for all Latin Americans, providing nutritional, health, and homemaking information and technical data on better farming practices. From the beginning, however, the program was concentrated in two countries: Brazil, because of its size and importance in hemispheric affairs; and Venezuela, because of its oil.

In 1945, Rómulo Betancourt's left-of-center *Acción Democrática* had come to power in Venezuela and immediately imposed an unprecedented 50 percent tax on oil company profits. To Betancourt's left, the Communist and other Marxist parties called for even more drastic action, including the outright nationalization of the oil companies. This provoked a response on many levels by Standard Oil and the competitors with whom it had a working relationship. The U.S. oil majors pushed harder on plans to open the Middle East as a potential alternative to deposits of Venezuelan crude. Meanwhile, in Caracas they strengthened contacts with right-wing military officers who were displeased by the "socialist" orientation of the Betancourt government, and embarked on an intense public relations campaign to convince Venezuelans that American oil producers were actually responsible corporate citizens interested in the nation's economic growth and social advancement.

It was a context tailor-made for Nelson's new organization. Every Venezuelan government since the Gómez dictatorship had pledged itself to a policy of *sembrando el petroleo,* "sowing the oil" profits in development projects. AIA identified itself as the spearhead of an effort to create a partnership between the "concerned" U.S. firms and the government's own development plans. Nelson approached the oil companies with the proposal that they back AIA programs to demonstrate their interest in the economic well-being of Venezuela. The proposal fell on receptive ears: the oil companies would ultimately account for nearly half of the $14 million AIA would raise and spend on technical aid projects in its twenty-year existence.*

---

*Rockefeller had less success, however, with U.S. firms not as threatened by expropriation as the oil companies, and not as directly subject to his family's influence. Robert Hudgens, a director of AIA, recounted the story of his efforts to raise money to support a farm credit plan from the Coca-Cola Company in Brazil. "The first thing I said was that I've never been to a crossroads in the Andes or anywhere else in Latin America that I couldn't buy a Coca-Cola.... Whether rightly or wrongly, if better living means the ability to buy

In pursuit of his partnership with Venezuela, however, Rockefeller was compelled to modify the original AIA concept, creating two organizations instead of one. The suggestion had originally come from John Lockwood. "One of these should be a Sunday company and one should be a weekday company," he had advised. "That is the historical, puritan, and Protestant tradition of this country—make money all week and tend to your eleemosynary operations on Sunday." On January 9, 1947, Nelson yielded to his attorney's wisdom and created the International Basic Economy Corporation (IBEC) as the profit-making companion to AIA. Creole and Shell Petroleum agreed to put up a total of $13 million for the first five years of operations, receiving preferred stock in the new corporation; control remained vested in the common stock, which Nelson and his family owned. To avoid charges of "Yankee imperialism," the IBEC charter eschewed the traditional business objective of making money; instead it defined its goal as promoting "the economic development of various parts of the world, to increase the production and availability of goods, things, and services useful to the lives of lifelihood of their peoples, and thus to better their standards of living." It was something new in the world of business: a corporation with a political ideology, apparently dedicated less to making profits than to propagating ideas—in this case, Nelson's fervid anti-Communism.

Some of his friends later theorized that Nelson's fixation with Marxism could be traced back to 1939, when he became embroiled in the furor surrounding the closing of Lincoln School, and decided that he had been "used" by Communists and fellow travelers in the ensuing controversy. Others say the formative experience of his ideological life was the Mexican government's nationalization of U.S. oil properties, which happened at about the same time. In either case, his almost obsessive interest in Communism was something new to those who had grown used to seeing Nelson suddenly embrace some new idea or concept and then just as quickly dis-

more Coca-Cola, then it's not only realistic for Coca-Cola to have an interest in it, but also gives this business organization an opportunity to make some contribution to the country in which it goes and sets up business." The Coca-Cola executive listened to the speech, but as Hudgens and Rockefeller came away from the meeting, they knew that the company would not make a contribution. Nelson said, "You know what that man is thinking now? He's thinking to himself, 'I'm not going to put my money into something that's going to prove that Nelson Rockefeller is a world-wide philanthropist.' "

card it. For a time in the days when he first became interested in Venezuela, he carried a copy of *Das Kapital* around
with him, quoting it and insisting that his aides become familiar with the tenets of dialectical materialism. As his Spanish
became fluent, he skirmished with Communist union organizers in the Maracaibo oil fields who sought to repeat in
Venezuela the triumphs of the left against oil companies in
Mexico and Bolivia.

His wartime work in the coordinator's office had provided
more fuel for the ideological fire that seemed almost to consume him, and gave him his first opportunity to enter the
fray at an international level. He insisted that the Nazis were
a short-range problem in the hemisphere and the Communists
an enemy that would remain to be dealt with long after Hitler had been vanquished.

Maintaining the labor, State Department, and intelligence
community contacts he had made in the coordinator's office,
Nelson became a key behind-the-scenes influence in America's anti-Communist effort in Latin America in the postwar
years.* He decided to carry the public fight through AIA and
IBEC, especially in Venezuela, which he seemed to have

---

*In 1944 the American Federation of Labor created a Free Trade
Union Committee, which, with CIA backing, would play a major role
in the postwar period, challenging Communist and leftist trade unions
around the world. To head the Latin American section, they selected a
man who had worked for Nelson in the coordinator's office, Serafino
Romualdi. For the next twenty years, Romualdi worked to create an
anti-Communist union movement in the hemisphere. In conjunction
with the CIA, he played an instrumental role in the overthrow of
leftist governments in Guatemala, British Guiana, Brazil, and the Dominican Republic, and in the abortive early efforts to topple Fidel Castro. Romualdi later wrote, "My two-year wartime association with Nelson Rockefeller, rather than coming to an end, was soon to be renewed
and transformed into one in which I have ever since received his sincere encouragement and effective support for every one of the many
labor, political and educational activities in Latin America in which I
later engaged." One branch of these activities was conducted through
the American Institute for Free Labor Development (AIFLD), created
in August 1961 with George Meany as president; David's friend Peter
Grace, of W. R. Grace & Co., as board chairman; and Berent Friele,
Nelson's chief Latin American expert, as vice-chairman. Funded primarily by AID and the CIA, though officially sponsored by the AFL-
CIO, the institute set up a training program for Latin American trade
union leaders. It was AIFLD programs and contacts that enabled the
CIA to utilize the Latin American trade union movement against democratic regimes in Brazil, British Guiana, and the Dominican Republic,
on behalf of conservative political forces more favorable to U.S.
business and policy.

selected as something like a research and development project
for his anti-Communist views.

Taking a $4.5 million investment from the Betancourt gov-
ernment in 1947 to go along with what he had already gotten
from the oil companies, he formed a subsidiary of IBEC
called the Venezuelan Basic Economy Corporation (VBEC).
The Betancourt government fell to a right-wing *coup* the following year, the new dictatorship crushing the trade union
movement and the left and initiating favorable policies for
the oil companies. Meanwhile VBEC moved ahead with its
idea that economic development could be promoted by importing U.S. techniques to improve food distribution, provide
cheaper services, and build new industries. From the beginning, however, VBEC ran into difficulties. Partly it was insen-
sitivity to local culture. (An elaborate and expensive attempt
to build a tuna fishery failed largely because key factors like
the place of fish in the dietary habits of Venezuelans were
not taken into account.) Yet the basic problem was the fact
that IBEC's personality was split between its corporate commitment to the status quo and its ideological commitment to
change.

The food distribution program showed the contradiction
most vividly. Nelson had decided to take over CADA, the oil
companies' vehicle for distributing food to their commissaries,
and build it into a wholesaler for all of Venezuela. (Because
of pressures from unions to lower workers' food prices, the
companies were grateful for the opportunity to turn CADA
over to someone else.) Yet IBEC quickly ran up against a
problem: to succeed would involve undercutting Venezuelan
businessmen in control of existing food wholesaling. One of
them was quoted in *Fortune* magazine: " 'This talk of lower
profits for the good of the economy is all very well for you,
Mr. Rockefeller; but do you really expect us to forego profits
of 30%, 50%, or even 100%, which are quite possible in view
of our capital shortages, in order to make 10%?' "

The last thing Nelson wanted to do was challenge the
structure of Venezuela's oil economy or its prospering
business classes. Especially after the nationalist and Communist forces in Venezuela had been subdued, he began to reevaluate his early ideas about the role IBEC would play. As
Fortune noted, "Rockefeller seems to have realized that the
IBEC companies, if they hope to engender large-scale emula-
tion, must make the normal Latin American profits." But before the company could take advantage of this new business

maturity and develop what Nelson now began to describe as a "more hard-boiled" formula of "good partnership," it had to reckon the failures of its launching period. By 1952, both the Venezuelan government and the oil companies had pulled out of operations there, the latter writing off an $8.6 million loss on their investment. In Brazil, there were also expensive losses and liquidations. Before it was over, the mistakes of IBEC's first decade would cost Nelson himself more than $7 million.

He went to Junior to try to get the cash he needed to replenish IBEC's losses. "Father," he said to the patriarch, "I need a million dollars to save IBEC." But the antagonism Nelson was provoking from Latin American nationalists for meddling in the country's internal affairs bothered Junior. And his fears were not allayed by Jamieson's reassurance that his son was "probably the number one North American in the eyes of the average Brazilian." Junior agreed to bail his son out, but on one condition: after IBEC was in the clear, he must wind up the operation. "All right, Father," Nelson answered coldly, and walked out.

Eventually Nelson raised the money from other sources, and IBEC started on a new and more conservative phase of its career. Having liquidated the failing enterprises, he strengthened the successful ones and began to look for new, more profitable avenues of investment, relying on Jamieson's public relations efforts to fulfill the corporation's anti-Communist mission. What happened to the CADA food distribution program was symbolic of IBEC's changed personality. Once committed to making "normal" Latin American profits, the next logical step was to maximize these profits by building a chain of supermarkets throughout the country, selling goods from U.S. producers, and driving small businesses to the wall. Rather than building up a native Venezuelan economy, therefore, his enterprises—working under the guise of American-Venezuelan cooperation—actually helped to make the country more dependent than before on U.S. corporations and the goods they offered.

Success was purchased at the price of the premise on which IBEC had been created, a premise that had distinguished it from other corporations. While changes in CADA and its other programs were taking place, IBEC acquired profitable U.S. manufacturing companies: a Cleveland producer of oil-extracting equipment; an Akron manufacturer of hydraulic valves; and a Connecticut poultry-breeding operation, one of the largest of its kind. The bulk of IBEC's impressive future assets thus came as the result of its acquisition of already existing, successful U.S. companies, rather than from the development of any new industries in Venezuela or Brazil. By the end of its second decade, IBEC would earn nearly half of its income in Latin America, but less than a third of its assets would be located there.

The company's turnabout did not come overnight. But its growth was steady. By its twentieth birthday, sales would have increased to more than $200 million a year, giving it a place on the prestigious *Fortune* "500" list, along with other giants of the U.S. economy. It encompassed more than 140 subsidiaries in 33 countries, operating mutual funds, insurance companies, housing construction corporations, and a galaxy of other enterprises. It had become a pioneer, although perhaps not in the way Rockefeller had originally projected. In fact, far from being a semiphilanthropy altering the fundamental realities of Latin American dependence, IBEC was an avatar of a new business form—the U.S. multinational with subsidiaries and markets flung far across the globe—which would be a primary fact in the economic life of the underdeveloped world in the second half of the twentieth century.

While Nelson was struggling to get IBEC into the black, President Harry Truman was organizing his second inaugural address around a three-point course of action in the area of foreign policy. The first two points were continuations of previous programs, but the third, promising a "joint agreement to strengthen the security of the North Atlantic area," represented a departure in American foreign policy—a peacetime military alliance (NATO) with transoceanic powers.

In the course of drafting the inaugural, a proposal for a fourth point was put to the President by Ben Hardy, a State Department official who had served under Nelson and Jamieson in the press division of the coordinator's office during the war. Impressed by the technical assistance programs of OIAA and the subsequent ones Nelson developed in the early period of AIA and IBEC, Hardy suggested that the President include in his inaugural an endorsement of a program of technical aid to the underdeveloped world. This would give the speech an idealistic touch and mollify the truculence of Point Three. At the last minute, Truman inserted the Hardy proposal calling for a "bold new program" of technical and development aid. In capitals all over the world there was praise for the vision and generosity of the proposal—known ever afterward as "Point Four"—which would be the only remembered part of the address.

When Nelson read the text of Truman's speech in the morning papers, he was delighted. No contact had taken place between him and the White House since Truman had fired him three and a half years earlier, but he immediately sent off a letter to the President saying that Point Four was the most significant thing that had happened in foreign policy for decades, adding the further blandishment that it would surely make Truman's position secure in the history books for all time.

The flattering phrases betrayed Nelson's eagerness to be back in Washington, but did not produce an invitation. In June, Truman asked for $45 million for the Point Four program, the relatively modest sum underlining the fact that he had been primarily interested in the program for its rhetorical effect. Fired with a new vision for an aggressive campaign to win the hearts and minds of the Third World, which was a compelling adjunct of his anti-Communism, Nelson went to Washington to testify before legislative bodies about lessons he had learned from his activities with AIA and IBEC in Latin America that might be relevant to legislation around Point Four. Time and again he returned to the need to create an agency for these programs that would not be under the control of the State Department.

The same summer, Nelson had occasion to visit the President. In the course of their talks, he suggested that the Latin American countries' solid stand in the U.N. favoring U.S. intervention in Korea warranted a speech of acknowledgment. Truman agreed, and Nelson, eager to be helpful, offered to "put together a few thoughts" that might be of assistance to him in making such a speech. The President gave Nelson's essay to his Secretary of State, Dean Acheson, who remembered his behavior in San Francisco when he himself had sided with Pasvolsky and the other members of State's International Division. Acheson received Nelson's suggestions politely, but no speech was ever made.

In November 1950, however, Truman appointed Nelson chairman of an International Development Advisory Board, which was to recommend policy in executing Point Four. Rockefeller's initial excitement at the appointment was increased when the President gave him to understand that he wanted the board to prepare the ground for the new assistance program in the same way that a committee headed by Averell Harriman had laid the foundation for carrying out the Marshall Plan. To ensure that it would indeed have such scope, Nelson insisted as a condition of his acceptance that the study would not be limited to technical aid, but would encompass the entire problem of economic assistance to the underdeveloped world.

For the working staff, Nelson recruited Stacy May, an old Dartmouth economics professor who had done much to educate him about Karl Marx and the Communist threat and on whom he had come to rely for economic advice in AIA and IBEC projects. He also sought out attorney Oscar Ruebhausen of the firm Debevoise, Plimpton and Gates, whom he more and more turned to for legal counsel as Lockwood was increasingly immersed in the affairs of the Family Office.

After five months' work, the International Development Board published its report, *Partners in Progress*, which stressed the importance of private capital as the key to development, supported by government aid for roads, ports, irrigation, and power facilities as a "base to build on." But the main recommendation, for which Nelson himself was responsibile, was to centralize all major foreign economic activities in one overall agency, a U.S. Overseas Economic Administration, headed by a single administrator and reporting directly to the President.

Point Four had already come under attack from the conservative right, which called it a plan to provide "a carton of milk for every Hottentot." Now, Rockefeller went to work on potential congressional opponents such as Senators Taft and Byrd. But while garnering support in these quarters, he failed to pay attention to a more formidable opposition building up in the higher echelons of the executive branch.

When he had secured the support of Taft, Nelson went to tell the good news to the President's special assistant, Averell Harriman, senior man in the area of foreign economic programs and head of the Economic Cooperation Administration (the agency administering the Marshall Plan), which Nelson's proposed agency would supersede. The meeting did not go well. Rockefeller's ebullience bounced off the stony Harriman, who had come into his own as a powerful foreign policy figure in the final Roosevelt administration (and had also been at San Francisco) and viewed Nelson's proposal as a bid to find a sinecure for himself. In measured tones, he told Nelson that he was going to continue the ECA (which had been set up as a temporary agency) and broaden its scope instead of setting up the new agency proposed in Nelson's report.

In limbo, Nelson was invited by Edward G. Miller, Jr. who had his old job of Assistant Secretary of State for Latin American Affairs, to testify before the House Committee on Foreign Affairs, then considering the legislation creating the Mutual Security Act. Supporting that legislation, he nonetheless would use the occasion as an attempt to create a groundswell of backing for his Overseas Economic Administration. After recounting his experiences in Latin American affairs, he launched into a prepared statement, which he called *A New Approach to International Security:* "As a nation," he began, "we have six percent of the population of the world and seven percent of the land area. Just before the last war we produced about thirty-three and a third percent, a third of the world's manufactured goods, and a third of the raw materials of the world. The two have been in balance." Then Nelson turned to the array of statistical charts his aides had set up to illustrate the comparative growth of industrial goods and raw materials from 1899 to 1951. These showed that U.S. industrial production had now increased to 50 percent of the world's total, while raw materials production was still only one-third. "Thus," Nelson explained,

> there is a gap between our manufacturing and our raw materials production. Now we are dependent on foreign countries for those raw materials to supply more than one-third of the raw material requirements for our factories... The question is from where do we get the raw materials we import. The answer is that seventy-three percent of our needs for strategic and critical materials come from the underdeveloped areas. We face the blunt fact that the United States no longer finds the base of its own security within its own border. That is a pretty startling fact in view of our own history of complete, as we thought, independence.

Nelson had, in a sense, been the pioneering architect of the system of alliances with which Washington was now encircling the globe. (The legislation he was testifying on was the Mutual Security Act, intended to begin a program of massive military aid to foreign countries.) In 1947 the provisions of the Act of Chapultepec had been realized in the creation of the Rio Pact, the first of the postwar defense arrangements, although some critics suggested that the threat of conflict in Latin America came mainly from its own numerous military regimes. But, while Nelson regarded military aid as essential to any security program, and so testified, he was also convinced it had to be integrated into a comprehensive plan that included economic and social efforts. Technical aid and public health programs were not only necessary to strengthen the U.S. image among the underdeveloped countries; they were essential infrastructures for the economic processes on which national strength and security were finally based. "For instance, you could not get rubber out of the Amazon during the last war because of disease, sickness, and lack of food," Nelson told the House Committee on Foreign Affairs. "Until you could lick those, you could not get the rubber. You find there is an interrelationship beween all these factors, particularly in the underdeveloped areas of the world."

Having thus built a forceful argument for technical assistance, Nelson concluded his House appearance by urging that a U.S. Overseas Economic Administration be created to orchestrate, and support with government aid and guarantees, the flow of billions of dollars of private U.S. capital into the underdeveloped world. The congressmen received the suggestion enthusiastically.

Rockefeller was not, however, invited to go on to the Senate to testify. And as it became clear that he had lost out in his bid to create and become the coordinator of a new agency overseeing U.S. foreign economic activities, he made an appointment to see President Truman and hand in his resignation from the International Development Advisory Board. Arriving at the White House, he chanced to meet Harriman, who was just leaving. As the two men shook hands and eyed each other with a circumspect cordiality, Nelson spoke: "I'm just going in to present my resignation as chairman of the advisory board."

"Oh, no," Harriman exclaimed. "The work is just beginning."

Rockefeller smiled knowingly and went inside to announce his decision. It recalled a similar meeting at the White House, six years earlier, only this time, there was no surprise for either man. "We had a wonderful talk," Nelson said afterward. "He couldn't have been nicer."

In March 1952, A. A. Berle, Jr., noted in his diary that Nelson had gotten Wally Harrison to help him fit out a "little house" behind the Museum of Modern Art as a "center for a very small and singularly esoteric group of serious thinkers." Remembering the heady days before the war, when he and the Group had independently forged policy that the government had no choice but to notice, Nelson was ready to try once again. Along with the Rockefeller Brothers, membership in this small club included Berle, Harrison, Jamieson, and the aging Ruml. The idea was that any outsider sponsored by two of the members could come by and discuss things over lunch. One of the understood topics of discussion was what the Brothers (especially Nelson) should do now that they were in control of the power and influence associated with their name. After recording Nelson's remark that "if the capitalist system has any way of getting things done, the Rockefeller brothers have access to it," Berle commented, "Nelson is seeking some method of giving some intellectual and philosophical direction to this blob of influence."

His recent experience in Washington had been disheartening. The Truman administration had accepted his ideas but refused him the role he felt he deserved in implementing them. Yet now that administration was nearing its end, and the Rockefellers were backing the candidacy of General Dwight D. Eisenhower as heavily as they had Willkie and Dewey in the past, and with far better chances of success. Nelson's Uncle Winthrop Aldrich had been crucial in persuading Eisenhower to run in the first place and then in organizing the financial community to back Ike over Taft at the Republican party convention. Nelson had every reason to think, therefore, that in the Republican era just beginning, he could overcome whatever anti-Rockefeller feeling lingered in Washington and rise to a position of importance in foreign affairs. And within a week of his election, Eisenhower appointed him chairman of a Presidential Advisory Committee on Government Organization charged with sweeping away the administrative debris of twenty years of Democratic rule. It began to look as though his time had indeed finally come.

It was not exactly the post he wanted. He was a man of strong opinions, and as the cold war heated up, his anti-Communism had begun to itch demandingly. He yearned to be in the front lines of policy, but the State Department was still filled with men who recalled his behavior seven years earlier in San Francisco, and the redoubtable Dulles (although long since reconciled to Nelson) was not about to let anyone interfere with his position as the President's lawyer for foreign affairs.* Yet while the post Nelson got was not glamorous, it at least placed him in frequent contact with the President and with his chief of staff, Sherman Adams, also an alumnus of Dartmouth whom he knew from their service together on the school's board of trustees.

As chairman of the President's Advisory Committee on Government Organization, Nelson was at least able to approach foreign policy obliquely. One of the first recommendations his committee made to the President-elect was the proposal for the creation of a supra-Cabinet post to coordinate the work of the nearly forty agencies engaged in some aspect of foreign affairs. But this plan ran directly into Dulles, who would be Rockefeller's chief nemesis in the Eisenhower administration, although not the only one. Dulles's Undersecretary, General Walter Bedell ("Beetle") Smith, who had just relinquished his post as head of the CIA to Dulles's brother Allen, was another. Formerly Ike's army chief of staff, "Beetle" was a key figure in the administration, the only channel of absolutely sure access to the President. (In addition to the relationship of trust that existed between the two men, Ike treasured Beetle's unique talent as the only man he knew who could "put the options on one sheet of paper.") In one of those bizarre contretemps that occurred frequently in the McCarthy era, "Beetle" was convinced that Nelson, despite his ardor for the free world cause, was a Communist or at least a left-wing radical and, while still head of the CIA, had told Ike so directly.

For the first few months of the administration, Nelson's committee turned out one reorganization plan after another, proceeding through the executive departments from Agriculture to Defense and eventually reaching the White House itself. One of these reorganization plans entailed welding the

---

*Dulles knew he had not been Eisenhower's first choice for Secretary of State. That had been John J. McCloy, but Senator Robert Taft had vetoed him as being too close to the "international bankers" and "Roosevelt New Dealers" and, by implication, to the Rockefellers. ("Every Republican candidate for President since 1936," Taft charged bitterly after his defeat in the 1952 convention, "has been nominated by the Chase Bank.") As chairman of the board of the Carnegie Endowment and the Rockefeller Foundation, Dulles, too, was part of the eastern establishment but had a more militant anti-Communism (particularly with regard to Asia, the favored frontier of the radical right) to recommend him over McCloy.

New Deal programs in health, education, and social security into a single Cabinet position, and when the Department of Health, Education and Welfare was formally approved by Congress in April 1953, Nelson was named Undersecretary to Oveta Culp Hobby.

When he became an administrator in charge of the new agency's $2 billion budget and 35,000-member staff, he began by immediately setting up a war room (as in OIAA days) and ordering the most up-to-date audio-visual equipment to use at weekly briefings. He was by all accounts the prime mover in the department during his brief stay. Yet his heart wasn't in it. William Mitchell, a Social Security Administration official, later said of Nelson's tenure at HEW: "He never impressed me as being either an effective or even particularly imaginative person ... and he seemed to work through advisors that were hazy figures on the periphery of the internal administration. They were people who apparently were tied in with the numerous Rockefeller outside interests, and I personally think he would have been a hell of a lot better off if he'd left them where they were."

Eighteen months after his appointment to the HEW position, which he had never regarded as more than a holding pattern, Nelson finally got his chance in international affairs when C. D. Jackson resigned his post as Special Assistant to the President and Nelson was named his successor. Jackson's full title had been Special Assistant for Psychological Strategy; Nelson's would be Special Assistant for Cold War Strategy. The odd designations reflected the peculiar nature of the post itself, which officially was to give "advice and assistance in the development of increased understanding and cooperation among all peoples," but was in fact that of Presidential Coordinator for the CIA.*

Reporting directly to the President, Nelson attended meetings of the Cabinet, the Council on Foreign Economic Policy,

---

*According to Dillon Anderson, who would eventually succeed Nelson, the post was necessary because when Congress had established the CIA it had been placed under the jurisdiction of the National Security Council, since, for constitutional reasons, Eisenhower had decided it should be under the President's jurisdiction. At the same time, however, he preferred not to know about clandestine operations such as the recent overthrow of the democratically elected Arbenz regime in Guatemala because of the difficulty he experienced in presenting the cover story at press conferences. To resolve the difficulty, he appointed a group to oversee these operations; it included the Deputy Secretary of Defense, the Undersecretary of State, and his own Special Assistant.

and the National Security Council, the highest policy-making body in the government. He also functioned as the head of a secret unit called the Planning Coordination Group, consisting of himself, the Deputy Secretary of Defense, and the head of the CIA. This unit was charged with implementing National Security Council decisions. It was a role that began to bring together some of the elements of the supercoordinator's position he had recommended. Yet Dulles was still a roadblock. Dulles remembered well how his own uncle, Robert Lansing, Secretary of State to Woodrow Wilson, had been outmaneuvered by Colonel House. While he didn't want an overt feud with Rockefeller himself, he did allow his underlings, especially Undersecretary Herbert Hoover, Jr., to frustrate Nelson. The most serious flare-up of tensions came in the "Open Skies" plan at the 1955 Geneva Summit.

During the first years of the Eisenhower presidency, there had been continuing conflict over the question of nuclear policy. As the Soviet Union began to narrow the atomic lead of the United States, Eisenhower came more and more to regard nuclear conflict as "suicidal." Dulles, however, adhered to the doctrine of "massive retaliation." In Asian policy, he had teamed up with Admiral Radford, Chairman of the Joint Chiefs of Staff and highest-ranking proponent of "preventive nuclear war," to advocate America's entry into the French conflict in Indochina. It was only with reluctance that he allowed himself to be dragged to the Summit, which was the first such meeting between U.S. and Soviet heads of state since 1945.

On May 10, 1955, Soviet negotiators had reversed nine years of disarmament history and accepted the Western plan for manpower ceilings, reduction of conventional armaments, and the Western timetable and technique for the abolition of nuclear stocks and for the reduction of all armed forces. Most unexpected of all, the Soviets agreed for the first time to Western plans for inspections, including on-site inspections with permanent international control posts behind the Iron Curtain.

Historians would later see it as perhaps the first and last opportunity to stop the escalation of the nuclear arms race. But at the Pentagon and in CIA headquarters at Langley Field, Virginia, the news of the Russian turnabout was greeted with suspicion. Determined to preserve the U.S. advantage in the arms race, yet apprehensive that a simple rejection of apparent Soviet concessions would give the

Kremlin an immense advantage in its current "peace offensive," they agreed that the problem before them was recapturing the political initiative. It was a task that appealed to the Special Assistant for Cold War Strategy.

Nelson's first move was to assemble a large staff of technical experts, researchers, and idea men in an atmosphere of secrecy at the Marine base at Quantico. After several days of deliberations, the panel came up with the Open Skies plan, under which the Soviets and Americans would be permitted to conduct aerial surveys of each other's territories as a measure against surprise attack. It was a plan world opinion could regard as bold and generous, but which the Russians were equally bound to resist as a retreat from the concrete disarmament measures already agreed to and as a scheme that would trade away their most important asset, secrecy, for no palpable return. (At the time, the Soviets did not have a delivery system for nuclear attack against the United States, although the Eurasian landmass was ringed by U.S. air bases.) For good measure, the Quantico panel threw in a proposal for exchanging the complete blueprints of all military establishments in both countries.

A few days before the President was due to leave for the Summit, Nelson presented the Open Skies idea in a terse one-page memo. The President agreed it was a good proposal and called Rockefeller to a meeting with Secretary of State Dulles the night before they were scheduled to depart. Dulles had viewed Nelson's moves with disapproval. "He seems to be building up a big staff," he had said apprehensively to Sherman Adams. "He's got them down at Quantico, and nobody knows what they're doing." Dulles did not see any particular value in proposing a "peace" plan. In his view, the Summit should be a forum for stating the principles and commitments that made the United States an opponent of Communism, and nothing more than that. "We don't want to make this meeting a propaganda battlefield," he said, deriding Nelson's Open Skies proposal.

The days before the Summit were filled with feverish intrigue, as the State Department tried to prevent Nelson from going to Geneva just as it had previously attempted to keep him from the U.N. Conference in San Francisco. The President was finally pushed to a compromise: Rockefeller could go as far as Paris to attend the preliminary meeting of experts who would go on to the Summit, but he would not go to Geneva itself.

Once on European soil, however, Nelson began lobbying for support of the Open Skies proposal. This time there was no individual of Vandenberg's stature to lean on, but Nelson managed to enlist the support of NATO Commander General Gruenther and of Admiral Radford. On the opening day of the Summit, Premier Bulganin drew attention to the Soviet acceptance of Western disarmament proposals and called for a dramatic reduction in the conventional forces of the great powers. The next morning, Dulles received a coded cable signed by Admiral Radford strenuously urging that he adopt Rockefeller's plan as a way of salvaging the Summit. Nelson (who had spent much of the previous evening with U.S. disarmament head Harold Stassen drafting the telegram) made sure the President received a copy via his aide, Colonel Andrew Goodpaster.

Nelson was called to Geneva, where Eisenhower took up the Open Skies plan once again with Dulles. The Secretary now admitted that circumstances had made him change his mind, and the next day Eisenhower stood in the magnificent Palais des Nations, looking down at the expectant faces. Staring squarely at the Russian delegation, he summoned all his Kansas sincerity and began, "The time has come to end the Cold War," and then went on to outline the Open Skies plan. Its success was instantaneous and complete, and Eisenhower became the hero of the conference. A month later, Harold Stassen, U.S. delegate to the disarmament conference, was able quietly to withdraw all the disarmament proposals that the United States had made over the previous ten years, and which had been substantially accepted by the Soviet Union.

A few sophisticated observers criticized Rockefeller's scheme as little more than a public relations gesture. (Richard Rovere called it "an instance of Batten Barton Durstine and Osborn's intervention in world affairs.") And Dulles himself remained skeptical from another vantage point. "Geneva has certainly created problems for the free nations," he noted apprehensively in a cable to all mission chiefs upon his return. "For eight years they have been held together largely by a cement compounded of fear and a sense of moral superiority. Now the fear is diminished and the moral demarcation is somewhat blurred."

But Nelson was already moving ahead. He persuaded Eisenhower to allow him to hold another seminar at Quantico (it would be known as Quantico II) on ways of implementing the cold war advantage gained at the Summit. Yet when its 41-page memo of recommendations was presented to the cabinet, he ran into a formidable wall of opposition.* The upstaged Dulles, who agreed with him on basic policy questions, was firmly against him. So was Treasury Secretary George Humphrey, a midwestern conservative and powerful opponent of "big spending." (He had bought Dulles's massive retaliation theory, in fact, because it had been sold to him as "a bigger bang for a buck" and a way of using the nuclear threat to economize on conventional forces.) It was Humphrey who used his status as Eisenhower's personal friend to block Nelson's programs and attack his ideas for their lavishness.

In the months following Geneva, as he found Eisenhower less and less available to him, Nelson began to consider resigning as Special Assistant. Then Secretary of Defense Charles Wilson asked Rockefeller if he would like to become his Deputy. Knowing that Wilson was about to retire from the Cabinet, and seeing the possibility of positioning himself to be chosen as his replacement, Rockefeller agreed. But within a week, Wilson was calling him back to admit that the appointment had been killed by Humphrey, who had told Ike it would be wrong to put a "spender" in a key defense post. On December 31, 1955, Rockefeller's third tour of duty in Washington ended when he resigned as the President's Special Assistant for Cold War Strategy. Wars—hot, cold, and internecine—had marked the high points of his federal service.

16

BY THE MID-1950s, the United States was locked into its global crusade and the Rockefeller family was established as an important resource in the life of the nation. If it was not quite the "Rockefeller conspiracy" some charged, it did have

*Still highly classified, Quantico II's recommendations involved a virtual master plan for the future conduct of the cold war and carried a price tag of $18 billion over a six-year period.

the appearance of careful organization. Through its connections with the Chase Bank and the Standard Oil companies, and its association with such great Wall Street investment and law firms as Kuhn, Loeb; Lazard Frères; Debevoise, Plimpton; and Milbank, Tweed, the family had its fingers on the pulse of the country's industrial and financial heartlines. Through the Rockefeller Foundation, the Council on Foreign Relations, and the Republican party, it was connected to the highest directorates of national policy. Whenever members of the power elite gathered to make the crucial decisions of the postwar period, one or two of the key individuals would inevitably be drawn from the executive levels of the institutions with which the family was deeply involved. Men like John J. McCloy, C. Douglas Dillon, James Forrestal, Robert Patterson, Robert A. Lovett, the Dulles brothers, and Winthrop Aldrich were never elected to office, but wielded a power that was in many ways greater and more sustained than that of the elected officials they served. While they shaped the contours of America's postwar strategy, the policy technicians who would succeed them—individuals like W. W. Rostow, Zbigniew Brzezinski, and Henry Kissinger—were busily working their way up through the complex of international institutes and think tanks the Rockefeller Foundation had played such a key role in creating.

The very environment—social, political, and financial—in which the Rockefellers moved was made up of those individuals and institutions that constituted a privately organized system of power defining the country's economic, political, and intellectual life. For the Brothers, as for those who surrounded them, the cold war was the time when this influence became truly global. Far from the haunted decade it would seem to the critical age of the next decade, it was rather an intoxicating moment of national triumph, a time when America emerged as the premier global power and their generation got its rightful turn to remake the world in its own image. Nelson was the Rockefeller most swept up in the maelstrom of this vision and these events, most intent on occupying the absolute center, but even the brother least like him was not far away.

JDR3 had come home from wartime Washington still lean and square-jawed, although his brown hair had thinned to a widow's peak and the onset of middle age had scoured away some of the naïveté that had been so noticeable in the first years after his graduation from college. He still slouched slightly to reduce his height and make himself inconspicuous, yet he seemed less apologetic about himself than he had in the past. It was as if the modest job he had had, shuffling military papers and writing reports, had offered him an important opportunity to inventory his character. He would never have Nelson's ability to win people over by grabbing them and sharing a joke, he now understood, but if his habitual seriousness could be proposed as sincerity, it might serve him just as well in the long run.

He had never really had a chance to declare himself before the war, but had passively (almost somnambulistically, some friends of the family thought) accepted all the responsibilities thrust upon him, the mundane with the momentous. He had been puzzled and pained when Nelson went off on his own—experimenting with varieties of independence that were frowned upon as irresponsible by his father—and then came back to the family center as the prodigal whose return seemed more important than his own years of steady effort. The navy gave him the time and distance to see that this uncomfortable period of his life had lacked something. One of his closest associates says bluntly, "John was in the padded cell from 1927 to the war." When he returned, he did not intend to be straitjacketed again.

His wife helped him in this resolve. An administrator in the Museum of Modern Art (whose president she later became) once said of her: "If there was ever a natural aristocracy—I don't mean an aristocracy of money but of pure quality—Blanchette would be my candidate for queen." If this was a kind of flattery that those who had been born Rockefellers soon learned to distrust, "Mrs. John" (as the Rockefeller staff knew her) did not. She was pleased by such compliments and seemed more at home in her husband's social world than he did. She was a stately and attractive woman who could affect an almost gelid elegance on official occasions. (Such occasions would multiply after 1959, when she was elected president of the Museum of Modern Art and took a position in its matriarchy similar to that once enjoyed by her mother-in-law.) Privately, however, she was sensitive to how deeply her husband had been wounded by being the oldest of the brothers and having all the pressures of the name and few of the prerogatives. She felt the anger he would not let himself express over Nelson's usurpation and fumed over the attitude, which she saw in some of the employees in Room 5600, that JDR3 was a dull man with few ideas of his own. She pushed him forward, yet pushed so inconspicuously that he thought he was moving himself. "Much of John's development," observes Donald McLean, the florid-faced, white-haired director of Boston's Leahy Clinic who was for fifteen years JDR3's closest associate, "is a result of Blanchette's interest in his career. She didn't attempt to take over his activities; she's more subtle than that. She tried to get him out of his shell and succeeded."

Even as he reached for independence, however, he did so within the framework that Nelson had established. His hiring of McLean to advise him and head his staff was itself telling. McLean had been a rising young attorney at Milbank, Tweed, working under John Lockwood, who was already Nelson's legal counsel. For a while, McLean had done odd jobs for the family and for JDR3, but then, as he recalls, "John got ahold of me and said, 'You know me and you know my family's affairs; I'm trying to strike out on my own and I'd like to have somebody work with me in this transitional moment in my life.'" McLean went to Lockwood and asked him whether he should accept the offer. McLean had been around the Rockefeller Office enough to know that it was a "complicated place," but he was persuaded by the senior man and comforted by the knowledge that "Lockwood would be my guardian angel."

JDR3 envied Nelson's ability to unify his life so that the public and private man were welded together. Before the war, he had tried to achieve this synthesis, but always found that the one was duty-bound to do certain things the other wanted desperately to avoid. Now he decided just to accept this schizophrenia and try to make the most of it. In the partial seclusion of the rambling château he had built at Pocantico, he began to construct the emotional base he had never had as a child because of his father's high expectations and his younger brothers' effervescence. In some sense, the family he and Blanchette raised at Fieldwood Farm (a daughter, Sandra, followed by the son called "Jay," and two more daughters, Hope and Alida) was an alternative to *the* family. He built a more ceremonial residence at 1 Beekman Place in New York, where he could play the Rockefeller in the life's work he now began to seek.

It started with Asia. Originally, he had been interested in that part of the world because his father was interested in it and because he knew his father wanted him to be interested in it. Yet it had something of its own that attracted him. In 1929 he had gone to Kyoto and wandered through the temples and shrines of carved and gilded wood and sat in the ornamental gardens talking to some of the old rulers who now held court in exile in this religious center of old Japan. Just as Nelson was attracted to the spontaneous enthusiasms of the Latin temperament and its cultural *machismo,* so JDR3 seemed to find comfort in the ceremonial understatement of the Oriental character.

In the navy, JDR3 began to see the Orient less as a family charity and more as an area vital to the balance of power. He had started in the Navy Bureau of Personnel, but had been transferred first to a job with the committee coordinating the efforts of the Departments of War, Navy, and State, and then to a position as Special Assistant on Far Eastern Affairs to Navy Undersecretary Artemus Gates. His continuing concern with Asia as a sphere of the national interest was in evidence when he attended the joint conference on the Far East the War and State Departments held in Honolulu after the victory.

In the summer of 1949, as the Russians exploded their first atomic bomb and the armies of Mao Tse-tung began their final sweep toward Peking, Secretary of State Acheson appointed a three-man committee to tour Asia on a fact-finding mission. Headed by Philip Jessup of the State Department and including Raymond Fosdick (now president of the Rockefeller Foundation) and Everett Case, a director of the Institute for Pacific Relations,* the team stopped off in Saigon to bestow official recognition on the Emperor Bao Dai, whom the French had just installed as a puppet to oppose Ho Chi Minh. On returning to the United States, the team submitted its findings to a round table of China experts convened at the State Department to recommend policy toward the Chinese Communists. JDR3 was among the select group of "China hands" present.

*When the United States entered the war after Pearl Harbor, the Rockefeller institutions with expertise in Asia became valued for the intelligence they could provide. The Institute for Pacific Relations, which had been launched in 1925 at one of John Mott's YMCA conferences with Junior's financial backing, provided the core of the U.S. intelligence network in the Pacific. So extensive was its monopoly of expertise in this area that virtually all Office of Strategic Services (OSS) chiefs with jurisdiction in East Asia were IPR members. The Rockefellers minimized their connection with the institute, however, when Senator Joseph McCarthy later attacked its policies and personnel.

The issue was whether to put maximum pressure on the new regime in an effort to promote its collapse (but thereby driving it also into the arms of Russia) or to maintain diplomatic and trade links with the mainland in an effort to encourage the forces of nationalism and wean Peking from Moscow's camp. In the discussions on these questions, JDR3 participated very little; but when he did, it was to come down on the hard side: "On U.S. trade with China," he offered at one point,

> my own reaction is that it should be terminated. It seems to me that the fastest way to contain communism is to discredit it in the eyes of the people of China. It seems to me that if the economy worsens, that this will arouse opposition to it, and as I see it, the opposition is essential if new leadership is to develop in China. . . . I appreciate that withholding trade will be a source of propaganda for the Communists to use. They will say we are starving the Chinese people by not continuing our trade, but it seems to me that whatever position we take in China, the Chinese Communists will develop propaganda that will be used against us.

It was, as he added, "a negative approach to the problem in China and I dislike very much negative approaches," but it was the consensus view of the men who gathered with him in the Council on Foreign Relations, and whom JDR3 regarded as peers. The round-table group was more disparate, more academic, and less socially distinguished. Their lack of enthusiasm for the hard line disturbed JDR3, and after returning to New York, he wrote a follow-up letter to Philip Jessup, who had chaired the meeting. He noted that there seemed to be pretty general agreement that even if China was not actually controlled from Moscow, its thinking and ideology were "in tune" with the Kremlin. The "big question" that remained was, Is China different? JDR3 was concerned that many of the experts at the round-table seemed to think so. "Much of the discussion at our conference was on the basis, it seemed to me, that China is different. In this assumption justified today, when totalitarian regimes have such effective methods of control as the secret police and the tommy gun?"

If this was not the most subtle view of the factors determining China's destiny, it was to be the prevailing one for the next two decades. With the isolation and encirclement of

Mao forming the backbone of U.S. Asian policy, the pivot of Washington's strategy in the Far East fixed on Japan. The time had come to negotiate a peace treaty so that the Japanese could become partners in America's Asian security system. To make the move bipartisan, Dean Acheson assigned John Foster Dulles, Dewey's foreign policy adviser, to negotiate the peace treaty.* Dulles asked JDR3 to come along.

Petty and insensitive, Dulles would never inspire a deep sense of loyalty among most of his colleagues. Yet something like an affectionate relationship sprang up between him and JDR3. They had known each other for years, moving in the same small social world of New York's most exclusive clubs, associations, and boards of directors. Dulles had been a trustee of the Rockefeller Foundation since 1935, and after he was appointed chairman of the board in 1950, he and JDR3 saw a good deal of each other, frequently meeting in Dulles's apartment over matters like the selection of a new president. (In 1952, they would decide to give the post to Dean Rusk, who, with the Democrats out of power, was then unemployed.) Dulles may have distrusted Nelson, but he took a liking to John. Possibly he saw a potential for development in the most repressed of all the Rockefeller Brothers; he certainly realized that such a person could be useful in negotiations where a cultural and philanthropic association with the Orient would be a rare asset.

The 1951 mission to Japan was a turning point for JDR3. Yet it was not because he was introduced to high-level diplomacy or policy making. His own job, as he recalled it, was far more limited than the hard bargaining Dulles was doing:

*Sixty-three at the time he was selected for this mission, Dulles's fortunes were at a low ebb. Having been the Republican foreign affairs adviser on bipartisan policy and appointed to a vacant Senate seat by Dewey (then governor of New York), he had recently been defeated in a bid for reelection by Herbert Lehman in one of the most inflammatory campaigns in New York history—and one that harped so bitterly on the failure of the Truman administration to deal with the "red menace" that it seemed unlikely Dulles would ever recover the reputation he had formerly enjoyed as a diplomat. He had gone to Dean Rusk, then serving as an Undersecretary of State for Far Eastern Affairs, and asked him to recommend him to Acheson, who decided to select him for the mission to Japan primarily because he could disarm the McCarthyite right. Yet, as it worked out, such caution would not be necessary: after the outbreak of the Korean War, the mission to Japan became a matter of national security.

I had very little to do in terms of actual negotiations. I was operating primarily on my own, first seeing a lot of Japanese, trying to get a sense of what their feeling was, what the prospects were for the future; and having done this, beginning talks with them in terms of what steps might be initiated in order to bring our peoples closer together in a positive fashion. . . . The six weeks I was there were [spent] getting background, developing my own thinking and preparing recommendations to Dulles.

Although he went to Japan as a sort of ornament for the mission, JDR3 had been assured by Dulles that his efforts would play an important role in future U.S.–Japanese relations. The view that cultural relations were an important aspect of diplomacy had become increasingly standard in foreign policy councils since Nelson's pioneering efforts in the coordinator's office. JDR3 assembled a small staff of his own and spent several weeks in Japan talking to political and cultural leaders all over the country. Then he came home and worked on his report along with a team of experts Dulles had gotten for him on loan from the State Department. The 88-page document proposed the creation of a cultural bridge across the Pacific: exchange of university students and professors, the establishment of Japanese-American cultural centers in the United States and Japan, and a continuing exchange of leaders between the two countries.

It didn't seem like much in comparison to the top-secret talk about nuclear submarine bases, tariff agreements, and the like, but Dulles appreciated the importance of Rockefeller's findings and of the course he prescribed. After reading it, he wrote in a letter to Paul Hoffman, late of the Marshall Plan and then with the Ford Foundation: "They [the Japanese] want to be a part of the free world. It is essential from our point of view that they attain this objective. . . . One of the most important factors is that they realize our long range interest in them. In my judgement a most effective way to bring this to their attention is through non-political, non-controversial channels. I have particularly in mind the cultural. . . ."

The mission to Japan was, as JDR3 now says of it, "a major step in my independence and a major step outside the family orbit." Self and family—the Dulles mission helped solve both problems. For it emboldened JDR3 to begin a series of projects on his own, all of them informed with the spirit of an American Mission in Asia to make the Pacific a breakwater against the Communist tide through efforts in the social and cultural realms.

By providing this outlet and direction, JDR3 had an alternative to working in Room 5600 and running constantly into Nelson. For, although the tension never became public, this was a time when antagonisms were hard to contain, let alone avoid. The contact that the Brothers did have in the Brothers Fund, for instance, showed these tendencies. JDR3, as the brother publicly identified as a philanthropist, had been the Fund's president since its creation. But Nelson dominated its activities. As Donald McLean remembers, "Nelson was a big bully. He was fast on his feet and Johnny wasn't, so it turned out that all of Nelson's ideas were picked up and not so many of Johnny's. When the Fund's meetings were over, the staff would be out there working on hot tickets for Nelson, but nobody was moving merchandise for John."

One of the careers that now stretched before him was that of an unofficial ambassador at large in Japanese affairs. Shortly after finishing his report for Dulles, JDR3 received a letter from the State Department urging him to continue his efforts at building U.S.–Japanese ties from within the "private sector." The Japan Society was the perfect candidate for such help. Founded in 1907, it had been precipitously suspended during the war, but was now back in business and looking for a new president. When JDR3 was offered the position, he accepted and immediately secured Dulles's participation as chairman of a reconstituted board of directors.*

As president of the Japan Society, JDR3 hosted the first dinner for the first postwar ambassador from Japan to the United States; over the next two decades he was to entertain every Japanese Prime Minister and member of the royal family visiting the United States. Raising that part of the society's yearly budget that he didn't contribute himself, he be-

---

*A year later, he wrote a letter to his friend John J. McCloy outlining his reasons for taking on the job and urging him to join the society's work: "My own decision . . . was based on three considerations: (1) My feeling as to the great importance of Japan in relation to the whole Asian area—it seemed to me that she had very substantially the same position there that Germany does in Europe; (2) My belief that the next three to five years would be critical so far as the future of Japan was concerned—that if she could weather this period successfully she would be a constructive member of the society of free nations; (3) My belief that an agency such as the Japan Society under imaginative leadership could make a real contribution in practicing respect and understanding between our two countries."

came a familiar face not only to the Japanese business leaders and statesmen who began streaming to the United States, but also to musicians, Kabuki troupes, and No players as well. He could often be found at Japan House, his tall figure draped in a kimono, hosting a tea for visiting dignitaries. He was so completely identified with the cause of bettered U.S.–Japanese relations that when producer Josh Logan received the completed script of *Sayonara*, he sent it to Rockefeller for his comments before starting to film.

The Dulles trip had opened other areas besides Japan. One was population. Neither JDR3 nor his family were strangers to that field. In 1925, Beardsley Ruml, then director of the Laura Spelman Rockefeller Memorial Fund, had written Raymond Fosdick to suggest that it was a field in which the Rockefellers could profitably involve themselves. Nine years later, in 1934, when the Memorial and the General Education Board were merged into the Rockefeller Foundation, JDR3 wrote his father of his concern that the sex education program of the GEB was not to become part of the Foundation, and suggested that he consider supporting it by private donations. "I take the liberty of making this suggestion to you," he wrote, "because of my very great personal interest in birth control and related questions. . . . I have come pretty definitely to the conclusion that it is the field in which I will be interested, for the present at least, to concentrate my own giving."

It was not then a popular cause. The Catholic Church opposed birth control with the intensity it would later marshal against abortion. The AMA did not endorse the practice until 1937, even then stipulating that it did so only on "therapeutic occasions." Yet by the 1950s some of the stigma would be gone, especially when discussions of birth control focused on countries in the underdeveloped world. Also gone was the notion that involvement in population was somehow "unmanly." As the field grew, it would attract business and military leaders such as Hugh Moore and General William Draper, who used "population bomb" and other apocalyptic metaphors when discussing the problem.

JDR3 was instrumental in making the transition. He had come back from his 1951 trip upset by the sight of Asia's teeming masses and convinced that the stability and economic progress of the underdeveloped countries would require attention to the runaway birthrate. He understood that to accomplish this, population research would have to be established as a science with a technology that could be exported.

The Rockefeller Foundation seemed like the logical place to launch a program in the population field. In 1948 its president, Raymond Fosdick, had sent a four-man research team on a fact-finding tour of the Orient. In a cautious set of recommendations, the team called for further study rather than action; yet even their modest proposals for a future program were rejected by the Foundation board.* Now JDR3 put his proposal before the Foundation.

He was the family representative on the board of trustees, becoming its chairman in 1952 when Dulles joined the Eisenhower administration. As such, he seemed in the key position to control policy. Yet the Foundation had come far since the days when Gates had built it and Junior had run it. Now it enjoyed a great international prestige and had incalculable social and political influence in the United States and abroad. Its leaders would be sought after for high government office: Dean Rusk, who became the foundation president the year after Dulles departed, would go to Washington as Kennedy's Secretary of State; *his* successor, J. George Harrar, would be offered the post, almost as if it were the Foundation's by hereditary right, when Nixon came to power. Nelson might have been able to bend the high-level trustees (when assembled, they looked like a combined caucus of the national scientific, university, and financial establishments) to his will, but not JDR3. He was a Rockefeller who could not get backing for a program he enthusiastically supported in an institution bearing his name. Looking back at it now, he shrugs and says, "Well, I pushed the subject as far as I felt I reasonably could, but I was unable to convince them."

Such a rebuff might have crushed him a few years earlier, but the Dulles mission had increased his confidence in his own ability to get things done. He assigned Donald McLean to pursue the creation of a program of research and development to increase and disseminate knowledge about population. While his chief aide was exploring the subject with Frank Notestein and others, JDR3 had a fortuitous meeting

*Frank Notestein, who had established the pioneering Office of Population Research at Princeton in 1936, was one of the members of this team and blames the church for the Foundation's hands-off attitude: "While we were out in the field trying to figure out what *ought* to be done. Cardinal Spellman was back in New York telling the Foundation trustees what *would* be done."

with Lewis Strauss in the only place on the 56th floor of Rockefeller Center where everyone, Rockefellers and non-Rockefellers alike, was equal—the men's room just off the main corridor.

A successful investment banker at Kuhn, Loeb and one of the original members of the Atomic Energy Commission, Strauss had left the Truman administration a year earlier to come to work in Room 5600. During their brief encounter, he mentioned that he had heard JDR3 was looking for a way to raise interest in the population problem. Why not call together a conference of scientists—not just the handful of people working in demography and birth control, but leaders from the related fields of conservation, nutrition, and agriculture? "It could be put together under the aegis of the National Academy of Sciences. Det Bronk is president, and I'm sure he'll be happy to sponsor it if we give them money to do it."

After talking it over with McLean, JDR3 agreed that Strauss's proposal was a good one. By sheltering under the wing of the scientific establishment, they could involve men like Bronk (who was later president of the Rockefeller Medical Institute) and Karl Compton of MIT, while also avoiding the sensationalism that had followed the birth control movement's feud with the Catholic Church. Working with Notestein, McLean put together a list of participants, and in June 1952 the conference was held at Basset Hall in Colonial Williamsburg. It went very smoothly, as Notestein remembers: "When some of the hard-liners like Kingsley Davis tried to inject the demographic problem into the discussion in crisis terms, the scientists jumped on them and put what they said into perspective. Things never got out of hand." At the end of the meeting, Strauss and McLean moved that a foundation on population problems be created. The motion carried unanimously.

At first, JDR3 hoped that the new organization might be run through the Brothers Fund. He was its president, and it had been formed for just such experiments in "venture philanthropy." Yet, with the passing of the years, it had become more conservative in the programs it supported. The Fund had inherited the personality of Arthur Packard, who, as Junior's principal philanthropy adviser, had been more anxious not to make a mistake than to back a new venture. As he fell ill in 1952, Packard turned the reins over to Dana Creel, a soft-spoken southerner (from the same part of Georgia as Ivy Lee) who had been hired in 1940 as a contemporary of the Brothers and who could represent their view in family giving. Creel had received a law degree from Emory and had then gone on to Harvard Business School; his approach to philanthropy was both legalistic and businesslike, dedicated to not rocking the boat, which was the way Packard thought it should be.

It was not surprising, therefore, that the Brothers Fund did not undertake the population project. Creel felt it would strain the organization, while Frank Jamieson saw it as political dynamite. A lapsed Catholic, Jamieson did not worry about JDR's proposed population organization because of religious scruples; rather, he saw it through the eyes of one who hoped someday to manage a Nelson Rockefeller political campaign. As McLean put it, "Even though Frankie was supposed to be the public relations director for the whole family, Nelson was all he really cared about. He didn't want anything to happen that might hurt Nelson's chances." Once more, John 3rd was on his own.

By November 1952 he and Strauss (with McLean doing the detail work) had set up a new organization that they called the Population Council. Contributing the first year's budget of $250,000 he took on the chairmanship of the board and picked former army General Frederick Osborn to be president.* Over the next few years, as dire statistics about the "doubling rate" of global population first began to worry the American public, the "Pop Council" (as it became known) played a crucial role in creating a professional establishment in the population field. The council made grants to universities and institutes, building the work of a handful of scholars into a full-fledged academic discipline. Gradually, the effects of its pioneering work began to be felt. Six years after its launching, a State Department digest of world population trends warned that rapid population growth might

---

*Self-made financially as well as intellectually, Osborn was markedly different from his celebrated uncle, Henry Fairfield Osborn, an outspoken pro-Aryan conservationist who had conceded to Junior in a letter a few years earlier that perhaps the time had come to have an "amiable Hebrew" on the board of the New York Zoological Society. Frederick Osborn had studied eugenics and written respected books on the subject. As Frank Notestein remarked, "There had been a lot of anxiety in the Rockefeller family about the appointment. John had to find somebody who wouldn't rock the boat and yet who could step up the technical competence of the Pop Council. Osborn was the perfect man."

prove to be "one of the greatest obstacles to economic and social progress and to the maintenance of political stability in many of the less developed areas of the world." The following year, 1959, a blue-ribbon subcommittee headed by retired General William Draper surprised the Senate Foreign Relations Committee by incorporating into its report on U.S. military preparedness a statement that long-term economic aid to the underdeveloped countries would fail unless population control was part of the program. By the end of its first decade, the Pop Council's success could be measured by the fact that the population question was not only an integral part of U.S. foreign policy operations, but that almost all of the council's $15 million annual budget was carried by the Ford and Rockefeller Foundations and the U.S. Government.

About the time that JDR3 launched the Pop Council, he also created an organization called the Agricultural Development Council ("John has always been big on 'council,'" observes McLean.) It expressed that Rockefeller yearning for balance: a negative approach, like population control, ought to be offset by a more positive approach, like increasing food production. Originally called the Council on Economic and Cultural Affairs, the ADC program was directed specifically to Asia and was a technical assistance effort to disseminate the research the Rockefeller Foundation had done on the so-called "miracle grains" and to hasten the coming of the "green revolution."

By the end of the fifties, JDR3 had come a long way from the days when he was a glorified clerk to his father. He was not very well known to most Americans and there were still small humiliations, as when an edition of the *Encyclopaedia Britannica* called Nelson "the eldest son of John D. Rockefeller Junior." Yet to a well-informed few, he was becoming recognized as someone who, while possibly not possessed by spectacular intelligence, was nonetheless able to use his name and connection and his native persistence to get things done. There was no doubt that he was the central figure in the population movement, and among those who counted, he was also becoming known as "Mr. Asia" (a term the *New Yorker* coined for him). There were frequent State Department consultations and requests that he entertain visiting dignitaries. In 1953, President Eisenhower's White House chief, Sherman Adams, called JDR3 to offer him the ambassadorship to Indonesia, but he declined, firmly believing in his father's principle that the man bearing the dynastic name should be above party, place, and politics.*

Mr. Asia took his obligations seriously. Almost every year he embarked on a trip to the Orient, often an exhausting tour of several months spanning dozens of countries. For another it might have been a junket, but not for the oldest Rockefeller brother. He resolutely refused offers from the Ford Foundation and American corporations to use the hospitality houses they maintained in countries on his itinerary, preferring to endure the hardships of local hotels in an attempt to be closer to the people.

Lewis Lapham, a journalist who accompanied JDR3 on one of these trips, recalls that it was a "grinding experience." It began in Tokyo, to pay respects to old friends; went on to Hong Kong; to Taiwan, to visit a small provincial town where the Pop Council was experimenting with the IUD; to Manila, where he visited the Magsaysay Foundation, which he had helped set up, and the Rice Institute of the Rockefeller Foundation; to Bangkok for an annual meeting of the Agricultural Development Council.

"We'd be up by seven every morning," Lapham recalls, "out visiting some clinic or rural project. Then there would be a long, exhausting ceremonial lunch with some head of state. Rockefeller sat in perfect humor through several courses, never losing his graciousness. He usually retired early, leaving McLean to stay up into the late hours getting down to the nitty-gritty with the local people and telling them what, for instance, they had to do to qualify for Population Council grants."

There was a strange epiphany in the streets of Dacca, an experience that seemed to epitomize JDR3 and his sense of things. "We went through the town on a particularly hot and awful day. It was crowded, dirty, squalid, smelly, poor, and absolutely swarming with people. They were lying in the streets; it seemed as though they were practically coiled around our ankles. I'll always remember Rockefeller standing there, very tall and gaunt, sweating in his crumpled drip-dry suit and hugging his briefcase. He was shaking his head slightly, but his face was immobile. Looking down at this

---

*Also, the manner in which the offer was made didn't particularly recommend the post. "One of the things that didn't impress John," Donald McLean recalls, "is that when Sherman called, he didn't seem to know whether it was the ambassadorship to Indonesia or India he was offering, and said he'd have to call back later on when he found out."

swarm of people, he said more or less to himself and in that quiet way of his. 'Well, that's the problem, isn't it?' Then he turned and headed off for his next meeting."

As the 1950s ground to a conclusion, JDR3 had achieved a kind of liberation from his family—not so much from the myth, which he continued to uphold, but from the fact. He traced it all back to Dulles. "I wrote Foster when he was dying of cancer to tell him how much the Japan trip had meant to me," he recalls wistfully. "But he never answered. I don't know whether he even read my letter." Whether he did or not, John D. Rockefeller III was named as one of the twenty-three honorary pallbearers by the former Secretary of State's widow, and when he appeared at the funeral, he was not just someone lending his symbolic name in tribute to the dead statesman but a public personality with achievements and an identity of his own.

17

It was in October 1954 that New York real estate promoter William Zeckendorf got a long-distance phone call from Spyros Skouras, head of 20th Century-Fox studios. A friend of Howard Hughes since his early days in Hollywood, Skouras said that the bashful billionaire was considering selling all his business interests so that he could devote his time and money to medical research. "Can you find a group big enough to handle this thing?" he asked.

After a brief pause, Zeckendorf answered dramatically: "It sounds like a Rockefeller proposition to me."

Zeckendorf had first become acquainted with the family when he negotiated the sale of the United Nations site to Nelson. But the brother he now called was Laurance, who had made a name for himself by the age of forty as a shrewd investor and the Rockefeller most concerned with business.

"Do you think Hughes really means it?" Laurance had asked in his deliberate, slightly nasal voice when Zeckendorf's call reached him in Room 5600.

The real estate man confessed that he didn't know, but thought it was worth pursuing. As Zeckendorf later recalled: "Laurance was intrigued. The whole thing appealed to his sense of humor and his spirit of adventure." Rockefeller agreed to fly to California to investigate.

Not long after, he and Zeckendorf were sitting with Skouras over lunch in the terrace room of the Beverly Hills Hotel discussing the security arrangements for the meeting with Hughes. The precautions amused Rockefeller, who thought nothing of leaving his office at Room 5600 in the early afternoon, taking a brisk walk down Fifth Avenue, and ducking into some side-street coffee shop for a quick sandwich. Yet he went along with the plan: at precisely one-thirty, Skouras would leave the table and take a taxi to a predetermined location where he would be picked up and taken to Hughes; at one-fifty, Rockefeller and Zeckendorf were to follow, driving to a certain intersection where a man in a red shirt would meet them and take them on to the rendezvous in his own car.

Arriving at a large house in a residential section of a Los Angeles suburb, they were escorted to the front door by one of the young guards patrolling the property and ushered into a room where Hughes sat waiting for them. He wore wrinkled slacks, dirty tennis shoes, and a three-day beard, and had a hearing aid whose receiver he pointed in the direction of whichever person was talking. Rockefeller, in contrast, looked like a European count—lean and impeccably dressed in a double-breasted suit, his features smooth and composed, with a watchful smile tilting the corners of his mouth into a disdainful look.

It was hard to imagine that the two men could have anything in common besides their great wealth. Yet both had been connected with the beginnings of commercial aviation—Laurance as an investor in Eastern Airlines, and Hughes as the aggressive entrepreneur who had built TWA into one of the biggest companies in America, and now owned it outright. Laurance had for some time been interested in engineering a merger between Eastern and a carrier with transcontinental routes, and the possibility that TWA might be up for sale alone made the trip west worthwhile.

Yet within the first few minutes of the conversation it became clear that while Hughes the eccentric was amused by the notion of having a Rockefeller come to him and Hughes the practical businessman was anxious to know what value a person in Laurance's inside position might place on his properties, neither of his dual personalities was really interested in selling. Zeckendorf mentioned the figure of $500 million; Hughes said it was far off the mark, but refused to name the price he had in mind. Laurance icily noted that he had not come along to make money for himself, but only because Hughes had said that the proceeds to be realized from the sale would be devoted to medical research. As a trustee of the Sloan-Kettering Memorial Cancer Clinic, he was of course interested for this reason alone. The meeting broke up with both parties promising to undertake further consideration of a deal they both knew would never materialize.

JDR3 might have been annoyed had he been euchred by a man like Hughes, but not Laurance. It was an experience, a good addition to his table talk. He prided himself on being able to tell a good story as much as on his individuality and his modern style, which showed in the graceful horizontal lines of Kent House and the silver Bentley that reigned over his stable of four cars, and even in the way he sped down the Hudson River to his office at Rockefeller Center during the summers in the converted PT boat he had moored at the Pocantico estate. It was a style that was low-keyed, often skeptical, and always contemporary. Even though his wife, Mary, had become almost obsessively religious, Laurance's children (Laura, Marion, Lucy, and Laurance, Jr.) grew up in a comparatively freethinking atmosphere without the family prayers that occurred in Nelson's household or the serious talks about duty held at Fieldwood Farm. It was a style that was introspective, remote, and—for the Rockefellers—uncharacteristically intellectual. Laurance was alone in being able to answer a question about one of his family with a *bon mot* that gracefully turned a defect into a virtue. (He once said of the underachieving Winthrop: "His continuity is the common man." And in defense of the hyperkinetic Nelson: "He's forever acting on his environment.") Sometimes, in fact, he seemed more style than substance.

Before the war his path had seemed less definite than any of his brothers'. But the time he served in the navy gave him an insight into investment opportunities that would be in the "national interest" as well as in his own. He had spent most of the war overseeing patrol plane assembly lines on the West Coast for the Bureau of Aeronautics. Then, a few months before Hiroshima, he was transferred to the Fighter Desk. He used this vantage point to help enterprises like the McDonnell Company, which he had become involved with before the war.* When J. S. McDonnell had heard that Laurance was conferring with Navy Secretary James Forrestal about a job overseeing production of naval aircraft, he wrote urging him to put in a good word about their joint venture. "Our company likes competition," his letter stated, "but during the emergency, we can service the Navy with the least waste of man hours, if the Navy could tell us person to person what new design of airplane they need most."†

Laurance may already have known about Forrestal's intention to get a commitment from Congress for postwar armaments while the war was still providing emotional leverage, but even if not, he had seen airplanes and other weapons on the drawing boards capable of revolutionizing not only warfare but the economy and possibly society itself. In order to have the sort of "preparedness" the military brass was pushing for (complementing the efforts of men like Senator Vandenberg and his own brother Nelson in international politics), the government could not wait for research and development to occur spontaneously. It would have to underwrite the costs and support the wartime mobilization on an ongoing basis into the postwar world.

He had set an explorer's foot on that virgin ground

---

*In fact, the future was writ small in the explosive career of the company he had helped begin in 1939. Carrying a staff of 15 when the war broke out, the McDonnell corporation had more than 5,000 workers when the fighting ended and had established itself as a center of research into jet propulsion. In 1943 the company got a contract to build the first carrier-based jet fighter, the FH-1 Phantom; it had completed its maiden take-off and landing from the deck of the U.S.S. *Franklin D. Roosevelt* by January 1946. Even before the Phantom had been deployed, McDonnell was already making it obsolete with a faster and deadlier successor—the Banshee, which would be the navy's workhorse jet during the Korean War. And by the time the last Banshee had left the flight ramp at the St. Louis plant, McDonnell had secured a contract for the Demon, the first navy fighter of the new era, with guns eliminated in favor of guided missiles.

†Laurance disposed of his entire holdings of McDonnell stock early in 1945, when he was moved to the Fighter Desk. When released from active duty, he had reacquired 73,000 shares (20 percent of the common) at a cost of $405,000. In 1946, government investigators contacted the McDonnell Corporation to inquire if Laurance had been influential in contracts awarded them. For a time it seemed that there might be an investigation, but when both McDonnell and Laurance wrote letters denying wrongdoing, the matter was dropped.

President Eisenhower would later name the military-industrial complex, and it left an impression on him. Like Nelson, whose lead he continued to follow, he made the transition from the World War to the cold war almost without taking time to discover that peace had broken out. ("I've never really demobilized," he later commented to a *Time* correspondent who asked about his peacetime contacts with the navy.)

McDonnell was only one of Laurance's links into the new military age. In 1946 the navy approached him with a problem. A helicopter company, which had been founded by Frank Piasecki, the son of an immigrant Polish tailor, and had received a contract to build twenty small craft in 1943, was foundering. Could Laurance help? After investigating, Laurance decided the company needed more capital and a firmer business hand. He agreed to head a consortium that included his friends C. Douglas Dillon and A. Felix Du Pont, and that purchased 51 percent of the Piasecki stock for $500,000. By the time war broke out in Korea, they had put Piasecki on a firm financial footing, and when a company representative went to the battle zone and was able to convince army generals that a helicopter his company had just built for arctic rescue under contract to the air force could easily be converted to use in troop transport, Piasecki became an important factor in the era of "limited war."

Investments in other young corporations with strategic potential soon followed. The navy was interested in Reaction Motors, a New Jersey company involved in classified research on liquid fuel rocketry. Like Piasecki Helicopter, it had fine engineering capabilities, but poor administration. Laurance purchased 21 percent of the company for $500,000 and sent his aides in to strengthen its managerial core. He also picked up a 20 percent interest in Marquardt Aircraft, which built ramjets; a 27 percent interest in Wallace Aviation, which built jet engine blades; a 30 percent interest in Flight Refueling; 24 percent of Airborne Instruments Laboratory; and 24 percent of Aircraft Radio, which specialized in electronic equipment.

To see his investments through what he called their "ten-year risk cycle," he assembled a group of employees to watch over his ventures and make them pay off. Names like Harper Woodward (a former secretary to the president of Harvard) and Teddy Walkowitz (a former air force R&D officer with strong scientific contacts) were not household words, even on Wall Street; but observers soon learned that their presence on a board of directors ("An Associate of Laurance S. Rockefeller" was how they indicated their affiliation) more likely than not meant that the company was young, that it had just had an infusion of Rockefeller capital, and that its new managerial team was hustling for government contracts while the directors were looking in a more leisurely way for an attractive merger with a larger company.

Laurance's associates were different from the employees the other Brothers had brought into Room 5600. They did not concern themselves with family policy or even with the personal career of their employer. They were money men, technicians who looked after Laurance's investments (as well as other family holdings) as his eyes and ears, bringing proposals for involvement in what they called "new horizons products"—the new technology ranging from optics to the computer science nurtured by fallout from the defense industry.

A rumor later circulated through Room 5600 that some associate of Laurance's had once turned down a bid to become involved in the early stages of Xerox. Whether or not this was true, most of their intuitions were sound.* In the early 1950s, even before the Atomic Energy Commission unveiled its blueprint for the peaceful use of the atom, Laurance's associates had convinced him to buy 17 percent of a young company called Nuclear Development Associates, which began work in nuclear fuels technology in anticipation of the day when there would be wide deployment of reactors. And in 1957 they convinced him to invest in a new Boston engineering firm called Itek, which would turn out to be one of the most phenomenal growth companies of the period.

He benefited enormously from contacts (his family's and his own) in government and finance, yet Laurance still prided himself on being the sort of man who could have made it even if he hadn't been named Rockefeller. And while he generally seemed to feel less of what he called the "missionary impulse" than his two older brothers (the extravagance of the family's rhetoric about itself, in fact, seemed to

---

*In 1950, however, he made a big mistake by selling off his shares in McDonnell. He made some $8 million on his $400,000 investment, but the company (whose sales were then at the $20 million mark) was just beginning its corporate climb. Eventually it would merge with Douglas Aircraft and become one of the three top defense contractors in the country, a multibillion-dollar giant in which Laurance's original interest would have been worth many times the profit he took.

embarrass him), he was involved in the dialogue about the direction the third Rockefeller generation should take. As in other things, he supported Nelson's view that the family should try to expand its influence: and he felt that the best contribution he could make would be financial—not only because the fortune had diminished from the time when Junior first began to disperse it ("We just don't have money the way people *used* to have it," Laurance once remarked with half-serious irony), but also because he felt that the technological advances of the postwar period would mean new centers of power with which the Rockefellers had to connect themselves if they were not to become a second-rate family.

Business, family, and mission had appeared to converge for Laurance in 1945 with the formation of Rockefeller Brothers, Inc. Although the New York *Daily News* greeted the announcement of the new enterprise with one of its trademark headlines ("Rock Mob Incorporates"), it described itself as "a holding company for ideas" and as "an attempt to achieve social and economic progress as well as a fair profit," with each brother investing an equal share of the $1.5 million initial capitalization.

Yet in Laurance's project, the crusading aspect was subordinated. Randolph Marston, one of his aides, wrote an executive of the Chase Bank: "This is just to give you an idea of the fields of investment currently of interest to the Rockefeller Brothers Company. The primary interest is in matters of aeronautical or air transport industries: other items of interest [include] industrial developments in foreign countries close to raw materials sources, particularly where there is an opportunity to produce something of real social benefit." For Laurance, the company never distinguished itself from his other venture capital projects.

One of its biggest projects came after Laurance sent a consultant to the Belgian Congo, the most fabled raw materials source and most notorious colony in Africa, "to make a study of the factors which relate to the establishment of a cotton textile mill. . . ." When the consultant was finished with his investigation, he reported back that labor was cheap (between 5 and 7 cents an hour) and that cotton could be obtained at half the U.S. price. Laurance then founded *Filatures et Tissages Africains* together with Belgian entrepreneurs (who controlled 60 percent of the stock) and family friend C. Douglas Dillon. A prefabricated mill was shipped from South Carolina, native labor was hired, and the company began production in 1955. It soon was making profits and having an impact on the consumption patterns of a select few Congolese who were in the money economy. "It was interesting to watch the changes as the women became style conscious," remarked one Rockefeller associate. "It seemed just like Fifth Avenue."

Other personal investments in the Congo followed: in Cegeac (an automobile distributor) in which Dillon also had a small share, Cobega (a metal can company), Anacongo (a pineapple processor), and Cico (a cement firm). But the investments—unlike the IBEC projects in Latin America—were never "political" in the sense that they would have been if Nelson had been involved: most of the holdings were sold in the first tumultuous days of Congolese independence.

Rockefeller Brothers, Inc., was only the first of several vehicles that Laurance would create over the years in order to guarantee that the family participated in new and potentially important business enterprises. Although modest in scope, this development was actually a significant change in the identity of the family. In Junior's time, the financial aspect of the office had been carefully controlled, reflecting his recognition that making money was a dangerous occupation for a Rockefeller. (The ritual emphasis on "fair" profit and social benefits in the public relations of RBI and other business projects in which the brothers engaged was a partial homage to this fact.) In the old days, the investments had been handled conservatively and discreetly; when a man like Bertram Cutler sat on a board representing Rockefeller interests, it was almost always a defensive maneuver designed to protect an old investment rather than to extend a new one. Laurance, however, had managed to place the financial concern at the core of the office, where it had been in his grandfather's day.

JDR3, who saw philanthropy getting shunted to the background, did not really approve of this new emphasis, and Winthrop, as he became more deeply mired in his personal problems and withdrew to Arkansas, ceased to participate very actively in RBI ventures. But Laurance had long ago understood that the momentum of the third Rockefeller generation would have to come from a triangulation of his interests and abilities with those of Nelson and David. Neither of them had any qualms about the fact the Family Office was undergoing a subtle change of character that would make it into an efficient money-making machine. Less involved in public affairs than the the the other Brothers, Laurance came to be the one in charge of Room 5600.

Bertram Cutler, who in 1902 had entered the office at 26 Broadway as a bookkeeper and stayed on to manage the family investments, was one of the old guard the Brothers retained both because they were valuable repositories of information and because of their longstanding loyalty to Junior. Yet, long before Cutler's retirement in 1951, Laurance, on the lookout for his replacement, was searching for a man who could oversee the development of the kind of office he had in mind. He thought he had found him, in fact, when he hired Lewis Strauss in 1950.

Strauss (he insisted on the pronunciation *Straws*, his detractors claimed, to deemphasize his Jewish origins) had a career that spanned two generations and several professions. He had served as secretary to Herbert Hoover during World War I and, while in France, had met Mortimer Schiff. scion of the Kuhn, Loeb banking dynasty who invited him to join the firm in New York. By 1928 Strauss had become a full partner in the investment bank. He had gone on to serve on the finance committee of the Du Ponts' U.S. Rubber Company (later Uniroyal), helped George Eastman patent and market the Kodachrome process, and backed the early inventions of Dr. Edward Land, the inventor of the Polaroid camera. An officer in the naval reserve (the navy was *de rigueur* for anyone with upper-class pretensions), he went into active duty after Pearl Harbor. Under the patronage of fellow Wall Streeter James Forrestal, he had risen to a position of influence in the Department of the Navy and was promoted to rear admiral two months after Hiroshima.

It was Strauss, as Laurance well knew, who had been instrumental in convincing Forrestal to ask Congress for postwar military appropriations in 1944 while wartime emotions were still high. Pointing out that the Allies were entitled to Germany's scientists and scientific advances as legitimate spoils of war, Strauss had managed to get a Naval Technical Mission sent into Germany on a talent-scouting expedition even before the surrender. When the war was over, he was appointed to the first Atomic Energy Commission and, before his resignation in 1950, had almost single-handedly convinced President Truman to overrule the majority of the AEC and proceed with the development of the hydrogen bomb.

Choosing the Office of the Messrs. Rockefeller (as Room 5600 was now called) for his return to private life, Strauss took over the Office Management Committee, a sort of executive group running the many operations. With his dual personality as an investment banker and former government adviser, Strauss was admirably suited both to oversee the growing portfolio of Rockefeller Brothers, Inc., and to suggest new areas where investment might intersect with trends in defense planning and spending. Strauss also went on the board of Rockefeller Center, the Brothers' most valuable joint asset, and spent much of 1952 in intricate negotiations with Columbia University for a renewal of the Center's lease. Although generally regarded as Laurance's aide, Strauss was a resource for all the Brothers. When JDR3 decided to move into population, Strauss was crucial in lining up the scientific establishment behind him. When the Chase Bank became the first to begin investigating the future field of atomic energy and investing in reactors, one of Strauss's old friends from the Manhattan Project, physicist Laurance Hafstad, came in to head the new division.

Strauss did not last long in Room 5600, leaving the Rockefellers in 1953 when Eisenhower called him back to Washington as chairman of the AEC in the new administration. But even in the brief time he was there, he had shown how necessary it was for there to be a strong man of the Brothers' age and outlook inside the office in a financial capacity. While a visionary entrepreneur (Gates) had been the main adviser to John D. Rockefeller, Sr., and a conservative attorney (Debevoise) to Junior, for the third generation it would be a financial man. After Strauss's departure, Laurance and David went on a talent hunt for a long-term replacement, finally settling in 1957 on a young Kuhn, Loeb investment banker named J. Richardson Dilworth. With Frank Jamieson and John Lockwood, Dilworth became part of a troika guiding the family, although it was clear that someday he would be the central power in Room 5600.

At the end of his "ten-year cycle," Laurance's venture capitalism began paying off according to schedule. The companies he had become involved in were now strong enough to be attractive merger possibilities. At about the same time that Piasecki Helicopter was bought up by Boeing, Reaction Motors was becoming part of Thiokol. Some of the maneuvers were more complex. In 1950, Laurance had bought 85 percent of Marquardt Aircraft. Four years later he sold enough of his stock to Olin Mathiesen to give them 25 percent of

Marquardt and him a seat on the Olin board. From this vantage point, he was able to help bring Olin Mathiesen's Chemical Division together with another of his investments, Nuclear Development Associates, to form United Nuclear, the largest private fuel business in the country.*

Yet there was no overarching strategy to these mergers, no effort to pyramid his holdings into a controlling position in the aircraft or defense industry. The pursuit of monopoly was a tabooed activity for a grandson of the first John D. The mergers he chose were generally with corporations too large for his own companies to be a significant factor in their future. Moreover, he usually liquidated his holdings after realizing a respectable profit. But in the case of Itek, which overnight became the premier developer of aerial reconnaissance and surveillance technology (providing the cameras for the U-2 planes and spy satellites) and reached the prestigious ranks of the Fortune "500" within the decade with over $100 million in annual sales, he didn't liquidate at all.

Itek was the first company that Laurance had gotten in on at the point of origin (on the advice of Teddy Walkowitz, he had put $750,000 in the Massachusetts firm shortly after incorporation), and it dramatically illustrated the peculiar caprice of success in the venture capital trade. For Itek had been conceived by its founders and sold to Laurance as a firm which would develop a version of the Kodak minicard for information retrieval in large libraries—a technology that had nothing to do with aerial reconnaissance, and which was never commercially developed. "The success of Itek," as former Vice-President Dr. Duncan ("Dunc") MacDonald, one of the firm's three founders (and a physicist who had headed a team working on aerial reconnaissance for the National Defense Research Committee during World War II), said, "came entirely from unplanned areas of operations."

The month after Itek was founded, MacDonald went on a trip to St. Louis to deliver a scientific paper and, on his return, decided to stop off at CIA headquarters in Langley Field, Virginia, for the odd purpose of picking up a fishing pole he had left there. (As a member of the air force Science

---

*As John Menke, head of United Nuclear, recalled: "Rockefeller and his associates were interested in what they saw as a wide open technology. They were instrumental in getting us together with the Olin people. They thought forming United Nuclear would make a profitable addition to the economy, but they were also interested in making a good profit. And they did."

Advisory Board and an export on optics and surveillance technologies, he was a frequent visitor.) While there, he received a phone call from his successor as head of the Boston University Physics Research Laboratory (which he had founded at the air force's request at the end of World War II to house its expertise in aerial reconnaissance). The caller told MacDonald that the cost-conscious Eisenhower administration had just given the government-created and -funded laboratory thirty days' notice that its contract was being terminated. The date was October 4, 1957, and the Russians had just launched the first earth satellite, Sputnik. MacDonald, knowing that the government would reverse itself, hurried back to Massachusetts to convince his colleagues to acquire the Research Laboratory for Itek. "Within six months," he said, "Itek had a three- or four-million-dollar backlog in government contracts, and we were going public on a rights offering at thirty bucks a share."

Up to this time, Laurance and his associates had remained well in the background, appointing a board of directors and insisting only that they approve the company treasurer. But now things began to happen. Laurance brought in Franklin Lindsay, a former CIA administrator whom Nelson had met in the first Quantico seminar, to head the company, firing the two other men who had joined MacDonald to found Itek. A new conservative program of acquisition and development was implemented. "As soon as the chips began to get worth something," recalls MacDonald somewhat ruefully, "the management was recycled and there was a shift to the principle of conservation rather than the innovative spirit that had made the company zoom. It became a company of skilled managers, but they had no idea of what they were managing."

In his first decade and a half of venture capitalism, Laurance had parlayed a $9 million investment into $40 million. While an increase of capital four and a half times was more than respectable, he could not help reflecting on the fact that the much larger amounts he had left in the blocs of conservative Socony Oil stocks had increased three times in the same period without any effort at all on his part. If, on the other hand, he attempted to measure his achievement by the fact that a high percentage of his investments were successful—that he had, as he said often, a ".900 batting average"—he came up against the awareness that what might be a gamble for an ordinary man could easily become a sure thing when a

Rockefeller exerted the force of his name, his connections, and his capital on it.

Laurance had reached a climax in his career. As a Rockefeller, he couldn't afford to go out aggressively and make a lot of money or reach for vast corporate influence. But as a member of the third generation of a public dynasty, he couldn't be totally happy in his accustomed position behind the scenes. By the end of this ten-year cycle, he began to move away from business in search of a field that would offer a better footing to build the public personality that every son of John D. Rockefeller, Jr., had to have.

It was natural that he should look to conservation. He had grown up more interested in the outdoors than his brothers, more aware of his father's contributions to the National Park Service as well. The men who were his father's chief advisers in conservation matters, Horace Albright and Fairfield Osborn (son of the New York Zoological Society's Henry Fairfield Osborn, "Fair" was author of the influential book *Our Plundered Planet* and considered the leading conservationist of his day), were his mentors as well. He would later tell his children that these two men, along with Captain Eddie Rickenbacker, had a greater influence on his career than anyone else.

In 1947 Laurance had become head of Jackson Hole Preserve, Inc., the foundation his father had established to pursue his conservation interests; the same year he helped Fairfield Osborn start the Conservation Foundation, soon to be one of the most prestigious organizations in the field. At the time, his involvement was limited because his own interests and the nation's had intersected in his venture capital investments. While it appeared that conservation was a good philanthropy (like his work as a trustee of the Sloan-Kettering Memorial Cancer Clinic), it did not seem important enough to warrant more than his passing interest.

At the beginning of the fifties, however, conservation had been dramatically elevated in the scale of national interests. The anxiety caused by the outbreak of the Korean conflict and continuing polarization of the world into two armed camps had created a near hysteria around the question of whether America's raw materials were sufficient to meet the coming crisis, particularly in view of the nationalist turmoil and neutralist tendencies of Third World countries. Nelson had warned of the future importance of the resources of the Third World countries ("Of the critical and strategic materials upon which armaments depend. they supply three-quarters of all United States imports"). Now his words were being echoed in the highest councils of state. In 1951, Truman appointed a blue-ribbon Presidential Commission on Materials Policy under the chairmanship of CBS head William Paley to study the country's present and future needs, not ruling out the possibility of war, and to make recommendations for policy. Along with Horace Albright, Nelson appeared before the commission to testify on the crisis.

The commission report, published in June 1952, as *Resources for Freedom*, began with a question: "Has the United States of America the material means to sustain its civilization?" Much of the five-volume work was a detailed inventory of each strategic resource located in the underdeveloped countries, which. in the words of the report, offered the best solution to the U.S. problem because they are blessed with "rich and relatively undeveloped natural resources often far in excess of their prospective needs." At home, the study called for an opening up of U.S. resources and federal lands to private industry, inveighing against "the hairshirt concept of conservation which makes it synonymous with hoarding. A sound concept of conservation, in view of this commission, is one which equates it with efficient management—efficient use of manpower and materials: a positive concept compatible with growth and high consumption in place of abstinence and retrenchment."

Laurance and his associates were enthusiastic about the conclusions of *Resources for Freedom*—by adding a national security component to the field of conservation, it had made it worthy of attention—and they joined the chorus of those who made the control of raw materials sources seem like a necessary preparation for Armageddon. Fairfield Osborn, who was awarded the Theodore Roosevelt Distinguished Service Medal a few weeks after the appearance of the Paley commission report, began his acceptance speech this way:

> We Americans do not even yet sufficiently realize that Conservation, meaning actually the intelligent use and development of national resources, must come to be thought of as essential to any national defense program. By this I do not mean merely military defense but the defense of every value that makes American life what it

is. It is a provable fact that no people, either throughout history or in modern times, can retain the qualities of inward strength or world influence if their resources fail them. As a present day example, the leadership of Great Britain has gone into eclipse because she no longer can depend upon the resources that were drawn from her colonial empire.

In December 1953 the Ford Foundation continued the dialogue by convening a Midcentury Conference on Resources for the Future. After President Eisenhower had greeted the 1,600 delegates, a working paper prepared by the Brookings Institution was passed around. "Can world development of resources keep pace in the long run with the growing needs of the American economy?" it asked. "To what extent will the aspirations and mounting requirements of people in other countries permit United States industry to attract as large a share of total production of raw materials as is now the case? What are the security implications of dependence on distant supplies and vulnerable supply routes?"

One of the results of the conference was Ford's decision to underwrite an ongoing organization to develop policy on resource issues and then make sure that this policy stayed in the frontal lobe of Washington's consciousness. Resources for the Future (as the organization was called) provided a think-tank atmosphere where social scientists could discuss pollution of the waterways of the Pacific Northwest one day and the extraction of raw materials from Southeast Asia the next. RFF stood on the crest of a wave. Not long after it was set up, in fact, President Eisenhower defended the new U.S. commitment in South Vietnam because it was first in a row of dominoes, and because "two of the items from this particular area that the world uses are tin and tungsten. They are very important. There are others, of course, the rubber plantations and so on."*

World resources loomed large in the deliberations of Resources for the Future (which invited Laurance to join its

*Resources for the Future was also the locus for an almost incestuous intermingling of the men who made up the Rockefellers' conservation family. "Fair" Osborn was on the original board of directors; when he resigned in 1953, the ubiquitous Beardsley Ruml took his seat. Horace Albright (of whom Laurance once said, "He is to our projects what yeast is to bread," adding the witty afterthought, "And father provided the dough") was chairman of the RFF board for its first half-dozen years.

board in 1958), but it was also interested in changes taking place in American society itself, notably the postwar affluence that had given the middle class the mobility and leisure previously reserved for the rich. This development was also the talk of the clubs and associations to which the Rockefellers belonged. But while some members may have fretted with a Tory hauteur about this invasion of their sanctuaries, Laurance was intrigued by the opportunity it offered to combine his entrepreneurial past with his conservation future. Claiming that he was interested in the art "of bringing man and nature together harmoniously," he began plans for a series of exclusive resorts in wilderness areas that had been too distant from the cities until the debut of the long-range commercial jets Eastern and other airlines were beginning to fly.

The seeds of the plan had been sown in 1951 by "Bee" Ruml, who at the time was the only North American on the Industrial Development Board that ran Puerto Rico's Operation Bootstrap, then trying to lure U.S. industry onto the island through "tax holidays" and an abundance of cheap labor. In his travels around Puerto Rico, Ruml discovered the beautiful Livingston estate on the beaches west of San Juan. The University of Puerto Rico was interested in converting the area into a botanical garden, but Ruml had an alternate plan—to develop the Livingston property under the aegis of Bootstrap into a large resort with golf courses and swimming beaches. He went to Laurance with the idea, and Laurance commissioned a study of the possibilities. When he received favorable recommendations, he went ahead with the construction of the elegant Dorado Beach Hotel, completed in 1956 at a cost of $9 million.

As a Rockefeller, he could not help having great peripheral vision, seeing as simultaneous developments what others would regard as unconnected incidents. For him, each venture led logically to the next; one field merged with its opposite. When he heard that the Caneel Bay Plantation, an exclusive resort on Saint John (most unspoiled of the U.S. Virgin Islands), was available, he bought it for $600,000 and immediately began purchasing the lands surrounding it. As in his father's decision decades earlier to protect his pristine Seal Harbor retreat by donating lands that became the nucleus of Acadia National Park, Laurance's decision to buy up the properties surrounding his resort was both a philanthropic gesture that would make the beautiful Saint John one of the jewels of the national park system and a pragmatic means of protecting an investment. By 1955, his Jackson Hole Preserve, Inc., had spent over $2 million assembling nearly 6,000 acres, which Laurance then turned over to the Department of the Interior. The Virgin Islands National Park was unveiled the following year in ceremonies that coincided neatly with the formal opening of the refitted Caneel Bay Plantation resort.

Laurance had inherited his father's need to see his character reflected in the buildings he placed on the landscape, and he was also heir to Junior's genuine, if somewhat abstract, love of the outdoors. Each summer Laurance took his family to his JY Ranch in the Grand Tetons. And while he personally was more comfortable sitting on a patio gazing up at the awesome mountains than hiking along their trails, the "renewing" quality of nature brought out the philosophical tendencies of his college days. "Close to nature," he said, "people find a mystical, almost physical kind of rapport. It is uplifting and creative."

In addition to its aesthetic dimension and its social and financial possibilities, however, the revitalized field of conservation filled a personal need. For years Laurance had been comfortable in the anonymity that allowed him to work behind the financial scenes. He had been successful, but not in the same way as his brothers. For the first time in his life, he felt the itch for the kind of achievement that would bring public recognition. This impulse had something to do with a biological clock—his fiftieth year was in sight—but it was even more the result of membership in a family that had come to depend on a certain annual quota of complimentary inches in *The New York Times* as an indication that it was doing right.

Characteristically, this did not manifest itself as some dramatic inner turbulence, self-doubt, or psychological crisis, but rather as a routine change in agenda in which conservation was elevated to the top of his priorities. As with other decisions, such a step was preceded by a study. At about the same time that unique Virgin Islands Park was being dedicated, Rockefeller aide Kenneth Chorley commissioned the public relations firm of Earl Newsome to conduct a study of the role Jackson Hole Preserve, Inc., might play in the growing conservation movement. The exhaustive report began by pointing out that the average American was on the verge of a momentous increase in leisure and income: "The trend is such that if some leadership does not emerge to provide the climate and facilities to make the most of the leisure, it could well turn out to be a besetting social problem." As a result, conservation would become important, although there was no "responsible" organization presently capable of exerting leadership. The sprinkling of small groups like the Sierra Club could be discounted because their existence was based on the voluntary membership of "zealots who characteristically become preoccupied with their individual view of the problem."

The Newsome study concluded that Jackson Hole Preserve, Inc., should change its name and attempt to move into a leadership position to give coherence to the developing conservation movement, because it "brings to the field a specific and positive experience . . . [and] has a record of known and valued achievement." More important, it reflected the personality "of the man who in his time has done more than any other individual to help. There is little likelihood that he will have an individual counterpart in the future."

Laurance was not inclined to reject a flattery that so coincided with his desire to play a public role as a "citizen-conservationist." Out of deference to the historical role Jackson Hole Preserve had played, he did not change its name. Instead, he created a new organization, the American Conservation Association. By 1958, his *curriculum vitae* was weighted toward his new career. He was a commissioner of the Palisades Park, a director of the Hudson River Conservation Society, and a trustee of the Conservation Foundation and the New York Zoological Society, as well as a director of Resources for the Future. His baptism into the world of official studies and commissions came this same year, when President Eisenhower selected him for his first important government post, head of the Outdoor Recreation Resources and Review Commission, which was to determine the nation's recreation needs to the year 2000. With this, the Rockefeller brother who had once humorously referred to his lack of a public voice by calling himself "the Harpo Marx of the family," was in a position to make a serious bid for fame.

18

FOR THE FIRST TEN YEARS of his career, he followed the same
morning ritual as other rising young executives—a quick
series of calisthenics, a light breakfast of toast, bacon, and
coffee, and then the brisk walk from his four-story red brick
town house on the upper east side to the Lexington Avenue
subway. Tall, looking heavier than he actually was, he would
have been easily reconizable to other junior executives riding
the IRT—not by name perhaps, but by such symbols of office
as the bulging attaché case, the *Wall Street Journal* tucked
under his arm, and the unvarying uniform of dark suit, white
shirt with a suspicion of starch at the collar, and shined (but
not shiny) wing-tip shoes. With the long nose poking outward, the round face was the sort that might have had a
jester's good humor if it had belonged to another man. But it
was the face of David Rockefeller, commercial banker, whose
philosophy of life was summed up in a comment he once
made to his oldest son: "Whatever you do, if you do it hard
enough you'll enjoy it. The important thing is to work and
work hard."

David had done just that, beginning his career (as Junior
proudly noted) "at the bottom." In 1946, while his brothers
were vying for position in the Family Office, he began work
in the foreign department of the Chase as an assistant manager, lowest of the junior executive positions. Two years later,
as a second vice-president, he was in charge of the bank's
business in Latin America, opening branches in Cuba, Puerto
Rico, and Panama, and starting an influential financial quarterly, *Latin American Highlights.* By 1952, he was one of six
senior vice-presidents of the Chase (although not yet a director like his brother Laurance, who was the only man under
fifty on the board).

In 1955 he became executive vice-president, and a year
later received his most important promotion—to the vice-
chairmanship of the Chase board. In addition to its other ad-

vantages, this position meant a full-time chauffeured limousine and the end to subway rides at rush hour. He could have bought such service anytime he wanted it, of course, but David had learned the unwritten law that unearned luxury was damaging to one's career, if not one's self-image.

It was a swift rise for a man barely forty years old, really more the grooming of an heir apparent than a Horatio Alger success story; still, it was not so swift that it could be said to have occurred *only* because of nepotism. With his youth, intelligence, and his Ph.D. in economics, David was exactly the sort of man (regardless of his name) that banks look for. While he did not plan to subject himself to the whole tedious process of rising through the ranks, he knew that he would never have the authority he wanted if he appeared to be merely the owner's son, and so he had made sure to pay his dues, for others' benefit if not his own. He had worked patiently in all the major areas of the bank (except for the relatively arcane world of trusts), including such unexciting departments as economic research and customer relations. Even though his own interests were strongly centered in international banking, he spent time organizing a metropolitan department and pushed for an expansion into branch banking. The Chase had previously ignored such innovation, concentrating instead on corporate and foreign business. In the intense competition for the saver's dollar that characterized the postwar banking world, the Chase had fallen from first to third position, disadvantaged by the fact that all but two of its twenty-eight branches were in Manhattan. Deciding to solve the problem through merger, it set its sights on the Bank of the Manhattan Company, only fifteenth in size but strongly represented by branches in the other boroughs of the city.* John J. McCloy, who handled the Rockefeller account at Milbank, Tweed and became chairman of the Chase board in 1953 when Winthrop Aldrich was appointed U.S. ambassador to England, used all his legal skill to bring the merger off, and in 1955 the new Chase Manhattan made its debut as the largest bank in the country.

David was only one of four executive vice-presidents in the newly merged institution, yet there was no doubt as to his fu-

*The Manhattan Company had been founded by Aaron Burr, Alexander Hamilton, and other leading citizens in 1799 to pipe fresh water into New York during a yellow-fever epidemic. Afterward its charter was expanded to include banking, and it was at the time of the merger the oldest bank in the United States.

ture. "Among the top men," commented *Business Week* at the time of the merger, "it is David Rockefeller who is heir apparent." Some of his colleagues may have seen that his almost perpetual smile had an element of the clenched jaw, but most simply accepted him as an inevitability. He accented the distance that naturally separated him from others by standing behind a polite yet awesome reserve that led one co-worker to refer to him as "the phlegmatic forty-year-old." He did not have Nelson's ability to simulate warmth and familiarity ("No one, and I mean *no one*, calls David Rockefeller 'Rocky,' " a Chase exec once admonished a newsman who had committed this unforgivable gaffe), yet he shared his older brother's Aldrich metabolism that allowed him to work all day, come home and change clothes, and then spend almost every evening in the entertaining that made him such an important asset to the bank.

Sometimes his activities stretched the working day to eighteen hours. "I'm appalled that anyone would want to work that hard," a Chase vice-president said. "If you were to see his schedule when he is attending the American Bankers' Association convention, you wouldn't believe it. I looked at it and told myself that if I were David Rockefeller, I'd just hand it back to the secretary. It would be difficult to find time to go to the bathroom." Yet no one pushed harder for the jammed routine than David himself. In rising to power at the bank, he had come to see himself as a "self-made man." Even his wife, Peggy, most critical and independent of all the Rockefeller wives, brought their children up to feel that they were different from their cousins because their father was the only Rockefeller who "had a profession."

As he grew older, David reminded family friends more and more of his father. He was methodical, orderly, reasonable, less excited by exercises of the imagination than by facts and blueprints. And there was something almost Victorian in his willful desire to leave the verities unchallenged. Although he eventually became a leading figure in the Museum of Modern Art (his involvement began when he asked MOMA President Alfred Barr to decorate his town house with some paintings that would provide an "esthetically stimulating" environment for his children), and would eventually assemble one of the finest collections of post-Impressionist paintings in the world, David's early interest was in collecting Chinese porcelains like those he had seen Junior spend hours admiring, arranging, and cataloguing at his Park Avenue apartment. He had also inherited his father's interest in real estate and building, and in seeing his will exemplified in the changes he could make on the face of a city. Unencumbered by qualms about his role or doubts about the family mission, in time he would become the complete Rockefeller.

In the general division of responsibility that ensued when Junior turned over to his sons the institutions he had built and the interests he had developed, David's combination of seriousness and competence made him the logical brother to take on the chairmanship of the Institute for Medical Research, perhaps the family's proudest creation. In 1950 he succeeded his father as its president, and in 1953 he surrendered that position to become chairman of the board. The vacant office of president was soon filled by Detlev Bronk. One of the half-dozen most powerful figures in the emerging scientific establishment, Bronk had been elected to the presidency of the National Academy of Sciences in 1950 after an unprecedented floor fight with James B. Conant, the candidate of the nominating committee, whose name had been linked to arms control. Engineering Bronk's victory had been Wendell Latimer, Edward Teller, Ernest Lawrence, and Luis Alvarez, all of the Berkeley Radiation Laboratory and all convinced that only the development of hydrogen weapons could answer the Soviet threat.

Under Bronk's leadership and with David's backing, a reorganization of the Institute was begun at once, transforming it into a graduate university and scientific research center. (Its official name was changed to Rockefeller University in 1965.) Specializing in advanced scientific research, it quickly became one of the half-dozen most prestigious and influential scientific institutions in the country, with a roster of Nobel prize winners on its faculty second only to those of Harvard and the University of California at Berkeley.

Of all the brothers, it was also David who took an active, if businesslike, interest in his father's investment in the institutions clustered on Morningside Heights.* As early as 1946,

---

*These included Columbia University, Barnard College, Teachers Colege, International House, Riverside Church, Union Theological Seminary, Jewish Theological Seminary, Juilliard School of Music, Corpus Christi Church, and the Cathedral of Saint John the Divine. It has been said that, like a modern Acropolis, Morningside combines more spiritual, cultural, and intellectual power than any similar area in the country.

he had become involved in discussions of the Morningside neighborhood, which was more and more dividing itself into two communities. Up on the Heights were the institutions of civilization and culture, their imposing architectures dominated by the Gothic bell tower of Riverside Church; below, in a belt known as the "Valley," were the residential dwellings of sixty thousand people, ugly, rapidly deteriorating structures packed with six and eight persons to a room. Socially and economically, the Valley was an expanding outer edge of Spanish Harlem.

The directors of International House decided to commission a study of the problem by William Munnecke, a University of Chicago urbanologist David, himself a university trustee, had brought to their attention. Munnecke's report called for a "total approach" on the part of the surrounding institutions to rehabilitate the area. In February 1947, David hosted a planning dinner. Attending were those who had been identified for years with his family's activities in the city, including Harry Emerson Fosdick of Riverside Church and Wally Harrison, along with representatives of the other Morningside institutions. Out of this gathering Morningside Heights, Inc., was formed, with David (who contributed $104,000 to help in the launching) as its president. His mandate was to put through an unprecedented scheme of "urban renewal," the first attempt to "remake" a major community in the United States.

The city agreed to condemn ten acres of "blight," inhabited by some 3,000 families, while Morningside Heights, Inc., raised $15 million to tear down the condemned dwellings and replace them with a modern apartment complex that would stand as a buffer against further incursions from the surrounding ghetto.* The program was not universally applauded. It soon became clear that only one thousand families would be accommodated in the new apartments, and since these were to be middle-income units, few of the dispossessed would qualify. Despite efforts to take the edge off local resentment by involving the community in decisions that had already been made and by finding housing elsewhere for those forced to move, there was bitter opposition to the plan.

---

*Twenty years later, using an analogy from the Vietnam War, striking Columbia University students would charge that the project was an "enclave" within the ghetto and point to the fact that one-third of the Morningside Heights budget was paid to police to secure its boundaries.

As in the case of Morningside Heights, the Trade Center was to be raised on land occupied by small businesses and some low-income housing; residents and shop owners joined to take the matter to court, charging that the project was designed less to stimulate trade than to elevate the values of property owned by the Chase and others in the lower Manhattan area. If David was invulnerable to such criticism, it was because he believed he was acting in the same spirit of public concern that had always motivated his father. If what was good for the city was also good for his bank, so much the better.

As he sat in his vice-chairman's office in the soon to be vacated Chase headquarters at 18 Pine, David could contemplate a grand future for the bank, and the financial community and nation of which it was part. The Chase was an overarching presence in the economic life of the United States—indeed, of the world. Alongside David on the board sat directors of Indiana Standard and Gulf Oil; International Nickel and International Paper; American Sugar and United Fruit; Time, Inc., and AT&T; in fact, of more than one hundred of the largest corporations and financial institutions of the country.

Within the family, David's leadership of the Chase made the offices he maintained in Room 5600 and at the bank the hub of the Rockefellers' economic power and influence. The network of the family's interests and those of the Chase were intertwined through trusts on deposit, through the Standard Oil companies it serviced, and, outside the bank, through the offices of Milbank, Tweed (which shared the talents of figures like partner John J. McCloy with the bank). The resources of the Chase, including its army of analysts, were always available to the financial men in the Family Office, and when Laurance sent his associates into the aerospace companies he invested in, they could usually count on a generous line of credit from the big bank to help in their efforts to turn the companies around.

It was, in fact, often hard to draw the line between bank business and family business, so persistently did they involve the same community of interest. Sometimes this overlapping

---

ten member banks of David's Downtown Lower Manhattan Association led by the Chase and the First National City Bank, which each received a 19 percent share.

became elaborate enough to draw the attention of regulatory agencies, as when the Civil Aeronautics Board ruled against the merger of Eastern and American Airlines.* But such action was rare.

Like its great rival, the First National City Bank, the Chase was an international bank, intensely concerned with the direction of government policy and its implications for business abroad. David's internationalism had been ingrained early (Junior's oft-repeated motto of concern for the "well-being of mankind" having been as much a part of his growing up as vacation retreats and governesses), and it was natural that he should be most drawn to this aspect of the bank's activity.

In 1948, returning from his tour of the bank's branches in Latin America, he had dictated a memorandum to his Uncle Winthrop Aldrich showing that he subscribed to his brother Nelson's philosophy of giving American businesses abroad protective coloration by identifying with nationalist emotion:

> Unquestionably the trend toward nationalism and all that it connotes is on the rise in Latin America. The day has passed when our Latin American neighbors will tolerate American institutions on their soil unless those institutions are willing to take an interest in the local economy. I believe that it is in our own interests, therefore, as well as others' that the Chase should rethink its policies with respect to Latin America in general. . . . I cannot see that the other North American branches have made much of a move in that direction, so we have an opportunity to be pioneers in the field.

---

*Although they were, respectively, the fifth- and third-largest carriers in the country, Eastern and American were losing money at the end of the fifties and, at the same time, were faced with massive capital outlays for a new generation of jet equipment about to hit the market. The negotiations were conducted for American by its president, C. R. Smith, and its director, Manly Fleischman, and for Eastern by Laurance Rockefeller and his aide Harper Woodward. Fleischman was also a director of the Equitable Life Insurance Company, which had lent Eastern $90 million and American $60 million, while Smith doubled as a director of the Chase, which had lent Eastern $28 million. David (who was also a director of the Equitable) knew that the merger would have the dual effect of bolstering his brother Laurance's position as Eastern's largest stockholder and protecting the outstanding Chase and Equitable loans.

Directors and officials of the Chase (and other big New York banks) shuttled regularly between Wall Street and Washington to advise and counsel the government and convey the interest of the financial community in the complex matters of state, particularly its international affairs.* One place where they gathered to discuss foreign policy and hammer out their consensus was at the Council on Foreign Relations, whose meetings were held in the old Pratt mansion Junior had bought and donated to the organization for its headquarters some years earlier.

David had been elected to membership in the council in 1947, joining John and Nelson (and such family and business associates as John Lockwood, Debevoise, Raymond Fosdick, Donald McLean, Frederick Osborn, Beardsley Ruml, C. Douglas Dillon, and John J. McCloy). But while his brothers attended only those meetings they could easily fit into their schedule, David characteristically became committed to the organization itself. He would later remark that the council represented his most important activity outside of the bank itself. He became involved in the council at all levels—as administrator, sponsor, and participant. In 1953 he gave $23,000 to help support a special council study on tariffs; the following year he participated in a panel on nuclear weapons and foreign policy led by a rising young Harvard professor and former intelligence officer named Henry Kissinger.

Once David decided to commit himself to the council, his

*David later said that it "was impossible to be involved in business with a great international bank without being involved in government and politics." The Chase was just the place to teach such lessons. Following his testimony on behalf of New Deal reforms which catapulted him to national prominence, Winthrop Aldrich had identified the bank so closely with national policy as to make patriotism almost a personal business style. During the war, the Chase had opened offices to accommodate the American expeditionary forces in North Africa (where David had been stationed as an intelligence officer) and, in 1944, had reopened its Paris branch on the heels of Eisenhower's invading armies. In 1947, at the suggestion of Attorney General Tom Clark, Aldrich had organized the American Heritage Foundation's "Freedom Train" sent around the country to display the nation's constitutional documents as an antidote to Communism. In 1948, following Tito's break with Stalin, the Chase became the principal banking connection with the Bank of Yugoslavia, and in 1950 it became one of the first banks to extend credit to Franco's Spain, now an important cold war ally. Twenty years later, it would be the first U.S. bank to open a branch in Moscow, and the first to move into China after Nixon's visit to Peking.

rise to its leadership was as inevitable as it had been at the Chase. He would not become chairman of the council board until 1972, but that was only because McCloy would hold the position for the preceding two decades. During the interim, David contented himself with a vice-presidency and with the fact that his closest friend and cousin George S. Franklin ("Benjy" to his intimates) was its executive director, heading the council staff, arranging the panels and study groups, and organizing the discussions and lecturers that made up the council activities.

In these activities, David failed to impress casual observers as a dynamic or dominating force; that was not his style. When a broad decision affecting finance or the budget was to be made, he would be actively involved and his considerable financial knowledge and incomparable access to resources and institutions would make his opinion both weighty and attended. But his real aptitude for leadership was different. It was, as one council fellow put it, to "articulate the informed consensus of the kind of people who gather at council meetings." He was a guardian of the establishment center, a fixed point of its moral order, not so much an architect or executor as a trustee of its informed and concentrated will.

His vantage at the council gave David an insider's view of the unfolding events of America's international policies. If there was a political crisis in the oil regions of the Middle East, Secretary of State Dulles (also a member) would brief his fellow council members on developments. When the African continent began to be the focus of increasing U.S. attention following the Suez affair, the council organized a study group under David's friend Harold K. Hochschild, head of the largest copper-mining interests in southern Africa, to discuss the situation and its options.

In September 1958, David and other members of Hochschild's group traveled for two weeks in Africa on a $45,-000 grant provided by the Carnegie Corporation to facilitate an on-the-spot study of the situation there. That same year, at the insistence of Nelson (anxious to have a cold war listening post on the Dark Continent), the Rockefeller Brothers Fund opened a branch office in Lagos, Nigeria. It was the only foreign office the Fund would ever have, and its budget of $250,000 was to finance feasibility studies for investment opportunities in Ghana and Nigeria. Functioning both as a channel of information and as a presence for the rest of Africa, the office was headed by Robert Fleming, a former U.S. information officer and Mobil Oil executive in Africa.*

In 1959, when the Aga Khan arranged to meet him during a visit to America, David had already achieved a record of dealing with the underdeveloped world in a way that combined bank business with larger geopolitical issues. In his frequent travels, he paid courtesy calls on heads of state in whatever countries he visited. Yet, as the Aga Khan knew, he had a special interest in Africa, where whole territories with great mineral wealth were in the process of freeing themselves from European colonial rule, thereby creating new opportunities for U.S. investors.

After lunching with David in the Chase boardroom, the Aga Khan asked for his host's help in connection with a cancer treatment center his Africa Research Foundation was building in Kenya. David made a contribution of $10,000. But the Aga Khan wanted more: use of Rockefeller's name as vice-chairman of the foundation board. This David would not donate. Afterward the Khan sent a letter urging Rockefeller, as one man of the world to another, to reconsider his refusal:

> I forgot to make a point which is growing in importance every day in East Africa: that African nationalist leaders such as Julius Nyerere, Tom Mboya, and Dr. Kiano are becoming more and more suspicious of newly formed foreign enterprises in East Africa.... In view of your interest in the Kitobere Sujar Valley scheme and the possibility that you may wish to go into similar projects in that area in the future, I cannot help feeling that it would be a well advised move if you were publicly connected with a non-political, non-racial organization. ... Perhaps you have been informed that the news of the Chase Manhattan Bank's substantial investments in the Union of South Africa had repercussions through the rest of the continent which were not entirely favorable.

*In his annual report to the Rockefeller Brothers Fund central offices, Fleming wrote: "One element in the Ghana scene, which may be worth noting in passing, is the growing importance of Eastern European influences. ... The director [Fleming] has made the acquaintance of the Soviet commercial attaché and, therefore, is moderately familiar with their plans and intentions with respect to Ghana's economy. This need not concern us except to note that it is a competitive factor, since the services being offered are the same as ours."

The Chase had indeed opened branches in Johannesburg, Cape Town, and the Transvaal, beginning a formal relationship with apartheid and white rule in South Africa that would eventually create a major crisis for David. The Chase and its Chase International Corporation were also becoming involved in Nigeria and East Africa,* and David was a partner in Laurance's textile mill in the Congo and had his own land speculations in Kenya. Yet he could afford to ignore the veiled threat in the Khan's letter. For the Rockefeller institutions had long since developed a wide-ranging spectrum of activities that allowed David to make contact with the leaders of the emerging nations on his own. About the same time the Aga Khan was writing him, in fact, David was sending a note to his friend Sir Ernest Vesey, a British colonial officer, in which he pledged a personal contribution of $10,000 toward the construction of the United Kenya Club, a Nairobi meeting place for business executives of all colors. Formerly Finance Minister of Kenya, Vesey had recently accepted a similar post in Tanganyika, in the government of Julius Nyerere. David, who had already made friendly contact with Tom Mboya through a student exchange program administered by Harold Hochschild's African-American Institute,† and had hosted Nyerere at his Pocantico estate, wrote Vesey: "I am very pleased that you have decided [to join the Nyerere government]—all the more so because I was greatly impressed by him on his recent visit to the United States. Perhaps by

*In 1959, Robert Fleming, writing in his capacity of director of the Brothers Fund branch office in Nigeria, reminded New York that October 1 would be Nigeria's Independence Day celebration. Emphasizing tha Nigerian orientation toward the politics of the West and conservative economic policies made it an important event, Fleming asked if one of the Brothers could attend. When the job fell to David, he wrote John Watts, a Chase employee in Nigeria, for his reaction. Watts's reply illustrates the pervasiveness of the bank's interests and how deeply fused they were with the Brothers': "If at all possible, I feel you should try to be present; you know and have entertained here at the bank most of the outstanding personalities in the country; you represent to them the Rockefeller Brothers Fund; the Chase has made an application to open a commercial banking operation in Nigeria; the Chase investment company has an important interest in a textile mill in the country; the bank and investment company have agreed to take $2.5 million of the early maturities of a port authority loan."

†The institute, whose programs accounted for 90 percent of the African students in the United States, had been set up with the CIA's support in the mid-1950s. In 1963, Dana Creel of Room 5600 became chairman of its board.

this time he may have told you that he lunched with us at my house in Tarrytown during my visit. . . . If Africa can develop more men of his caliber, I feel very hopeful of the future."

By the end of the decade, David had emerged as a banker-statesman in a class by himself. Jetting from continent to continent in the family's fifteen-seat Caravelle, he negotiated with monarchs and ministers with a cachet normally possessed only by high-ranking diplomats. He had a card file at the Chase with twenty thousand names of people he knew in high places around the world, and whom he thought of as "personal friends." He was all the things that such a man was supposed to be: fluent in three European languages; a wine connoisseur with part interest in a vineyard in France and, in his Pocantico home, a renowned temperature-controlled cellar sealed with a bank-vault door; a yachtsman with three 40-foot boats he sailed off the Maine coast from his elegant Seal Harbor estate; possessor of a major collection of Impressionist and post-Impressionist paintings; and enough of a gourmet to walk casually through a wall of French paratroopers during the Algerian crisis to get to a favorite Paris restaurant. His six children (David, Jr., Abby, Neva, Peggy, Richard, and Eileen) would have glimpses of the private person in uncharacteristic moments, as when he invited such intimacies as joining him in the bathtub; but for them, as for the world, he was primarily a banker and a Rockefeller.

In 1960 the New York *Post* suggested David as the ideal fusion candidate for mayor. David's interest was piqued, yet he was not really tempted because he knew he was already able to achieve political ends (be it remodeling New York City or making foreign policy) without the necessity of submitting to the political process. Not yet forty-five, he knew he could soon expect to be president of the Chase and chairman of its board. There was the possibility of taking a high appointive post to cap his career later, he told intimates, but for now he could serve himself and his family best by staying in the institution that was the cornerstone of their power.

19

NELSON WAS PLEASED by the achievements of David and his
other brothers, if for no other reason than that they were like
jewels surrounding his own career and setting it off to better
advantage. Yet after his experiences in the Eisenhower administration, it was not clear exactly where his career would
lead. When, late in 1955, he left Washington for the third
time, he felt that he would never return as Secretary of State,
as he had once hoped. He had burned too many bridges for
even a Rockefeller to repair. Nor was he the sort of man to
mend fences or, like Dulles, to spend half a career in intrigue
and humbling maneuvers within the Republican party to
achieve a high policy-making position. He returned to New
York, therefore, at a crossroad in his life. It was as his friend
and adviser A. A. Berle, Jr., noted in his diary after a telephone conversation with Rockefeller on April 4, 1956: "With
Nelson . . . the question is what to do with his life; and with
the most magnificent 'do-it-yourself' kit ever provided; only it
has no plans or suggestions."

While making up his mind, Nelson resumed his old positions of influence in family institutions as president of Rockefeller Center, chairman of IBEC and AIA, and president of
the Museum of Modern Art.* He again became a presence in
the Family Office, which had grown along with the Brothers'
careers to the point where, in 1956, there were more than
one hundred employees in the major departments of taxes,
accounting, investments, public relations, and philanthropy.
The Office now handled every aspect of the family's life—
from paying the small army of gardeners and groundskeepers
in charge of Pocantico and the other estates, to scheduling

*In 1957 he also established the Museum of Primitive Art to house his
extensive collection. After his son Michael's death on an anthropological expedition to New Guinea in 1961, the collection was named in
his honor. In 1969 Nelson donated the Museum of Primitive Art to the
Metropolitan Museum of Art, which built a special wing to house it.

travel on the family's three airplanes. Unofficially it was "Room 5600," although it had long since expanded beyond the 56th floor to parts of the floors above and below.

In the decade since the war, the Office had taken on the Brothers' personality—not only in decor and style, but in the fact that year by year the old men dressed solemnly in black suits and wearing the look of formidable discretion marking them as Associates of Mr. Rockefeller, Jr., had begun to disappear through death or retirement.

The Rockefeller Brothers Fund (or "RBF," as it had become known in the family's burgeoning system of acronyms) had also expanded in size and influence. In the growing bureaucracy of the Office, it had become the premier institution of the third generation, and Nelson settled into its presidency along with his other high offices. The Fund was the perfect place for him. Under JDR3's administration, it had not developed any strong identity that would restrict him when he sought to make it conform to his purposes. And unlike the Rockefeller Foundation, it had not become an independent foundation with an independent board of trustees. It existed to serve the Rockefeller Brothers, and its philanthropy was still conceived primarily as advancing the specific causes associated with their personal careers and interests.

From the moment in 1956 when he replaced his older brother as its president, Nelson proceeded to transform the Fund into a personal instrument reflecting his new realization that the kind of power he aspired to could come only through an electoral mandate. It was not a new idea. As early as 1949, it had been suggested that he run for mayor of New York. (One of his aides responded, "He doesn't want to be Mayor, he wants to be Pope.") Seven years later, Republican leaders had actively considered him as a possible candidate for the U.S. Senate seat being vacated by Irving Ives. But Nelson had made up his mind that he was going to run for the governorship, a stepping-stone Al Smith, FDR, and Tom Dewey had used before him in their bids for the presidency—the only goal worthy of his ambition.

The gubernatorial elections were not to be held until 1958. In the interim, the Rockefeller Brothers Fund was a perfect vehicle to keep Nelson's name before the public.* By far the

* And before important individuals as well. One of the grants RBF made under Nelson's reign was $300,000 to the Sam Rayburn Foundation in Texas to help establish the Rayburn Library as a repository for the speaker's personal papers. The museum consultants hired by the

most ambitious effort he undertook was assembling the Rockefeller Panel Studies, an enterprise that brought the four Brothers together for a climactic show of their joint ability to influence national policy. When, three years later, the studies were completed and published under the title *Prospect for America*, the directors had spent over a million dollars in gathering nearly a hundred of the most illustrious and influential names in America for the project. It may have originated in a sense of pique at having been shunned by the Eisenhower administration, a determination to go ahead and create a personal manifesto for a Rockefeller party. But by the time six panels had produced their reports, the recommendations would be incorporated into both party platforms in the 1960 presidential elections and would exert a profound influence on the course of America's military policies and domestic affairs over the next troubled decade.

Chairman of the panel on foreign policy was Rockefeller Foundation President Dean Rusk, shortly to become Secretary of State in the Kennedy administration. Heading the panel on education was Carnegie Corporation President John Gardner, shortly to join Rusk in the Kennedy-Johnson admistration as Secretary of Health, Education and Welfare. There was a panel on foreign economic policy for the twentieth century (on which David sat) and one on the domestic economy. But the panel that was to have the greatest impact by far on the whole fabric of American society in the ensuing years was the panel on international security headed by the director of the Special Studies Project, Henry Kissinger.*

Fund to assess the project advised that it had virtually no value as a museum or library and was little more than a personal monument. Nelson, however, was interested less in the philanthropic than the political proprieties, and the gift was made.

*Like Nelson himself, Kissinger was just then at a critical juncture in his career. Two years earlier, as an ambitious young instructor in government at Harvard, he had looked beyond the academic world for the experience and exposure that would allow him to return to Cambridge as a tenured faculty member. Early in 1955, he had been considered for the vacant managing editorship of *Foreign Affairs*. But while his Teutonic literary style had disqualified him for that post, Harvard Dean McGeorge Bundy had recommended him as rapporteur for a Council on Foreign Relations study group on nuclear weapons. Working with men like General James Gavin, Roswell Gilpatric, and Paul Nitze, Kissinger had used the group's deliberations in his book *Nuclear Weapons and Foreign Policy*, which argued the feasibility of "limited nuclear war" and which, surprisingly, made its way onto the best seller list. Kissinger had worked with and become close to Nelson during the Quantico seminars. As one of the future Secretary of State's colleagues

Panel II (as it was called) was in many ways an elaboration of the Council of Foreign Relations study group on nuclear weapons Kissinger had headed. Six of its members were
alumni of the study group, including its chairman, Gordon
Dean, a former AEC commissioner who was presently vice-
president for nuclear energy of one of the big defense contractors, General Dynamics. They were joined by nuclear
physicist Edward Teller, who, with Lewis Strauss and Dean
and air force brass, had won the 1950 battle to overrule
AEC majority and forge ahead with the development of the
H-bomb in a fight that split the scientific-military establishment for more than a decade. Teller's views on nuclear
weapons and the necessity of achieving absolute supremacy in
the arms race closely paralleled Nelson's, and the two were to
support each other in varying capacities in future political
campaigns.

The entire Special Studies Project reflected Nelson's apocalyptic vision of the cold war. ("At issue is nothing less than
the future of America and the freedom of the world," he announced in the preamble to the final report.) But international security was the object of his keenest interest. The Panel
II report could be easily interpreted as a point-by-point rejection of the Eisenhower defense policies and, particularly, of
the administration's efforts to impose budgetary limits on military spending. "When the security of the United States and
of the free world is at stake," Panel II declared in one of its
most memorable passages, "cost cannot be the basic consideration." In a direct challenge to the President's military
prestige, Panel II charged that present defense spending was
"insufficient to maintain even our current force levels" and
recommended "successive additions on the order of $3 billion
each year for the next several fiscal years." Pressing priorities
included missile development and antimissiles, the expansion
of conventional mobile units "essential for limited war," and
the initiation of a national civil defense program of fallout
shelters to prepare the country for all-out nuclear war.

Nuclear weapons were a special preoccupation of Panel II,
and the only source of internal dissension came when some

would later write, "Nelson Rockefeller became a trusted friend. Rockefeller liked Kissinger, admired him for his intelligence and wit. . . . Because he learned best through personal encounters, Rockefeller spent a
great deal of time with Kissinger. Kissinger enjoyed the association. . . .
He knew how much Rockefeller esteemed him, and it was impossible
for him not to be moved by that knowledge."

members questioned the efficacy of "tactical atomic bombs" for fighting "limited wars." Such doubts were overruled and overwhelmed by panel Chairman Kissinger (although he would later recant this position). "Very powerful nuclear weapons can be used in such a manner that they have negligible effects on civilian population," the final report claimed, in what Washington gadfly I. F. Stone later called its "most wondrous sentence." Among Panel II's specific recommendations was that the way be cleared to give nuclear weapons to the NATO allies and that the capacity be developed to use nuclear weapons in conflicts ranging from "minor police actions" to small-scale, limited wars.

The issue of developing the capability for fighting limited wars, with either conventional or nuclear weapons, was a crucial point of conflict with the Eisenhower administration. As Nelson's old antagonist, Treasury Secretary George Humphrey, put it, the United States had "no business getting into little wars. If a situation comes up where our interests justify intervention, let's intervene decisively with all we have got or stay out." Panel II envisioned a different order of intervention, which foreshadowed the next fateful decade in Southeast Asia. "Our security can be imperiled not only by overt aggression but also by transformations which are made to appear, insofar as possible, as not aggression at all. These 'concealed wars' may appear as internal revolution or civil war; they may be instigated by outside forces or exploited by them. Greece has furnished one example; Vietnam another."

One external reason for the far-reaching impact of the Special Studies Project report was undoubtedly its timing. Dissatisfaction with Eisenhower's efforts to hold the line on military spending and with his search for some accommodation with the Russians was growing within the Pentagon and from all sides of what the President in his Farewell Address would describe as the "military-industrial complex." On October 4, 1957, the Russians had startled strategists in the West by launching the first earth satellite and thereby demonstrating a small, but unexpected, lead in one aspect of the arms race. Amid the uproar following the launching of Sputnik, when every Pentagon general seemed to be clamoring for funds to make up another military gap, Nelson rushed the Panel II report to completion.

Galvanized by the national excitement surrounding the launching of the Russian spacecraft, Rockefeller arranged to take a preliminary memorandum of Panel II's findings (especially prepared by Kissinger) to the President. He called on General Lucius Clay (a panel member and Eisenhower's old comrade-in-arms) to run interference for him at the White House. He also called on his former colleague and fellow Dartmouth Trustee Sherman Adams in a vain effort to get the panel's recommendations on defense reorganization inserted into the 1958 State of the Union message.

On January 10, 1958, despairing of Washington's ability to act quickly in what he believed was a national emergency, Nelson, on the verge of declaring his candidacy for governor, appeared before the Senate Armed Services Committee, chaired by Senator Lyndon Johnson and issued a dire warning: "Ever since World War II the United States has suffered from a tendency to underestimate the military technology of the USSR. . . . Unless present trends are reversed, the world balance of power will shift in favor of the Soviet bloc. If that should happen, we are not likely to be given another chance to remedy our failings."

All that could be accomplished by a "private citizen" had been done.* Moreover, he had come to a familiar point in his projects where, having gotten something going, he began to lose interest and was content to turn things over to others. In the spring of 1958, with most of the panel reports either published or close to publication, he released Kissinger to return to Harvard and then stepped down himself, leaving Laurance, as the new chairman of the Special Studies Project and president of the RBF, to finish up the details. As for himself, he was now ready to turn his full attention to the electoral struggle ahead.

At first he met with unexpected resistance. Some members of the family, notably JDR3, sensed a great difference between public service, as exemplified by sitting on commissions

---

*Panel II's final report would stand as the Brothers' ultimate monument in the sense that Rockefeller Center was Junior's. Nelson would force Nixon to accept it in 1960; JFK would accept it voluntarily. (Journalist Tom Braden remembers traveling on the Kennedy campaign plane during the primaries: "When some foreign policy question came up, Kennedy yelled to Salinger, 'Hey, Pierre, get the Rockefeller Brothers Studies. It's all there.'") One of the passages in the report might almost as easily have applied to the Rockefellers themselves as to the nation: "A sense of being watched—in an almost Biblical sense of being judged—has remained with the United States . . . Americans have cared what history thought about them, what the ultimate judgement would be upon their work. They have known that the hopes of the world were, in some sense, bound up with their success."

and accepting appointive posts, and the aggressive pursuit of office through public combat that would revive old antagonisms. The impulse to shield the family from publicity was shared to a degree by David, and by the female members of the family, who had no direct voice in the councils of Room 5600. But for Nelson these were qualms not worth considering.

Nineteen fifty-eight, the experts agreed, was going to be a "Democratic year." Tom Dewey told Nelson to forget it. Even Frank Jamieson, who had been guiding Rockefeller toward a political career for more than fifteen years, agreed that he should bide his time. Yet, ironically, the incumbent governor, Averell Harriman, helped make up Nelson's mind. Having noted ironically in 1957 that the Republican chances were so dim they ought to try a long shot "like Nelson Rockefeller," he also appointed him head of a bipartisan state commission, delegated to resolve a dispute between the parties over reapportionment. The Commission on a Constitutional Convention (its published findings would eventually run to seventeen volumes) allowed Nelson to travel around the state talking to local political leaders and becoming associated in the voters' minds with state problems.

By spring 1958 he had definitely decided to make his move. He formed a campaign committee whose nucleus included such trusted advisers as Jamieson, Lockwood, Harrison, and Stacy May, along with newcomers like William Ronan, a former professor at NYU whom Nelson had met during the work of the Commission on a Constitutional Convention, lawyer George Hinman, and Assemblyman Malcolm Wilson, a widely respected party conservative whose support was crucial in helping Nelson counter charges that he was a New Deal liberal at heart. Standing beside a bronze bust of his grandfather in Room 5600, he declared his candidacy before a battery of television cameras. "What we need is a transfusion of political courage to grasp the opportunities and the ideas of men who have convictions and creative talent and faith in the future." Then with Jamieson and Ronan coordinating the campaign from New York, he set out in a Buick driven by his son Steven and accompanied by Wilson to tour the state and convince county chairmen that he was such a individual.

His identification with the New Deal and with massive federal spending did not make him a favorite of upstate New Yorkers. Yet potential primary opposition to Rockefeller, never strong to begin with, was demoralized by the prospects of battling Rockefeller money and by gloomy predictions of a Democratic landslide. In August, when the Republican state convention met, no other name was entered in nomination against him.

The election, as events later turned out, was decided on the last night of the convention, but not because of anything that Nelson had said in his acceptance speech or put into the party platform. His campaign committee was in his hotel suite listening to radio coverage of the Democrats' convention in Buffalo when it was reported that Tammany boss Carmine DeSapio had forced Governor Harriman to accept his candidate, Manhattan District Attorney Frank Hogan, as the party's nominee for U.S. senator. "That's it," Jamieson said, jumping up from his chair. "There's our campaign issue."

Later Malcolm Wilson realized that everyone in the room looked at "Jamie" as though he were touched. "We said to ourselves, 'Oh, no, not again.' We'd been beating Tammany to death for as long as we could remember and where had it ever got us?"

Grasping the bossism issue was an instinctive choice for Jamieson, who still had a journalist's reflexes and remembered the campaign he had run more than twenty years earlier to elect Charles Edison governor of New Jersey against the Boss Hague machine. Yet, this would not be another attempt to bait Tammany Hall, as Wilson feared. It would be a campaign to undermine confidence in Harriman's moral authority. They would contrast Harriman's position with the 1924 convention, when Tammany had tried to force William Randolph Hearst on the ticket and Al Smith had locked himself in a hotel room, threatening not to run rather than capitulate. Discarding hundreds of position papers on the issues researchers had spent months preparing, Rockefeller—who started the campaign with 35 percent of early polls—began to crisscross the state comparing Smith's "courage" to Harriman's "surrender."

When he went upstate before conservative audiences, Rockefeller hammered away at the Harriman administration's deficit spending. But the Democratic stronghold of New York City provided a milieu that drew out the many facets of his political personality. There he campaigned as a liberal, drawing on the connections and alliances his family had established in three generations of living and giving. Negroes were reminded that the Rockefellers had funded Spelman

College, built the Paul Laurence Dunbar apartments, and kept the Urban League alive. Jews knew that the Rockefellers had been generous in purchasing Israel bonds and had contributed to Jewish philanthropies. Union members were made conscious of the high regard their leaders had for Nelson. The average person was surrounded by the family's building projects—Rockefeller Center, the Cloisters, and the Museum of Modern Art, the massive Lincoln Center project JDR3 had helped begin, and David's ambitious plans for the restoration of the downtown area.

Nelson did not impress anybody by his ability as a platform speaker. From the beginning, the professionals on his staff had cringed when he began to read prepared remarks, his dyslexia causing him to stumble over words, invert phrases, and look generally puzzled as he tried to decipher the paper in front of him. (Eventually he would partially overcome this difficulty by memorizing key sections of his speeches.) Yet he had an asset that overcame all this—the ability to participate in politics as a contact sport. The excitement of the crowds he plunged recklessly into was not in thinking him a common man, but in the fact that he was willing to drop the posture of a frigid aristocrat and, for a moment at least, act like one of them. It was a special charisma, drawn out of the name. They liked to see him and touch him. He knew they liked it and played it to the hilt.

He was the perfect candidate for New York City's multiple personalities. He campaigned through Harlem on a flatbed truck with Count Basie sitting at the piano beside him; he spoke to Puerto Rican audiences in Spanish that was by now fairly fluent, telling them he wanted to have a chance to become an *"auténtico representante del pueblo"*; his already nasal voice developed a more pronounced plebeian twang when he spoke to workers on the job. The issues of the campaign became secondary when Nelson arrived at a crowd gathered by his advance men and treated it to the spectacle of a Rockefeller donning beanies, twirling Hula-Hoops, eating any kind of ethnic food in sight. (A Democratic party leader would one day scoff at Nelson's presidential ambitions by saying, "What's he ever done besides eat knishes, anyway?") Tom Morgan, later an aide to Mayor John Lindsay, watched Nelson on the campaign trail in 1958 and wrote: "He made crowds quiver. He demonstrated that vaunted, celebrated, feared Rockefeller personality which, like beauty in women, was both given and self-conceived."

As in the old days at the coordinator's office, he drove himself remorselessly, getting at most six hours' sleep a night as he toured nearly 8,500 miles throughout the state and made more than 100 formal speeches. Jamieson, to make sure Rockefeller's odyssey was fully covered, organized what for its time was an innovative media campaign: he assigned a television crew to accompany Nelson and hand out film of some aspect of the day's campaigning each afternoon to local television stations that might not have been able to cover it themselves.

Another Democrat might have used Rockefeller's wealth against him, but Harriman too was the scion of a robber baron fortune and spent as much as the Rockefellers in what the papers billed as "the millionaires' sweepstakes." The governor tried unsuccessfully to make the election a referendum on the Eisenhower administration, but Nelson stayed on the offensive. By the end of the campaign Harriman's tall patrician figure was wilted by fatigue and his gaunt features sagged in defeat. Nelson appeared even more youthful and vigorous by comparison.

It was still early on the evening of November 5 when the governor left his suite in the Biltmore and was convoyed down to the ballroom to make a concession speech. Just blocks away, Nelson was pushing through crowds and flashing the toothy grin that pulled his eyes into slits. Surrounded by his wife Tod and his favorite son, Michael, he surged forward to claim victory. History was present a few weeks later when, on New Year's Eve, he paid homage to the tradition that had produced him by taking the oath of office with his right hand resting on his Great-Grandmother Eliza's Bible.

It was hard to tell, so completely had he perfected the suppression of emotion, but no one was more profoundly moved by Nelson's swearing-in than his father. Now eighty-five years old and growing feeble in body if not in mind, Mr. Junior was proud of all his sons—less specifically for what they had accomplished, perhaps, than for the way their success vindicated his own efforts as a parent. In 1955, after reading a collective portrait of the boys that had recently appeared in *Fortune*, he wrote them a joint letter (as he often did on important occasions). "What you are doing for the well being of mankind throughout the world is breathtaking," he said.

It took these articles to bring me up to date on your many activities. How proud I am of the contribution you are making to your day and generation, of the wise, intelligent, unassuming way in which you are making it, and above all, of the kind of men you are! To our family have come unprecedented opportunities. With the opportunities have come equally great responsibilities. Magnificently and modestly you boys are measuring up to those opportunities and responsibilities.

When they first came back from the war and began taking over the Office and other institutions he had built, Junior had been disturbed, feeling once again that he really didn't know his sons and hoping that *their* associates would help explain them to him. In effect, they were telling him that youth must be served and that he had to stand back even though he felt in the prime of his life. They rejected advisers like Debevoise, who had served him long and faithfully, and began changing the nature of the family's identity, doing things that were foreign to him and ignoring others he thought were important. He could have stopped them; yet the fact they should *want* to shoulder the responsibility, he knew, was the fulfillment of the hopes he and Abby had had when raising them. He had tried to step gracefully into the background, not leaving the family concerns, but rather narrowing the scope of his interests so as not to conflict with them.

Throughout the early fifties, Junior continued to come to the Office whenever he was in town and sit for long hours at the great Jacobean desk taking care of business he thought important and trying to get an idea of the affairs in which his sons were gradually involving themselves and the family. If nothing else, he still had the power of the purse, controlling the almost $200 million of the great fortune not set aside in trust funds for his descendants. If his sons wanted ready money for one of their projects and did not want to invade the principal of their trusts, they still came to him. He was the one who paid the bills of the Office. He was still the patriarch, as he had in a way been since he was a young man, yet his powers were fading day by day.

For years he had shunned public recognition. But by the mid-1950s he capitulated to becoming a celebrity, acknowledging the fact that the apotheosis begun some forty years earlier by an obscure chain of events on the wind-swept plains of southern Colorado was now complete. His name was the best one an organization like the United Negro College Fund could have on its letterhead; his presence at a ceremonial occasion gave the event a moral authority nobody else could have provided. In 1956 his friend Henry Luce put him on the cover of *Time;* the feature story, entitled "The Good Man," noted that "it is because John D. Rockefeller Junior's is a life of constructive social giving that he ranks as an authentic American hero, just as certainly as any general who ever won a victory for an American army or any statesman who triumphed in behalf of U.S. diplomacy."

Always more a Victorian than a modern man, in the bustling post-war world of his sons he seemed very much the survivor of a bygone era. In 1952, David Lillienthal, former commissioner of TVA and the AEC, met Junior at a dinner party at JDR3's house at 1 Beekman Place and was struck by the antique quality of his appearance and conversation. When he came home that night, he recorded his impressions in his diary:

> He sat down next to me in the library after dinner, as curious about me as I was about him. I don't know what he found interesting about me, if indeed anything, but I confess fascination for his shoes. They were *high button* shoes! Beautiful of course, and polished to a glint. . . . What he did say was rather anxious, worried sort of thinking, restraining himself from expressing too strongly his disappointment of the short hours of labor for example, lest I think he approved of excessively long hours— but, he said, what good is leisure anyway if people don't know what to do with it?

He had been devastated by Abby's death. Not long after the funeral, he had invited the entire staff of Room 5600 to Pocantico. With a black shawl on his shoulders he had shown them around the house and gardens, talking incessantly about his dead wife and telling them how much he had cared for her. He was terribly lonely, almost lost, without her, and his sons had breathed a sigh of relief when, in 1951, Junior married Martha Baird Allen, 56-year-old widow of Arthur Allen, an old college friend from Brown. (In an act of rare whimsy he entered "real estate developer" as his profession on the marriage license application.) His new wife was a former concert pianist who had made her professional debut with the Boston Symphony, had been a guest soloist with Sir Thomas

Beecham's London Symphony, and in 1940 had composed "Win with Willkie," adopted by the Republican standard-bearer as the official song of his campaign. All the Brothers liked "Aunt Martha," although later, as their father got weaker, relations became strained when they felt she monopolized Junior and made it difficult for them to see him. They knew the remarriage was no slight to their mother's memory. It provided Junior with companionship, as well as a way of arranging his residual estate for tax purposes. (Experts in the Office had arrived at a means for avoiding any estate tax at all, by stipulating that half would go to his wife and half to the tax-exempt Rockefeller Brothers Fund—a device that became known in the accounting trade as a "Rockefeller will.")

Yet as he grew older Junior had not completely embraced that autumnal period of reconciliation said to come with old age, at least not as far as his errant son, Winthrop, was concerned. Winthrop's early failures, his playboy antics, and his climactic fall into disgrace with his marriage and divorce, might be forgiven but would never be forgotten. When Winthrop picked up and left for Arkansas, far from appeasing his father, he only added a blow against the concept of family that Junior had spent his life building.

There was no open break between them; in fact, relations were cordial during Winthrop's frequent visits to New York. Yet both men knew that an invisible boundary had been crossed, creating a breech in their relationship there was no way of repairing. Junior never went to Arkansas to see Winrock Farm, or to appreciate his son's other achievements in his new home. It was clear to everyone that Winthrop needed his father's benediction to help resolve the guilt that still lingered from his past; yet Junior always declined his invitations, saying that it was far too demanding a trip, even though he and Martha traveled to Arizona each winter. It seemed a particularly harsh punishment, and one observer close to the family later said, "Mr. Rockefeller would go the ends of the earth for the 'well-being of mankind,' as everybody knew, but he wouldn't go three hundred miles out of his way for the well-being of his son."

The patriarchy Junior still exercised at Pocantico revolved around Sunday dinners, which were held in the Big House, with each of his son's families alternating in attendance. When he gave his grandchildren money for their birthdays, the check was usually accompanied by some bit of homiletic advice through which he attempted to transmit the ideals of the family mission to the new generation. The young people meant a great deal to him. Once his friend Fosdick found him unusually happy and asked why. Junior replied that he had just gone out to buy twenty-two Bibles, one for each of the grandchildren. When he agreed to allow his biography to be written, he stipulated that it was only so that his children could "know the sort of man I tried to be."

His life was as regular as it had always been: rise at seven, breakfast at eight, work until noon, then lunch and change into pajamas for an hour's nap, followed by a drive with Martha in the Cadillac limousine. Part of each winter was spent in Tucson, in the little inn he and Abby had found years earlier, and where they had passed some of their most tranquil moments. Spring and fall were passed in Pocantico, with interludes at Basset Hall where he could watch Williamsburg bustle as it had in colonial times. In the summer he went to Seal Harbor; there he would sit in the almost Oriental splendor of the living room, working at the kneehole desk and gazing out the window where, in the distance, the Atlantic extended into the horizon.

His last years were given over to thoughts about the family name now that he had finished his own mission. Although to the public he was the anonymous Rockefeller, little more than a bridge between a notorious father and famous sons, he had done his part. He had protected and replenished his inheritance, but also used it so that future generations would inherit an awesome name. It might not have occurred to him to use the word "dynasty," yet there was something—a moral and social ambience—stemming from his own efforts that distinguished his side of the family from his Uncle William's—the Stillman Rockefellers—and from other families of great wealth who might have bequeathed large gifts to society but never dedicated themselves to the merger of national and personal ambition in quite the way he had.

In 1959 he had a prostate operation. By early 1960, he was eighty-six and increasingly feeble, the bones sticking out prominently from his face, and his knobby fingers shaking so badly from palsy that he could hardly write. He often sat by the window, a blanket tucked around his knees, the spring sun streaming in to warm him as he received old friends, for what they both knew were last visits. His work done through his sons, he suddenly seemed to have little use for them and bewildered them by his desire to be alone. On May 11, 1960,

Mr. Junior died, having paid so long and so well for his father's transgressions that the world was now in his debt.

The archetypal Rockefeller, his passing came at a time when his greatest creation, the family itself, was at its high point. Yet it was possible for some to see that his death left the family poorer than it had been, and weakened it against the future. His grandson, John D. Rockefeller IV, who flew home from studies in Japan to attend the memorial service, recalled later: "It was quite powerful, the whole experience of grandfather's death. I remember feeling strongly the idea that more than my grandfather had died. It was the end of an era. It was history itself passing on."

20

JUNIOR'S PASSING did not affect his sons the way their mother's had. The bargain between the old man and his boys had hinged on achievement, not affection, a contract involving the fulfillment of his family design. He had been a sponsor and a Pygmalion; in return, they had taken on the responsibilities he had accumulated. They mourned discreetly, yet far from being overcome with grief, the third Rockefeller generation seemed to heave an unconscious sigh of relief with the passing of the man who had been father, taskmaster, and symbol. As Nelson's son Steven commented later on, "Grandfather's death did not have the emotional element that Grandmother's did. I think one of the reasons was that there were these five Brothers, all champing at the bit. They had been held in very sternly by him. They were all bigger than he was and they outnumbered him, but he had kept them in line."

For Nelson, who had flown with Laurance to Tucson to be with Junior in his last hours and bring his cremated remains home to New York for the family memorial service, the loss had in fact been easier to bear than one he had suffered a few months earlier. Then it had been Frank Jamieson, the man who had been closer to him than anyone else except

Laurance for the past twenty years in a friendship that had penetrated the final layer of suspicion isolating the Brothers even from their most trusted aides. "Frankie" had been the rock on which Nelson had built his career. Now he was dead of lung cancer at fifty-five, gone before he had a chance to enjoy fully the fruits of his complex labor in shaping Nelson's political career. It had been painful to watch Jamieson drag himself to meetings at Room 5600 in the last weeks of his life; it was as if he fought to forestall death just a little while longer to help Nelson through a critical moment in his political life.

For Nelson had hardly achieved his first electoral triumph, than he was running for office again. In his inaugural address as governor, he had urged New Yorkers to show the way to a better world, as though they were but the advance guard in his larger constituency. Barely two months after spending his first full day as governor arranging his favorite Picassos and Légers on the walls of the Executive Mansion, he had converted a pair of town houses he owned on 55th Street into a New York political office. There he installed a large staff with the go-ahead to pursue discreetly the 1960 Republican nomination for him. The operation was soon in high gear and running so well that, as T. H. White later remarked, John F. Kennedy's own efforts that same spring were "by comparison a Montana roadshow."

Nelson knew he had ignited the fancy of citizen Republicans all over the country in his 1958 campaign; and he knew, too, that a poll commissioned by Nixon's own people showed him leading the Vice-President 40 percent to 38 percent among rank-and-file voters. The question was how the party bosses would regard him and his upstart challenge. Beginning in May, he embarked on a highly publicized national speaking tour that also offered occasions to duck into smoke-filled rooms and receive his answer.

Nelson's eye had been on the White House at least since leaving the Eisenhower administration. The thought of the alternative, Richard Nixon, had only strengthened his resolve. Nelson had not been reluctant to make his low opinion of the Vice-President well-known. "I hate the idea of Dick Nixon being President," he told a friend. Nixon had the wrong ideas, the wrong friends, the wrong reasons for seeking power. He had no vision of the Republican party, let alone the presidency. In challenging the iron law of politics that said Nixon was heir apparent to the nomination, Nelson felt he was justified because, as T. H. White later wrote, the party was "almost a dependency on the Rockefeller family, like the Rockefeller Foundation or Rockefeller University." Nelson was not above taking the skeptical aside, pulling a neatly folded piece of paper with a dollar figure on it out of his breast pocket, and telling them that the astoundingly high sum they saw written on it in blue ink was the Rockefellers' bounty to Republicans over the years.

The people who came to see Nelson on his tour liked his enthusiasm and the populist twang in his voice. Yet the county chairmen and other party caciques were less enthusiastic. Nixon had sedulously worked the vineyards of state and local campaigns during the previous six years as a stand-in for a President who was not, in their oblique phrase, "politically conditioned." They owed him, and payment of their debt was the oil that made party machinery work. Yet they might have been persuaded to forget this if they had not had doubts about Rockefeller's version of Republicanism, which seemed so far from the cautiousness of the midwestern heartland that Ike had tapped for eight good years.

For the first time in his political career, Nelson began to feel the latent strength of that wing of the party for which Robert Taft had long been spokesman—oriented to the middle of the country; suspicious of internationalism, Wall Street, and the East; not comfortable with big ideas and big budgets. Even Wall Street, his own natural constituency, however, was not willing to gamble on him. One of Nelson's first probing acts had been to get his brother David and J. R. Dilworth of the Family Office to canvass the financial community. They found big business Republicans solidly behind Nixon. It was not because they especially liked him (they knew, in fact, that there was little ideological space between the two men and that Nixon, of all the Eisenhower administration, had been most receptive to Nelson's hard-line ideas); it was rather that they saw the Vice-President as a political *tabula rasa* on which they could write their own interests. A Rockefeller, on the other hand, immune from controls imposed by begging for contributions, might be destructively headstrong.

The route was still open for Nelson to enter the primaries and prove what he had been saying all along to party professionals—that Nixon couldn't win with the voters. Yet this would have involved running head-on against Eisenhower himself. As much as he felt that the administration had been an indecisive and incompetent interlude between the New Deal and the future—which he had limned out in the panel reports—Nelson didn't need Frank Jamieson to convince him that it would be political suicide for him to repudiate publicly the past eight years.

The campaign committee he had assembled continued to work for some kind of leverage. Emmet Hughes, a prominent journalist and former Eisenhower speech writer, joined Henry Kissinger as Nelson's chief ideologue and worked to establish positions that would put Nixon on the defensive. Yet toward the end of 1959, after six discouraging months of "taking soundings," Nelson realized he was in a no-win position. The day after Christmas he read a statement prepared by Hughes announcing his withdrawal from a contest he had never formally entered. When an invitation came from the Republican National Committee to serve as chairman or keynoter at the convention, he refused, saying he didn't even plan to attend; and he added that in no case would he be interested in the vice-presidential nomination.

Yet he still hoped. From time to time he would snipe at the party bosses who were barring him from the nomination. One revealing piece of evidence that he continued to consider himself a potential candidate came later in the spring, when he met Nikita Khrushchev during the Soviet Premier's visit to the United States. It was the first by a Soviet head of state since the revolution and a dramatic step in the thawing of the cold war which Eisenhower had made possible, despite great political pressure, by his enormous personal prestige. Meeting Rockefeller, the Soviet Premier proposed a toast to "peaceful coexistence," but Nelson refused to join him, stipulating that he would drink only to "cooperation" and allowing himself to be photographed with Khrushchev only with reluctance. Later he explained to journalist Chalmers Roberts that he did this because he was convinced that the Russian's entourage included psychologists sizing up possible future Presidents, and hadn't wanted to appear weak in front of them.

When the Summit meeting of heads of state collapsed on May 17, 1960, following the downing of a U-2 spy plane over Russia and Eisenhower's refusal to apologize for the incident, Nelson saw the chance he had been waiting for. He had his friend and adviser Oren Root study the possibilities of organizing a draft movement like the one Root had as a young man put together for Wendell Willkie; and he allowed his operative L. Judson Morhouse to spread the word he was available, and that he had decided to attend the convention after all. On Memorial Day, only seven weeks before the delegates were scheduled to meet in Chicago, Nelson closeted himself with Hughes for a long brainstorming session. He emerged to launch a *Blitzkrieg* against the Republican party and Nixon. "I am deeply concerned," Rockefeller told the press in his opening barrage on June 8, "that those now assuming control of the Republican Party have failed to make clear where this party is heading and where it proposes to lead the nation." Referring to a "dangerous missile gap" between the United States and the Soviet Union, he called for a $5 billion increase in defense spending, a $500 million increase in civil defense, and a stepping up of the national growth rate by 50 percent.

Rockefeller's divisive assault on the Republican party and its heir apparent continued right up to the convention. Nixon, who had justified his nomination by a series of victories in the primaries, viewed the governor's attacks with mounting apprehension. Then, only a few days before the convention opening, Rockefeller announced that the party platform—a document which in normal circumstances would get little public attention—was unsatisfactory and indicated that there would be a floor fight to change it. Desperate to avoid any disunity, Nixon instructed former Attorney General Herbert Brownell to call the governor's aides and request a meeting to talk things over. Rockefeller then laid down the conditions that would continue to rankle his rival in years to come, as their political paths and personalities became more deeply entangled than either then imagined possible: the Vice-President would have to call Nelson personally to request the meeting; it would have to take place at a location of Nelson's choosing; and Rockefeller would control the press release announcing the outcome.

On July 23, two days before the Republican convention was scheduled to open, Nixon made the humiliating journey to New York. Starting with dinner at Nelson's 32-room *pied-à-terre* apartment with Nelson flatly refusing to consider taking the vice-presidential nomination, the two men worked until three A.M. rewriting the platform to include fourteen of Nelson's points—among them his tougher defense position and more liberal posture on civil rights. When they were finished, they relayed the decision over a special telephone trunk line Nelson had had installed for the occasion to the astonished platform committee, which had already wrapped up its work after deliberating for weeks in Chicago.

The Compact of Fifth Avenue, as it was called, angered Eisenhower because it seemed like a repudiation of his eight years in office, and seemed especially harshly critical of his handling of foreign and military affairs. From the conservative camp, Senator Barry Goldwater called it "the Munich of the Republican Party." To Nelson such charges only confirmed the fact he had won. Waving the agreement in front of newsmen when he arrived at the convention in Chicago, he said, "If you don't think this represents my views, you're crazy." Not bothering to calculate the number or the bitterness of the enemies he was making, Nelson climaxed a virtuoso performance when he agreed to appear before the convention on the final night (he had refused to nominate Nixon) to introduce the candidate. With the audience gasping in surprise, he capped the usual litany of hortatory clauses by saying, ". . . and the man who will succeed Dwight D. Eisenhower next January—Richard E. Nixon!"

Yet despite the gaffe (which he would arrange to have corrected in the official transcript of the speech), Nelson returned to New York jubilant. If Nixon was elected in November, he could take credit for having steered the party in the right direction; if Nixon lost, he could say that it was because he had not leaned far enough in his direction. Either way he would stand in a commanding position the next time Republicans selected a presidential nominee. His friend A. A. Berle, Jr.—a Democrat—congratulated him for "a good hand, well played." Nor was Nelson's prestige hurt when John F. Kennedy told confidants after his election that if Rockefeller had been his opponent the Republicans probably would have won.

It was a heady time for Nelson. His popularity was still high in New York, despite a tax increase, and his administration was embarking on a program of public construction that would change the state's physical appearance almost as drastically as its finances. Some of the commitments he undertook in his first term as governor seemed calculated as demonstration projects for the rest of the nation. He moved to make New York the capital of the nation's nuclear industry by creating the State Atomic Research and Development Authority. He also prepared for the possibility of less peaceful uses of atomic energy by proposing a $100 million bomb-shelter program.* The New Frontier could not help being interested in what he was doing. After all, many of its characteristic innovations were based on programs and ideas Nelson had done much to pioneer. In fact, the Kennedy administration's main effort—a dramatic escalation in the country's military posture including a multibillion-dollar annual increase in defense spending, emergency step-up in ICBMs, and the development of a counterinsurgency capability that would shortly be tested in Vietnam—was almost a point-by-point implementation of the recommendations of the Rockefeller Brothers Panel Studies.

Nelson was flattered by the President's evident regard. But he was also more obsessed than ever with the dream of someday having his own inaugural parade down Pennsylvania Avenue, especially since Nixon's loss had left the party leadership open. A week after Kennedy's election, Nelson sat down at Pocantico with Emmet Hughes, Harrison, Lockwood, George Hinman, and other trusted aides to begin long-range planning for 1964. The group became a sort of shadow Cabinet; its regular meetings were based on the assumption that Nelson's only problem would be overcoming the Kennedy charisma in the general election. Yet Nelson had earned himself a reputation as a renegade and had made a lot of enemies among party regulars and conservatives in Chicago. Bridges had to be repaired, and under the tactical

*In a series of almost frantic moves, Nelson ordered a $4 million bunker built in the state capital capable of housing 700 key public officials for at least two weeks. A storeroom under his Pocantico house was remade into a shelter, and a basement in his Manhattan apartment was converted for the same purpose. (Laurance built a submarinelike blast shelter under his home at Pocantico and connected it to a fallout shelter stocked with goods for several months of underground life.) Meanwhile Nelson was pushing his friend Edward Teller's plan for a $200 shelter in the home of every family in New York, bullying the legislature into granting a large tax exemption for any home with a shelter. Former New York State Senator Jack Bronston said of the obsession: "It was the single policy most consistent with Nelson's real personality. Despite strong opposition, he fought for his plan with everything he had. I remember one afternoon he invited a bunch of us to the red room in his mansion in Albany. He had these maps all over the wall with nuclear bombs exploding on them in color. He gave us a long, emotional lecture on how many lives the shelters could save in case of nuclear attack. I think he was more sincerely committed to this program than to anything since." Rockefeller even pushed shelters in a meeting with Nehru during the Indian Prime Minister's visit to New York in 1960. "He talked to me about nothing but bomb shelters," Nehru later said. "Why does he think I am interested in bomb shelters? He gave me a pamphlet on how to build my own shelter."

guidance of George Hinman, Nelson set out on the campaign trail once again, this time to woo the Republican right.

His series of carefully calculated moves began with Barry Goldwater, who was then the leader of the conservative wing of the party. Nelson invited the Arizona senator to intimate lunches at the Foxhall Road mansion in Washington he still maintained from OIAA days, to explain his political philosophy and views. By the beginning of 1962 (according to Washington reporter Robert Evans) Goldwater was telling his conservative friends, "Rocky's really not such a bad fellow. He's more conservative than you would imagine. You ought to talk to him someday." Less than a year later he was ready to fade out of the presidential picture because of his newfound faith in the New York governor.

Publicly Nelson paid his dues to the Republican right wing in a fierce attack on Kennedy when the President proposed the creation of a new Urban Affairs Department, which as a big-state "liberal" he was expected to support. Nelson denounced it in a speech in Des Moines as a threat to the Constitution and condemned the proposed appointment of Robert Weaver to head the department (who would thereby become the first black cabinet member in U.S. history) as "political fakery." By 1963 he was sniping at Kennedy's foreign policy for its "soft" attitude toward the Communists and for making "concessions" to the Russians on atomic testing, which, he said, "endangered national security." Half-heartedly endorsing the proposed Test Ban Treaty, he was quick to indicate reservations: "The administration should take every step to preserve the ability of our military establishment to deter and defeat Communist aggression against free peoples everywhere. Specifically there should be a national commitment that . . . we must at all times be prepared, able and willing to use nuclear weapons to repel aggression, alone or with our allies." Then, in a move that pleased his new allies on the right and disturbed the liberal press, he lashed out against what he called Kennedy's "failure" on Cuba: "It is very hard for me to understand why we are supporting in Vietnam freedom fighters and why we are holding them back and preventing them from operating on Cuba. . . . I hope it is not to placate or appease the Soviets."

His ambitions were coming to fruition with a speed that satisfied even him. Yet those who were close to Nelson knew there was a time bomb in his personal life that might well go off at any moment. It was his marriage to Tod, which had been on the rocks for some time. Over the years, she had withdrawn more and more into the role of Calpurnia, the features of her long face congealing into a stoical mask as rumors of her husband's persistent infidelities circulated just within range of her hearing. She had grown accustomed to walking into suddenly hushed conversations about her husband—who he was with now, how he had sent so-and-so on some elaborate fact-finding junket to countries where IBEC did business so that he could enjoy the man's wife during his absence.

It could be accepted as part of the seemingly inevitable pornography of political life, although it made the role of Caesar's wife even more unbearable for her than it in any case would have been. Everything in her upbringing recoiled at the vulgarities of the political arena, the meaningless pleasantries of the reception line and of official dinners and entertainments. She was not, in campaign language, "a political asset." Moreover, she could not accept what family friend George Gilder describes as the Great Man Complex: "Tod was smart—smarter and wittier than Nelson, in fact. As he became absorbed in his political career and started believing his campaign literature, it was increasingly difficult for him to come home every night to an amused skeptic, who knew him as he used to be, before he was great."

Nelson himself had long since realized that the marriage was not working and had settled instead for an arrangement in which appearances would be observed: publicly he would play the role of husband and father; in return Tod would cause no scenes. Privately they would each go their way. But shortly before his first campaign for governor, the rules under which they had managed to live for years ceased to apply when Nelson fell seriously in love and decided that he had to have a divorce. In 1957, prior to the gubernatorial campaign, he had told Jamieson that he had made up his mind to go through with the divorce. But, in the course of a long meandering automobile ride, he allowed himself to be convinced by his friend that it would be political suicide. ("Frank felt it would be the end for Nelson politically," Jamieson's widow, Mrs. Linda Storrow, recalls. "Nelson knew it too, but Frank had to work very hard to change his mind.") Now Jamieson was gone. Nelson's children were grown, and even though he had vast resources for carrying on his current affair, including a "hideaway" on the Pocantico estate, the whole thing had become clumsy. As his emotional and political waves crested together, he felt that it was time to clear the decks.

The first public sign of his troubled marital life came on March 3, 1961, when the Executive Mansion caught fire late one night, and observers noted that firemen escorted Tod to safety from a wing opposite the one where her husband slept. After that, she never returned to Albany, although the separation was not announced. It went unnoticed that Nelson was living alone and shunning social occasions because attention was focused on his entrance into New York City politics, where he hoped to elect Attorney General Louis Lefkowitz mayor and thus not only improve his own chances of carrying the city when he ran for reelection but also show that he was the one Republican capable of dueling JFK for the urban centers in 1964.

On Saturday, November 18, 1961, after this adventure in king making had been beaten back by Mayor Robert Wagner, Nelson officially announced the separation from Tod. He knew there would be repercussions. It was one thing for someone like his brother Winthrop to marry and divorce a lower-class fortune hunter. It was something else entirely for the governor of New York to leave a wife of more than thirty years and the mother of his five children.

Yet the next day something more dramatic forced the separation out of the headlines. Nelson was lunching with his brother David, discussing the impact the news would have on his political future, when the telephone rang. There was a scrambled, terrifying conversation with Dutch officials in New Guinea. It was about Nelson's son Michael, who, with Dutch anthropologist Rene Wassing, had been on a field trip into the Asmat, a remote jungle area rarely visited by white men. The two had rigged a catamaran and begun sailing down the coast of the Arafura Sea, when their craft had been blown off course and out into the open sea. Voices on the other end of the echoing telephone connection said that three days ago Michael had strapped two empty gasoline cans to his back for flotation, left his partner clinging to the wreckage of the boat, and plunged into the shark-infested waters, beginning the eleven-mile swim to shore. Although Wassing had been rescued, nothing had been seen or heard of Michael since.

With this news flaying him as if in retribution for the previous day's announcement about the breakup of his marriage, Nelson chartered a plane and hurriedly left for New Guinea with Michael's twin sister, Mary. For a week they combed the area, coordinating with Dutch search parties as they hedgehopped in light planes over the impenetrable jungle, hoping for some sign that the 23-year-old youth was alive. On November 26 they gave up and began the long return home. Mary stopped off in Manila to visit her husband, navy Ensign William Strawbridge, and Nelson continued on to Idlewild, where he was met by family, state officials, and some two hundred journalists. Unable to bring himself to use the past tense about the son he now knew was surely dead, he spoke briefly of Michael at an otherwise silent press conference: "Ever since he was little, he has been aware of people, their feelings, their thoughts. He is a person who has a tremendous enthusiasm and drive, love of life. . . ." Afterward he went to his estranged wife's apartment to meet with her and his children. "You had a hard trip, Nels," she greeted him.

"Yes, I'm sorry to bring home such bad news, Tod," he replied.

The broken family was momentarily knit together again by the tragedy as Nelson spread a map of New Guinea on the floor in front of the fireplace and told of the search. After it was over, he got up looking gray and worn, kissed Tod on the cheek, and went home alone.

Michael's death placed an unspoken moratorium on discussions of Nelson's marital situation. In February 1962, Tod went to Reno to file for divorce on grounds of mental cruelty. Nelson brushed off rumors that he was romantically involved with someone else and set out to win reelection (reporters might have been more inquisitive had they known that he had the official history·of the Executive Mansion rewritten to eliminate Tod's name), hoping for such a large plurality over his little-known Democratic opponent, Robert Morgenthau, that it would prove conclusively his appeal had not been lessened by the divorce.

Although failing to achieve the million-vote margin he had expected, or even to equal the margin by which he had won in 1958, Nelson was reelected by more than 500,000 votes. Coupled with Nixon's loss in California's gubernatorial race and his vituperative withdrawal from politics, Nelson's triumph in the midst of personal problems that might have sunk another politician gave him an aura of invincibility. Walter Lippmann looked ahead to 1964 and wrote that he was "in the position of a man so certain to be nominated that he could not prevent it if he wanted to." Yet even before the assassination of Kennedy altered America's political course forever, Nelson made what hindsight would prove to be the most disastrous decision in his life: to marry the woman he had loved secretly for more than five years. The last step on the path that began with his separation from Tod, this decision might have had the portentous quality of a trope from classical tragedy if Nelson had possessed the self-recognition necessary for heroic stature. Even though he didn't, the act would come in time to seem as though it contained an element of fate.

The family took the news as a severe blow. Winthrop flew up from Arkansas to argue against it. David was devastated. His daughter Abby recalls: "The remarriage was the most distressing thing to him that ever happened in the world. Nelson was supposed to be the pivot around which the family would build its identity. That was why they all saw it as such a disaster." Neither Winthrop, nor David, nor John attended the wedding, nor did Nelson's children, Rodman, Mary, Ann, and Steven.

It took place at high noon on May 4, 1963, in the living room of Laurance's home at Pocantico. Nelson seemed younger than his fifty-four years as he stood in front of the minister from the family church at Pocantico Hills exchanging vows with Margaretta ("Happy") Murphy, a pretty 36-year-old society matron with honey-brown hair and a fresh-scrubbed, almost virginal look set off by a blue silk afternoon dress with a demure bow at the neck.

She and the husband she had divorced a month earlier were no strangers to the Rockefeller family. Dr. James ("Robin") Murphy was the son of an old friend of Junior's, and when he had married Happy in 1948, the couple had journeyed to see the Rockefeller patriarch at the Eyrie in Maine. Junior had been much taken with the attractive young couple and took them under his wing, arranging to have the ambitious Robin appointed to a research project of the Rockefeller Medical Institute in San Francisco. The following year Robin wanted to move to New York, and David, who was now the head of the Rockefeller Medical Institute, got him a permanent position at the Institute headquarters. In time, David arranged an unprecedented privilege for the young couple: Happy and Robin would be invited to build a home within the Pocantico Estate. As the family's architect in residence, Nelson naturally conferred with the Murphys at length about the sort of home they planned to build, and later went over the blueprints closely with Happy at David's Seal Harbor home.

Outwardly Happy and Robin were the perfect couple, their relationship seemingly cemented over the years by four children. They were among the few outsiders allowed within the Rockefellers' charmed circle. Yet the taste of intimacy only created an appetite for more. Ironically, it was Robin Murphy who took the lead. As a close Rockefeller friend recalls: "Robin was the chief force in courting Nelson. He truckled to him, laughed too hard at his jokes, praised his art collection too unctuously. He was obvious. Usually the Rockefellers saw through such fawning."

One of the reasons Nelson bore it was the liaison with Happy, begun in the mid-1950s and intensifying after she went to work as a volunteer in his gubernatorial campaign and stayed on as a paid member of his staff. To facilitate the arrangement, Nelson appointed Robin—who privately raged at Happy, but attempted to maintain outward appearances— to a position in the state health office in Albany. "I'm not sure I really deserve it," he confided pathetically to a family intimate. "I don't know how I'm qualified for it. I guess I must really have impressed Nelson with my work at the Rockefeller Institute or something."

Happy was different from the other women with whom he'd been involved. "Nelson was really deeply in love, and would get terribly romantic, almost sentimental, in talking about Happy during those years he thought he couldn't have her," recalls Frank Jamieson's widow. Happy had youth, beauty, and the rare ability to embody the unattainable.

"She was just dazzling in those days," George Gilder remembers. "She had a way of glowing at you, and her glow made you feel you were the most brilliant man in the world." She took on an almost symbolic quality in Nelson's life. Like Fitzgerald's Daisy Buchanan, she was "that spectre of womanhood that for a little while, makes everything else seem unimportant." Yet, as Nelson would discover, Daisy pursued was one thing and Daisy attained was quite another.

Even as the couple jetted off for a seventeen-day honeymoon at Nelson's 18,000-acre Monte Sacro estate in the Venezuela mountains, Rockefeller's conservative opponents in the GOP—never fully convinced by his attempts after 1960 to mend fences with them—began to see that they might bring him down from his high perch in the party's future by pin-ning a morals charge on him. Divorce was one thing; remarriage was something else again, especially when the bride had to give up custody of four small children in her hasty trip to the altar. A Gallup Poll taken three weeks afterward confirmed that it had indeed done significant damage to Nelson's political hopes. The 43 to 26 percent lead he had enjoyed over Barry Goldwater before the wedding announcement had now vanished, and he trailed the Arizona senator 35 to 30 percent.

As columnist Stewart Alsop observed at the time, Nelson could have remarried or run for President, but he couldn't do both. He might have tried some variation of Edward's "the woman I love" speech, played the kingmaker in 1964 by anointing someone like Pennsylvania Governor William Scranton as the moderate candidate early in the campaign, and waited for 1968 to make a bid against Lyndon Johnson. Such a course would have been a reasonable one for him— leaving his options open—and a practical one for his party. It would have provided, moreover, a considerate release for his family, which was still in a state of shock over the divorce and remarriage, and for Happy, who did not want to continue her public ordeal. Yet he had always found it hard to accept the constraints that governed the actions of other men. In the months that followed he did not slacken his pace. If he could no longer have the nomination for the asking, he would take it through the primaries, regardless of the consequences. If there were still some doubts about his remarriage, he would take his now-pregnant bride across the country and compel the public to bless their union at the ballot box.

The new situation would have demanded a new strategy. He could not promote party unity as he would have if he had been the favorite; only a bloodletting could win him the prize. He would now declare war in the name of liberal values on the right wing he had covertly courted for the past two years. On July 14, 1963, he unveiled his new position with a bombshell declaration against Goldwater (whom he did not yet name) and the "well-drilled extremists" whom he had suddenly discovered "boring from within the party." Calling his declaration "A Matter of Principle," he said:

> I am now convinced that the Republican Party is in real danger of subversion by a radical, well-financed and highly disciplined minority.... Completely incredible as it is to me, it is now being seriously proposed to the Re-

publican Party as a strategy for victory in 1964, that it
write off the Negro and other minority groups, that it
deliberately write off the great industrial states of the
North. . . . The transparent purpose behind this plan is to
erect political power on the outlawed and immoral base
of segregation and to transform the Republican Party
from a national party of all the people to a sectional
party of some of the people.

The destiny of the Republican party, he concluded in a typi-
cally apocalyptic thrust, "is to save the Nation by first saving
itself."

By September 15 a Gallup Poll showed that Goldwater
was leading Rockefeller by a 59 to 41 percent margin among
Republican voters. Yet the Rockefeller camp, fueled by its
leader's inexhaustible determination and resources, was em-
phatically optimistic. "There is nothing wrong with Rockefeller," declared Charles F. Moore, who had left a spectacular
career at Ford to manage Rockefeller's public relations in the
primaries, "that can't be cured by a win in New Hampshire."

By early 1964, as the primaries were about to begin,
Rockefeller had assembled the most elaborate political apparatus ever seen for a primary struggle in the history of
American presidential elections. Before it was over, his official campaign would spend $8 million, the bulk of it from his
own and his family's funds. He would get Laurance and the
crestfallen David to make generous contributions, and he
would receive others from Junior's widow, Martha Baird.
Once he officially announced his candidacy, his paid campaign staff was increased from seventy to three hundred, and
it was operating out of Rockefeller Center, the West 55th
Street brownstones, an entire floor of an office building at
521 Fifth Avenue, and a suite of rooms in the United Rubber
Building on West 49th Street. Emmet Hughes was gone,* but
old Rockefeller hands like Lockwood, Harrison, and Kis-

*Hughes had been Jamieson's replacement for three years in the public
relations post of Room 5600. ("Hiring him was Nelson's attempt to
keep his hand in the affairs of the Office from afar in Albany, but
Hughes never took," says John Lockwood.) Yet even in his absence,
Hughes's association would weigh heavily against Nelson. Eisenhower
would never forgive his former speech writer for publishing *The Ordeal of Power*, which he regarded as a malicious kiss-and-tell memoir.
Nelson's patronage of Hughes, combined with memories of the Compact of Fifth Avenue, kept the former President from yielding to pleas
that he stop Goldwater by an early endorsement of Rockefeller.

singer remained from the brain trust that had been meeting
regularly since the Kennedy inauguration.

New Hampshire was supposed to be a political weather
vane, showing how public opinion would sort out Nelson's remarriage and his attacks on Goldwater's ideology. In the
weeks preceding the primary, the right-wing Manchester
Union Leader printed front-page editorials denouncing
Rockefeller as a "wife swapper." Yet Goldwater made some
of his most stunning gaffes during his appearances there.

Rockefeller spent weeks slogging through the snows of the
state with the pregnant Happy beside him. It was a bone-
wearying effort that wound up inconclusively. Rockefeller
forces spent hundreds of thousands of dollars, but when the
votes were in, Henry Cabot Lodge, a write-in candidate, had
scored 35 percent of the vote, Goldwater 23 percent, and
Nelson 20 percent.

Yet he was undaunted. Setting out for Oregon like a driven
man, he waged an exhausting campaign that left him gray
and drawn, but rewarded him with a bracing primary victory
over Lodge, whose campaign was dealt a crippling blow. The
stage was set for the climactic battle in California.

Nearly half of the $3 million Nelson had budgeted for the
primaries was spent in California, publicizing select Gold-
waterisms about the bomb, Social Security, Medicare, and
civil rights. One of these, a pamphlet titled *Whom Do You
Want in the Room with the H-Bomb Button?*, was distributed
to two million California voters.*

It was a cruel campaign for Rockefeller, who had to run
through the heartland of the John Birch Society and the radical right in Orange County. There were bomb threats; a tea
party attended by Nelson and Happy was crashed by thugs;
and there were endless organized calls to radio talk shows
complaining about the remarriage and describing the liberal
Republican candidate as morally unfit for the presidency. But
for a while, especially after a late and restrained intervention
by Eisenhower on behalf of responsible politics, it looked as

---

*Yet the answer to the question, which might have seemed obvious to
those who knew only of the Arizona senator's celebrated faux pas, was
not so obvious if Nelson's own record was examined. In pushing the
fallout shelter program and in promoting the defense strategy of limited nuclear war, Nelson more than any other politician of national
stature had put his political weight behind policies designed to make
nuclear war a practical option. He and Goldwater even shared an adviser on nuclear matters, Dr. Edward Teller.

though Nelson might pull off his miracle. The Friday before the primary, the prestigious Field Poll showed Rockefeller leading Goldwater 49 percent to 40 percent. But then came the final ironic twist in the crooked path leading from the decision to divorce Tod. On Saturday night, three days before the primary, Happy Rockefeller entered a New York hospital to give birth to a son—Nelson, Jr. The following day, a new Field Poll showed Rockefeller and Goldwater even. And when the voters went to the polls on Tuesday, the momentum caused by this reminder of Nelson's marital escapades gave his opponent a narrow victory and the 1964 presidential nomination.

Thrust into the unaccustomed role of loser, Rockefeller returned to San Francisco a month later as titular head of the anti-Goldwater forces at the convention. When he stood defiantly before the convention whose candidate he had denigrated and whose philosophy he had mocked, he was even more the enemy than Democratic candidate Lyndon Johnson. It was as if Nelson had decided that if he couldn't have their affection, he would at least have their hatred, and he baited them into howling at him and interrupting his speech ("This is still a democracy, ladies and gentlemen," he lectured them) as if to prove on national television that they were the wrathful, intolerant zealots he had all along claimed them to be.

If 1964 was a time when he won a large following among those who interpreted his confrontation with Goldwater as a courageous moral stand, it also seemed to be the end of whatever realistic hopes Nelson may have had of being nominated by his party for the presidency. He would never be able to give up his quest, but he could no longer believe as he had that it would naturally come to him.

It was as if a malignancy had been discovered in his career. To those who had jeered him in San Francisco, he would always be the Great Wrecker—not just of Robin Murphy's home and family, but of the campaign of Barry Goldwater, whose steps Nelson had dogged all the way from New Hampshire to California, reminding audiences of his extremism, goading him into even more extreme statements, and creating doubts about his stability while also perfecting the vocabulary of attack the Johnson forces would use so effectively in the general election.

Now it was time to pay the penalty. The call came from an unexpected source: the liberal wing of the party, whose leadership he had assumed in 1958 by right of conquest. After the November Democratic landslide, old comrades like Senator Jacob Javits urged Nelson to remove himself from future presidential contention. They didn't want a repeat of 1964. And they told him so.

Always before, Nelson had expressed candid optimism about his dreams for the White House. "Being President?" he once said. "Well, I'm a politician. That's my profession. Success in politics, real success, means only one thing in America." But now he became more self-protective. Responding to questions about his future plans, he would say that the dirty character of the '64 campaign had soured him on national politics, and he was no longer interested.

The people who knew him well doubted this, yet they could not deny he had changed. The ebullience, the appearance of innocence that had tended to take the sharp edge off his drive for power when he first appeared on the political scene had vanished. In its stead was a hardness, a cynical and querulous quality. He now seemed a prisoner of the drives that had once been the essence of his freedom. It was a quality Norman Mailer had sensed toward the end of the 1964 primaries when he wrote of Nelson: "He had a strong, decent face and something tough as a handball in his makeup, but his eyes had been punched out. . . . They had the distant lunar glow of the small sad eyes you see in a caged chimpanzee or gorilla. Even when hearty he gave an impression that the private man was remote as an astronaut lost in orbit."

Politics, which had always been enjoyable for him, a true recreation, now came to seem a harsh exercise in survival. At the 1965 Governors' Conference, he announced his withdrawal from national politics to help unify the party. But this gesture got him little thanks from those whom he had used so cavalierly for his own ends. When, that same year, he gave John Lindsay half a million in loans, which Lindsay had demanded to run as Nelson's hand-picked candidate in the New York mayoralty race, it was because he knew that the glow had worn off his own administration, especially with upstate conservatives irritated at the massive debt with which he was saddling the state. He would have to count on heavy support from the city in his next campaign.

When he himself entered the 1966 gubernatorial contest, it was against a Democratic candidate who was far ahead in the polls. It was not that Frank O'Connor was popular, but that Nelson's appeal had slipped to the point where early polls had shown him getting only 25 percent of the vote against *any* candidate. His brother David tried to dissuade him from running, but that was never an option.

The polls showed that crime was the uppermost issue in the minds of the voters, and in 1964 Nelson introduced the "no-knock" law, which allowed police to enter a house without bothering to announce themselves first. (He had already enacted a "stop-and-frisk" law allowing police to dispense with probable cause provisions and search anyone suspected of bearing weapons.) And as part of his campaign against O'Connor, a former district attorney, he had promised a new $400 million Narcotics Addiction Control Act, setting up a system whereby addicts would be committed either civilly or after trial in state facilities he proposed to build.

Realizing that he was in the fight of his political life, Nelson spent an incredible $5.2 million on the gubernatorial race, almost ten times as much as O'Connor's $576,000. The focus of Nelson's campaign was a devastating two-stage media attack. In its first weeks, when he was 26 percentage points behind O'Connor in the polls, Rockefeller advertisements stressed the achievements of his two terms: overhauling and dramatic expansion of the state university system, building tens of thousands of miles of new highways, and the like. Then, in the last weeks of the campaign, as he began to pull even, he turned to attacks on his opponent, who had failed to adopt his "tough" attitude on urban crime. (O'Connor, for instance, had come out for a modified version of the English technique for dealing with drug addiction, saying that one of his first acts as governor would be to throw out Rockefeller's Addiction Control Act.) During the final days of the campaign, television viewers were blitzed with commercials showing a syringe entering the main line, or hoodlums walking menacingly on dark, rain-slicked streets. The voice-over was that of Nelson, and it rasped: "Want to keep the crime rate high? Vote for O'Connor."

Nelson's media blitz would later be studied as a textbook example of the way an unprincipled use of television could affect the outcome of a campaign. Yet the campaign itself, regarded as one of the most ruthless in recent New York history, was successful. The usually infallible New York *Daily News* straw poll picked O'Connor, but Nelson's narrow victory proved it wrong for the first time in thirty years.

In postelection statements, Nelson again disclaimed any intention to run for the presidency in 1968. It seemed plausible, given the 1964 disaster and his narrow victory in New York. There was an understandable mood of resignation in the answers he gave to questions about the future: "There are things that happen inside. I'm not a psychiatrist or psychologist. I can't analyze it for you exactly. But I just don't have the ambition or need or the inner drive—whatever the word is—to get in again."

Yet Bill Moyers was correct in his assessment of these weary disavowals of ambition: "I believe Rocky when he says he's lost his ambition. I also believe he remembers where he put it."

A week after his defeat of O'Connor, in fact, Nelson was running again. In the past he had been described by George Hinman as a polar bear. "You shoot at him, and he just keeps coming on." Somehow, he knew now, this technique wouldn't work. But he had no compensating motion. So he continued to lurch forward. He ran, to begin with, as a man must who has been rejected and then formally and unequivocally taken himself out of contention; by supporting someone else. Of the new generation of Republican moderates clamoring for a chance at the nomination in 1968, Governor George Romney, who had won resounding victories in Michigan in three successive elections, was the leader. And it was Romney that Rockefeller invited to join him at his brother Laurance's Dorado Beach Hotel in December for conversations about the party's future.

Romney was far and away the leader in the polls. It was true that he had a reputation for making confusing statements and lacked a clear perspective on foreign affairs, but since he was the front-runner, and the last thing Nelson could afford was to create a schism within the moderate wing of the party, he urged him to get his candidacy going early. During the days they talked in the Puerto Rico sun, Nelson promised Romney the backing of the Republican governors (whose titular head he was) as well as money, workers, and the wide range of other resources that went into a typical Rockefeller campaign. Nelson's chief speech writer, Hugh Morrow, was donated to the Romney campaign in the early months of 1967; George Gilder, godson of David Rockefeller and co-founder of the liberal Ripon Society (and, in 1964, a speechwriter for Nelson), also joined the Michigan governor's staff; Henry Kissinger was made available for day-long foreign policy briefing sessions and went over Romney's major statements on Vietnam (trying to bring them into line with the more hawkish views he and Nelson shared). If, later, George Romney decided that Rockefeller had probably hoped to hang him all along, he couldn't say that he hadn't been given the best rope money could buy.

One Republican leader later said that the Michigan governor's campaign for the presidency had been like "watching a duck try to make love to a football." His most inept maneuver (although events would ultimately vindicate him in an odd way) had been his offhand statement in August 1967 that he had been "brainwashed" by U.S. generals while touring Vietnam. By the end of 1967, his credibility had sunk so low and he was lagging so far behind Nixon in the polls that he came to Nelson and asked to be relieved of his commitment to run. But Rockefeller, fearing that a premature Romney withdrawal could result in the moderates' anointing someone like Charles Percy, held him to his word and urged him to hold on through the New Hampshire primary. Only after he was humiliated there did Nelson release him from his obligation.

Yet Rockefeller, still gun-shy from 1964 and aware that he could not risk a primary loss to Nixon, hesitated about his own candidacy in what would strike some of those close to him as an odd and disturbing indecision. In March he formally took himself out of the contest. In April, after LBJ's withdrawal, he announced with equal suddenness that he was a candidate and tried quickly to reassemble his dismantled campaign team, conscripting Emmet Hughes and Kissinger once again as the top men.

They were an odd couple—the liberal journalist who had opposed the lassitude of the Eisenhower presidency and then committed the indiscretion of writing an intimate memoir about it, and the pragmatic professor, still committed to the diplomatic minuet of the cold war and completely loyal to his sponsors. The central drama in Nelson's on-again, off-again 1968 campaign was a struggle between Hughes and Kissinger over the candidate's Vietnam position. Hughes wanted Nelson to come out for immediate and total withdrawal, but was blocked and isolated by Kissinger to the extent that he could only use his power as chief speech writer in a negative way. Yet on the surface there was peace between them. It was Hughes who made the top-secret trip to California to meet with Ronald Reagan and form the strategy of cooperating to try to squeeze Nixon out of a first-ballot victory. Meanwhile Kissinger attempted to create a Vietnam position for Rocke-

feller that at least *seemed* different from the Johnson administration's policies,* and prepared a highly confidential "Black
Book on Nixon" as a casebook for Nelson to use in attacks
on his old rival in the months between April and the convention. (This document, with provocative chapter headings like
"The Tricky Dick Syndrome" and "The Loser Image," would
remain locked in a closet in Room 5600 long after Kissinger
had become the brightest luminary of the Nixon administration and Nelson one of the President's staunchest supporters.)

Yet until June 5, the Rockefeller campaign suffered from
an indecisiveness that had uncharacteristically overtaken the
candidate. It was as if his political personality, so sharply defined by events four years earlier, was now out of focus. He
searched for a foothold in space that other politicians occupied more dramatically. It was only when news of Bobby
Kennedy's death flashed through New York that Nelson saw
an opening in the role of charismatic maverick bucking the
establishment and quickly decided to fill it.

His son Steven recalls how Nelson came to him after the
assassination to ask for his help, saying that while he didn't
have the answers himself, he believed he could put together a
coalition of minorities, young people, and liberals. "He
wanted to go to the people, to get the nomination by a great
public outcry," says Steven. "He's always loved the street, the
crowd, shaking hands, dealing with hecklers. He just eats it
up. Going to the people is his thing; he loves the applause.
Going to the delegates was not his thing."

Within forty-eight hours of the assassination Nelson had
prepared a speech to be followed by a series of newspaper
ads saying that he alone now offered a choice between "a
new leadership and old politics," and he began a whirlwind
tour that would take him into big cities all over the country,

---

*In March 1968, when his candidacy was off, Nelson responded to a
journalist's question for a summary of his views on Vietnam as follows: "My position on Vietnam is very simple. And I feel this way. I
haven't spoken on it because I haven't felt there was any major contribution I had to make." After he had changed his mind and gotten
his campaign going, he had Kissinger create a plan for a four-part operation beginning with the withdrawal of 75,000 troops and eventually
involving an international peace-keeping force. Kissinger worked hard
between Nelson's announcement of his candidacy and Miami, holding
four-hour foreign policy briefings daily with the press and smoothing
over his patron's confusing statements. Journalists requesting clarifica-
tion of Rockefeller statements would be told: "Go see Henry. He's the
only one around here who can explain what our position is and make
it come out sounding right."

where he would plunge recklessly into crowds, allow young people to rip off his cuff links, and try to build pressure on delegates from below.

Yet if the style of Kennedy politics suited him well enough, he was unable to embrace its substance. It was only through violent infighting that the younger members of his staff were able to defeat Kissinger's insistence that Nelson issue a major policy statement supporting the antiballistic missile system. On the question of the war, Nelson continued to vacillate. He had supported the Johnson administration's Vietnam policy from the beginning. (In the 1964 campaign he had said, "Winning the fight for freedom in Vietnam is essential for the survival of freedom in all of Asia. The communist Vietcong guerrillas must be defeated.") Now, with something like a national referendum taking place on this issue as he sought the old Kennedy constituency, the best he could do was to streamline his stand without breaking with the hardline attitudes that had always been the spine of his political philosophy. The result was often confusing. On one campaign swing, he made this statement in answer to a question about the war: "I think that our concepts as a nation and that our actions have not kept pace with changing conditions. And therefore our actions are not completely relevant today to the magnitude and complexity of the problems that we face in this conflict." When a *New York Times* reporter asked, "Governor, what does that mean?" Nelson snapped, "Just what I said."

By the time he got to Miami, Nelson's attempt to ride past the party bosses on the shoulders of the people had clearly failed. He had managed to capture the diminished crest of the Kennedy wave but never its basic energy. He had spent $8 million in an effort to wrest the nomination away from Richard Nixon, but all he had really done was to help dramatize a convention whose conclusions had been foregone for months, since those crucial moments earlier in the spring when he had equivocated and lost the support of figures like Spiro Agnew who might have helped put him over despite the united opposition of the party regulars who remembered 1964.

Nelson had come a long distance from that time eight years earlier when he had been able to rewrite the Republican party's platform to suit his pleasure. But most of the way had been downhill. As Nixon was nominated on the first ballot, the prize Nelson had been striving after for more than a decade seemed finally out of his reach. If Nixon defeated

Humphrey, as seemed likely, there would doubtless be a
clamor among party regulars for four more years in 1972. By
1976, Nelson would be sixty-seven years old—young for a
Rockefeller, perhaps, but old for a presidential hopeful. It
seemed that he, like Tantalus, would have to learn to live
with a raging thirst even while standing waist-deep in the
lake.

21

NIXON'S INAUGURATION coincided with a moment when the
Rockefellers passed over an epic cusp into an age with new
laws of motion slowing the movement that had elevated the
family with such velocity during the previous half-century. As
if overnight, they began to realize that something had gone
out of their world; the pinnacle they had strained so hard to
attain was suddenly now behind them, and in the future their
children would handle the name and its responsibilities far
differently from the way they had. They still had the power
they had been born to, but in exercising it they were filled
with a foreboding that affected them all in a deep and personal way.

If they did not confront the crisis directly, it was not because they were strangers to crisis. The family had faced and
overcome awesome dilemmas in the past. But what they
faced now was nothing like the furor over the South Improvement plan, or the "tainted money" controversy, or even
Ludlow. It was no crisis that they could stage-manage in such
a way as to turn guilt into redemption. In fact, there was no
single event they could focus on and hold responsible for the
malaise that now took hold of them. It was something that
was happening *to* them, not *because* of them.

One of its manifestations was the resurgence of an anti-
Rockefeller zeal that had not been seen since World War I.
The revival was due partly to Nelson's political campaigns,
his readiness to use the immense resources at his command to
achieve ends that were obviously connected to his own ambi-

tions and desires. In his reckless flaunting of self, as in his opting for a political career in the first place, he had violated his father's lessons in pragmatic morality. Only if the Rockefellers stayed in the background and strenuously drained personality from their acts could the hatred of the Rockefeller wealth be kept dormant. Junior had been right: Nelson had produced a reaction and stirred up sleeping dragons.

The conservative Republican heartlands, which periodically had seen their presidential favorites blocked by the powerful caucus of eastern finance, had come to see that power personified in Rockefeller and the Rockefeller institutions. A pamphlet that served as the call to arms of the Goldwater campaign described how "the secret New York kingmakers" had controlled every Republican nominee since 1936, "to insure control of the largest cash market in the world: the Executive Branch of the United States Government," and how Nixon's 1960 "surrender in Manhattan" to Nelson was but the latest phase of their long, undemocratic *coup*.

Nelson was the immediate target, but in the long run such arguments were aimed at the name itself as the symbolic expression of forces drastically affecting American life. Whether the discussion was about big government or big business, the Rockefellers were potent representatives of both. Even the bizarre linking of the Rockefellers with the Communist conspiracy in right-wing demonologies seemed to make sense when it was coupled with the view that Socialism was not a share-the-wealth program but a method to consolidate and control economic life.

Underlying this unease was a sense that things were increasingly out of control, that "insiders" manipulated the government through interlocking directorates and elite organizations, like the Council on Foreign Relations, which dominated policy while operating outside the democratic process. "They" controlled things but were not accountable. And among those who conspired to run the world from behind the scenes, the secretive Rockefellers ranked at the very top.

Nor was the right wing alone in seeing the family as a symbol of unchecked plutocratic power and conspiratorial control. The left also revived the anti-Rockefeller tradition going back to the muckrakers and the Walsh Commission, as the cold war consensus that had dominated the thought of the preceding decade foundered on the shoals of Vietnam, broke up, and readmitted critiques of wealth, power, and corporate predation into the cultural mainstream.

Consequently, although they were doing nothing different from what they had done for decades, the Rockefeller Brothers suddenly found themselves demonstrated against and denounced, the subject of "underground" exposés and ingenious diagrams which showed the interests and institutions interlocking them with apartheid in South Africa, militarism in Latin America, war in Indochina.

The family's secrecy and its global involvements could plausibly suggest a Byzantine network of control, feeding the right's fear of conspiracy on the one hand and left-wing paranoia about the Rockefellers on the other. When economist Victor Perlo claimed that the family directly controlled financial and industrial corporations worth more than $60 billion, this improbable figure was quickly accepted as an article of faith. When Ferdinand Lundberg theorized, in *The Rich and the Super-Rich*, that the family fortune itself amounted to some $5 billion, others said this was a gross understatement. Out of style for some fifty years, Rockefeller baiting had become fashionable again.

If they had not been so conditioned to accept the mythology that enveloped their lives and careers, the Brothers might have realized that a critical juncture had been passed in the dynasty they now controlled. They might have convened a summit meeting at the Playhouse (as they often did to discuss personal matters), away from the employees who stood guard over the Rockefeller myths like harem eunuchs, and tried to unravel the process that was cutting a jagged swath through American history and dragging them behind it. They would have had to step out of the ceremonial roles they had learned to play, and look at themselves objectively—as they might at the priceless artifacts they collected. They would have had to discard the books written by authors they had paid or sanctioned, and try to strip the presumption of manifest destiny from their history and come to grips with the peculiar series of events that had produced their unique family.

It would have been like reconstructing a true version of the family dialectic. It would have to begin with the grandfather—not the venerable old eccentric they had known as boys or the moral paragon their father had spoken of reverently, but the flinty industrialist who had terrorized his competitors and bent the country's economic system to his iron will, even at the cost of becoming a national outcast, as hated as he was feared. Next had come their father, the prim little man who had dedicated his life and the tainted fortune he inherited to changing the adverse view of the family created by the excesses of the Standard trust. He found that he could best ensure against the future hatred of the Rockefeller name by welding the family's destiny to the new political and economic order propelling the nation to a position of global leadership and empire. As he did so, something seemed to lock, and a myth of epic proportions began to take shape.

Far from questioning the symbiosis between their family's destiny and the country's, the Brothers had devoted their careers to forging even stronger links that allowed them power of a kind their grandfather never could have hoped for, and also a kind of invulnerability, as the family's identification with America became so strong that it almost seemed treasonable to attack them. The fifties had been *their* era— the time when they came of age and first began to know the impact they might have on the world—and the sixties had begun even more auspiciously. Kennedy was President, but the Brothers had spent years building outposts in that area he now proclaimed a New Frontier. They were representative men of an aristocracy of wealth and power that would influence his administration, and the others to follow.

Like their father, the Brothers had not made rash decisions. Each step along the way had been carefully weighed by them and the elite team of experts they had assembled to advise them. None of them could have foreseen that by the mid-1960s the country would be convulsed by race riots, generation and credibility gaps, and a genocidal war in a distant land: phenomena that hastened the destruction of the national consensus the Rockefellers had not only helped create, but also benefited from in a unique and compelling way.

They were still regarded as a valuable national resource by the people who counted. Their access to the important nodes of social and economic power was undiminished. Yet there had been a fundamental change in the way the world perceived them. No longer were they knights *sans peur et sans reproche,* as they had been when they were young men making their debuts. Now they were simply men of power, and they found it increasingly difficult to use the myth their father had created to avoid being called to account for its exercise.

Not only were they suddenly questioned about things for which they were in some sense responsible—the policies of Standard Oil, the Chase Bank, the Rockefeller Foundation, and other institutions they were involved in—but they were also attacked for the sins of the system itself. They had become the most visible embodiments of that sinister power implicit in the "establishment," "power structure," "ruling class," and the host of other terms used to describe the continuum of economic interest and ideological commitment people could not see but felt was responsible for the social and moral chaos of the times. The Rockefellers were influence, money, control, policy. They were power.

To understand all this and grapple with it would have been a major task and perhaps beyond the Brothers' conceptual range. If they *had* attempted to come to terms with the process that produced them, it would have destroyed the elaborate edifice supporting each of their personal lives. Yet, although they dared not ask precisely what the problem was, they could not help knowing that something was wrong. The symbolic identity they had pursued so long had taken over their private as well as their public selves, and they had become shadows on the wall of the cave, the logic of their acts illumined by the fires that burned all around them.

Of all the Brothers, John 3rd seemed least to deserve this harsh treatment. Most of his life had been devoted to philanthropic service. The money he had given—far greater than the contributions of his brothers—had generally gone to causes he was involved in; but it was not at all unusual for him to make modest grants to movements outside his field of interest. In 1970, for instance, he gave $25,000 to the students of Massachusetts's Hampshire College for a local environmental project. But when the gift was announced, along with the fact that he was coming to Hampshire to speak to the student body, there was a minor furor. Students debated whether to accept his grant. Some resurrected the term "tainted money" to describe it; others said the real issue was JDR3's role as an "architect of U.S. imperialism."

When JDR3 arrived for his visit, his entourage was forced to pass a demonstration in which five students wearing grotesque costumes (including oil-derrick hats) portrayed him and his brothers playing Monopoly for the properties of the world. Blanchette Rockefeller became livid with rage when she saw her husband's impersonator as a smiling hypocrite tending his Asian real estate, and angrily shouldered her way through the skit. But JDR3 paused for a moment to study the scene. It was not that he wondered if there might be an element of truth in the exaggeration, but that the principles he believed he stood for, principles of reason and decency, demanded he give even these students the appearance of a hearing. Only after this duty was discharged did he pass on.

The eldest Rockefeller Brother had learned over the years to carry himself in a way that was at once poised and self-effacing, grandfatherly and naïve. Everyone agreed that he had grown more than anyone had expected him to, yet some of his acquaintances found him disconcertingly similar to the awkward youngster who had emerged from Princeton some forty years earlier. He still fretted endlessly over even the smallest obligation, as though the twinge of anxiety was the only sure sign that he was doing the right thing. He still found it hard to be at ease outside the Rockefeller milieu. (One associate remembered JDR3 at a barbecue during his son Jay's 1972 campaign for the governorship of West Virginia. One of the locals with whom he was making halting small talk discovered that Rockefeller was staying at a hotel in town and protested: "Next time you come down here, you-all be sure to come stay with *us*." After hesitating for a moment in search of the proper response, JDR3 blurted out, "And if you ever come to New York, you-all come stay with *me*.")

Although Nelson had formally moved into the role of family patriarch after Junior's death, JDR3 had continued to feel that the title he bore made him the ultimate guardian of the Rockefeller name. It persisted like a secret fantasy, even though he knew he could not command enough power in the family to exercise his birthright. Yet the impulse to assert the authority that should have been his surfaced at odd moments, even if only in a negative way. Displeased by the Happy Murphy affair, for instance, he had spent the day of the marriage in seclusion at Fieldwood Farm, less than a mile from the ceremony, entertaining Tod Rockefeller as his house guest.

When he was a younger man and his energies were being dispersed in dozens of different directions (none of which, he feared, really reflected *him*), JDR3 had worried that his ceremonial identity as heir to *the* name might smother his personal growth. The problem had been a difficult one and had left scars on his character. (He probably would have agreed with his daughter Hope's diagnosis of him as "one who loved a good joke but couldn't bring himself to tell one; one who loved to have a good time, but didn't really know how to;

one who suffered from never doing things just for enjoyment and not because he had to.") Yet in the delayed flowering that started with the Dulles mission, he had found a way of reconciling the conflict between self and duty—not by constantly litigating their respective claims on his life, but by simply embracing the Rockefeller role and trying to express himself through it. Like the Christian paradox of freedom within servitude, this solution allowed him the illusion at least that he was doing what he wanted at the same time that he was satisfying the father, who even after death, continued to peer over his eldest son's shoulder to make sure that he did what was required.

It seemed fitting that he had devoted so much of his time to Asia, for the ceremonial mask he wore and the part in the country's affairs he played seemed more in keeping with the symbolic movement of a character in Oriental drama than one wheeling and dealing on the American stage. The role he would play had been foreshadowed in his early attitudes toward China. In 1949, when the tide was running toward isolation and containment and he had spoken up against recognition of the People's Republic, his voice was less that of an individual than of an informal consensus. By 1967, when his speeches began to drop broad hints that the United States might have entered an era when it could "welcome a peaceful China back into the community of nations," it was not that John D. Rockefeller 3rd had personally changed his mind. Rather, it was an indication that the laborious machinery of foreign policy with which he was intimately connected by name and association was about to slip decorously into another gear. Endless hours of Council on Foreign Relations seminars, informal club discussions, and State Department dialogues had created a context in which Rockefeller's speeches were the responsible gestures for a patrician leader to make. In 1969, three years before Nixon visited Peking, JDR3 prefigured the event in an address he gave while presiding over the keynote session of the National Committee on U.S.–China Relations. "For the past twenty years," Rockefeller began, "we have had no relationship with mainland China at all. During this time our thinking has been dominated by fear, so much so that in the recent past many regarded it as virtually treasonable to even raise the question of rethinking China policy. This sort of rigidity has no place in a democracy."

Had he chatted with the Hampshire students demonstrating against him, JDR3 might have responded to charges that he was an agent of imperialism (with the candor that was one of his most appealing characteristics): "Listen, I'm not really like my brother Nelson in Latin America or David in Africa. I've never really *done* anything in Asian affairs outside of greeting diplomats and being a sort of ambassador of goodwill, things like that." In a way, he would have been right. Yet it wasn't that simple. Perhaps he did not realize the uses to which his good offices had been put. The fact was, he had been thrown into the middle of a brier patch of espionage and intrigue soon after the Dulles mission.

On one occasion, at least, his staff had saved him from a disastrous blunder. It was in 1954, when the Asia Foundation (as the right-wing Committee for Free Asia had recently renamed itself) invited him to become its president. CIA chief Allen Dulles wrote JDR3 to urge him to accept the post, adding his voice to his brother Foster's. But Frank Jamieson counseled aginst it. "My principal reservation," he wrote JDR3 in a memorandum, "is the Asia Foundation's origin. It is my understanding that the Committee [for Free Asia] has been regarded with varying degrees of resentment in Asia because it spends a lot of money and is regarded as a propaganda device of the U.S. government. . . . Therefore, it seems to me you would not want to jeopardize your own activities in the Far East by closely associating with the Asia Foundation." JDR3 would have good reason to be thankful for this advice fifteen years later, when the Asia Foundation was revealed as a CIA front whose operatives had been spying in countries throughout the Orient.

Yet it was harder to say no when it was not an odd collection of former OSS men and out-of-pocket journalists asking for help but one's own brother representing a more respectable view. In 1957, Nelson (recently returned from his stint as Eisenhower's Special Assistant for the Cold War, where he oversaw CIA operations) reacted to the sudden death of Ramon Magsaysay by asking JDR3, who had known the Philippine President, to put his reputation as a philanthropist behind the creation of a monument to Magsaysay in the form of a foundation that would make annual awards in the manner of the Nobel Prize.

At first, Nelson had considered awarding the citations for "public service and the maintenance of democratic ideals" to men and women throughout all of Asia. But then he had decided that it would be better to limit the effort to the Philippines, where it appeared that Magsaysay's death might lead to renewed political instability. After writing Allen Dulles and Deputy Undersecretary of State Robert Murphy to get clearance, Nelson decided on a course of leaving the mechanics in the hands of his older brother, or, as he chose to formulate it, "letting Johnny run with the ball." Johnny's growing reputation as a philanthropist in Asia was perfectly suited to the job, and Nelson put him in touch with Colonel Edward G. Landsdale for background.*

On April 12, 1957, Landsdale sent JDR3 his reactions in respect to the Magsaysay Foundation: "Any organized means to further strengthen freedom, this cherished ideal of man, would be truly reflecting the real heritage of Magsaysay in Asia." JDR3 traveled to Manila, came back, and dispatched two aides to do the groundwork in setting up the foundation. Then he returned to the Philippines once again to make the first presentation of the awards.

It seemed odd that a man who saw himself as an international philanthropist should become a partner of the real-life prototype for *The Ugly American*. Yet it was a natural alliance, given the fact that the mission of American power in Asia and what Junior might have called "the well-being of mankind" had been welded into a single purpose during the postwar expansion, and all the authority figures in JDR3's life—the Dulles brothers and his own brother Nelson—pushed him in that direction.

If he did what he was asked, however, he was unlike Nelson in that he never was emotionally caught up in the conflict with Communism and revolution and never became a political crusader. He was one of the founding members of the special study group on Southeast Asia that the Council on Foreign Relations formed in 1954 in the wake of the French disaster at Dien Bien Phu, but though the question of American involvement in Vietnam soon became a burning issue for it and for policy makers generally, JDR3 attended few of the

---

*A romantic, almost legendary figure in the Saigon of the late 1950s, Landsdale had played an equally important—although less well-known—role in the Philippines earlier in the decade. The CIA had posted him there to help then Defense Minister Magsaysay fight the Huk guerrillas. It had been Landsdale who perfected the strategy of combining token land reform with well-financed psychological war operations against the Huks to crush the insurgency and give Magsaysay the prestige leading to his election as President.

group's meetings over the years, even after the initial intervention had escalated into a major commitment of U.S. forces. On the other hand, when Ngo Dinh Diem made his first trip to the United States as President of South Vietnam in 1957, JDR3 gave a luncheon in his honor which was attended by men like John J. McCloy (then chairman of the Chase Bank), and he later joined with his brother David to host a reception for Diem at Pocantico at which members of the Asia Society mingled with assorted bankers and businessmen.

Later, after the war in Vietnam had begun its long escalation, the State Department turned to the philanthropist for aid. In May 1963 the Asia Society (up to that point concerned only with arranging for Asian cultural exhibitions and acquainting Americans with the riches of Oriental art) convened a meeting "to reappraise the whole pattern of United States policy in Southeast Asia." A conference paper delivered by William Henderson (soon to become an "adviser on international affairs" for the Socony Mobil oil corporation) warned that the United States would ultimately fail to secure the basic objectives of its policy in Southeast Asia "until our commitment to the region becomes unlimited." This was a position strenuously backed within the Kennedy administration at the time by Kenneth Todd Young. A former State and Defense Department official (he had written the famous 1954 letter from Eisenhower to Diem pledging U.S. support after the French pullout) and former vice-president of Socony Mobil who had wound up his official career as the ambassador to Thailand, Young became part of JDR3's personal staff after retiring from foreign service. In 1963, at the suggestion of the State Department, Rockefeller made him president of the Asia Society.

Young's chief act as president was to convince the society to take under its wing an organization called SEADAG (Southeast Asia Development Advisory Group) and to locate it in Asia House, the society's four-story exhibition center and headquarters in New York. Unlike the Asia Society, whose funds were provided mainly by JDR3, SEADAG was financed by the government through the Agency for International Development. SEADAG had been created by the government (as one of its former members observed) "as part of its expanding effort aimed at cooptation of the academic community and its more general intention to use academics as a cover for covert activities in Southeast Asia."

As the war in Vietnam became increasingly unpopular, especially on the nation's campuses, SEADAG inevitably became a target of protest. Its Council of Vietnamese Studies was headed by Samuel P. Huntington, a Harvard colleague of Henry Kissinger who developed a theory rationalizing the terror bombing of the South Vietnamese countryside as "forced urbanization." In 1969 a SEADAG meeting chaired by Huntington in Boston's Sheraton Hotel was broken up by a demonstration of Concerned Asian Scholars. Inside the Asia Society itself, the demonstration fanned the fires of a smoldering rebellion on the part of cultural experts and scholars connected with its activities, and spurred perhaps by the irony of their complicity in a war that was destroying the art and culture of Indochina along with everything else. The rebellion focused on Kenneth Young, and was deep enough to force his replacement and to pressure SEADAG into moving its headquarters out of Asia House.

Through all the controversy and furor that rocked an organization which he had created and to which his identity was intimately bound, JDR3, who had inherited his father's ability to touch pitch and not be defiled, remained steadfastly aloof. Joe Fischer, an Indonesian expert who had once convinced JDR3 to help restore the Burmese Temple of Pagan, later complained: "Rockefeller's style does not include staying on top of things. The irony was that the Asia Society didn't need AID money, didn't need SEADAG. In fact, SEADAG had absolutely nothing to do with the society's work. What always bothered me was that when things got serious as a result of his having brought Young in and making him president of the society and the crisis came, Rockefeller was nowhere to be found."

During the next decade, JDR3 continued to be "Mr. Asia," greeting diplomats, making his annual Pacific tour, and carrying on as an ambassador of goodwill. He donated $1.8 million for Japan House, the Japan Society's permanent new home in New York, and when it opened in 1971, the Emperor's son, Prince Hitachi, journeyed there for what was not only a celebration of strengthened ties of U.S.–Japanese relations, but also a kind of tribute to Rockefeller himself.

Yet, gradually, his personal interests had refocused on America. "I had been much more active on the international front," he later explained his decision, "and because of my sense of responsibility, I felt I should do something for my home community." The advice to look for a project closer to home had come from his close aide Donald McLean, who saw Lincoln Center for the Performing Arts as the most promising candidate for Rockefeller's efforts.

The Lincoln Center project had first been broached in 1957 at a Council on Foreign Relations meeting in the Pocono Mountains, when Charles Spofford (Wall Street lawyer and board member of the Metropolitan Opera Company) took JDR3 aside and described what he called "three coincidences." One was the Met's plan to build a new home to replace the 39th Street opera house; another was the fact that the Philharmonic was being evicted from Carnegie Hall; third was the fact that Robert Moses had recently undertaken a project to clear a few blocks of urban "blight" at Lincoln Square. (Another, not mentioned by Spofford, was the fact that it represented a chance to finish old family business, begun with the early plans for Rockefeller Center, which had been linked to the opera house and never realized.) It was, JDR3 later said, "a fascinating set of circumstances," and when Spofford asked him if he would be interested in heading an exploratory committee made up of like-minded figures (Devereux Josephs, an eminent figure in the Council on Foreign Relations and in Wall Street circles, and C. D. Jackson, whom Nelson had earlier replaced in the Eisenhower administration, were among the names Spofford mentioned) to look into the prospects, JDR3 said he would.

He applied himself to the project with characteristic diligence and soon had expanded the original concept from a music center to a center for all the performing arts. In 1957 the chairmanship of the exploratory committee led to the presidency of Lincoln Center, Inc. In 1960, following the groundbreaking, JDR3 moved up to the chairmanship of the board.

In many ways, the undertaking was a new experience for him. There were endless meetings and trips abroad to study the great concert halls of the continent. For the first time he entered personally into a vigorous and complex world where his name did not awe people into automatic respect and his staff could not always be there to protect him from too much contact. He had to deal with a host of strong and often abrasive personalities in the city bureaucracies, and among the real estate interests and New York's civic-minded elite.

In the past, his remoteness and caution had occasionally elicited critical remarks (and crass ones as well, as in William

Zeckendorf's comment, "Frankly, I wouldn't be surprised if he sits down to pee"). Yet, for the most part, the majestic role he had been born to protected him. Now, he entered a situation where people saw warts on a face that from a distance had seemed unblemished. The patronizing slowness with which he discharged the dictates of duty, which had been borne patiently by supplicants who came hat in hand for his philanthropy, was infuriating to men of action with independent resources and bases of power. In their eyes, his stubborn hesitation and ponderous self-inquiry merely wasted their time. Speaking to a *New Yorker* reporter, New York's crusty master builder Robert Moses complained: "John . . . has a veneer of humility. I've never been able to figure out how deep it is. One inch?"

Yet he persevered, making virtues out of those qualities that men like Moses and Zeckendorf saw as weaknesses. As costs rose from an estimated $75 million to $185 million, he took on the task of raising the deficit. A large portion of it came from the family itself. The Foundation gave $15 million; Junior contributed $11 million before his death; the Brothers Fund gave $2.5 million. In 1959, when Muriel McCormick Hubbard (daughter of the errant Edith Rockefeller McCormick) died and left a $9 million trust fund to her four adopted children, JDR3, as her cousin and head of the committee of trustees at the Chase, contended that the children were not legal issue as defined by the terms of the trust and asked that the money be given instead to Lincoln Center. (The matter was eventually settled out of court, with the children getting $3 million of the money and Lincoln Center the rest.) JDR3's own personal gifts to the project were estimated at nearly $10 million, far more than any of the Brothers had hitherto given personally to any single project.

All this came from a man who was neither a first-nighter, nor even very familiar with the performing arts, a man, who, unlike his brother Nelson, took no particular joy in creating concrete monuments, especially one that inspired as little enthusiasm as the Lincoln Center structure Wallace Harrison designed, which then dragged on thirteen years before completion. "I was exploring for something to do and it seemed right. I had no idea what I was getting into. It was infinitely larger, more complex and full of anguish than I had anticipated. . . . I had no love of opera or dance. For me it was more a chance to do something that would be a major contribution to the community."

The almost Gothic nature of this sense of obligation was illustrated by a unique meeting that took place on February 11, 1958, at the swank George V Hotel in Paris, between Rockefeller and J. Paul Getty. As avid a collector of art as of wives, Getty would have been a natural target for the fundraising effort even if he hadn't been the world's richest man. As it was, JDR3 was almost sure that Getty would recognize his obligation and make a generous contribution to the new center for the performing arts, even though he had been noncommittal during lunch, listening politely and promising to make his answer by mail. Yet, when the letter came, it simply said no, without further elaboration. In an uncharacteristic expression of pique, JDR3 fired off a reply by return mail. After expressing shock that Getty should decline to contribute to something so important, Rockefeller's letter concluded abruptly, "And I am sorry for your children, if you have any."

Bringing the sprawling, stubborn Lincoln Center project to a successful conclusion was a major step in JDR3's development. It was the first time he had ventured into an area that had not in some sense been inherited from his father, and it encouraged him to venture out farther from the family umbrella.

He had been upset with the direction the Brothers Fund had taken. It was giving away huge sums of money, yet the giving was somehow impersonal, more a necessary adjunct to the Brothers' complicated tax liabilities and a conduit to causes they were interested in, than an expression of their philanthropic interests. (Emmet Hughes remembers from his three years as senior adviser to the family on public affairs, "The Fund had gotten to be little more than a sort of cash register; a couple of times a year the Brothers would get together and decide how to cut up the pie.") Still laboring to be worthy of his father's trust and of the name that set him apart from his brothers, JDR3 felt that philanthropy should be a more sincere pursuit of the third generation, although he knew that this belief alienated him even further from Nelson, Laurance, and David, the triumvirs who had taken over direction of the family.

In 1963, therefore, he created the JDR3 Fund, his own private foundation into which he would put some $5 million over the next five years and around which he would organize his own philanthropic activities. It was the final indication that he was stepping out of the family situation in which his personality had so long been submerged.

He returned to population. The Pop Council, which he had launched a decade earlier, was now the most prestigious institution in its field, operating on a multimillion-dollar annual budget in a dozen foreign countries. But its scope was limited to research; it avoided policy recommendations that might jeopardize its work in this still sensitive social area. Yet a change was taking place in the population movement and in JDR3 as well. Fred Jaffe, vp of Planned Parenthood, recalls: "John had dropped a lot of the cold war rhetoric of the fifties. Now when he saw bodies floating down the Ganges, he still worried about the possibility of a Communist takeover of India, but he was as concerned for the victims and their families."

After the 1964 elections, JDR3 tried to get an appointment to discuss the population issue with President Johnson. When LBJ declined, JDR3 lunched with Secretary of State Dean Rusk and asked him to urge the establishment of a presidential commission to study the question. Replying that this was premature, Rusk did promise to try to get some mention of population in the forthcoming State of the Union address. As it came out of the typewriter of speech writer Richard Goodwin, it was not more than a mention—one brief sentence, alloyed by emphasis on resources: "I will seek new ways to use our knowledge to help deal with the explosion in world population and the growing scarcity in world resources." But it was a beginning, the first time an American President had included population in the official agenda of problems with which the country had to deal.

Toward the very end of his administration, partly as a result of his friendship with Laurance Rockefeller, LBJ finally agreed to appoint an Advisory Committee on Population and Family Planning. JDR3 was made cochairman along with former Secretary of Labor Wilbur Cohen. After meeting for several months, the committee made its recommendations, and most prominent among them was the suggestion that the President appoint a special commission on population. Johnson did not have an opportunity to act on this matter before leaving office, but after Nixon's inauguration, JDR3 brought the subject up again. After a period of uncertainty and an unexpected assist from presidential adviser Daniel P. Moynihan, the President set up the Commission on Population, Growth and the American Future in the spring of 1970, with JDR3 as its chairman.

It was the sort of opportunity he had been waiting for. The prestigious post conformed perfectly with his new mood of independence, and for the next two years he worked hard, flying back and forth between New York and Washington several times a month and often descending from his ceremonial perch as chairman to take part in his commission's acrimonious debates over the issues. When the final report was released in three parts, beginning in March 1972, it surveyed the whole field of population and made dozens of recommendations, ranging from restriction of immigration to passage of the Equal Rights Amendment. Although many of the report's recommendations (that contraceptive information and services be made available to minors, that private and public forces join to provide adequate child-care services to all who might want them) were in advance of the national consensus, the commission entered a real political minefield only with its recommendation that "the matter of abortion should be left to the conscience of the individual concerned . . . and that states should be encouraged to enact affirmative statutes creating a clear and positive framework for the practice of abortion on request." It was a stand that collided head-on with Nixon's election-year strategy of building a "new majority" on the cornerstone of ethnic Catholic support. When he initiated the commission, Nixon had described the problem of population growth as "one of the most serious challenges to human destiny." But as the report was published, he maintained a stony silence.

If he had not put much original thought into the report, JDR3 had put his heart into it. He took pride in the fact that it was the first presidential commission on the population problem in the nation's history, and he had given it his time and money and the sanction of his name, elements that he was used to having count for something. Instead, when he finally obtained an audience at the White House to present the commission's findings formally, he was received in a stiff and somber atmosphere mirroring official displeasure with the findings. In a situation where small gestures count greatly, Nixon failed to invite JDR3 to sit on the sofa in the Oval Office, as he was known to do during interviews which he meant to be cordial, instead receiving him sitting at his desk. JDR3 was dismissed after a perfunctory conversation, and as he was leaving the White House, a presidential aide caught up to give him a copy of Nixon's official reaction to the report, which had just been released to the press. It left no doubt as to where the President stood: "I consider abortion an unacceptable form of population control. In my judgment unrestricted abortion policies would demean human life."*

JDR3 showed his hurt over the President's treatment only to his family. "He thought it very shabby," his daughter Hope recalls, "but he didn't really feel he could express his feelings." Not really up to what he saw as Nixon's unprincipled tactics or suited for open political struggle, he was at a loss to know exactly how to respond to his spurned labors. Yet the shrug with which he replied to questions about Nixon was eloquent, as if to say, "Well, what can you expect from such a man?" He confided to Hope that he would even have been willing to break a lifetime rule and family tradition and endorse Democrat George McGovern in the 1972 election except for the embarrassment it would have caused Nelson.

As the sixties ended and JDR3 turned sixty-five, the metamorphosis that had left him gaunt and silvered was completed. The stoop of his shoulders had decreased his height; the face was now a fragile composition of bone protruding from shadow. The insularity and shyness that had afflicted him as a younger man had been worn down by the years, replaced not by urbanity exactly, but by an air of paternal concern that mitigated his ineffectuality. It was a true *noblesse oblige*—the belief that responsible people like himself must act, because if they did not, affairs would be left to those who were irresponsible. It showed through his every gesture, as in his 1969 testimony before the House Ways and Means Committee on behalf of a bill requiring some tax payment by everyone. Speaking with his thin voice and seeming to look down at the congressmen over his reading glasses, Rockefeller explained that even though he could arrange tax-deductible con-

---

*While Nixon was snubbing JDR3, he also struck a glancing blow at Nelson. As Right-to-Life groups worked to repeal New York's "model" abortion law, which Nelson had backed, the President wrote a well-publicized letter to Cardinal Cooke calling the campaign "truly a noble endeavor" and applauding "the decision to act in the public forum as defendants of the right to life of the unborn." When the New York legislature passed the repeal bill, however, Nelson vetoed it with a message defending the position he and his older brother had taken: "I can see no justification now for ... condemning hundreds of thousands of women to the Dark Ages again ... I do not believe it is right for one group to impose its vision on the entire society."

tributions so that he did not have to pay any taxes at all, he himself, "voluntarily gave" 10 percent of his adjusted gross income each April 15.*

He had aged into the sort of man who managed to create sympathy not because of what he had actually accomplished in life, which was modest enough when measured by the material resources he had available, but for the sizable psychological obstacles he had overcome in accomplishing anything at all. He had begun as the Brother most bound by tradition and had ended as the one receptive enough to new ideas that he appeared to have undergone a remarkable transformation even on the threshold of old age. At the same time his brother Nelson's outlook was calcifying with reaction, JDR3's was in the process of a liberalization that surprised even those aides closest to him and made some of them speak of his being in his "second childhood." This process was reflected in the task he set himself at the beginning of the seventies, of studying and understanding the "youth revolution."

In part it was an increased sensitivity to his own children. His global responsibilities had kept him away during much of their growing up, his trips to Asia alone occupying several months at a time of each winter. When he was home, he had been insulated from their childhood and adolescence by nurses, governesses, and private schools, not to speak of his own formidable reserve. He was alarmed by what he saw in their young adulthood, at a time when he happened to be refocusing his attentions closer to home. His oldest child, Sandra, had shocked him and his wife by her reaction to growing up Rockefeller, which was to become a recluse, attempting on more than one occasion to give away her name and the millions in trust funds that went along with it. Then his youngest child, Alida, came home from Stanford during the late 1960s terribly upset at the distrust and hostility she experienced because she was a Rockefeller and therefore assumed to be genetically complicit in all the ills that affected the world.

*John Hodgkin, former Rockefeller family treasurer, says: "John the third had an interesting way of approaching taxes. At the end of the year he'd look at his income and say, 'I want to pay ten percent of that in taxes. Give away enough to reduce my income to that point.' The other Brothers would want to pay as little as they had to—or nothing if they could, though this was usually impossible for Nelson because of his large political contributions. Their father would pay taxes one year and then have it arranged so that he would pay none the next."

If it had been only his own children, JDR might have brooded silently over the problem as he did with others involving the family. Yet, since his own discomfort happened to coincide with the wide-spread social dislocation called "the generation gap," he decided it was his obligation to try to do something about it. The first impulse was to institutionalize the response to the crisis by suggesting that the Rockefeller Foundation take it up as a program. As Hugh Romney, vice-president of the Foundation, says, "He tried to get us more interested in the youth thing than we were willing to be. We could see the relevance of research on youth and drugs, or youth and international relations. But youth as youth, we couldn't see." As in the case of the rejection of his proposals for a population effort some fifteen years earlier, JDR3 decided to undertake the problem by himself. This time he had a ready-made, if modest, agency available for the task. A few months before he was confronted by student protesters at Hampshire College, he set up a Youth Task Force within the JDR3 Fund.

It was not surprising that he should choose to see the problem as youth's disaffection from the "establishment" and to make seeking out areas of possible cooperation and communication the primary work of the task force. Pollster Daniel Yankelovich was hired to do extensive surveys of the attitudes of young people and of their elders in the business world, concentrating especially on the changed values on U.S. campuses in the wake of the invasion of Cambodia and the Kent State murders. Dialogues were staged between select activists and major business leaders, like A. W. Clausen of the Bank of America, in six metropolitan areas. The intent of the meetings, in the words of the fund's 1971 report, was "to give business and community leaders a better understanding of youth's diagnosis of society and to give young people greater insight into the process of getting things done within the constraints of established institutions."

Yet by the end of this program, some of the young people involved in the task force were disillusioned by the fact that the efforts seemed to be striving for a predetermined result, and that there had never really been any intention to study the problem in depth. As one task force member later said, "The problem was that the whole thing began with certain cant assumptions: that the 'generation gap' was just a problem of *communication* and that if people would just talk to each other, everything would be okay. Rockefeller was really trying on this one. But the problem was that he didn't want to believe that there were any real or fundamental reasons for young people to be estranged from authority—especially businessmen and parents—so that it was never considered in our work. I got the impression that it would have been personally threatening to him to even entertain this possibility."

After the Youth Task Force had completed its work, it was succeeded by the Youth Project, which was to implement areas of concern that had been uncovered. JDR3 took part in the discussions and participated in the deliberations over grant proposals and policy. Jerry Swift, 36-year-old former Youth Project head whose job was terminated in 1973 after he was quoted by the *New Yorker* to the effect that JDR3 was "conscience ridden," recalls one occasion when there were two $5,000 grants under consideration, one for a group proposing to set up a legal aid office for Vietnam veterans, and the other for a study on the problems of amnesty.

"He went over these proposals with unbelievable care. None of us on the panel cared all that much. Either one of them or neither would have been all right with us. But the arguments pro and con went on for about four hours. Then he finally asked to be allowed to sleep on it. He came back to the office the next day and said that he'd made up his mind: he would okay the amnesty study and not the legal aid. We all said, 'Okay, fine, that's a good choice.' But that wasn't the end of it. Later on he came into my office, sat down, and once more went over all the reasons for his choice in great detail. I said that it wasn't important, but he insisted. It was like he was almost pleading for understanding. Dammit, he *is* conscience ridden."

Whether or not JDR3 was pricked by the imputation of guilt in his young aide's remark, the fact that he wanted to be understood by the younger generation and in some way identified with its energies was evident. He consulted his college-age daughter Alida when making important speeches, altering them occasionally to meet her objections. He conducted numerous "research" lunches, at which he talked with the teen-age children of his acquaintances. He was fascinated with the rebelliousness of youth and its willingness, as he put it, "to try the new and question the old." Yet he could not wholeheartedly embrace its passions, especially when they came in conflict with the proprieties that formed the core of his life.*

---

*He had written that the most critical challenges facing the nation were the problems "of population growth and environmental damage."

As a result of the work of the Youth Project, JDR3 wrote a short book called *The Second American Revolution*, which he described as "one of the toughest assignments I have ever undertaken," and which, though impersonal on the surface, was in its way a succinct revelation of self. It was a book in which issues were not so much joined as melted into one another, where a social synthesis was perceived "which blends the values of the American Revolution and the Industrial Revolution, the humanistic and the materialistic values as we think of them today." It was an endorsement of youth, but a statement of age; it appeared to welcome change, but reaffirmed conservative principles. In it he preached his philosophy of stewardship as a doctrine for what he termed an "emerging revolution": "My thesis is that instead of being overwhelmed by our problems we must have faith that they can be resolved ... the justification for this faith will depend on Americans generally feeling a sense of responsibility for what happens in their country."

The Second American Revolution was a peculiar book, but it aptly expressed the peculiarities of JDR3's lifetime dilemma. It was determinedly about "revolution," but a revolution taking place almost as a passage of generations; a revolution, moreover, which would fulfill the promise of an older heritage. "The name Rockefeller does not connote a revolutionary," JDR3 wrote in unnecessary note of apologia, "and my life situation has fostered a careful and cautious attitude that verges on conservatism. I am not given to errant causes. I have quite a consistent record as a Republican. ... But once one accepts that a revolution of positive potential is emerging, it is time to stop worrying about scare words and to start thinking about what one can do to help ensure that positive outcome."

The reviews, which remarked how out of character it was for a Rockefeller to be expressing such support for the rebellious complaints of youth, were pleasing to JDR3, whose discomfort under the Rockefeller identity fashioned by his brothers had become more and more apparent over the years. The symbolic link he made between the generational crisis of

---

Yet when one of his nieces proposed to give proxies in support of a stockholder resolution criticizing the management of Standard Oil of California for opposing pollution control legislation, she received an unusual long distance call from her Uncle John, who spent nearly an hour trying to dissuade her from getting involved in the conflict, which he said would be "embarrassing to the family."

the family and of the nation took a new turn in early 1974
when his office received a call from Leonard Garment of
Nixon's White House staff. Garment was asking for help in
connection with the planned Bicentennial Celebration, which
was floundering badly in the wake of the Watergate revelations. After consulting with his aides, JDR3 agreed to join
the Bicentennial Commission to provide it with some financial support in an effort to rescue the event from the odor of
scandal and from the crass marketeers of the national history
who had been previously solicited by the Nixon staff. "The
idea was not just that the Bicentennial would be a nonevent,"
explains John Harr of Room 5600, in recalling the reasons
for their willingness to take on the project, "but if the responsible people didn't do something about it, it was going to be a
disaster. This was when we began to get interested. We didn't
just go rushing in."

It was patriotic. (In fact, with a top hat, a tailored suit of
stars and stripes, and a tuft of beard, JDR3 would have
looked a little like the allegorical Uncle Sam.) But there was
also a leaven of pragmatism that would have made his father
proud. It was as if John D. Rockefeller 3rd had understood
in his own oblique way that, since his family was stuck with
its close identification with the nation, he now had the obligation to show it wasn't as bad as it seemed. The task, in a
sense, was to make America live up to the Rockefellers.

22

IT WAS EARLY IN 1973 that the Rockefeller Brothers agreed
to grant CBS permission to film a documentary about their
lives. They had always rejected such proposals in the past;
but now, with the Watergate crisis and the disarray of the
Republican party sharpening Nelson's presidential ambitions
once again and with news of Winthrop's terminal illness reminding them of their mortality, they decided that the time
had come for a summary of their joint and individual accomplishments.

Once the decision was made, the filming itself became just another item on calendars already tightly scheduled far into the future. Over a period of several weeks, the Brothers allowed network crews to trail them through their crowded lives. They knew how to put themselves in the hands of experts when their purposes so required. They sat docilely where they were told, posed for background footage when asked, and answered Walter Cronkite's questions on cue. All but Laurance. He wanted to stage his own scenes, setting up his entrances and exits and suggesting that his career might be summarized by vignettes showing him emerging from a swim near his Virgin Islands resort, talking over problems with administrators at the Sloan-Kettering Memorial Cancer clinic, or in some other moment of crucial self-dramatization.

The role of director suited him. He liked orchestrating things and appearances, and a hint of theatricality had always been submerged just below the calm surface of his personality. Each of the Brothers had arrived at his own way of coping with his special vulnerability as a Rockefeller. Laurance's solution had been to create a mask through which he could look out at the world but not really be seen. The idea was to seem more formidable and mysterious than he was, and he had worked as a young man to fashion the poker player's eyes, the mouth turned up at the corners in an enigmatic smile, and the unruffled look of someone more interested in the mechanics of a problem that the morality. It was a face that had served him perfectly in the years when he was just back from the navy and making his mark as an entrepreneur in the interstices of the military-industrial complex. He had assumed automatically that it would work just as well when he decided to go public as a conservationist. It was a rare miscalculation.

Laurance was quick to recognize that the Outdoor Recreation Resources and Review Commission, to which President Eisenhower appointed him in 1958, could be the bridge leading him from his enterpreneurial past to his conservationist future, and poured more of himself into it than he had previously into any other activity. He spent time in Washington getting to know the congressional leaders and private conservationists serving with him on the commission, the Interior Department sachems, and key businessmen. He smoothed the interfacing between the commission's work and his own private efforts, augumenting the commission staff with aides from his two conservation organizations, Jackson Hole Preserve, Inc., and the American Conservation Association. In 1962, after three years of hard work, he delivered a thick report and twenty-nine supplementary studies to President Kennedy.

Cursed by an ungraceful acronym (ORRRC) and working from a relatively narrow mandate—to inventory the nation's recreation needs and potential to the year 2,000—the commission was not one whose work captured the public imagination, particularly amid the dozens of more glamorous activities and programs of the New Frontier. Yet the conservation establishment around Washington, recognizing it had been several decades since so thorough an evaluation of the nation's Great Outdoors had been made, knew that ORRRC's findings would have resonance in the years to come—especially its recommendations to emphasize the urban centers instead of the western states in future spending for parks and recreation; to adopt a policy of "multiple use" encouraging mining, lumbering, grazing, and other industrial activities on recreation lands; and to create a Bureau of Outdoor Recreation within the Department of Interior to handle work formerly spread among more than twenty different federal agencies.

Laurance moved quickly to capitalize on ORRRC's impact. Even as the report was being delivered to the President, his own American Conservation Association (which would spend nearly $800,000 between 1962 and 1964 promoting the commission's report) gathered over 150 leaders from business, labor, and public affairs into the Citizens' Committee for the ORRRC Report; its aim was to make sure the recommendations got the widest possible circulation and acceptance. If it kept the commission's work in public view, this sort of publicity also kept Laurance's name in front of those who mattered, and when President Kennedy announced a Cabinet-level Advisory Council on Recreation, he appointed Laurance its head.

The Outdoor Recreation Resources and Review Commission was the vehicle by which Laurance transformed himself from a gentleman conservationist into a statesman in the emerging environmental movement. It was the kind of change in direction (or at least unexpected augmentation) that he liked to make; it was a demonstration of his freedom—the art of *becoming*—to confound those who claimed that to be a Rockefeller was to be locked into a role. Yet, if he alone of all

John D. Rockefeller, Sr.
Date Unknown.

Laura Spelman ("Cettie")
Rockefeller. Date Unknown.

Forest Hill, Cleveland.

10 West 54th Street, New York City.

Senator Nelson Aldrich.
COURTESY OF THE
ROCKEFELLER FAMILY ARCHIVES.

Abby Aldrich Rockefeller.
COURTESY OF THE
ROCKEFELLER FAMILY ARCHIVES.

The children of Junior and Abby. From left: Abby ("Babs"), JDR3, Nelson, Laurance, Winthrop, and David.
COURTESY OF THE ROCKEFELLER FAMILY ARCHIVES.

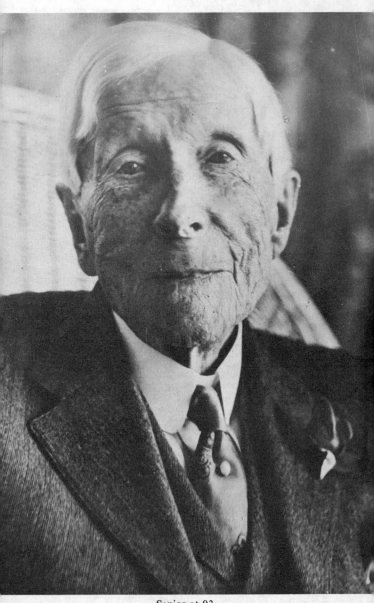

Senior at 93.

Junior's office at 26 Broadway before he had it redesigned in 1924.
COURTESY OF THE ROCKEFELLER FAMILY ARCHIVES.

Summer of 1920, Seal Harbor, Maine. From left: Laurance, Babs, JDR3, Abby with David, Winthrop, Junior, and Nelson.
COURTESY OF WIDE WORLD PHOTOS.

The wedding of Mary Todhunter Clark and Nelson Aldrich
Rockefeller, June 23, 1930.
COURTESY OF WIDE WORLD PHOTOS.

Junior and his sons awaiting the funeral train bringing Senior's
body home. From left: Junior, David, Nelson, Winthrop, Laurance, John D. III.
COURTESY OF THE ROCKEFELLER FAMILY ARCHIVES.

JDRIV ("Jay") campaigning unsuccessfuly for governor in 1972. In 1976 he was elected as the Democratic Governor of West Virginia.
COURTESY ELIZA DAVISON.

Nelson with Happy, May 4, 1963.
COURTESY OF WIDE WORLD PHOTOS.

Dr. Lucy Hamlin, daughter of Laurance S. Rockefeller.
COURTESY OF WIDE WORLD PHOTOS.

Hope, daughter of JDR3.
COURTESY OF WIDE WORLD PHOTOS.

The children of David and Peggy.

the Brothers could savor the existential implications of such a midlife transition, he hadn't become involved in conservation because of strong ideas or compelling personal vision. In some sense, conservation had been a natural area for him to expand into, not only because of his father's long identification with that cause, but also because it was a field that had touched on so many sensitive areas that it was obviously destined to play a significant role in the future life of the nation.

By the time ORRRC made its recommendations, in fact, the conservation movement was already developing. When it had first attracted Laurance's serious attention in the mid-1950s, it had been an adventitious outgrowth of the cold war and America's concern about strategic materials. But in the years since the Materials Policy Commission first raised the specter of a resources famine, the emphasis had shifted. The crisis of the next decade would not be based on strategic foreign materials like tin and tungsten, but on the basic resources of air, water, and land, which were increasingly threatened by pollution. The crisis was summarized in the phrase "quality of life," which John Kenneth Galbraith, among others, saw as threatened by a business economy that created artificial consumer wants and failed to calculate the social costs of its production.

Laurance accepted without reservation the idea that growth and conservation could be familiar bedfellows. And, as one straddling the fence between business and environment, he knew he could be an effective salesman of the concept of conservationist concern, allaying the fears of industrial leaders that the push for protection masked an antibusiness attitude. In a 1963 address to the seventieth annual meeting of the Congress of American Industry in New York, he tried to assure businessmen that nothing in the new concern for pure water and air threatened them. "Business can take this development in stride," he counseled, "in the same way it has, over the years, taken in its stride other steps which seemed like broad social rather than economic obligations. Like so many of the others it will turn out in the end to be just plain good business."

During the months that followed the ORRRC report and his appointment to the President's Advisory Council on Recreation, Laurance made similar speeches to other groups of business executives. In a movement characterized by what many industrial leaders feared was anticorporate hysteria, he seemed almost too good to be true: a Rockefeller and yet a legitimate spokesman for the "public interest" in matters of conservation. One of those impressed with his performance was the new President, Lyndon Johnson, who had announced his own intention to take conservation seriously in the Great Society speech he made in the spring of 1964. When, the following fall, the President appointed a series of task forces to chart the course of his administration, one of them was on natural beauty, and he named Laurance a member.

While this task was meeting, Lady Bird Johnson became interested in beautification and indicated it would be her own special area of concern as First Lady. She sought out Laurance's advice. He enthusiastically supported Mrs. Johnson's ideas and helped launch the campaign, traveling with her in her "beautification bus" and later inviting her to become a trustee of Jackson Hole Preserve, Inc.

Soon Mrs. Johnson was introduced to the Rockefeller family and allowed to enter the charmed circle within which they conducted their private lives. She became an intimate, witnessing the minutiae of their daily life, which came out vividly in the diary she kept during her White House years. She remembered staying with Laurance's family at the Mansion, his home in Woodstock, Vermont. Coming down early one morning, she found the pious and withdrawn Mary French Rockefeller alone in the prayer room, head bowed and Bible on her lap. She was flattered when Laurance invited her and daughter Lynda Bird to be his guests at his JY Ranch in the Grand Tetons. (After accepting the invitation, Lady Bird noted with maternal cunning that "it would be very pleasant for [Lynda] to meet some young Rockefellers." Yet, while Jay and Laurance, Jr., most eligible of the young men of the fourth Rockefeller generation, were all there during the visit, no romantic attachment came of it.)

When she visited Pocantico, Lady Bird recounted the experience as breathlessly as some matron from the Pecos on a Grayline tour of Versailles:

> The great stone house where Nelson Rockefeller now lives .. commands a hilltop and is surrounded ... by a frieze of beautiful American elms. You wind up a driveway past statuary, some of it wildly modern. There are two great torchieres at the entrance of the house and at night the Tiffany amber glass must look like twin flames

when you drive under the porte-cochere. As I mounted the steps I could see down the length of a hall, a graceful, elegant statue—ancient Eastern art—and ... downstairs there was a ... sort of gallery full of way-out modern things.

Lady Bird became one of Laurance's greatest boosters, speaking glowingly of his contributions to beautification and calling him "that number-one conservationist" and "America's leading citizen-conservationist." Early in 1965, after the Task Force on Natural Beauty had delivered its report, which was largely a rehash of ORRRC's recommendations, and while Laurance was working with Lady Bird on her campaign, LBJ sent Congress a strong message making it clear that conservation would have a high priority in his administration and announcing a White House Conference on Natural Beauty, to be headed by Laurance. One of the conference's results was the creation of a Citizens' Advisory Committee on Recreation and Natural Beauty, with Laurance serving as chairman and charged with advising the White House on environmental matters.

His ascent into the upper reaches of public policy as the President's privy counselor on the environment was remarkably rapid, even for a Rockefeller. He had penetrated officialdom deeply enough to be mentioned as a possible future Secretary of the Interior. But even as he was reaching this pinnacle, his name had ceased to inspire confidence among rank-and-file conservationists, who had turned out to be far more stubborn and independent than was ever contemplated. The grass-roots movement that emerged during the social turmoil of the sixties had a systemic view of the crisis (and a new concept—"ecology"—to describe it), which was not quite what Laurance, "Fair" Osborn, and the others had in mind when they helped christen and launch the bandwagon for environmental quality. Yet when they realized that the movement that had once been made up of weekend hikers and bird watchers was out of their control, it was too late to do anything about it. The genie was out of the bottle.

Most of the great conservation battles of the mid-1960s would involve Laurance in some way or another. A harbinger had come in the controversy over Storm King, the massive granite bluff looming up dramatically at the gateway to the Hudson River Highlands. Local residents admired the mountain's weather-beaten face and were unaware that Consolidated Edison had drafted plans to drill into Storm King and hollow it out for a huge hydroelectric pumping station whose reservoir and generators would stand in reserve in case of emergency power needs in Manhattan.

By mid-1962, when the plan was finally made public, Nelson enthusiastically backed it, having been recruited to the project by Building and Trades Union boss Peter Brennan and others whom he had come to depend on as his political base inside organized labor. Nelson praised the plan as "an imaginative, long-term solution for the energy problem"; Laurance followed suit. After meeting with Con Ed executives to make sure that they did not intend to intrude upon the lands of the nearby Palisades Park and to convince them to change plans that had originally called for stringing unsightly transmission lines across Storm King gorge, he announced that he felt the utility's project could actually be "an exercise in democratic planning." Laurance brought his growing national reputation and his prestige as a Palisades Park commissioner and as head of the State Council on Parks (a post to which Nelson had appointed him in 1963 after forcing the aging Robert Moses out of the job) to the decision to back Con Ed. Moreover, as a trustee of the respected Hudson River Conservation Society, a patrician organization that had stood guard over the river since the early 1900s, Laurance was able to persuade its president, William Osborn (cousin of Fairfield and brother of JDR3's population associate Frederick), to endorse the plan.

Support for Storm King by the state's leading conservationist and the region's leading conservation organization seemed to give the project an indisputable seal of approval. But there were some residents—the sort of people who could generally be counted on as conservative and Republican on most issues—who had doubts. Tentatively at first, and then with growing certainty, they began speaking out against the project, forming an organization they called the Scenic Hudson Preservation Conference. Later they would develop impressive data showing how the pumping station would destroy the Hudson's marine environment, but they began with the same opposition to the disfigurement of the area that had led a wealthy man like John D. Rockefeller, Jr., to begin buying up the Palisades decades earlier to save them from the quarryman's dynamite.

The controversy simmered for a year and then erupted into

a *cause célèbre*. As the public became aware of its fight, Scenic Hudson was joined by celebrities like James Cagney, Pete Seeger, and Nelson's son Steven; it hired attorneys to take the matter into court. Meanwhile, its publicists made much of such ironies as the fact that it would take one and a half times as much energy to pump water up to the storage reservoir as would be generated when the water was released. In March 1965, however, the Federal Power Commission ruled against Scenic Hudson, granting Con Ed permission to proceed with construction; one factor that weighed heavily in their decision was the backing Laurance had given it.

In explaining how the man who had been called the country's leading conservationist could be in the opposition camp, Scenic Hudson researchers raised the question of conflict of interest. "Governor Rockefeller and his brother Laurance agreed to that plant through private negotiations with the company," charged one of the organization's founders in the *Cornwall Local*. The purpose of the secrecy, he implied, was to conceal the connection between the agreement and a substantial stock interest in the utility company. Nelson and Laurance's Great-Uncle William Rockefeller had been, in fact, one of the original owners of Con Ed, and based on figures Junior had given TNEC investigators in 1937, the family's current holdings would amount to better than $10 million. Yet financial advantage—which in any case would have meant only a fractional increase in the Rockefeller fortune— was not the source of their support for Con Ed. A more plausible reason was later offered to author Robert Boyle by a prominent New York Republican: "The people who own Con Ed are his [Laurance's] people. They're in the same club." It was a philosophical kinship with the project, a belief in the "efficient use" of natural resources and the importance of industrial growth, that committed Nelson and Laurance to their course.

The Storm King battle would rage on in the appeals courts for the next decade. By early 1965, however, the issues it had already raised led an ambitious young Westchester congressman named Richard Ottinger to demand that the Interior Department make the Hudson River Valley a federal preserve, implying it was not safe in its present hands. Later in the year he introduced a bill to make the Hudson and a one-mile strip on either side a national scenic riverway under jurisdiction of the Interior Department.

The Rockefellers responded quickly to what they regarded

as a challenge to their proprietary authority. It was, after all, an area where their father had invested millions in projects like the Palisades Interstate Park and the Sleepy Hollow Restorations (which included the purchase for public use of the famous Philipsburg and Van Cortlandt manors, and Sunnyside, Washington Irving's home) and where he had helped build their family demesne. With $25,000 from his executive chamber budget, and a matching grant from Laurance's American Conservation Association, Nelson created a state watchdog agency called the Hudson River Valley Commission "to protect the river and its surrounding area." Made up of leading citizens like Averell Harriman, IBM's Thomas Watson, and Ford Foundation head Henry Heald, the commission was an attempt to head off federal intervention. Laurance, whom Nelson had named chairman of the new agency, said, "It's a matter of who can best save the Hudson. The Federal government acts in default of state responsibility. The burden should not be shifted to it as long as the State demonstrates the capacity to do the job."

The struggle for authority over the region came to a head in 1965 when the state of New York announced that north–south traffic between the Hudson Valley and Manhattan was becoming a problem and, since Route 9A could not handle it, a superhighway connecting New York City to Croton-on-Hudson must be constructed along the bank of the river. With this, the Rockefeller family's past and present conservation philanthropies—which had made conservationists reluctant to suspect their motives at the onset of the Storm King struggle—ceased to shield them from attack. Conservationists opposing the damage the highway would do to the Hudson were quick to point out that the planned road had apparently been drawn with the family's Pocantico estate in mind. Indeed, in 1957, when Interstate 87 (as the road was known) first entered the state Department of Transportation's long-term planning, the idea that it might be built along the Hudson, involving an expensive dredge-and-fill operation, was not even seriously considered. At that time, it had been thought that the most economical and logical route would be up through the Pocantico Hills area. The version of I-87 planned during the Harriman administration would have bisected the Rockefeller estate so neatly that Nelson's house would have been on one side of the road and Laurance's on the other. Immediately after Nelson's election, needless to say, these plans were scrapped and the redrawn proposal for I-87 (now called "the Hudson Expressway") moved it five miles west of Pocantico, which placed it parallel to the east bank of the river.*

A confidential Interior Department memorandum done at the height of the highway controversy and entitled "Benefits to the Rockefellers from the Expressway" said: "Probably the greatest financial benefit to the Rockefeller family would accrue from the fact that the Expressway, together with the extension of Route 117 from the Expressway to U.S. Highway 9, will open up the Rockefeller holdings to people, as far away as New York City." Their father had been interested only in keeping people *away* from Pocantico. Yet Nelson and Laurance were looking ahead to a time when taxes and upkeep would make the family's 3,600 acres a financial burden. Land for residential development in the area was selling for as much as $100,000 an acre, and the two brothers were intrigued with the idea of Pocantico's potential for tasteful condominium and single-family dwellings. Underpinning this idea was the fact that the proposed expressway would make the area more available to Manhattan executives.

But the expressway was another of those projects Nelson and Laurance would have supported even if personal considerations had not been in the background. In their view, it was a case where growth was not only desirable but inevitable, and could best be handled by careful planning. "Compatible development" was the term Laurance used to defend it, arguing that the Hudson River area would certainly develop, if not under the state's master plan, then in a spontaneous sprawl. In its 1966 report, the state's Hudson River Valley Commission, as was to be expected, backed the project, claiming that it would "not constitute a significant impairment of the natural resources of the river," but would in fact increase and improve the public's access to the Hudson.

*While they were at it, the Rockefellers took advantage of the opportunity to finish some unfinished highway business. It concerned the old two-lane Route 117, which at the time meandered through the heart of Pocantico, connecting Route 9 in North Tarrytown to Route 9A east of the estate. Junior had always been distressed by the number of motorists who used the road primarily in hopes of catching a glimpse of a Rockefeller in habitat and, in 1932, had offered to pay half the cost if the state would relocate 117 away from the estate. The offer had been refused, but now Nelson was able to accomplish the same end free of charge. Route 117 would be moved up a couple of miles so that when it did cut through Pocantico to connect with the new Hudson Expressway, it would be in a relatively unused part of the estate.

The commission scheduled public hearings on the expressway and was undaunted when all but two of the forty-three people testifying were vehemently opposed to the development.

The Rockefellers too were oblivious to opposition. New York state Assemblyman Laurance Cabot later told of one occasion when he personally brought a load of antiexpressway mail from his constituents to Nelson's office. Rockefeller glanced perfunctorily at the huge mound of letters, listened to Cabot's speech, and then shrugged. "That's odd," he said, "I haven't heard a single objection to the expressway."

Charles Stoddard, then executive director of the Citizens' Advisory Committee on Recreation and Natural Beauty, recalls also getting a great volume of mail on the issue. "People were begging Laurance to do something about the highway. But he never really considered it. He didn't see it as a conservation issue."

Because of the Hudson River Compact (Ottinger's bill had passed into law in 1966), the Interior Department had to approve the project and grant the U.S. Army Corps of Engineers permission to issue a permit for the construction. Conservationists had assembled a compelling case suggesting that while people would no doubt use the expressway once it was built, there was not enough real demand to justify its construction. They had also commissioned studies from fisheries experts showing how silt deposits from dredge-and-fill operations would devastate the spawning runs of the shad, striped bass, sturgeon, and other game fish of the area, while also wiping out the propagation beds of native shellfish. Interior Secretary Stewart Udall seemed persuaded; he was already on record as opposing the road and had written: "Such an expressway in the highly scenic and significantly historic corridor along the Hudson River would seriously impair the values we are all trying to preserve." But as the infighting intensified, the Rockefellers began to exert leverage on the Secretary. It would have taken a stronger man to withstand their pressure.

Udall had already begun to waver on January 25, 1968, when he was summoned to New York for a meeting at Nelson's apartment with the Rockefellers and their aides. Even if he had been willing to buck the governor, it would have been hard to deny a man like Laurance, who was known to have the President's ear on conservation matters. As Udall now says, "It seemed to me that Laurance and the governor were wrong. I didn't really like the highway. But at that meeting they came in with all kinds of charts and reports. It was the *complete* presentation. During the meeting and after, Laurance leaned on me very hard not to interrupt the plans he and Nelson had for the Hudson. He picked up all the outstanding due bills on this one." It was not long after the meeting that Udall told Ed Crafts, director of the Bureau of Outdoor Recreation and a long-time friend of Laurance, that he had now changed his opinion and would no longer oppose the expressway.

Still, seven months later, Udall's conversation had yet to be made public. On August 20, Laurance called the Bureau of Outdoor Recreation. In Crafts's absence, Associate Director Lawrence Stevens took the call. The memorandum of the conversation he kept gives a glimpse into the Rockefeller style of operation:

> Mr. Rockefeller said that he was with his brother, Governor Nelson Rockefeller, and he was calling to find out the status of Interior's review under the Hudson River legislation of the application . . . for a permit to construct the Hudson Expressway. . . . They wanted to be sure that Interior had not lost track of the application. . . . He added that he understood Congressman Ottinger was putting great pressure on Secretary Udall to oppose the Expressway and implied that Governor Rockefeller was prepared to exert counter-pressure if necessary.

Only after Stevens assured him that "the matter had not fallen between the cracks at Interior" was Laurance satisfied.

When Udall publicly announced his decision to allow the Corps of Engineers to grant a dredge-and-fill permit, the Sierrra Club and Citizens Committee for the Hudson Valley (an *ad hoc* group formed in 1965 in Ottinger's district to fight the road) moved into federal district court and were granted an injunction prohibiting construction. The complex legal battle that followed finally ended two years later in 1970 when the U.S. Supreme Court declined to hear New York's appeal on the matter, thus driving a final nail through the heart of the Rockefellers' highway plan.*

---

*The indefatigable Nelson ordered his Department of Transportation to draw up plans for several alternative routes far enough from the

Laurance's role in these struggles over the Hudson had been hard to pinpoint. His influence was felt, yet he was very much a background figure in a group photograph. Compared to the other starkly defined people, he seemed slightly out of focus, his motion not quite frozen by the camera's shutter. When he was captured, it was not looking ahead full face, but glancing over his brother's shoulder at someone else in the group, the habitual look of detached amusement on his face. In the case of the fight for California's Redwood National Park, however, his role was clearer.

By the mid-1960s, this park was high on the conservation agenda of the Johnson administration, but it was mired in controversy. A National Park Service study had agreed with the Sierra Club's recommendation that Redwood Creek—with the most extensive stands of virgin forest and the largest individual trees—would be the ideal site for the proposed park. But by 1967, timber companies and other opponents of the plan had decided that, if there had to be a park, it should be in the Mill Creek area. Mill Creek was not only smaller than the Redwood Valley, but already had two state parks. The lumber companies joked among themselves that by putting the national park there they would stop the spread of "park blight." As the controversy heated up, Udall stood back from the issue and gave it to Ed Crafts to handle. Two competing bills were introduced in Congress: one for Redwood Creek by Senator Lee Metcalf on behalf of the Sierra Club; the other by Senator Thomas Kuchel on behalf of the Johnson administration. Orchestrating the forces for the Mill Creek site within the Johnson administration, among the lumber companies, within California's Republican administration, and among select conservationists was Laurance Rockefeller. He earlier had made several trips to northern California to soften industry opposition to the park and had satisfied himself the Mill Creek site was a good compromise, all that could be hoped for without a long and bitter struggle. He had then played a significant role in getting President Johnson to commit himself to the Mill Creek legislation.

In doing so, he was not only placating the lumber companies, he was also responding to the Byzantine political situa-

river to avoid being defeated by the new environmental impact proviso involved in approval of such legislation. But when the $2.5 billion transportation bond he submitted to the voters in 1971 was overwhelmingly rejected, even he had finally to admit that the highway was a "dead issue."

tion within California's Republican ranks. Governor Ronald Reagan's attitude toward the park might have been presumed from his celebrated statement, "If you've seen one redwood, you've seen them all." He supported the Mill Creek site because the lumber industry did, and as part of a deal in which the Interior Department agreed not to oppose his plans to build a state highway across part of Sequoia National Park to provide access to the Mineral King resort planned by Walt Disney Enterprises, which had backed his 1966 election. In sponsoring the Mill Creek bill, liberal Republican Senator Kuchel, marked for defeat by the state's right-wing Republicans because he had headed Rockefeller's 1964 primary slate against Goldwater, hoped to curry favor with Reagan and ensure his neutrality in the upcoming 1968 primary. As an added twist to the situation, there was the emerging understanding between the California governor and Nelson which would lead to their alliance in Miami in an abortive attempt to block the nomination of Richard Nixon.

To forestall criticism that this juggernaut was anticonservation and to offset Sierra Club opposition, Laurance enlisted the prestigious Save-the-Redwoods League.* In an atmosphere of almost Alexandrian intrigue, he shuttled back and forth between the various principals. It was a diplomatic offensive anticipating those his brother's adviser Henry Kissinger would later wage on a global scale. He was known to be the President's ambassador, and not surprisingly, the mood of compromise he represented was strongly represented in the final park legislation. Only a small part of the Redwood Creek area made its way into the bill brokered through conference committee by House Interior Committee czar Wayne Aspinal.

Several years later, reflecting on the chain of events that led Redwood National Park to be smaller and less breathtaking than it might have been, former Interior Secretary Stewart

---

*The Rockefellers had given several million dollars to the Save-the-Redwoods League in the years since Junior first journeyed to northern California in 1926 and became impressed with the organization's plans to assemble small areas of the redwood forests and turn them over to the state for parks. The league had ample reasons of its own for supporting the Mill Creek bill over and above its debt to Laurance's family. The two state parks within the Mill Creek site were its creation, and it was anxious that they be protected from incursions like those that had occurred in the late 1950s when the state built a freeway through park borders. They hoped the federal aegis would keep that from happening again.

Udall was still resentful of Laurance's actions. "This park was the one area where he really outflanked me," he says. "From the beginning he was for the kind of compromise that was finally made. I had begun by being undecided, but increasingly I realized that the Sierra Club was right in their request for a large park. I was restrained to some extent by the Bureau of the Budget, but the real problem was Laurance Rockefeller. He went behind my back to President Johnson and worked out the compromise. His idea was that everybody had damn well better be content with half a loaf.

"Laurance had close ties with the people at Weyerhauser [Timber Company] and prided himself on the fact that he could talk to them as one businessman to another. He prided himself on being able to go up on the Hill and reason with conservatives like Congressman Aspinal. He prided himself on his ability to get everybody to agree. Having this kind of power was very important to him, more important than aiming for what was right. It was all done with great delicacy, of course. Laurance doesn't like controversy. Now that I think of it, I don't believe that he's ever gotten blood on him in any of these fights. It's almost instinctive with him: never to get bloodied."

By the late sixties, conservationists were beginning to wonder if Laurance might not be one of those friends who make enemies superfluous. He had sponsored growth at the expense of the environment; he had been part of deals undercutting the bargaining power of groups working in the public interest. Moreover, even as he was giving money to create parks—and this seemed the biggest contradiction of all—he was carving luxury resorts out of the wilderness.

In his mind there was no inconsistency. Conservation was just one side of the equation; the other was jobs, growth, development, and profit. He saw his task as balancing the scales. He had gotten involved in the ORRRC study not only because of his conservation background, but also because he was interested in the leisure revolution and the new possibilities that it implied. If increased leisure promised to put new pressures on the nation's recreation lands, it also meant new investment opportunities in the tourist and hotel business.

The continuity he saw between conservation and tourism was apparent in the way he had timed the opening of his Caneel Bay resort to coincide exactly with the dedication of the Virgin Islands National Park, whose lands he had do-

nated. Laurance had gone so far as to have his aides draw up
a plan to formalize the connection between the two events.
After specifying the key guests—from the press, the Department of the Interior, and Congress—to be flown to Saint
John at his expense, there was a summary of the plan's intent: "Purpose—to transfer the title of lands to the government in such a manner as to emphasize the economic and
conservation benefits to the islands and the nation. To
properly launch a unique resort achievement with maximum
impact for promotional carry-over and simultaneously under-
scoring Caneel Bay's unique appeal."

The hotels themselves were only part of a larger picture.
Opened in 1957, Caneel Bay Plantation had helped make
tourism a $100-million-a-year business in the U.S. Virgin Is-
lands by the mid-1960s. This meant a dramatic increase in
the value of the 4,000 acres Laurance held jointly with his
brother David on the still undeveloped Virgin Island of Saint
Croix. In Puerto Rico, the Dorado Beach Hotel, which had
cost him $9 million, had so prospered that 1,500 surrounding
acres of land Laurance owned with his partners were used in
creating the Dorado Beach Estates (high-priced, one-acre
executive retreats with frontage on Robert Trent Jones's
spectacular golf course) and the Villa Dorado Condominium
sitting on 31 elegantly landscaped acres. Laurance had also
broken ground on a sister resort to Dorado Beach, the Cerromar Beach Hotel, where gambling tables and nightlife would
attempt to promote San Juan as the new pre-Castro Havana.

By 1965, in addition to holdings in the Virgin Islands and
Puerto Rico, Laurance was proprietor of the posh Little Dix
resort in the British Virgins, the Grand Teton Lodge in Yellowstone, and the Woodstock Inn in Vermont. It was in this
year that the centerpiece of his resort developments—the $20
million Mauna Kea Beach Hotel—had its grand opening,
with Treasury Secretary C. Douglas Dillon (Laurance's sometime partner in venture capital), former CIA chief and
Standard Oil Director John A. McCone, Leonard and Harvey
Firestone, Henry Luce, and Senator Daniel Inouye among
those attending the festivities.

First struck by the stark grandeur of the leeward Kohala
coast during a 1960 trip to look over the development potential of the big island of Hawaii, Laurance had bought land at
Kaunaoa Beach and then employed the architectural firm of
Skidmore, Owings and Merrill to work with him on the
design. With its high vaulted ceilings and enormous terraces

looking up at the snow-capped volcanoes and down at the surf, it was to be the *pièce de résistance* of his hotels and he wanted it to dominate the surrounding land- and seascape. No expense was spared in the Mauna Kea's construction. The architects' first prototype of a guest room—an igloo-shaped structure costing $200,000 to build—didn't please Laurance, and he scrapped it after one night's trial. He orchestrated all aspects of the hotel's development and construction, from the design of the closets to the itinerary of experts sent to scour the Orient for statues and artifacts for the main lobby.

In the year following the Mauna Kea's opening, Laurance formed Rockresorts, Inc., a management company set up to run all his resorts and streamline their operations. Richard Holtzman, former president of Sheraton's operations in Hawaii, was named head of the new company. Laurance retained the role of presenting the philosophical aspects of his hotels. ("This is an uplifting, creative environment," he told a journalist present at the Mauna Kea's grand opening, "and my hotels are designed to keep people as close to nature as possible.") Holtzman's job was to talk business. Pointing out seven years later that the Mauna Kea had one of the best occupancy rates in the industry and indicating that he expected it to reach a profit position in 1973, Holtzman said: "Mr. Rockefeller insists on very high standards because he believes that adherence to quality standards is ideologically sound, but also because it finds its way to the bottom of the P&L statement."

If at the onset the hotel was still a long way from running in the black, it seemed the adjacent lands that came with it would make the Hawaiian investment pay off sooner. From the beginning Laurance had hoped to use the Mauna Kea to open this remote part of the island of Hawaii to tourism, and then to carve a whole new city out of the jungle. He had acquired rights to some 12,000 acres in the vicinity and, even as the Mauna Kea was going up, he had blueprinted a massive development keyed to his grand hotel (and six others less grand and catering to a downwardly sliding scale of clientele), which would be at the center of the new town at Kavahae. In addition to the hotels, there would be recreational areas and a large shopping center serving the 20,000 people who would live in housing Laurance proposed to develop.

Such a plan required extensive maneuvering. By 1967, knowing that a Civil Aeronautics Board (CAB) recommendation had given Eastern Airlines the inside track in the hotly contested trans-Pacific air routes, which President Johnson would soon act on, Laurance had traded Eastern an 80 percent in his Dorado Beach venture and 60 percent of the Mauna Kea in return for $22 million of the airline's stock. He used this stock to join Eastern and the Dillingham Development Corporation (a construction firm specializing in high-rise buildings) in establishing Dilrock-Eastern, which was to undertake his $250 million recreational, tourist, and residential development on the Kohala coast.*

Laurance's endeavors set off a development fever that swept through the island of Hawaii, bringing Boise-Cascade, Signal Properties, and several large Japanese developers trailing in his wake. Because development had managed to spoil the tropical beauty of some of the other islands, Laurance changed his development hat for his conservation hat. When it appeared that a unique rain forest area on the neighboring island of Maui was endangered, Laurance donated 54 acres he owned in the Seven Sacred Pools area, and convinced the Nature Conservancy to buy up the surrounding 4,000 acres and donate it all to the adjacent Haleakala Volcanoes National Park. Yet the time had passed when such gestures could erase the impression made by his hotel developments. The difference in emphasis was shown by the price tag. In the last decade his resorts had cost him an estimated $40 million; during his lifetime he had spent less than a quarter of that amount on his conservation philanthropy.

If environmentalists had come to be wary of him, even those who had dealt with him at a higher level—as co-conspirators in the politics of ecology—had become progressively

---

*Getting the Hawaii air routes was crucial to Eastern's participation. As a major stockholder in the company and personal friend of LBJ, Laurance was in charge of lobbying the President. To offset the fact that he was a Republican and the other airlines had front men who were Democrats (Clark Clifford for Continental and Abe Fortas for Braniff), Eastern hired the prestigious Washington law firm of Revis, Pogue, and Neal, one of whose senior partners, Welsh Pogue, was a former head of the CAB and also a prominent figure in Democratic party politics. Robert Beckman, a Washington attorney specializing in air route litigation who had an insider's view of this battle of titans, says, "It was well known that Rockefeller had several private audiences with the President on this. The investment in the trans-Pacific route was staggering. Each of the major contenders spent a minimum of $1 million on their campaign. You need a figure like Laurance just to be in the game; but even so it doesn't guarantee success once you get out on the field."

more disenchanted. Stewart Udall, who went along with Laurance—and was as often dragged along—on many of the crucial battles of the 1960s, has since reflected on the experience. "Laurance is a curious study," he says. "I've always thought that the hotels are examples of the basic conflict in him. Take the Virgin Islands. In his interests there you see the two elements of his personality—the selfish and the public-spirited—right on the surface. On the one hand, he sees this little island and says, 'Now this is one of the finest things under the U.S. flag, and it ought to be a park.' But then he ties it all together with buying up some plush resort right in the middle of all this beauty, but out of the reach of the ordinary person. It makes you wonder where his commitment is. It's symbolic of the contradiction at the core of Laurance's life."

Charles Stoddard, who worked closely with Laurance for over a year before resigning as executive chairman of his Citizens' Advisory Committee, says, "If anybody but a Rockefeller did what Laurance has—donate land for national parks and then develop them and build large hotels nearby and hold a lot of land for development—it would not only be in obvious bad taste, but a conflict of interest too. But as a Rockefeller he seems to be able to get away with it. The truth is that basically Laurance doesn't have a very long attention span. It's helpful to his image to have a do-gooder approach, but let's face it—the environmental problems facing this country aren't a very zealous concern of his."

In the summer of 1968, when Senators Henry Jackson, Edmund Muskie, and other conservation leaders in Congress joined in a special meeting to discuss formulating a national policy on the environment, they invited Laurance to be the opening speaker. In his remarks he suggested that the President should appoint a special Commission on Environmental Organization. His listeners assumed that Laurance would be the ideal man to head such a commission. It would have been a final feather in his cap, and a way of recovering the prestige lost in the conservation infighting of the past few years. But the President was deeply mired in his own difficulties over Vietnam and never got around to setting up the commission. It was the second rebuff of the year for Laurance, who had earlier seen American Airlines and Braniff chosen over Eastern for the coveted trans-Pacific air routes to Hawaii.*

Laurance would continue to be an important figure in Washington's environmental establishment. He was a large contributor to Nixon's 1968 campaign, and after the new administration took office, he remained head of the Citizens' Advisory Committee on Environmental Quality (as the new President had renamed Johnson's Committee on Recreation and Natural Beauty). He continued to have a formidable reputation in government circles. In the early 1970s a discreetly unsigned memorandum circulated through the upper reaches of the Interior Department regarding Laurance's influence; as author Allan Talbot observed, it sounded like an FBI dossier on some Mafia don. The memorandum noted that he "controlled" two conservation organizations and had "infiltrated" eleven more, while eight others were "suspect." He had the same sort of proprietary relationship with the increasingly important Bureau of Outdoor Recreation that his father had had with the National Park Service. He also had close relations with individuals like Russell Train, former president of the Conservation Foundation (one of the organizations he had "infiltrated" by helping Fairfield Osborn found it in 1947, giving it annual gifts averaging $50,000 a year ever since), who began the Nixon years as an Assistant Secretary of the Interior and later became head of the Environmental Protection Agency.

Yet, the memo was already behind the times. Though it might be difficult to see with the naked eye, Laurance's stock as a conservationist, which had risen precipitously in the gogo years of the Johnson administration, had begun a slow decline. After Earth Day, 1970, brought ecology to the foreground of the public conscience and stimulated the growth of environmental action groups all across the country, Laurance's dilemma became clear. He may have privately abhorred the oil spills that blackened the beaches of Santa Barbara and San Francisco, but he could not publicly align himself with people picketing the oil companies and making antibusiness statements. He found himself involved in negotiations for a Golden Gateway National Recreation Area to preserve San Francisco Bay at the same time that his brother

---

*After the air route decision, the Dilrock-Eastern partnership was terminated. Laurance reacquired the 60 percent of the Mauna Kea the airline had obtained in 1967, exchanging for it his remaining interest in the Dorado Beach and Cerromar resorts in Puerto Rico.

David was involved in Westbay Associates, a joint venture with Lazard Freres and the Crocker Land Company that proposed to fill in 4,800 acres of the bay to provide a foundation for a $3 billion real estate project. (When, after holding hearings, the San Francisco Bay Conservation and Development Commission sidetracked the Westbay project, Warren Lindquist, David's chief aide, charged that a good plan had been sabotaged by "articulate and rabid conservationists.") While environmental organizations like Friends of the Earth (which he purported to admire) were fighting to make the public aware of the potential disasters inherent in plans for the commercial use of nuclear power, Laurance continued to put venture capital into nuclear technology,* and, along with Nelson and David, fully backed the efforts of Con Ed and other utility companies in their deployment of nuclear reactors.

It had always been Laurance's special pride both to be in the avant-garde of whatever movement he happened to be involved in and to feel that he had mastered the contradictions in his life by a sheer act of will. Yet now, at least in the conservation movement, his ideas and style of operation were passé. And as for the contradictions, they seemed to have slipped out of control.

His life had taken on a strangely circular quality. He had begun his career without any particular commitment, made a serious bid for fame and influence, and, when this entailed more controversy than he had anticipated, retracted back into the "creative dilettantism" of his younger days. He continued to be active in environmental affairs, but it was primarily as an emeritus removed from the everyday struggles. (Though his aides would deny it. "Just because he isn't in the headlines anymore doesn't mean that he isn't working effectively behind the scenes," Gene Setzer, Laurance's chief conservation aide,

---

*In the fifties he had been instrumental in putting together United Nuclear Corporation. In the sixties he led several family members into an investment in New England Nuclear, which became a leading producer of radioactive drugs. The investment was one of the best performers in the venture capital portfolio of Room 5600, returning the family $1,982,000 on an initial investment of $160,000 in a ten-year period. The company was reprimanded time and again in the late sixties by the AEC for discharging potentially disastrous levels of radioactivity into the air and sewers of Boston. After these incidents became public and one New England Nuclear employee contracted leukemia as a result of severe exposure to plutonium inside a laboratory and died within three days, the family reluctantly decided that the public relations risks outweighed the profits and got rid of their stock in the company.

says. "That's always been what he does best anyway.") He gave himself over to sudden enthusiasms like reconstructing a nineteenth-century model farm near his Woodstock Inn as part of a "living museum." He continued to dabble in business, watching over his hotels and continuing as the "anchor man" in the Family Office.

Outwardly he was much the same as he had always been. His features had been sharpened by the onset of old age, and the side of one cheek was occasionally blotched below his ear from a skin cancer Sloan-Kettering doctors assured him was under control. He was pipe-smoking and philosophical, always ready with a graceful quip and anxious to keep up with the trendy epiphenomena of pop culture. (During a 1971 visit with one of his daughters, Laurance surprised dinner guests by mentioning that he had just finished Theodore Roszak's *The Making of a Counter-Culture*, and that it had had a deep impact on him.)

Yet inwardly he had changed. From his youth he had been the Brother with the best chance to step outside the viscous mystique with which Junior had surrounded the Rockefeller family. This latency, the sense that he could be different if he *wanted* to, had always marked Laurance off from the other Brothers who accepted the Rockefellers' manifest destiny and its implications for their personal lives as an item of faith. Yet, as this latency remained bottled up in Laurance, it fermented into a cynicism.

Beneath the debonair manner was a nihilism none of the other Brothers was capable of, perhaps because none of them was as aware as Laurance of the awesome price he had paid to be a Rockefeller. It was a quality he generally subdued, yet occasionally it slipped out. One of the employees of Room 5600 remembers sorting through Laurance's memorabilia with him and coming across the Medal of Freedom President Johnson had given him in his last days in office. Laurance picked up the nation's highest civilian honor, looked at it for a moment, and then handed it over. "I guess we ought to put this someplace," he said. Then he added the irony, "Lyndon gave me that instead of the Hawaii air route."

Laurance's life continued to be encased by the insulation common to all men of affairs: endless conferences, board meetings, and briefings. There was a continuing commitment to his brother Nelson. (When his daughter reproached him for allowing himself to be used as a fall guy when Nelson's confirmation hearings hit a snag because of the Arthur Goldberg biography, he shrugged. "Well, no politician is perfect. But if you look at the batting averages over the years, Nelson's is pretty good.") But otherwise all his activity rotated around a core of emptiness. Off the record, some of his aides admitted as much, although to say so publicly was impermissible.

His children were under no such constraints. His daughter Laura says regretfully, "I feel sad for him in a way. He missed the boat. Daddy could have been creative."

Her sister Marion agrees. "He depends on specialists and experts for everything. They block off reality while he goes faster and faster. He's always getting off one jet and onto another; hasn't got time for anything, especially for understanding himself."

Laurance was aware of the fact that his life lacked a center of balance. He referred to it obliquely in comments which had once seemed nicely ironic, but as he grew older acquired a tone of desperate flippancy, as in the reply he gave when an interviewer noted that his career seemed to lack a plan: "Yes, my life has been almost Zen-like, finding without seeking." Since his undergraduate days at Princeton, Laurance had always professed to believe that a man was the sum of his contradictions, yet in himself it was increasingly difficult to tell what exactly it all added up to.

23

IT WAS EARLY FEBRUARY 1974, and David Rockefeller was off on another of his globe-trotting journeys. This time it was to the Middle East, where the highlight of his trip would be a visit to Cairo to confer with Egyptian President Anwar Sadat and the completion of negotiations for the opening of a new office of the Chase, making it the first U.S. bank in Egypt since the 1956 invasion of Suez. The trip would include conferences with oil company personnel about the dramatic rise in prices initiated by the producing countries in the aftermath of the October War with Israel, and about its effect on the international economy.

Midway through his visit, David got a telephone call from the White House chief of staff, General Alexander Haig. The President had just received the resignation of Treasury Secretary George Shultz, effective as soon as a replacement could be found. Haig's voice quavered over the connection; could David fly back immediately to talk about taking the job? Speaking in the precise manner that made his ordinary conversation sound as if he were dictating a business letter, David replied that he would come to Washington as soon as he could, but thought that it would be in the best interest of the country if he remained a few more days in the Middle East and finished his work there.

While David was flattered by Haig's offer, it was no novelty for him to be called for this job. He had been sounded out for the Treasury post by Kennedy and offered it outright by Lyndon Johnson. He had accepted neither, however, because at the time he didn't want to interrupt his rise to the top at the Chase with a term of government service, and also because his wife, Peggy, was adamantly opposed to living in Washington.

With the economy badly shaken by the oil crisis and inflation, and with the Watergate scandal poisoning the atmosphere in Washington, the post was in many ways less attractive than it had been. It was no secret, moreover, that President Nixon did not like Rockefellers. In 1968 the Washington grapevine had flashed the story of how Nixon had reacted on a flight to Key Biscayne when an aide tossed out David's name for the Treasury post. Another of the President's men, recalling that Nelson's name had already come up for Secretary of Defense, quickly pointed out that this would make two Rockefellers in the Cabinet. Nixon had grimaced and said, "Hell, I don't know why there even has to be *one* Rockefeller."*

Still, as he flew back to the United States in his private jet, David found himself seriously considering the offer. If nothing else, the magnitude of the task made it tempting. The country needed someone with his standing to restore the credibility of Washington. The Herculean labor involved in cleaning up the economy was a challenge fit for a Rockefeller.

*Yet, the realism of power, in which Nixon was steeped, would eventually result in his offering David several positions: the Treasury post, Secretary of Defense, and the Ambassadorship to Moscow.

He arrived home in New York at eleven P.M. on a Wednesday night. By nine-fifteen the next morning he was in Haig's office in Washington talking about the authority he would insist on having and demanding assurance that he would be allowed to make economic policy free from interference by tactical considerations stemming from the Watergate affair. That night, leaning toward accepting the job, he went to a state dinner on the Middle East attended by Secretary of State Kissinger and the President. The President greeted him and shook hands cordially, but there was no mention of the new post, nor were there the expected words of encouragement urging David to come aboard. Things did not seem right. Within the next few days, the two men had occasion to meet again, and the President again failed to mention the post. David went back to his advisers to reappraise the situation. Perhaps it was just a mental lapse by Nixon, a result of the stress that had been so visible on the drawn grayness of his face; yet without the President's firm encouragement, the offer seemed too dangerous, given the risks.

The next day David called Haig from New York and told him that he would have to decline the offer. When the chief of staff pressed for his reason, Rockefeller paused for a moment, then with his usual diplomatic tact said that his decision was based on his fears that too many people secretly blamed his family for the energy crisis for him to be able to do an effective job at that point in time.

Others might have swallowed their doubts and taken the job on faith, but David didn't operate that way. In the nearly two decades he had worked in the Chase, he had long since come to occupy—in the words of *Finance* magazine—"the equivalent of cabinet rank in the society of his peers." This was a status that didn't change when a new administration moved into Washington or the nation's economy tumbled into chaos. It reflected a basic reality of the systems of power guiding the nation, and his own place in that arrangement.

In David's world, institutions occupied a primary place; and after the family, the Chase was the institution that mattered most of all. When he first decided to accept his Uncle Winthrop Aldrich's offer to go to work for the bank, it was because he realized that it was the kind of institution, perhaps the only kind, where he could have both the authority and the social position he wanted. (He had already noted the disorienting effects that being *just* a Rockefeller had had on his older brother John.) There was something especially appealing about the bank, moreover, in the way it matched the shape of his personality and ambition. He could see from his uncle's career that bankers were the statesmen of the business world. Insofar as the private sector had a general interest, bankers expressed it; their very boards were gathering places for corporate collectivities of power. As holders of credit, they were the moralists of corporate behavior and the guardians of the economic future.

David realized that while he had been making his way up the executive ladder of the Chase, a crucial drama was taking place in the postwar American economy. It was the growing dominance of financial over industrial institutions, and of large institutional investors over shareholding individuals as the legal owners of the country's leading corporations. These trends intersected in the emergence of banks as the epicenter of the economy. Controlling huge trusts and even larger pension funds, they had become the great powers of the economic order. Among the powerful, the Chase Manhattan ranked very near the top. At the time David was deciding to turn down Nixon's offer of the Treasury post, he chaired a board of directors interlocked with the boards of Allied Chemical, Exxon, Standard of Indiana, Shell Oil, AT&T, Honeywell, General Foods, and dozens of other corporate giants. The Chase was a leading stockholder in CBS, Jersey Standard, Atlantic Richfield, United Airlines, and a galaxy of other corporations—from AT&T and IBM to Motorola and Safeway. The power this stockholding position conferred was immense.*

The fruits of this brave new world of banking were still before him in 1960, when at the age of forty-five David Rockefeller was appointed president of the Chase and given a one-

---

*The bank had used its stockholding position to become especially influential in the transportation industry. In addition to being the leading stockholder in two major railroads and two large trucking firms, the Chase had substantial holdings in the airlines industry. It was the leading shareholder in United (8 percent), Northwest (9 percent), and National (12 percent). It also had large holdings in TWA, Delta, and Braniff. The reason that a bank acting in trustee capacity would choose to invest in relatively stagnant airlines stock was the airlines' frequent need for new generations of extremely expensive equipment and the financing required for its purchase. In this connection, it was no accident that by 1974, 14 major airlines had a total of $275 million in outstanding loans from the Chase.

half share of the chief executive officer's job. The other half went to the man who had succeeded John J. McCloy as chairman of the board, George Champion. Tall, graying, distinguished, Champion had gained a solid reputation over the years as a commercial banker. He was more than ten years Rockefeller's senior, and in many ways his intellectual opposite. Yet the two men agreed on the basic issues confronting the bank. Almost immediately their new regime surprised the business world by acts that were out of keeping with the Chase's patrician image: giving away bayberry candles to lure new accounts, flooding the media with a multi-million-dollar ad campaign centered around the slogan, "You have a friend at Chase Manhattan."

Their amiable relationship was based on the understanding that there were things about which they must simply agree to disagree, notably Champion's religious fundamentalism and David's penchant for modern art. When Billy Graham came to New York, David's contribution to his campaign was generous enough not to seem perfunctory; when Rockefeller and his art acquisition committee (which included Alfred Barr of the Museum of Modern Art, Robert Hale of the Met, and other family advisers on aesthetics) began filling the bank with abstract expressionism, the traditional-minded Champion insisted only that the avant-garde sculpture constructed of auto fenders and other materials he considered unseemly be kept out of view of his office. (Aside from Champion's cavil, which was aesthetic, there were stockholder concerns that were financial. When the question was raised at one of the annual meetings whether the money might not better be distributed in dividends, David met the philistinism head on by pointing out that the 1,600 art works in the Chase collection, which had cost less than $500,000, had appreciated in value to more than $3 million by 1972.)

The relationship between the two men was smoothed by the fact that they knew their joint tenancy would be over in seven years when the 58-year-old Champion reached the mandatory retirement age and David assumed the full control of the bank he had been destined for from the moment his Uncle Winthrop had hired him. The Chase's new headquarters at 1 Chase Manhattan Plaza, in fact, seemed an aluminum and glass monument manifesting his destiny. (In that respect it was like Nelson's Albany Mall and quite different from Laurance's imitation of Rockefeller Center's move across Sixth Avenue in 1960 to build first the Sperry-Rand

Building in association with Uris Brothers, and then other structures.) Sixty stories high, David's $150 million slab jutting up above its neighbors was the first skyscrapper completed in David's planned renovation of lower Manhattan. It was the biggest bank building in the world. It had the biggest battery of computers and the biggest vault. It was a superbly equipped machine able to handle any sum of money or power.

On the 17th floor, guards moved inconspicuously up and down the corridors while executives sat in the barber shop getting their weekly trim or waited for the express elevator to whisk them to the aerie high above, where they lunched in executive dining rooms. Here David might be glimpsed darting out of his own private elevator—he moved with surprising quickness for a big man—and disappearing through the push-button, sliding glass doors into his private office, an opulent mélange of Cézannes, Wyeths, Rothkos, Etruscan pottery, and African sculpture. He was probably oblivious to the fact that the three hundred vice-presidents working under him regard this as the *sanctum sanctorum,* a spot not approached without a properly humbled heart. Yet Richard Reeves, former *New York Times* political writer, recalls the effect mere proximity to the president's office had on David's underlings: "I'd go down to One Chase Plaza several times a month. The thing that always struck me was the absolute terror of the subordinates where David was concerned. They creep silently in and out of his office. Almost every time I interviewed him, some vice-president would come up to me before I went and say, 'Look, you're not going to ask about his daughter Abby and her women's lib or anything like that, are you?' "

He seemed naturally to inspire this sort of hushed decorum. Just as "orchestrate" was his brother Laurance's favorite concept, so "appropriate" was David's. He was unique among the Brothers, as his friend and godson George Gilder says, because "he holds to all the stern precepts in which the family was raised justifying his power and position by trying to be somehow morally superior to other rich and powerful families. It is this sense that justifies his wealth and allows him to sleep easily." Perhaps the deepest wound David ever suffered was caused by the absolute *inappropriateness* of Nelson's divorce and remarriage. "Rockefellers just don't do things like Nelson did," Gilder says. "This is what Hollywood rich people do." It was a sin against the moral structure of the family. ("Marriage is the cornerstone of civilization," David would say to his daughter Abby when she announced her intention to remain single.) He moped for weeks over the divorce, one of his children says, but was so trapped in his sense in propriety—it was one of those things one simply doesn't talk about—that he couldn't bear to mention it to the brother he had always worshiped, and in the end he had no alternative but to acquiesce.

He was the most peculiar of the Brothers, strangely vacuous for an important man, and definitely a throwback to his father's Victorian *beau ideal* in which emotion is always submerged beneath the agreeable formal facade of the rational man. ("To our loss," David's son Richard would say looking back on his childhood, "emotional was seen as the opposite of reasonable, which made it bad.") He seemed almost characterless, someone whose views were bounded by what men of his station were supposed to say and whose acts were dictated by his sense of what it was appropriate to do. But if this made him frustrating for family and close friends, it also made him the perfect man to head one of the most powerful financial institutions in the world. That predictable, carefully measured quality that made him privately appear to be manipulated by some hidden ventriloquist also made him the consummate public spokesman for the community of which the Chase was a part. He knew the language and forms of the communication required of him and could articulate the point of view with perfect impersonality. He had learned well how to envelop himself in the double majesty coming from being a Rockefeller *and* head of the Chase, and how to use this institutional, semisymbolic power his own personality alone might not have won him.

David's voice had been muted in the 1950s, when he was working his way up through the Chase's executive ranks and it was only proper that he should defer to those who were technically his superiors. But his arrival at a position of power in the Chase coincided with the advent of the New Frontier and created a situation in which he could begin to act as the leading oracle of the business world, wielding some of the influence latent in his position.

From the business community's point of view, the most pressing issues facing the Kennedy administration were a sluggish growth rate and a weakened dollar. The "key importance of economic growth" had been the incessant theme of the Rockefeller Brothers panel study on the economy. Its goal of a doubled growth rate had been explicitly endorsed by Nixon and forthrightly defended by David. "Economic growth," he summarized in one of his speeches, "although not the complete answer to human happiness, has commanded the highest social priority because it provides the essential ingredients for improving the well-being of society, as well as the well-being of the individual."

Although the new President also endorsed the goal of economic expansion, the New Frontier had begun by challenging the idea that simply putting more goods on the market would bring the good life to Americans. In his best-selling book *The Affluent Society*, Kennedy advisor John Kenneth Galbraith had decried the condition of "private wealth and public squalor" produced by previous increases in the GNP and called for a program of government spending to "redress the social balance." Much to the concern of the business community, Kennedy himself had taken up these ideas in his campaign, declaring that the problem of providing enough consumer goods had already been solved, and that what remained were "those problems which lie largely in the realm of public action—bad housing, poverty, recessions, unemployment, discrimination, crowded and obsolete schools. . . . polluted air and water." The first major political struggle of the Kennedy administration polarized the liberal advocates of more federal spending to stimulate the economy and the conservative advocates of a major tax cut favoring potential investors. In this arena, David stepped to the fore as a spokesman for the business viewpoint.

For the first two years of the Kennedy administration, David's speeches reflected a near-obsession with the necessity of a tax cut to stimulate the economy. "President-elect Kennedy has stated that he favors liberalizing the treatment of depreciation for tax purposes," he told an Ohio audience late in 1960. "That may not be enough. As a nation we may have to face up to the question as to whether a corporate income tax that takes 52% of all earnings is consistent with a national objective of a more rapid rate of economic growth." In 1962, after complaining that "the role and influence of business on the American scene has declined relative to that of labor and government," David told a reporter from the *Wall Street Journal:* "It is clear that the nation suffers from an outmoded tax system which holds back tax investment. . . . Here again sound policy is often at odds with what is made to have popular appeal from the soapbox."

That same year, David attended a White House dinner honoring André Malraux. As David and his wife were leaving, Kennedy took him aside and asked for his views on the balance-of-payments situation and the current attitude the business community was taking toward the economy in general. David responded in a 3,000-word letter, which was featured, together with the President's answer on a facing page, in *Life* and covered throughout the press in a way that confirmed his role as the emerging spokesman for the responsible business viewpoint. In his own way, he had become as representative a figure for the era as Floyd Patterson or John F. Kennedy himself.

Like his friend C. Douglas Dillon (whom Kennedy had appointed Treasury Secretary after David made it clear he wasn't interested), David urged the President to keep the federal budget in check and even reduce government spending in nonmilitary areas. (Both David and Dillon were prepared to accept the New Frontier's massive increase in military spending in connection with Vietnam, however.) It was, in fact, with "concern and dismay"—the strongest expressions David allowed himself—that he viewed the increase in government spending relative to private investment in the previous five years. "Of course, I recognize," he said, "that we cannot reduce government expenditures and reduce the tax burden in one easy stroke. But the very difficulty of the task requires that we undertake it at once."

By this time, however, the chief exponent of the spending policies that in David's view would weaken the dollar was safely appointed to an ambassadorship in India. "I am not sure," John Kenneth Galbraith said of the tax cut Kennedy subsequently enacted, "what the advantage is in having a few more dollars to spend if the air is too dirty to breathe, the water too polluted to drink, the commuters are losing out on the struggle to get in and out of the cities, the streets are filthy, and the schools so bad that the young, perhaps wisely, stay away, and hoodlums roll citizens for some of the dollars they saved in taxes." He had no hesitation in assigning motives for those, like David, who favored lightening the tax burden of the wealthy while opposing a government-funded effort to redress the social balance: "That is because public services, though extremely important for people of moderate incomes, are not nearly so essential for the rich. And the rich pay more [in taxes]. The rich and articulate accordingly oppose public spending. That this policy encounters resistance means only that it is painful to the selfish."

David Rockefeller would have been pained to be thought of as a selfish man. It was not part of his sense of himself and his function; nor was it the way others in his circle thought of him. His friend André Meyer, head of Lazard Frères and Company and a colleague on the Chase board, had been quoted in the *New Yorker* saying how different David was in precisely that respect. "There's nothing on earth I wouldn't do for David. It's not because he's a Rockefeller but because he's the kind of human being you want to do something for. I've never seen him mean. I've always seen him acting with poise and class, and greatness. In this financial jungle, you have all kinds of animals. He's the best." Walter Heller, who was liberal chairman of Kennedy's Council of Economic Advisers, adds: "He's just a helluva nice guy, easy to deal with, easy to communicate with." Yet the measures David helped convince Kennedy to adopt (a 1962 investment credit and accelerated depreciation allowance, along with a tax cut two years later) represented a massive redistribution of income from the poor to the wealthy. Forty-five percent of the tax cut was earmarked for the top one-fifth. (A family earning $200,000 a year got $32,000 in return, while one with a 3,000 income got $60.) Corporate taxes were slashed as much as 23 percent, while profits rose 57 percent. Dillon was able to announce with pride that government expenditures on nonmilitary programs had increased one-third *less* in the first four years of the Democratic administration than during Eisenhower's final term of Republican fiscal conservatism.

David's vantage at the Chase made him feel that it was his duty to be a guardian of sound economy not only at home but in many countries abroad as well. Nowhere did he feel this responsibility more than in Latin America. His own career in international finance had begun in the Latin department of the Chase, already at that time a power in the hemisphere; and with his brother Nelson he had embarked on several projects south of the border, including a ranch and a financial venture with IBEC in Brazil, and had participated with Laurance in development schemes in the Caribbean. The very *milieux* in which he moved, moreover, were made up of the stewards of Latin American finance and industry: friends like the Peter Graces, with whom he yachted in the summers at Seal Harbor and whose family firm dominated Latin American shipping, or colleagues like André Meyer and Doug Dillon, whose investment houses underwrote Latin American governments and paved the way for such corporate giants as Standard Oil and ITT to advance in Latin American markets.

The sixties had begun with an unsettling event for this social circle. It occurred on January 1, 1959, when Fidel Castro's guerrillas marched into Havana to end the dictatorship of Fulgencio Batista, under whose rule the billion-dollar investment of U.S. business in Cuba had thrived. Although David personally might not have condoned the corruption that kept the Batista regime afloat and responsive, the Chase had been one of a handful of New York banks holding the strings of credit on Cuban governments and dictators for half a century. Rockefeller himself was a director of the Punta Allegre Sugar Corporation, second-largest of the U.S.– owned companies that produced Cuba's most important export. A. A. Berle, Jr., the family's adviser (shortly to be appointed by Kennedy to head a task force developing policy guidelines on Latin America), was chairman of the board of SuCrest Corporation, the largest sugar refiner on the East Coast and a Chase customer. When the National Security Council made its decision to invade Cuba, five of those present were David's close friends or associates (Secretary of State Rusk, Secretary of the Treasury Dillon, CIA chief Allen Dulles, Presidential Assistant McGeorge Bundy, and Berle).

Even before the Kennedy administration had launched its ill-fated invasion, a long-range program had begun to contain the Cuban heresy by making an "Alliance for Progress" with the other Latin countries. Announced by the President in March 1961, the idea for the Alliance had been generated by Berle's White House task force and formalized at the elegant beach resort of Punta del Este on August 17, 1961. There Douglas Dillon had pledged $10 billion in U.S. aid to Latin countries promising to undertake social reforms that would make possible a 2.5 percent annual growth rate over the next decade.

Despite the presence of Dillon, the U.S. business community was uneasy about social reformers of the Kennedy administration like Deputy Assistant Secretary of State Richard Goodwin, who saw economic development and social change commitments. Moreover, they felt the New Frontier had not shown the proper eagerness to bring business into the initial planning of the Alliance. It was not, for example, until about three days before the Punta del Este Conference that a White House aide called David's cousin Richard Aldrich (a director of IBEC) to organize a business delegation to the meeting, and then they were invited only as observers.

The gap between Kennedy and the business world presented David with an opportunity and responsibility which he undertook with characteristic dedication. He joined the Commerce Committee for the Alliance and criticized the program for not insisting strongly enough that the Latin nations promote the expansion of private U.S. capital. ("The United States," he said, "should concentrate its economic aid program in countries that show the greatest inclination to adopt measures to improve the investment climate, and withhold aid from others until satisfactory performance has been demonstrated.") As head of the U.S. Business Advisory Council for the Alliance, he took the position that there should be a move toward a common market in Latin America to ease the efforts of U.S. multinationals to expand their operations. And in sessions with business groups, he stressed the importance of the Alliance as security against the spread of Castroism. A year after the Bay of Pigs, he told the Economic Club of Chicago, "We have made a firm commitment to Latin America for economic aid and for assistance in containing communist imperialism. I think the situation warrants substantial expenditures on both fronts on the scale proposed by President Kennedy."

To placate the business community, Kennedy asked David to organize the Business Group for Latin America. Composed of nearly two dozen heads of corporations doing business in Latin America, it was to meet regularly with Washington officials and discuss policy.* That same year, David proposed an International Executive Services Committee, which would be the businessmen's equivalent of the Peace Corps (referred to by its members as the "Paunch Corps"), sending retired or on-leave executives to assist their opposite numbers in the developing countries. The program, launched officially in 1964,

---

*In 1965, David merged this group with two older business organizations (the U.S. Inter-American Council, founded in 1941 by Nelson's office, and the Latin American Information Committee, founded in 1961) to form the Council for Latin America, its more than 200 member corporations accounting for over 80 percent of U.S. investment below the border. David arranged to have the council located in a six-story town house across from the Council on Foreign Relations.

would eventually be sponsored by more than 175 U.S. multinational corporations.

By the end of its first year, the Alliance was in serious trouble. A Chase Manhattan report issued on the anniversary of the Punta del Este Conference observed that the tendency of the Alliance to stress government projects was likely to discourage private incentive. Three months later, *The New York Times* reported that the flow of U.S. investments to Latin America was "drying up." Opposition to the Alliance, the *Times* reported in a special review the following April, had emerged "from conservative Latin American groups—mainly land-owning and traditional business classes—that feared the reformist ideas of the Kennedy planners ... [and] United States business interests concerned about the safety of their traditional investments." The most articulate expression of these views, the *Times* observed, was contained in a recent report of David's Commerce Committee for the Alliance, which proposed, in effect, a switch from governmental aid to private investment.

By 1965 the Alliance in its original concept was a dead letter. Especially after the appointment of Thomas Mann as Assistant Secretary of State for Inter-American Affairs, official policy stressed the primacy of protecting U.S. private investments and disclaimed any responsibility for promoting democratic government in the hemisphere. Two weeks after Mann announced these policies, a military *coup* toppled the democratically elected reform government of Brazil in what Secretary of State Rusk hailed as a "move to ensure the continuity of Constitutional government."

If the new military regimes that began appearing on the already bleak political landscape of Latin America dealt harshly with their opposition, they also brought a certain stability. It was for this reason that David welcomed the new conservatism of Washington's alliance with the Latin republics. Writing in *Foreign Affairs*, the house organ of the Council on Foreign Relations, in 1966, David observed that the revised and scaled-down version of the Alliance for Progress was better than "the overly ambitious concepts of revolutionary change of the program's early years, because it created a climate more attractive to U.S. business."

David himself had never ceased to work on behalf of that climate. A year earlier, he had been to Peru to talk with officials about the Peruvian government's dispute over back taxes and royalties with the International Petroleum Company, a subsidiary of Standard Oil. A week after this visit, Bobby Kennedy, then a U.S. senator, arrived in Lima. With him was former Alliance Administrator Richard Goodwin. At an intimate gathering of Peruvian intellectuals, Kennedy was asked about the conflict with the oil company. "This is your country," he answered, "and how you handle the dispute is your business."

One of the Peruvians objected: "David Rockefeller was down here last week, and he told the government that if they didn't give in to the International Petroleum Company, they wouldn't get any aid from the United States."

Kennedy leaned forward, the muscles of his face tensing, and replied: "Well, we Kennedys, we eat Rockefellers for breakfast."

"Someone at the gathering leaked the incident to the press," Goodwin recalls, "and it got around. When we stopped in Argentina, a reporter rushed up to Bobby and said [in a mistranslation that nonetheless managed to capture a sense of the way Latin American policy was made]: 'Senator, is it true that you have breakfast with Rockefeller every morning?' "

The arena in which Kennedy was proposing a contest was far from the touch football fields of Hyannis Port; it was not even the battleground of party politics. Nor was David Rockefeller a Richard Nixon or a Jimmy Hoffa. He appeared in the national and international arenas as the representative of the most powerful and most permanent order of social authority and influence. When he spoke, it was with the voice of powers and institutions that Presidents themselves came to, to get sanction for their programs. The Kennedys were not even in his league.

David did not think of himself as an idealogue on Peru or on any other issue. He liked to imagine himself as a person who judged things on their merits; a truly reasonable man devoted to the commonweal and possessed of *gravitas*, that weightiness of judgment so prized by the Romans. Yet he had, like his brothers, grown up in the shadow of Nelson's political philosophy; but while JDR3 merely paid lip service to it and Laurance uncritically accepted it as an article of faith, David believed in it perhaps even more deeply than Nelson himself.

He had become an early and enthusiastic backer of Kennedy's decision to send advisers to Vietnam, a move foreshadowed in the Panel Studies. By 1965, David had joined his fellow Chase board members Eugene Black (of the World Bank), John J. McCloy, and C. Douglas Dillon to form the Committee for an Effective and Durable Peace in Asia, in order to press for support for the war throughout the financial community. The year had begun with the bombing of North Vietnam; in July President Johnson had made the fateful decision to commit the first 200,000 U.S. ground forces. These actions were strongly supported by David and other financial leaders concerned about the political instability of the Pacific area. Indicative of the attitude of these men were the words of one senior Chase official. "In the past, foreign investors have been somewhat wary of the over-all political prospect for the region," the vice-president in charge of the Chase's Far Eastern operations had reported.

> I must say, though, that the U.S. actions in Vietnam this year—which have demonstrated that the U.S. will continue to give effective protection to the free nations of the region—have considerably reassured both Asian and Western investors. In fact, I see some reason for hope that the same sort of economic growth may take place in the free economies of Asia that took place in Europe after the Truman Doctrine and after NATO provided a protective shield.

On September 9, a full-page ad appeared in *The New York Times:* signed by David and other members of the Committee for an Effective and Durable Peace, it endorsed Johnson's escalations and asserted the right of the South Vietnamese "to choose a government of their own, free from assassination, threats of violence or other forms of intimidation."

As part of its stepped-up involvement in Vietnam, the government asked the Chase to open a branch in Saigon to handle U.S. embassy, AID, and military funds that had previously been dealt with by French and other foreign banks. The new bank office rose up out of a neighborhood of GI honkytonk bars like a modern fortress in granite and sandstone. Built especially for wartime conditions, it had glass blocks instead of windows, and walls designed to withstand mine explosions and mortar attacks. In 1966 David flew to Saigon to open the Chase officially and to have a private conference with Premier Nguyen Cao Ky, in which he assured the

Saigon leader that influential Americans like himself had no intention of turning their backs on his country.

To have entertained doubts about the official assumptions on the war would have involved questioning the basic structures of his life—inner as well as outer—which David was less capable of doing than any of his brothers. In fact, he would continue to support the Johnson policy in Vietnam long after many of his colleagues in the financial community had recognized it as a defeat and were ready to write the war off as a bad investment, particularly in the light of the damage it was doing both to the domestic economy and to the political and social fabric of the country.

But while he was unwavering in his belief in the causes for U.S. involvement in Vietnam (as late as 1968 he would call for a tax increase of "at least $10 billion" and for "several billions" to be slashed from domestic spending to help wage it), this war did not define the contours of his character the way it did for men like Bundy, Robert McNamara, and Lyndon Johnson. In that respect, David's Vietnam took place in South Africa.

In March 1960, 50,000 blacks had gathered before police stations across the country in a nonviolent gesture against the South African regime that prevented them from living, working, or traveling freely. On March 21, in the Transvaal town of Sharpeville, police fired on one of these demonstrations killing 69 Africans and wounding 180. Most of those killed were shot in the back.

All over the world there was a wave of outrage over the Sharpeville Massacre. From London, Winston Churchill denounced it as "the most frightening of all spectacles—the strength of civilization without its mercy." Suddenly, the South African regime appeared isolated in the international arena, and shaken at home. A flight of capital lowered reserves below minimum levels, investors curtailed their activities out of apprehension about the stability of the regime and the possibility of economic boycotts, and Johannesburg entered a period of economic and political crisis.

It was at this point that a consortium of U.S. banks, fearful of the consequences of the collapse of the regime for the vast investments of their clients throughout the subcontinent, undertook a crusade to restore confidence in the government. The Chase had opened its first South African office in 1959, a year after the U.N. General Assembly had voted to condemn the country's racial policies. Along with Dillon, Read and Company (the firm of then Undersecretary of State Douglas Dillon and investment bank for Charles Engelhard, biggest U.S. diamond and gold magnate in Africa and prototype for James Bond's nemesis, Goldfinger), and the First National City Bank,* the Chase had been a prominent member of a consortium offering $40 million in revolving credit to the South African regime. Now, in the aftermath of the Sharpeville crisis, the revolving credit was quickly renewed and an even larger consortium provided $150 million in loans to the government. Buoyed by this support, Prime Minister Hendrik Verwoerd told his House of Assembly: "We want to make South Africa White. . . . Keeping it White can only mean one thing, namely White domination, not leadership, not guidance, but control, supremacy."

The wave of investment that poured into South Africa touched off an economic boom, with the Chase assuming a new level of involvement. By 1965, David and the other directors had voted to purchase a major share in the Standard Bank, Ltd., the biggest British bank in Africa, with over 800 of its 1,200 branches in South Africa, where it was the second-largest bank. As a result the Chase had a greater stake than ever in the stability and prosperity of the regime.

Awareness of the revolving credit loan and its significance for the survival of apartheid had begun by this time to spread to the American civil rights movement, and the Chase found itself the target of sit-ins and pickets by the Students for a Democratic Society and the National Student Association (which had joined religious groups and small lobbies like the American Committee on Africa). In 1966 a Committee of Conscience headed by A. Philip Randolph assumed leadership of the protest against the consortium loan. In addition to picketing and demonstrations, a campaign was launched to convince individual and institutional customers (churches and universities) to withdraw funds from the ten banks backing the South African loan and to divest themselves of stocks in complicit corporations.

Eventually, some $23 million was withdrawn from the ten banks, but this was far less important than a variety of public

*On March 30, 1955, the National City Bank was merged with the First National Bank of the City of New York, becoming the First National City Bank of New York. In 1962 the name was shortened to the First National City Bank.

relations problems caused by the campaign against apartheid, some of them within the bank itself. For while demonstrators were chanting outside the Chase, blacks inside were beginning to speak up about the bank's discriminatory practices in hiring and promotion in America. Seizing on the relationship between South African and American racism, they initiated a legal action with the Human Rights Commission, and when David hired Jackie Robinson as his special consultant on urban affairs in 1967, the former Brooklyn Dodger and racial pioneer spent most of his time fielding complaints from blacks in the Chase headquarters.

By 1967, Chase stockholders were confused and upset, especially when their annual meeting was surrounded by a line of pickets displaying signs parodying the bank's advertising slogan: "Apartheid has a friend at Chase Manhattan." As the meeting opened, a stockholder from Philadelphia offered a resolution calling on the Chase to withdraw from South Africa, which was brusquely ruled out of order by Chase Chairman George Champion. David then took the floor as the bank's president and presented a carefully formulated justification of its position. It had been prepared for him by the Chase public relations department, but bore the unmistakable stamp of his personality. "None of us holds any brief for apartheid. In fact, we regard it as a dangerous and shocking policy," he began, and then went on to say that, all the old colonial powers having left Africa, it was clear the United States must now play a more significant role there. It was in fact its solemn duty to help people who were attempting to develop their country. If this were not enough, there was the relationship with the Standard Bank. David continued in a speech rich with unintended irony:

If we were to pull out of Africa, it would be a great blow not only to Standard Bank, but to the development of the continent as a whole. . . . Not long ago, I discussed the problem with President Kenneth Kaunda of the Republic of Zambia. He expressed the belief that U.S. business pulling out of South Africa would be a bad thing because the greatest impact would fall on blacks. . . . No matter what one may think about the moral or ethical implications of apartheid, one must acknowledge that the black people of South Africa are far better off economically than the black people anywhere else in the African continent. . . . We at the Chase Manhattan have never felt that doing a bank business with a particular country necessarily implies any endorsement of that country's social or political policies. Our practice has been to follow the State Department's lead. If they maintain friendly diplomatic relations with a country, we ordinarily do banking business with that country. We have talked to the State Department on the question of South Africa and they have told us it would not be a helpful thing for us to withdraw.

This argument was already familiar to family members who had been troubled by the linking of their name to apartheid through the Chase. Laurance's daughter Marion remembers writing David to protest the bank's support for the South African regime. Prepared to be ignored or to get back the equivalent of a form letter, she was surprised to receive a lengthy reply by return mail, which David had obviously composed and then typed himself. If we who care about blacks pull out of Johannesburg, he wrote, we will be replaced by others who don't care; just by our presence we can fulfill our duty of helping better the lot of blacks and work against prejudice from within.*

David could not seriously entertain the possibility that charges regarding his bank's complicity with racism on South Africa might have even a tincture of truth in them. Yet the attacks had made him uneasy and anxious to demonstrate he was on the right side of the question. As the consequences of the Vietnam War began to make themselves felt at home in the long, hot summers following the explosion of the Watts ghetto, he got his chance. It was in April 1968, after Martin Luther King, Jr., had been murdered and the nation was bracing for another season of racial warfare. The Urban Coalition, of which David was a charter member, stepped forward to undertake "significant programs" with the $200,000 donation it had obtained from the Brothers Fund. "The mo-

---

*The suggestion that South African blacks were "better off" as a result of the Chase's help was something David relied on in his defenses of his position. Yet it was not a very plausible idea. As Chase Vice-President Stephen Pryke later admitted to Washington *Post* writer Jim Hoagland in 1970, "There is no way you can point to something concrete and say that our presence is having a positive effect on the racial problem." In this Pulitzer Prize-winning book, *South Africa: Civilizations in Conflict,* Hoagland later quoted one South African economist on the net effect of the Chase's "progressive" presence: "More economic progress means the government can buy more guns, bigger tanks, and pay its spies among the Africans a lot better."

ment has arrived," David declared, "when the American business community must become a leader rather than a follower in the identification and solution of our nation's challenges. We must meet our social responsibilities sooner and more massively and aggressively than we are now."

Housing was the area in which he decided he could make an impact. Drawing on the reputation in urban affairs his work in Morningside Heights and the Downtown Lower Manhattan Association had given him, David called on the federal government to begin immediate action in low-cost housing for the poor, including the initiation of a privately run National Urban Development Bank to help rebuild the inner cities. In the meantime, he announced that his own bank was joining with eighty others in New York in pledging a $100 million mortgage pool to help residents of the Bedford- Stuyvesant ghetto in New York.

David's program was to be a demonstration project, indicating what the socially conscious private sector could do to narrow the gap between black and white. Yet, like most of the Urban Coalition's other efforts, it failed to sustain its promise over the next two years, as summer riots did not materialize and the economy entered a recession. In 1970, black leaders called a news conference to point out that although the Chase claimed to have set aside $5 million as its share of the pool, loans actually made in the two years amounted to hardly more than a tenth of that sum. Moreover, they charged that even in its conception, the program was a sham, pointing out that only buildings housing four families or less qualified for the loans, which automatically excluded 80 percent of Bedford-Stuyvesant's structures.

These leaders saw a dramatic contrast with other building programs with which David was publicly involved. While low-cost housing loans languished in the Chase bureaucracy, the Downtown Lower Manhattan Association (which he still headed) had summoned a great deal of energy for projects like the midtown expressway. Cutting across the city and making lower Manhattan into an enclave more easily protected from the depredations of urban blight, the proposed expressway would also have created huge new sums of bonded debt for the banks to service and the public to pay. And the Chase expeditiously found money to help build Manhattan Landing, a $1.2 billion apartment project to be constructed on platforms over the East River. While these plans to make lower Manhattan into a "gold coast" were proceeding at full

speed and developers were using tax abatements and mortgage subsidies to make what was in effect low-cost luxury
housing available to executives earning up to $56,000 a year,
areas dozens of blocks square in the heart of the city were as
desolate as a town hit by air raids.

At the height from which David surveyed the world, such
voices of outrage were annoyances to be suffered, but not
worried about. Nor would it ever have occurred to him that
there was more than a perfunctory connection between the
Chase's impact on the black populations of South Africa and
New York City, or between his own lobbying on behalf of
fiscal responsibility and a trim federal budget and the legacy
of economic misery and aborted reform that was the lot of
the black and urban poor. He was protected from such insights both by his character and by the men and institutions
that surrounded him and his family like a placental lining.

Each time it seemed that he might be called to account for
his beliefs and the policies of the bank, some retainer interposed himself between David and his punishment. The National Urban League's 1970 convention provided a clear instance of this. Hardly among the more radical blacks in the
country, the 4,000 delegates who gathered at the New York
Hilton were angry enough to entertain a motion that the
Chase Manhattan Bank be condemned and expelled from the
league's activities for its domestic racism and its sorry role in
South Africa. It was league President Whitney Young—for
many years a protégé of Room 5600 and a recipient of its
largesse—who rose to argue against what would have been a
serious blow to David's prestige. Young pointed out that the
Rockefeller family, which had given so much to Negro betterment, could hardly be accused of racism. David Rockefeller had just informed him, as a matter of fact, that a black
executive named Thomas Woods had been appointed to the
board of the Chase the previous afternoon. Using all of his
considerable power of persuasion, Young succeeded in preventing the Chase's expulsion from the league (though he
could not prevent the delegates from censuring the bank,
thereby saving David a significant embarrassment.

In David's ledger, the other side of every social dilemma
was a business opportunity, especially if one looked pragmati-
cally to the more tractable aspects of the problem. In his
speeches on the urban crisis, he would often cite statistics
showing that just to keep up with the population explosion, it

would be necessary to build the equivalent of 650 new municipalities of 100,000 people by the year 2000 and 10 new urban centers of over a million. He was keenly interested in new towns and satellite cities (the Chase had already helped to finance the planned community of Columbia, Maryland), and his own private investments were increasingly calculated to take advantage of this area of growth.

Although he did not take the pleasure in erecting buildings that Nelson and Laurance did, never lingering over the aesthetics of plans or landscaping, his personal real estate holdings were greater than those of either of his brothers. In addition to residences in Manhattan and Pocantico, he had vacation homes at Seal Harbor and on the island of Saint Barthélemy in the Caribbean; he had a 15,000-acre sheep ranch in Australia, part interest in a French vineyard, and several thousand acres of future development on Saint Croix in the Virgin Islands and in the Brazilian interior.

Real estate, in fact, was the focus of his private investments. Forming a syndicate with André Meyer's Lazard Frères and Company and George Garrett, a Washington businessman, in 1965 he had acquired a one-third interest in the $100 million L'Enfant Plaza development in Washington, D.C. It was a venture in which all that was required of David was his participation, including a third of the capital and his ability to commit the Chase to a line of credit. William Zeckendorf's firm of Webb and Knapp had already invested a dozen years in planning and negotiation to bring the project to the threshold of completion, and had then gone bankrupt on the edge of success. (At the 1969 ground breaking ceremonies, a Washington *Star* reporter asked Zeckendorf how it felt to watch others take the honors and the profits of a project he had worked so hard developing. The old tycoon glanced over at David's associates and shrugged. "Well, I'm the guy who got the girl pregnant. Those fellows you see around here are merely the obstetricians.")

Many would say that a spider in a web was a more appropriate metaphor than midwifery. By and large, David allowed the building deals to come to him. In 1966, at about the same time he was obtaining a one-third interest in the ill-fated plan of Westbay Associates to build a mammoth development on landfill in the San Francisco Bay, David accepted the invitation of the development firm of Crow and Trammel to become part of the Embarcadero Center, a huge commercial construction project on eight acres in the heart of San Francisco. In return for an investment of $2 million and the use of his good offices, he received 25 percent interest in the $200 million venture. His good offices had a high value—most obviously with the banks and insurance companies financing the project, but also with its critics. His background in urban renewal helped to satisfy the qualms of the San Francisco Redevelopment Agency, and on one of his trips to the Pacific, he paused long enough to testify before the San Francisco Board of Supervisors on allowing the Embarcadero Center to exceed the city's height limit. David pointed out that the developers planned to put more than $1 million worth of art and sculpture into the project, implying that this should more than compensate for the damaged skyline.

Behind this development was the ghost of his father's great construction project in the heart of Manhattan. (It stood as the unattainable model for all the Brothers in their varied ventures into construction.) James Bronkema, executive director of the Embarcadero, says: "Although our buildings are different in style, they're supposed to call up the precedent of Rockefeller Center. In fact, at one point we almost named it Rockefeller Center West."

If San Francisco had Rockefeller Center West, Rockefeller Center South was to be in Atlanta, a city where the family foundations had invested extensively in education and which David's experts at the bank assured him would have one of the greatest growth rates in urbanization during the next two decades. He began investing there in 1967 when he joined Greek shipping magnate Stavros Niarchos in the development of Interstate North, a $50 million, 240-acre commercial and residential development 10 miles outside the city. Six months after beginning this venture, David obtained a 50 percent interest in Fairington, a $90 million, 700-acre residential community of apartments and condominium town houses 13 miles from the downtown area.

"When I worked for the *Times*," recalls former political bureau chief Richard Reeves," I was constantly amazed that whenever David made a statement—even if it was a speech at the opening of an art show or something like that—I'd be asked to cover it like it was a political event. Abe Rosenthal would come running up to me and say, 'Look, Dick, this is terribly important. I want you to drop whatever you're doing and get over there.' I'd say, 'Come on, Abe. I'm into a story on how three hundred thousand dollars just went out of the city budget,' or something like that. But he'd say, 'That's okay. Drop it. Just call the guy David has writing this speech, will you?' So I'd call the guy and he'd offer to show the first draft to me like it was the Declaration of Independence or something like that. After I'd written the story and the *Times* editors had carefully taken out the one or two barbs I'd tried to sneak in, it would appear on the front page under some kind of bland headline like *David Rockefeller Says People Should Be Nice to Each Other.*"

David had become a figure whose almost metaphysical relation to private and public power made him listened to as no one else in the business world was. Enemies like Congressman Wright Patman might criticize his pompousness, but Rockefeller was fond of appending terms like "city planner" and "spokesman for corporate responsibility" to the list of accomplishments that trailed and stabilized his career like the tail of a kite. Yet, however important a bellwether he was in domestic finance, foreign affairs remained his specialty. His home at Pocantico often seemed like a mini-United Nations, with Philippine President Marcos touring the area in a Rockefeller limousine one day, and King Faisal walking over the golf course built by the world's first oil mogul the next. Every year David hosted a board meeting of the World Bank, many of whose members he had worked with personally at the Chase. On his dozen or so trips abroad each year to attend monetary conferences and meet with executives in the Chase's foreign branches, he was accommodated by heads of foreign governments as if he were a Secretary of State. And as he ran across young and promising politicians and businessmen in the countries he visited, David put their vital statistics in his card file, by then containing the names of 35,000 "friends."

His international contacts gave David an edge on his competition he didn't hesitate to use. Yet the affairs of the Chase involved more than accounts and deposits. The Chase was an oil bank; its business was often indistinguishable from foreign policy itself. In his efforts in international banking and oil, national policies were crucial elements of the framework in which the complex private deals and tremendous corporate projects took place. Because he represented such prodigious consortiums of power in these undertakings, David so came to anticipate the trends in foreign policy that it almost seemed possible to predict them by simply charting his movements. He was like the figurehead on the prow of a Yankee clipper: always seen first, but only because he was pushed by a mass from behind.

The question of détente was a case in point. As Nelson's brother and a formidable partisan of containment in his own right, David could hardly be accused of being soft on Communism. Yet the seeds of future "cooperative" U.S.–Soviet relations were contained in his 1964 visit to Russia when he had a two-hour conference with Khrushchev in Leningrad, although *Pravda*'s account of the meeting was restrained: "N. S. Khrushchev and D. Rockefeller had a frank discussion of questions that are of mutual interest."*

By 1970 the international moves that would come like thunderbolts midway through Nixon's first term were already consuming much of David's time. In October he hosted Romania's President Nicolae Ceausescu at the Chase (which was the leading correspondent bank for Romania) and spoke out in favor of granting Romania the most-favored-nation status that would pave the way for U.S. trade, also letting it be known that his bank was considering a large equity investment in the country.

It was also in 1970—while Secretary of State William Rogers was preparing his Mideast accords—that David returned from a long trip to Egypt to tell President Nixon of his private conference with Nasser in which the Egyptian President had claimed to be saddened by deteriorating relations between the two countries and said he would actually prefer a relationship with the United States to one with the Soviet Union. A year later, in March 1971, this diplomatic campaign in the Mideast went a step farther when Egyptian newspapers carried a large front-page photo showing the new President, Anwar Sadat, and his wife smiling broadly with American visitors David and Peggy Rockefeller. On his return from this trip (which also included conferences with heads of state in Jordan, Lebanon, and Israel), David told a press conference that the political climate in the Mideast was "more conducive to peace than at any time since the Six Day War," and predicted that there would soon be enough stability in the Persian gulf (where the Chase was about to open a

*Ever after, David would have a special cachet in Moscow. After the 1968 elections, the Russians let it be known through diplomatic channels that chances for reapprochement would be dramatically increased if David were ambassador. George Gilder says: "David goes through Russia and is treated royally. Ironically, nobody knows how to revere, blandish and exalt a Rockefeller half so well as the Marxists."

branch in Bahrain) for foreign economic investment. It was only a matter of time, he said, until there were similar conditions in the eastern Mediterranean.

David was also looking farther east. On March 5, 1971, he told a select group of European businessmen meeting in Rome that there must be more U.S. trade with the Soviet and especially the Chinese governments and that the "iron curtain must be replaced with a plate glass curtain." Four days later he told a financial forum in Singapore organized by the Chase that it was unrealistic for the United States to act "as if a country of 800 million people did not exist," and said that we must "establish contacts with the People's Republic of China."

When détente was officially ratified by Nixon, David's work had a payoff, although that had not been the primary reason for his efforts. The Chase was selected by the Soviet government to be the first American bank to open a representative office in Russia. (The official address of the Moscow branch, somewhat incongruously, was 1 Karl Marx Square, and it was located one block from the Kremlin.) Then, after David's lengthy audience with Chou En-lai in Peking in 1973, the Chase was named correspondent bank for the Bank of China. In the wake of bettered relations with Arab nations, the Chase moved into the Mideast, opening its Cairo office in 1974 and making an $80 million loan to Egypt for the Suez–Mediterranean pipeline, while also entering into discussions with King Faisal over what might be done with the huge foreign currency balances Saudi Arabia had accumulated as a result of the international crisis in oil. It was a diplomatic accomplishment that happened less because of David's skill than his position, yet it still impressed even his brother's friend Kissinger.

David was like his brothers in that he had been prepared by his unique upbringing for every kind of adversity in life except failure. As he drew close to his sixtieth year, however, this possibility had begun to penetrate his unflappable exterior. It was nothing to put a finger on, but there were signs that things weren't quite turning out the way they should according to the unfinished idyll his father had scripted for the family. The virulence of the attacks on the Rockefeller name upset him and the irreverent attitude of his children, which he took to be a repudiation of his values and family traditions, wounded him deeply. "I think I have as interesting and

exciting a job as anyone could have," he said plaintively to
an interviewer, "but I don't think I have really convinced my
children of the fact, at least not to the point where they're
anxious to go into business." Yet these factors could be accounted to irrationality—the common reaction to public figures and parents.

The bank was finally the high ground where he chose to
make his stand. His character was submerged in its conservatism, and he took a special pride in the fact that (as he put it
to an interviewer) he was "the first member of the family
since Grandfather who has had a regular job in a company
and has devoted a major part of his time to being in
business." If there were a tangible measure of his achievement amid all the ceremonial distinctions conferred on him
and all the consensual authority he wielded without in some
basic sense having earned, it was the enterprise in which he
had spent a quarter of a century of his life and which was
the well-wrought platform from which he had made his public ascent. His ability as a banker was that part of his life
which had to be completely certain; failures that occurred
here could not be rationalized.

Yet failure was in the air at three-thirty P.M. on the miserably chilly and rainy day of October 12, 1972, when David
strode into the Chase boardroom, the muscles in his cheek
twitching from the clench of his jaws. He glanced at the flock
of reporters who had been summoned only three hours earlier
by the public relations staff for what was billed as a major
announcement. They had quickly noted that David was not
accompanied by the bank's president, Herbert Patterson, appointed with great fanfare only three years earlier when
George Champion had retired and David had made his final
move to the top as chairman of the board and chief executive
officer.

Those assembled knew that the Chase had not been doing
well lately. In the first six months of 1972, its earnings had
increased only 1 percent as compared to 16 percent for its
great rival, the First National City, now incorporated as the
Citibank. This was just part of a larger trend. Among the articles appearing recently in the pages of the financial press
about the bank's difficulties, the most widely discussed had
been a feature in *The New York Times* financial section,
which had run underneath the foreboding headline, "The
Chase at Ebb Tide?"

It took David only a moment to drop the expected

bombshell. In view of the slipping competitive position of the Chase, its executive committee had decided that Patterson should be replaced as president by Vice-Chairman Willard Butcher. "It was a stunning move by Rockefeller," commented *Business Week,* "—indeed a brutal one by the standards of big business and big banks, where discarded top managers are allowed to gently fade away." Wall Streeters were critical of the way the matter was handled, especially given the fact that Patterson, a Chase officer for twenty years, so clearly appeared to be a scapegoat for ills that proceeded from sources higher up. "Somebody had to take the rap," a dealer in bank stocks observed, "and it wasn't going to be the guy who owns the bank."

David's fellow bankers were not so circumspect in assigning responsibility for the Chase's problems. John R. Bunting, chief executive officer of the First Pennsylvania Bank, one of the largest financial institutions in the country, says of David: "He's got the best name in the world, the absolute best name in the world, or at least the best name in this country. Rockefeller. . . . He's got the bank with the—I would say—most prestige in the country going for him. And he's running a third-rate bank. Walter Wriston in First National City is beating the hell out of him."

At the end of 1968, just before David took over as chairman, the Chase's assets were $19 billion. It was slightly less than Citibank's $19.6 billion, but the Chase was slightly ahead in total deposits. Yet, by the end of 1973, after five years of David's chairmanship, and a year after Patterson's replacement, Wriston's Citibank had built an enormous lead in assets ($41 billion to $27 billion), in deposits ($32 billion to $26 billion), and in profits, which, at $250 million, were 50 percent more than those of the Chase. "At the Chase," one Wall Street analyst quipped to a *Newsweek* reporter, "you feel like you're in a bank. At Citibank, you get the feeling that you're in a profit-making organization."

It was already several years since the Chase had lost its position as New York's largest bank to First National City because of the latter's commanding position in overseas areas. As an added humiliation, it had also lost the lead in domestic banking that it had always enjoyed among the giants of New York's money market. More recently, it had fallen behind in correspondent banking (banking for other banks, an area it had long regarded as one of its greatest strengths) to Manufacturers Hanover Trust, an institution with only half the overall volume of the Chase. At the same time, a number of key senior Chase executives, including a vice-chairman, several executive vice-presidents, and a number of senior vice-presidents, had left the bank for other jobs. As one of them told the *Times:* "These offers come in all the time; you don't listen to them when you're happy."

The very fact that the Chase's difficulties extended across such a wide range of activities indicated the basic nature of the problem: for many years the bank had simply been outmanaged, outclassed, and outdone as a profit-making institution by its rivals in the commercial banking field. "The Chase of late, has come to resemble a lumbering giant—huge but neither quick nor shrewd," commented *Business Week.* "It has lost its verve, it's momentum, its fine competitive edge." The Citibank had beaten the Chase into the bank holding-company field and its diversification moves had set the pattern that other banks were copying. It was ahead in moving into the fields of mortgage banking and management consulting, and its lucrative traveler's check operation had no equivalent at the Chase. Even where the Chase had taken an innovative lead, it lacked the will to carry its vision through to successful completion. In 1958 it had been a pioneer in starting the first bank credit-card system the Unicard. But having gotten in a little too early, the Chase management lost its nerve and sold out to American Express for $9 million, taking a considerable financial loss. Then, after Bank-Americard, and Master Charge (in which the Citibank had been a founding participant) showed a few years later how lucrative credit cards could be, the Chase had to pay $50 million to American Express to get Unicard back. Chase hoped to make Unicard a rival to the two leaders, but finally in 1972 was forced to throw in the towel, joining its regional system to Bank-Americard under the logotype of one of its major competitors.

It was ironic, however, that it was in David's speciality—international banking—that the Chase should be most significantly outdistanced. While David was visiting with heads of state of various countries in meetings where the advantage to the Chase was often in intangible goodwill, Walter Wriston was moving ahead without fanfare all over the world. In an area where bank profits were growing twice as fast as at home, the Citicorp had three foreign offices for every one belonging to the Chase. The Chase had attempted to cut the effects of Citibank's lead in foreign branches by making investments in 17 subsidiary banks (like the Standard group) with operations in 74 countries, but the strategy had not paid off. It was hard for the Chase to control banks in which it had less than a majority interest, and in some cases where there were both subsidiary banks and Chase foreign branches in the same area, Chase executives found themselves in the odd position of competing against themselves.

Inevitably David's extrabanking activities came in for some sharp criticism as a source of the Chase's difficulties. "Rockefeller is viewed by the investment community as a great world figure, a friend of kings and presidents," *Business Week* summed up, "but not as a skilled commercial banker." A harsher judgment was made by *Fortune* senior editor Sanford Rose: "David Rockefeller knows the banking business and the monetary system of this country very well. The central problem is that he doesn't pay attention to the Chase Manhattan. He is best described as a man who goes from global concern to global concern in an air-conditioned limousine, and occasionally in the midst of these global considerations, pauses to make a decision about the bank, and goofs. You can't spend all that time being head of the Council on Foreign Relations and being an important international figure and still run a bank like the Chase. Rockefeller has permitted a situation to develop at the Chase that has led to widespread demoralization."

David faced the storm with the same placid exterior that he brought to every other potentially trying situation. Three months before firing Patterson, he had told the *Times*: "At no time in the twenty-six years I've been with the bank have I felt more optimistic about its future than I do at this moment." Sanford Rose responds: "He's totally unflappable. You could come up to him and say, 'Listen, I just heard that your wife is sleeping with Walter Wriston,' and he'd look back at you and say, 'Well, I'm sure there are rumors to that effect.' "

By the 1970s, David had become an almost allegorical figure: Chairman of the Board of the Establishment; Midas at the top of the power structure; a pudgy Cardinal Richelieu in a three-piece suit implicated in events as diverse as the Sharpeville Massacre and the overthrow of Salvador Allende. He was the long historical shadow of his grandsire, and as events inexorably dragged the Rockefellers back toward the controversy with which they had started, David's name was

used to conjure up the specter of irresponsible power for the
Age of Aquarius in the way that the first John D.'s had been
for the Gilded Age.

His power—less as a man, perhaps, than as an idea—was
such that he had become the archetypal Rockefeller. His
brother Nelson was still the dominant figure inside the family
and always would be. Yet in his public life Nelson had spent
himself too prodigally over the years. The lines and wrinkles
on his face mapped all the frantic campaigns for the
presidency and indicated a sharp yearning that lacked fulfillment, even after his selection as Vice-President. Nelson's
strength was in the sheer animal force with which he assaulted his environment; David's in the more passive way he had
allowed himself to be the lightning rod of discharging the
static energy hanging in an immense cloud above the Rockefellers' family, financial, and policy-making institutions. The
power he wielded cost him far less than that which Nelson
had sought. And while his older brother was soaring like
Icarus across the fiery horizon of American politics during
the sixties—peaking, stalling, and then gliding downward and
only partially recovering—David was always moving methodically up, usually in the shadows, always building a solid
foothold before taking the next step, and never allowing his
task to get out of hand or become swollen with existential implications.

Nelson reveled in the image, yet for David the open aspira-
tion to power was unseemly and vulgar. (David's wife,
Peggy, despised Nelson exactly because of his unregenerate
lust for power; not only was it inappropriate in itself, but she
recognized it as giving the lie to the myth by which the rest
of the family tried to justify their unique stature in American
life.) The lesson David learned from his brother was the obvious truth about power and money: they stained anyone
grasping them too avidly. Yet like money, power had its perverse fascination. An enterprising publisher had managed to
promote a book about David onto the best-seller lists by
quoting its line that "for David Rockefeller, the presidency of
the United States would be a demotion." Despite the book's
inaccuracies and distortions—it was a diatribe done from
newspaper clips—David still seemed to take a secret pleasure
in the *fact* of the book. When his son Richard asked how he
stayed calm in the face of such abuse, David told him the
family had long since learned it was best not to dignify such
attacks with a response. Then he added, "People will believe

what they will believe, and if people believe I'm powerful, that's useful too."

The unspoken assumption that he was indeed as powerful as others thought, stood behind a ceremonial meeting that took place each year in the private office David maintained in Room 5600. "Dick" Dilworth was always there, along with Donal O'Brien (the young attorney from Milbank, Tweed that John Lockwood had brought in as his replacement), and Dana Creel. Joe Reed, David's chief of staff at the Chase, and other bank aides were there. Peggy Rockefeller was present, too, in her capacity as David's wife and adviser. The subject was always the same: how David should budget his time for the upcoming year; what responsibilities would advance his career.

This illusion that they controlled their lives was important to all the Brothers. It was especially important to David. Yet for all the discussion and apportionment of time and energy, his career really had no plot; there was no sense of a man working through obstacles to discover unexplored aspects of his character. The central lesson of his life had nothing to do with power corrupting, but rather with the fact that at the level at which he moved there is often a yawning gap between men and what they symbolize. David was a man respected by heads of state all over the world, yet thought of as unimaginative and obtuse by his children; a man who could influence the shape of the globe, yet could not control the destiny of his own bank; a man who prided himself on his ethical sensibility, yet was constantly being accused of complicity in immoral acts. If there was a force that sustained him, it was not his power, but his deep and unquestioning belief in his own destiny and the divine right of his family and its history. The increasing absurdity of these beliefs could not penetrate his opaqueness.

24

ON JANUARY 12, 1971, the governor of Arkansas stood before the state legislature to deliver his farewell address. Gripping the podium with whitened knuckles and speaking in halting sentences, Winthrop Rockefeller was much changed from the man who had taken the oath of office four years earlier. Confidently youthful in that brief moment of triumph and vindication, he had since put on pounds and lost hair; tiny networks of ruptured capillaries reddened his puffy face; his jaundiced eyes seemed covered with a thin film, giving him the look of one who was getting more information than he could process. The optimism of the first inaugural was gone too, having been scaled down by what for any other man would have been called sobering experiences. This farewell speech had a plaintive quality. "When the history of the last few years is written," went the phrase that particularly stuck in listeners' minds, "I hope the historian will think of me as more than a political phenomenon."

It was more than the usual political valedictory. Those who had followed Winthrop's career and knew his background realized it was a deeper appeal—not merely for applause, but for understanding and even forgiveness. It was clear to everyone that the brief rebirth he had enjoyed in Arkansas was over now; much had happened in his seventeen years in the state, yet it all seemed a fairy tale. That tale had ended, leaving him in the condition in which he had arrived in Arkansas: defeated, divorced, revealed as an alcoholic, and hoping that those who judged him (surrogates of the father who withheld approval on into eternity) would weigh his human qualities in the balance and not be too severe.

In the beginning, his naturally genial nature had bloomed in the red dirt of Arkansas. It was far from the family and the standards he had never quite managed to live up to. He was no longer the least successful of a remarkable group of

Brothers. He was *the* Rockefeller and he could make his own way at his own speed. And for the backward state of Arkansas, the mark he had made was very broad indeed. It was as if some giant had come to live there; Arkansans had watched in awe as he sliced off the top of Petit Jean Mountain to build his immense home of stone and glass, raised barns, outbuildings, a huge auditorium where he kept his collection of antique cars, built homes for his chief assistants and apartments for the other help—all of it equal to a good-sized Arkansas town. Winrock Farm had its own airfield, fire department, and shortwave radio; it flew its own flag. The flamboyant initials WR were branded onto objects all over the 900-acre estate—from the coasters on which the perspiring martinis appeared early every afternoon, to the shining rumps of the prize-winning Santa Gertrudis cattle, which breeders from all over the world came to bid on at auction time.

It began as an exile from failure but developed into a time of reorientation and success. Winthrop's personal life seemed to straighten out. In 1956 he had flown to Idaho to marry 37-year-old Jeannette Edris, who brought a ready-made family of two children by a prior marriage (Bruce and Anne Bartley) back to Winrock with her. Winthrop adopted them as his own. The photographs taken at the time show him standing beside the immense swimming pool with his new family, looking prouder and more confident than ever before.

Inside the Rockefeller family, Winthrop's primary virtues—simplicity and a capacity for spontaneous warmth—had always been seen as a weakness, and he had grown embarrassed by these feelings, hiding them as if they were overlarge hands or some other clumsy defect. But in Arkansas he found a kind of space he hadn't had before, and was no longer forced into the role of Mr. Junior's ungainly, wastrel son. His natural warmth reappeared. After Frank Jamieson's death, it was Winthrop of all the Brothers, who became concerned about the family he left behind. Mrs. Linda Storrow, Jamieson's widow, recalls: "Winthrop got us to come down to the ranch. He *insisted* that we come. Then he went on the wagon, which wasn't easy for him, kept regular hours, and spent time every day for two weeks going horseback riding with my two children. It was a kindness so sincere and totally uncalled for that I've never forgotten it."

But it was not enough merely to give these feelings free rein. And from the moment he arrived in the state, Winthrop had begun looking around for a way of achieving what he had not been able to back in New York. It was clear to everyone in Arkansas that he represented a political potential. In 1955, Governor Orval Faubus tried to capitalize on it for his administration by making Winthrop chairman of the Arkansas Industrial Development Commission (AIDC). This gave him a chance to do something about joblessness, the most urgent of the state's many problems. Mechanization of the cotton farms had thrown large numbers of people out of work. What industries there were—lumber, clothing, and furniture manufacture—were so underdeveloped, depressed, and low paying they couldn't attract skilled workers. College graduates routinely went to other states to find work fitting their education. With little industrial growth, Arkansas was steadily losing population and, next to Mississippi, had the lowest per capita income in the nation.

Winthrop threw himself into the task with a gusto he had not been able to summon for the responsibilities his father had thrust on him after he returned from the army. It was *his* job to succeed or fail at, and there was no abstract standard by which his performance would be measured. The impoverished state treasury couldn't devote much money to the commission, so he underwrote much of its efforts himself, beginning by adding enough to the $8,000 that had been allotted for personnel so that he could import a pair of New York executives recommended by brother Laurance to head his commission. While they were working to compile an impressive record during their first year—73 new plants located in the state, creating 7,236 new jobs—Winthrop formed Winrock Enterprises, a multimillion-dollar venture capital company involved in agriculture, the manufacture of plastic pipe, and housing developments. Its demonstration projects were intended to show interested corporations that Arkansas's attractive tax laws could support industrial innovation.

It was also in 1956 that he began his Rockwin Fund to handle his philanthropy. Arkansas was unlike New York in that even relatively small sums could have a large impact. A $1.5 million grant built and equipped a model school in Morrilton, a small town near Winrock; it soon became a sort of educational laboratory for the state. Winthrop also equipped and supported a Perry County medical clinic, gave a series of college fellowships, and raised $1 million to help build the Arkansas Art Center while also buying an Artmobile to carry culture to the hills and hollows of the Ozarks. His arrival in Arkansas seemed a godsend. It was as Orval Faubus had said at a conference of southern governors when one of them asked how a person might go about getting a Rockefeller for his state. "I don't know," the Arkansas governor replied, "but you keep your cotton-pickin' fingers off mine."

Winthrop reveled in the acclaim his efforts brought him. It was a far cry from the humiliation of his past, and he gave his move to Arkansas a finality by transferring all his personal papers there and taking his investments and trust fund out of the management of Room 5600, putting them into the hands of the team of personal advisers he assembled in Little Rock. (They signed themselves "An Associate of Winthrop Rockefeller.") Yet his move out of New York was never quite complete. His work in Arkansas was in some sense a mime performed for the approval of a faraway group, which would ultimately have to sanction his new identity. However much he liked to travel through his adopted state in a stetson and hand-tooled cowboy boots, Winthrop would always be involved in what his advisers called the "pin-striped suit syndrome." Several times each year he got into the Falcon jet and flew east for family reunions, meetings of the Rockefeller Brothers Fund, and other family affairs where he found, if not respect, at least a surprised relief on the part of the family. As George Gilder says, "Because he broke all the rules, the family thought he couldn't make it. They had given up on him as though he were the bad seed."

He had been seen as a potential candidate for governor since settling in Arkansas, and as the impact of his AIDC work and his Rockwin Fund philanthropies reverberated through the state, it became merely a question of when he would make his bid. Arkansans recognized what an anomaly he was: a Republican among Democrats, a liberal among conservatives, a rich man from the big city among rural populists, an impulsive and self-indulgent man among people whose circumstances had made them taciturn and self-denying. Unaware of the specifics of the family conflict that had bankrupted his life in New York and sent him fleeing to their state to lick his emotional wounds, Arkansans wondered why anyone should leave such a world of boardrooms, yachts, and nightlife to build a rambling aerie on top of a desolate mountain and spend his money and energies on their impoverished state. What was it he *wanted?*

Yet if they were suspicious of him, as of other "carpetbaggers," they also knew not to look a gift horse in the mouth—

even if he was a thoroughbred who had been a trustee of the Urban League and had publicly criticized Governor Faubus in 1957 for using National Guardsmen to prevent the integration of Little Rock's Central High. A certain pride went hand in hand with the suspiciousness. What other Arkansan could be seen on the front pages of newspapers across the country riding in a carriage with Queen Elizabeth and Prince Philip during their 1957 royal visit, or would be visited by Edward R. Murrow's "Person to Person"?

Despite his resources (and it would later be estimated that he had poured more than $10 million into his political career during the 1960s), Winthrop faced a formidable task. Changing over to the Democratic party would have been a greater break with family tradition than leaving New York and Room 5600, and was additionally impossible because of the adverse effect it would have had on Nelson's political career. So Winthrop undertook the rebuilding of the state Republican party, the tiny vestige of Reconstruction now shrunk to the point where it was little more than a tattered umbrella under which a few individuals collected every four years to receive patronage from the national party apparatus, although they rarely managed even to field a complete slate of candidates for state offices.

Winthrop phrased his early efforts in loftier terms than personal ambition, forming the Committee for the Two Party System in 1960 and throwing a gigantic "Party for Two Parties" at Winrock with a guest list reading like a *Who's Who* of Arkansas's business, political, and social life—mostly Democrats—paying $50 a head and crowding into tented pavilions to feast on barbecued Santa Gertrudis beef and be entertained by Edgar Bergen and Charlie McCarthy, Tex Ritter, and others. Yet it was always clear what he meant by the two-party system—a party other than the Democratic party, a party in which he could run. In 1961, Winthrop was elected Republican national committeeman, and he began crisscrossing the state in what was billed as "an effort to rebuild the Republican party from bottom up," but was actually an early campaign tour. In 1963 a gala dinner in Little Rock commemorated Winthrop's tenth year in the state and reminded voters that he now must be considered one of them.

Shedding 35 pounds to reach a trim 207, Rockefeller began a tradition he would follow three times in the future when, in 1964, he journeyed to the small Arkansas hamlet of Winthrop in Little River County to announce that he would run for governor. Rockefeller had proved his loyalty. It was through his efforts that the AIDC had brought 600 new businesses into the state, providing 90,000 new jobs and $270 million in payrolls and being largely responsible for the fact that per capita income had risen 50 percent in Arkansas in the previous eight years. But while he could hardly call Winthrop a carpetbagger, Faubus could exploit his great riches and the civil rights issue. Although Winthrop told voters that he, like Barry Goldwater (whom he endorsed in San Francisco after vainly trying to steer the immovable Arkansas delegation to his brother Nelson), would have voted against the Civil Rights Act of 1964, Faubus made much of the fact that Rockefeller was the sort of man who had once addressed a national convention of the NAACP and was known to have Negro friends.

Winthrop lost to Faubus, but he got 43 percent of the vote, a respectable enough showing for him to assure supporters, even while conceding defeat, that he was ready to begin the next campaign immediately. And for the next two years he continued to travel through the state, the closest thing to a celebrity Arkansas had. By 1966 the civil rights issue had been cooled somewhat by the humiliating national publicity the South had received. There was a widespread feeling that Arkansas must cultivate a more moderate image. Faubus was retiring after six terms, but old-guard Democrats managed to nominate an even more rabid segregationist in his place, James D. ("Justice Jim") Johnson, former state supreme court judge, founder of the White Citizens' Council, and ardent backer of Alabama Governor George Wallace. If Johnson, who opened and closed campaign rallies with rebel yells and taunted Rockefeller as a "liberal lush" and a "prissy sissy," came to personify the strong gravity of history attempting to pull the state back into the heyday of Jim Crow, Winthrop willingly adopted the role of Arkansas usher into the twentieth century. Traveling through the state in a bus that was modest on the outside, but fitted with elaborate sleeping quarters, bar, and kitchen inside, he put together a fragile coalition of blacks, liberals, moderate Democrats, urban dwellers, and mountain Republicans. He beat Johnson with 57 percent of the vote to become the first Republican governor since Reconstruction. On January 1, 1967, he took office in a jubilant mood of vindication—it seemed more a personal than a political triumph to him—taking his oath of office with his hand resting on his mother's Bible.* It was as if he had at last joined the Rockefeller family, although his close friends would soon be looking back on the ceremony and saying that it was probably the high point of Winthrop's life.

Given that only 3 of the state's 135 legislators were Republicans, it was clear from the outset that Winthrop's legislative plan—a country-cousin version of Nelson's program in New York—would have troubles. Arkansas was too impoverished for such high-rise dreams, and the legislators were unwilling to raise taxes to make them a reality. At the very beginning of his governorship, therefore, Winthrop saw it would be necessary to substitute a symbolic program of crusades for a real legislative effort.

The first such crusade was the Arkansas penal system, renowned as the most barbaric in the nation. News of the atrocities in the dark recesses of Arkansas prisons had begun to leak out toward the end of Faubus's last term in office, and though only a few details were known, it was enough to suggest an American Devil's Island had grown up in the heart of the state.† The work gangs labored under heartless conditions; torture was an everyday occurrence; a vicious and corrupt trusty system was the means of maintaining internal order. Winthrop had said bluntly, "Our prisons stink," and he hired Thomas Murton, a young criminologist from Illinois, to supervise reforms.

Meanwhile, the governor's office had also declared war on gambling operations. Winthrop put a former FBI man named Lynn Davis in charge of the state troopers and sent him on

*One small insight into his feelings may be found in the fact that he had scorned Raymond Fosdick's authoritative biography of his father when selecting campaign literature—he thought it too pompous and not sensitive enough of his mother's contributions. He chose instead to hand out hundreds of copies of Mary Ellen Chase's slender and sympathetic book about Abby Aldrich Rockefeller.

†Massive documentation had been gathered in 1966 by the Criminal Investigation Division of the state police (and suppressed by the Faubus administration). One of the dozens of case histories investigators had gathered went as follows: "LL-33 [the CID used a code to protect the identity of informants] was stripped of all clothes. The warden then stuck needles under his fingernails and toenails. His penis and testicles were pulled with wire pliers and he was kicked in the groin. Two other inmates then ground cigarettes in his stomach and legs, and one of them stuck him in the ribs with a knife. The *coup de grâce* came from an inmate who squeezed his knuckles in a nutcracker." This story was verified by the CID after lengthy interviews with other inmates.

an assault against illicit gambling throughout the state. For weeks, Arkansas newspapers were filled with pictures of the flamboyant Davis in full dress uniform raiding gambling establishments in Warm Springs and elsewhere, dismantling slot machines with sledgehammers, and feeding them to raging bonfires.

The conditions he exposed shocked Arkansans, and they gave Winthrop their support on penal reform and gambling. On the question of civil rights, however, they did not. Nonetheless, although he eventually recanted his probussing stand and minimized the degree to which he had been involved in organizations like the Urban League, Winthrop did begin his administration by forcing state agencies to hire blacks in professional and supervisory jobs, and for the first time the state civil service in his administration had a sprinkling of black faces. When the legislature refused to give Winthrop the civil rights commission he had requested, he created one by executive order and gave it space in his own offices. After Martin Luther King's murder, he went to the steps of the state capitol building and joined hands with black leaders in mourning there.

There were tangible accomplishments that came from this reforming atmosphere, and his efforts did purge the state of the last barbarous elements of its antebellum past. Yet as his reformers uncovered more and more of a systemic evil, Winthrop's commitment to change began to flag. Thomas Murton and the prison system was a case in point. It was clear that the problems went deeper than had been imagined when, in early 1968, inmates led Murton to unmarked graves containing the decapitated skeletons of prisoners who had been murdered by authorities during the previous warden's term of office. A national news story, the discovery intensified demands for a thorough overhaul of the prison system. Yet Winthrop, anxious about his 1968 reelection campaign, tried to softpedal the issue, suppressing a report on prisoners secretly murdered in the Arkansas prison just as Faubus before him had tried to suppress a report on atrocious conditions in the prison system. Shortly after Murton presided over the grim ceremony of the exhumation of the shallow graves, he was fired (joining trooper Lynn Davis, who had also been dismissed). As he left, the state prisons slipped a step backward toward the dark ages from which he had struggled to free them.

Winthrop was reelected in 1968, but by a narrowed majority and without appreciably increasing Republicans' strength in the legislature, as he had hoped to. Aides began to get the impression that he had wanted to be *elected* governor more than actually to *be* governor. Reports of his immoderate drinking filtered into the public press. In reporting on Winthrop's appearance before the state legislature on behalf of a mixed-drink bill, the *Pine Bluff Commercial* of June 2, 1968, noted that "the legislators were paying little attention to his message. They were snickering over what they assumed to be the governor's inebriation."

In addition to drinking, Winthrop rarely came to the governor's offices on the second floor of the capitol building, preferring to stay at Winrock, rising late in the morning and working late into the night in his office there or climbing aboard his Falcon jet for the five-minute ride into Little Rock, where he was chauffeured by his bodyguard in a maroon Lincoln limousine to the suite of offices he maintained in the Tower Building (the city's first skyscraper, which he had built).

It was as if dark forces beyond his knowledge, much less control, were pulling him back into that vortex of failure which had dizzied him most of his life. He almost seemed to expect to fail. When his bills were rejected by the legislature and he ran into problems that couldn't be solved with a flourish, it started a disenchantment that finally avalanched into a despair smothering all aspects of his life.

After the 1968 reelection, it was clear to close observers that his marriage was feeling the strain. For Jeannette Edris, Rockefeller politics had been an enemy, stirring up forces in her husband she thought were buried for good and destroying the life they had enjoyed in their first years at Winrock. As the moodiness, drinking bouts, and fits of bitterness increased, the mutual friends she and Winthrop had made began drifting away. She tried to accompany him on his political tours in and out of the state, but the large retinue traveling with them had proved too unwieldy and the pleasures of the rubber chicken circuit too sparse. Soon she began staying home. By 1969 she and Winthrop were living apart and had agreed on a divorce.

As Winthrop and his wife eyed each other coldly from opposite wings of the house, Winrock became less a home than a tourist attraction and convention center. There were banquet-sized dinners two or three times a week, and continual meetings, not only of political organizations, but of groups in which Winthrop was interested personally or which he thought might benefit the state.* The climactic event of the year was the weekend of the annual cattle sale, when Winthrop flew in hundreds of VIPs in his private jet, housed them at Winrock, and fed and entertained them at opulent buffets in the huge circus tents set up in the "backyard." One part business and one part bacchanal, these weekends were renowned throughout the Southwest and attracted an exotic mix of celebrities, business people, and the social set. (A reporter from *The New York Times* society section, dispatched to cover the affair, was less interested in the guest list, however, than in the triumph of art over nature embodied in a gardener whom she watched spend a half-hour carefully brushing a bald spot in the lawn with a can of green paint.)

Defying all political auguries as well as the increasing chaos of his private life, Winthrop decided to run for a third term in 1970. If nothing else, his presence in the state had forced the Democratic party to streamline its image and structure, and purge the old guard from its leadership. This time they put up no Jim Crow reactionary, but a young moderate named Dale Bumpers.

Bumpers clearly outcampaigned Winthrop. Previous opponents had called attention to his notorious drinking problem, but Bumpers didn't have to; audiences saw ample evidence of it for themselves in Winthrop's personal appearances and on television. At best he had been an undistinguished speaker, so halting and tongue-tied that reporters—most of them friendly because he was both amiable and available—often left his press conferences in bewilderment, wondering how to reconstruct what he had just said. But in 1970 it was not just sentences left dangling perilously in the air or metaphors twisted into exotic shapes. (Journalists collected and traded them like Confucian gems; one of the acknowledged classics of Winthrop's political career was "You could have

*Mrs. Margaret Black, for fifteen years Winthrop's housekeeper and confidante (and increasingly, in Jeannette's absence, his official hostess), says that life at Winrock was "one thing after another. There was never the idea of just enjoying yourself." Mrs. Black recalls a time when Winthrop invited a select group from an international conference on air technology meeting at Warm Springs to come to Winrock for dinner. Present were Tojo (son of the Japanese warlord), A. E. Russell (developer of the Spitfire), and Messerschmitt of Germany. When she asked him about seating arrangements, Winthrop told her: "I don't care where you put the German. I didn't fight him in the war. But put Tojo down at the other end of the table, away from me. Those were the people shooting at me in the war."

knocked me over with a fine-toothed comb.") But now it was the serious incoherence of a man who was often not sure what he was saying.

Winthrop, beaten badly by Bumpers, made his farewell to the legislature and withdrew to Winrock. If he had little hope of the eventual comeback that eases most defeated politicians' reentry into private life, he did have a complex empire of investments and interests in the state that could occupy him. Winrock Farms—which had purchased nearly 50,000 additional acres of grazing land in Texas and Oklahoma—was now producing revenues of $20 million a year. Winrock Enterprises had grown from a demonstration project into a large, diversified corporation building shopping centers in Albuquerque and elsewhere in the Southwest, producing trailer homes and plastic pipe, and leading Arkansas in the construction of single-family dwellings.*

Yet his financial affairs did not really interest him. For six months he looked for a vehicle through which he could express his opinions on the changes that would affect Arkansas and other southern states being hurled into modern times. Then he decided to set up an organization he called the Coalition for Rural America to be made up of agricultural, livestock, and other groups with an interest in the development of rural society. Winthrop hoped to weld these elements into an organization capable of exercising an authoritative voice in directions the New South would take. But the coalition was not well-built; soon after it was established, the individual interest within it began to struggle among themselves for precedence, and Winthrop disbanded the organization.

By 1972 he was sixty years old, although with his teeth mottled brown from years of smoking unfiltered Picayune cigarettes and a tic making his head bob and weave as he began sentences, he looked older. Falling into the role of the old man on the top of his mountain, he cultivated a flowing gray beard peppered with black that set off the sad and pensive eyes women had once found so attractive. He told aides that he felt he was on the threshold of the most creative period of his life. Yet a kind of resignation and randomness had crept into his days. In between drinking sprees he walked

---

*In the early fifties, Winthrop had worked briefly as head of the housing division of Nelson's IBEC, which possibly accounted for the emphasis of Winrock Enterprises. The Arkansas corporation also paralleled IBEC's career in the way it made the transition from a semi-altruistic enterprise to a profit-seeking one.

around the farm by himself, occasionally standing at the long flagstone walk with biblical questions set in stone or walking over the grounds strewn with statues that had once belonged to his mother, carrying pruning shears to sculpture the trees and improve the view of the Arkansas River snaking through the valley below Petit Jean Mountain.

His 24-year-old son, Winthrop Paul, the relative stranger who was the first descendant of Mr. Junior to grow up outside the Rockefeller ethos, had come to Winrock to work his way into his father's affairs (after being "sent down" after a few months at Oxford). Winthrop spent time trying to get to know the boy and find ways of integrating him into his own large activities and into the Rockefeller family as well.

In the summer of 1972, the former governor went to Miami as a delegate to the Republican convention. A few weeks later, after returning to Arkansas to help set up the campaign that would allow Richard Nixon to become the first Republican since U. S. Grant to carry the state in a presidential election, his private physician discovered a cyst under his arm and removed it. After a biopsy showed it to be malignant, Winthrop flew to Sloan-Kettering for extensive surgery and a course of chemotherapy. He returned to Arkansas late in October looking thin and shaky, although he buoyantly told reporters who met his plane the doctors had probably stopped the cancer.

Privately he knew that they had not, and that his time was short. Over the next few months he worked to get his affairs in order, knowing that his son would be first of his generation to take control of a share of the awesome fortune history had created and maintained. He remade his will so that while Win Paul got the large '34 Trust, much smaller trusts would go to Jeannette's two children, Bruce and Anne Bartley. The rest of his property, stocks, and land went into a charitable trust, among whose executors were his brother David and, from Room 5600, J. R. Dilworth and attorney Donal O'Brien. (The pin-striped-suit syndrome asserted itself strongly toward the end, Winthrop's Arkansas advisers felt.)

By New Year's he had grown weak. Margaret Black remembers him spending much of that cold month staring bleakly out at the snow and dragging himself through the many rooms of the huge house to sort out clothes and personal belongings and tell her who they should go to in the ritual lottery he knew always followed death in the Rockefeller family. The chemicals pumped into him at Sloan-Kettering to fight the spread of the cancer made him feel constantly chilled, and in mid-February he flew to his vacation home in Palm Springs to try to warm himself in the desert sun. While there he lapsed into a coma, and on February 22, 1973, the Rockefeller brother who had been last all his life was the first to die.

The funeral was a state occasion, taking place on top of Winthrop's mountain in the huge hall housing his collection of antique cars. The governors of Arkansas, Virginia, and West Virginia were there, along with Vice-President Spiro Agnew and his squad of Secret Service men, and various state dignitaries. Winthrop had scripted much of the funeral service before his death—one last attempt to control his image—and it was primarily a family drama. Rockefellers came from all over the country—Charleston and Cambridge, Palo Alto and Pocantico—setting down in a drizzling rain on the slick runway of the Petit Jean airport in commercial planes and private jets. The Brothers and their wives were ushered to the front row. Behind them were the larger group of fourth-generation Rockefellers known as the Cousins. Sitting behind them, in their accustomed role of buffer between the family and the rest of the world, were key members of the staff who had been flown down for the occasion from New York. The pathos of the situation was clear to Laurance's daughter Marion: "He was always issuing these general invitations—'y'all come down.' He was terribly lonely. Yet the only time the family showed up was for his funeral."

William L. ("Sonny") Walker, whom Winthrop had made the first black to head a major Arkansas state agency, centered his funeral remarks on the dead man's commitment to racial equality. There had been compromises, yet Winthrop had been the only governor in the South to join in mourning when Martin Luther King was murdered. Beginning to cry as he spoke, Walker recalled that day in 1968, when Rockefeller had come down to the steps of the state capitol building, holding hands with weeping blacks and saying in his brief speech: "I am not my brother's keeper; I am my brother's brother."

The use of this phrase hung heavy in the service, unintentionally establishing a motif for what followed. It built into a major, although unannounced, theme by the time Nelson rose to give the main eulogy. Where had Winthrop fit among his *own* brothers? The governor's remarks struck listeners as almost too smooth and polished, lacking any felt sense of loss. What few people in the room knew was that the words he read had been written a few days before the funeral by one of his speech writers, who had been instructed to call the Rockefeller Family Office to get the pertinent facts about Winthrop's life. Nelson had not seen the speech until midnight in flight between Albany and Winrock.

Yet it hardly mattered. Winthrop was gone—in death as in life a sacrificial offering confirming the unity of the rest of his brothers. It was with a realism absent from the funeral oratory that his longtime friend and assistant, Margaret Black, later pointed out the only truth to be learned from his passing. "That poor, poor man," she said with an edge of bitterness in her voice, "he was just fair game for everybody—for strangers and family too."

25

To THE ROCKEFELLERS, Arkansas was *terra incognita*, a haven for exiles who could not function in the world of affairs. Winrock Farm had the eerie feeling of a place built by someone who seemed to have a detailed knowledge of what it was to be a Rockefeller but had not quite been able to attain their exquisite taste and sophistication. With its biblical quotations set in stone, its sculptured trees and other arabesques, Winrock seemed less a successful imitation of Pocantico than a parody of it, slightly embarrassing in the way Winthrop himself had been.

The Rockefellers felt the pathos and waste of their dead brother's life, yet they had grown so accustomed to regarding themselves as the type and him as the variant that it was hard not to share the attitude lying just below the patina of polished impersonality in Nelson's eulogy. As a direct descendant of the first John D., Winthrop had to have a state funeral; but whatever the words said over him, the family knew that the terminal disease had not been cancer at all, but weakness. In death, as in life, he had broken ranks and compromised them all.

Yet in this most final of analyses, how different were they really from the one Emmet Hughes had called "the brother apart"? Winthrop was their *memento mori,* and in the cold light of his death they saw change written boldly on each other's face—not the benign change that works its way unobtrusively through the decades, but change as a harshly final, completed act.

It was noted by J. Richardson Dilworth, head of the Family Office. "I think this generation has not tended to think of itself as mortal until now," he said shortly after the funeral. "This is why Winthrop's death was a great blow. You act one way if you assume twenty years is ahead of you; another if you realize time is shorter than that. Winthrop's death instilled a sense of urgency in the remaining brothers."

Soon after returning to New York, JDR3 began tidying up his affairs and readying his collection of more than three hundred pieces of Oriental art for donation to the Asia Society. Laurance startled his children at a family gathering celebrating his fortieth wedding anniversary by telling them what each one's share of his estate would be. Not soon after, David began to do the same in individual conferences with his children.

Nelson could not help making some of these deferential gestures toward mortality. He seemed already to have lived two lives, one that ended in the late fifties after he left the Eisenhower administration, and the other that began when he became governor. He had watched the associates and friends of the earlier era die or wear out. Jamieson, Ruml, and Berle were all gone now; Wally Harrison, balding and gaunt at seventy-seven years, was nearly deaf; John Lockwood had passed the mandatory retirement age and returned to Milbank, Tweed to take up an emeritus's desk, his weak eyes shaded by dark glasses and his working day kept purposefully short. The children of Nelson's first marriage had grown up, married, and had children of their own and, led by Rodman (age forty-two), were now themselves poised on the edge of middle age.

Nelson was no longer the handsome, blue-eyed, irrepressible young man who had popped like a champagne cork into public life thirty-five years earlier. Liver-spotted and wrinkled despite being hovered over by personal physicians, he now looked his sixty-six years. His features had settled into the square mass that recalled his father in old age, and with his heavy black-rimmed glasses and his gravelly voice, he looked and sounded like a WASP George Burns.

Yet at a profound level of his character, he could not accept growing old. As the elaborate machinery sustaining his public and private life wore down, he replaced it, finding younger people to serve as prosthetic extensions of himself. He had gotten a new set of young aides. He had a young wife (though even she had not been able to keep his amorous eye from wandering) and two young sons (Nelson, Jr., ten, and Mark, eight) on whom he lavished rides in the family helicopter, moments alone with him in his office sharing Oreo cookies, and other evidences of an almost grandfatherly affection. He was fond of saying to those who asked him about his age, "My grandfather lived to be ninety-seven and my father to be eighty-six. I plan to make it to a hundred." As friends watched the husky figure walking with Happy and the children along the beach at Seal Harbor, the rolling flat-footed gait reminded them of an old boxer who knows only one way to move—forward.

In him the unsated hunger of most politicians was enlarged several times, yet Nelson's quest had been different. He had begun by looking for goals worthy of him and of the family tradition he had come to embody. His political career had involved a flirtation with the apocalyptic that was unique in American politics. In foreign affairs, it had been the cold war, bomb shelters, nuclear weaponry—that most fearful apparatus of modern life that normal men approached only with awe. In domestic politics, it had been his epic plans for tearing apart and reconstructing New York; the scope of this privately conceived system of public works was unrivaled anywhere in the nation. And all of it had been aimed at the presidency—potentially, the most apocalyptic job in the world, and certainly the only one that could complete his sense of his destiny.

His friend Jacob Javits had once said: "Nothing stands in Rockefeller's way. Nothing. He always gets what he wants."

When Nelson was asked if he felt this was true, he responded with a parable. "I remember bidding at an auction on a Modigliani once and losing to the Museum of Modern Art, of which I was then president. And years later another one came on the market and I was fortunate enough to get it. So it shows if you've got patience and persistence, even though you're thwarted at one point, you can [get what you want]. I'm a great believer in that."

Yet patience and persistence, he had to believe after 1968, would not get him the prize he had sought throughout his political career. For one of the rare times in his life he was in a position of having no alternatives. He could not let go of the ambition that had driven him through public life, but its fulfillment now clearly depended on some miracle that he was unable, as had always been his custom, to *make* happen. He could only wait for some divine intervention and prepare to take advantage of it—should it occur—by supporting and even toadying to Richard Nixon, a man he not only loathed but also felt was mentally unstable. And as the presidency receded from his grasp, a new element of bitterness entered his character. It was as if the world had undergone an elementary mitosis, splitting into the two opposing camps of friends and enemies.

He had the wealth to buy loyalty and the breeding to buy it in such a way that neither party in the transaction had to admit a deal had taken place. Rockefeller loyalists could count on jobs not only in the state government but also in the larger world of private patronage that Nelson controlled.* If he had always known how to reward his friends, after 1968 he began to take a new kind of pleasure in finding ways to punish his enemies.

The celebrated feud with John Lindsay was a case in point. At the core of the conflict was a question of loyalty—personal and political—regarding how much exactly the mayor owed Nelson. The beginning of their struggle went back to 1965, when Rockefeller had helped convince Lindsay to abandon his congressional seat and enter the mayoralty race. In agreeing, Lindsay stipulated that he had to be assured of a campaign war chest of $1 million. When the primary neared and he had accumulated just half of this sum, one of his

---

*Robert Douglass, former Rockefeller chief of staff, later went to Milbank, Tweed and the N.Y. Port Authority; Alton Marshall, former secretary to the governor, became head of Rockefeller Center and Nelson's representative on most New York City committees on housing; Frank Willey, former counsel to the governor, became state superintendant of banks and later a Chase Manhattan executive, to cite only a few examples. Richard Reeves formerly of *The New York Times* says of Nelson: "What does he get from these people besides service? Well, there's never been a single defection from him or the family in twenty years of vicious politics—no books, no memoirs, no nothing. Think about it. It's unique."

campaign lieutenants, Bob Price (the man credited with organizing Nelson's "miracle victory" in the 1964 Oregon primary), made the trip to Pocantico to get the rest.

In giving the $450,000 he raised from his family, and in the other help he gave to make Lindsay's victory possible, Nelson naturally assumed he had gotten something he had been hoping for since first becoming governor: a Republican mayor of New York through whom he could control the city *in absentia*. Yet Lindsay soon began to go his own way, with youthful vitality, charisma, and an apparently bright future—exactly those things Nelson's own life now lacked. There was an almost sexual jealousy in Nelson's reaction to the new glamour figure of New York Republicans, the leader protecting his supremacy. (In the narrower arena of the Rockefeller family, Nelson would later feel something like this emotion over the success of his nephew Jay, who seemed to be upstaging him from West Virginia.)

"At least Rockefeller thought he was in command of Republicans in New York," remarks Ripon theorist George Gilder in explaining the origins of the feud. "It was the least he could be. If he couldn't rule the world, he had those New York Republicans. And then Lindsay began maneuvering around, getting his own base, making his claim on the progressives. Nelson liked to maintain that he was the most liberal figure the Republicans could accommodate and also that he was extraordinarily virtuous in some sense, and here Lindsay was on his left offering another kind of motif. Lindsay, moreover, had a certain disdain for Rockefeller, and he couldn't disguise it. Rockefeller couldn't bear the idea that he could succeed. Rockefeller's reaction was fanatical."

The flash point came in 1968, when Rockefeller not only ignored Lindsay's request to call out the National Guard to pick up the mountains of garbage left by striking city sanitation workers, but settled the strike over the mayor's head. In return, Lindsay denounced Rockefeller for "cowardice" and "capitulation to blackmail." Nelson chose to believe that Lindsay's outburst had been calculated to embarrass him and that it had actually been a critical factor in his loss of the presidential nomination to Nixon at Miami Beach. The following year he refused to endorse Lindsay in his reelection campaign, and the mayor reciprocated by endorsing Democrat Arthur Goldberg for Governor in 1970. From then on it was open warfare, with Nelson using the full reach of his official and private leverage in the struggle that ended with

Lindsay leaving the Republican party and, ultimately, public office.

It was not unique that Nelson should be involved in a struggle for power, but the amount of personal venom this particular conflict brought out in him did surprise those who had watched him over the years. He not only wanted to defeat Lindsay, he wanted to crush him as well. Congressman Ogden Reid (another former ally who also felt Nelson's wrath when he followed Lindsay in switching to the Democratic party), says, "The Nelson I once knew is no more. He has gotten increasingly monomaniacal. During the height of his quarrel with John Lindsay, I've seen Nelson have his whole day absolutely made by just being able to outflank the mayor on a press release, or something petty like that. It's hard to believe."

Nelson had spent an immense amount of family money on his own political career,* and had always helped strategically placed Republicans in states where he wanted influence (as in California, where first Senator Thomas Kuchel and then gubernatorial candidate Houston Flournoy were seen as "Rockefeller's men"). Now, however, he began to use his money to defeat opponents and punish defectors as well. This was true of the New York mayoral race of 1969; it was also true in 1972, when half the proceeds of a $2,000-a-head fund raiser at Pocantico went into the campaign of the opponent of Richard Ottinger, whom Nelson still blamed for the defeat of his expressway, and the other half to Congressman Ogden Reid's opponent. (Reid's office estimates that in all—cash and paid workers—Nelson contributed over $100,000 to defeat him in 1972.)

People who had been in politics with him for twenty years began to see a new side of Nelson that was far different from the young man whose sins had once seemed to spring only from an excess of enthusiasm. He had grown irritable and wintry, and a calculating vindictiveness joined thwarted ambition as his prime traits. He ruled New York like a modern pharaoh, cajoling, wheedling, threatening, and intimidating legislators into supporting his programs and doing whatever was necessary to gain his ends—casually giving powerful Assemblyman Meade Esposito a Picasso print he had admired

*He spent $21 million by his own account; $27 million according to CBS News; $48 million by the reckoning of George Thayer, author of *Who Shakes the Money Tree.*

and just as casually breaking the power once enjoyed by Robert Moses.

He had grown increasingly cavalier and arrogant. His first move against Moses—for decades regarded by many as the most powerful man in the state—was not begun for any reason of policy, or even of personality. Nelson simply wanted the chairmanship of the State Parks Commission for his brother Laurance. Nelson got the resignation from Moses, but it would be several years before the struggle between the two came to a head. When, in the late sixties, Nelson decided to centralize a state transportation empire under his aide William J. Ronan, Moses's last and seemingly most impregnable fortress—the Triborough Bridge Authority—stood in the way. The wall around this fortress consisted of the bondholders' covenants, which secured Moses's position and which not even a governor backed by the legislature could break—except that in this case the bondholders' trustee was the Chase Manhattan Bank. When the time came to merge the Triborough Bridge Authority into Nelson's superagency, he sat down with David in his 55th Street town house and within an hour concluded the arrangement.

There was nothing new in this mutuality. Nelson had always been ready to help David while advancing his own best interests. From the outset of his first administration, he had pushed for a liberalization of the laws on bank mergers and branch banking, and for the creation of bank holding companies, which would allow the banks to expand into other forms of business. Nelson also stepped in when the World Trade Center seemed about to become a costly white elephant. Though the Port Authority had floated $850 million in bonds to build it, and David and the Downtown Association had pressured the city into taking some major planning decisions to make it possible as it neared completion it was finding it difficult to attract tenants. Nelson helped out by moving more than two dozen state offices into the Center buildings, taking out a 40-year state lease on 60 full floors of one of its 110-story twin towers. By 1974 the state was paying $18.3 million a year in rent to the Port Authority, and an investigation by the Comptroller's Office was already under way to look into why the state was paying $4 million more annually on its 2.3 million square feet of rented space than private tenants were paying for comparable footage.

All of this was done with a brazen indifference for the consequences and regardless of whether the victims were powerful, like Moses, or impotent, like the vast unfathoming public who paid the bills. It was as William Farrell, former *New York Times* Albany bureau chief, said: "Nelson is a true democrat. He has contempt for *everyone* regardless of race, color, creed, religion or anything else." Aides who felt the sting of his increasingly foul moods called him "Fang" behind his back. Political opponents, T. H. White remarked, "called him simply the most ruthless man in politics."

The anger and spite were signs that he had not given up. Restless as ever, he was anxious to have a hand in the foreign policy of the Nixon administration.* He arranged to get himself appointed to the Foreign Intelligence Advisory Board (where he would soon be hearing of the CIA's concern about the Allende government in Chile, and its plans to "destabilize" it). And on the new President's first day in office in 1969, Nelson called on him; after an hour's discussion, he came away as the head of a presidential mission that would visit all the countries of Latin America and then make recommendations for a new policy toward the hemisphere.

It seemed natural that he should turn again to Latin America. It had, after all, been the launching pad for his career almost thirty years earlier; perhaps it might now serve to reinvigorate his political fortunes. But the days when he had been the hemisphere's golden boy were long gone. Both he and the continent were changed, and a closer reading of the current scene would have warned against any facile expectations of repeating earlier triumphs. He was no longer an unknown quantity, a young man starting out with ideas that were fresh

---

*Nelson's primary contact with the administration would soon be Henry Kissinger. As his protégé rose higher and higher in the Nixon Cabinet (ironically, displacing Secretary of State William Rogers and attaining that position of "coordinator" or First Secretary of Foreign Affairs Rockefeller once visualized for himself), Nelson became more and more solicitous toward him. Nelson had always been a patron, supporting Kissinger as a consultant at $12,000 a year since the days of the Panel Studies and later setting up a trust fund of $65,000 for him. Kissinger had delayed going into the Nixon administration until it was clear that Nelson would not become Secretary of Defense, as he had momentarily hoped to in 1969. Even after Kissinger was a national celebrity, the relationship was unchanged. In 1973 Nelson accepted the Family of Man medal for the absent Secretary of State and said (in a characteristic coupling): "He's never let me down and he's never let the country down." It was Nelson who got the honor of announcing Kissinger's engagement to his own former aide Nancy Maginnes, and gave them the use of one of the family's planes for their honeymoon trip.

and disarming, especially for a scion of Standard Oil. As for the hemisphere itself, it had been fired by the passions of the Cuban revolution, by its urgent demand that the weight of poverty and oppression be lifted. Characteristically Nelson met this challenge with his own hard line, deciding to take General Robert W. Porter, Jr., who had directed the counter-insurgency operations against Che Guevara two years earlier in Bolivia, as the military adviser of the 27-man entourage he assembled to accompany him at a personal expense of $750,-000.

He planned to cover the Latin American countries in a series of four trips (one week on the road and then one week back home to handle state business). In May of 1969, he began his first visit. Instead of hearing the old cries of *"Viva Rocky,"* his arrival in Honduras was met with angry demonstrators who raised the shout that would be the watchword for his trip—*"Malvenido Rockefeller."* By the time he returned from the last of the four visits in July (only to be greeted by a noisy confrontation with SDS demonstrators at Kennedy airport), Rockefeller's embassy of goodwill had provoked the deepest display of anti–U.S. sentiment in the history of the hemisphere, and the most spectacular rejection of any U.S. representative on record.

At that first stopover in Honduras, police had killed a student during anti-Rockefeller demonstrations. In Ecuador, Rockefeller's visit sent the capital of Quito into a paroxysm of disorder; while demonstrators battled police in the central part of the city, Rockefeller's entourage was hustled through the backstreets (with a military helicopter riding shotgun from above), finally meeting the presidential delegation at a hotel cordoned off by a thousand troops. Because of a conflict with the State Department over tuna fishing, Peru canceled the visit. Bolivian officials felt that Nelson's safety could not be guaranteed inside their country, so they restricted his stay to a quick three-hour meeting at the airport. Venezuela and Chile canceled his visit outright. Brazil's government prepared for Nelson by rounding up three thousand dissidents and putting them in preventive detention. Before he even arrived in Uruguay, a General Motors plant was burned, causing one million dollars in damage. In Argentina Nelson's stay was marked by the bombing of thirteen IBEC supermarkets and the assassination of a labor leader who had opposed his coming. The Rockefeller party's exit from Santo Domingo, last stop on the tour, took place in a bus convoyed by armored personnel carriers along a route lined by soldiers and police who had already killed four demonstrators. On the entire tour of twenty countries, only Paraguay and Haiti, the oldest and most ruthless dictatorships on the continent, were enthusiastic, large crowds turning out by presidential order to greet Rockefeller.

It was unlikely that any other U.S. figure, even Richard Nixon, could have provoked such a demonstration of hemispheric resentment, for no one was so closely identified with the smothering "special relationship" (as Nelson's report was to describe it) by which the United States had maintained its hold over the hemisphere. Yet, far from seeing the reaction as a plebiscite on policies he more than anyone else had been instrumental in establishing, Nelson used the chaos and bloodshed that marked his tour as grist for his ideological mill: "Forces of anarchy, terror and subversion are loose in the Americas," he warned portentously in his report. "Doubt and cynicism . . . have grown in other American nations as to the purposefulness of the United States in facing this serious threat to freedom, democracy and the vital interests of the western hemisphere."

To remedy this situation and to meet the challenge of "communist subversion," the report urged a reaffirmation of the "special relationship" and an acceleration of Washington's efforts to maintain security in the hemisphere. There were the usual Rockefeller recommendations for new bureaucratic structures and administrative centralization, including the creation of a Secretary of Western Hemisphere Affairs to "coordinate . . . all U.S. government activities." But the main thrust of the report was to urge a more "pragmatic" approach to the Latin American military regimes and a more decisive retreat from U.S. policy commitments for social reform from the early days of the Alliance for Progress. Lamenting the fact that U.S. military assistance had fallen from $80.7 million in 1966 to $20.4 million in 1969, Nelson argued for a dramatic increase. He suggested military missions be streamlined to lessen their numbers and visibility and to further Latin-Americanize the conflict against Communism. He complained that the United States did not have "a full appreciation of the important role played by the police," and urged that the government "respond to requests for assistance of the police and security forces of the hemisphere nations by providing them with the essential tools to do their job."

He criticized the "paternalism" of the Agency for Interna-

tional Development program, yet the larger paternalism behind it went unchallenged. The prize was not Latin American
welfare or freedom, but Latin America itself, both as a symbol and a reality: "Failure to maintain that special relationship would imply failure of our capacity and responsibility as
a great nation.... Moreover failure to maintain this special
relationship would create a vacuum in this hemisphere and
facilitate the import in the region of hostile foreign powers."

The lines could have been taken from some position paper
for the coordinator's office, or a memorandum prepared
twenty-five years earlier for the Chapultepec Conference and
the beginnings of the post-war obsession with hemispheric
security.

President Nixon did not cold-shoulder *The Rockefeller Report on the Americas* the way he would JDR3's population
report. He simply did not act on it. He did not reorganize the
Latin American bureaucracy in the State Department, or embark on any grand hemispheric security schemes as Nelson
had recommended. He just followed the drift of U.S. support
for the hemispheric status quo and concentrated his presidential energies on the war in Southeast Asia.

Since the 1964 primary campaign, Nelson had seemed to
develop a persecution complex and a tendency to see himself
as the symbol of an embattled establishment. In a fundamental way, this had always been his operating assumption; but
now he began increasingly to confuse the political corner in
which he found himself with the dilemma of established social order. He *was* order; those opposing him were representatives of anarchy. (This binary code of morality would lie at
the heart of the Attica tragedy later on.) His strength had
never come from reflection but from the raw energy with
which he assaulted his environment, and, no sooner had he
completed one thing—a program, a building, or a tour—than
he immediately began looking toward the next. Even before
delivering his report on the Americas, he was already pointing toward what he knew would be a hard reelection campaign against Arthur Goldberg.

Nelson's name and wealth provided him with a nimbus of
gentility that never dimmed. Yet the fact was that he had
long since developed beyond that neophyte "citizen politician" who took office in 1959. By 1970 he was an extraordinarily savvy operator, wielding the powers of the governorship with a flair and cunning no predecessor since Al Smith
had managed. (Kissinger had once observed, Nelson may

have had a "second rate mind" but he made up for it with a "first rate intuition about people.") Over the years he had mastered the resources in and out of Albany and had developed the most crushing political style in the nation. He had taken over the machinery of state government and made it *his* machinery, forcing his personality into every crevice of state government and using to advantage the nearly forty thousand jobs said to be affected by his patronage. The fact that he did not have to beg for contributions made him even more powerful.*

Nelson helped dozens of party figures to high nonpartisan office. (The most flagrant example came when he made former Republican State Chairman Fred Young a presiding judge, allowed him to step down to work in a campaign, and then reappointed him afterward.) In the words of one reluctantly admiring Democrat who later surveyed the Rockefeller years as governor: "Nelson out-Tammanied Tammany." His administration was unique in statehouse politics: a governorship whose sweep and power was almost as imperial as the presidency itself.

Rockefeller still mixed with the people every four years, presenting his stage version of a plebeian style and filling up on ethnic foods; yet he realized as well as the voters that the persona of "Rocky" had become something like a joke whose punch line was too well known. He was almost as tired of running for office as New Yorkers were of having him run, and his campaigns came more and more to rely on massive infusions of money and lavish use of the media. Once gala affairs, they had now come to have a predictable certainty: a tank corps offensive rolling inexorably across the desert.

A more imaginative opponent might have taken advantage of New Yorkers' readiness to be convinced that Rockefeller was not an inevitability. Yet Arthur Goldberg's starchy pompousness only made Nelson seem more colorful than he was. The inability to take advantage of Rockefeller's weaknesses on issues went deeper than the yawning gap in resources between the two campaigns, although this was a large factor in

---

*He could get away with egregious acts such as pardoning L. Judson Morhouse, his friend and onetime political mentor. Morhouse, who had been state GOP chairman and a longtime Rockefeller aide (as well as the recipient of some of the loans that were to cause a furor in vice-presidential confirmation hearings later), had been sentenced to prison in the wake of a bribery scandal that swept through the State Liquor Authority he headed.

Goldberg's defeat.* The former Supreme Court Justice's ineptitude seemed to spring from a more profound source. Long after the campaign was over, aides were still speculating about it. One of them, speech writer Paul Weissman, feels that a vision of the family's awesome power had given Rockefeller a kind of political voodoo over Goldberg: "I frankly think the campaign was over when Arthur was invited up to Pocantico late in the primary. The note came after it was pretty clear that he was going to be the Democratic nominee. It was cordial and handwritten, and Arthur accepted. He came back from the meeting terribly shaken. It was not, as some of us assumed at first, because of threats or anything like that, but just because for the first time in his political life he had seen what *real* power was, what it could buy, how it lived. Really, I don't think he was ever the same afterwards."

If Goldberg was overawed from on high, he was outflanked at the grass roots level as well. At crucial nodes of the traditional coalition that Democrats must put together to win in New York, Goldberg found himself blocked. White ethnic groups were attracted by Nelson's hawkish views on crime. Though he was running against a former Secretary of Labor and a famous union lawyer, Nelson was endorsed by the state AFL-CIO representing over one million workers and anchored by the Building Trades Union, which had profited immensely from the governor's long series of construction projects. Nelson's ability to assume a familiarity with caciques of the state AFL-CIO was also a tremendous asset in his attempts to woo organized labor. Victor Gotbaum, head of New York's District 37 Municipal Employees Union (and one of New York's labor leaders who didn't support Rockefeller), says, "He is able to 'lower' himself to the level of the 'average guy.' You have no idea the impact just being 'one of the boys' has on labor people. We were once having a Central Labor Council meeting, I remember, and all through the cocktail party that preceded it, the guys were standing around

---

*Goldberg had 35 paid employees, while Rockefeller had over 350, 38 on leave from state jobs. Goldberg campaigned most often by regularly scheduled airlines, while Rockefeller zipped around the state in the Grumman Gulfstream 2-jet or the twin-engine Fairchild, taking his press entourage along with him. Rockefeller spent twice as much on media alone—$3.5 million—as Goldberg did on his entire campaign: it was later estimated that his campaign message—"He's done a lot for New York, and he'll do a lot more"—reached 95 percent of all state households; the average New Yorker saw 9.4 Rockefeller commercials. In all, he reported expenditures of $7.2 million.

talking about 'Nelson,' about what a cocksman he was and all
that. They were getting a terrific thrill out of the fact that
here was one of the richest, most powerful, most cultured
guys in the world, and he encouraged *them* to call him by his
first name and allowed them to get in on his sexual exploits."

By early fall of 1970, Rockefeller had pulled even with
Goldberg in the polls and in November he easily won an unprecedented fourth term. As always, victory was sweet, yet it
was not like old times. People voted for him, he understood,
but they didn't particularly like him. His status as the golden
boy of American politics had long since slipped. As late as
the 1968 presidential campaign, this diminished appeal had
enough vestigial strength to inspire talk in political circles
about how the country *needed* Nelson. His appalling record
on civil liberties in New York was minimized, and his hard-
line views on Vietnam were discounted the minute he began
to make his ambiguous overtures to the antiwar sentiment
that had crystallized around the candidacy of Robert Kennedy. People had willingly suspended their disbelief and
made the sort of allowances for him they would not have
made for any other politician in America. (His association
with culture, philanthropy, and national policy acted like a
centering device whenever the untamed element in his character reared itself and appeared to lead him off course.) Underneath the pragmatism necessary to his profession, they
said, there was a man of basic humanity and liberal instinct,
a man who just might be able to pull the nation out of its
self-lacerating trauma and bind up its wounds.

As the seventies began, this myth of Nelson's liberalism
could no longer be sustained. During the campaign against
Goldberg, Nelson had emphasized his support of Nixon's Vi-
etnamization plan, and when Senator Charles Goodell (whom
he had appointed to Bobby Kennedy's seat in 1968) introduced his troop withdrawal plan, Nelson opposed it, saying,
"It can only undermine the effectiveness of the President's
bargaining position in negotiations with the North Vietnamese." In domestic affairs, he had inveighed against "welfare
cheats," ordering audits of the relief rolls. He had announced
cuts in Medicaid. Appealing to the silent majority in New
York, he would remind audiences on the hustings that he had
been "Spiro Agnew's first choice for President."

Political observers interpreted these moves as a calculated
"turn rightward," an attempt to make peace with the conservative wing of the Republican party and to accommodate the

new interest in "law and order." Yet the thrust of his statements, particularly on Vietnam, was not wholly determined
by expediency. He had always been, in the words of his one-
time friend Congressman Ogden Reid, "a hardliner on anything involving negotiation." This quality had previously been
more or less absorbed by his foreign policy positions—the
Test Ban Treaty, détente, Vietnam, and so on—but now it
broadened to include all the dissident groups in the country
who challenged the views and prerogatives of men of his
status and class. Under the pressure of domestic radicalism
and in the face of the broad protests of the sixties, his hard
line had taken over his political personality. In this sense he
was ideologically prepared for the nightmare of Attica long
before it happened.

Nelson was in Washington D.C., on September 9, 1971, attending a meeting of the Foreign Committee on International
Intelligence, when he first got word from Commissioner of
Corrections Russell Oswald that a rebellion had occurred at
the state prison at Attica, and that 1,300 prisoners were holding 38 officials and guards in D Yard. Assuring Oswald that
he had faith in his ability to handle the situation but caution-
ing him to avoid the appearance of "vacillation and indecision" in negotiations with inmates, Rockefeller told him that
he would return to Pocantico the next day and assign his
chief counsel "Bobby" Douglass to stay in contact with the
situation. But when Oswald was unable to make headway in
the discussion of inmate grievances, negotiations were taken
over by an informal team of observers that included Congressman Herman Badillo, *New York Times* editor Tom
Wicker, black state Assemblyman Arthur Eve, attorney William Kunstler, and others.

Discussions broke down on the issue of amnesty, which became especially crucial to inmates after a prison guard died
of injuries suffered in the takeover. Equally crucial was
whether Nelson would come to the scene of the crisis. On
Sunday, four days after the rebellion first erupted, it appeared
that troopers would be ordered to storm the prison. The observers broadcast a message over New York radio begging
Rockefeller to intervene: "The committee of observers in Attica Prison is now convinced a massacre of prisoners and
guards may take place in this institution. For the sake of our
common humanity we call on everyone who hears these
words to implore the Governor to come to Attica."

That afternoon, Wicker, Badillo, and State Senator John

Dunne (who had Nelson's private phone number at Pocantico) talked with Rockefeller by phone for two hours, stressing that they wanted him on the scene at Attica. The conversation became a mini-campaign speech, as Tom Wicker later recalled in his book *A Time To Die*.

" 'Governor,' said Wicker, 'I'm up here at Attica.'

" 'I know you are,' Rockefeller broke in, 'and I just want you to know how grateful I am and how much I really admire what you and the others are doing up there. I know you've all worked hard and I appreciate it. I really do. It's just great. Just great.' "

But the bottom line was that he wasn't coming.

That evening Oswald too called the governor to ask him to come to the prison. Rockefeller replied that he had been in touch with Bobby Douglass and they had decided that he didn't have the constitutional authority to grant amnesty to the prisoners, so that a visit would be pointless. "In life," he told his commissioner of corrections, "it's not easy to face a hard decision, particularly when human lives are involved. . . . But I think that we have to look at these things not only in terms of the immediate but in terms of the larger implication of what we are doing in our society."

The next morning Oswald called Nelson once more to ask if his mind was still made up. When Nelson said it was, orders went out to begin the offensive against the inmates assembled in D Yard. Without warning, a helicopter swooped down over the yard dropping a thick cloud of pepper gas. At this signal, snippers atop the prison battlegrounds let loose a hail of fire against the prisoners trapped in the yard, and an army of hundreds of state troopers and correction officers armed with shotguns and high-powered rifles began a volley of concentrated gunfire that lasted six minutes. When it was over, and the ceasefire order given, ten of the hostages and twenty-nine inmates lay dead or dying in the yard. (In all, forty-three would die at Attica at the hands of the assault squads and eighty would suffer gunshot wounds.) As the McKay Commission, which investigated the events afterward, commented, it was "with the exception of Indian massacres in the late 19th century . . . the bloodiest one-day encounter between Americans since the Civil War." When the smoke cleared, and the observers outside knew that their worst fears had been confirmed, Congressman Badillo summed up their feelings. "There's always time to die," he said in disgust. "I don't know what the rush was."

From the governor's office, a press release was issued following the attack; even those who had been sympathetic to Rockefeller's dilemma found it chilling: "Our hearts go out to the families of the hostages who died at Attica. The tragedy was brought on by the highly organized, revolutionary tactics of militants who rejected all efforts at a peaceful settlement, forced a confrontation and carried out cold-blooded killings they had threatened from the onset." When Rockefeller met the press two days later, however, autopsies had revealed that hostages did not die from having their throats slashed by their captors, as had first been suggested by prison officials, but from the troopers' deadly fire. Yet Nelson was not going to relinquish an inch of the ground he had staked out. He noted that when he was telephoned with the news that the remaining hostages had been brought out alive, he was "absolutely overwhelmed" with joy.

A reporter interjected, "What does this tell you about the prisoners, the fact that so many men [hostages] emerged unharmed?"

Rockefeller snapped back, "What it tells me is the use of this gas is a fantastic instrument in a situation of this kind."

Tom Wicker, one of the team of observers, testifying before the New York State Special Commission on Attica (the McKay Commission), said that he had hoped Rockefeller would come to the prison for two reasons: "First, it would be a symbolic gesture to the inmates of his concern; second, if he would come, we could break the impasse in negotiations. Something might give." Yet Nelson remained adamant on his reasons for not coming. "If the Governor has to be the one who negotiates," he said in a statement that showed where he placed himself in the great chain of being, "... we may find ourselves in a position where next time they say, 'We won't negotiate with anyone but the President.'"

The final words on the matter came from the Special Commission on Attica. Concluding that the governor's presence would have had a stabilizing effect on the troopers and correction officers during the assault, and in containing the rampage they went on afterward, it said: "The governor should have gone to Attica not as a matter of duress or because the convicts demanded his presence, but because his responsibilities as the state's chief executive made it appropriate that he be present at the scene of the critical decisions involving great loss of life."

Nelson's actions had a political reference that was wider

than Attica, and which he never lost sight of. Throughout the events, he was in constant touch with the White House, where the rebellion was seen as a test case in the mood of insurgency spreading through prisons across the country. It was also looked on as a test of Nelson's new commitment to conservative politics. Shortly after the uprising was quelled, Nixon sent Rockefeller a telegram praising his "courage." William Safire, then still a Nixon aide, told political writer Richard Reeves: "The assault on Attica was a moral disgrace, but politically he did what our people wanted."

Many called it "Rockefeller's Bay of Pigs." If they had known the history of his family, they might have more aptly called it his Ludlow, for Attica had an almost eerie resemblance to that day over fifty years earlier, when troopers, perched on a rim overlooking the camp of the striking miners, trained their Hotchkiss guns on the tattered tents and opened fire. They might have noticed the same procrastination, the attempt to stay aloof from the crisis while taxing others with ultimate responsibility for the life-and-death decisions that had characterized his father's behavior. Former Lindsay press aide Tom Morgan (now Nelson's son-in-law) says, "Attica is the symbolic Rockefeller act. He delayed and hung back at each critical moment until all the 'liberal' options were exhausted and he was able to choose the reactionary solution, which was the one he had wanted all along."

Yet Nelson was unlike Junior in one key way: Attica left him with no queasy aftertaste, no fear for his public image, and he had no intention of making anything like the pilgrimage of atonement his father had taken to Colorado.* The lesson Nelson drew out of the Attica tragedy bore closer resemblance to the propositions Junior had taken into Ludlow than those with which he had emerged. "Of course there was more at stake than saving lives," he had assured Commissioner Russell Oswald in a telephone call after the assault. "There was the whole rule of law to consider. The whole fabric of our society, in fact."

---

*On the contrary, the adverse criticism seemed to bring out the vindictive element in his character. He appointed a special prosecutor, Deputy Attorney General Robert E. Fischer, to investigate and prosecute all crimes committed at Attica. Operating on a budget that reached $3 million by 1974, Fischer and his aides returned 42 indictments against 61 Attica inmates on charges ranging from kidnapping to murder. No indictment was returned against prison officials, guards, or the assaulting army that had engaged in an orgy of brutality after the storming of the prison.

For everyone involved—prisoners, observers, and executioners—Attica was one of those rare events that manage to heighten aspects of individual lives submerged in their daily existence. For Nelson it was the completion of an apotheosis. Henry Adams's famous statement might almost have been made with Junior's most irrepressible son in mind: "The effect of power and publicity in all men is the aggravation of self, a sort of tumor that ends by killing the victim's sympathies."

Attica was an ultimate indication of the extent to which Rockefeller had made his peace with the Republican party's mainstream. He could even veto antibussing and antiabortion measures passed by the New York legislature without being accused of backsliding, so firm was his conversion. On the larger issues—war and peace, crime and punishment—he was, in a favorite phrase of the Nixon's administration, "on board." At the 1972 convention he was chosen to nominate Nixon for a second term. This time he got the name right.

He worked hard for the President against McGovern and shared the satisfactions of the unprecedented Republican triumph. Yet folded in the small creases of that election was the event that presidential Press Secretary Ron Ziegler would later immortalize as "a third rate burglary," and which would dramatically alter Nelson Rockefeller's political fortunes along with the rest of his party's. As Watergate developed, crippling the Nixon presidency a little more with each passing month, Nelson realized that he had reason to hope again—not much, perhaps, but enough to make him begin looking toward 1976 with a rejuvenated eye. He watched as the clouds of scandal drifted over Washington and cast shadows over the lives and careers of his possible adversaries. They seemed to go one by one. As Spiro Agnew fell, Nelson maneuvered vigorously to create a groundswell of support in the party that would force Nixon to name him as the replacement. But the old bitterness had not faded, and the President instead chose Gerald Ford. The next casualty of the spreading scandal was John Connally, Nixon's own choice as heir apparent. It seemed for a moment that 1976 might come down to a choice between Rockefeller and California's Governor Ronald Reagan in a replay of Nelson's hoped-for scenario at Miami in 1968.

Nelson became obsessed with taking advantage of the strange turn of events that had suddenly changed the entire atmosphere of American politics. He assembled the nucleus of a campaign staff at Albany. Throughout the last part of 1973, he toured the country on behalf of Republicans whose *bête noire* he had once been, even flying to Arizona to be the featured speaker as a testimonial dinner for Barry Goldwater. Although he would not have admitted it, his activities constituted a belated pilgrimage of expiation for 1964, and he stopped at every station of the cross. Speaking to the Southern Republican Conference, he commented on his old fight against the conservatives: "I don't think the ideological differences were as important as they seemed then, or as some of us made them out to be." In December 1973, Nelson took the last step toward freeing himself to seek the presidency by resigning the governorship he had held longer than any other man in modern New York history.

Trying to assess the impact of the Rockefeller years in New York was like trying to analyze the aftereffects of a tornado. On coming to the governorship, Nelson had quickly grasped that there were two kinds of money available from the taxpayers: money for social services and money for construction. It was the second type that interested him. Like his father, he was intrigued by the sight of buildings going up, especially buildings that bore his stamp. (When someone at a testimonial dinner once praised Junior as a great philanthropist, Nelson had smiled and answered: "Father was a development man . . . an all-out exponent of economic growth.") And he realized that this kind of money had greater velocity and passed through more hands than social service money, reaching more of the people likely to help him in organizing a power base in the state. Construction money, as one person noted, could act "like a shot of cortisone on New York's metabolism." Never mind that too much cortisone might weaken the defenses of the body politic, as it could the human body. On coming to the governorship, Nelson had assumed that he wouldn't be in Albany long enough to face the consequences.

His administration started out with flair and innovation; the conspicuous and well-publicized successes would make his early years in Albany seem a model for what an imaginative and activist executive might accomplish. One of his first acts as governor had been to appoint a committee to study higher education. Its report concluded that if something were not done immediately, students would soon be unable to obtain a quality education. Nelson began a unique program that coupled upgrading of academic facilities with a massive building expansion.

Fearful that the voters, already chafing at spiraling government costs and rising taxes (which he had pledged to hold down) might reject the bond issue (the usual means of financing such a project), he cast about for an alternative. The plan he came up with was conceived by a man then known best as an attorney with the blue-ribbon firm of Nixon, Rose, Mudge—a specialist in municipal bonds named John N. Mitchell. The idea was to set up a semi-independent agency, the State University Construction Fund, authorized to issue construction bonds with little more than the state's "moral pledge" behind them. Tuition, fees, and all other university receipts would then be used to pay the debt service. From the governor's office it seemed to be the modern equivalent of El Dorado: something for nothing. ("The greatest system ever invented," Nelson exulted.) The cost would be over $1 billion, yet none of it would appear to come out of the taxpayer's pocket. And clearly it was a case in which the ends justified the means: in 1958 the New York State University system had 38,000 students attending classes on 28 campuses. By the time Nelson left office, after a decade of his unusual financing scheme, there were 246,000 students attending a vastly expanded and upgraded university system comprising 71 campuses.

After this, Rockefeller announced a major new program every year. He may have had to renege on his ironclad pledge not to raise taxes, but to New Yorkers—initially at least—the results seemed worth the cost. They helped sponsor his ambitious legislative program by voting for huge bond issues and applauding those cases when he bypassed them by setting up authorities. The state's economy, which was sluggish when he took office, started to boom. Everywhere there was evidence of the growth and progress he had promised. New state office buildings, mental hospitals, schools—the New York landscape was filled with construction projects. He built roads as well as buildings. He lost out on the Hudson Expressway, but by the time he ran for his third term in 1966, his television commercials could claim that, if the highways he had built were set end to end, they would stretch from New York to Hawaii and back again. In urban transportation, he campaigned for a $3.5 billion bond issue to provide financing for a newly created Metropolitan Transportation Authority, which would take control over all subways and bus routes in New York City, as well as bridges, the Long Island Railroad, and parts of the New Haven and Penn Central, all of which he predicted would be upgraded and expanded into the best transportation system in the world.

In housing (again relying on the advice of John Mitchell), Rockefeller created a Housing Finance Agency early in his first administration and made $1 billion available to it to stimulate middle- and low-income housing. Eight years later he replaced it with the Urban Development Corporation (UDC). Its enabling bill had been bottled up in the state legislature until Martin Luther King's assassination. Nelson flew back from King's funeral to make a plea for the UDC, and it was swept into existence with broad powers allowing it to do everything from condemning and razing old structures to overriding local building codes and zoning laws and undertaking the construction of apartment projects or new towns. In 1965, partly in response to adverse publicity generated by the Storm King affair, Nelson sponsored another ambitious program with a $1 billion Pure Waters Act. The funds were to allow local governments to build modern sewage disposal plants and thus clean up the state's waterways in six years.

The "all out war on drugs and addiction" he declared in 1966 also had a building component. When he created the Narcotic Addiction Control Commission (NACC), the idea was that offenders should receive compulsory treatment and civil commitment. Once committed, the addicts were to be sent to one of the dozens of facilities the NACC was slated to build. In a sense, the program would rise or fall on these facilities, for two-thirds of its budget went into their construction.

Some began to complain that buildings were not programs; by the mid-1960s many wondered about the real benefits Nelson's expensive efforts were buying. State Comptroller Arthur Levitt was worried for a different reason, and he began to issue periodic warnings about the state's fiscal condition. "All of these financing schemes," he said of Nelson's unorthodox techniques for financing his campaign of public works, "have been adopted in the name of necessary public projects, but all of them are in derogation of the right of the people to vote upon the indebtedness of the state of New York."

What Nelson had done was to break off functions of state government and set them up as quasi-autonomous units, selecting their administrators and the interests that would be represented on their boards of directors. To head the MTA,

Nelson appointed his secretary, William J. Ronan, who had been a university professor before joining the Rockefeller campaign in 1958. Not only had Nelson made Ronan's political career, but, as would be learned later at the vice-presidential hearings, he raised him up socially and economically as well, providing him with personal capital of over half a million dollars. At the head of the Urban Development Corporation he placed Edward J. Logue, an urban planner from Boston who was also personally indebted to the governor for a huge cash sum. The creation of these authorities was in effect a personal appropriation of the functions of government by the most powerful political figure in the state since the bygone era of Boss Tweed.

Yet the event that came to symbolize the Rockefeller governorship was not a program but a giant complex of buildings—the Albany Mall. Shortly after taking office in 1959, Nelson decided that the area between the Executive Mansion and the state capitol buildings—a run-down site inelegantly called "the Gut"—might be made into what he called "the most spectacularly beautiful seat of government in the world." The project was to cost $250 million, but Rockefeller (who had his mind's eye on Brasilia, the capital being carved *de novo* out of the Amazon jungle) assured his constituents that it would be "the greatest thing to happen to this country in the last hundred years." Fearing they might not agree, however, he was reluctant to submit the mall to a referendum. He adopted an unusual financing arrangement suggested by Albany Mayor Erastus Corning II (whose firm was to write the insurance on the buildings): bonds would be floated not by the state, but by the county of Albany; after construction, the state would rent the buildings from the county, with rental payments amortizing the bonds in some thirty years. (Corning later noted that Rockefeller went for the plan "like a trout for a fly.")

This plan was a chance, perhaps the final one, for Nelson and his old friend Wally Harrison to collaborate once again. As the two men stood looking at the construction site a half-mile long and a quarter-mile wide, they visualized a final tribute to a relationship that had begun thirty years earlier with Rockefeller Center. What they saw was an imperial capital for the Empire State: a 44-story office tower, four identical 23-story agency buildings, buildings for the legislature and the juidiciary, a headquarters for the motor vehicles department, a museum and library. The building plans called for flying buttresses, splayed columns, sheaths of Italian marble, and other epic devices. The major architectual innovation was to be the interconnection of the structures through the Main Platform, a five-level plaza with meeting complexes, reflecting pools, restaurants, parking areas, and a bomb shelter.

The mall was more than a series of structures, more even than a state capital. It was part of Nelson Rockefeller's apocalypse, another indication of the large hungers rumbling in the pit of his being that he tried to satisfy first with his grandiose plans for global organization, then for the cold war and an arms race, and finally with millions of tons of concrete and glass.

Yet the mall was an ambivalent symbol. If its scope showed the extent of Nelson's vaulting imagination, its implementation came to stand for the forces of gravity that inevitably pulled that imagination to the ground. What was to be his final tribute to himself became just another of the occasions conspiring to inform against him. It was as if his personal demon had been loosed in the ground breaking ceremonies.

Long before construction on the mall began, Nelson's own planning commission had predicted grave difficulties, noting that among other things there was not enough skilled labor in the area to complete it. From the outset, the project was hindered by the odd state administrative procedure whereby the contracts for each individual structure were let to different contractors, who in turn made dozens of subcontracts, with the results that there was little in the way of overall coordination and workers were often stumbling over each other and competing for materials and machinery. As construction finally got under way, it was discovered that the original designs (some based on drawings and dimensions Nelson himself had hurriedly scratched on paper cocktail napkins when seized by some idea, later relaying the results to Harrison) were inadequate. As they were revised, so were the buildings' estimated costs. (The museum and library, for instance, went from $52.6 million to $73.4 million.) There was also the problem of the grand architectural style chosen for the mall. The cost of the average Manhattan skyscraper was $35 per foot of usable space, but a structure like the mall's domed meeting center (nicknamed "the Egg") cost $263 per usable foot. Changes in the project seemed to embody Nelson's own priorities: acknowledgment that the mall had been trapped in an inflationary spiral caused him to eliminate the low-income housing project (which had been inserted into the plans as redeeming social merit to make up for the 3,000 families bulldozed from their homes before construction began), but the 13,000-square-foot bomb shelter stayed.

The mall had become bogged down in massive delays and slowdowns by the mid-1960s, at about the same time that Nelson's sense of destiny itself had encountered immovable obstacles on the national scene. The mall's completion had originally been set for some indeterminate point in the late sixties. By 1965, however, it had been rescheduled for 1971, later for 1972, and finally for 1976. Meanwhile the original estimate of $250 million skyrocketed: by 1965 the estimated price tag of the mall was revised to $400 million; in 1972 it was revised again to $850 million.

Even when the buildings finally did begin to take shape, New Yorkers were scornful of them, coining such names as "Instant Stonehenge," "The Hanging Gardens of Albany," "Rocky's Folly." (One critic said they smacked of "Stalinesque Moderne.") The *final* cost, according to a distressed announcement by the state comptroller's office, would be $1.2 billion. This was enough to build a high school in every school district of the state of New York—31 in the city of New York alone. It was eerily close to the total benefactions of the first John D. Rockefeller and John D. Rockefeller, Jr., given over the course of nearly one hundred years—now taken back in one daring raid by the leader of the third Rockefeller generation.

Nelson not only ignored the bitter criticism caused by the mall, he seemed to revel in it. Wallace Harrison tells of being with the governor in Albany during a press briefing about the mall: "I'll never forget it. Some reporter said something about him being a 'frustrated architect,' and Nelson paused for a minute, then gestured out the window at the mall and said, 'I'm not frustrated anymore.'" In November 1973, as one of his last acts before resigning, Nelson dedicated the yet unfinished capital city. Rebuking the lilliputian mentality that had criticized his dream, he said: "Mean structures build small vision. But great architecture reflects mankind at its true worth. We are creating a capital that expresses our faith in ourselves and our belief in the future."

Nelson may have had a pharaoh's faith in his future, yet as he left office the future of the state was doubtful. The programs that had begun during the balmy days of his governance were, like the mall, stacked up in various stages of incompletion and disillusionment, as it became clear that his massive building program was not only not a people program, it wasn't even a good building program. The $1 billion Pure Waters Act, which he had claimed would restore the state's waters in six years, had created large numbers of sewage treatment plants, but water quality itself had declined and revised estimates called for the goals of 1965 to be met in 1992 at a revised cost of $4.35 billion. In housing there had been 105,000 units built the year he took office; a decade later, after millions of dollars had been spent, 67,000 units a year were being built. Far from solving transportation problems through the MTA, things had grown worse: subways were dirtier and more dangerous than ever; shortly after Nelson predicted that it would "be a race between the Penn Central and the Long Island Railroad to see which is the best commuter train in the country," the one was bankrupt and the other was crippled by delays and charging higher fares per commuter mile than any other railroad in the world.

The accumulation of public debt to finance his schemes and the increased revenues required to pay for it had begun to build up a wall of taxpayer resistance. In the spring of 1971, when Rockefeller submitted an $8.5 billion budget (up a half-billion from the previous year, based on a projected tax increase of $1 billion), the legislature reacted by trimming his figures by half and forcing him to decree sweeping cuts in his programs. He accepted the rebuke only as a mandate to cut back on the state's welfare program by 10 percent.

In 1960 he had vetoed a bill establishing residency requirements for welfare recipients, citing "our state's heritage with its respect for the dignity and worth of each individual." Now, to cut the welfare bill, he introduced a residency requirement, even though the U.S. Supreme Court had ruled two years earlier that such requirements were unconstitutional. A 1970 report of the State Department of Social Services had indicated that "of the 1.8 million persons who received some type of assistance only about 6 percent were considered employable," yet Nelson made the center of his welfare "reform" package the requirement that "employable" welfare recipients seek work, requiring all redefined welfare recipients to report twice a month to the state employment offices. (In practice, the program failed to place significant numbers of recipients in jobs, but it managed to disqualify a much larger number from receiving welfare benefits.) Nelson even proposed a version of his grandfather's Ledger A for the poor, which he called the Incentives for Independence program. Under this program a family of four would receive a basic yearly payment of $2,400 instead of the current $3,900, but could then "earn" the remaining $1,500 by attending school, taking part in training programs, or participating in community improvement projects. The proposal was widely derided as "the Brownie point plan," and overwhelming opposition combined with the difficulties of administering it resulted in its redesign.

During nearly four terms in Albany, Rockefeller had repeatedly defended his increase of state expenditures as an effort to enhance what he called New York's "proud progressive tradition of services to our people." Yet the bulk of the monies he had spent had gone into monuments that had little relation to the pressing needs of New York's population. In the field of narcotics, his failure in this regard was perhaps even more vivid than in the construction debacle at Albany. The 1966 civil commitment law was a shambles; the Narcotic Addiction Control Commission was itself a travesty of its original intentions. By 1972, almost three-quarters of the $224 million it had spent had gone into the construction of residential facilities. Some of them never opened; those that did spent $30 million a year on payroll and had more employees than addicts, although only a tiny fraction of the employees were physicians and psychiatrists. Of 5,172 individuals treated and released under the NACC's compulsory treatment program, only 141 managed to stay drug-free at the end of a year and a half, which meant each cure had cost New Yorkers about $1.6 million.

In his 1973 state of the state message to the legislature, Rockefeller acknowledged that the program had been a failure, that despite the nearly $500 million spent on drug control during his years in office, heroin-related deaths had risen by 32 percent and drug use had reached "epidemic proportions." Yet if the compulsory commitment program of 1966 had struck many New Yorkers as an extremist measure, he now proposed to replace it with one that was if anything even more severe. Almost in the same breath as admitting the failure of the 1966 law, Nelson announced a new program based on giving mandatory life sentences for persons convicted of possessing or selling drugs, with "bounties" paid to informants whose tips led to drug convictions.*

As Nelson left office, draconian drug laws and other stiff rhetoric could hardly divert attention from the fact that the state was in moral and fiscal chaos; its political functions had atrophied and its future was weighed down under the burden of financial obligations that would tie its legislators' hands indefinitely. New Yorkers were already paying dearly for his public and private works—those they had approved at the ballot box and those on which they never had a chance to vote. Taxes of one kind or another had gone up in 8 of his 15 years in office, although his earliest and firmest pledge to New York voters had been that there would be no increases. Taxes amounted to $94 per person when he came to power, $460 per person when he left. When he came to Albany, there was no state sales tax; now there was one of 4 percent; the 3-cent cigarette tax had jumped to 15 cents a pack; a 4-cent-a-gallon state gasoline tax had doubled.

The state budget had increased by 300 percent, but the state debt had increased by 400 percent. The semipublic authorities Nelson had brought into wide use now operated, according to State Comptroller Arthur Levitt, "on a scale so massive that, in some instances, they overshadow the fiscal operations of the state itself." By the time Nelson left office, these authorities had an outstanding debt of $10 billion, with $50 million a year required merely to pay the interest.

Things had come to a standstill. It was as if Nelson had taken a huge mortgage on New York's future to finance the expensive therapy required by what was now widely recognized as his "edifice complex." There had been no new or innovative programs since his fourth inauguration. Even his special pride, higher education, had felt the pinch. (Nelson had announced gloomily in 1971: "The problem of financing

---

*Widely criticized as an "Archie Bunker law," this proposal raised even the eyebrows of *The New York Times*, which until Attica had backed almost all of Rockefeller's ambitions for the state and the nation. (An editorial stated: "Rockefeller's simplistic, lock-em-up-for-life-for-everyone proposal is a gross disservice, making adoption of a responsible program less likely than ever.") Yet, as with Attica, Rockefeller's polls of people across the nation showed strong support. On May 8, 1973, after whipping the plan through the legislature with the incentive of 100 new judgeships (which, according to one legislative analyst, "had a lot of Democrats drooling in the aisles"). Nelson signed it into law, taking the occasion to vaunt over "the strange alliance of ... political opportunists and misguided soft liners who joined forces and tried unsuccessfully to stop this program."

and operating higher education . . . has continued to intensify. The fiscal plight of private institutions worsens while
funding for public higher education is jeopardized by the general fiscal crisis.")

It was all like a huge house of cards built only to fall. Nelson blamed the federal government for the state's fiscal
chaos. Noting that New Yorkers got only fourteen cents returned from their federal tax dollar in services, he went to
Washington and became a persistent witness at congressional
hearings into revenue sharing. Yet even here he was trapped
in his own history, which prohibited him from seeking a real
solution, for while he favored transferring services provided
by the federal government to the state, he opposed any cuts
in the defense budget—which accounted for most of the tax
dollar and which he, as much as any living American, had
helped elevate to its outrageous levels.

Nelson displayed his new hard line in a series of town
meetings convened throughout the state in 1972. Mobbed by
heckling crowds attacking every aspect of his governorship,
Rockefeller fought back like the seasoned political street
fighter he had become, spitting back insults at his detractors
and appearing to take perverse pleasure in the truculence and
confusion in appearances caused. Journalist William Kennedy
captured Rockefeller at bay in his reply to a young radical
who, having taken the microphone during a meeting on Long
Island, had proceeded to harangue the governor and his
family: "OK, wise guy, now let me finish, OK? Thanks, sure,
beautiful, beautiful. . . . I happen to believe in open discussion. That's why we're having this meeting. . . . I broke
ground at Stony Brook. . . . Only because of this administration do *you* have a chance to get a college education. Look at
me, please. I'm talking to you. . . . I deplore what you said,
but I fight to the death for your right to say it. . . . You
wouldn't be in college in any other country. . . . You ought to
be glad you live in a democracy. . . ."

Yet it was not just radicals, Gay Libbers, and Right-to-Lif-
ers who were disenchanted with Nelson. When they had a
chance, the mass of New Yorkers were increasingly voting no
on Rockefeller. Two transportation bond issues he had
deemed especially vital—one for $2.5 billion in 1971 and one
for $3.5 billion two years later—were roundly rejected by the
electorate. The machinery seemed to be slipping out of his
control. Even institutions like the Museum of Modern Art
that had always been under his family's and his own control

began to get obstreperous. At a 1971 exhibit of kinetic sculpture, one of the pieces was a whimsical voting machine designed by sculptor Hans Haake: people passing by could pause, look, and then cast a vote *against* the governorship of Nelson Rockefeller.

In December 1973, Nelson announced that he was resigning from the governorship before the expiration of his term. By resigning when he did, Nelson accomplished several things at once. He spared himself from having to run for reelection in 1974 and defend his record in New York, although his control over New York politics was by now so complete that he probably didn't have to worry. To Lieutenant Governor Malcolm Wilson—described by Albany Mayor Erastus Corning as a man who had spent fifteen years "playing second fiddle in a one man band"—he gave the chance to run as an incumbent. He nonetheless still maintained control over the Republican state organization and delegation for the 1976 convention. Finally, he freed himself to spend the next three years gaining national visibility and meeting potential delegates across the country as chairman of two important federal commissions.

One was the National Commission on Water Quality. Established in 1972 with the budget of $2.5 million, it had a mandate to investigate the implementation of water pollution control standards and to report in two years. The other and more important was the Commission on Critical Choices for Americans. It had begun as a state commission studying New York's planning for the future, but as the convulsions within the Republican party gave Nelson new hope for 1976, he persuaded President Nixon to give it federal standing and a new mandate to report on the nation's prospects as it entered its third century. He hoped for federal money too, but when the Senate Appropriations Committee killed an initial request for $1 million of the estimated $6.5 million budget, Nelson began raising money himself. He gave $1 million to the tax-deductible Third Century Corporation and got Laurance to contribute a like amount, an indirect way of circumventing the new law that a candidate for federal office can accept only $100,000 in contributions of his own money and his family's.

The efforts of the commission would involve an encyclopedic technique reminiscent of the Panel Studies. The inquiry was to be broken primarily into three fields—growth and resources, individuals and institutions, and international security—with each field studied by a panel consisting of old Rockefeller advisers like Edward Teller and new faces like Bess Myerson and Vice-President Gerald Ford. Hired consultants to the commission included former White House strategists like Vietnam hawk W. W. Rostow and social policy specialist Daniel Moynihan; the panel on international studies was headed by Nancy Maginnes Kissinger, Nelson's longtime staffer. In all, 139 aides were hired for the first year of the commission's work (at a cost of slightly under $1 million), constituting an array of talent and expertise on major policy areas that dwarfed the President's personal staff and anything he might wish to assemble without extraordinary congressional authorization.

Just as the Panel Studies had set the guidelines for the course of government policy when they had appeared a decade earlier, so Nelson felt this new commission could fill the vacuum that had developed as a result of the cumulative crises and conflicts of the sixties, the doubts that afflicted the country's sense of itself and its global mission, and the crippling of its leadership as a result of the Watergate scandals. The commission's goals were stated in even more cosmic terms than its predecessor's had been:

> A review of the fundamental philosophical and moral considerations of man and his institutions. . . . A projection of present trends in the U.S. and other areas of the world to 1976 and 1989, including political, economic and military developments. . . . Development of alternative conceptual approaches to deal with these emerging forces. . . . New concepts relating to the structure of our federal system and our domestic and international institutions.

The idea was that, as Nelson was now free of Albany, he could crisscross the country in his capacity as commission chairman, holding public hearings and allowing potential convention delegates to catch a glimpse of his new conservative ideas and image. And by July 4, 1976, when the nation was celebrating its two-hundredth anniversary and Republicans were getting ready to select their standard-bearer, Rockefeller's commission would deliver the first part of its report prescribing a "way out" of what Americans had grown used to as their perennially changing and deepening national crisis.

The scenario might have been scripted in Hollywood. There was no margin for error; everything depended on Nixon's success in stone-walling through the Watergate investigations and surviving to the end or almost the end of his second term so that Gerald Ford could not establish himself as a legitimate national figure. (As late as February 11, 1974, Nelson was still defending this position, telling journalists that those who would "harass and drive a President out of office by resignation would not only circumvent but abrogate the Constitution of the United States.") He had been identified as a wrecker so long that he could no longer take his chances in mounting an insurance campaign for the nomination at some future time. For Ronald Reagan, perhaps, such a campaign could be interpreted as an exercise in conviction; in Rockefeller it would only rattle old skeletons in his political closet. As it became clear that Nixon's days were numbered, Nelson decided to seize the main chance and began lobbying vigorously to fill the soon-to-be-vacant number-two position. After Nixon resigned, the newly inaugurated Gerald Ford held a *pro forma* consultation with party leaders and surprised nobody by announcing that Nelson Rockefeller was his choice as Vice-President.

When the call came on August 21, Nelson was vacationing in the Seal Harbor house Wally Harrison had designed for him in 1939. Built of wood and stone, the house perched on a spit of land above the water; below, a weathered boathouse containing five boats (ranging from the 65-foot yawl, *The Nirvana*, to a rubber lifeboat) and a study hung with Picasso tapestries. Along the beach was a cavity hollowed out of the rocks allowing waves to lap in and fill a heated swimming pool.

The summons was not unexpected. Nelson had managed to stay on the periphery of the scandals rocking Washington. His long career in national politics and especially foreign affairs balanced the new President's obvious parochialism. His "progressivism" would be a counterweight to Ford's ultraconservative voting record in Congress. Ironically, his wealth was perhaps his greatest asset, apparently putting him above suspicion in the "post-Watergate" morality.

On August 22 he posed for photographers on the sandy beach below his house. After telling reporters how pleased he was, he and Happy went across the bay to join Douglas Dillon and his wife for lunch with David and Peggy at *their* Seal Harbor house.

Nelson's acceptance of the vice-presidential nomination was oddly anticlimactic. How many times had he claimed that he was "not cut out to be Number Two"? How often had he scoffed at the idea that he, a Rockefeller, should become "standby equipment"? Yet his moment of truth had come; he knew this was his last, best shot at the prize he otherwise had little chance of winning. This way he would at least have a seat at the table where the high-stakes game was going on and be in a position to take advantage of the country's volatile politics.

If he had not learned humility over the past fifteen years, he had at least become more of a realist about party affairs. He knew he was reduced to taking what he could get now and hoping that the nation's economic crisis, a lack of stomach for the pressures of the presidency, or something else (soon the illness of his wife, Betty, would be added to the list) might persuade the former Michigan congressman to bow out in two years, leaving his loyal Vice-President on the inside track. Even if Ford did seek another term, there was still 1980. When one of the reporters who had flocked to Seal Harbor noted in passing that he would then be seventy-two, Rockefeller summoned a fey look and reminded listeners of the advanced ages his grandfather and father had attained, noted the Golda Meir and Konrad Adenauer had both governed well into their seventies, and added that he himself fully expected to live to be a hundred.

If there was any surprise at all over Nelson's designation as Vice-President, it was that the explosion anticipated from the Republican party's right wing never came. Barry Goldwater noted in passing that perhaps it would be wise for Rockefeller to be omitted from the 1976 ticket if Ford sought the nomination; but the pragmatic sense that the party was in shambles—the fall of Agnew and the guilt of Attorney General Mitchell in particular having drawn the right wing into the Watergate cauldron—counseled a discreet silence. There was also Nelson's own political shift over the years. The fact that those who had howled in execration when he stood before them in San Francisco in 1964 now found no plausible reason for rejecting him was a testament to the kind of man he had become.

In his first days in Washington, he barreled through the Capitol, shaking hands and exchanging pleasantries, lunching with Henry Kissinger and Soviet Ambassador Dobrynin, jousting with members of the press who accosted him on the subject of his family's great wealth, and making visits to legislators in anticipation of the beginning of confirmation hearings. Moving swiftly in his rolling, seaworthy walk down the halls of Congress, pausing to stick his head into each congressman's office (except for those inhabited by Ogden Reid and others high on his personal enemies list), he reminded aides of the old campaigner who had plunged joyously into the streets of Manhattan. Seeing Peter Rodino in the corridor, he went up and grasped him, saying loudly, "Hiya, Pete! I want to tell you how grateful I am for what you've done for the country," then dashed off for his next appointment.

The chairman of the House impeachment hearings, recalling Rockefeller's strategic silence throughout the Watergate inquiry, shook his head and rolled his eyes in disbelief. He said to one of the newsmen for whose benefit the little charade had evidently been staged, "Did you hear *that*?"

As so often in the past, however, Nelson's euphoria about his political career was not shared by family members. Laurance, as always, was an exception, and David was able to accept it reluctantly as part of the necessary burden of his family's stewardly responsibility. But the rest of the Rockefellers were not very pleased; many were not even particularly proud. For the Cousins—most of whom were actively opposed to Nelson and his politics—the nomination meant only an annoying alteration of their life-style. They must now become conscious of security (the Secret Service had soon contacted them all) in a way that further emphasized the vast distance between them and others, a distance they had spent much of their lives trying to narrow. It had been one thing for Nelson to be elected to office; it was quite another to accept an appointment that meant submitting to a nationally televised grilling which would inevitably involve the rest of them, their careers and riches. As one aide in Room 5600 put it, "There is a strong feeling among the Rockefeller family that they want their privacy. And they would rather that Nelson was not Vice-President if the central trusts were exposed."

Yet it was with relish for exactly these details that the capital waited impatiently for hearings to begin. Nelson was not just another rich man like John Kennedy—he was part of a vast agglomeration of wealth and influence. As *New York Times* Washington correspondent William Shannon wrote, "Not since Lady Godiva rode naked through the streets of Coventry have the inhabitants of any town itched to see something usually hidden as people here now desire to see the extent of the Rockefeller fortune." But those who hoped the hearings would become a significant inquiry into the way the premier family in America used its immense wealth and power to influence national policy soon found that Nelson's strategy was to give the senators just enough hint of his family's fortune to awe them into submission.

Dressed in one of his inconspicuously elegant dark blue pinstriped suits, he sauntered into the Senate caucus room on the morning of September 23, occasionally breaking out of the flying wedge of aides to grab at some legislator or friend with the two-handed handshake he uses when he wants to emphasize the warmth of his feelings. Sitting in the same red leather chair where witnesses little more than a year earlier had begun the long death of the Nixon presidency, he spread a jumble of scrawled notes to himself on the green table, checked with aides as to what files they carried, and smiled at a phrase in Senator Jacob Javits's introduction: "If you gave a civil service examination for President, at the head of the class would be Nelson Rockefeller." The only sign of nervousness was the speed with which he attacked the carafe of water in front of him, emptying it in the first two hours of his testimony; yet there was no hesitancy in the 72-page history of the Rockefeller family that stood as his opening statement.

He had largely written it himself, using the family archives for summaries of information about the achievements of his forebears. In his version they were part of a pantheon of American virtues. His paternal grandmother's family, the Spelmans, stood for racial justice. His maternal grandparents, the Aldriches, had roots that went back to the *Mayflower*. Gread-Grandfather William Avery Rockefeller, the bigamous cancer quack, became in Nelson's presentation "a gregarious, adventuresome, and fearless man who worked hard and paid his debts promptly. Among other things he got interested in botanic medicine, the selling of which occupied an increasing amount of his time." The first John D. was a benign, diligent man who created Standard Oil and then spent the rest of his life giving "help to those who were in need." Then there was Junior, a man who followed what Nelson called the "family ethic," which, he went on to define, meant devoting oneself "to the service and well-being of others throughout the world."

It was the Rockefellers' money that people were primarily

interested in. The figures had always been held on to as tightly as classified government secrets. How much exactly had Senior left Junior? What had he done with it? How much did the Brothers have? What had they done with it? How much of the American economy did they now control with their purse strings?

The family had always avoided rendering an accounting not only because to do so would be to violate the most guarded principles of individual privacy, but primarily because it would involve giving up some intangible yet essential part of their power, draining a crucial element of mystery from it and robbing the myth of part of its animating spirit. Yet this secrecy now stood as an obstacle in Nelson's way, and he did not hesitate to sacrifice it. As he told the senators, "This myth about the power which my family exercises needs to be brought out into the light. . . . It just does not exist . . . I have to tell you I do not wield economic power."

All during the week before he began his testimony, Rockefeller had been chuckling to reporters who asked him about his personal fortune, hinting that they should be prepared to be disappointed in their extravagant expectations. One unconvincingly low figure of $33 million had been leaked. Now it was time for the truth. After finishing his historical sketch, Nelson turned to the financial data. Junior had gotten $465 million from Senior. Of this he had put $240 million into the Chase in trusts for his sons and grandchildren. Nelson's own share of these trusts, which had grown huge over the years, was $116 million in a depressed market. (The '34 Trust had, in fact, dropped $20 million in two months.) In addition, he itemized $62 million in personal assets, which was in the main made up of his huge art collection ($33 million), real estate ($11 million), and securities ($12 million); added to the trusts, this made a total of almost $179 million. Later, an IRS audit would raise the value of his real estate, and his total fortune would then stand at $218 million.

It was a phenomenal sum by most standards. Senator Byrd calculated that these assets—which he mistakenly raised from $179 million to $182.5 million—amounted to $1 a minute for every minute since 1627. Yet by other standards it was disappointing, for it was dwarfed by the billion-dollar personal fortunes of a J. Paul Getty, Howard Hughes, or H. Ross Perot. (Nelson's brother David was often heard to complain to intimates that he and his brothers weren't really rich when compared to people like Greek shipping magnates Aristotle Onassis and Stavros Niarchos.) The Rockefellers had a lot of money, but it certainly wasn't equal to the reputation for riches it carried; nor was it enough to control the economy in the way it was alleged that they did. This became even more evident (and the revelation even more disappointing) as Nelson went on to describe the current state of the family's holdings in Standard Oil.

In the TNEC hearings of 1937, the first and last time an effort was made to determine the ownership of the American economy, it was disclosed that between them the Rockefellers held from 8 to 16 percent of the various Standard companies' stock. Nelson now pointed out, "The total holdings of all the living descendants of my father, both outright and in trusts, do not amount to more than 2.06 percent of any of these companies." (The exact figures were 1.0 percent of Exxon, 2.06 percent of Cal Standard, 1.75 percent of Mobil, and 0.23 percent of Indiana Standard.) He continued, "None of these descendants of my father serve on the boards of any of the oil companies and we have no control of any kind over the management or policies of any of them." As an added caveat, he revealed the family's share in the Chase, where the entire family holdings amounted to 2.54 percent of the outstanding stock. (They were still, in the case of the oil companies and the bank, however, the possessors of the largest blocs of private stock.)

One important reason for the decline of the family holdings in the stock of the Standard companies was the economic impact of the tax laws, which made it almost profitable for them to make their philanthropic gifts in the form of Standard shares. The stocks had appreciated more than ten times over the years. Thus, if they sold such a stock, which might have cost $10 originally, they would have to pay a capital gains tax on $100. If, however, they gave away the same stock, they could take a $100 tax deduction and avoid capital gains taxes altogether. They would end up making a gift worth ten times the original cost to the family while receiving a tenfold tax break into the bargain. As a result, Rockefeller gifts were commonly in the form of shares of the companies that their grandfather had built.

Even had they been more anxious to retain their Standard shares than they in fact were, their economic hold on the Standard companies would have eroded as a result of the large underlying trend in the control of the American economy, which passed from individual to institutional investors in the postwar years. (The Rockefeller trust funds were themselves no exception, being voted not by the family but by the Chase.) In 1974 the top three shareholders in Mobil Oil—the second-largest of the Standard companies—were three New York banks (Bankers Trust, 6.1 percent; Chase Manhattan, 5.2 percent; and Morgan Guaranty, 2.9 percent). New York's "Big Seven" banks controlled a total of 17 percent of the shares of Mobil, or more than the Rockefeller family and its foundations held in 1937.

Nelson's disclosures exploded the myth of the family's megawealth and its vast portfolio power. Yet the point was not, as he implied, that they lacked the power attributed to them, but that this power lay elsewhere. Its nature was far more potent and complex than indicated by net worth. In a striking consensus of views, Wall Streeters interviewed by *The New York Times* in the wake of Nelson's statement agreed that the Rockefeller portfolio was only the merest tip of the iceberg. "If you go just on his holdings of stock," commented one investment banker talking about the family influence, "it's piddling. But let's face it, the Rockefellers are the Rockefellers." Another financier observed, "In family power in the United States, there is nothing that even faintly resembles the Rockefellers. They have tremendous power."

The nature of the power showed how successful Junior had been in his attempt to consolidate the dynasty. It did not spring from money, but from the unique network of Rockefeller institutions and associations, beginning in the economy but now stretching across all the political, cultural, and intellectual boundaries of the national enterprise. As a result of Junior's colossal investment in diverse fields and institutions and the Brothers' lifetime of activities in an even more kaleidoscopic range of endeavors, there was hardly a significant arena of decision making in which their employees, protégés, or institutions did not exert a major influence. Even the Rockefeller Foundation, in which they were no longer paramount, was run by men they had had a hand in appointing and who had experienced a profound sense of obligation to the family for its largesse. If the underlying trend of power in the nation was from individuals to institutions, the dynasty Junior had created was enmeshed in the syndication of such networks and gave the Brothers an unrivaled influence in national affairs. The Mellons and a few other American families may have been richer, but among the power elite whose rule stretched from Wall Street to Washington the Rockefellers were without peer.

Yet no one on the Senate Rules Committee could (or would) pierce the veil. West Virginia Senator Robert Byrd, alone in appearing not totally awed by Nelson, attempted to get the witness to be more candid about his family's power, but the line of questioning was spiked by Senate Minority Leader Hugh Scott, who acted almost as Rockefeller's attorney on the committee. His support made Nelson even bolder in his evasions of the issues at hand. When pressed by Senator Byrd about potential conflicts of interest should he be confirmed, he began by denying the existence of a "Rockefeller empire" and proceeded to confuse the issue with a lecture on the American system itself. The free enterprise system had made America "the greatest nation in the world," he said. "This system is not an empire. It is a democracy."

This was the characteristic way Nelson dealt with the conflict-of-interest question when it reappeared throughout the hearings. He would simply assert that he loved his country, or that he would take an oath of office and this in itself would dispose of the issue. Did the senators mean to be so discourteous as to imply that he who had dedicated his life to public service could intend anything venal or self-interested in fulfilling his duties? Rockefeller's assumption of a posture of almost divine rectitude and innocence made the questions about power appear increasingly defensive and apologetic. After several frustrating attempts to establish that the accession to the vice-presidency must result in a vast concentration of Rockefeller power, Senator Byrd finally reduced his interrogation to a modest effort to pry from Nelson the admission that the combining of his great economic wealth and the great political power of the office would mean "a far greater power" for him than "for the average occupant whose financial means is much less than yours." Yet Nelson's reaction was so obtuse that he answered even this in the negative. From that point it would have been embarrassing to proceed, and no one was willing to cause embarrassment to the meticulously courteous figure before them. The issue of power and its potential for conflicts was left behind, everyone realizing that the Rockefellers' conflicts of interest were so pervasive and in a sense unintentional that they exemplified the conflicts inherent in the system itself.

At the end of the first day of testimony, Nelson gathered up his papers, put his silver pen in his pocket, and told reporters, "I thought it was great," as the television klieg lights went off and he pushed his way out of the room. The next two days went equally well. He presented his family as people so deeply involved in their individual pursuits that they had no time to come together for the sort of planning for control that only the paranoid could assume they did. In addition to their relatively "small" holdings in the Chase Bank, the Standard companies, and some other industries, and except for IBEC and some of Laurance's venture capital companies, there was no enterprise in which they held more than 2 percent. With Republican Senators Scott and Marlow Cook running interference, Nelson was not only able to fend off questions concerning individual and family conflicts of interest, but also such suggestions of failure as the handling of Attica, the virtual bankruptcy of the state of New York, and other matters involving his record. Questioning on his commitments in the field of foreign affairs, the most crucial part of his political personality, was almost nil. When Senator Mark Hatfield asked him about the CIA (with which he had been involved since at least the Eisenhower administration) and specifically the propriety of its intervention in Chile, Nelson produced a yellow-jacketed book called the *Art of War*, a 2,500-year-old Chinese classic which, he said, contained "a whole chapter on secret agents." The message enfolded in his response seemed to be that spies, like the rich, ye have with ye always. He endorsed the CIA's activities in Chile and elsewhere: "I assume they were done in the national interest." Answers like this, in addition to his backing increased aid to the Thieu regime in Vietnam, later led *New York Times* editor Tom Wicker to recall his record as "the coldest Warrior of all" in a column charging that the perfunctory, almost apologetic, questioning in this area of foreign policy was one of the major failures of the hearings.

By September 15 the senators had finished. Immediately after Ford had nominated him, White House and congressional mail had been overwhelmingly opposed to the choice, but the only noteworthy opposition during the hearings came from Angela Davis, the Liberty Lobby (which remained convinced that the Rockefellers had bankrolled the international Communist conspiracy), and Right-to-Life groups still seething over his veto of the repeal of New York's liberalized abortion law. This strange mélange seemed only to underline his inevitability.

Feeling he was as good as confirmed, Nelson took a quick vacation following the Senate hearings. He could not really chart a campaign for imperiled Republican candidates in the upcoming election, much as he would have liked to, but he could be a national presence. On October 4 his entourage boarded his 18-seat $4.5 million Grumman Gulfstream 2 jet to fly west for speeches at Brigham Young University and in San Francisco. For some members of the press, it was the first chance to see the style that had always made New York newsmen glad to be assigned to a Rockefeller campaign. When you traveled with Rocky, you traveled first class. The jet's interior was fitted out like a living room, with couches and reclining chairs; a steward pressed drinks on the passengers from a well-stocked bar and meals from a small kitchen. The Grumman flew 115 miles an hour faster than commercial jets, and the Secret Service agent who checked out the plane pronounced it "in better shape than Air Force One."

It was while Nelson was on the West Coast that disquieting leaks began to appear. New material had turned up in investigations by Congress, the IRS, and the FBI (which would ultimately have 300 agents on the Rockefeller case). In quick order it was revealed that audits showed he owed nearly $1 million in back taxes; that in 1970 he had gotten his brother Laurance to put $60,000 into a dummy corporation to finance a derogatory biography of gubernatorial opponent Arthur Goldberg by right-wing columnist Victor Lasky; that he and his family had spent some $20 million on his political career alone, not to mention contributions to other candidates; and most damning of all, that he had made loans or gifts (or some combination of the two) to public officials totaling several millions including $50,000 to Henry Kissinger, $250,000 to New York Urban Development Corporation head Ed Logue, and $625,000 to MTA chief William Ronan.

On October 20 Nelson's staff released a list of his philanthropies over the preceding seventeen years. It was a use of the philanthropic gesture which his grandfather would have approved, yet the total of $24.7 million illustrated how diminished charitable activity had become in the family over the years. The list itself hardly showed a broad-gauged interest in the well-being of mankind. About 70 percent of Nelson's giving involved what were basically gifts to himself, his family, and their institutional extensions, including AIA, Jackson Hole Preserve, Inc., the Rockefeller Brothers Fund, the Museum of Primitive Art, the Museum of Modern Art, the Government Affairs Foundation (created by Nelson), the Third Century Corporation (the funding body of the Commission of Critical Choices), the state of New York (to landscape the grounds of the Executive Mansion, build a swimming pool, a pool house, and furnish the governor's quarters in the style to which he was accustomed).

The publication of the list and the illness of Happy served to dampen some of the mounting criticism against him, but he was worried. The news leaks breaking all around him had managed to levitate the unexorcised ghost of Watergate, and Nelson now found his nomination in trouble. Appealing personally to Committee Chairman Howard Cannon, he tried to get the hearings rolling again. He publicly demanded that the Senate Rules Committee reconvene to allow him a chance to answer charges against him. But he had to wait for the completion of the elections, and for a month he was like a beached whale. All he could do was wage a war of press releases, finally using even the news of Happy's operation to board the brief wave of sympathy Betty Ford's mastectomy had won the administration.

It was not until November 13, after the Republican debacle that had swallowed up his friend Malcolm Wilson and many others, that Nelson was back on the stand. Unruffled, his opening statement was to remind people that he was no Nixon operating in the back alleys of the system, but a member of the mainstream. "It is the unbought voice of the American people that here ultimately determines everything," he lectured.

> And when you are in office, true authority ... comes only through public support and the cooperation of all three branches under our separation of powers. ... That is what I have in mind when I say that the American constitutional system is the greatest arrangement ever devised for taming private power and moderating it into public authority. ... In corrupt or tyrannical systems, those with power rule and they rule corruptly or tyrannically. But here in America, it is the magic and majesty of our constitutional order that all of the sources of private power are in the long run tamed or domesticated. I believe my life demonstrates that my purpose has always been to serve the best interests of—and hopefully to earn the good opinion of—my fellow citizens by a devotion to public service.

Yet in the material that had emerged, the public got its first chance to see the approximate features of the real Rockefeller. The face was far different from that of the sophisticated charmer of the first round of hearings. The issues had been placed into a new framework. Nelson was no longer "clean as a hound's tooth," in the phrase so frequently used in the days following his selection by Gerald Ford. Nor could he continue to press the implication that the great advantage he offered over other politicians was that he was too rich to be bought. What had been shown was something more sinister (yet ironically less blame-worthy, according to current political standards) than being bought: being rich enough to do the buying. The information that had surfaced between the first and second rounds of hearings showed him to be as much a ruthless operator in politics as his grandfather had been in oil.

Of the charges that had been made against him, taxes were the easiest to field. In the past 10 years, he had paid more than $11 million. The additional $1 million the IRS now wanted came from exaggerated deductions for office expenses (including such items as the cost of the entire staff he had taken with him on his ill-fated Latin American tour) and for costs claimed for the management of his investments. In some sense it was palliated by Nixon's recent tax innovations. As *The New York Times* wrote: "In dollar terms, Mr. Nixon's big tax reducing devices were the illegal ones. It appears that the amounts Mr. Rockefeller saved in taxes by pushing right to the outer limits of the law—and possibly past them—were small compared with those he saved simply by using the special privileges that were available to him within the law." His financial statement indicated that he received about $1 million a year in interest on tax-exempt municipal bonds, some of them from the very authorities by which he had built his expensive public works monuments while governor. (His trust, held by the Chase, included $3,-254,000 worth of New York State Housing Authority bonds; $3.2 million worth of New York State Power Authority bonds; and $1 million worth of Port of New York Authority construction bonds.) Other rich men's deductions Nelson was able to use included his art and his Standard Oil stock. When he gave a painting to a museum (even though he usually stipulated it would remain in his possession for the rest of his life), he deducted the market value instead of the purchase price. Overall, *The New York Times* estimated that the true cost of his $24 million in charitable donations from 1957 to 1974 was closer to $8 million, since if he had not made them, in his tax bracket he would have paid somewhat over $16 million more in federal taxes.

The Lasky book may have been poorly researched and shoddily written, as Nelson claimed, yet it smacked of one of Donald Segretti's dirty tricks. Moreover, Nelson's denial of knowledge of the book was as much an issue as his commissioning of it. When first asked about it under oath by the FBI, he had denied any knowledge of or involvement with the biography. On October 10, after information leaked to the effect that he had indeed been involved, he issued a statement to the press again denying responsibility, this time blaming Laurance for backing the project in an excess of brotherly loyalty: "Evidently what happened was that my brother had agreed to participate as an investor in underwriting a book that was expected to sell well. . . . Had he only told me about it at the time, I would have been totally opposed to it and would have strongly advised against his participation in any form." In the same press release Laurance validated this statement to cover for his brother, although privately he had been upset by the attempt to make him a fall guy. He visited his daughter Lucy in Washington shortly after the announcement and (in her words) "appeared extremely downcast." He told her that he had not masterminded the Lasky book and promised that the blame would soon be taken from his shoulders. When he reappeared before the committee, Nelson issued a "clarifying" statement completely changing his position and admitting that it was actually he who had recommended Laurance make the investment in the book.

If it had been another man, the perjury and the lies might have been taken seriously. But when Nelson took the stand, he described the bewildering maze that had led to the "unfortunate" decision: how Jack Wells (Lasky's attorney and an old political operative of Nelson's) came to him with the proposal, was sent to family attorney Donal O'Brien, who got Laurance involved and then got J. R. Dilworth to set up the investment through a dummy corporation in Philadelphia. The message seemed to be that this was the way decisions got made in the rarefied atmosphere of Room 5600, where another man's perjury was a Rockefeller's bureaucratic snafu. After being led through that bureaucracy, the senators tired of the matter and gave up. When Arthur Goldberg appeared at the hearings to testify, Nelson rushed up to shake his hand

and said, "Thanks for coming." It was as if his former opponent had come to a Rockefeller testimonial dinner.

It was the question of political contributions that tended to contradict most dramatically Nelson's previous testimony that the economic power of his family was a myth. By his own figures, Nelson had contributed some $3,265,373 in his years in politics, much of it to himself. (To appreciate this figure it need only be pointed out that the entire Du Pont clan, whose legendary political power has made the state of Delaware into something like a wholly owned subsidiary, has spent just barely $3 million on political contributions during all of its seven generations.) Yet Nelson's own giving was just the beginning. Other family members had chipped in every four years (or every two when he was running for President) as if by prescribed tithe and regularly enough to refute Nelson's previous testimony that the family rarely acted in concert. In all, they had contributed something over $20 million, with JDR3 giving the least and Laurance the most, and with nearly $11 million coming from the Martha Baird Rockefeller trusts, which had been established under the Brothers' control to handle their stepmother's residual estate.

Yet it was the series of gifts and loans that most showed the Rockefeller style. When news of the several millions given to aides and operatives first broke, it conjured up visions of a Renaissance prince throwing bags of gold to his retainers and awarding small kingdoms to his liege lords. "Rockefeller benefactions to federal officials," editorialized *The New York Times*, ". . . are aspects of private government more appropriate to Florence in the days of Lorenzo the Magnificent than to democratic America." Although subjected to staff questioning, however, Nelson insisted these were the result rather of simple human decency stemming from the family's philanthropic ethic and the "American tradition" of sharing. He had been taught, he told the senators, that when he had a basket of apples and others did not, he ought to share his apples with them.

> My sole intent was to respond to cases of personal hardship, family need, or out of pure friendship. Whatever successes I may have had, in both public and private life, have been due to the character, brilliance and continuing sense of common purpose with those with whom I have been associated. What kind of human being would I be if, under the circumstances, I had not re-

turned their confidence, attention and commitment; if I
had not welcomed opportunities to be helpful to them in
their needs and problems.

As far as his penchant for lending money and then
canceling the debt was concerned, Rockefeller had another
bit of treacly sentiment for his audience: "I would like to just
recall that a large percentage of the American people say, either in the morning or the evening, the Lord's Prayer. And
the Lord's Prayer says: 'Forgive us our debts as we forgive
our debtors.' And I do think that has got some relevance
here."

From what he said, it might have seemed that the men he
had gathered around him had been victims of contagion or
disaster. Yet on the whole, they were not poor men. William
Ronan, for instance, was making over $100,000 a year while
getting the last of his hardship loans from Nelson. It was the
case of L. Judson Morhouse, however, that was most indicative of the puzzling and disquieting nature of Nelson's
largesse.

The relationship went far back—to 1958, when Morhouse,
as chairman of the State Republican Committee, played a key
role in getting Nelson the gubernatorial nomination. After he
was elected, Nelson lent Morhouse $100,000 for a business
investment and persuaded Laurance to lend him $49,000 to
buy some stock in a gas transmission company whose shares
would soon yield a $100,000 windfall profit when put on the
open market. Before the committee, the reason given for this
charity was that Morhouse was unable to make ends meet;
yet, between 1959 and 1963, he had made $231,000 as a lob-
byist in Albany.

In 1966 Morhouse was convicted of taking a bribe in a
scandal surrounding the State Liquor Authority. In 1970, after appeals were exhausted and he was about to start serving
a term in prison, Nelson pardoned him because he had terminal cancer; at the time of the hearings, nearly five years later,
Morhouse was still alive. In 1973, Nelson forgave him the
$100,000 he had lent him. This caused some to wonder what
it was Morhouse had done to deserve this loyalty and
whether the gift had played any role as hush money in the
Liquor Authority case. In any event, Morhouse managed to
get from Rockefeller what the Watergate burglars were never
quite able to extract from Nixon: a full pardon and a cash
payoff.

The discussion in the hearings revolved around the question of what exactly Nelson had gotten from Morhouse and the others to whom he had made immense loans and gifts, and whether this largesse put them on call should he ask for favors afterward. Yet the hearings never really penetrated to the deeper commitment, for these monies represented far more than a simple cash transaction. Nelson did not make the deals in order to buy Kissinger, Ronan, Logue, and the others: in a large sense he already owned them as the patron of their rise to the heights they now enjoyed. The cash was more a reminder of who was lord and who the vassal. It was as *New York* magazine wrote:

> Rockefeller and his gifts ... managed to eliminate the countervailing forces that should surround an elected official. Elliot Richardson can quit, Gerald terHorst can quit, and other men can whisper to the press or competing politicians that the emperor has no clothes. Bill Ronan and Ed Logue are not people who can do that—in fact they're not people, they are property. A $625,000 I.O.U.—which Rockefeller held before forgiving Ronan his debts, certainly carries more weight than the signed but undated resignations that "tough" bosses keep in their desks.

By the end of the Senate hearings, Nelson had managed to dissipate a good deal of the myth his father had devoted a life to building. It was not the sense of the family's power that had been destroyed; if anything the mystique had been augmented by the spectacle of U.S. senators paying such deference to it. It was the philanthropic core of the myth that suffered by Nelson's exposure. His father had labored a lifetime to prove that Rockefeller gifts were something more than bribery; in a few memorable moments of the committee hearings, by presenting what certainly appeared to be political payoffs as pure-minded philanthropy, Nelson undid the effort.

In part because of this, in part because of the ill will stirred up by the disclosures, the rest of the Rockefellers had become increasingly agitated as the hearings progressed; their anxiety increased as it began to seem possible that one or more of them in addition to Laurance (who had appeared with his usual obtuse urbanity before the Senate Rules Committee) might be called to testify. An employee in Room

5600 captured their state of mind when he said, "This is a family that had always guarded its privacy. Way back to John D. Senior they've tried to avoid too much publicity. Then something like this investigation comes along. You could say that they've been deeply disturbed." His words were echoed by Nelson's 38-year-old son Steven: "The family is going through a radical shakeup as a result of this dragging out of their dirty laundry." In other circumstances, JDR3 might have headed a delegation to plead with Nelson to withdraw his name from consideration and thus spare the family its agony. But the family knew that, were Nelson to do so at this point, it would only confirm all the charges that had been made.

Nelson himself didn't seem much to care. There was a certain relish evident in his manner during his second appearance before the Senate Rules Committee. It was like the inquisitions his grandfather and father had gone through over such epic events as the consolidation of Standard Oil and the Ludlow Massacre. His personal crisis now resonated in the great historical tradition.

His answers to the questions flung at him did not remove the shadow of doubt that now covered his career and personality. Far from it, the image remaining after the hearings were over was that of a ruthless man of power possessed by an almost obsessive ambition. But it was not that of a corruptionist. Moreover, if great wealth in itself was not a disqualification for the office (as all the senators agreed), then there was finally little to be said. For everything Nelson had been and done had resulted from the immensity of his resources and his resolution to use them in a maximum way.

By the time the hearings passed on to the House on November 21, all doubts about confirmation had disappeared. It was nearly two months since the original revelations—if they could be called that—had placed his career in a moral penumbra. Rather than beginning an avalanche of damning corroboration, the original news leaks had summarized what was to come. Nothing further had been revealed. There was a growing mood to speed things up and get Nelson into the vacancy, especially as Gerald Ford floundered in his first months in office. Whatever his personal defects, so went the one myth left standing, Nelson had access to the "best people" in the country. Perhaps he, with his immense resources, could shore things up at the White House.

Nelson was to get his stiffest questioning in the House hearings, where he was handled with less deference than in the Senate. Yet with the doubts about confirmation all but gone, he gave back as good as he got, as he sat joking and sipping at a glass filled with Gatorade. Questioned pointedly on Attica by Congressman Charles Rangel, he admitted to making what he called "a serious mistake"—not in ordering the assault, but in overriding Corrections Commissioner Russell Oswald when he wanted to storm the prison early in the rebellion. Questioned about his hard-line view of drugs by Representative Paul McCloskey, Rockefeller noted in a heavy-handed aside, "I have a feeling that had the Founding Fathers been on marijuana, we would not probably have the United States or the Constitution."

Casual observers couldn't have known it, but the climax of the hearings came midway through the House inquiry. Two University of California professors, Charles Schwartz and William Domhoff, had sent each congressman a paper entitled "Probing the Rockefeller Fortune." The paper laid out the thesis that the Rockefeller fortune, though vested in individual members of the family, was actually centrally coordinated by Room 5600 and represented a vast concentration of economic power. They had determined that 15 employees of the family working out of Room 5600 sat on the boards of nearly 100 corporations with combined assets of $70 *billion*.

The rebuttal witness was the silver-haired head of the family office, J. Richardson Dilworth. In the Senate hearings, he had appeared as one peripherally involved in the corporate subterfuge surrounding the Goldberg book. Here he was appearing as the head of Room 5600, and the material he presented was a sop thrown to those who might otherwise have clamored for an appearance by David to testify about the uses of his power at the Chase, and respond to persistent rumors that Rockefeller political allies and friends had been given preferential treatment by the bank in a wide variety of services.

For three days beforehand, Dilworth had been on the phone with his clients, the Brothers and the Cousins. He had called to inform each of them that he would be a witness and that circumstances now compelled him do something he had hoped would not be necessary, in fact something that went profoundly against his grain—list all the family's property and holdings as a way of laying to rest the questions that had arisen as a result of rumors and the Schwartz-Domhoff testimony concerning the family's economic power. It was Tuesday morning, November 26, when Dilworth came before the House Rules Committee armed with five charts showing the way Room 5600 managed the $224 million in charities under its control and how it manipulated the family securities. The assets of the 84 family members (the figure was intended to make them seem more diverse and numerous than they were; the 84 actually amounted only to Brothers and their wives, Babs, and the Cousins and their spouses and children) calculated from Dilworth's figures and from previously provided information came to nearly $1.3 billion. The list of securities that Dilworth presented was an unprecedented accounting. Never before in the history of America's great fortunes had any of the proprietors disclosed the true extent of their ownings and wealth. "It may be of interest to this committee," Dilworth observed, underlining the obvious, "that this is the first time that any attempt has been made to aggregate the financial holdings of this family in this or any other manner." Dilworth's testimony left many questions unanswered, but it did show what basically had happened to the fortune that had once been America's greatest.

Although the $1.3 billion it came to was less than a quarter of the sum that had generally been projected (Stewart Alsop had even theorized that it amounted to $10 billion), it was hardly a case of "shirtsleeves to shirtsleeves in three generations" as Junior had once worried might be the case. He and his father had given more than $1 billion to the great corporate philanthropies which had brought unparalleled acclaim to the family name. He and his sons had probably spent an equal sum supporting themselves in a style of regal splendor and in maintaining the dynastic retinue that operated out of Rockefeller Center and extended their reach into the vast complex of establishment institutions and associations that constituted a private caucus on the nation's destiny and progress. And yet, as a result of the surplus the fortune continued to generate, its total was slightly more than it had been at its highest point sixty-five years earlier. It was having your cake and eating it too on an epic scale.

Although many of Dilworth's answers were evasive in a manner not unnatural for a man whose responsibility was managing a great accumulation of wealth, his data were such as to confirm the impression previously conveyed by Nelson that the Rockefeller family holdings were diffuse and did not represent the vast concentration of ownership control in major American corporations that Rockefeller critics had talked about for years. Among the Rockefeller holdings in corporations with over $300 million in sales, only three amounted to more than 2 percent of the stock (IBEC, 78.60 percent; Rockefeller Center, 100 percent; Allis-Chalmers, 3.45 percent). As Dilworth himself noted, this contrasted with other great families who were known to hold controlling shares of 10 to 20 percent in four or five corporations more than twice the size of these.* Excluding their holdings in IBEC, the Standard Oil companies, the Chase, and Rockefeller Center, the Rockefellers' largest cash investment was the more than 300,000 shares they held in IBM. This stock was worth more than $70 million; yet this amounted to only one-quarter of 1 percent of the outstanding IBM shares. Nor was the overall situation altered significantly by taking into consideration the shareholdings of the Rockefeller University and Colonial Williamsburg endowments, both of which were managed by the Family Office and therefore might be coordinated with the family holdings.

In his testimony, Dilworth also sought to pare down the number of interlocking directorates generated by the economic power of the family. He picked Nelson's aide George Hinman as an illustrative case, since Hinman's directorship of IBM accounted for several billion of the $70 billion aggregate of corporations listed by Domhoff and Schwartz. It was true that Hinman had worked for Nelson for years and was still a consultant to the Office and even designated to inform the Office of the situation of the company. Yet, as Dilworth explained, Hinman was a director of IBM not because of his Rockefeller relationship, but because his father-in-law was Thomas Watson, the founder of IBM.

Dilworth's observations were meant to lay to rest the ghost of the Rockefellers' "empire." In a sense they did, yet they

*On the other hand, it was not always necessary to have a large cash investment in order to exert control over a large corporation. Not included on Dilworth's list, for example, was Eastern Airlines, an omission he justified by the fact that Laurance's 216,000 shares of preferred stock—convertible at 63—was not marketable in 1974's low prices, and failed to meet the $1 million cutoff point for "major stock holdings of the family." Yet this stock represented 100 percent of the company's preferred. Laurance was undoubtedly the most powerful shareholder in a company with well over $1 billion in assets. As Malcolm MacIntyre, former president of Eastern, says: "Let me put it this way. If I had Laurance's man [Harper Woodward] with me on an issue, I wouldn't care if all the rest of the board was against me."

also raised the specter of a much more imposing network of interlocking relationships than was intimated by shareholdings in the Rockefeller portfolio. If the son-in-law of the founder of IBM and one of its biggest stockholders considered working as a Rockefeller aide a worthy career, what did that suggest about the reach of Rockefeller power? This power was certainly based on the primary place the family had long occupied in international banking and oil. But clearly it did not end there.

The contrast was best made by their cousins, the Stillman Rockefellers, whose roots were in the same oil and banking institutions as theirs, but who failed to exert anything like their influence in national affairs. In one sense the powers of the John D. Rockefellers were the generic powers of the rich: possession of the means by which individuals rose, institutions developed, and elites prospered. But there was another dimension of their power, one that made them different from even the wealthiest of their peers. If it had a corporate identity, it was the billion-dollar investment that Junior and Senior had made in the superstructures of the social order. Directorships in one or a hundred business corporations had little to do with the ability of the Rockefellers to lift an academic like Henry Kissinger or Dean Rusk into the stratospheres of national power and policy, or to put together a prestigious body like the Rockefeller panels and establish the framework of national defense strategies over a decade.

If there were interlocking relationships that reflected their influence, they were the interlocks with government and philanthropy, with the scientific and cultural establishments, with top leadership in business and politics, which made the descendants of John D. Rockefeller more potent as a family than the richer Du Ponts and Mellons. In the end it was the dynastic ambition, the lifetime spent in "public service," and the active assumption of leadership roles that tied these threads of influence together and knit them into a formidable social force. It was the network of interconnections *across* the realms of business, culture, and politics—all of it institutionalized in Room 5600—that gave them what one Wall Streeter described to *The New York Times* as "a position in the sun." This position was beyond the will or ability of the Congress to probe. The House hearings finally dragged to a conclusion. Shortly afterward, Nelson was confirmed. The doubts remained, but there was nothing that could be done about them. On December 10, with his young sons Nelson, Jr., and

Mark squirming alongside Happy in the gallery, Nelson placed his hand on his grandmother Cettie Rockefeller's Bible—the one he had used four times previously in Albany—and took the oath of office. Reporters present claimed that they saw him lift his glasses and wipe a tear away before he began his speech accepting the great responsibility now officially thrust upon him.

It was clearly a climax in his career. Where did it go from the vice-presidency? That was the question that haunted the political pundits after Nelson's confirmation. Would Betty Ford's cancer force her husband out of the 1976 race? (It was a measure of Nelson's ambition that no one would have asked this question about Happy's even more serious brush with the disease.) Would the economic situation worsen to the point that the Ford presidency would be irremediably crippled? But Ford showed more strength than had been anticipated and ambition to be more than a caretaker President. As the threat of a serious insurgency by the Reagan forces began to loom up on the administration's right, the question regarding Nelson's future was dramatically rephrased. Was he a political asset? Would he be the sacrifice conservatives demanded as the price of a unified party in 1976, delayed payment of the old debt?

Nelson had reached a vantage point he badly wanted, however ambiguous his triumph would become over the next few months. To get to the vice-presidency, he had looted the family mythology, trading the awe and mystery of the Rockefeller name for the satisfaction of this last ambition. He had picked up the last remaining IOU, scraped up the last of the goodwill his father had stored up for the family. His ambition and the question of the Rockefellers' future had been fatefully entwined since he was a young man musing on the coincidence that he had been born on the same day as his famous grandfather. Now he had dealt the tradition that flowed from the first John D. a mortal blow even as he was fulfilling its dictates. He was, in a sense, the last Rockefeller. As he was making his way toward the summit one last time, a new Rockefeller generation was watching from below with something like revulsion for the spectacle he had made of them all.

PART IV

The Cousins

"*The younger generation coming along, they've got to do their thing. And they'll rise, like a balloon, until they hit their own ceiling.*" —NELSON

"*Most of the younger people are not interested in going into business. And I think in a way it's too bad· but with so much to do. you can't do everything, and they're interested in environment, they're interested in philanthropy, they're interested in government and politics.*" —LAURANCE

"*Because there are twenty-three of them and six of us, inevitably that combined with estate taxes is going to mean that they will necessarily have less than any one of us will have.*" —DAVID

"*The world is in a state of rapid transition and I think that at present we as a family are in a transitional state too I'm not sure yet just what it will add up to in the end.*" —JDR3

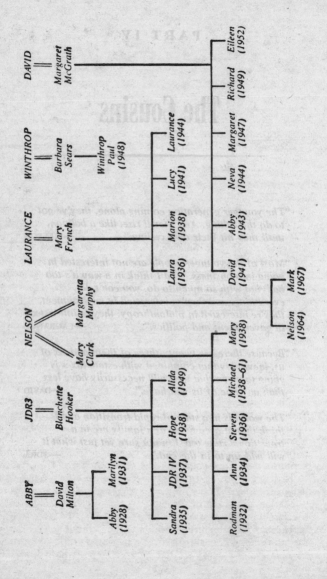

26

LOOKING AS THOUGH it had somehow run off the tracks of Western Pacific's Feather River line and tumbled to a stop in the freshly mown field, red caboose number 694 stands rusty and flaking in the moist warmth of the northern California summer. Smoke curls out of a stovepipe poking up from its roof. The only sounds are the busy noise of bees from a nearby hive, the territorial screech of red-winged blackbirds, and the muted bump of a car driving up a nearby dirt road.

A blond woman emerges from the back of the caboose where she has just finished cooking over a wood-burning stove. Her hair is gathered off her pretty sun-freckled face into an old green cloth serving as a bandanna: a thin coating of dust clings to her handmade ankle-length skirt. Trailed by a barefooted four-year-old with light hair and faded blue eyes that resemble her own, she spreads some dinner scraps on a compost pile and then walks over to shade herself for a moment in a stand of locust trees. Sweating slightly and looking out over the mesa rising above the California coastline, she resembles a character from *The Emigrants*, as content in respite as in labor.

Someone who knew her might easily shatter the illusion by asking what the great-granddaughter of John D. Rockefeller and potentially one of the richest and most powerful women in the country is doing in a place like this. But for Marion, second daughter of Laurance, the answer comes easily and without affectation. "It feels good here," she says in her soft, serious way. "Very good. The work, everything. Things seem to be coming out all right. More and more I feel that I control my life, that it's *my* life and not in hock to the family."

Marion lives here in the caboose only on weekends and in the summer. The rest of the time is spent in Berkeley, where her husband, Warren, is finishing a Ph.D thesis in English at the university. The plan is to move here permanently when he finishes, and complete the organic farm foreshadowed in

503

the two acres of pumpkins and cherry tomatoes whose fruits are sold in the fall at a roadside stand. In the meantime, they work hard to be self-sufficient and to keep a tight budget. So far they manage on $700 a month for a family of four, the first Rockefellers in more than a hundred years to live below the national average. The next goal, when they move to the farm, will be $300, bartering their produce with neighboring farmers for eggs and meat, and then as close to absolute self-sufficiency as possible. It is close to the spirit of the first John D.'s Ledger A, except that Marion, unlike previous Rockefellers, is trying to be free of the money, not worthy of it. A convert to Thoreau's idea that one is rich in proportion to the number of things he can do without, she supplements Warren's income as a teaching assistant by babysitting and weaving, and by growing comfrey in the backyard of the Berkeley house and selling it to local health food stores who have no idea that they are paying 50 cents a plant to a Rockefeller with a $10 million trust fund and the promise of many times that to come.

Although she is perhaps stronger in her determination to establish her own relationship to the world, she is like her other cousins in her attitude toward money: the wrestling is symbolic of an effort to gain control over the terms of her life: its aim, as she puts it, is "to get off the breast." Most of the fourth Rockefeller generation have spent long years with psychiatrists in their efforts to grapple with the money and the family, the taint and the promise. Marion explores inner space in her own way—among other things by attending to the promptings of an uncreated consciousness that finds expression in her dreams. Many of them are explicitly about her family, and almost literary in their attempt to fix the dilemma.

"Our family was all together," she recounts one of them. "We were dressed in flowing and very expensive clothes, with golden thread and thick, rich fabric. We are all walking down this road: it is beautiful, smooth, and very pleasant, and we're gliding over it. But suddenly I see out of the corner of my eye that there are people in the pastures on both sides of us, people we never knew were there, just regular people looking at us with envy and curiosity. I feel embarrassed and want to tell them something. Somehow I manage to get away from my family. Then, the next thing I know, I'm in the field with the regular people, watching the Rockefellers on parade. I feel glad that I'm not one of *them*."

But the biggest dream of all takes place in her waking hours. It is to have the Rockefeller identity totally behind her. "The fortune should be made extinct," she says passionately. "I was with my father in Woodstock recently, and he was talking about making up his will. I don't want his money passed on to me. I don't want it passed on to my children. I don't want them to have to deal with what I've had to deal with. I hope the social revolution will come soon and take away from us the necessity of having to deal with it."

The extremism of the formulation might bother some of her cousins, but she is far from alone in her desire to experience the Horatio Alger myth in reverse. To some degree they are all princes and princesses yearning to be paupers.

Speaking of the contemporary Vanderbilts, Cleveland Amory once said that it was "impossible to tell them from anybody else." When the Cousins (as the fourth generation is known) gather at Pocantico every June and December for their semiannual meetings, there is no doubt they are Rockefellers. Running like leitmotifs through their faces are the telltale square jaw of John D. Rockefeller, Jr., and his wife Abby's generous mouth. Features from the Brothers' generation are also present in new combinations: the pointed nose and high cheekbones of the David family; the greyhound leanness and regal bearing of JDR3 and Blanchette; Nelson's solid body and Mary Clark's long face and jutting chin; Laurance's steady eye and rising forehead.

Yet this group of Rockefellers is separated from the past by facts that have played a large role in their unusual development. There are twenty-one Cousins,* as dramatic an increase over the previous generation as one of the population charts from JDR3's desk. Only one-third of the Cousins are males, in a family that has always been patriarchal. Only four of them live in New York City. And finally, there are substantial differences in age and outlook that not only divide them into two groups on opposite sides of the generation gap (the oldest Cousin, Babs's daughter "Mitzi," 46, could be the mother of David's youngest, the 22-year-old Eileen), but also preclude the unified view of things that led their fathers into public life.

---

*This number does not include Nelson, Jr., and Mark, Nelson's sons by his marriage to Happy; any of the fifth generation of second cousins (so far numbering thirty-eight); or Michael, Nelson's son, who died in 1961.

Rodman, 42, Nelson's son and oldest male, is the president of IBEC, a dedicated businessman, and the only member of his generation living off his salary. The 37-year-old John D. Rockefeller IV ("Jay") is the Cousins' most famous member because of his career in West Virginia politics. Marion's sister Lucy, a Washington, D.C., psychiatrist, is interested in the La Leche League and other organizations having to do with parenthood. David's daughter Peggy, 27, has been involved in Cambridge's radical circles since the early days of SDS.

Political opinions range from the conservative Republicanism of Winthrop's son, "Win Paul," to the Marxism of David's daughter Abby; life-styles, from Marion's part-time existence in caboose number 694 to the Oyster Bay opulence of Mitzi, or the upper east side chic of Nelson's daughter Mary. Yet they are united by something thicker than blood itself: a searching look, an unremitting seriousness, a wariness so habitual and ingrained that it cannot be relaxed even in each other's presence. They have the look of people who have grown up with a burden they still aren't sure how to handle even though most are well on their way through adulthood. Whether to pick it up and heft it gingerly, or to decide in advance that it is too heavy and stand back from it: this is their choice.

Except for a few, like Marion, who have chosen the path of most resistance. Not only has she walked away from the family responsibility she was supposed to accept as a sacred trust, but she has come to see the mission itself as corrupt and destructive, and has spent much of her life scouring the missionary impulse and imperative out of her temperament. The path to the caboose standing in solitude in the shadow of the California mesa was a tortuous one. It led from the Brearley School for Girls to debutante balls, through periods of dark self-questioning and a strange kind of penance as a volunteer worker in madhouses and hospitals. "You grow up feeling that you can't ever make up for all the guilt and all the evil, and that you just have to be saintly," Marion says. "So you martyr yourself. That's how I entered the adult world. I wanted to be near people who were suffering, and to help them in some way. I worked as an art therapist in a home for retarded adults. Then I did the same thing in a terminal cancer ward in Cambridge, and then I worked in a sort of ghetto situation. Just the scarier the better. It was the only way *I* could feel better about things.

"The whole name problem is so strange. To be truthful, it

was a great relief for me when I got married and didn't have
to carry it around anymore. Now it's not the first thing that
hits somebody when you first meet them. It's great to be free
of that. I make my friends and later on my background seeps
out and it's okay because we've had time to get to know each
other on a different level. But it has been terribly hard to get
to this point. And then with ourselves, we don't even get that
far. Within the family, one hardly ever talks directly about
who we are without our Rockefeller identity, our social identity, very little about love or hate or anger, without all these
other damned attachments. It's really tragic. I think that's one
of the sadder things about our family."

For each of the Cousins, being a Rockefeller has seemed
like an Oriental puzzle of shadow and act, of opposites flowing into and out of each other. It is a blessing, bestowing more
wealth and power on one at birth than most others accumulate in a lifetime; it is a curse, for the riches can be possessed
only at an awesome spiritual cost. All of the Cousins have
been tantalized by the Rockefeller identity, yet all have
thought at one time or another that to be born into this dynasty was like having an exotic and utterly incurable hereditary disease.

"It's a preposterous name." says David's oldest daughter,
Abby. "I remember as a child having it whispered that we
were rich." she recalls. "I have vague memories of my classmates talking and then all of a sudden, of the name Rockefeller looming as something beyond. Very quickly I came to
feel that it wasn't my name. I never felt integrated with it,
never felt connected to it. I always said it as if everyone
would know it wasn't my name, and eventually I came to
dread saying it, because of the fear of being seen as some
other *thing*."

The Cousins are not a rebellious generation, and yet in
their paralysis and painful attempts to locate themselves in
the middle of the drama that has been unfolding over the last
hundred years, they have surprisingly brought its plot to a
sudden end. It is a peculiar finish for the morality play which
had the first John D. representing Worldly Riches, redeemed
by Junior's Good Works, with the Brothers stepping forth as
gilt-edged Everymen. One thing the Cousins could be said to
agree on is that to be an Everyman is finally to be a kind of
no man. and that to put on the Rockefeller role is ultimately
to drain oneself of humanity, concreteness, and connection. If
they are part of the drama, it is only as a kind of Gothic epi-

logue, played out in cabooses settled down into western soil and other exotic settings. The action of this part of the plot is summarized by Abby: "The problem of disentangling oneself from a tradition and creating a new sense of self is unbelievably difficult and confusing. If you're a Rockefeller it is doubly so. You need an exorcism."

Marion's dream work, abounding in family images, often settles on Pocantico. "I was a stranger in some foreign land. I was the only blond—everyone else had black hair—and I was definitely a stranger. I sat at a table with those cold black-haired people I didn't know. At one point the women among them were picking up bouquets and throwing them in a heap, as if at a funeral. They asked me about myself, and I told them the truth. I also told them what my feelings were now. They asked, 'And who owns the estate now? Do the Cousins own the estate?' And I said, 'No, no, the uncles own the estate, and it's going to be sold.' As I said this I was flooded with a bittersweet feeling. I was glad that we were getting rid of it, but nostalgic because I remembered my childhood there."

The Cousins grew up as their fathers had: weekdays were spent in New York City, yet every weekend, vacation, and summer was spent at the estate. It was where the free time, the time that mattered, was spent. Though they would later reevaluate their growing up, there would always be good memories.

Mitzi, Rodman, and a couple of the other older ones have vague recollections of great-grandfather—the thinly delicate, parchment-skinned founder of Standard Oil. Yet for most, he was only an image in the old Pathé newsreels the Family Office had spliced together in a kind of elaborate home movie to show at Christmas parties—an oddly Chaplinesque figure doffing his hat and dropping dimes into the outstretched hands of children. For most of the Cousins, the earliest memories were of the period just after the first John D.'s death, the war years when their own fathers (with the exception of Nelson) were gone for long periods, suddenly reappearing in striking dress uniforms, their arms filled with presents. Only their Uncle Winthrop had any war stories. The Cousins who were old enough to remember recall the excitement caused by news that he had been wounded in the battle for Okinawa.

Pocantico felt the pinch of the war only slightly. The

Rockefellers had no stamp books and carried no grease to the butcher. It literally took the family three days to open all their Christmas presents. Yet fear of rationing did midwife the rebirth of farming at Pocantico, which had declined since the days when Senior had insisted on having produce from the estate shipped to him whenever he was at his three other homes. An immense vegetable patch was planted—the Rockefeller variant of the victory garden. Junior bought ninety head of beef and sundry other livestock, which were housed in the rambling structure known as the "farm barns." The Cousins often went after milking time to get the still-warm milk or newly churned butter. Sometimes they stayed to watch in fascinated horror as a steer was slaughtered, dressed out, and then smoked or placed in the estate's large freezers to be apportioned among the families or shipped by railway express to their homes in the city or to the vacation retreat at Seal Harbor.

During the war and for some time after, Pocantico was a society of women, children, and servants. The Cousins went with head groundsman Tom Pyle each spring to dig out fox dens and see the newborn kits. They were taught to ride by the Prussian riding master Joe Plick, who kept their grandfather's stables and named the newborn colts "Roddy," "Mitzi," and other Cousins' names. Bouncing up and down in English saddles behind him on the elaborate network of bridlepaths, they learned the rules for riding, which were broken the moment they were on their own. There were jumping and steeplechase competitions organized by their grandmother and by Aunt Blanchette and in these there were always the same number of ribbons as entrants in each category.

There were certain things that didn't make sense, such as the time Nelson's son Michael was attacked by one of the savage guard dogs patrolling the periphery of the estate and suffered a badly mauled arm. This and other similar incidents would cause them to look back later and wonder (in the words of one Cousin) if Pocantico had been a paradise or a prison. Yet when they were young, there was no doubt. It was Eden, and they were innocent. Marion remembers: "It was carpeted in green and very beautiful. I had my cousins for my friends, and the beauty of the place was wonderful. There were deer, raccoons, foxes, other animals living in our woods. We were almost like Indians. We roamed and roamed at will on our horses. Mine was named 'Queenie,' a raggedy palomino I got when I was ten. When I got Queenie I'd take off by myself without saddle or bridle. Just take off. Somewhere I'd meet my cousins and we'd just go all day. We took off most of our clothes and rode half-naked. We covered all the trails. Sometimes we rode on Great-Grandfather's golf course. Once our horses' hooves gouged great chunks of sod out of his putting greens. We laughed."

They occasionally played in the Playhouse that had been built for their fathers. But not squash and the other sports for which it had been designed. They allowed the Gothic interior with its deep, echoing shadows and splotches of black at the stairwells to dictate the nature of their games. One of them was called "Murder in the Dark," played in the dimly lit corridors with new improvisations each time, but usually climaxing with rolling around in the giant handwoven Indian baskets their Uncle Nelson had bought in the Southwest. The older Cousins introduced the younger ones to the subject of sex in the Playhouse, whispering about it in the closets and accompanying the discussions with furtive, groping explorations of each other. They occasionally took this mood outdoors. In one well-remembered incident, the children of Nelson and Laurance stripped naked and joined in "raiding" the gardeners at work. They were apprehended and given the stiff punishment of being forbidden to play together for a week.

Only the boys were allowed to have friends visit them from the nearby hamlet of Pocantico Hills. Yet the parents' fears of exogamy were unnecessary. The Cousins felt more comfortable with each other than with outsiders. For them the word "Cousin" was more than an anthropological designation; it described a bond cemented by the fact that they had only each other. There were pairs of best friends within the group even closer than brothers and sisters: Marion and Nelson's daughter Mary; Nelson's Steven and Laurance's Laura; Laurance's Lucy and David, Jr. They formed cliques and built clubhouses with cabalistic initiation ceremonies and caches of contraband comic books resting in orange crates.

This desire to build, to seize a piece of ground for their own and claim it with a structure, sprang from a feeling universal among them that the large, formal homes that operated with the effortless precision of hotels, with servants whisking in and out of rooms, meals magically appearing and dishes disappearing, guests coming and going according to schedules in leather-bound appointment books, and clothing never being allowed to linger long on bedroom floors, did not really reflect *them*. "With servants, you can't do anything but it is brushed away or it is picked up; you don't really make a mark," complains Marion. "I never was allowed to make my room my own," her older sister, Laura, agrees. "I hated evey place we lived. There wasn't a comforable chair in any of them." Building was an attempt to ground themselves in something of their own. "We were always trying to make some cozy little place that belonged just to us," recalls Laura. "We went from one chicken coop to another, and we built shacks as clubhouses."

These projects ran afoul of the rigid inspection code of their grandfather. Junior stopped short of totally forbidding their construction, but did insist that they must not be visible from any of the roads that laced the stately grounds. He liked the estate to look formal and neat. And his word was to be obeyed on such matters. (The Cousins knew that their Uncle Nelson had managed to pressure him into allowing an outdoor pool near the Playhouse only after much argument.)

Their Grandmother Abby Aldrich had died too soon for most of the Cousins to have any more than a slender memory of a handsome woman smelling of lilac and wearing extravagant hats, who became thick at the ankles and frequently ill in her last years. She loved painting and automobile rides, and made no attempt to hide her preference for male offspring, whether her own or her children's. "I don't know why the Lord has decided that I should have more granddaughters than grandsons," she had said, "but I suppose there must be some good reason."

Yet memories of their grandfather—Mr. Junior—were firm. Even when well into his eighties, he controlled Pocantico with an iron hand, acting as "the Laird of Kikjuit" in a way his own father had not. He was generous with the cornucopia of good things at the estate, but left no doubt that they were his to give or withhold. The shiny, perfectly combed and cared-for horses Joe Plick kept in the central stable were taken out only by Grandfather's permission. The armada of electric cars sailing soundlessly over the estate were his to command. The bounty of food every family received from the farm barns and vegetable garden came from him. He alone controlled the allegiance of the small army of workers tending the estate.

The Cousins noted that this arrangement did not satisfy their fathers, and that they chafed under Junior's rule. Yet they themselves rarely experienced their grandfather as a disciplinarian. To them, he was a shy and increasingly fragile man whose uniform of dark suit and tie and starched white shirt was unvarying whether he was meeting with associates from New York City, or going for a Sunday afternoon drive with Martha Baird, the old family friend he had married after Abby's death.

He was like a gentleman from one of the old books their nurses read to them: proper, precise, dignified. His clothes, the formal way he addressed people he'd obviously known for decades, the obsessive desire to have naturally fallen trees and underbrush cleared from the forest floor lest they "spoil the view" of Pocantico (in his last years he frequently annoyed their fathers by casually driving around the estate marking certain "obtrusive" standing trees for the groundskeeper's ax), even the way he sat in the small Pocantico Hills church in the left front pew reserved for the family, twiddling his thumbs in satisfaction during the sermon—any one of these things taken by itself might have seemed trivial or ridiculous, but they united in him to form a man left like an artifact of a prior age.

Nelson's son Steven later reflected on the generalized graciousness that was so great a part of Junior's personality in his old age. "He didn't like to speak badly of anybody. If he said anything that was in any way critical, he would quickly soften it with a little laugh. He'd tilt his head and smile as if to say, 'Well now, we all have our little weaknesses, don't we,' and then he'd find something nice to say about the person he'd criticized. His way of relating to the world was somehow distressing to us. We noticed that nobody ever called him by his first name." Yet like the other Cousins, Steven learned that it was irrelevant whether one loved Grandfather; the important thing was that he must be respected.

They could tell they represented something special to him. There was a tenderness in his manner toward them that never entered his relations with their fathers. Occasionally he would appear like a ghost at the window of the Big House and beckon one of them playing alone outside to come in to have a cup of tea. Once Sandra, JDR3's oldest daughter, got an invitation to spend two weeks with Junior at Seal Harbor. This earned her their envy. Seeing Grandfather alone or having a moment of personal contact that broke through his reserve was an experience so rare that it became the most precious coinage of their youth. Steven remembered one such moment long after with the clarity of a religious epiphany. It had occurred because he had become stricken with grief at Grandmother Abby's funeral, sobbing uncontrollably. "Afterwards Grandfather called me on the phone and said that he understood why I cried, that he'd cried a great deal himself. He said he was sending me a little present. It was a World War I machine-gun shell with a gold pencil inside. A friend of his had given it to him, he said, in 1917. This episode was the only time he related to the uniqueness of my life—that is, to something that was happening to *me*—and allowed me to have an intimacy with him. It meant a great deal to me."

For the most part, the Cousins had to be content to experience Junior in groups at the punctual intervals of every fourth Sunday, when it was their family's turn to go have Sunday lunch at his house. These dynastic meals were anticipated with excitement and a measure of dread. Without ever being told exactly why, the youngsters understood that Grandfather was a man who embodied the past history of the family as much as they themselves did its future hopes. Being with him was like standing in the presence of a living idea, almost a continuation of the experience of having gone to church. The wild behavior of the week was put away for a few hours: hair was braided and cowlicks subdued; clothes were flawlessly pressed and crinkled with starch. When they sat down at the long dining room table, there were always flowers floating solemnly in crystal finger bowls. The polite adult conversation hummed above the click of silverware on china.

After the Sunday lunches were over, Junior would push away from the table and sit down on the floor to play with them. His own father had often put on an antic disposition for the amusement of the Brothers when they were young, but this was not Junior's way. (His rare attempts to be amusing were flat, almost painful. JDR3's daughter Hope recalls: "Once in a great while, Grandfather used to decide to try and tell us a funny story: he'd stand up and start it, and then suddenly he'd get terribly nervous and begin to blush.") His preferred mode was the didactic. Often he would join them on the floor and play Musical Authors, an Old Maidlike game that gave him a chance to correct their phonetic pronunciation of names like Beethoven or Bach. He would often read from some book like *Tom Brown's School Days*. He had an affecting way of dramatizing a piece of fiction, assuming the characters' various voices and carefully developing the suspense or humor. One of his favorite texts was an obscure Victorian novel about a boy whose high spirits always got him into trouble. At the end of each chapter he would get caught and Junior would smile as he lowered his voice to read the father's invitation to get caned: "I will meet you in my office, sir."

He was the center of the world of Pocantico. Either in the massive stone house or driving around the estate in a horse and buggy or a limousine with a blanket over his lap (often stopping and walking with Martha into the fiery autumn woods with the uniformed chauffeur waiting a discreet distance away beside the idling black Cadillac), he was the patriarch. If anyone told them about their duties as Rockefellers, it was he—yet not in so many words. Direct indoctrination was not his way. There was just an air about him, the peculiar pride in his voice when he talked about the way "our family" went about things. What he said had a compelling ring to it, especially in the handwritten letters he sent them on their birthdays. On his tenth birthday, Nelson's son Steven received this note from Junior:

Dearest Steven:

Tomorrow is your birthday and here is my birthday check. You have had presents like this before so you will know what to do with it. I wonder if your mother or father give you an allowance and whether you write down in a little book what you are given and what you spend? If you do not do this, someday you will. Your father did it, and all of your uncles. It helps to keep track of money, to know how much one has and how one spends it.

Money is a useful thing to have. You can buy candy with it, and tops, and marbles and boats and many other things you may like to have. But it has other uses. When there are children who are hungry or who need clothes or who have no homes, it helps to get for them what they need. . . . You will enjoy the tops and the marbles much more when you have given something he needs to another boy who has less than you. . . .

The massive fortune he had inherited intact from his father had been distributed. Much had gone into the corporate philanthropies and institutions that had been his lifework. It had bought important future assets like Rockefeller Center, and created the huge trusts for his sons in 1934. Yet he realized that being a Rockefeller involved having a piece of Standard Oil. In 1952 he took 120,000 of his remaining shares of Standard of New Jersey stock and set up trust funds for each of his grandchildren.* When they reached their twenty-first year, they learned about the trusts, as part of their "financial rights."

That the trust had the desired effect is suggested by a letter Nelson's son Michael wrote Junior in 1959:

> Dear Grandfather:
> On my twenty-first birthday, my father made known to me the trust which you have established out of consideration for me and my future. For this I am deeply grateful. It is unique and extraordinary that the third generation after Great Grandfather will be able to share in the privilege and wonderful opportunities coincident with taking responsibility over a trust which he made possible. . . . I will become that much more a part of a wonderful tradition, one which has already exerted a profoundly broadening and morally inspiring influence upon my upbringing.

None of them ever really got to know this prim little man very well. Yet if not in his life, then in his death they grasped his meaning. After he was gone, the central stables, garden, and livestock operation of Pocantico were all shut down. Each individual family retreated a little farther into itself. It was as if the force holding them all together had gone out of the estate—and the world.

Winthrop's son, Win Paul, grew up in his mother's custody and away from the other Cousins. Babs's daughters, Mitzi and Marilyn had grown up as Miltons, not Rockefellers, and were more like visitors at Pocantico than residents. Of the four Brothers whose families lived there, JDR3's was farthest from the others, both in terms of space and emotion. The children who grew up at Fieldwood Farm were more a self-contained unit than the others. The firstborn was Sandra, who

*This amounted to 20,000 shares for each family, split evenly between the children in it. In David's family of six children, for instance, each one got proportionately less than in JDR3's family of four or Babs's of two. But in any case all would have a comfortable sum of $5 million to $9 million each on attaining their majority.

as a child seemed wispy, easily frightened, almost neurasthenic. Next came a boy, "Jay," only half a namesake because his father (in a covert act of rebellion against the responsibility he had borne so faithfully and at such a cost) named him simply John Rockefeller and said he could have the option of adopting the dynastic designation carried by the middle name Davison and the number IV when he came of age. Hope grew into a tall, statuesque blond. Alida, born eleven years later in 1949 when her father was nearing middle age, had the same aristocratic good looks. All of the children had a regal quality; it was instilled by Blanchette, who seemed to hope to recapture in their generation the rule of primogeniture she felt Nelson had stolen from her husband.

JDR3 was away during much of their youth. "He traveled at least three months a year while I was growing up," Alida says. "Every winter he and mother went to Asia for a couple of months and I stayed with a nurse." Yet the psychic distance was always greater than the actual miles. Hope recalls him as always being in between appointments or projects. "One of the things I remember best about my father was the careful measuring of time. There was a certain time set aside for exercise, a certain time for receiving guests, and so on. If someone stayed too long, for instance, I noticed that my mother got extremely nervous."

When he was with them, he resembled his own father in that the role that was most comfortable for him was that of instructor. Hope recalls him setting out to teach her to drive in an old Jeep and retaining his serene patience as the vehicle gnashed gears and bucked like a Brahma bull over the dirt roads behind Fieldwood Farm.

Like his brothers, JDR3 felt that there were certain stones in the family past better left unturned. His daughter Alida remembers being twelve and pulling into a Mobil station for gas with a carload of her friends; when they started making the inevitable jokes about how she wouldn't have to pay, she couldn't understand and had trouble convincing them that she really didn't know that the family fortune was connected with this company. Yet her father was the one Rockefeller Brother sincerely interested in passing on the tradition of philanthropy to his children, even if only as an exercise in *noblesse oblige*. "Ever since I was very young," Alida says, "I remember Father talking to me about responsibility. I was made to think I was special from the beginning, that I had a special duty. From the time I was five years old I got an allowance that gradually increased from fifteen cents to five dollars a week. There were three little jewelry boxes. I got fifteen cents to spend, fifteen cents to save, and fifteen cents to give away. Every Christmas season, my father would sit down with me and we'd decide who I'd give the money in the third box to. Usually some went to Riverside Church, and always to one of the one hundred neediest cases in *The New York Times*. We read the cases together and decided which to give to. It was a real ritual, one of the times we were closest."

Laurance's children were more tentative than JDR3's. To the degree that their father did not know himself, he cut the ground from under them: it was as if they were confused by his ironies and kaleidoscope of moods. Laura, the oldest, dealt with Laurance by trying to master his casuistry; she debated him constantly. Marion was as withdrawn and mystical as her mother. Lucy showed some of the independence of her namesake, the half-deaf and aged Great-Aunt Lucy Aldrich. She defied her father, who thought that everything she wanted (her own pets, her own friends, and her freedom from family rituals) came too soon. The boy, Larry, grew up extremely cautious watching his mercurial father occupying all the spaces where he tried to expand.

Like JDR3, Laurance was absent during much of their growing up. Yet he was a power to be reckoned with even when gone, protean in the psychological shapes he could assume, hard to pin down, able to cut down a child's adventuresome inquiry with one quick stroke. He was the dominant fact in their lives, yet the tone of the family came from the mother. Mary French Rockefeller, in odd complement to her agnostic and very secular husband, spent much time reading the Bible and meditating by herself. If Laurance defused emotion through irony, she suppressed it through silence. "She never raised her voice when we were young," her daughter Marion recalls. "She never said much at all, the idea being that if you were in communication with God, you didn't *need* to communicate. During the family arguments she never said a word. We practically used to hurl things at her—words and objects—and she'd just take it stoically."

The children of the Laurance household would look back in a kind of anger at their growing up. Lucy, now a Washington, D.C., psychiatrist, lives in a stylish Chevy Chase house whose front yard is littered with children's toys. Along with her involvement in the La Leche League (which seeks to promote the breast feeding of infants) and in organizations emphasizing parental responsibility, this hints at the fact that she is still sorting out the past. "We were not so much isolated as children as we were encased in a vacuum," she said. "Nobody wanted to communicate. Nobody bothered to orient us to the world. Nothing was really talked about at home. They operated on the theory that you don't talk about important things to your animals, or servants, and you don't tell them to your children."

In each of the households, servants and nurses provided the close contact, while the mothers orchestrated and the fathers came and went. This too had an impact: "My struggle is for recognition," says Laura. "I was never recognized for myself by my parents. The servants gave us individual presents. Our parents gave us tons of presents, but never any that were for *me*. I became fond of the maids and the servants, and then when I heard my parents talk to them as though they were nonpeople, I vowed I would never treat anyone like that."

Laurance's children were inevitably drawn to Nelson's house. It was warmer and more open than their own, yet hardly informal by any standards other than those their grandfather had established as the norm of Pocantico. As Steven recalls, "Our lives were actually highly regulated. If you didn't show up in time for a meal, you didn't get it. Bells were rung and then you had five minutes to show up. If you didn't make it, you didn't get fed."

Rodman was somewhat detached from his brothers and sisters and also the other Cousins, made haughty (they felt) by his status as first male of their generation. Ann was the quietest of Nelson's children; Steven a natural leader in a way Roddy was not. Everyone was especially fond of the twins, Mary and Michael, whose high spirits and constant exuberance reminded relatives of Nelson when he was young.

Nelson dominated his family, much as he dominated everything else, with his steamroller enthusiasms. (Not without a faint irony his sons called him "Chief.") His brothers John and Laurance let the forms of their own growing up slide in their children's youth, but Nelson did not. He made his children sit still for the Sunday devotions and Bible readings he himself had so chafed at under Junior's regime. Although they took lunches and dinners with their nurses, he made a point of being present—as Junior had—at breakfast. He explained about Great-Grandfather's Ledger A and made them keep accounts of their own. ("He was not overly strict," his son Steven recalls, "but he definitely implanted the idea in us that accounts were very important. The threat was mainly that if they didn't balance, we wouldn't get our allowance.") He was nonchalant about material things, and his children could lose a tennis racket and expect that another one would replace it. This contrasted with their mother's attitude, which was that they should not be spoiled just because they were Rockefellers, and if they carelessly broke something, they should repair it.

Nelson was insistent about what he regarded as moral questions, and his displeasure was withering. His daughter Mary recalls: "I've never heard Father raise his voice to any one of us. When he got angry he'd just turn to stone. He would go cold and this stone quality would just enter his voice and manner. It was terrifying."

All the Cousins (but especially Laurance's children) were fond of Tod. Aunt Mary (as they called her) had an athletic grace and whimsical good humor the world at large didn't often see. Marion remembers seeking her out time after time, while she knelt at work in her gardens, to ask her questions and wait for the amusing replies to float up like bubbles from under the voluminous sunbonnet. A good part of what the Nelson children were to become stemmed from their mother's quiet, intelligent strength, which was unique in the increasingly diverse society of Pocantico. The qualities that made Tod fail as Nelson's wife helped her succeed with the children. "In Mother," Steven recalled later, "there is a liking and respect for books and learning that is absent in Father. Father likes his art and so forth, but even there his appreciation is completely intuitive, based only on immediate reactions. Wham! That's it. Who did the painting, why, or what it means—all these intellectual questions don't interest him."

But it was "the Davids" who were generally reckoned by family observers to be the most interesting group at Pocantico. David took fatherhood seriously in a way that JDR3, Laurance, and Nelson did not, perhaps because he was the only Brother to accept uncritically the Rockefeller myth and to assume the necessity for instructing the young to shoulder its burdens. Yet he was absent from his children's growing up even more than his brothers were—especially during their childhood, when he was traveling in the foreign department of the Chase. With characteristic obtuseness, he emphasized these absences by bringing home toys he had obtained in the countries he visited.

It was, however, the mother who had the greatest impact on the children. Peggy McGrath Rockefeller was perhaps not as intellectual as Tod or as sophisticated as Blanchette, but she was by far the most independent and spirited woman to marry into the Rockefeller family. Blessed with resilient good looks, she came into the family an intuitive rebel with an often violent temper, an unadmitted hunger for independence, and a secret skepticism regarding much of the Rockefeller pomp. The other Brothers' wives were from pedigreed families; Peggy McGrath's was well-off, but several rungs down the social ladder. To her, marriage to a Rockefeller had been a dramatic step up, and though she understood that it had involved something of a Faustian compact in regard to her private life, she never seemed to make her accommodation complete. In some sense she remained ambivalent, fearful that she might become a concubine to the famous name, poised for flight from its complexity to something simpler. While her husband was on one of his globe-circling tours, she would often be on Buckle Island, a small seven-acre island a half-day's sail from Seal Harbor. She had bought it with her own money; the only structure was a small prefab house she had built, where she stayed alone, away from the retinue of servants, gardening in solitude.

"Mother is terribly intense," says her daughter Neva. "It never occurred to her to surrender to the Rockefeller personality." Indeed, she seemed to be fighting some invisible opponent all through their youth. Only when they came of age themselves would they begin to understand the snarling moods, closed doors, meals taken with gritted teeth. She was the only one capable of open rage, of living in flamboyantly contradictory terms. On the one hand she understood that the expectations held up for her and all other Rockefellers were ridiculous and inflated; on the other, she could not stand deviations from duty or from aristocratic standards the family set for itself, and she despised Nelson for the public flaunting—"vulgarity" she called it, summoning her most damning epithet—of the family tradition and morality. In her effort to keep her children from being spoiled, she reminded them constantly that being born into their unique status did not make them particularly special. "It's an accident," she would say of the wealth. "It could just as easily have fallen on anyone." Yet she also insisted that they strive to live up to the ideals (artificial though they might be) on which the family was founded. She made existentialists of them all.

She was capable of breaking through the *noblesse oblige* that hung over the family like a fog with one swift gesture. It was in contrast to her husband's remote and condescending good manners, a veneer of humility whose solicitousness toward lesser beings seemed actually calculated to prove the reverse—how much better he was and how deserving of the privilege he enjoyed. Peggy treated the servants with a hauteur that earned her their hatred. She assigned her children to weed pulling and other tasks, as if unconsciously trying to sweat the Rockefeller pretension out of them.

"When we were young," says Abby of her mother, "she was the center of everyone's interest and of our frantic desire to win approval." But the attitude toward the father was more complex, especially since his mood of equanimity was taken as the family norm mother and children were guilty of violating. The children coveted his attention when he was available. Every Friday afternoon, when the family tumbled out of the Manhattan town house and piled into the large limousine with nurses and pets to begin the trip to Pocantico, there was a struggle among them for the privilege of sitting next to him in the front seat. Yet they had what approached disdain for him as well. He was good on beetle-collecting trips, where the information he dispensed was crisp and specific and gained him their complete respect. But otherwise he seemed to convey attitudes rather than data, speaking in the code of platitudinous gentility that was totally different from Peggy's continual attempts to define and discriminate. He seemed predictable, superficial, obtuse, his religious observances and ideas on the sanctity of the family almost comical. More than any of the other Cousins, David's children had the impulse to probe and understand; yet when they managed to penetrate their father's placid reserve, they found only give. There was one uniform mood, one tone of voice that carefully skirted conflict. "To our loss," said his son Richard, "*emotional* was seen as the antithesis of reasonable, which made it bad. Repress emotion. Control yourselves. These were the lessons we learned."

There were few offenses grievous enough to suspend David's rule of reason. One memorable farce occurred when their mother was in the hospital having Eileen. Abby, Peggy, and David, Jr., let the sheep out of the corral and one became lodged in a drainpipe and suffocated. David called his wife at the hospital in consternation at the idea that he would have to take responsibility for the punishment. She said that the children must certainly be spanked. In a panic he called her back three times for instructions before he could bring himself to carry out the sentence, finally paddling each of them gently with a soft old slipper as a way of carrying out the letter of the law while avoiding its spirit.

Within this scheme, the rare event of violence was both a shock and a kind of relief. All of the children recalled a time when they had been on a family walk with their father at the Seal Harbor vacation home. They had gone through the Hidden Gardens their Grandmother Abby Aldrich had built, and when they passed a statue of Buddha a second time, David noted that a dime placed in the outstretched hand long ago was missing. He turned to his son, David, Jr., accused him of stealing it, and later beat him with a rage that was not only uncharacteristic (it was the only violence his children ever remembered from him) but wholly out of proportion to the alleged crime. His son remembers the incident ruefully: "He had no intention of ascertaining the truth when he called me to witness. As far as he was concerned, I had profaned the treasured object of his mother and must suffer for it."

David commanded them to go to church even though his wife's absence—she was an atheist—silently condemned it as hypocrisy. As in other matters, however, they tried to serve mother and father at once. They dutifully squirmed through the sermons at the Pocantico Hills church, watching rainbows of sunlight stream through the stained glass windows Henri Matisse had done as a memorial for their grandmother; then after the service was over they chivied the Reverend Hansen with youthful Humean skepticism about the existence of God.

If the religion that had been such a great factor in the Rockefeller saga was breaking down, the great fortune was not. It represented an even more fundamental puritanism. They learned early that it was a threat to those who dared approach it too directly. "I remember when my brother David had just learned that our father was a millionaire," Abby recalls. "He was ten or eleven. He took a vulgar enthusiasm in telling the rest of us about it. We listened with as perverse and lustful an interest as we did when we heard for the first time about sex in the Playhouse alcove. It was wildly illegitimate and pleasurable." When David, Jr., later asked his father how much money he had, the response was cold and angry. Abby says, "My father said that such talk was *not nice*. The way he said these words made me glad I had not been the one to ask the question. Early on I picked up the signals that I shouldn't be proud of the money. Should I be grateful? No, that was wrong too. So was pride, and contentment. There was no attitude in our childhood that we were allowed to have with respect to that money that was appropriate. We weren't allowed to discuss it; we weren't allowed to gloat; we couldn't do anything. And so it was like a festering sore. Like a thing that was going to pop later on."

Money (and the desires it represented) was an urge that had to be controlled. If it was not, then it could be destructive—not only of self, but of the family. ("If you let it control you," David, Jr. notes wryly, "then you become a philanderer instead of a philanthropist.") The message had not changed much since Junior's youth, and neither had the prescribed technique for sedating the desires the money incited. It was the account book. Laurance and John had let this tradition slide altogether. Nelson had gone through the motions with his children. But David took it seriously. It was something his father had done and his father's father before him. He had done it himself. His children, therefore, would keep their generation's version of Ledger A.

With David, Jr., he was fairly successful; but his daughters rebelled against the idea and became masters of fabrication and deceit. Abby and Peggy both took advantage of the long train rides home from boarding school at vacation time to fictionalize several months' accounting of their weekly allowance. They filled the lined pages with expenditures on brassieres and Tampax, hoping to embarrass their father to the extent that he would fail to carry out the audit.

The David family was marked by insight and intelligence. Yet its unique atmosphere created hungers that it could not satisfy. As Peggy recalls of her growing up, "We ate shepherd's pie with our nurses in the kitchen while our parents ate steak in the dining room. When we went in to say good night, we would hang on them, begging for food off their plates. Strangely enough, we had a sense of there not being enough to go around—not enough food, not enough love."

The Cousins' growing up had been in many ways idyllic. Yet there were elements of uncertainty from the beginning, questions that began increasingly to demand answers as they grew older. Why should relatives be their only friends? Why did they play behind patrolled gates? Why was family history a tabooed subject? (As Lucy later said, "It was considered indelicate to ask about our past. It was like sex, a forbidden topic. And like sex, we found out about it piecemeal from other sources.")

The Brothers had the same sort of protective impulse toward their children as Junior had had toward them. As late as 1968, JDR3 replied to Henry Luce, who had written about the possibility of *Life*'s doing a feature story on the family: "We have reluctantly come to the decision that we would ask that the proposed article be postponed. One main reason for this is the children. We feel very keenly the importance of their growing up as normally as possible." Yet by this time most of the Cousins were well past their twenty-first year and their growing up had been far from normal.

Nelson's oldest children, Rodman and Ann, followed in their father's footsteps to Lincoln School for a few years. After he moved to Washington to become Coordinator of Inter-American Affairs, they went to the progressive, liberal Sidwell Friends School, although Nelson would have preferred them in a less exclusive setting. As Ann remembers, "He wanted us in the public schools. If the Washington, D.C., school system had been better academically, that's where he and Mother would have put us."

The other Brothers did not share Nelson's belief that the children should have their instincts for survival and competition sharpened in public school. Lincoln School, which had been so important a part of the Brothers' youth, finally closed down in 1948. Even if it hadn't, the other Cousins probably would have gone to schools more befitting their class. For the boys it was grade school in institutions like Buckley, then on to Exeter, Choate, or Deerfield. For the girls, it was fashionable schools like Brearley or Miss Chapin's School for Girls,* then on to a prep school like Milton or Farmington Academy. Their parents thought they might be sheltered by such schools, but being there only added to the cognitive dissonance of their youth. It had been emphasized that they

---

Fortune magazine wrote about Miss Chapin's, calling it the "smartest school" in New York City: "Nowhere else will you see so many limousines, such smart governesses waiting to take their charges home, such elegant parents escorting offspring to luncheon. . . . Here they learn not to cook, but how best to budget a household and estimate their legitimate number of servants, to keep accounts, to speak French, to read Latin . . . and above all else to have Poise."

were normal children, no better than anyone else except perhaps in the extent of their obligation to benefit their fellow man. Yet now they found themselves in institutions training them to rule.

Even among the children of Du Ponts and Fords, the Rockefellers bore a special name. It was like being a crown prince or princess, but their parents had not prepared them for the notoriety they encountered. JDR3's daughter Alida recalls: "When I was about eleven and at a summer camp in Maine, people found out who I was. One kid came up and asked if I lit my cigars with million-dollar bills. Another came up and asked for my autograph. I gave it to her."

Whatever their school, the problem was the same. They were curiosities. They had the sense that they were constantly on stage, that other people were watching them and evaluating their actions for signs of selfishness or pride, on the one hand, or artificiality on the other. Everyone they met seemed to know more about them and their family than they themselves did. Upon being introduced, they became accustomed to the name producing a flicker in the eye of the beholder. It froze them and instantly set them apart. From the time they entered grade school, they were the focus of hostility, obsequiousness, and ironies that were felt but often not understood. The extent to which they were different was something communicated silently, almost subliminally, by teachers and schoolmates. As Lucy later said, "It seemed as though my friends were always apologizing because their china wasn't as fine as ours." It was a situation calculated to drain their attempts to create distinct personalities and to set up walls between them and others. As Abby says, "Being a Rockefeller was an enormous, pervasive, and central issue for me. From the second grade onwards, it had me worrying all the time. My whole being was organized to try to repulse situations created by it."

School was an ordeal. "When I heard the family name mentioned," says Lucy, "I used to just blank out. I didn't take American history for that reason: I didn't want to hear about the Rockefellers." Her sister Marion's recollection of driving to Brearley in a chauffeured Cadillac is far different from the carefree days when her father and uncles had skipped or rollerskated up Fifth Avenue until they were tired and then climbed into the limousine Junior had ordered to crawl along beside them. "The closer we got to school," Laurance's daughter remembers, "the lower we sank into the back seat of the car. By the time we were almost there, we were begging the chauffeur to please drive a few blocks further and then let us out so we could arrive at school on foot, anonymously."

It was all the worse because it could not be discussed. The Brothers continued to promote the idea that being a Rockefeller was actually no different from being a Smith or a Jones, except that you were to be more responsible, and—it was never spoken, but always understood—better. Yet their children couldn't buy either the expectations or the illusion that they were the same as any other teenagers. On the contrary, for no reason they could quite pinpoint they began to feel ashamed of their name and connections. They were attracted to the privilege and the power, but ashamed of succumbing to such a base emotion. "The problem," recalls Abby, "was trying to figure out where the balance lay between the perverse pleasure of the magic in it, and the pain of alienation from it. I never got anything but a shameful pleasure from my name. I never got a clean sense of pride. To the extent that I ever felt privileged, I felt guilty and ashamed and embarrassed for the privilege."

They all experienced the Rockefeller name as an awesome obstacle. The signals they got from others were reinforced by subtle messages from their parents and the advisers their parents provided for them. Lucy says, "We were counseled not to make loans to friends. Why? 'Because your father and his brothers did so when they were young and they were not paid back.' Like other Cousins, I disregarded this advice a few times and found that sadly enough it had been right. I didn't get paid back. It wasn't losing the money; I didn't care about that. It was just painful to get treated like a nonperson, especially by people you thought were your friends."

Hope, now a writer contributing articles to magazines like *New York* on abortion and other subjects, echoes this feeling. Apologizing in advance for the fact that it sounds absurd, she compares their youthful perception of their situation to that of racial minorities. "In growing up a Rockefeller, I lived with a tag, just like a Jew or black. I'm not by any means suggesting I suffered in the same way, but it is true that when people heard the name Rockefeller, there was no way they could see the person named Hope."

For some of the Cousins, however, the problem was being bothered all the time. Alida, for instance, was trailed over the Stanford campus for several months by an unstable young man who wanted to be a writer and felt this Rockefeller could be his muse and ensure that his works were published. For her sister Hope, it was just the opposite. "When I was at Smith," she says, "people shunned me. It was the exact opposite of what you'd expect. When I saw how reserved they felt about contact with me, I just withdrew. In a situation like this, you finally stop trying and just burrow down into yourself."

It was an odd predicament. They had private planes, yachts, constant travel abroad, servants, vacation homes from the tip of the Caribbean to the Maine woods, from Venezuela to Wyoming, dinner conversation with princes, prime ministers, and some of the most celebrated commoners in the world; they had more than any other group of young people in America. Laura, an attractive 38-year-old woman with three children, who is finishing a Ph.D. and writing a brief history of the Rockefellers, summarizes the problem: "How in the world do you ask for sympathy when you've got all the things that are *supposed* to make you happy?" They were conscious of falling into the melodramatic stereotype of the poor little rich boy or girl and felt that they could not talk about their troubles. Yet their friends understood their dilemma, probably better than they imagined. A confidante of Peggy's who knew her well during the difficult period of her early womanhood, says: "Despite what would appear from the outside to be one of the most secure and attractive situations possible, there was a real human vulnerability. I remember her telling me once in the course of a conversation, 'Look, nobody's ever gonna want to marry *me*.' You *know* that the costs in human terms have got to be great when you say something like that and are in analysis five days a week for several years to work out things that most people wouldn't have to bother to deal with or could resolve by themselves."

As this confusion surrounded them, it naturally altered their view of their heritage. Laura was popular enough to be elected president of her class in high school, yet during those years and the college years that followed, she was almost afraid to bring people home with her. "You had the awful feeling that when you invited friends home and took them through the gates at Pocantico, they wouldn't love you anymore. Those goddamned gates! The messages they conveyed about the world. The world must be a pretty scary place if it is necessary to have police dogs and armed guards prowling around behind closed gates!"

It was possible to rebel against aspects of their growing up. As in the David family, they could flaunt the tradition exemplified in the account books, the church-going, and even ridicule some of the more fatuous aspects of their father's behavior and beliefs. Yet questioning the accumulated weight of the name they had been born with made about as much sense as questioning their height or facial structure. The Cousins' anxiety, therefore, was not in rejecting the family and its role and privilege but in safely finding a way to accept it. The Rockefeller image might be swollen as from elephantiasis, making living up to it impossible, but in the unrelenting system of moral accounting perfected by their grandfather, this debt was owed.

The Cousins couldn't behave as if their name were Smith and quickly finish college so they could get jobs and begin making money. They had to have plans worthy of them. There were pressures—especially on the males—to take posts of responsibility in the family empire, to flow smoothly into the dynasty and do their part to enlarge its influence. Some of the older ones tried to live up to the challenge; but most of them perfected strategies for stalling, creating alternatives, gaining time to organize their lives and prepare for the big decisions ahead.

If they had been born a little later and with different names, they might have taken off with backpacks for Nepal or Tierra del Fuego. But they were Rockefellers, and even their escapism had to be of a high moral order. During or after college, many of them paused to spend a season in obscurity among the poor, dispossessed, or disadvantaged, or occasionally among some unknown culture on a distant continent. These trips were times when they could lose themselves—often quite literally as far as their Rockefeller identity was concerned. The form varied from one Cousin to another, but these pilgrimages into anonymity all shared the same motive. It was a legitimate excuse for flight; it was a way of proving to themselves that others' assumptions were untrue and they really didn't think themselves superior.

When Nelson's daughter Mary was in her first year at Vassar, she discussed her depression and unhappiness with her twin brother, Michael. After they had talked for hours about the wall that existed between them and others, Michael suggested that she get away for a time, go someplace where nobody knew who she was. (Her sister, Ann, had already spent time doing social work in London's East End.) In the turmoil of her freshman year, her uncertainty had so disoriented her and sapped her vitality that she had been put on probation. She agreed that she needed a change of scene. She didn't actually have to look for something to do; as soon as the word went out that there was a Rockefeller looking for a summer's obscurity, she had alternatives to choose from. She decided to join a team of Cornell researchers setting up a public health project on a Navajo reservation. Even now, after fifteen years, Mary becomes animated when discussing the experience. "We lived in a trailer and ate out of cans and lived among people who had never heard of a Rockefeller." She calls it, without qualification, "the turning point in my life."

Peggy went to Brazil, a country that knew of Rockefellers through Nelson's IBEC and David's travels for the Chase. For three summers while she was an undergraduate at Radcliffe, she did social work there. In the third summer she moved from the mansion where she'd lived with friends of her father, to a *favella*, existing amid grinding poverty. When the local press found out about her and arrived at the shack of the poor family with whom she lived, she and a friend escaped through the back door to avoid being interviewed, taking a 1,200-mile bus trip through the Brazilian countryside to preserve her incognita.

Jay Rockefeller spent three years in Japan, mastering the language and culture in anonymity while living with a family in Tokyo. Marion went to territory as distant when she spent months working in hospitals for the retarded and terminally ill. After graduating from Harvard, her brother, Larry, lived in an East Harlem tenement for three years while working as a VISTA volunteer.

"It's hard work for a young person to be a Rockefeller," says Hope. "You have to get to the point where you can take it all the time. The weight of it is such that we all at different times have had a tremendous urge just to get away from being a Rockefeller for a while." In her own case it involved living for more than a year in Nairobi with former husband John Spencer. Later, in a book titled *East African Diary*, she wrote with trepidation about how the local newspapers had reported JDR3 and Blanchette's visit to the Spencers. "This was the first public revelation of my 'identity,' as some of my friends phrased it afterwards. . . . John and I think that now is as good a time as any for our friends to learn about it ... I think our relationships with most of our friends are fairly established and am confident we will not need to alter in any way the informal pattern of living we have followed here."

These odysseys were not purely escapism. They were also calisthenics for the future, part of a search for the "real" self the Cousins felt must exist beneath the artifice of their Rockefeller-ness. It was in this context that Michael decided to get away from his family.

He was accounted one of the "best adjusted" of the Cousins, a favorite of everyone in the family. With sandy hair, thick glasses, and an unaffected warmth, he was an athletic youth (he had lettered in lacrosse and was an excellent swimmer) who reminded family friends of the young Nelson. Although his temperament lacked his father's sharp edges, he seemed to have Nelson's ability to project himself past the obstacle of the name. "When you first enter a group," he once said, "people are curious; but when they find out you're human, it's okay again."

Michael, the most purely aesthetic member of the family, according to his sister Ann, had hoped to study architecture, but had been forced to yield to parental pressure and take up economics. He was just finishing his senior honors thesis at Harvard on his Great-Grandfather Nelson Aldrich and banking reform when a roommate told him about an expedition planned by the Film Study Center at Harvard's Peabody Museum. A small group of anthropologists and a film crew were going to the Baliem Valley in Dutch New Guinea to make a record of tribes whose primitive agricultural society was as yet untouched by Western culture. It was a rare opportunity to set foot in a place where few whites had ever gone, to step back into the Stone Age.

Michael had worked for IBEC in Puerto Rico and served as a ranch hand at his father's Venezuelan estate during summer vacations. He had once told his parents, "I want to do something romantic and adventuresome now while there are still faraway frontiers to explore." This seemed exactly the opportunity he had been waiting for. He was an accomplished photographer, and this competence (along with the influence trickling down from his Uncle David's status as an overseer at Harvard) helped him finesse his way aboard the expedition.

For different reasons, his older brothers, Rodman and Steven, had not worked out as heirs to Laurance's role as the

Rockefeller who kept an eye on the family business. Michael knew that he had now become the male Cousin the Brothers agreed was best suited for leadership of the family in the coming generation. To his father and uncles, he explained the trip as a valuable experience for the future, as well as a chance to obtain artifacts for the Museum of Primitive Art, of which he was already a board member. His brother Steven later said, "The trip was acceptable to the Brothers because they were made to feel that it might be a prelude to a career in international business. Actually to Michael it was a way of buying time."

From the moment the expedition took off, Michael was galvanized by the prospects ahead. He carried out his job of photographer with zeal and also took on the job of sound man. He impressed his colleagues with his appetite for work and his lack of pretense. As one of them later said, "He suffered from the family complex of feeling that he had to work even harder than the rest to prove himself." If they noted any flaw at all in his character, it was a failure to calculate consequence, a kind of recklessness.

He managed to pack a lot of observation of life and death into his few weeks among the Kurelu tribesmen, photographing babies being born, warfare with other tribes, the death of wounded warriors, and the ceremony preparatory to the cremation that sent the dead to oblivion. He enjoyed observing and trying to understand the human cement that joined tribesmen to others. "Michael really found himself over there," one friend in the expedition later told a reporter. He grew a soft, dun-colored beard and decided that when he returned home he would enroll as a graduate student in anthropology.

Having heard of the art of the Papaguan tribes in the coastal Asmat, he went there on a side trip in mid-August and became "wildly excited" by the artifacts he saw. The Peabody expedition had officially concluded, but Michael decided to put off his return to America. He was making preparations for a second, longer trip into the coastal area when he received a cable warning that his parents had decided to make public their intention to seek a divorce.

Michael immediately returned home. It took him only a week in New York to recognize that there was nothing he could do for them. He told them about his decision to become an anthropologist and then hopped aboard a plane and flew to Hollandia (now Djajapura). There he met with Dutch anthropologist Rene Wassing, and together they went on to New Guinea to begin two months of field work.

Moving in and out of the rivers of the Asmat in a catamaran powered by two 18 horsepower motors and able to carry a large load of trade goods, he and Wassing covered a lot of territory. The artifacts they collected—exquisitely carved shields and canoe figureheads, along with a good selection of shrunken heads—made Michael dream of returning home in triumph with the most complete record of primitive life ever assembled. This letter home to his parents testifies that he was secure enough in his own ideas to sideswipe his father's vision of the world:

> The Asmat is filled with a kind of tragedy. For many of the villages have reached that point where they are beginning to doubt their own culture and crave things western. There is everywhere a depressing respect for the white man's shirt and pants, no matter how tattered and dirty, even though these doubtful symbols of another world seem to hide a proud form and replace a far finer ... form of dress. ... The West thinks in terms of bringing advance and opportunity to such a place. In actuality we bring a cultural bankruptcy which will last for many years. ... There are no minerals; and not a single cash crop will grow successfully. Nonetheless, the Asmat like every other corner of the world is being sucked into a world economy and a world culture which insists on economic plenty as a primary ideal.

On November 18, after several weeks in the field, Michael and Wassing decided to travel to a large village on the other side of the South Eilander River. Instead of going by way of the complex system of inland waterways, they thought to save time by venturing out into the coastal waters and then going up the South Eilander. In the middle of this passage, which local traders had warned them was a dangerous one in the best of circumstances, a large wave swamped the catamaran, drowning the engine and sweeping most of Michael's field notes overboard. The two men clung to the foundering craft overnight, slowly being carried out to the open sea by the tide. The next morning Michael decided to try to make the eleven-mile swim to shore. Wassing pleaded with him not to, pointing out that the crocodile- and shark-infested waters would make it an almost impossible task to reach the shore.

But as the middle-aged Dutch anthropologist later said, "He listened to me, but I knew in advance that he would go ahead. It was very difficult to make him change his mind." Stripping to his undershorts, tying his glasses around his neck, and strapping old fuel cans over his shoulders for flotation, Michael looked at Wassing one last time, said, "I think I can make it," and then plunged into the sea. He was never seen again.

Nelson and Michael's twin sister, Mary, flew to the area and participated in several exhausting days of searching along with elements of the Royal Dutch Air Force. There was no sign of him. Finally they returned home having accepted the verdict of authorities in the area. The official view was that Michael had almost certainly drowned in the treacherous tides; yet almost immediately rumors began filtering out of the wild, impenetrable jungle and were carried to civilization by Dutch missionaries in the area. One that gained some acceptance was that Michael did indeed make it to shore and, as he emerged from the exhausting swim, stumbled onto a party of warriors from the village of Otsjanep. He assumed that they would be friendly to a white man and hailed them, not knowing that Dutch soldiers had earlier killed several members of their tribe in a pacification campaign. According to this version, he was killed on sight and later eaten. For years travelers returning from the Asmat brought back lurid stories of having seen natives wearing Michael Rockefeller's broken glasses around their neck and of having been shown what was purported to be his shrunken skull.

To the world at large, Michael's disappearance was a compelling interlude in the drama of Nelson Rockefeller's divorce and remarriage. It was the story of a romantic, daring young man who had lost his life in pursuit of adventure. Only the Rockefeller Cousins could appreciate the true nature of his quest. They decided to pay tribute to his memory by endowing the Michael Rockefeller Fellowship at Harvard. It was the first institution they had formed and funded by themselves. (They did not ask the Brothers to contribute to it until it had been going for several years.) The language in the statement of intent (written by Steven) had a special meaning to them: "The primary purpose of the Fellowship is the development of an individual's understanding of himself and his world through involvement with people of a culture not his own."

Michael would always be the special Cousin, loved and admired by the others for daring to journey to the heart of darkness in pursuit of selfhood. (And perhaps secretly envied because his early death came at a time when he was not yet compromised by the decisions they would all soon have to make.) His death highlighted the necessity of reaching some sort of accommodation with their dilemma. "Every one of us has thought at one time or another of getting away from the name, the whole thing," Hope says, "yet we all know deep down that there's no escape."

27

IN MIDSUMMER 1970, Room 5600 arranged to have a number of questions regarding the Rockefellers inserted into the regular Gallup Poll. From the responses, they extrapolated what they called "The Public Attitudes Toward the Rockefellers." Bound, stamped "confidential," and handed out to family members, its findings showed that although Nelson was the only Rockefeller with whom the public was very familiar (respondents had difficulty distinguishing the other Brothers from each other and from their father), the public image of the family, because of the philanthropies with which it was associated, was generally good. The report concluded with an exhortation aimed indirectly at the Cousins:

> Here is a family whose vast wealth might be expected to generate envy, jealousy, and hatred; but instead it is seen predominantly by now as a dedication to public and humanitarian service for the good of mankind. . . . The current generation of the family and their advisors have done their job, have made their impact; they have scaled about as far up their heights of esteem as it is humanly possible for the Rockefellers to attain. What is most needed now is that the younger generation proceed to carry on, with devotion, the good work—and good works—of their forebears.

This was an exact summary of their dilemma. The good works expected of them could take place only within the context of institutions pioneered by their grandfather and perfected by their fathers. Even if the Cousins hadn't had doubts about the enterprise, they would have felt that the heights had been scaled and the possibilities for self-discovery exhausted. Much of their reluctance about the tradition into which they had been born centered exactly on the fact that its epic bulk smothered their individual attempts to locate themselves within it. Yet, whatever doubts they had about being Rockefellers, they did want to *do* something with their lives. To accept the scenario implicit in the survey's conclusions, however, would be to become little more than curators in the museum of past Rockefeller accomplishments. It was not enough.

Even had the Cousins been able to formulate this sense of dread, the Brothers would have had trouble understanding, let alone accepting it. They found it hard to accept the fact that the Cousins had been scarred by growing up Rockefellers: it was as if to do so would somehow equivocate their own lives and accomplishments and call for a reevaluation of the tradition and responsibility they had accepted. *We were up to it, why aren't you?* This was the attitude the Cousins—particularly the male Cousins—sensed in their fathers and uncles. To refuse the responsibility embedded in the fortune was made to seem the ultimate ingratitude and elicited a sense of guilt equal to that of having the privilege itself. It had all been summed up in the Creed that Ivy Lee had helped Junior write as a summary of his philosophy: " *'Every right implies a responsibility/Every opportunity an obligation/Every possession a duty.'* That is pretty heavy stuff, especially when you're just a kid and you know you've got all those millions coming," says Steven, quoting the lines from memory. "If you believe that to justify wealth you have to do good works, and then you have this tremendous fortune, you have to become a kind of messiah to justify it."

As one after another of his and the other Brothers' children went into therapy, Laurance (who had refined his own tenuousness into a life-style) sneered that they were "copping out." In few areas was the generation gap felt more acutely than in the question of seeking psychiatric help. David's younger son, Richard, smiles bitterly: "My father doesn't understand what a hang-up is. He and his brothers feel that if you're down, you should go and clean up your room and then you'll feel better. For that generation it seems to work: if they 'clean up their rooms,' they *do* feel better."

If the Brothers didn't understand how their children felt oppressed by the Rockefeller identity and all it portended, they also failed to calculate the extent to which the Cousins were children of their own time, an era of protest over imperial war, racial inequality, and social injustice. The generation they identified with was challenging exactly those powers and assumptions on which the family tradition was based. The Brothers' insistence that the Cousins should be Rockefellers in the same sense they had been, showed how isolated the third generation had become.

It seemed natural that the female Cousins should take the lead, running interference for their more cautious and in some ways more burdened brothers. They were more numerous and had grown up knowing they would someday lose the name by marriage. If they felt less pressure, they also were less firmly anchored. They sensed that little was expected of them, which increased their unexplored outrage. Many of them were attracted by the political consciousness ushered in by the New Frontier, and even to its more radical fringes. The idea they picked up from activist students—that what their fathers had taught them was a social harmony was actually a violent union of the powerful and the powerless—appealed to realities they had perceived from their own status in the family and smoothly meshed with their own inner turmoil. Their dilemma also expressed itself in polarities: liking the privilege and possessions that Rockefeller money bought, yet feeling somehow tainted by them; respecting the family's "good" accomplishments in philanthropy, yet fearing that this was only one side of a coin whose obverse was not altruistic.

One Harvard SDS friend recalls how David's daughter Peggy, an early supporter of the Cambridge antiwar movement, came to his room, tears streaming down her face. It was 1966, at the time of the Vietnam teach-ins. He asked her what was wrong. "My father just asked me to go abroad with him to attend an opening of a branch of the bank," she replied.

"What's so bad about that? You've done it before," he comforted her.

Peggy answered, "The branch is in Saigon."

Peggy's older sister Abby was the only Cousin whose life would ultimately be profoundly changed through her involvement in the new politics. For many of the others, however, such involvement would be an important step in their struggle to locate themselves in the context of the family and to win freedom from its oppressive expectations. Like Abby and Peggy, Laura became an early sponsor of SDS during its participatory democracy stages (and remains a funder of the Cambridge Institute, which specializes in designing decentralized alternatives to capitalist forms of business and social organization); nearly a decade later, Alida, one of the last of the fourth generation to reach college age, stood sympathetically on the periphery of the Third World movement that swept over the Stanford campus. In between, Rockefeller women poured hundreds of thousands of dollars into movement causes ranging from *Ramparts* magazine and the film *Milhouse* to the *Venceremos* Brigade and Vietnam Veterans Against the War.

In some of this there was an element of "radical chic." Yet for this family above all others, politics is a metaphor for identity; it summarizes in solemn mummery the differences in sensibility and world view between the generations. The dialogue was particularly lively in the David family. He was not only the Brother most completely identified with the "system," but also the one who most felt that it (and by implication himself) must be defended against the onslaught of the younger generation. Peggy remembers heated discussions about the Chase Bank's involvement in South Africa and David's defense of reactionary regimes in Brazil and elsewhere around the world. "He always tried to justify support for dictatorships via the notion that the economic growth which stability brought to these countries made the average person there better off," she says, with a smile that betrays her embarrassment at the naïveté of it, and a certain shame at the complicity it defends.

As the war in Vietnam escalated, there were ever more violent discussions about it. They usually ended with Peggy shouting or bursting helplessly into tears while her father continued to defend some particularly indefensible aspect of official policy, like the domino theory, by claiming that he got his information from privileged communications with "Bob" McNamara or someone else who represented what he called the "horse's mouth." Peggy says, "He always insists that he gets his facts from some high-up source. This was true about Vietnam and later about Watergate. He claimed that McGovern had inflated the break-in out of all proportion and that people around the President had personally assured him that Nixon knew nothing about any part of it."

It was in part her activities around Cambridge radical

circles that led Peggy to drop her last name. "My brother Dickie was always getting in political hassles because of the name," she says. "It got in the way of things I was trying to do. In this country, Kennedy is the only other name I associate with such hassles: money, power, politics, philanthropy, buildings all over the place. The name got in the way of things I was trying to do."

Always, whatever was involved, it came back to the name. Sandra, JDR3's oldest child, had been the first to jettison it, becoming plain Sandra Ferry in 1959. It was an attempt to solve the dilemma in one swift move; at the same time she dropped her last name, Sandra also tried to give away her money. Yet the trust fund was more firmly affixed to her than the name. She became the eccentric among the Cousins, the one whose name always brought a raised eyebrow or a shrug of incomprehension. By the early sixties she had moved to Cambridge and become a recluse and valetudinarian, still avoiding the family and the name, although now accepting the money. She lived behind multiple locks like a woman twice her age, being visited regularly by a psychiatrist and a music therapist. According to family lore, she once spent five years recovering from a broken toe.

In the completeness of her flight from the world the Rockefellers had been born to rule, Sandra represented the opposite extreme of Michael's aggressive search for self. The Cousins accepted her as an equally symbolic figure. As Abby says, "Sandra is the extreme reaction against the notion that a Rockefeller *must* be responsible and concerned. Her rebellion has been to become totally centered on herself."

Most of the female Cousins took a less direct route of changing their name: they married. Throughout the early sixties, formal weddings were becoming frequent affairs at the small Pocantico Hills church, brides being given away by their celebrated fathers to a series of commoners. Soon there were announcements heralding the arrival of the fifth generation of Rockefellers, bearing names like Case, Hamlin, Kaiser, Strawbridge, and Spencer. Yet time would show that more had been involved than young love. Since divorced and remarried, Laura now says, "I got married when I was nineteen because it was a way to lose the name. I copped out."

The wives of the Brothers had played a certain role as Rockefeller consorts, "fitting into their husbands' lives, managing their homes, entertaining their guests," as Nelson's son Steven characterizes it. Yet the Cousins couldn't do this, and not only because of the coming of women's liberation and the destabilization of traditional roles. They were, after all, Rockefellers by blood; their mothers were Rockefellers only by law. After making their marriages, they were faced with the impossible task of having to learn to express their Rockefeller ambitions through domesticity. While some of them were comforted by the protective coloration of the housewife's role, they still had the need to *do* something. There was also the unspoken but disquieting problem that their marriages were morganatic and that they had to live with what David, Jr., calls "the odd fact of having more power than their men."

Marriage got rid of the name, but at awesome emotional costs. By the mid-1960s, the handsome young couples who had said their vows a few years earlier were breaking up. Of seven such marriages launched in this period, five resulted in divorce.* The process became not a solution but another step in the search. As Lucy, one of the victims of a hasty first marriage, explains, "When I got divorced, I went into analysis. I wanted to find out about myself. My first husband had been a good person. There was something wrong with *me*. I didn't know how to think things through. I didn't know how things worked. I didn't know how anything related to me as a Rockefeller."

The Brothers were puzzled and even saddened by what they saw as their daughters' chaotic lives. Yet in some sense it was not unexpected. There were precedents in the two previous Rockefeller generations—their errant Aunt Edith and their own sister, Babs, neither of whom managed to stay married or happy for long. For the male Cousins, the expectations were different. The structure was designed for them to move into, as the Brothers themselves had; it was a reality and a lifework. Awaiting them was a multiplicity of institutions ranging from Rockefeller University and the Riverside Church to Rockefeller Center and the Chase. Perhaps they had faced difficult adjustments growing up but by the early sixties, as the last of them emerged from college, all that was behind them; the stage was set for the genteel Darwinism by

---

*Laura married James Case in 1956, divorced in 1970; Hope married John Spencer in 1959, divorced in 1969; Ann married Robert Pierson in 1955, dovorced in 1966; Mary married William Strawbridge in 1961, divorced in 1974; Lucy married Charles Hamlin in 1964, divorced in 1969.

which the fittest among them would be selected to lead the family in the coming generation.

Their options were not kept secret. As Steven recalls, "The older generation expected us to continue accepting responsibility for the family institutions and programs just as Grandfather had expected them to do. I had meetings with my father and uncles on the question of following in the family tradition. Nobody ever said, 'I expect you to do this or that.' It was not that explicit. The message was more like this: 'The Rockefeller family has all this wealth to use for good social programs, and it is your duty as a male member of this family to take a position of responsibility.' "

The male Cousins did not rebel as forthrightly as their sisters. It was only through small gestures that did not necessarily have to be interpreted as antagonistic ones, that they made their feelings known. Larry, for instance, who had inherited an interest in conservation from his father, gave $10,-000 to the Sierra Club Legal Defense at about the same time the organization was fighting his father on the Redwood National Park issue. But for the most part it was as if Nelson had gathered all the Rockefeller energy, ambition, and *machismo* to himself and burned it out in his own incandescent quest for power. His son Steven was an omen of things to come. After his graduation from Princeton in 1957, he went to work in the rentals office of Rockefeller Center. This is where his father had started twenty-five years earlier. But while renting space had offered the eager young Nelson a chance to prove himself to his father by helping make the family's riskiest venture work, Steven found dealing with the successful Rockefeller Center absurd and demeaning, and soon resigned.

Steven's older brother, Rodman, the first male of his generation, had been the logical candidate for leadership. He had an interest in it, along with an aptitude for business. Closer in outlook to the Brothers than to most of the Cousins (he once said to someone who had asked him how it felt to be a Rockefeller, "I really couldn't tell you, as I've never been anything else"), he had mastered whatever doubts he had about being a Rockefeller long before graduating from college and apparently without a struggle. Speaking from the president's office in IBEC's suite in Rockefeller Center, Rodman sits with one long leg hooked over the other, not noticing that his pants cuff is hiked high above the top of his sock. Blinking bookishly out of thick glasses, he has the appearance and bearing of someone caught between two worlds. His face is utterly unlined and oddly boyish for a 42-year-old man; the shock of hair is gray, yet tufted in tight, youthful curls; he is the chief executive of one of the biggest corporations in the country, yet people call him Roddy.

Rodman talks about his life as if it were a junior version of the Brothers', inflating the tale at certain points to try to fill the space of the role. He was very happy as a young man, as he says, "because Father always included me in his interest areas and therefore I was never alienated from him." He followed Nelson to Dartmouth (where a former classmate, filmmaker Bob Rafelson, recalls sitting behind him in class and gazing wonderingly at the long cashmere scarf with the name RODMAN C. ROCKEFELLER emblazoned in heavy block lettering down its edge). During the summer vacations he went with his father on trips to South America, and when he was sixteen Nelson put him in a Venezuelan agricultural school for several weeks. The Latin American influence manifested itself in the subject of Rodman's senior thesis in economics: "The Effect of U.S. Decisions on the Balance of Payments in Brazil."

After graduation, he spent two years in the army stationed in Germany. On his return he entered the Columbia Business School. He had listened earnestly to the advice Nelson gave him. "Get into one of the family institutions and use it as a vehicle for your personal interests." There was some talk about bringing him into Room 5600 to understudy Laurance, but the Brothers finally agreed that he did not have the temperament or command sufficient respect among the other Cousins for this role, and turned their attention to Michael. Steven, and Jay. His Uncle David thought Rodman might be a good candidate for an executive position with the Chase and offered him a job there, but he had already gotten an offer he couldn't refuse—from Nelson himself. In 1960 Rodman joined IBEC as head of its Housing Division, working his way steadily up the executive ladder until 1969, when he was made president of his father's company.

Along the way he had adopted certain Rockefeller mannerisms which might have fit prior generations but in his seemed painfully out of place. One of his father's old friends, Frank Jamieson's widow Linda Storrow, recalls meeting Roddy at a summer home in Nantucket. She invited him and his wife out for a drink. When getting ready to pay the bill, she asked his advice on tipping. He replied that 10 percent was right. She remarked that this seemed rather low. He answered, "My Great-Grandfather tipped 10 percent, and what was good enough for Great-Grandfather is good enough for me."

Rodman became an enthusiastic worker in the New York Republican party, campaigning loyally for his father in Spanish among the Puerto Rican community every four years. He became a leading member of Riverside Church. After his Uncle David had gotten involved on the fringes of the concerned businessmen's movement, Rodman formed an organization to help gain corporate positions for minority executives. There are few things about the family he did not embrace, his only cavil being that the Brothers have not accepted him as a full and functioning partner in their enterprise. "Far from being a problem," he says, "the Rockefeller identity has allowed me to spread my wings. I never went through a period of questioning about being a Rockefeller. I was once referred to as 'moneybags,' I believe by a young Du Pont, but I guess we all have our crosses to bear. I'm like my Father: I can honestly say that being a Rockefeller has never been a burden. It's one thing I have no doubts about."

The other Cousins feel that Roddy has made these choices to avoid conflict with Nelson. For them, the very fact that he never went through "a period of questioning" was reason enough to reject his clumsy bids to become the leader of their generation and their spokesman. That he could claim to find a kind of fulfillment working within the institutional Rockefeller identity made him almost as much an eccentric among them as Sandra's paranoia made her. This was especially true because such strict adherence to the letter of the Rockefeller law—demanded of the previous generation by Junior—was no longer entirely necessary. None of the Brothers was sufficiently enthusiastic to take upon himself the role of guardian of the family tradition; none was ready to excommunicate anyone for falling off. Thus, in Rodman, it seemed an almost gratuitous sacrifice, a stubborn decision *not* to find himself.

It was something no other male Cousin would do. They would equivocate, temporize, hide, and use a variety of other techniques to avoid an outright break with the family, but none of them would embrace it so uncritically or claim, as Rodman does, that the family helped them spread their wings. On the contrary, the others felt that being *that* kind of Rockefeller was either too ridiculous (in Steven's words), or simply unthinkable in post-Vietnam America. Within the family, it is generally assumed that Roddy, like his Uncle John, was victimized by being the first male of his generation.

Unlike his cousin, "Young David" (as he is called by the Office, the term managing to conjure up the image of the pretender to some throne) is both subtle and tactful. At thirty-four, the oldest son of the president of the Chase Manhattan Bank is not portly in the manner of his father, but he does have a soft layer of flesh, which inflates under psychological pressure. For almost a decade, this pressure has been to decide what he finally is going to do with himself.

Sitting in his personal office in downtown Boston, David, Jr., gives an impression that is somewhat casual for the former assistant general manager of the Boston Symphony, a post he occupied for six years before recently leaving to rent this room to "figure things out." Music has been a central part of his life. An accomplished baritone, he organized an acclaimed Bach chorus in Boston called the Cantata Singers. He is also one of the sponsors of the experimental Kodály method for teaching music to very young children, which is being funded by the Ford Foundation. (When Mrs. Kodály, widow of the Hungarian composer, came to Boston, David, Jr., arranged to hire a pianist so they could sing to each other.) "Music is an intense interest of mine that has led me into administrative responsibilities as a performer and a trustee," he explains. "It is the thread of my life. In a way it is soul food enough, but whether or not it takes care of the sense of responsibility is another question. The big issue for me is how I spend my life."

After being discouraged from an early interest in poetry, which flourished at Exeter, Young David dutifully entered Harvard for a degree in economics that his father approved, then attended Harvard Law School, following that with a year's graduate work in economics at Cambridge, and, at last, ran up against the conflict between desire and duty that no amount of education could make disappear. For six years he postponed the decision about which course his life would take by becoming assistant general manager of the Boston Symphony (in charge of marketing and public affairs) and even participating in seminars at the Harvard Business School, presenting papers like "A Decision Point in the Symphony's Recent History" to make his job seem weightier to his father.

Yet he always felt his father's silent reproach condemning his involvement in music as a mere hobby—something like beetle collecting—not worthy of a life's dedication, particularly not a Rockefeller life. The one thing that could make his father truly happy, however, was the one thing that was totally out of the question. "I think there is a nepotism rule at the bank," David, Jr., replies with muted sarcasm to the inevitable question about a future at the Chase. "And if there wasn't such a rule, I'd invent one." In his carefully chosen rationale to explain his adamant stand, he shows that he has mastered his father's tact. "From the point of view of morale inside the bank, I think it would be a disaster for me to get involved there. One thing this family does not need to do is make itself resented by thousands more people. The issue of whether we make it by pull or merit is complicated enough."

If the Chase is out, so is Rockefeller University, on whose board of trustees David, Jr., has agreed to sit in another gesture of compromise. Here the question, as he puts it, is one of leadership. "My father succeeded his father as chairman of the board. There never was a non-Rockefeller chairman of the board, I think. Under this direction the institution has done very well, so you can conclude that that was a healthy feudalism, or you can conclude that it was healthy then but not now, or that it was never healthy. I lean toward the conclusion that for its time, it was healthy. As for now, it's not my issue to answer. It's the university's issue. For myself, I don't see my interests involving being the chairman of that university. It's a huge institution and to assume its leadership, I'd have to be deeply committed to what the university is about. But I don't see my own life interests going in that direction."

The issue finally is one of time and one's sense of self: "One of the most valuable things that's happened to me in the last few years is that I have learned how to say no without guilt. When a request gets really big in terms of time, I can't see it, unless it feels personally right. Where our generation assumes positions of authority as a proving ground of personality, it'll work out. Where these commitments are predominantly brought about through the sense of responsibility, they're not going to work out. None of us are going to live our lives with a sense of responsibility hanging over our heads like a cement block."

David, Jr.,'s younger brother, Richard, is at this point the only other potential male "heir" to the bank, which has during David, Sr.,'s time become the cornerstone of the family's financial power and influence. A gifted photographer and amateur pilot, Richard lives in an apartment on one of Cambridge's tree-lined residential streets. It has the unmistakable quality of student housing. In the bedroom, a pair of giant elephant tusks rises vertically off pedestals to a height of five feet, just enough for him to hang his shirt on, revealing an athletic build which seems a reproach to his father and older brother. The tusks, he explains, were a gift from his father, who was presented with them on a recent trip to Africa. He got them, he says with a laugh—enjoying the absurdity but failing to escape embarrassment completely—because his father "already had a pair."

Richard knows what is expected of him but is less guarded than David, Jr., in expressing his opinion of it. "I feel severe pressure not from my father directly, but from associates of his, to control either the Family Office or the Rockefeller Foundation," he says. "I have to ask myself if I've got the ability to bridge the gap between being a dilettante and being a Renaissance man. That gap can't be bridged by money." Discussing a project he had been contemplating in the field of education (in which he has spent several years as a graduate student at Harvard's Ed School), he says with vehemence: "I wouldn't touch the Rockefeller Foundation in seeking funding. To do so would prevent me from ever establishing my identity. How would you even know why people are listening to you? Other family members have run things, but never *produced* anything. If I did it, I would want to do it on my own. I want to know that I can do it on my own."

The project Richard had contemplated was that of writing a critical study of American universities, something he thought of as a sort of Michelin guide to higher education. Like his older brother's poetry, however, this did not fit the definition of the kind of work that justified not being involved in some family institution, and his father in particular did not think much of it. Richard hesitated as long as possible. Then, in the fall of 1974, following a banking trip with his father to the Middle East, he told his family that he had made a decision about the future: to enter medical school. This solution ingeniously satisfied his own requirement that he develop an expertise along with the Rockefeller obligation to do something for others, while putting him beyond the reach of family ambitions that he enter the Bank, the Office, or the Foundation.

Richard and the other male Cousins have been aided by their sisters' rebelliousness (politically and personally), which provided a kind of protective coloration for their more moderate efforts to find a spot for themselves outside the family. The sons had also discovered that the Brothers themselves had unwittingly expanded the area in which a Rockefeller could maneuver without being guilty of an outright break. It had not been intentional, but occurred as a by-product of *their* accommodation to the name and the role as younger men. In a sense, Laurance's irony had been a kind of rebellion, enlarging the inner space permissible for a Rockefeller to explore and making possible a kind of bemused detachment from the high seriousness with which Junior had surrounded the family mission. By subordinating everything else in his own career, Nelson had created a precedent for the Cousins' struggle to pursue individual goals. Most of all, there had been Winthrop. Although the moral of his flagrant behavior was not lost on them, the male Cousins were grateful to him for stretching the lengths—spatially and behaviorally—to which one could go without being completely cut off. As Steven says, "Win paid a great price for it, but he rebelled rather forcefully and went his own way. Without breaking completely, he attempted to start a whole new life for himself. In a certain way, he was a model for us all. This is especially true of someone like Jay, of course."

The smoothly handsome 37-year-old Jay would agree that he is the most direct beneficiary of Winthrop's small rebellion. He recalls spending long nights with his lonely uncle at Winrock, watching him drink Scotch from water tumblers, listening to his rambling stories, and feeling his pathos. A towering six foot six, Jay is so thin that West Virginians call him "the beanpole politician." Yet he moves with a kind of grace befitting one who played basketball at Exeter and then on Harvard's freshman team. Eased into a chair in the office he currently occupies as president of West Virginia Wesleyan College, he looks out the window at the students walking up the streets of Buchanan. When he speaks, it is with the pleasantly familiar manner of someone who has worked hard to exercise all vestiges of the seigneur from his manner. He is not above saying "bullshit" and knows far more about the inner workings of professional baseball (his knowledge of this sport's trivia is almost encyclopedic) than about what takes place in the Rockefeller Family Office. While he goes out of his way to affirm his closeness to his Rockefeller elders (it is primarily a political decision, an understanding that his present ambitions demand that he keep closed ranks with them), the story he tells of coming to West Virginia shows how he declared a separate peace from the family.

He had gone through Exeter Academy in a kind of haze. The extent to which he was out of touch with his father was emphasized by his fanatical interest in sports: JDR3 had managed to grow up in the middle of New York without ever having seen the Giants, Yankees, or Dodgers play. Jay, on the other hand, benefited from his mother Blanchette's natural athletic ability; *her* father had hired a tennis professional to come and live at the Hooker estate in Greenwich to perfect the game of his four daughters. In his first year at Harvard, Jay enjoyed playing on the freshman basketball team because it gave him a chance "to associate with fifteen other guys from totally different walks of life." Yet after this experience he found himself walking an automaton's path toward involvements more in keeping with his background and future. He joined one of Harvard's most exclusive clubs. It was as if he had no real alternative to choices whose banality he fully recognized. "I was unable to keep myself from being pulled along this route. It was more or less expected of me to do certain things, and I did them. I really didn't like doing them, but I couldn't have admitted it then, let alone done anything about it."

In his third undistinguished year at college, as he began to feel that he was falling into the narrow part of the funnel and would soon find himself out of school and working in the Office if something weren't done, things came to a head. Feeling miserable about what he calls "the general sludge of Harvard," he went to see Professor Edwin O. Reischauer, former ambassador to Japan and a friend to JDR3. "I told him I really wasn't happy with my life and didn't feel I was doing the right thing with it. I told him I wished I could get off the track I was on, and do something different, something that was not just pushing blindly ahead." It was natural that their conversation should get around to the Orient. Jay had gone there with his father on one of JDR3's annual tours, and mentioned that he had most enjoyed Japan. Reischauer suggested that he consider taking a year off to go there and study. It was the perfect solution: it had the feel of comforming to family tradition, yet he would be going there not as a symbolic figure interpreting America to the Japanese, as his father had, but as an anonymous American student. It was what, in the football jargon Jay had mastered as well as any other armchair quarterback, was called a "good lateral movement."

He left in 1958 and moved in with a middle-class family in Tokyo. He could come out of hiding and use the Rockefeller identification to his advantage when he wanted to attend diplomatic functions or needed respite from anonymity. Otherwise he was like anyone else. "When I got there," he says, glancing involuntarily at the large handpainted Japanese screen on the wall of his office, "I worked hard. I threw myself into it totally. I was like a monk. Every morning I was up by five-thirty sitting crosslegged on a bamboo mat in my room, surrounded by books. I took courses, talked to students, read constantly. After a while, things began to change for me. I began to feel better about things."

The three years he spent in Japan were a respite during which he prepared himself for the ordeal ahead, the lifetime of being a Rockefeller. Yet it was also a time when he began to understand that if he could claim some territory that was uniquely his, the name might be as much a help as a hindrance. He says, "It wasn't on the surface of my mind, but I suppose I was resolving whatever doubts I had about being a Rockefeller. All the problems I'd had before seemed to get taken care of, although I don't recall really *doing* it myself." At about the same time that his sister Sandra was trying to renounce her name and heritage, Jay embraced his. John Rockefeller became John D. Rockefeller IV.

The first of two trips he made back to the United States during his stay in Japan came when his father wrote asking him to visit his namesake, who was critically ill. The second trip came when he was cabled of Junior's death. The way the news reached him seemed itself an epiphany of the miraculous power in the name to which he was now at least nominally committed. "I happened to be in the middle of the Ceylon jungle—quite. literally in the middle—visiting an old friend. I still don't quite know how they located me, but some way or another this native came walking up in the middle of this God-forsaken place and asked me if I was Mr. Rockefeller. I said I was. He gave me a telegram from my father."

He got on a plane for New York, attended the memorial services for Junior, and hardly pausing for breath, flew back to Japan. The sleeplessness helped give the whole experience a kind of hallucinatory quality, convincing Jay that he had done the right thing in deciding not to swim against the current of the tradition that bore him along. "It was a powerful, intense moment in my life—one of those experiences where a great deal is happening inside and out, and which you later have trouble expressing in words. It was all tied up with me—with who I was and where I came from. I remembered writing Grandfather when I was twenty-one, asking him for formal permission to use the whole name. He'd written back a very strong letter, proud of my request. It was very powerful, the whole experience of his death. It was more than a man passing on: it was history itself."

Part of the history that passed on, as it worked out, was that which in his father's generation had entailed a special obligation on the man bearing the dynastic name. Jay might now feel positively about being the fourth John D. Rockefeller, but this didn't change the independent course he had set himself. Though he knew that the Brothers felt he was an ideal candidate to go to work in Room 5600, when he returned from Tokyo it was not to New York but to Cambridge. Reentering Harvard in 1961 as a serious student, he quickly went through all the Japanese language, literature, and history classes the college offered, while also beginning to study Chinese. He was in such a big hurry that he went down to enroll in Yale (where he had been admitted as a graduate student in Oriental Studies) even before Harvard's commencement ceremonies.

He had originally planned to finish his Ph.D. in four years, but after the first year he lost the enthusiasm as suddenly as he had gotten it. It was as if the obsession with things Oriental had fulfilled its task, burning out his uncertainty about being a Rockefeller male, and could now be discarded. As Jay says, "It was like the fever had passed and I didn't need that kind of intense involvement anymore." Understanding intuitively that he had passed the stage where his only two choices were the equally impossible ones of turning his back on his family or being used by it, he cast about for ways in which his status as a Rockefeller might satisfy his inborn need, as he puts it, "to do something worthwhile," if not for all humanity—in traditional Rockefeller fashion—at least for himself.

As a good example of what passed for involved youth in the early 1960s (he had written an article for *Life* while in Japan pointing out the reasons for the restlessness of radical Japanese youth), Jay had been selected by the Kennedy administration to be on the advisory board of the new Peace Corps after he returned to Harvard. ("Out of deference to my Uncle Nelson, I had first registered as a Republican—any news to the contrary would have embarrassed him politically—but I'd voted for Kennedy and considered myself part of the new things happening around the Democratic party.") The New Frontier was a logical beginning for someone with Jay's ambition and connections. In 1962, leaving graduate school, he took a job as Sargent Shriver's special assistant. One of his tasks was interviewing people for Peace Corps staff positions overseas. He recalls one occasion when he got a phone call from Attorney General Robert Kennedy, who said he was sending over a good candidate for a choice Peace Corps position. Jay interviewed him, but wrote him off. "About ten days later, I got another call. The Attorney General said, 'Look, I feel pretty strongly about this.' I told him I felt pretty strongly too. We agreed to a standoff. It was the beginning of a pretty good relationship with Bobby."

For a young professional, as Jay had by that time begun to regard himself, the Peace Corps was perfect. "Papers moved fast, so did promotions and careers. Since going to Japan, I had fantasized constantly about being the first U.S. ambassador to the People's Republic—fantasized so much that I actually believed it would happen. I left the Peace Corps for the State Department to get some 'real' experience in foreign affairs." This was in 1963. For the next few months he worked as special assistant to Roger Hilsman and third man on the Indonesia desk. "Basically my job was to arrange Hilsman's desk for him every morning, getting the top-secret cables in order and that sort of thing."

When Hilsman was fired by Lyndon Johnson for not exhibiting sufficient enthusiasm about Vietnam, Jay was faced with a decision. He could have had a career in foreign affairs; his father's connections in the State Department guaranteed that. Yet it would begin at a lower level than he was interested in, and it would not give him the sense he was his own man. His movie star's good looks had made him one of the most active and successful bachelors in recent Washington history—he lived in a fashionable town house with a heated pool in Volta Place and shuttled between parties in his XKE escorting a variety of young women—but he was not really comfortable in the nation's capital. He was too much a Rockefeller.

He was attracted to the world of politics, and he convinced himself that it was not the same world inhabited by his Uncle Nelson, but the newer politics of the Kennedys, which had transformed Washington society and given an existential touch to the wheeling and dealing and frantic mobilization of personal power that went on there. Politics was now a world better reported by a Norman Mailer than a Joseph Alsop, an ideal arena for any ambitious young man trying to choose from among an embarrassment of riches. Jay decided he'd like to return to Washington someday—by election.

The question was where he should begin. He realized that it had to be removed from the New York–Washington axis—removed spatially and intellectually—if he were to keep from constantly tripping over his family. (He had agreed to join his father as a trustee of the Rockefeller Foundation; but it was as a useful connection, both familial and financial, rather than as a primary responsibility.) While he was pondering this question, an old friend from the Peace Corps, Charlie Peters (subsequently editor of the *Washington Monthly*), suggested West Virginia, whose Appalachia had become a highly symbolic area as a result of the cooperation between Michael Harrington and the Kennedys. Peters arranged for Jay to fly over the countryside and see the devastation. He was suitably impressed. But he was also considering working in Southern California's Mexican-American community. He flew out there to see the *barrio* in Los Angeles. "Coming back on the plane," he recalls, "I made a check list with the plusses and minuses for each area, West Virginia versus Los Angeles. It was a very Rockefeller thing to do, I know, but actually not very characteristic of me." Either place would do: both communities had such problems that someone dealing with them as he proposed to would become immediately visible. Yet the fact that West Virginia's people—31 percent of whom were officially "poor"—spoke something close to his language finally made up his mind for him.

The decision came before OEO or VISTA had been created. Getting to West Virginia in some legitimate capacity that did not have the word "carpetbagger" written in golden letters all over it was a problem. But as his goals became clearer, any reluctance he might have had to pull Rockefeller strings to get what he wanted was disappearing. He called Bobby Kennedy, who arranged to have him appointed to the Presidential Commission on Juvenile Delinquency, which had an agency (Action for Appalachian Youth) in West Virginia.

He arrived in Charleston in 1964 to find a desk job waiting for him in the state office building. Yet the kind of future he envisioned depended on being about among the people. He picked an area fifty miles away from the state capital. It was

Emmons County, where (he says) "only thirteen of the two hundred fifty-six families weren't either ex-employed or working in some nonunion doghole." He bought and parked a small house trailer there so he could stay longer hours and work to overcome the suspicion these mountain people usually reserved for Republican organizers and revenue agents.

His time there stretched into two years. He says, "Not necessarily because of me, the community began to get together. Once we found out that a nearby town had condemned an elementary school and was going to tear it down. We bought it for seventy-five dollars, brought it back to Emmons on flatbed trucks, and reassembled it as a community center. From then on, except for Sunday mornings, there wasn't a day it wasn't filled." Such work was the initiation providing Jay with the credentials and the excuse—clearly, there were systemic problems community organization could not change—to do what had been in the back of his mind since he first came there: run for elective office. Early in 1966 he had changed his registration to Democratic; in November he was elected to the state's House of Delegates by a large margin.

He was a West Virginian in the way his Uncle Winthrop was an Arkansan: admired as a celebrity; coveted as a resource; tolerated as an outsider. If he didn't control enough of the great family fortune to focus it on the state's problems as Winthrop had in pumping some $35 million into his adopted home, it was widely *assumed* that he could, and that the magic of the Rockefeller name would attract a cornucopia of investment capital and government grants. (But he did have enough money to spend $300,000 a year on a private staff studying the state's problems and possibilities.) Jay also performed a similar symbolic function to Winthrop's in indicating that the twentieth century had finally come to West Virginia and in bringing glamour to the state. He was certainly the only resident who could have been involved in the Wedding of the Year.

It came in 1967 when he married Sharon Percy, the honey-blond daughter of the Illinois Senator whom Jay had met when she was working in the office of then-Congressman John Lindsay. The wedding showed that Jay had not completely forsaken his family identity for the hills and hollows of Appalachia. Although he gallantly insisted that it was a "Percy affair," its ritual was distinctly Rockefeller. It was performed in the Rockefeller Chapel of the University of Chicago, named after his great-grandfather. The wedding march was played on the huge carrillon donated by Junior. The gathering of notables—the Mark Hatfields, John Lindsays, George Romneys, and various Rockefellers—were guided to their seats by Amyn Khan, son of Ali Khan and a JDR IV classmate at Harvard.

Jay did not follow his Uncle Winthrop's example and build himself a Jayrock. Even if he had had the money, which he didn't, this was not the style of his generation; none of the Cousins had the need to re-create Pocantico. Instead he and his bride moved into a relatively modest—for a Rockefeller—rambling country home on Barberry Lane in Charleston (the lotus fragility of the Oriental art he had collected in Japan was mixed with Early American antiques by a New York decorator to create what Sharon Percy Rockefeller called "a young house"), and he bought a thousand acres in Pocahontas County where he would eventually build a country home. In 1969, after Jay had been elected secretary of state and was clearly pointing toward the governorship, Sharon had their first child. He was named John (to be called "Jamie") and would also have the option of including "Davison" and "V" when turning twenty-one.

If Jamie does decide to adopt the name, the decision will be less tortured by far than it was for his father. For him, the question of being a Rockefeller will be like choosing a fraternal lodge or some other pleasantly voluntary association. This will be true because his father has arranged his own life so that he is, in a manner of speaking, a Rockefeller in name only. "It's funny about the name," he says casually. "It's like the money: you come to the point finally where you just accept it and quit worrying about it. The thing is that I know it's part of me and I'm part of it, so there's no use sweating it one way or another."

Yet most of Jay's cousins continued to sweat it. By the late sixties, they were like him in that they were finally beginning to put their individual lives in order and decide at least about some of the things they *wouldn't* do. Yet few had gotten as far as this celebrity of their generation. For most, finding a way to relate formally to the machinery of the family remained to be settled. What "identity" would the Cousins as a group assume? How would they relate to Room 5600? In these questions their individual dilemmas were writ large.

28

THE FAMILY OFFICE had changed greatly from what it had been when the Brothers returned from the war. Then it had still been a relic of Junior's years of achievement, an extended personal staff designed to serve him and achieve the ends to which he had devoted his life. The Brothers had remodeled it, making it a better receptacle for the increased wealth and influence their careers were designed to accumulate. When they finished, it was as if its Victorian structure had been streamlined by the Bauhaus technicians of whom Nelson was so fond: the Office had become a thoroughly efficient instrument suited to modern occasions. By the time the Cousins came of age, its structure was less that of a group of personal Associates than of a corporation operating by flow chart and the committee system, holding significant power and conscious of its own bureaucratic ends.

To the world at large, even the skeptical world of Wall Street, the combination of secrecy and mystique attached to its operations imparted an air of Byzantine intrigue: the *mysterium tremendum* of the Rockefeller Dynasty. Room 5600 was the place where the Brothers gathered with their illuminati of friends and advisers to make the decisions that would shake the world; it was Merlin's cave, where proposals for new ventures were carefully screened and the decision made to apply the alchemy the Name possessed above all others in the country and thereby turn the lucky few to gold. The mystique was enhanced by the fact that few had ever passed behind the glass doors of Room 5600, walked down the long halls lined with art works, and sat in the boardrooms where decisions were made regarding its unique product—the Rockefeller family.

The nerve center of the power radiating through the corridors of Room 5600 is the private office of J. Richardson Dilworth. Looking more like a scholar's study than an executive suite, the decor is consistent with the personality of a one-time investment banker whose responsibilities now include trusteeships of Rockefeller University and Princeton's Institute for Advanced Study (a Rockefeller beneficiary). Calf-bound editions of Elizabethan voyages stand on bookshelves in the faint disorder of works actually read rather than purchased by the linear inch from the interior decorator. Above the massive Chippendale desk is a portrait of a balding, obviously prosperous burgher whom Dilworth identifies as a great-grandfather and the man who gave young Andrew Carnegie his first job when he arrived in the United States.

After being lured away from Kuhn, Loeb in 1958 by David and Laurance, Dilworth became part of the troika running Room 5600 that included John Lockwood and Frank Jamieson (and, for a time after Jamieson's death, Emmet Hughes). By the early sixties, as the Office took on more and more of a corporate character, Dilworth emerged as its "chief operating officer" responsible to a board of managers, which included the five Brothers and a few Cousins, and involved working closely with Laurance.* Dilworth is in charge of the total daily operation of the Office, although his specialty is the heavy financial matters the Brothers have gotten into over the years. Former Eastern Airlines President Malcolm MacIntyre says, "Dick Dilworth was brought into the picture when we were in the final stages of trying to work out our merger with American; he only steps in at critical moments in the Rockefellers' affairs." It was Dilworth who advised the family to buy a large bloc of Chrysler at a 1961 low and then took a seat on the board of directors as a family representative.

Lean and gray and looking like a model for older executives' clothes despite the shirt monogrammed with the initials JRD on the pocket, "Dick" Dilworth lacks only a dueling scar on the cheek to indicate membership in some aristocratic caste. With the same remote charm he displayed to the House Rules Committee during Nelson's confirmation hearings, he tilts back in his swivel chair and speaks of his role: "I'm a quondam lawyer and I think of myself more as a family solicitor in the English sense than as a corporate head. Sometimes the problems I deal with are financial; sometimes

---

*His emergence was, John Lockwood says, largely due to the fact that "Nelson was busy in Albany and had no candidate of his own to propose for the job. If he had still been involved in Room 5600, Dilworth never would have had the independence he needed, and ultimately he would have quit."

they're human. Frequently the human ones are the more complex."

As the Brothers' chief aide and heir to the role of confidant and privy councilor played by the Reverend Frederick T. Gates and attorney Thomas Debevoise in the previous two generations, Dilworth affects a bemused distance from the Cousins' difficulties. ("In a sense at least," he says in the genteel, highly qualified language used by all family aides, "the pressure they feel is a figment of their imagination; actually their parents are enormously supportive of their children's difficulties.") Yet clearly the fourth generation has been foremost among the "human problems" the chief operating officer has faced.

Not without an eye toward its own survival, the Office has attempted to make itself amenable to the Cousins. Realizing their skittishness and anxiety about being swallowed up in its machinery, it has tried to accommodate to them, making itself into a place they can "plug into" if or when they want, yet not coercing them into involvement. In December 1965, when most of them were well into adulthood, the letters on the directory of 30 Rockefeller Plaza were changed from "Office of the Messrs. Rockefeller" to "Rockefeller Family and Associates" to invite a broadened participation. An attempt was made to hire aides of the Cousins' age in important roles. As family attorney John Lockwood approached retirement age, he reached back into his old firm of Milbank, Tweed for his replacement—a ruddy-complexioned, personable, 34-year-old banker's son named Donal O'Brien, who was thought capable of winning the trust of the fourth generation at the same time he was serving the Brothers.

The Brothers and their advisers recognized that whether or not individual Cousins stepped forward to take over in the Office, the Chase, Rockefeller Center, and other institutions, it was still necessary to link the members of the generation to each other and to the family. The best way to do this was to give them their own institution, following the precedent of the Brothers Fund. In 1968, with grants from three of the Brothers totaling more than $300,000, the Family Fund was begun.* It started on a very modest basis; yet, as in everything else, it was recognized that there was more to come. A staff generally reflecting the Cousins' outlook and interests

---

*The contributions were as follows: $152,742 from David; $101,042 from Laurance; $25,259 from JDR3; $25,445 from Junior's widow, Martha Baird.

was hired to work with them in designing a philanthropic program. Dana Creel, head of the Rockefeller Brothers Fund and, next to Dilworth, the Brothers' most important adviser, explains why the Family Fund was created instead of simply integrating the Cousins into the operation of the Brothers Fund: "The Brothers Fund is a major foundation playing in the big leagues in terms of the number and sort of projects it develops. It was not in a position to take a lot of the Cousins on the board or to deal effectively with young organizations. But the Brothers realized the need for another institutional vehicle to get the current generation into things. This is why the Family Fund was created: to give them a situation where they could have personal involvement."

If the meager sum with which the Fund was endowed expressed the fathers' caution in making even this gesture to their reluctant children, the fact that David, Sr., was its first president and that Laurance also sat on the finance committee made its purpose clear. Alida calls it "a training institution to show us how it's done." It was a clever stroke. The Family Fund did indeed give the Cousins a financial stream where they could get their feet wet, and it soon became a neutral ground which some of them occupied when returning to the family fold after years of radical activity and criticism. The Family Fund developed five areas of emphasis (education, institutional awareness, women, conservation, and the arts) so that it would not overlap with the Brothers Fund and so that each Cousin could find something in the program he or she could become enthusiastic about.

Yet the problem of Room 5600 remained. The Cousins had managed to extricate themselves from their families and begun to pursue individual lives and careers, but the Office continued to function *in loco parentis*, a bureaucratic guardian of elaborately complex proportions handling everything legal and financial for its wards, from the doling out of their income to preparing their tax returns, and even to relatively simple tasks like the purchase of automobiles and house insurance. (Except for spending-money, they hardly had to touch their fortunes.) By insulating the Cousins from the facts and process of their wealth, it made them dependent to an extraordinary degree, adding a sense of helplessness to the sense of guilt they already felt as recipients of the awesome legacy.

When solicited for a gift, a Cousin needed only to phone the appropriate person in the Office to decide the form in which the gift would be made, whether and how tax advantages would be derived, and the details of its transference. Or if the individual did not want to be bothered with such decisions in the first place, the Office offered the services of its philanthropic staff to suggest areas and projects in which the tax-deductible portion of one's income might be invested.

The operation of the Office had a dual effect. On the surface it made the Cousins' relationship to their wealth appear casual and it encouraged them in the comforting illusion that money really mattered less to them than to their fathers, who were preoccupied with its getting and spending. Yet in the end, they could not suppress the realization that their ignorance did not make the money insignificant, and that they were as dependent on it for their survival as they were on the Office for making it work.

The very manner in which they received their income symbolized the predicament. The Brothers had given each of their children a sizable sum on their coming of age, but the bulk of their income came from the "Fidelity Trust" (so called because it was held in New Jersey's Fidelity Union Trust Company), which Junior had set up in 1952 with 120,-000 shares of Jersey Standard stock.

The terms of the trust vary among each of the Brothers' families. The income is graded, almost as if to assure a slow maturing of the recipient's sense of responsibilities. In Laurance's family, for instance, the Cousins receive $5,000 a year income from the trust on turning 21; by the age of 24 it has risen to $10,000, increasing at the rate of $5,000 a year until age 30, when it jumps to $65,000. After that, or upon marriage, the heir can get all the income from the trust, ranging from $200,000 to $300,000. In David's family, by contrast, a stipulation limits the amount of income receivable, and the trustees are mandated to reinvest a portion of it. It is David's way of inculcating the puritan ethic, and although he did not follow it in practice, Laurance approves. When some of David's children pressed for a greater share of income from their trusts, Laurance supported his brother's refusal. Remarking that for years he had to pick up the crumbs from his father's table, he asked, "What's all this talk of wanting it now?"

Anyone over thirty can invade the principal of the trust, but only for approved purposes and only after solemn application to the trustees, headed by Amyas Ames, the president of Lincoln Center, and including such notables as William

McChesney Martin, former head of the Federal Reserve; Albert L. Nickerson, former president of Socony Mobil; and Nathan Pusey, former president of Harvard. The idea behind all the majestic legal machinery is that that part of the great fortune which was bestowed on each of the Cousins was not really *theirs*, but only held by them in trust for their children—whether or not they had or intended to have them. It was like a particularized expression of Junior's philanthropic idea that the great Standard Oil fortune was held by the Rockefellers in trust for the benefit of mankind. The Cousins were confronted by this limitation of their inheritance whenever they sought money in excess of the trust income (which, in the case of the David family, was quite modest, but in all cases hardly up to the Rockefeller standard set by their parents) for purposes not approved. "I was given a severe lecture by an accountant in the Office," recalls one of the Cousins about one such occasion, "for having spent what I had spent previously in the way that I had spent it. I was told explicitly that the money was not mine, that the trustees were responsible for what they did, and that if they approved something irresponsible they would be held accountable."*

Just as the small army of accountants, analysts, and lawyers controlled the Cousins' trust, so a public relations department in Room 5600 controlled their official statements and vital statistics, and the archives controlled their history. Larry, Jr., came into the archives one day to look through his file and was surprised to find a cache of letters he had written as a boy after Abby's death addressed "To Grandmother in Heaven." Along with other personal information and material, he had no recollection of writing them, much less any idea that they had been kept. Often the Cousins worried that the Office seemed to know more about them than they knew about themselves.

*Senior's attorneys had identified the value of a trust as a holding company for vast corporate undertakings. It took a loophole in the tax laws to show that a trust could be a holding company for dynastic purposes as well. For what seemed to the Cousins like the optical illusion of their inheritances—that the money should be theirs but yet not really theirs—was simply the consequence of their construction as generation-skipping trusts to avoid the estate taxes that would otherwise have been due. The same arrangement and the same set of ironies made them the beneficiaries of the mammoth '34 Trusts, whose multimillion-dollar income allowed their fathers to live like Rockefellers, but which would not pass on to be divided among them until their fathers' deaths.

Yet for all their doubts, they found it hard to wean themselves from the benign management of Room 5600. They had grown up relying on Office staff to be the buffer between them and the world at large in ways they hadn't fully realized; they had allowed it to take care of the problems in their daily lives, and it had become an addiction. But if they were addicted to the Office, they resented it. They were ambivalent about Room 5600, and the Office (for it was almost impossible not to personify it) was equally so about them. It wanted them to be involved, yet it also wanted to keep them passively vibrating the strands of the web. Abby recalls an instance when she went to Room 5600 to find out exactly how much money she had, how it was invested, and how she went about getting control over it. "There was a surreal meeting with Don O'Brien, Dilworth, seven or eight assorted people from the Office, and an accountant named Joe Lee. They handed out a little red portfolio with all 'my' investments in it. Everything was so altogether done that I could hardly feel like a participant. Dilworth suggested to Lee that he run through my investments. He did, giving me a little synopsis of what each one was doing. He got to Exxon and said, 'Well, here's an old friend.' Then came Mobil, and he says, 'Now Mobil is a kind of little sister to Exxon.' That kind of stuff. Good-humored, but clearly meant to put distance between me and the money and to leave in question the degree to which it is *mine*. It worked. I felt like I had a mask over my face and was being laid out ready for an operation. Room 5600 is an institutional replica of my father's manner; it prevents one from asking questions that might explain its inner logic."

In Abby's opinion the Office is composed of two separate classes, which she calls *obsequiators* and *patronizers*. "The obsequiators are usually the junior members. They fawn over anyone whose name is, was, or even might be Rockefeller. They do it, but feel demeaned by it. They try to do the Cousins' will and the Brothers' at once, not admitting the conflicts that exist between them. The Brothers pay the bills and are in charge now, but on the off chance that we might take over someday, the obsequiators have to hedge their bets. The patronizers are those like Dilworth for whom the Office *is* the Brothers—they are men without qualms about power. To them, the Cousins are just aging wards incapable of making a serious bid for power, and are to be treated as such."

Other Cousins are similarly wary about Room 5600. When Marion asked Dilworth why she got such a small percentage of her trust at a time when she wanted income to further a land reform project she was interested in, she got a phone call from Dilworth. "He started talking and I said, 'Excuse me, I'm going to get Warren,' because I really couldn't believe what he was saying. He was the epitome of indirectness, the epitome of a language that I hardly even understand."

As much as anything else, it has been the shared problem of the Office that welded the Cousins together into a group: the desire to face Dilworth and the others with a united front that would keep them from being overpowered as in their one-to-one dealings. It was a desire that dominated the mood, if not the actual discussions, of their annual meetings at Pocantico.

These Cousins' meetings had begun as informal get-togethers, presided over by Mitzi and Rodman as the elders of the generation and originally intended as initiation ceremonies meant primarily to induct Cousins who had reached their majority into the mysteries of their "financial rights." As time passed and more Cousins turned twenty-one, the meetings took on a social quality, and an attempt was made to forget the past few years of individual anguish and recapture some of the closeness of their youth. By the late sixties, however, as almost all of the Cousins began attending the meetings and the external pressures on them became severe, they began to discuss issues.

Some were internal matters, like the Brothers' plans for Pocantico. Although no Cousin except Rodman was interested in maintaining a home there in the style of the Brothers, some of the Cousins indicated they would like to have home sites, especially if the isolation of their youth was replaced with a more open situation. (One suggestion was to allow small communities of a few hundred people each to locate throughout the 3,600 acres.) Since this expression of interest came at a time when Laurance and Nelson were interested in developing parts of the estate, the Brothers agreed to commission a study of the possibilities. The Rouse Plan, as it was called, proposed that some "Cousins' Sites" of 20 acres each be developed around the "park" area, and that some 650 acres in the northern part of Pocantico be developed into two good-sized towns with 7,500 people, schools, recreational areas, and other support facilities.

Even for Laurance and Nelson the question was not so much making money from Pocantico as properly disposing of it after their generation was gone. After the Rouse Plan (whose attempt to accommodate both Cousins and Brothers had pleased neither group), Nelson Aldrich, the Brothers' cousin and David's architect-in-residence, was called upon to propose a comprehensive scheme that was to eliminate the idea of having planned communities in the estate. Yet a third plan was broached in 1968; this one was not architectural but financial. It called on stockholders of the Hills Realty Company (namely the Brothers), which owned Pocantico, to sell their stock to the '34 Trusts; the trusts, in turn, would hold it until they were dissolved in the fifth generation.

It was at this point that Steven and, to a lesser extent, Larry began arguing against the Brothers' plans. "In order to inherit Pocantico," Steven recalls, "the Cousins would have had to pay such heavy taxes that it wouldn't really be worth it. The question was whether to sell it and make as much money as possible, or to just agree that this extremely beautiful piece of land should be preserved for everyone to enjoy. I argued that the family didn't need the money. For us to divide Pocantico and sell it would be as great a crime as breaking up a work of art and burning it for the heat it would give during one evening."

The Cousins agreed. So did JDR3, who had always been against the kind of development Laurance and Nelson (with David's acquiescence) had been considering for Pocantico. The issue became symbolic of the differences in philosophy between the generations. Finally, architect Harmon Goldstone (who had worked with the family in other matters over the years) was brought in as a mediator to conceive a plan acceptable to all. The idea of ultimately giving Pocantico to the state for public use—announced in 1970 by Nelson in his role as family spokesman—was the resulting compromise between the Cousins and Brothers.

The estate, however, was a unique issue. When Steven and other Cousins tried to mobilize the fourth generation for a public stand against the war in Vietnam, they got nowhere. As a group they were fearful of doing something that would be interpreted as a repudiation of their fathers, all of whom supported the war. Yet the problem remained: in the criticism of the family that cropped up with increasing frequency in the late sixties, the Cousins were implicated as Rockefellers along with their elders; and unlike their fathers, they were not intellectually sealed off from the effects of this criticism, nor content to bifurcate reality so that wielding power was separate from doing good.

The issues were very much on Steven's mind and also Marion's. She and her husband had already informed the Internal Revenue Service of their intention to stop paying that proportion of their taxes that went to what they called, in their letter, "this government's murderous violence in Vietnam and other parts of Indochina." Telling the IRS it would have to get its taxes without their cooperation, they sent the money instead to antiwar groups. In 1971 Marion wrote a letter to Dana Creel, head of the Office's philanthropic division, in which she raised the issues of the lack of coherence in family policy:

Dear Mr. Creel,

My sister Laura just sent me a copy of her letter to you and I want to say that what she had indicated about the necessity of inter-relationship beween the philanthropist and the investor parts of us is, I believe, extremely important. I join her in feeling that we must take a hard look at our investment policy. . . . For example, I am very anxious to see this war end and the amount of money presently spent on defense decrease. I have given part of my income toward the work of various peace groups. But part of my income comes from dividends from investments in industries such as Westinghouse, Dupont, General Electric and Dow—companies who help make this war possible and hold substantial defense contracts. Likewise I am concerned about pollution and I support with part of my income various ecological groups and yet such a large part of this income results from investments in Standard Oil of New Jersey. I think as a family we could put pressure on Standard Oil to mend its ways. . . . I think our consciousness as a family will slowly grow as to the necessary relationship beween our responsibilities as investors and philanthropists. It should become increasingly evident that it is nonsense to create with one hand and destroy with the other. I would appreciate your thoughts on all this.

The answer was not forthcoming, and other Cousins fretted about the same issues. If taking political stands as a group was out, they nonetheless felt that they had to at least try to seize the initiative over their money from Room 5600 and make sure it was not invested in corporations profiting from the war, supporting the South African economy, or exploiting the environment.

It was in their Cousins' meeting of June 1972 that these issues interacted with the personal anguish they had hacked their way through as individuals. Arriving from all over the country with their families, the Cousins' invasion made the estate look as though it had been rented to a summit meeting of McGovern staff workers. Some of them wore faded denims and long air and had scruffily dressed children in tow. Most had, in fact, contributed generously to the campaign of the Democratic candidate, but this weekend they were worried only about family politics. It was on their minds from the moment that Sharon Percy Rockefeller, their elected president, stood up in the Playhouse Junior had built for their fathers half a century earlier, to call the meeting to order.

It was as if the doggedness with which they had borne their dissatisfaction for so many years suddenly collapsed, allowing the unhappiness to escape. There was resentment over the way the Office was organized to keep them infantilized. As the employees from Room 5600 appeared at the estate to make their yearly presentations, they were surprised to find themselves grilled with unusual force. The Cousins requested that Dilworth prepare a family directory completely blueprinting the workings of the Office. They talked about their individual frustrations in trying to manage their own money. The discussion snowballed until they found themselves appointing an Investment Committee of four Cousins instructed to work with Room 5600 in figuring out ways to bring their portfolios into line with their social values. The committee was headed by Jay, who had good reason for concern: he was in the middle of a race for the West Virginia governorship on a platform of independence from the mining interests that controlled the state, and had already faced a crisis when critics pointed out that the Rockefeller Foundation, of which he was a trustee, was a large shareholder in the Consolidation Coal Company, one of the biggest of the coal operators and a company that had been charged with lax safety regulations in respect to the prevalence of black lung disease among the miners.

Once the genie was out, it seemed impossible to entice it back into the bottle. After discussing investments, the Cousins broke up into men's and women's groups. In the men's group, the "in-laws" spoke up about the problem of having the money and power reside with the women (even those husbands who had been divorced from Rockefeller women had gotten "alimony" in the form of property settlements), while the male Cousins compared notes on how they had avoided involvement in Room 5600.

But it was the women's group that provided the real drama. The women discussed their broken marriages and the question of women's liberation. One of Laurance's daughters said that their troubles sprang from a confusion that was learned in the family—or, at least, that the female role learned in her family was quite simple: "Daddy likes his women quiet and religious."

Laura, who was gathering data on the early childhoods of the older generation and therefore knew with what reverence the Brothers regarded their mother, observed that Abby Aldrich had been a wonderful person, who seemed to handle the role well.

She was immediately challenged by Babs's daughter Abby ("Mitzi") O'Neill, who stood up under the portrait of her mother and said with an ominous tone in her voice: "You don't know what grandmother was like." And then, with tears in her eyes, she talked about how her mother's life was "ruined" by Abby because, from the time she was a little girl, she was put off in a corner; it was only her sons that Abby cared for. As a result, her mother had no avenue of self-fulfillment or self-esteem; she had become reclusive and ineffective, as one of the other Cousins later observed, "an addendum to the Brothers' generation."

As the meeting concluded, the Cousins were left in a state of surprise over what had happened. At first there was euphoria. Hope said soon after, "There's an impulse not to take orders anymore or to agree automatically that this is a good firm and that a good investment, just because Room 5600 says so. This was the first time we flexed our own judgmental muscles."

Her brother, Jay, agreed: "As the Cousins come to see each other with mature curiosity and affection, we are better able to handle our relationship to the Office. It used to be that the Cousins would always be calling up Room 5600 and saying, 'I've lost my dog, what shall I do?' or 'I need a new refrigerator, how do I go about getting one?' No more of that."

At the time it occurred, the 1972 meeting was seen as a breakthrough by the Cousins, both in terms of the level of personal revelation—a mode not easy for any Rockefeller—and in terms of the challenge to the Office. Yet there was an uneasiness as well, a feeling that they had overreached, a sense that this meeting had really been a delayed reaction to the ferment of the late sixties and that they had spontaneously taken a more extreme position than they really meant to follow through.

Those who misinterpreted the signs and thought that their generation was ready to issue a serious challenge to the Brothers soon found that the last thing the majority of the Cousins wanted was for their meetings to become a Jacobin Society. Marion and her husband, who arranged to show a Quaker-supported research group's slide presentation of the effects of the air war on Vietnam, were not encouraged in their efforts to follow it up. They found themselves continually frustrated when it came to any action, however modest, the Cousins might take as a group. When Alida, the youngest Cousin present, saw the film *State of Siege,* she became upset because Rockefeller was the only U.S. name introduced in the panorama of brutality and repression. "I wrote a letter telling the Cousins that everyone should see it before we have our next meeting, just because I think it's really a super eye-opener about the family and the possibility of how our money might be influencing things in ways we're not even aware of. It was like an accusation of murder." Yet when Alida attempted to get a discussion of the movie put on the agenda at the next Cousins meeting, she was told that it was not the place for "personal hobbyhorses," and that she should talk to the Cousins individually.

Even the Investment Committee's visit to Dilworth resulted in little or no tangible result. There was no change in the management of the portfolio, but a woman, Catherine Tracy, was hired to work in Room 5600, gathering information about developments in the field of corporate responsibility. She was to keep abreast of all the stockholder resolutions proposed by church and consumer groups in their efforts to change or modify corporate policies. Several times a year she sent summaries of these struggles to the Cousins so they could act if they wished.

Far from advancing the Cousins' cause, her presence seemed meant only to disarm their concern. As an employee of the Brothers responsible to Dilworth, she had certainly not been hired to encourage the Cousins to assert themselves on behalf of greater conscience in the management of family finances. Her officially formulated memos, summarizing in neutral tones the views of the corporate managements she contacted alongside the views of the corporate rebels, both complicated the issues and removed from the Cousins any sense of moral crisis they might have had. After passing over her desk, the burning social issues of the time came to seem like complex problems of social management in which there were no simple rights or wrongs. At the same time, by making contacts herself with the young activists in church and consumer groups, she insulated the Cousins from having to experience the urgent concern of their peers and prevented them from having to confront the issues directly.

When a few of them decided to act in spite of this, they found their freedom to do so severely limited. Thus, when Marion, in the spring of 1974, requested that the shares in one of her smaller trusts at the Chase Manhattan Bank be voted on behalf of several stockholder resolutions, including one inspired by the Watergate revelations then reaching their denouement, she received the following communication from Catherine Tracy: "Chase Manhattan Bank—Mr. Daniel Dorney—advises me that they voted for proposals 2 and 3 [as per Marion's request] on the IBM proxy. However, they would not take our suggestion that they vote in favor of the Project on Corporate Responsibilities resolution prohibiting corporate campaign contributions on the ITT proxy. Sorry!"

Though the Cousins were forced to backtrack, the reverberations from the June 1972 meeting continued to spread long after it was over. By the fall, the Cousins received one of the items they had requested from Room 5600. It was a detailed thirty-page family directory, which showed the form and function of Room 5600.* It was accompanied by the

*The report showed the Office broken into several major departments. Accounting and Taxes, headed by Treasurer David Fernald, involved 15 accountants, 6 bookkeepers, 10 clerks, and 5 computer experts. The Investments Department, headed overall by J. R. Dilworth, is broken into subdepartments: Standard Investments (managing portfolios of family members and also Rockefeller University, the Rockefeller Brothers Fund, and other boards), with 9 managers and their secretarial and clerical help; Venture Investments, headed by Harper Woodward, with 6 other executives who also screen proposals and sit on the boards of firms in which the family has made investments; Real Estate Investments, managed by David's aide Leslie Larsen. The Legal Department consists of 5 attorneys headed by Donal O'Brien. The Philanthropic

caveat, "As you might suspect, the confidential nature of the work performed by the Office presents problems in delineating each job." Yet even the part of the leviathan it showed was impressive. There were more than 200 employees. The exact figure of the budget was not given (one of Laurance's aides, Peter Crisp, noted that "it is confidential in nature") but was an estimated $6 million a year. The charts illustrating lines of authority showed how completely the Office personality had come to be dominated by investments. The Brothers Fund and Family Fund were not independent, as was implied, but subordinate to Dilworth. The division of the budget dollar (the percentages were given even though the total expenditures were not) also reflected the proportionate importance of philanthropy in Room 5600: investment accounted for 30 percent of the budget; accounting and taxes for 20 percent; the Legal Department for 18 percent; management and public relations for 8.6 percent; rent and telephone for the Brothers' offices, 5.8 percent; miscellaneous, 9.2 percent. This left a little over 8 percent of the total expenses of Room 5600 devoted to the philanthropic unit.

These facts were sobering for the Cousins. They showed how vast and complex was the operation which they presumed to alter to conform to their sensitivities and tastes. The Cousins realized that the Office was too formidable an enterprise and too strongly headed in the direction their fathers had sent it to be purified in the manner they wanted. The issues they had raised in their 1972 meeting would now be disposed of once and for all, ironically enough, in the one institution in the Office the Cousins theoretically controlled.

In the years since the Family Fund had begun operation in 1969, it had grown into a fairly large foundation, the result of a bequest of $10 million in Martha Baird's will. (When she died in 1970, Junior's widow left all of the $72 million he had willed her to various family philanthropies.) From the beginning, some of the Cousins feared the Fund would become just another Rockefeller institution. Marion and her

Department (the Brothers Fund and the Family Fund) headed by Dana Creel has 45 full-time aides and associates. Other departments are Travel and Public Relations. Room 5600 also houses the Brothers' personal staffs; Rockresorts, Inc.; the JDR3 Fund; Jackson Hole Preserve, Inc.; the American Conservation Association; and other boards, all of which have their own staff. Overseeing the whole operation is the Board of Managers comprising the Brothers, Dilworth, and a few Cousins.

husband wrote the other Cousins when its five areas of emphasis were being decided upon: "We are quite excited about the possibilities of the Family Fund. We hope very much that it will serve as an alternative to the usual channels and mode of giving. Focusing on environmental ecology, for example, is in our opinion a marvelous idea, but only if this (or any other cause the Fund supports) is not treated as though it were an area of concern like education, the arts, health and so on. In our view, to adopt such an attitude, which we sense in the communications we have had about the Fund so far, is merely to play the old role of philanthropist with a somewhat new twist. The times demand something more than one more tax deductible foundation. The task as we see it is often to attack the very political and economic forces which perpetuate the deductible contribution. . . . We think the Fund has an obligation to seek out organizations like American Friends Service Committee, Friends of the Earth, Pacifica stations, American Documentary Films et al. and support them regardless of their tax status."

Yet most of the Cousins were not ready to insist that these principles be adhered to, especially if it meant once again troubling the smooth waters they had so recently passed into. They accommodated themselves to what they felt were the realities of the situation. One of these realities was the presence of David, Sr., and Laurance on the board of trustees and Investment Committee of the Fund.

By the spring of 1974, Catherine Tracy had sifted through the proposals of various insurgent stockholder groups and presented the Cousins with some they could act on with respect to the Fund's portfolio. The three issues addressed by the stockholders' resolutions were strip mining in the Rocky Mountain area by Exxon; insufficient minority hiring by General Electric and Caterpillar Tractors; and the South African policies of IBM. The Family Fund's Investment Committee dealt with these questions in executive session. There was unanimous agreement that Exxon's explanation of its strip-mining policies and its promise to reseed the gouged-out areas were adequate. On the question of minority hiring, the committee accepted David, Sr.,'s suggestion that instead of giving proxies to the church groups challenging GE and Caterpillar, they should vote with the management, while also writing a letter for the record emphasizing the Rockefeller family's commitment to equal opportunities. When it was suggested by one of the Cousins that the letter also be used to request that the companies put the results of minority hiring programs in future annual reports, David objected, saying that he thought this was really "asking too much." Jay agreed, seconding his motion not to make this request part of the letter, which then passed unanimously.

At issue in the IBM stockholders' resolution was whether or not there should be complete disclosure of information on the company's activities in South Africa. David brought up a *Fortune* article stating that IBM was one of the more progressive firms in South Africa. The members of the Family Fund Investment Committee agreed with him when he then stated that if they were to vote with the dissident stockholders in favor of compelling disclosure, they would appear not to support IBM's progressive stance on some of South Africa's internal matters. The Fund voted only to write a mild letter outlining their views.

In addition to setting the tone for the Family Fund's responses to these specific stockholder issues, David also settled the general problem of the Fund's investment policy. The Cousins had assumed that the organization's investment would be consistent with its philanthropic policy, and had moved to instruct the company managing the Family Fund's portfolio to do so in a way that would reflect their generation's commitment to "corporate responsibility." However, "Uncle David" again interposed a strong opinion: if they didn't give the investment company a free rein to make as much money as it could, they wouldn't get anything out of it at all and the Fund's endowment might diminish. Unless they were willing to contest the assumptions behind this statement, which they weren't, they couldn't argue against its logic. In the end, they deferred on this question too.

In 1972, David, Jr. (who had succeeded his father as president of the Family Fund), noted during a speech to a New England Conference on Foundations that his institution's uniqueness came from the fact that it was devoted to "venture philanthropy," perhaps not realizing that exactly the same term had been used by his Uncle John some thirty years earlier to describe the newborn Rockefeller Brothers Fund. Except for the difference in the size and emphasis of its program, the Family Fund had, in fact, become very much the obedient child of the parent institution. The reality of the situation was that, instead of helping free the Cousins, the Family Fund had put them on trial: if they performed "responsibly," their philanthropy might become the beneficiary of the Brothers' wills, or receive the endowment of the Rockefeller Brothers Fund after the last remaining Brother had died. ("The Brothers are watching us," David, Jr., confirms somewhat sheepishly. "It's as though they've given us a chunk of gold to see what we'll do with it: whether we'll turn it into lead or make it something better, in which case there'll be more to come.")

Some of the Cousins were bitter over what they saw as the Family Fund's capitulation to the fantasy that the temporary compromise was worth the increased wealth and power to do good works it might someday bring. As one of them said, "The only difference between our generation and theirs is that for the Brothers, the gestures toward 'good works' were a way of deflecting attention from the other things they were doing. For us, the gestures are just gestures, nothing more."

The Brothers had resignd themselves to the fact that the Cousins' group identity would be in philanthropy and that if they were to extend the family's influence, it would be in that way. To a certain extent, the Cousins were like Junior. In the strange dialectic expressed in the alternating generations of the family, their role was to atone for the sins of their fathers. Yet unlike Junior, their giving was not part of anything more than personal redemption. They had no dynastic objectives. Their philanthropy was actually only an aspect of a continuum of behavior in which they sought "liberation." One of them might occasionally make a gesture of bravado about philanthropy, as in the case of Laura's statement: "It's very hard to get rid of the money in a way that does more good than harm. One of the ways is to subsidize people who are trying to change the system and get rid of people like us." Yet in the last analysis giving occupied only a small part of the Cousins' energy.

They did not intend to reopen the Pandora's box they had peeked into in 1972. The minutes for their 1974 meeting show that they were more concerned with the Symbionese Liberation Army and other matters than with corporate responsibility:

> We then turned to a discussion of family personal security. Mary said she was especially concerned with kidnapping but that there was not much she could see that we could do except to prepare our children and safeguard our homes. Ann had understood that the Office

had drawn up a list of guidelines, but it appears that no one has gotten anything. Rod pointed out that 70% of the kidnapping is of adults, not children. . . . Win suggested the possibility of having a shadow, but Tom [Tom Morgan, Mary's second husband] pointed out that it is dangerous to have a kid followed by security people—too many guns go off accidentally. Sharon [Jay's wife] suggested that we have the head of security at the Office come to talk to us at Christmas, and people generally agreed.

We then went on to talk about the investment policy at the Office. Rod had been talking to the uncles and the Office about investments and the relationship between income and expenses. Where is our income going to come from for the future? Our generation has been trained to consume and donate, but not to produce. The stock market is no longer enough to mobilize the increase we need, and we must now concern ourselves with the production side of the equation. . . . Rod went on to outline the "vertical organization of family planning" as opposed to overall family planning (that is for dollars, not children). Resistance among the Brothers to our even talking about it is high. Ferguson Reed was hired by Dilworth to deal with the Cousins on business problems. He is an investment banker and would like to meet with us; the question is, is one person adequate to meet what seem to be growing needs. An ultimate issue we might all consider is why do we need to replenish family resources? That becomes a personal decision to some extent. . . . Steven was more concerned with the fact that our children on our death and our parents' deaths will have far more money than us and how will they be able to deal with that? . . . He pointed out that the problem of generating more cash was a problem only in relation to the personal living habits of some of the Cousins. He raised the question of whether the family beyond this generation wants to continue to function as an institution.

Steven's question was well put. For the issue had gradually shifted in the years of their growing up from whether and how they would participate in the Rockefeller dynasty, to whether or not the dynasty itself had a future. The Office, which had always been the engine powering the dynasty, was itself faced with this problem. Winthrop's death had shocked everyone concerned into the realization that Room 5600 was every bit as mortal as the Brothers themselves. It was expensive to operate. The Cousins weren't aggressively generating the income that would justify an effort to keep it going. Increasingly there was talk about the Office's being dissolved or radically modified after the next Brother died.

J. R. Dilworth attempts to discount the talk. "There's really no accurate way to predict what will become of the Office. It depends on the future. Even if the Cousins decided to go off on their own entirely, they'd have to come back at least once a year—at tax time. We've got services here for the next generation that they couldn't normally find, services they couldn't get by going off to any ordinary banker or lawyer. It's all here in the Office. We seem to have the best way of handling the complex business situation they're involved in— investment of their funds and, from a separate pocket, giving away a certain amount of their money. If by some catastrophe, all the remaining Brothers died today, moreover, it would take seven or eight years just to disband the present operation and unravel things satisfactorily."

Yet despite this, there was a feeling of waiting for the second shoe to fall. After the funeral at Winrock, the long corridors of Room 5600 were filled with speculation. Would the investments be curtailed and the Office consolidated into a philanthropic and accounting operation, the minimum functions necessary to handle taxes? Would the present scope of operations be maintained in skeletal form? There was a kind of *fin de siècle* mood that was heightened by Nelson's unraveling the family secrets before Congress in a last desperate attempt to gain national office, and by the pain his confirmation hearings caused them all. Whatever the Cousins did or didn't do with the Office, its days seemed clearly numbered.

This might have caused pangs of nostalgia among others, but not among the Cousins. Even if they were not prepared to stand up against the family juggernaut, they were more than willing to be the passive beneficiaries of history. They thought what prior Rockefeller generations would have regarded as unthinkable. Steven says, "Someday somebody is going to have to go down there to Room 5600 and figure out what to do with the Office. That's the main reason our periodic Cousins meetings are important. We're learning to work together, to make decisions, so that we'll be ready when the time comes. The question ultimately will be whether or not the family will be preserved as an institution in the form of Room 5600. The Cousins will decide that sometime in the next twenty years as Fate determines—Fate in the form of the passing of the Brothers. The majority of the Cousins are unwilling to subsume their individual personalities inside this joint one. My own attitude is that I've got my own goals in life, and I won't sacrifice them to the Family Office."

As he talks, the words begin to sound like a benediction. "The family institutions—first the Foundation and now increasingly the Brothers Fund, which the new laws say must put outsiders on the board—are getting out of the family's control. As with these institutional children so with the real children. They're getting out on their own now, away from the family; and once they're out, I don't see any way to get them back."

29

For the Cousins who journeyed to Arkansas early in 1973, Winthrop's funeral was an emotional moment. It was not so much grief for his passing: with the exception of Jay, Larry, Steven, and one or two others, none of them had really known the sad-eyed giant of a man, although they could feel the pathos of his last days when he had seemed to contract, his wasted body becoming the battleground where alcohol, chemicals, and cancer fought a last, awesome battle. It was more that this uncle's death and strangely antiseptic last rites seemed to mark the exact moment when time slipped out of one frame and into another. It was an event that moved them all a quantum jump closer to the time when the hard and yet inevitable choices would be made about the future of the family, choices in which they would play an as yet undetermined role. They were interested to see how their cousin Winthrop Paul would handle things. He was the first among them to take the big step.

For the first few weeks the only information from Arkan-

sas was confused indications that the changing of the guard
was not going smoothly. His heart may have been at Winrock, but a large part of Winthrop's soul had remained in
mortgage at Rockefeller Center; and the dichotomy was reflected in the disposition of his affairs. In his last months,
when he knew that he was dying, Winthrop had turned to the
Family Office for advice. His final will had named five executors to oversee the disposition of his estate and to try to
smooth a path before his son's youth and inexperience. Two
of them (former chief adviser Max Milam and personal
friend Marion Burton) were trusted associates from Arkansas; but the strong hand would be held by a New York triumvirate composed of David Rockefeller, J. R. Dilworth, and
family attorney Donal O'Brien.

The heir, 24-year-old Win Paul, was a big, broad-shoul-
dered, handsome young man who looked good in western-
style suits and square-toed cowboy boots. He had his father's
openness, and except for thick black hair and a dark
moustache curling over his upper lip, he looked like Winthrop about the time he left Yale to go to work in the oil
fields.

Yet Win Paul was really an unknown quantity to family
and friends alike. Not only was he the first descendant in the
male line from John D., Sr., to grow up outside Pocantico,
but his childhood had been spent with a mother who loathed
the Rockefellers and his youth in a series of European
boarding schools far from the family's ideological reach. He
was an outsider, a fact that hadn't been changed by spending
summers and vacations at Winrock. Win Paul stayed in Europe for college at Oxford. When he flunked out and came to
Arkansas for good in what proved to be the last year of his
father's life, he got married and settled down as if he had always been a functioning member of the family. Yet he was
different, totally, without the anxiety and ambivalence present
as a common denominator in the other Cousins. It was as if
they were the control group and he the experiment.

Having grown up without being exposed to the system of
debt and obligation that bristled like thorns all around the
Rockefeller privilege, he did not see his inheritance as a burden. On the contrary, almost immediately after the funeral he
began to move in and take control of the empire his father
had built, indicating that he had his own ideas and a new
team of advisers to implement them. The old guard of his father's associates, headed by former Professor Max Milam,

didn't feel he was ready. The immediate issue centered on which of the parties was to handle the papers left on Winthrop's desk at the time of his death. Milam finally scooped them up and put them in a safe deposit box. This touched off a struggle for power that perplexed those watching the situation in Room 5600.

Later one former family employee would say with more truth than his light-hearted tone intended, "It was like the State Department keeping on top of a *coup* in Latin America; we had people down there who were reporting what was going on to us." The reason for the Office's interest in Arkansas was clear. Unlike the other families, in which the inheritance would be divided between four to six Cousins, Win Paul was the only heir, which made him theoretically as wealthy as one of the Brothers. If he were to disengage himself completely from the family, the impact of the approximately $125 million trust would be subtracted from institutions like the Brothers Fund, where it had always been an important factor. Win Paul had to be brought into a firm orbit around the family.

By appearing to side with the heir in the struggle with his father's old retainers, the Office began the process of winning him over. Winthrop's will itself was a help in this regard. It was an ingenious instrument, solving several problems at once. Win Paul was made the beneficiary of the '34 Trust; he also got his father's sprawling ranch house and the "homestead" immediately surrounding it. But he didn't get what he wanted most—the rest of Winrock Farm, the livestock and lands, and the corporation itself.

Winrock was more than a major company valued at some $50 million. It symbolized the power and prestige Winthrop had built during his years in Arkansas, and was the embodiment of the roots he had set down. Winrock was willed to a charitable trust that the executors were to administer "for the benefit of the people of Arkansas." This solution avoided taxes and emphasized the permanence of the former governor's commitment to his adopted home. Yet it didn't entirely exclude the possibility that Win Paul might someday control the corporation. In fact, the way Winrock had been disposed of deferred Win Paul's gratification in a way that could help in his "Rockefellerization," a task his dying father had not had time to complete. The executors indicated that in disposing of Winrock to benefit the people of Arkansas, they might well decide to sell it. If so, why not to Winthrop's flesh and blood? Win Paul had the money; they were certain that his trustees would give permission to invade the trust principal for the funds necessary to finance such a purchase. But first there had to be some indication that Win Paul was committed to this valuable property and able to manage it.

For the year after his father's death, he proved himself by moving to Fort Worth to take a crash course in ranch management at Texas Christian University. While there, he made visits to New York in his father's private jet to talk to the executors. The Brothers always found time for him. They hosted him and his wife and child at their vacation homes, made him feel a part of the great tradition, and began to find ways to allow him to participate in the operation of the Office. He joined Laurance and David as a member on the board of managers in charge of overseeing the operations of Room 5600. He became a trustee of the Family Fund and began attending the Cousins meetings.

By 1974, Win Paul had embraced the Rockefeller myth with the zeal of a convert. He tried to convince his Cousins to fly down to Winrock for their annual meeting. He wanted to know all about the foundations and boards that were the institutional musculature of the Rockefellers' influence. He told his uncles that he wanted to get "more involved" in the family and in the direction of its affairs.

Win Paul's enthusiasm to step into his father's shoes (he had already told Arkansas newspapers that they could assume he was a likely gubernatorial candidate for the future) and his flamboyant arrival in the family fold did not really tell the Cousins much about how they would handle the problem of inheritance when their time came due. Yet they did learn something. Seeing him carrying on a flirtation with the myth they had spent half a lifetime trying to get free of made being a Rockefeller in the traditional sense seem even more an absurdity, like a scene in some Broadway musical spoofing money and power. To Winthrop Paul, the Rockefeller family was the Big Rock Candy Mountain. Watching his impatience to start his climb up its gilded slopes, the Cousins realized the extent to which they themselves had reached an angle of repose in their long fall away from it.

This was not to say that they had arrived at the same place at the same time. Far from it. There were an adventuresome few who had managed to come a great distance, and some

stragglers who had not gotten very far at all. The others
strung out along the way.

There was much that could be said against the Cousins. As
a group they had bungled their halfhearted attempt to alter
the Family Office so that it conformed to their morality. They
had grasped at the straws offered them, like the Family Fund.
They had settled for appearances, more often wanting to do
what made them feel good than what they knew was right. In
some ways, they were a collection of timorous souls permanently juvenilized by their relations with their fathers and
their dependence on Room 5600. They admitted as much:
the family struggle was unresolved because they did not want
to have to deal wih it.

The Cousins were a well-educated, good-looking, accomplished, and—for all the associations attached to their
name—rather unremarkable group of people. But even so,
something quite dramatic had happened. They had put themselves first. In any other context this might have been simply
selfish. But, for born Rockefellers, it was the most subversive
thing they could possibly have done. None of them were
willing to nourish the family dynasty they knew had begun to
wither and would probably die in their own time. Most were
content to be passive spectators of this decline for which they
were at least partly responsible. Three or four of them were
determined to work through the decaying family structure to
achieve something like a full personal liberation.

It was hard to tell how it had happened. In some sense, the
tumultuous age they had been born into helped spring them
from the dynastic grasp. Their fathers had assumed that the
strength of the family myth would tie them to the family in a
way that couldn't be changed. Yet it hadn't worked, and partly because they *knew* what they were missing. Abby says,
"It's as if someone told the Brothers, 'Look, let your kids
grow up knowing ordinary people so they'll be able to deal
with things and act ordinary themselves.' The trouble is that
once you've experienced what it is to be ordinary, you can't
stand to be treated like a freak anymore. You want to be *absolutely* ordinary. It's like an Ivy Lee recommendation that
backfired."

To the average person, of course, the Rockefeller Cousins
are about as ordinary as a tribe of Martians. There is a kind
of glamour attached to them that no casual manner or old
clothing can cover. It is the kind of glamour usually associated
with movie stars and politicians, something that comes from a

source not consciously controlled and not rational. Alida discovered this when she went to West Virginia in 1972 to work in her brother's gubernatorial campaign. She was not just another 22-year-old college student. "I discovered that, like it or not, I was a professional Rockefeller. Some people get interviewed for having written a beautiful book or for being an accomplished actor or for climbing the Matterhorn. The reason I was interviewed wherever I went—my uniqueness—was being a Rockefeller."

Nor do they live like ordinary people. Whatever radical styles they affect, their life-styles range between comfortable and sumptuous, although perhaps not exactly what one might expect of multimillionaires. The possibilities are summarized by the Cousins living in Cambridge, spiritual center of their generation in the way New York City was for their fathers. Here Sandra lives behind locked doors, alone, in suspicious comfort. Often wearing blue jeans and an old shirt, Peggy comes and goes from a run-down graduate student apartment complete with secondhand furniture. Her brother Richard lives more pleasantly not far away on a tree-shaded street in a modest white clapboard house whose hall is lined with exquisite photographs he has taken of the brooding Maine coastline.

Neva, another of David's children, owns a two-story wood frame house just off Brattle, the most elegant street in Cambridge. Surrounded by spacious lawns and set back discreetly from the sidewalk, it looks like the kind of home that is within the reach of a successful attorney or stockbroker (her husband is an English professor). But stepping inside is like entering another world. Oriental rugs sit like pools of color on the lustrous geometry of parqueted floors. The paintings on the walls are chosen to set off the rich tones and textures of the wood and fabric in the furniture. The interior of Neva's home cost $600,000 to remodel and redecorate into what she herself admits is a near-perfect imitation of her father's Manhattan town house.

Laura lives near Neva in a similar house whose interior is warm and tasteful but not nearly as opulent. She says, "What Neva has done is incomprehensible. It's absolutely unthinkable to me to want to live like my parents." Yet she recently did something her cousins regard as equally extravagant when she spent over a million dollars buying thirty choice acres on Martha's Vineyard. Nor is she alone. Richard rides around Cambridge on an old bicycle, but on weekends he often goes out to the airport and climbs into his single-engine airplane for a short flight to Maine, or boards his $20,000 sailboat for a cruise in the bay. His sister Abby drives a well-used VW squareback, but one of the places it takes her is the New Hampshire farmhouse on a hundred acres of rolling land for which she paid several hundred thousand dollars cash.

They are attempting to secularize the money, separating use and enjoyment of it from acceptance of the obligation to make it increase and multiply and to wield their power for "the well-being of mankind." Laura's statement stands for stark historical counterpoint to her great-grandfather's claim that God had given him his fortune: "There's no way to justify the money. My liberation came when I realized, 'Well, you've got it. It's yours. It's not your fault that you've got it. Go ahead and do the best you can with it.'"

They have discovered that spending their money doesn't increase their indebtedness to its source. Yet spending it is rarely accomplished without a degree of self-scrutiny that, depending on the Cousin, ranges from true metaphysics to casuistry. Alida, last-born child of JDR3, recently decided to replace her beat-up old Volkswagen. "It took me a year or so thinking about it. Finally I just went out and bought this BMW I'd wanted for a long time. I'd never done anything that extravagant. I don't feel guilty, yet buying the car was quite traumatic for me. I could never have bought a Mercedes or anything like that: that's a rich person's car. But I really dig my car and don't regret spending the money. The notion that it's not inherently mine to enjoy is one of the hang-ups of the money. I think you should be able to enjoy it. But you should keep it in balance."

Yet the money is still a powerful totem, to be approached with anxiety and caution, if not reverence. "The major area in my life I learned to be unconscious about," says Abby, "was money and the material conditions of my existence. It was an area of calculated, contrived, un-self-consciousness." This tendency to envelop the family legacy in a fog of not knowing is a striking characteristic of the Cousins' generation. One measure of its density is that although well into adulthood as a group, the Cousins first learned about the size and extent of the fortune they would inherit as a result of Nelson's public disclosures of the family's financial data in his pursuit of the vice-presidency. Until that moment, this family, one of the most secretive in America, had been in this respect a secret also to itself.

Most of the Cousins were even then unaware of the contours of the family epic. "I have a tendency to hide from the family history," says Nelson's daughter Ann, who was once embarrassed to discover on a tour of Versailles that her grandfather had financed its restoration. "The more you discover what grandfather did, the littler and littler you feel. Nobody ever talked to us about his life and achievements. My father certainly wouldn't tell us."

It is a refrain heard throughout the generation, and none of the Cousins is quite sure of the reasons behind it. Perhaps as another Cousin observes, it was the very ambivalence of the Brothers toward *their* father's achievement—they still lived on the estates he had built and operated from the institutions he had created or acquired—that made them reluctant to speak. As though the telling would make them seem littler too.

Not knowing and not *wanting* to know, however, are often hard to separate in this family. "It's threatening to find out about the money," Lucy says flatly. "It's awfully hard to figure out." One of the most sensitive and self-assured of the Cousins, Lucy has developed a kind of tunnel vision in which the disorienting, almost metaphysical complexities of her background are filtered out as if by Polaroid lens, enabling her to locate and proceed on a forward path step by step. "Being a Rockefeller is like being a cripple," she says. "No matter what you do with your crippled arm or leg, it's still crippled. What you try to do is develop the rest in such a way that the disability is not really *you*."

In Lucy's own case (as for most of her cousins) psychiatry has been important in coming to terms with her dilemma and in fact led her to become a psychiatrist herself. "The best thing about money," she says sardonically, "is that it buys good analysis. It was in analysis that I learned how to think. I hadn't been exposed to thinking things through before that. I never knew how anything worked or how it related to us." When she got things straightened out, she remarried and had children. As with other of the female Cousins, the first marriage seems to have been a needed sacrifice to make the second work well. A parallel development was that she found she wanted to acquire a skill, to specialize and not be dependent on experts in the way her parents were. "If I'm going to do something, I'm going to do it well, instead of being a pseudo-expert, or surrounded by a lot of pseudo-experts," she says. "Except for David, the Brothers haven't mastered a particular area; I wanted to master a particular area. Something about Mummy, especially, impelled me in this direction. She was floating. Her friendships weren't particularly clear. Without Daddy or us, I felt she would be helpless. I wanted to avoid that. I wanted to be able to call my own shots."

It was difficult. She went to medical school and had a very hard time doing biology and the physical sciences. The medical school board said that though she had passed, she would have to repeat her first year. "They hoped it would make me quit. A member of the committee later told me that it was one of the most unfair things he'd ever seen the committee do, and that they were doing it to me because I was a Rockefeller and they thought that someone with so much money shouldn't be in medical school. But I went ahead and did it anyhow. I studied my head off—had no time for anything else—and I made it."

Her sister Marion's solution is also a reaction against the family. By making her goal doing everything for herself, from growing her own food to earning her own money, she has tried to get far away from a life where everything was done for her, where everything was perfectly symmetrical, almost clinically expert, and without the mark of a personality on it. Doing for herself and doing competently is a victory. It is something that started in her adolescence when she got her first horse. "Queenie was different from the horses in Grandfather's stables. They were kept smooth and sleek, just perfect. Queenie was all raggedy. But I took care of her. I did it myself. When I first realized that I was actually doing it, I couldn't believe I would succeed. But oh my God, the joy of it when I did. My parents enjoy things that are beautiful, well-done. There is no conflict in their lives. Everything has to fit together smoothly. Everything is taken care of for them. They're like prisoners. I've completely rebelled against that. I'm very extreme, but I want to be away from that whole world where you never really *know* anything, where you're a child no matter how old you are. There have been times in my life when I wanted to be a lamb almost, just to raise the wool so I could card it, and spin it, and make it into a blanket for myself."

To some extent the Cousins exemplify the truth of one of Oscar Wilde's witticisms: "Children begin by loving their parents; as they grow older they judge them; sometimes they forgive." Most of them would be reluctant to use the word "forgive" to describe their current attitude toward their parents, yet there is a new mood of acceptance among many of them. Their quest for normalcy has come up against the fact that ultimately, no matter what they do to prove themselves as individuals, they are marked out as members of a special caste and they fear that the consequence of the angry attempt to win independence is to be cut off from the only community where they are not regarded as oddities. As the cost of rebelliousness becomes clear, many have drawn back and reached an accommodation with the only group in which everyone is an oddity.

Laura, who is finishing a Ph.D. in psychology, has turned from her early radical activity with SDS to become involved in education. It is a "more acceptable avenue" of social change. "I now accept many or most of the values or goals that come to me by way of my family," she says. "But with the means I part company, especially that patronizing dimension that says we Rockefellers can know what is good for somebody else."

It is characteristic of the artificiality of this solution that one of the positions Laura accepted upon her "return to the fold" was a trusteeship of Spelman College in Atlanta, most poignant symbol of Rockefeller paternalism. Yet she attempts to resolve the contradictions just as her father did when he was younger—by an act of will. When Laurance appeared before the House Rules Committee to defend himself and his brother against charges of collusion in dirty tricks in the matter of the Goldberg book, he asked to read a note one of his daughters had written him on the question of "the Rockefeller empire." The author was Laura:

> The vision of "empire" . . . can only seem ironic to someone who happens to be a Rockefeller. This human plurality called "the Rockefellers" is not an "empire" but a family. There *are* ties that bind this family together. However, these ties have little to do with the exercise of business power and almost everything to do with having a shared set of common experiences. Although the public stereotype of "the Rockefellers" has changed from decade to decade, most of us have shared the experience of struggling to cut through that stereotype and to be recognized and valued as useful and responsible individuals. An inventory of the vocations of members of this family indicates that most have succeeded in finding a

way to do his or her "own thing" rather than a "family thing." Those who are younger are still engaged in a search for a separate identity.

Her cousin Peggy has also moved back into the family orbit from a radical past. Yet even more than Laura she remains a study in ambivalence. On the one hand, she maintains an assumed identity, having dropped her last name because she values the sense of privacy and self-satisfaction it seems to give her in her work. "My interest is in working with public schools to try to create alternatives," she says. "I looked for a job—without my Rockefeller name to help me—for five months. At one point, Bill Dietel [vice-president of the Brothers Fund and one of the associates employed by the Family Fund] suggested I could get involved in high-powered things in education, like the National Educational Association, which needed someone to run it. It was the kind of thing I never could have gotten without connections. I turned it down and went on looking. I wanted to get a job without using the name in any way." She finally did—in an experimental school. Yet the irony of working and living under an assumed name is not lost on one of her closest friends. "The one way for Peggy to test whether people will like her for herself is to see if they will like her without the name. Yet it's ultimately impossible for her to know, because no relationship can be *real* until they know who she is."

Peggy is now active in the family: secretary for the Cousins meetings, an influential member on the board of the Family Fund, and once more in close contact with her father. "He doesn't exasperate me anymore," she says, "although the whole issue of my changing my name he can't understand at all, can't accept or deal with. I used to follow the party line and was upset by any opposition. Now I have a much clearer sense of issues and am not so threatened by disagreement. He isn't threatened by education, which is what I'm into now. He's pleased that I've decided that education is the route to change society rather than revolution. Things are going my way in our discussions. We talk about Watergate, which he used to say was blown up by the Democrats and for which he's now apologizing. I'm mellowing. When I was in SDS, they used to say: ultimately you rich people will go back to your establishment ways. I'm pained that that's exactly what I'm doing. My superego is a straight Marxist line."

Yet the difficult problem of attaining a rapprochement with

the family is not that easily overcome for others. "My father," says Peggy's sister Abby, "doesn't try to bridge the gap between us. He must know that my life expresses different values from his, but he doesn't acknowledge that, doesn't want the tension of it. He tells me what *he's* doing and hopes I will be pleased. He doesn't even attempt to say that if I were to take a different attitude I might see that what he's doing constitutes a bridging of the gap. All he does is hope that what he's doing will simply bridge *me*."

In the Cousins' generation there has been a great deal of movement, shifting of positions, and changing of commitments. The degree to which this has gone on seems a function of the individual families. The odd chemistry of David and Peggy's marriage seems to have encouraged rebellion. In JDR3's there has been more of a calm acceptance than in Laurance's, where the children's real anger often bubbles to the surface of their attitudes. Nelson was the most expansive and supportive of the fathers, yet ironically the least tolerant. With the exception of Steven, this has produced children who seem content not to question their circumstances. For Rodman, the solution has been to try to imitate the manhood of the previous generation even at the risk of rattling around in a form that is too large for him. For the daughters, Ann and Mary, the solution has involved simply stepping to one side and watching.

Like others of the Cousins, Mary continues to be strongly involved with the Rockefellers' household gods, as the decor of her upper east side apartment indicates. In her library, there is a complete set of *En Guardia*, the Latin American magazine Frank Jamieson produced for her father and the Office of Inter-American Affairs when she was a child living with her parents in wartime Washington. On an end table is a photo of Nelson and one of Junior, along with a small wooden bust of Senior. She glances at the picture of Nelson and says, "It's hard for us to break away from the light of his image." After a moment's pause, she continues: "In a way it's easy, comfortable, compelling to have one's identity joined to an institution and to find oneself within it. I've never had the feeling that I needed to rebel against being a Rockefeller. My quest has been to get outside the family institution and find my identity that way."

She gestures at the icons on the table. "I'm not sure why I have them there. It gives me a perspective on my heritage. I admire the ingenuity of my great-grandfather. My grandfather stands for moral purpose. My father, well, I love him for his warmth. But he stands for power, and I think it's very important how one relates to power. It stands as a warning." Mary may think of herself as someone who has never questioned her commitment to family and father, but her personal life offers an example of an unannounced rebellion. When she recently remarried, her new husband was Tom Morgan, former chief aide to John Lindsay, author of essays strongly critical of Nelson in *Esquire* in the early sixties, and currently an associate publisher of *New York* magazine, a publication strongly critical of Nelson's governorship and quest for national office.

Jay, too, has embraced the family, although for reasons that are as much political as personal. He says, "When I was at Exeter having a difficult time with my father, I spoke to one of my teachers about it. He said something to the effect of, 'Well, finally it's the son who has to initiate improved relations with the father, not vice versa.' I didn't believe him at the time, but now I realize he was right. Things have gotten better and better between us over the last few years. I'm not naïve about the family, but I accept it. I've worked things out in human terms with the people who are my relatives. Everyone always says my Uncle David is the most powerful and busiest man in the country. He probably is, but he always makes room to see me when I'm in New York. I admire his terrific energy. I used to like going out to Jackson Hole to be at the ranch, but now it's to see Uncle Laurance. I admire him for the way everything he is or isn't is right on the table. I admire Uncle Nelson for being such an embracing person, I mean literally."

Jay has realized that making a separate peace with the family by moving to West Virginia was not enough, because he still wanted to use the family and the myth for his own advancement. There is private competition and bitterness between him and Nelson, yet he knows it would not do to wash this linen in public. He knows, too, he has gotten where he is because of who he is. As he once exclaimed to a *New York Times* writer, "If I was John D. Smith IV, where would I be?"

Jay has used the "good" things in his background to give a resonance to his own personal ends. It is like skimming cream off the top of the milk bottle: the trick is to do it so deftly that nothing has a chance to bubble up from below. "I've read the first volume of Nevins's life of my great-grandfather and enjoyed it, although not enough to compel me to finish the second volume. I've also read Fosdick's life of my grandfather and like it too. At times I can get terribly involved in being a Rockefeller. Not long ago I was in Florida and took time off to go to the Flagler Museum there. I was intensely curious about everything to do with my family. I saw Great-Grandfather's private railroad car and I began to fantasize about it like crazy. It was the same way I used to fantasize when I was a kid about someday inheriting and living in the Big House at Pocantico."

JDR3 had once been angered by a magazine article about the family in which Jay was referred to as Nelson's son. Yet there is perhaps a larger truth here about inheritance of family traits. Nelson had expanded the permissible level of personal ambition in the family. In his own case, however, it had still been entwined with the family—as an ambition drawing in its wake the hopes and compassion of all the Rockefellers. In Jay, the ambition is similar, but it has been divorced from the family. He is like any other politician with a famous name and lots of money. (In 1972 he spent nearly $2 million, over half of it his own money and most of the rest coming from his family.) Yet in his losing gubernatorial campaign, which he ran as a candidate independent and critical of the West Virginia mining interests, he learned he couldn't just pick the "good" element from the Rockefeller myth. At a time when he was attacking the lack of safety measures, citing this as a source of black lung disease among the miners, it was revealed that the Rockefeller Foundation (of which he was a trustee) held 300,000 shares of the Consolidation Coal Company, the biggest of the operators. And toward the end of the campaign, the past he had tried ambiguously to embrace at arm's length came to haunt him when bumper stickers appeared throughout the mine fields where he was counting on support. They read: "Remember Ludlow."

The temptation for the Cousins is to allow themselves to be carried along on the calm waters of the tradition, to save themselves and allow the Devil to take the hindmost. Yet for a few this is not enough. For them, the pursuit of an occupation as the means of breaking with the encumbrances of the legacy is at best only a partial solution. It rescues one element of the self, but it leaves another behind. A few of the Cousins have come to the realization that personal liberation can occur only when they have fully understood and exorcised the destructive powers of the tradition. Marion is such a one. So are Abby and Steven.

The newest Rockefeller business is headquartered just off Harvard Square in a slightly run-down four-story office building whose hallways sponge up the pungent aromas of the lunchroom on the ground floor and whose windows look down on the smoky gray streets below. The offices of Clivus Multrum, USA, are clean and tidy; the only hint of what business it is involved in is a three-foot-high blue fiberglass box sitting atop a radiator between two desks in the main office. With pipes coming up through the top and a door at one end, it looks like an oven for rectangular foods, or a high-school student's modernistic interpretation of a time machine. In point of fact, it is a Swedish composting toilet, and the Rockefeller who is president of the company holding the exclusive North American license to manufacture and sell the Clivus is Abby.

The oldest daughter of David has close-cropped hair and the fresh, freckled features of her mother. She is attractive in spite of a stubborn refusal to allow that attractiveness to be conveyed in conventional terms; solid, athletic, she projects a sense of physical competence and even power. She is dressed in a pullover shirt, jeans, and boots (it is ten years since she last put on a dress) that are reminders of the fact that she has been involved in radical politics for the last decade. She is aware that the fact that someone who is a professed Marxist and feminist should start a business allows her family to gloat and may seem to connect her to her family's commitments in a way she does not intend; this complication annoys her, as does the way the particular business she has chosen exercises the fancy of newspaper feature writers. Yet she accepts it all as an occupational hazard. The "clivus" is something she feels is eminently defensible and consistent with all the ideas she has been connected with in the past. "I guess I have a romantic sense of its possibilities," she says, leaning back in her chair and bringing her feet to rest on the top of her desk. "I have a sense that people would be better off if they did not feel their existence to be in fundamental conflict with the life cycles. To have your shit go out to sea produces melancholy. There must be some Rockefeller left in me because I see the clivus as a way, God forbid, of helping restructure the world."

Exactly how much Rockefeller Abby does have in her is problematical. Perhaps more than any of the other Cousins, her life has been a struggle against the name, a painful, almost violent effort to burn the Rockefeller compulsions and obligations out of her personality, including the guilt that is the most prominent features of the fourth generation. ("The Cousins don't want to get down to the sense of superiority they all feel. So instead of rooting that out, they use guilt as a shield to obscure it. That's why they are so willing, even eager, to express their guilt: guilt is socially acceptable; arrogance is not.") When she talks about herself, it is in a spontaneous recollection, so well-digested and precisely delivered that it seems almost a prepared text, as though each insight had been won by an intense and anxious labor. The sentences swarm around themes that for Abby are interconnected and flow in and out of each other—politics, family, feminism, self.

"I guess you could say I started to become a rebel when I didn't want to wear girls' clothes, which is since I can remember. My younger sister Neva and I were the same in this. We felt ourselves humiliated by girls' clothes—the very term was repugnant to us—and we disdained the girls who liked to wear them. This attitude was carried in the air in our family. It came from my mother. She was the center of everyone's interest and of our frantic desire to be approved of. My father, of course, liked these frocks. But he was somehow peripheral. My sense as a child was that his work was boring and that his manner was remote. Everything except his interest in insects, which was concrete and specific and a source of real contact with us, was tedious and formal. He dispensed allowances and made us do meaningless things like going to Sunday school, a job which fell to him because my mother wouldn't have anything to do with that. The fact that he liked dresses was not comforting.

"I wore boys' pants, undershirts, all those things. These clothes felt good, natural, self-respecting. But then suddenly I was a teenager and was told that I ought to wear all this other stuff. I found the change of rules and the meaning of the rules at first confusing, then intolerable. My refusal to accept the rules was distressing to my parents; their distress was distressing to me.

"There was a quick period when I was thirteen and I tried lipstick against my better sense. I gave it a try against a sense of great shame, great fear. I wanted to test it out and waited, terrified to see how the world would take it and what it would mean about me. And then, I got some remark from my mother—I've forgotten it exactly, but the gist was that because I was too young it was *vulgar* for me to be doing it. 'Vulgar' was the principal term of disapproval for my mother, the opposite of 'fine.' Vulgar is not knowing your place either way, of pretending you're something you're not. If you behave as if you are more than you are or less than you are, you're vulgar. If women who are well-bred dress in a sexy way, that is vulgar. So I dropped lipstick, flatly gave it up and everything that went along with it. But then, lo and behold, I got another sign. My mother said she was very upset that I did not wear girls' clothes and that if I didn't get to like being a girl I was going to be a very unhappy person. That's what she said, and I can remember thinking: it's too late, that kind of talk."

Abby was sent to Miss Chapin's School for Girls. She was stubborn, often miserable, and, especially when she got to be a teenager, things got bad at home as well. The signals were contradictory. "We have been raised to sew and draw and make our own presents at Christmas, and were praised for it. Then one year I was told out of the blue that I did seem a little old not to be spending my own money on presents—the implication was that I was being ungenerous."

She was in a perpetual rage because other evidences of self were constantly eradicated. She left her room messy and was beside herself when servants cleaned it, as they regularly did. She balked at the family rule of a daily bath and once, when she went away to summer camp, didn't bathe for six weeks. Her rejection of decorum—in neatness, table manners, dress— she now sees as "the first level in the development of my refusal of the class ideals behind the decorum. Making the connection was difficult and tense, a long process for me."

When her parents took her to Europe in her eleventh year, she hid in the bottom of the limousine that drove them to the presidential palaces and finest restaurants. "Part of it was to annoy my parents. I was disdainful of the Cadillac, of the hotels we stayed in, of the fawning we got everywhere. Nevertheless I was outraged that I had to hide in the bottom of the car, and it began to strike me that I was going to have to take a position on the whole thing. There was something in the Cadillacs, the estate, that went with being a Rockefeller, all that fancy stuff. It was vulgar, embarrassing; it made people have a funny attitude towards me—inflated, fawning, and yet despising. It was like a joke on me."

Abby was not a successful student and had a variety of tutors and remedial teachers; meanwhile, she poured her deflected desire to learn into the cello, which she began studying at the age of twelve. "I studied the cello with an intensity which I guess I hoped might somehow redeem my awkward failures everywhere else to be what others wanted me to be." After Miss Chapin's she went to Milton, a highly rated coed prep school, which ominously allowed the boys to watch from their dorms as the girls lined up every morning as if on display. She sank deeper at Milton and did poorly, living in terror of flunking out, although suspecting guiltily that her name would protect her from such a trauma. "It would be inexcusable, inconceivable, that someone like me should not pass such a school. That's why we were sent to these schools in the first place: they were to give us the sense that we were not only going to pass, but we were going to go on and run the world; that's the sense that was communicated to us. I got together with my friend Nan, who was doing as poorly as I. We fantasized about grotesquely celebrating our failure by going to graduation naked. Those were crazy, unhappy years for me. The only thing to be said in my behalf is that I was not afraid to be neurotic, the only female in the family, I think, who refused to be a debutante."

Abby spent the two years after she graduated from Milton living in a family friend's home in Cambridge playing the cello, recovering, and taking writing courses at night. "I was struggling with the whole thing—God, money, the name. How was I to stand towards these things? By now the choices had begun to jell. If it should seem to be true that there was a God, that would make sense of everything, make me, the money, and everything part of a divinely given order. If I took the view that there was a God, then my whole sense of myself, of other people, of the world would be affected. I would devote myself to using this Rockefeller name and money 'wisely.'

"On the other hand, if there were no God, then it would follow that the whole thing was capricious, accidental, arbitrary, and I could act in either one of three ways. I could use the money and the power that I had been born into for myself—just accept the accident and take pleasure in it. I could do 'good works' with it according to some system. Or I could give it all up on the grounds that it was illegitimate, unjust. Beneath the formality of the considered alternatives was an anxiety and ambivalence. I wanted to be rid of the false and immoral trappings of my life. But I could not do that without giving up the power, status, and luxury of those trappings. This is the madness I tried to deal with, even though I think that more than the rest of my cousins I was successful most of the time in blacking out the fact that Rockefeller was my name."

During this period of recovery and reflection in Cambridge, she entered psychoanalysis, which lasted seven years. It was more than passive free association. "I used to argue with my psychiatrist, struggle with him. I claimed that all women hated being women, that in some way it enrages them, embitters them. What is there to like about it, the way men have defined it? I claimed a woman was crazy, self-destructive, if she liked being female. These are the things I'd say to him. He'd answer, 'Maybe some women, even most women, hate it, but not all of them.' This would drive me into a fury. I'd say it was impossible that this should be so, because the rare woman who didn't hate the role must understand the degrading things she had to do to reach her 'good' position. He felt that until I saw the problem in my own terms, as *my* special problem, I couldn't deal with it; but I felt that I couldn't deal with it until the situation of women was generally changed. It was around this time that I wrote a long, impassioned letter to James Baldwin laying out what I thought the similarities between being black and being female were. I never sent it, as I sensed that he would feel insulted by the analogy."

Ultimately, the emergence of the feminist movement would allow her to integrate her dilemma, and help her in her efforts to dig her way out of the family problem. But other elements of a political consciousness came first. There was an interesting foretaste in 1959, when she was sixteen and happened to be spending the weekend with her father's close friend, Harvard President Nathan Pusey. That weekend Fidel Castro came to Boston. As his motorcade passed by Quincy Street, Abby climbed up on to the fence to see him. "It was my first political thrill. I knew nothing about him, nothing at all, but something exhilarated me. Where politics before had bored me, I was excited by this, and I went over to Soldier's Field at Harvard where he was speaking and stood on a chair for four hours to listen to him speak in broken English and tell what was going on in Cuba. And I was moved, extraordinarily. I was beside myself; it seemed to me so good. It was the first piece of political, moral sense which put things together that I ever heard. Then I went back and I spent another couple of hours telling Mr. Pusey what a fantastic person Castro was, and I assured him, naïvely, that from everything I could see, what he was doing was excellent. Mr. Pusey just shook his head and said with a worried tone. 'Well, Abby, I hope you're right; I hope you're right.' Then I repeated the performance with my father, and told him what an extraordinary person Castro was, and that he was good. Afterwards, after the break in relations, when it was said that Castro was a Communist, I can remember my father telling me: 'Well, he didn't turn out so well, did he, Abs?' I couldn't answer, because I didn't know anything still, I remember feeling ashamed of my wayward judgment."

It would be another two years before things began to sort themselves out. She was constantly fighting against family, status, sex, the orders that violated her sense of self; yet there was a numbing uncertainty at the heart of her struggle. Perhaps it was not the world that was crazy in paying deference to Rockefellers; perhaps, after all, it was she who was neurotic and arrogant for raging against something others appeared to accept so easily. Her father lectured her obliquely on that subject when she was eighteen, saying that to dress the way she did in old and often ill-fitting clothes was merely a way of demonstrating the fact that she could get away with it. David was the abiding force—as father, man, symbol—that gathered all the contradictions of her life to a luminous point. "From the time I was little I vacillated between thinking that my father was either silly or a god. The peak of the tension over this issue came in 1963, in my freshman English class at the New England Conservatory, which I had just entered. The class was taught by a Marxist, and one day, by way of jumping into the question of the logic of values, he asked each one of us to give an example of a person we thought was great. The students were naming people like Jesus, Moses, Gandhi, etc. I started to stew. I was sitting in the front row, as I always did, and suddenly I felt I was going to have to choose between oscillating views of my father: whether he was tedious, boring, impervious to the meanings in everything that went on around him, as in my rage I had seen him—or a god, which is the way his subordinates and associates and my family saw him. If this were the case, then it was I who was a fool, a child.

"At this moment, the 'mature' part of me asserted itself. It was the part that had been thinking all along that in the *real* world, which had a far greater complexity than a child's view imagined, most people were brutal, violent, or vile to each other, and my father—wielding enormous power, as he did—seemed respectful and kindly in his relations with everyone. It was a mode of behavior—I hadn't yet seen what it really meant—that expressed a kind of heroism, a kind of greatness, a kind of magnanimity.

"All the confusion of my life came to a head at this moment, and seemed to drive me to the test. If I really thought all this stuff about my father, then I ought to say it, even in public, even though he was my father. Yet, to do so was anathema; it was the opposite of everything I'd done, thought, and been so far in my life, which had meant hiding, concealing, minimizing everything to do with my name and my connection to the family and its worldly glory.

"Trembling and in a sweat, I gave my father as my choice of who was great. I said, 'My father.' Then I sort of blacked out. It was a big moment in my life. I had exposed to the fire this way of being, to see it go up in smoke. It was an exorcism, a stage in my release from the terms in which I had seen my dilemma. Now, having passed as it were to the other side, I was able to separate out the love I had for my father from the sense I had of the banality and injustice of his role in the world. I saw that to be great and powerful in the world's terms, as the world was presently structured, was a sham. The problems I had wrestled with were more complex now, but also more manageable."

Not long afterward, Abby met her instructor in the conservatory cafeteria. They got into a discussion, which she remembers as another pivotal moment. "As an adolescent, I'd always been extremely violent in my political fantasies, insofar as I had them. But I had changed by this time, at least on the surface, muddling my way through to some kind of liberal pacifist position. We began talking politics, and I think I was saying that there shouldn't be any violence, as though there could be a political system that was dedicated to the absence of violence. I remember his answer. He said that violence or the use of violence depended on the willingness of anyone to use it. And that if anyone was willing to use it, that settled its occurrence; and furthermore, anyone who was willing to use it settled pretty much the terms of it, and how much there would be. Then he threw in the clincher. He said that it was those who were in possession of the goods, of society's wealth, who established the terms for how much violence was used in the world. They did so in their efforts to maintain their possessions, and they did so in two ways: through the act of maintaining their possessions, depriving other people of them, and in the act of repressing those who rebelled against this order itself. This discussion marked an important day in my life, although I was miserable for a long time afterwards because of it. It pierced through those immature political ideas I'd held, and I couldn't go back to them. It was like some fundamental truth."

The next few years involved a process of reorientation. One important element was the analysis she argued her way through. "For me the fundamental part of this whole experience was the sense that everything was connected, inexorably connected, and that there was nothing inconsequential in the psychic life. That was a big step for me; that drove me to take seriously the implications of my behavior in a way I think I hoped I could get by without doing. I saw that I had wanted to do what everyone else does—to mystify the meaning of what I was doing in a complete and fascinating way, so I wouldn't really have to confront it.

"Combined with this was the Marxist method. It was even more striking than these psychic revelations: the view that history, societies, the world situation—everything was related in an intelligible way. I had thought that it was possible to believe that people came to be where they were as a consequence of arbitrary forces, accidental and independent strings pulled without relation to each other, certainly without any systematic interrelationship. Consequently, I could have the sentimental pity for the accidental poor, and the sentimental gratitude for the accidental rich. The idea that riches and poverty were interwoven, that one fed on the other, that the many suffered because of the few, that good and bad fortune were inextricably linked—this was new to me. It was compelling.

"Naturally I tried to explain it all to my parents. I assaulted them with it. But I knew so little: I could assert only the skeleton of the argument, the first principles. Even so, we had terrible, violent discussions. We would have the capitalism versus communism scene quite regularly. I would argue the idea of communism as I had read it in Marx's *Manifesto*. My father would doggedly bring in all this 'factual' stuff he knew about Russia in order to defeat me. He came to Cambridge once—it was at one of the points where warfare was so bad between us that I didn't want to see them in their house—and we went out to dinner. It was touching in a way, because he started out by asking me why it was that I believed as I did—it was the only time he's ever done that. He asked me how it was that I had repudiated everything he believed in; how could that have happened? I said that I thought I had learned a lot of what I thought from them; that I thought I had learned, especially from my mother, that there was no order to the fact that we had all this money, that there was no justice to it. And I said that I had learned from him that people should be decent to each other, and that it now seemed to me that the only thing systematic about our wealth was the indecency of it.

"I think he asked me directly why did I prefer communism, how could I think that it would be appropriate? I answered that it was really a question of two things: one's view of human nature and one's view of which system would bring about decent human conditions the quickest. So we got to talking about human nature, and he said that he believed in the carrot-and-the-whip theory. Just like that: carrot and whip. That he believed people needed to be prodded and then rewarded to be made to work. That those two stimuli would keep people going. In effect, he absolutely corroborated that capitalism is based on laziness and greed.

"I said I disagreed with his view of human nature. People were capable of being made like that, but they were also capable of being otherwise. It seemed to me true that people were capable of behaving in a variety of ways, and that the systems could elicit either the good or the bad, and that it seemed to me that capitalism elicited the bad. And he just said, well, he disagreed.

"Yet, shortly thereafter he invited me to come to Saigon with him to open a branch of the bank. It was 1966 and I was doing draft resistance. It was preposterous that he should have invited me, of course. But that was exactly the manner which had always seemed to me obtuse. I had thought the discussion had settled everything; it had aired our differences; it was civilized and friendly and real, and I was delighted. But I remember, afterwards, he was sad. There was no mention of his thinking that that was a good time, as he usually expresses one way or another. And in fact, with absolute regularity, the more tedious and formal I find an occasion in which we're together, the more he has liked it. Invariably. The more substance it has, the more disturbing it is to him.

"It's even worse when we don't meet on neutral ground. Everything is run and governed in my father's household, and if I do things out of step of the smallest kind—if I come down wearing the same clothes twice in a row—never mind that they are jeans instead of dresses—I feel the weight of that; that makes my father unhappy. There are almost always other people present, business friends, politicians, college presidents, for breakfast, lunch, dinner, in Maine, New York, even the Caribbean. My parents always take people with them. There is no room, there is no opportunity or desire for real talk. Real talk would mean that differences, conflicts would be brought to the surface. My father's idea is that there should be no conflicts. He can't see why there has to be tension of any sort. For me to accommodate myself to that order and that attitude feels like a betrayal of myself. But for me merely to express the tension that I feel is taken as a betrayal of him. It's impossible."

About a year before the discussion with her father, Abby had met and talked with a young man selling *The Militant* on a street corner; as a result of the discussion, she started going to Socialist Workers party meetings. ("Lord knows what I must have looked like to them. Their meetings were so boring. I think they may have thought I was stupid.") Over the next few years she became more deeply involved in antiwar activities. She augmented Marxist literature with extensive reading on Southeast Asia, including Bernard Fall's books and other early classics on the war which she found herself using as texts to pierce the myths about Vietnam and the U.S. intervention. She primed herself to counter the notion of her father and his friends that Vietnam was just another case of "Communist aggression." She also studied the intricacies of the Selective Service system, becoming a counselor in the Boston Draft Resistance Group.

Politics provided a framework and rationale for the revolt she had begun in childhood. It also had begun to give a sense of clarity about the Rockefeller money. "Getting rid of the money as some act of purification began to seem foolish, like an act of cowardice. I began to get this sense that I wasn't just on my own trying to be pure, but that what I had was a tainted but nonetheless powerful tool and that it made good sense to use it in behalf of the things I thought were good. I gave to everything: civil rights, draft resistance, teach-ins, radical education, everything. I was getting about twenty-five thousand a year then. I used very little of it for myself; most of it I gave away."

For years she was known as one of the easiest touches on

the left. In a crunch, Abby Rockefeller could be relied on for a few thousand. Her money found its way into everything from SNCC to the anti-Nixon satire *Milhouse*. Although she avoided open confrontations with her family and its institutions, which might be exploited by the press, there were inevitably times when her radical philanthropy would obliquely touch the Rockefeller edifice. Some years later, for example, when James Forman read his Black Manifesto from the pulpit of Riverside Church and demanded $400 million in reparations for 400 years of servitude, few in attendance realized that the chief financial support for Forman's organization came from one of the granddaughters of the man who had built this pillar of the Christian establishment.

Although Abby sometimes adjusted the amount of her offering because of the limits of her resources, she never refused a request. "I don't ever remember saying no. Literally never. I couldn't, really. The money didn't really *belong* to me in the sense that I didn't really *belong* to myself. I had a way to go for that to happen. At this point in my life I felt this way: Why *not* give it? What do I know? So what if they're hustling me? In their hands the money might at least do some accidental good."

Late in 1968, she was visited by a different kind of supplicant. It was Roxanne Dunbar, and she was requesting funds to send a delegate to a forthcoming feminist conference in Chicago, the first major gathering of its kind. Together with Dana Densmore, Betsy Warrior, and a few other harbingers of the new women's movement, Roxanne had already founded and put out the inaugural issue of *The Journal of Female Liberation*,* a seminal publication of the emerging feminist movement. Roxanne was a mover, a doer, and Abby realized that her visit would end in something more than the usual request granted. "I'd considered myself a feminist all my life, although I never would have used the word, because I hated anything involving the word '*female.*' Not exactly a case of self-loathing, just the realization that there was nothing in what I'd been given as a woman to like. All the associations were repellent to me. All 'feminine' mannerisms—making

---

*Also called *No More Fun and Games*, it is described in the *New Women's Survival Catalogue* as follows: "One of the earliest feminist groups in the country, Cell 16 has published since 1968 six Journals of Female Liberation. Theoretical statements by Lisa Leghorn, Roxanne Dunbar, Dawn Warrior, Dana Densmore, Betsy Warrior and others are some of the most articulate, provocative and most often reprinted of any magazine in the course of this second feminist struggle."

oneself up, wearing clothes men had designed, acting the way men said they had to—seemed part of a setup to make women contemptible for men, so that men could hate them. Given this sort of thinking, obviously, Roxanne's visit was a striking event, especially when you consider that this was a time when the women's movement consisted of little more than Betty Friedan's book."

With Roxanne and the others, Abby started Cell 16, soon one of the premier feminist organizations. There were endless meetings in the basement of her Cambridge apartment. The group began to put out the *Journal*, along with pamphlets, papers, and miscellaneous propaganda. They organized meetings around the Cambridge area. In the spring of 1969, Cell 16 sponsored the second major feminist conference. Held in Boston, it included an exhibition of *Tae Kwon Do*, a Korean variant of karate Abby had been studying for over a year. Although the press had been officially barred, one journalist from *New York* magazine got in and filed a story, which played on Abby's prominent role. "It was a really bad article," says Roxanne Dunbar. "It just set us up, saying how one woman would walk into a corner and break a board with her head. Stuff like that. As though we were a bunch of idiots or something. It really zeroed in on Abby of course, because it was newsworthy that this was Abby Rockefeller. It really put her down."

After the story appeared, there was a call from her parents. Her mother did the talking. "She said that my father was just sick at seeing his mother's name being dragged through the mud. I answered, 'Well, why did you name me after her then?' And she said, 'How could we have known you'd be doing *this* sort of thing?' "

Roxanne Dunbar recalls how upset Abby had been. "Her mother said that she was hurting the family. She reminded her of what had happened when Nelson married Happy and told her she was hurting them all when she allowed a spectacle to be made of something she did."

The incident rankled, as did other *contretemps* with her parents. Abby had not intended to wound them, only to try to establish her own prerogatives and do what she felt was right. As she says, "The family—the Brothers really—get to say what it means to be a Rockefeller and then expect the rest of us to live with it. For me to even name my values or interests, should they be different from *the family's*, constitutes a betrayal. Acting them out is unthinkable."

Abby quickly realized that the emerging feminist movement was the catalyst she needed, providing a position from which she could break with her history in a way that radical politics had not: it gave a perspective and a context that allowed her to stop her primary reactive gestures and plant herself. "It was good to see that vigor, violence, and rage could be associated with all the things I had been bothered by all my life; that you didn't have to sit back and take it neurotically; that there could be fundamental changes in marriage, child rearing, the family, and a whole range of other institutions that affected how women lived and what they thought of themselves."

Once, the violence came to the surface in a dramatic way. "About eight of us were walking along the street in Boston after a meeting. It was late and there were very few cars. Suddenly a car with two guys in it started crawling along the curb beside us. They were saying, 'Hey chicks, wanna ride?' and other obnoxious stuff. This kind of thing had enraged me all my life, but it had seemed like there was nothing that could be done about it. But this time Roxanne ran at the car and jammed her fist in the open window. Then she jumped back and taunted them: 'Who do you think you are, anyway?' Instinctively, I moved closer to the car and adopted a threatening posture to prevent the driver from getting out. While Roxanne was taunting him, I could see him fumbling under the seat. All of a sudden he opened the door and came at me with one of those four-way tire irons and tried to hit me over the head. I deflected it with an upperparts block. He was so terrified at the idea that I had defended myself that he jumped back in the car and screeched off. When he got a couple of hundred yards away, he abruptly stopped the car and he and his friend started shouting 'Fucking lezzies!' and other nasty stuff. It was an absolutely mad, ugly moment, yet I must admit that it felt like a breakthrough of sorts."

Throughout 1969, she was involved in intense, exhausting activity at Cell 16. At the beginning of 1970, the group began to break apart, fragmenting in a general cannibalism that would soon destroy the movement. Roxanne left for an organizing tour. The rest were tired. When the group was sufficiently feeble, the Socialist Workers party packed the membership well enough to stage one of its "democratic takeovers." When this happened, Abby and a few of the remaining members of the original group launched a midnight raid on the office she had paid for and equipped, "stealing" typewriters she had bought a hundred times over, taking back issues of *No More Fun and Games*, and other materials; they packed it all in a borrowed van and a rented taxi and spirited it away to safety.

She remained a free-lance activist in the women's movement, confronting baroque elaborations of its decay such as Radical Lesbianism. "This solution to the problem did not make visceral sense to me, but the logic in its favor was hard to argue against. If the problem was that women had been living with our enemy, then why shouldn't we stop doing this and start living with our friend? The reason women had never gotten out of their predicament was that they were so intimate with their oppressors. There was nothing comparable to it in history. Even slaves had separate quarters from their masters and could occasionally get away from this punishingly intimate connection. Yet we, the remnants of Cell 16, warred with the lesbians and everybody else because of our line on the question, which was that women should have the right to choose *no* sex if they wanted it that way."

Yet even as she fought, Abby, like many other militants, was on her way out of active participation in the feminist movement whose center of gravity was itself moving from the radical collective to the middlebrow mainstream. She spent a year concentrating her energies on Tae Kwon Do, playing the cello, and teaching classes at the New England Conservatory for which her favorite texts were Marx, Dickens, and Flaubert. She found that she had changed without really knowing it. "Before the feminist movement, I was vulnerable to many things—appeals for money, appeals to guilt, appeals to go out on dates. I had no system for saying no to any of it. I had no sense of right, of limit, over myself. I learned to say no in stages. I started saying no to men who'd been asking me out at the beginning of Cell 16. That was a huge relief. I knew that the next time I accepted such invitations, it would be on *my* terms. In the course of this I was able to come to the conclusion that I should give selectively and then only to feminist causes. That was good too, at least at the time, although when the women's movement started to decay, I felt the same *usedness* I had before; so I learned to say no there too. It may be, in fact, that being mature—at least for a fourth-generation Rockefeller—is learning to say no well. This involves an understanding of what your personal boundaries are, your desires and limits."

The thinking she had done in Cell 16 was continued in intense and exhausting study groups, and the views she evolved were distilled into a long essay she wrote for the spring 1973 issue of *No More Fun and Games*, the title of which was "Sex: The Basis of Sexism." In it Abby argued that the reason for the oppression of women was the greater and less discriminating nature of the male sexual need. "Men almost universally have a greater desire for sex than women [and are] less discriminating in terms of time, place and choice of object." Men know that they cannot get either the kind or amount of sex they want if the female's will is to be considered. Therefore they find it necessary to dominate and oppress women in order to satisfy their need. Consequently, "feminism is not just a 'war between the sexes,' it is a war over sex itself." Men should be prepared "to emulate women and learn to sharpen—and obey—their sense of when sex is appropriate or inappropriate." When female power is a reality, she concluded, "which is the same as to say when the female sexual sensibility is the universal one, although sex will be better, there will most certainly be less of it."

Even as the essay was appearing, she had moved past the period in her life that had begun five years earlier. A kind of equanimity had entered her days, as if she had gotten basic principles established and planted herself to such a degree that she could now do something other than worry about her emotional state. Some wound seemed healed. She bought a farmhouse in New Hampshire and spent her time and money (the first she had lavished on herself) remodeling it and making it into a working farm.

In the course of this she happened to see an article in *Organic Gardening and Farming*. Inauspiciously titled "Goodbye to the Flush Toilet," it was a description of the clivus, a compost system developed by Swedish engineer Rikard Lindstrom. It was able to handle excrement and household garbage without smell or mess, breaking down an average family's yearly waste into about three pounds of composting material. "I was struck by the idea that modern technology didn't have to deal with our waste products by polluting the environment but could instead be used to turn those products to a valuable form, positively beneficial rather than positively harmful."

Intrigued by the radical ecological implications of the clivus, she ventured to Sweden in spite of a long-standing fear of flying. She inspected the methods of construction and signed a contract licensing her to manufacture and sell the clivus in America. By the summer of 1974 she had installed the first two of these systems in America, one in her house in Cambridge and the other at the New Hampshire farm. Raising money from her trust and from other members of the fourth generation, she began the operations of Clivus Multrum, USA.

The new venture has not closed the gap with the family. Abby has always been the troublesome Cousin, the one who might do anything, whose words carry a critical sting against the Rockefeller enterprises as sharp as anything hurled from outside the family walls. When she first started the business, with technical advice from Room 5600, there was a gloating that she had come over to capitalism, even if the business she had chosen was the excrement business. Yet the amused tolerance for Clivus Multrum, USA ("I guess we've finally flushed her out," says Rodman in a labored pun), has been succeeded by a puzzlement over Abby's new incarnation. Should she be patronizingly encouraged, or should they worry that she mocks them through this new twist on the symbolic connection of feces and money?

Recently she bumped into her Uncle Laurance during a rare trip to the Family Office to try to get more money out of her trust to expand her business. She hadn't seen him for eight years. "He was charming as usual, although aged in a way I didn't expect, as though his particular brand of cynicism hadn't kept him afloat. He kept saying that he and I were both in the same thing, except in separate ways. Kept saying it over and over. He wanted to demonstrate to me that he knew about the clivus. Acually, he did. He ran on about how the bacteria operate to aid composting, what composting is, and why it's important. Hardly without drawing breath, he told me he's got MIT—of which he's a trustee—working on some river in Vermont which will be cleaned up by such and such a date with central sewage treatment plants. He suggested the clivus might be added to this system to take the sewage after it was treated. And then he was gone to another appointment. I never got a chance to point out that the whole purpose of the clivus is to *replace* sewage treatment plants, which are environmentally disastrous. It was a classic confrontation."

For Abby the problems are far from solved, particularly the sorting out of human relationships within the family from the institutional aspects of its fame and power, which she completely rejects. Her dilemma is poignant, especially because she feels that open warfare against the family is a posture that would confuse and demean all the dimensions of the Rockefeller problem. Yet the closer she attempts to draw to personal connections, separating them from their social husk, the more clearly she is forced into the realization that the taint of the fortune is an inextricable part of the family structure itself. The irony is summarized in a recent incident, which she tells with a melancholy air:

"Other members of my family had been pushing my parents to tell them how much money they were going to inherit, on the grounds that it would be embarrassing for them to read about it in the papers, a disclosure which for a while seemed likely as a result of Nelson's upcoming vice-presidential hearings. The reason my father and mother had not wanted to talk about it was apparently the fear of having their children eager for their deaths. That idea repulsed me, made me sick; I had been thinking that it would be good not to have the whole thing hanging over us, not to have that money coming, with all its attendant problems. Then, when I was at my father's house one evening, he called me in to his study and started to tell me about the money. He was tremendously tense as he explained to me that my grandfather had set up a trust which would be handed down upon his own death, and he added that of course he didn't have any expectations of dying soon. He must have said that three times. It was very painful for me, to hear him feel compelled to say this. And then he explained what the arrangement was: that when the time came, it would be divided six ways, and that we would each get twenty-five million dollars.

"When he was finished I said, 'Well, you should know what my view of this is.' I said that I thought that I would prefer not to have it. I said that what I did not like was the idea of it hanging over me, affecting my future and my present, affecting my relations with people, and affecting my relations with him. I said that I thought that it was just bad for relations. I thought we had enough to deal with between us without this sort of thing.

"I didn't say this with any antipathy. But he looked stunned, upset, and he said, 'Well, I'm terribly sorry to tell you, but there's nothing I can do about it.' And then it was clear, and it became clearer with each word that he said afterwards, that he took it as an absolute accusation and expression of the most extraordinary ingratitude. It was like so many of our other arguments. There was no way I could make him see my view—that it was not a question of gratitude but a question of history. I was to receive the consequences of history, not of someone's generosity—as even he admitted when he said he could not alter the terms of the trust. I said I could understand how he might have felt connected to his own grandfather, whom he had known; how he might have some feeling for the handing down of the fortune; but that I had no such sense (even without the politics of it, which I didn't go into) and that in fact I thought the burdens of it were greater than the advantages, though they were many.

"But it was no use. There was no way he could see around the whole institutional framework of the family and its history. He was hurt and angry at me for being ungrateful."

In a way Abby has given up any hope she ever had of resolving the tension with her family. For her the only posture seems to be the calculated disequilibrium of the dissident. "My being is tormented in their household," she says. "Yet not to go there ever again, to cut ties completely, would be to decide it simply doesn't matter where and what one comes from. It would be to deny the very meaning of the ties. Going to that house a couple of times a year at the very minimum lets me see where I am in my life. My behavior— how I deal with the Rockefeller outrages—is the clearest barometer to my general condition. My family is the constant—the yardstick by which I measure my own movement."

Except for the Judy Collins album *Wildflowers*, which is visible in the window through a gauze of curtain, this two-story white frame house is like a hundred others in the small town of Middlebury—well-kept and sturdy, private but not unfriendly. It is obvious that its owner knows and admires Vermont's sober Yankee virtues. A tall, thin man with thick glasses and a full beard fringing a boyishly angular face, he comes out of the front door smiling pleasantly, extending a wiry arm from rolled-up white sleeves for a handshake. "I'm Steven Rockefeller." The famous name is said without evasion or self-pity, without the spiritual flinching of some of his cousins. It is announced with the calm knowledge that it is bound to hit the listener, but that after the reaction has passed the two of them can go on from there.

There are recollections of Nelson's features around Steven's eyes and jaw, yet the hardness is not there. The eyes that look out from behind horn-rimmed glasses express the vulnerability that disappeared early in his father's life. The total impression is of a paring away—of flesh, pretense, ambition—and of hungers understood and controlled, as if this Rockefeller had gone through some arduous training and come out toughened, yet paradoxically more human. When he speaks, it is as a survivor, not an exile, in contact with and often speaking for his generation of Rockefellers and its concerns. "I've followed the same path as many of my cousins," the 38-year-old son of the Vice-President says. "Circumstances have forced us to come to terms with our inward life in a way no other group of Rockefellers ever had to. There are exceptions, but most of us have seen that there is no sense in living as robots of a great institution called the Rockefeller Family and constantly paying dues to a guilty conscience."

Born the year before the death of the first John D., Steven felt connected to Rockefeller traditions in a way some of the younger Cousins did not. Unlike Abby, for whom the role of female Rockefeller led to an early struggle against the family, Steven was a potential inheritor for whom everything was smoothly arranged. When he looks back, it is without sentimentality or bitterness, and without the aid of the family icons that are spread throughout his sister Mary's house. His recollections have the same stripped, pared-down quality as his person.

"My grandfather was a very determined little man, very much in control of the critical aspects of the family structure until the very end of his life," Steven says. "Don't let anyone tell you that he didn't decide exactly what went on at Pocantico. He did. This idea that my grandmother was somehow the stronger of the two is pure nonsense. She was intelligent and extremely warm. My father has some of her qualities, which he uses politically; you can feel it coming off him whenever he's functioning, and it's very seldom that he's not functioning. Junior was reserved, tighter than Abby Aldrich, but he had a very definite sense of himself and what he expected of the people around him. That included his grandchildren."

Junior didn't talk much about his past on the occasions Steven spent alone with him. Nor did Nelson or his uncles talk about Junior's life, which in effect summarized the history of the family up to that point. Steven only realized why later on. "Grandfather set a pretty fast pace around the track, you know. Father and his brothers seemed to feel that he was everywhere. They had a terrific burden on them to try to outdo or at least equal him. They all seemed to feel that if they dwelled on his accomplishments, it would only make their task harder."

Less awed by Nelson's image than his older brother, Rodman, and not captivated by his father's magnetism in the way his sisters, Ann and Mary, were, Steven grew up with questions, which was one of the few things Nelson definitely discouraged. "Father never aggressively tried to oppose what I thought. The only problem we had as kids was that he didn't like to be questioned about his beliefs, so that kind of confrontation was prevented. He is expressive and emotional, but only on his terms. There was no discussion of issues in a critical way, no dialogue. If we didn't like the way things were being run, we were free to say we didn't but that was the end of the conversation. In short, the technique was that people were allowed to say what they thought, but they were also made aware that they would be frozen out if they did. We learned early what the consequences were for deviating from the established position."

Inside the family, Steven was strengthened in the course of independence he would eventually choose by his mother's understanding. "She wanted to be supportive, even though she may not have understood the dynamics of everything I was struggling with. She's extraordinarily open-minded for a person of her background and class." And in an ironic way, Nelson too contributed to the breaking of the dynastic mold. "Father himself cut *his* own way," says Steven. "He has his own goals, his own ambitions, and one of the things he said to me once that has really stuck in my mind, was that if you want something in your life, set your eye on it, go after it, and don't let anything distract you. That's the way he's been all his life; he went his own way; he's done what he wanted to do."

Steven emerged from childhood believing in and wanting to serve the party line. He took Nelson's strongly put ethics very seriously. "When we were given our allowance, there was a very clear understanding that we were going to give away twenty percent of it," he remembers. The view that money means responsibility was "hammered into us." Steven came to know and memorize his grandfather's "creed." In fact, the only annoyance produced by his legacy in these early years, as Steven passed through Deerfield Academy with good grades, was the assumption of his schoolmates that the prizes he won were in some way purchased by his status as a Rockefeller.

He entered Princeton and in a small rebellion won the right to major in history. ("Actually I was interested in philosophy, but as a Rockefeller male I should have majored in economics.") After completing his senior thesis on the role his father's old adviser A. A. Berle had played as a Roosevelt braintruster, he was awarded the Taylor Pyne Prize given to that senior exhibiting "excellent scholarship and manly qualities" as well as the Class of 1901 Medal.

With his education apparently complete, he went up to New York City to begin the future that had been laid out for him. It was not laid out in quite the way it had been for the prior generation, but then his father was not Junior and made few demands that his sons pay tithes to the family as such. Nelson's philosophy on the subject was summarized in a comment he had made to Rodman on his graduation: "You should use the family institutions as a base from which you can operate. Get into something like IBEC, and use it as a vehicle for what you want to be."

More than Roddy, Steven was seen by his uncles as a promising candidate for their future plans. "I grew up with the idea that I had a responsibility to become like the Brothers—to be a leader in family institutions and then to go out into the world and assume a social and political leadership role in society at large." Winthrop asked him to go on the board of Colonial Williamsburg, and there was general pressure from Room 5600 to get involved in the administration of Riverside Church. He turned both of these positions down, but did accept his Uncle Laurance's invitation to go on the board of trustees of Jackson Hole Preserve, Inc., and the American Conservation Association.

There was not much time for him to get involved in these institutions, however, before he was swept up in his father's first campaign for governor. The 1958 campaign was a contrast to the reelection steamrollers Nelson would launch with crushing regularity every four years after gaining the office. There was no lack of money in 1958, but the campaign had a personal, almost amateurish quality that gave it a spark never again captured. The 22-year-old Steven was able to assume a position as one of three critical people in the actual daily campaign, the other two being Malcolm Wilson and Nelson himself. After Princeton's commencement ceremonies, the three of them got in Nelson's Lincoln and went all around the state, Wilson using his contacts as a long-time Republican assemblyman to line up county chairmen and local leaders for Nelson to meet. Young, earnest, believing that his father did have something unique and valuable to bring to the stagnant waters of American politics, Steven was the driver and detail man.

After being elected, Nelson asked Steven to come to Albany with him, but he refused, still remembering the charges that prizes he had won could be attributed to his family's power. ("I didn't want anyone to say I had a job because my father was running the show.") He decided to fulfill his military service requirement instead, joining the army reserve and going on six months' active duty. He had signed up for ROTC at Princeton on older brother Rodman's advice, but hadn't been able to stand it and, after a confrontation with the dean of students there, had deliberately flunked out. But now the army gave him a welcome opportunity to glide for a moment while he made up his mind about the future that loomed before him. "I enjoyed it, being a nobody, a private first class," he says in a statement recalling his Uncle Winthrop's experience in the service. "It was nice having no responsibility. It was a vacation. I enjoyed going to the PX and drinking pop."

Yet there was something going on behind the scenes. In 1956 his mother had hired a new maid, Anne-Marie Rasmussen, a pretty blond woman from a small fishing village in Norway. Two years younger than Steven, she had come to America in search of the excitement described by an uncle who had emigrated to the United States years earlier. Her difficulty with the language ("Hello, Rockefeller President," she had answered the telephone at Pocantico, mistaking the magic word for "residence") was an asset as far as her new employers were concerned. In all the Rockefeller households, foreigners were preferred as domestic help: they could not carry tales over the language barrier.

Steven didn't get to know Anne-Marie until the summer of 1957, when he startled everyone present at the annual Fireman's Ball at Seal Harbor first by appearing and then by asking his family's attractive servant to dance. He began dating Anne-Marie frequently and taking her for drives in his beat-up, used Volkswagen. By the time he returned to Princeton for his senior year, it was an established romance which Tod, who would later become one of Anne-Marie's staunchest defenders, found discouraging.

Finding it difficult to dine with the Rockefellers as Steven's "date" and then go back to work in the kitchen, Anne-Marie left their employ. She took other jobs, first as a clerk at Bloomingdale's and later in a New York insurance company. Early in 1959, while Steven was in the army, she returned to Norway. In August, after his discharge, he flew there to meet her, sending his parents a cable to announce that he planned to marry. Billed as an international Cinderella romance, news of Steven's engagement quickly found its way to the front pages of *The New York Times*.

Steven now admits what was not quite obvious at the time: that the marriage was an indication of the rebellion that had been percolating in him but had not yet built enough pressure to break through the rational crust of his upbringing. "I guess it was an attempt to get out of the social world I'd been part of. In terms of values, what appealed to me about Anne-Marie was that she seemed to offer a way of getting back to elemental values lacking in my own life. She came from a tightly knit community on a small Norwegian island. I was trying to sink my feet into the earth somehow, to get out of the formal, tightly controlled world of my childhood into something more fundamental and real."

Later in the year, the couple were married in a small Lutheran church in Anne-Marie's birthplace of Soegne, which had overnight metamorphosed into a cosmopolitan center. Former United Nations Secretary-General Trygve Lie was one of many prominent personalities present. It had been falsely rumored that President Eisenhower would attend. But even if he had, it is likely that he would have been upstaged by the bridegroom's father. Nelson had taken time out from his search for the Republican presidential nomination to jet to Soegne. As he stepped off the plane and yelled "Hiya kids" to Steven and Anne-Marie, a crowd as large and frenzied as any drummed up by advance men back home chanted "Rockefeller, Rockefeller, Rockefeller." The Norwegian Cinderella wasted little time in trying on the glass slipper. Shortly after the wedding ceremony, Anne-Marie told reporters in her rapidly improving English, "This will change my life completely. Everything now will become new and different for me."

The fact that he had married a commoner made his marriage the most notable social landmark for the family in the period between Winthrop's divorce and Nelson's remarriage. Steven and Anne-Marie returned to Pocantico to find a traffic jam of reporters and television crews milling about near the estate's main gate. Their car slipped unnoticed through David's private entrance near his house. They spent their honeymoon at Hawes House, where Nelson and Tod had first lived when they came to Pocantico as newlyweds. Secluded, it was the most romantic of the homes on the estate. During the day, the two of them rode together on Steven's motorcycle over the miles of bridlepath, often stopping to go off alone into the woods. At night there were occasional crank calls. Steven was used to hearing anonymous voices filled with impersonal hatred on the other end of the line, but Anne-Marie was not. Some of their first nights together were passed with an old groundskeeper, who had worked for the family for years, sitting alone in the kitchen with a shotgun in his lap keeping vigil over their bridal bed.

Aside from the fact that he had married a serving maid instead of a socialite, Steven's life began to resemble his father's. Like Nelson, he had overruled family opposition in getting maried early, and spent the first year after graduation in indecision. Now, he was ready to buckle down. "I was conscious of the previous career of Nelson Rockefeller. I felt somehow that it was my responsibility to go and do likewise."

He literally did, taking a job in the rentals office of Rockefeller Center, the point at which his father had entered the dynastic enterprise some thirty years earlier. But there the similarity stopped. While Nelson had enjoyed the sense of power and maneuverability filling the vacant offices of Rockefeller Center had given him, Steven felt simply foolish. "I found myself going around knocking on doors and saying things like, 'Hello, I'm Steven Rockefeller and I'm here to raise your rent.' It was ridiculous. I had to admit that I was far more interested in other questions. I had just finished working for my father's campaign and studying history for four years. I was interested in politics and religion, in questions about the moral basis of democracy and the nature of the 'good society.' There's a basic conflict between this level of thinking and going around trying to raise somebody's rent, especially when it didn't seem to me that the family needed much more money. I didn't need more money, didn't need more than I already had. I already sensed an injustice in us having all that we had, in the midst of a world with such great need on the part of so many."

Steven tried to make the job more meaningful by doing things like convincing the family to place a bronze plaque bearing Junior's creed over the ice-skating rink, which forms the Center's main courtyard. Yet this kind of gesture did not satisfy him.

During the time he was working at Rockefeller Center, he was moonlighting at a most un-Rockefeller endeavor: reading Paul Tillich and other contemporary theologians and trying to piece together a vision of the good society as it related to individual fulfillment. His realization that the family business was not for him was hastened by his interest in moral questions. "I had begun to wonder if I was going to sneak this interest into small openings in my spare time. I said to myself, 'Look, you're going to spend the rest of your days reading these books during your lunch hour and in the evenings, and come to the end of your life regretting that you never pursued it.' I decided to leave Rockefeller Center and enroll at Union Theological Seminary. I still felt, though, that it was irresponsible of me to do so. My real responsibility was to in some way serve the family, or to serve its principles. So I told myself that I wasn't breaking away. My plan was to go there for a year, get all the answers I could, and then come back out and go into politics as an effective social leader."

Yet right from the start he realized that things might not work out so simply. When he was applying for admission, he had lunch with Union's president, Henry Pitney Van Dusen, a longtime friend of the family and a Rockefeller Foundation trustee. "I said to him that it seemed to me that a good deal of the way our society was run was not in keeping with the very Christian tradition which was supposed to be at the foundation of it. And he said, 'Well it's obviously in plain contradiction to it, isn't it?' My initial reaction," recalls Steven, "was well, that's too harsh, too strong. It's not a contradiction. But soon I was beginning to see that he was right."

The year stretched into three. Instead of emerging into the world as a politician, he withdrew deeper into himself, following the dictates of a quest whose ends he didn't quite understand. "I was trying to make sense out of what I saw. I started from the bottom and tried to examine the religious ideas at the foundation of our society, ideas which articulate the basic values of Western civilization. I studied Old and New Testament theology. I went deeper into the assumptions I'd had about my relationship to society. A lot of this went into a thesis I wrote on the thought of Reinhold Niebuhr. I considered the ministry, but I wasn't really a believing Christian, so that was out."

It was about this time that his brother Michael was lost in

New Guinea. To the world at large it might seem the tragic accident in a young man's romantic quest. But Steven knew better from his own increasingly painful confusion. He knew the expedition Michael had allowed his anxious father to rationalize as the prelude to a career in international business was something else. "Michael saw the trip as an acceptable way of buying time. He had the courage to go out to follow his interests and desires. From everything we know about his last weeks, he was intensely happy over there. His independence helped convince me that life was too short to compromise on the things that really matter to you, and that if you do, then you're finally no good to your society, your family, or yourself. One of the things I believe deeply, by the way, is that Michael would have broken out of all this if he had lived. He would have made it."

As he finished his third and final year at Union, everything seemed to be happening at the same time. His parents had split and his father was carrying on a clandestine romance with Happy Murphy that wasn't nearly as secret as he thought. Michael was dead. Steven himself was increasingly unsure where his own life was leading. And not surprisingly, the marriage with Anne-Marie was coming apart. "She was not interested in the radical social and individual questioning that I was going through. She wasn't prepared for long years of graduate study and moral angst. Our relationship became as confused as everything else in my life."

For Steven there would be no escape by going abroad, living incommunicado, or doing social work among the disadvantaged. He had begun a cerebral odyssey as forbidding and fraught with dangers as Michael's. When Steven emerged from his jungles, he would be the most admired Cousin, Jay and others going so far as to call him the "conscience" of the fourth Rockefeller generation.

"I went through a period of major confusion. I became unsure about everything I had grown up believing. I became obsessed with the problem of my own identity. I became obsessed with God—the central symbol of values in any society. How had I come to believe what I did? Why did society believe the way it did? It was at this time that I began to question the core of the family myth: that the Rockefellers are superpeople. I had to deal with the problem of wealth and guilt. The Rockefeller mentality grows out of the notion that our money is justified by doing good. Having wealth is unjustified, but the Rockefellers justify it by doing good. I had to cut through all this and understand that there is *no* rational justification for my family having the amount of money that it has, and that the only honest thing to say in defense of it is that we like having the money and the present social system allows us to keep it."

He decided that reason alone could not help him in his crisis. He began sessions with a psychoanalyst that would last for five years. Inevitably the repression of emotion which was so central a part of all the Cousins' experience became the central theme of his therapy. Like everything else, it led not away from the family, but back into it. "I think this repression is closely tied to the awesome sense of responsibility toward this awesome *thing* that is the Rockefeller family. The family is something you dare not violate. It incarnates itself in certain figures toward whom you *must* act in a reverent, respectful fashion, the way people act when they go to church. Walking around with their hands folded, trying to look pious and good. Worshipping God, well, it's worshipping the family. It's the same. The family is a holy thing: you dare not transgress against its principles, standards, ideals, and so on. The result of all this is that a lot goes unsaid. Hostility toward the family or severe questioning of it is just not tolerated. It is a very tough system. You get indoctrinated when you're a kid and it takes a lot of will and energy, guts and lonely moments to move out of it."

Shortly after entering analysis, Steven enrolled as a graduate student in philosophy at Columbia, systematically reading through the history of Western philosophy wih John Herman Randall, beginning with the pre-Socratics and making his way to John Dewey, a task that would take another three years and lead to a doctoral thesis on the ethical foundation of Dewey's thought.

There was no sudden moment of clarity. Steven remembers many evenings spent walking alone or driving aimlessly through New York in his Volkswagen looking at other lonely people he imagined to be similarly lost. Whatever tendency he once had to feel above the common man's troubles had disappeared; on the contrary, he felt triumphant that he now felt no worse off than they. "I took some comfort in the fact that we were all members of the same community of confused seekers," he says now.

It was during his deepest despair that he began consciously moving away from the family. As he remembers, "All during my confusion I hadn't been able to put away my 'Rockefeller conscience.' I was still working at projects in the community as a responsible Rockefeller. But I had come to the conclusion that I really wasn't doing anything for anyone—myself most of all—when I acted only from some abstract sense of duty. I realized that it had to be out of some more genuine emotion, love or some other variety of personal commitment; that the only kind of experience that can generate a good society is when people act out of inner conviction, not an inherited sense of duty or fear. I gradually found myself going my own way where family affairs were concerned, starting to do only the things I believed were right and most important to me personally. I got off Laurance's boards and got clear of most of my Rockefeller responsibilities."

The distance he had come in the independent course he was charting for himself was manifest for the first time publicly in 1967. He had been working on a poverty project in Tarrytown while finishing his Ph.D. thesis at Columbia. One of his co-workers, a nun from nearby Marymount College, asked him if he would like to give a commencement address as a "neighbor" of the college. He agreed. At a time when his father and uncles were all firmly pushing the escalation of the war in Vietnam, Steven made what for any male inheritor in his family, but especially for the son of New York's governor, was an outspoken declaration. "If I were in Vietnam," he said in a voice recalling the reforming zeal of his abolitionist Spelman ancestors, "I would be haunted by the question of the justice and intelligence of U.S. policy. . . . It does not seem possible that we will win any significant victory over the real problems that face our nation and mankind by what we are doing there. The world cries out for new life and a new creation, and we are expending our resources on a hideous destruction."

His wife, Anne-Marie, later noted that the speech caused more controversy among the Rockefeller Cousins than any event since Jay's decision to change his registration from Republican to Democrat. Looking back on it, Steven says, "Stating my position publicly made the differences between my views and my family's real in a way that they hadn't been before. It was the first expression of the increasingly wide gap between what I thought and what my father thought. I valued the family community very much, but what was more important to me was the integrity of my own mind. I knew that to surrender that for the price of the family community would only leave me as a person without self-respect."

When reporters asked him about his son's speech the following day, Nelson snapped back, "It's a free country," in obvious irritation. Yet a year later, after the Kennedy and King assassinations, when "the Chief" was entering the final phase of his off-again, on-again campaign for the Republican presidential nomination, he came to Steven to ask for help in building a coalition of liberals, minorities, and young people that would be able to "bring the country together again."

It was not so much that Nelson literally needed his son's help as that he had come to regard him as a moral touchstone and needed his blessing on beginning his new crusade. Anne-Marie got involved, helping organize Scandinavian Americans for Rockefeller. Steven had changed in the ten years since the first gubernatorial campaign in ways that Nelson would never be able to understand. In 1958, Steven had really believed that his father was the best man for the job. In 1968, he helped set up People for Rockefeller more out of a sense of loyalty tinged with compassion than any political conviction. He looks back on those days: "If you analyze the sixty-eight campaign, with the assumption that Father really wanted the presidency, you've got to conclude it was a very peculiar campaign. He spent a lot of money for nothing. All he did was give the appearance of conflict, which was good for Nixon. Father's period was the fifties, the cold war. The Brothers Reports represented the high point of his leadership and impact. If he was going to do it, he should have done it when Kennedy did. He hasn't given up trying, but that time in his life has passed."

The following year, 1969, Steven announced his separation from Anne-Marie. The marriage had been shaky since before the birth of their third child, Jennifer (preceded by Steven, Jr., and Ingrid) in 1964. Tiring of being a Cinderella wed to such a reluctant prince, Anne-Marie had decided to change worlds. While campaigning for Nelson in 1968, she had met Robert W. Krogstad, a Wisconsin manufacturer of Norwegian descent serving as head of Scandinavian Americans for Rockefeller. Three months after her separation from Steven was announced, she went to Juárez for a Mexican divorce and then married Krogstad early in 1970. Steven says, "She was as badly misled in our marriage as I was. She had come off an island to marry a Rockefeller and thought she would have wealth, social life, glamour—all the things I was rejecting."*

Part of Steven's "solution" to the dilemmas of a Rockefeller heir is to wall off his principles from any direct encounter with the family. Yet despite this self-imposed limit, his perspective cuts to the core of the dynastic theme of the family epic and philanthropic thread that runs through it like a gold filament. It is articulated in a monologue that binds the history of four generations into a simple and compelling unity, and more than anything else tells why the tale is finally at an end:

"I'm not interested in passing judgment on what anybody else did in the past. That's a problem for the historian, not for me. For me the problem is 'What do I want to do personally?' and here I find that I cannot continue to try to play the role of the Rockefeller as it has been defined by my great-grandfather, my grandfather, and the Brothers, while remaining an individual at peace with myself. I would hope that I can continue to play a constructive role in philanthropy as long as the family's resources remain, but only in areas where I am actively interested and not necessarily as a trustee of funds that bear the Rockefeller name. The thing that I don't ever want to let happen to me personally is to be useful solely because someone dumped a bag of money in my lap. This is a major problem for all the Cousins. They don't like to be related to as a dollar sign. The issue is one of having something to offer that comes out of your own individual self, your own understanding, humanity, and creativity, and not just out of your bank account.

"For my grandfather, it was a somewhat different situation. He faced the question of the whole fate and future of the fortune. There was a certain creativity in the way he handled it, and swung things decisively in the direction of philanthropy. It began with his father, but it was he who emphasized the tradition of giving and social service, which was so terribly important in the development of the family.

"But there was a contradiction in all of this which I've never been able to fully understand. It's always troubled me and it's simply this: we were brought up as children to be-

---

*Anne-Marie divorced her second husband after two years of marriage in 1972. Emphasizing the fact that some part of her would always be involved with the Rockefellers, she built an estate in the manner and style of Pocantico, named it "Ras-Rock," and settled there with her three children.

lieve that as long as there was need in the world among other people, we should give a sizable portion of our money away. And for me personally the implications of this were quite simple: if we should in fact give money to other people who don't have sufficient money to take care of their own needs, then it's also true that there is something wrong with the world as long as these other people have such great needs when we have so much more than we need. If you really believe that there's a claim on your life from these other people who are in need and you really take that claim seriously, then where do you draw the line? And if you grow up in a democracy and believe in equality and you're brought up in a Christian church which tells you that God is love and the highest form of self-realization is self-giving, to draw the line at twenty percent or thirty percent or fifty percent (which in fact means no sacrifice to you personally at all) doesn't really make much sense. Proceeding from the logic my grandfather established, you really ought to be giving away as much as you possibly can. Your obligation is an open-ended one.

"Perhaps I took the ethic of philanthropy far more seriously than I was ever intended to. It became a logical bind for me. And I remember Reinhold Niebuhr commenting once about philanthropy that it was in many ways a form of paternalism in which a privileged class tried to preserve its own status by paternalistically doling out funds to a needy group. When I originally read that statement, I was somewhat offended. But I think I was basically offended because I knew right at the beginning there was a truth in it. I still think within the framework of American society, philanthropy is an important vehicle for sponsoring creative leadership, and I'm all for it; but at the same time I think you've got to create a social system that provides for the citizen's basic needs.

"For myself, I'm still trying to draw the line. I'm very uncomfortable with the wealth that I have, but of course it's made even more complicated by these trusts. I am firmly convinced that there is no rational justification for extreme privilege and the accumulation of vast sums of wealth. You cannot rationally justify it or give a good moral reason for it. You cannot defend it as socially good that some people should accumulate huge piles of money and live in great comfort and wealth, while other people live miserably wretched lives. You cannot. All you can say in defense of your living that way is 'Well, the social system makes it possible for me to enjoy this and I like it. So I support the social system that makes this possible.' But I don't consider that a rational argument. It's just a selfish declaration of one's own preferences.

"For myself, I live comfortably but not extravagantly; I haven't resolved all the personal and social difficulties that would be involved in an adequate solution. But what I try to do with myself is be honest about the problem and not pretend that I'm living according to some values when in fact I am not. The family has given away something like a billion dollars, but obviously, as any observer could see, it has not caused any great sacrifice to the family. They've done it because they've been interested to do it, and I believe they've done a lot of good works with it. But it certainly hasn't been a sacrifice. Giving away a million dollars when you've got a hundred million doesn't make you a better person than others. Yet this is what has given rise to the whole notion of the Rockefeller family as somehow superior to everyone else. Part of the problem for the Cousins in trying to establish their own identity, in fact, is that they believe in their heart somewhere that there *is* something very superior about the Rockefellers. Part of the myth that they've accepted is that the Rockefellers *are* the royal family of America, that they *are* superior. I don't buy that."

On a good day, as the famous Green Mountains of Vermont loom up like icebergs behind Middlebury, Steven often jogs and bicycles through the campus as he has since coming to the college in 1969, taut and sparse in a windbreaker and gulping in the almost mentholated air. He is just an assistant professor nodding at the colleagues and students he passes, his mind often locked on unfinished chapters of the book on the early career of John Dewey he must complete before his tenure review. While he feels he is probably only at the midpoint in his quest, he appreciates the sense of balance in his current life. "I enjoy teaching. It satisfies my social conscience and keeps my sanity at the same time. Sanity comes from having real relationships with other people."

This includes his family. Rejecting the Rockefellers has never been a serious option for Steven. Even though they set limits to his freedom and deprive his perspective of completeness, he feels that he can afford to accept them as a given, and that he has a positive duty to function effectively inside the family structure, as he has as a leader of the Cousins.

Yet the word "leader" implies an ongoing Rockefeller dynasty. Steven doesn't want this role and doubts that it will be necessary in the future. He sees himself more as a supervisor in the dismantling process that is bound to take place in the Rockefeller family during his own lifetime. "There are those in the family—even in my own generation—who feel that the Rockefellers have some special role to play in history. I feel there are just too many of us for the family members to go parading around talking about our special identity. With me the family is not primary. It has become a practical question: What can the Rockefeller family as an institution do to further *my* interests? What can it do for my children to ensure that they will grow up good democratic citizens in this country? Can it really help them or isn't it really just an anachronism, a dinosaur that is trying to keep them from going out and getting involved in American life like everyone else? My feeling is that the family as an institution was the creation of a certain culture and a certain time in the history of this nation. It has had its day. Once the original generating energy goes out of an institution, it just dies. That's the way it is and ought to be. The dynasty stuff—that's all finished."

He says this with the same pleasant, unflinching, and matter-of-fact tone that he uses to introduce himself. It is not a melodrama or a tragedy; it is a fact. The Rockefeller dynasty ends neither with a bang nor a whimper, but with a shrug and a smile.

Perhaps the ability to say "Steven Rockefeller" without shrinking is related to the ability to foresee an end to the history that has made what Abby calls "this preposterous name." Normally it is the sort of conundrum Steven likes to discuss. But on this particular day he is taking care of his son, Steven, Jr. He begins to rummage around for the boy's jacket so the two of them can walk up to the campus and see a Middlebury soccer game. Looking out the door, he says, "One of the best things in my life is living here and being able to walk down Weybridge Street and say hello to my neighbors. It may seem like a small thing, but it was denied me as a child, you know."

Epilogue

AT LEAST since William Avery's brushes with the law in the wilds of upstate New York, the fate of the Rockefellers has been synthesized out of the unpredictable chemistry of parents and children. Even more than their predecessors, however, the Cousins have grown up in an oedipal brier patch. For them the simplest acts have been fraught with heavy significance; the paths to maturity have been strewn with the emotional detritus of past struggles between fathers and sons. Repossession of self is not only a rebellion against the parents; it is magnified into a killing blow against the family, its rules and traditions. In their world of shadow and act, where each gesture is inflated out of all human proportion, the symbolic parricide becomes an act of murder against history itself.

Living in a family of immense silences where there are abundances of everything except feeling, the Cousins have tried to make as few decisions as possible. But even their modest desire to be individuals first and Rockefellers second has been interpreted as a mortal affront to the dynasty their grandfather consolidated. With an unintended acuity, this desire has cut through the religious awe surrounding the family and its special mission. In standing back from the responsibility of the role and the obligations of the power, the Cousins—without meaning something so portentous—have pierced the dynastic illusion. As if by some monstrous Freudian slip, the intention to say that the only thing they want is to be themselves has come out sounding like the last thing they want to be is Rockefellers. Apart from the human aspects of their dilemma, the Cousins have become a sort of living fossil preserving the skeleton of a unique history.

At the core of Mr. Junior's dynastic project was a shrewd piece of moral calculation. Through his philanthropic efforts, the taint in the family fortune would be expunged, the blot on the name scoured away. Beginning with an obsessive need to believe his father pure, Junior's life gradually developed into a prolonged exercise in self-justification. The family became the vehicle of his quest to prove that the money, of which he was now the custodian, was not only fairly gotten, but well-deserved. Junior's idea was that future Rockefellers would earn their inheritance by assuming responsibility for what the Reverend Gates had called "the well-being of mankind." Instead of wealth coming, however obliquely, as a reward for individual effort, the individual would pay a life-term debt of service to the wealth itself and thus earn it after the fact. The concept of stewardship implied in Senior's claim that God had given him his money was refined by Junior into a comprehensive morality whose terms his heirs would come to understand quite well: power, like money, was an obligation; like money, it was a necessary part of the legacy.

Junior was a classicist, shaping nature to his requirements. Construction was always his favorite outlet: the materials were inert and tractable, willing co-conspirators in the process of creation. He did well also in those vast fields of endeavor his Associates discovered for him; these too could be shaped by careful infusions of capital and the gardener's clinical detachment. But while he might order and even alter the nature of things, he could not control human nature. *That* would be the only volatile element in the Rockefeller enterprise.

The problem cropped up immediately, among his own sons. They would roam freely in the epic space that Junior's judicious use of the first John D.'s fortune had created. They would be borne aloft, socially and politically, on the buoyancy of the institutions he had built and the connections he had made. They never really questioned the inflated roles they had been allotted in life; they simply failed in the end to fill them, or to endow the Rockefeller identity with survival potential by paring it down to realistic, intelligible, and durable dimensions.

JDR3's foundering in the role of heir apparent would become obvious when he tried to grow beyond it, beyond the task of being his father's representative. The meaning of Laurance's inability to step decisively from the background and of Winthrop's self-destructiveness would become clear toward the end of their lives. The message of David's stately rise at the Chase was that finally Junior's institutions supplied the energy for the Rockefeller aura, not the other way around. And Nelson's ambition, like some devouring metabolic disorder, finally turned upon the traditions at the very marrow of the family's morality, consuming them indiscriminately along with everything else.

Part of the Brothers' failing was their unblinking acceptance of the sense of manifest destiny with which their father had imbued the family. They believed in it completely, not only for themselves, but for their children as well. They ignored the impact of the social upheavals of the sixties on the Cousins, assuming that their alienation from the family myths was a temporary phase in their development, a sort of stage fright comparable to their own youthful hesitation to step into the giant future that had awaited them. They failed to see that, without really willing it, their children had been severed by events from the sense of family mission which, in the harsh light of Vietnam and then Watergate, would itself come to seem not only exaggerated and archaic, but culpable, even tainted. The peculiar burden of the fourth generation would be to look with a kind of nostalgia at past Rockefeller power and grandeur and yet realize that it was not for them. They would be forced to see the family and its myths with the eyes of outsiders and thus to realize that the family's place in the sun was an achievement of power, not of desert. And this perception was the single ragged threat that unraveled the whole fabric of Mr. Junior's elaborate moral tapestry.

As David Rockefeller's sons drift away from careers at the Chase, heading into fields like art and medicine, an epic moment passes. For unlike wealth or property, power must be exercised to be possessed. Whatever the family's influence as stockholders in the bank, without a Rockefeller at its head, the Chase will no longer lend its magnificence to the dynastic idea. It will be no more an instrument of family power than the Citibank is personally used as a vehicle by the Stillman Rockefeller clan. Like its rival, the Chase will become part of the continuum of interlocking institutions whose ultimate owners include the Rockefellers along with other families of great wealth, but include them only as legal titleholders, not active potentates; as repositories rather than sovereigns of power.

The Rockefeller Foundation is the paradigm for the fate of the institutions designed to buttress Junior's dynasty into eternity. Though no longer within the closed circle of the family proper, it continues to stand at the epicenter of American wealth and power, its trustees drawn from among Rockefeller friends and institutional kin. It is *by* the family, but no longer *of* it, a formula that applies even more strongly to the syndicate of companies led by Standard of New Jersey, now, more than a generation after the last Rockefeller has left it, once again the biggest industrial corporation in the world. The dynasty is mortal; the institutions have a life of their own.

The process that began when the commission merchant firm of Clark & Rockefeller made its first venture into oil is far from over, yet the shape it will ultimately take is foreshadowed in the attitudes of the present generation. Perhaps some of the Cousins' children will retrace their Uncle Jay's course and harness the considerable energy lingering in the money, name, and connections to achieve positions of personal power. Others will be content to enjoy the wealth, at least to the degree that such enjoyment is possible for a Rockefeller heir. A few will persist in the eccentricity of rebellion. Meanwhile, the critical mass will move toward a merger with the nation's general aristocracy of wealth, and the benign drift away from dynastic imperatives will continue year by year.

Room 5600 will be forced to scale down its activities to concentrate on giving and taxes, two inseparable functions required by the still significant residue of the great fortune. That part of its identity concerned with directing the family's destiny will atrophy along with the sense of destiny itself. The Rockefeller Family Office will no longer attract the services of men ambitious to climb the interface between public and private power.

Instead of *the* family, there will be five families—those of each of the male heirs of the Brothers. Long after the Brothers have died, their grandchildren—the fifth generation—will finally inherit the vestige of Senior's fortune, the '34 Trusts, which terminate by law when they reach maturity. The aging Cousins will no doubt worry over the impact this sudden wealth will have on their children and what it will portend for the Rockefellers and their concept of service. But by that time the sense in which this has been the most royal of America's families will have passed, and the question will be largely academic.

There is thus a strange circularity to the Rockefeller saga. It is as if the entire effort since the founding of Standard Oil were an extravagant mummery on the theme of the vanity of human wishes. Junior set out to prove to the world that the wealth he inherited was morally just; in the end his efforts failed even to convince his grandchildren. He built a dynastic identity meant to close the distance between the Rockefellers and the rest of mankind; in the end his efforts only magnified the space separating the Rockefellers from everyone else and, in a final irony, divided the family even from itself.

The Cousins' attempt to recapture a personal identity from the family is too tentative and stumbling, and finally too mundane, to be seen as a heroic enterprise. Yet the end of this dynasty does have an epic quality, even if it is as symbol rather than event. For more than a hundred years, the Rockefellers have molded their ambition to the imperial course of the nation itself. Now their decline comes into view at the time that the American Century too is ending, over fifty years before its term. Far from what Junior envisioned, in neither fact is there much cause for regret.

Bibliographic Note

Public opinion has been an overriding concern for the Rockefellers almost from the beginning—at least since the South Improvement plan put John D. on the front pages for the first time in a black-bordered box containing the names of conspirators. Senior reacted to this attack the way he would when savaged by the press in years to come—with a policy of silence. But it backfired, and by the time Junior had retained Ivy Lee, the problem had become critical.

Successfully disentangled from Ludlow, Junior realized that the Rockefellers could avoid similar errors by applying Lee's deceptively simple formula for public relations success: take popular opinion into account *before* beginning any new act or policy, not afterward when it was too late. But the problem of the past remained. Lee and Junior both knew that the family's reputation for good works would never be secure until the air was cleared of ill will against Senior. They agreed that the best way to accomplish this was to mold public opinion in a way the old man had disdained—with a detailed, factual, and (inevitably) positive biography of the first John D. that would replace the efforts of the muckrakers. During the nearly twenty years that Lee worked for Junior after Ludlow, this project would occupy a surprising amount of his energy. By the time this ideal biography of Senior was published, it would stand as a case study of the family's obsession with controlling America's attitudes toward it.

Senior was not particularly interested in the project. Unlike his son, he was not anxious about what others thought. Satisfied that he had done right, he frequently advised Junior to keep his own counsel and "let the world wag." Lee realized, therefore, that he must move carefully if he expected any cooperation at all. After some searching, he selected William O. Inglis, a reporter from the New York *World*, to become the old man's Boswell. Not a particularly distinguished writer or thinker, Inglis was tactful and pleasant, a man who could both tell and appreciate a good story; even more important, he was a good golfer. The Pocantico golf course was the place where Lee planned to smuggle his agent into the old man's confidence. It was a shrewd maneuver. After a few rounds, Senior agreed to reminisce in semiformal sessions with Inglis. He understood how much it meant to his son ("I know he is getting together this record out of devotion to me," he told Inglis in one of their early conversations, "which I deeply appreciate") and was touched by Junior's need to believe the best.

Inglis's association with the master of Standard Oil would last ten years, from 1915, when he first began his conversations, to 1925, when he turned in the completed manuscript of his biography. He was paid what for those days was the substantial sum of $8,000 a year. In addition to interviewing his subject, he traveled throughout upstate New York talking to the few individuals who remembered the Rockefellers from the old days. He also interviewed Senior's sister Mary Ann, his old partner, Maurice Clark, and other family members and close friends who were survivors of the past age.

It was an invaluable body of research well worth the considerable investment Junior made in it. It would not be long before it would be impossible to expect the aging Rockefeller to make the effort of the detailed and lucid recollections Inglis extracted from him. But even after his memory and interest failed, there was a fat typescript titled "Conversations with John D. Rockefeller Senior." Soon all the other old-timers who remembered the bygone days would be dead. But their reminiscences would be preserved in "Conversations in the Moravia Neighborhood," and other materials Inglis had assembled. To a degree that would not be fully appreciated for another fifteen years, Inglis had succeeded in trapping quicksilver.

When Inglis turned in his completed manuscript, Junior immediately sent it out for review to Raymond Fosdick, George Vincent (then president of the Foundation), and others of the discriminating men who made up his inner circle. In an egregious turning of the other cheek, he even sent it to the aged Ida Tarbell, who had mellowed into a defender of the corporate world whose scourge she had once been. Miss Tarbell liked Inglis's work, but Junior's own perception—shared by most of his associates—was that the manuscript was far too flattering to be taken seriously. It didn't have the requisite air of authenticity necessary to impress the intellectuals and opinion-makers who would have to validate it as the "standard" biography. Along with the research materials gathered over a decade of work, the manuscript was shelved. Inglis was taken off the payroll. The project momentarily lay dormant.

Yet there was no cessation of literary hostilities against the family. In 1919, John Winkler's *John D. Rockefeller: A Portrait in Oils* was published. Although irritated by the fact that it gained a wide audience when serialized in *Cosmopolitan*, Lee realized that this book would not have a lasting impact. Published three years after Winkler, John T. Flynn's *God's Gold* was another matter. In the grand tradition of muckraking, it won a large and enthusiastic following, and was a sharp reminder of the urgency of getting the "right" book on Senior.

With Junior's blessing, Lee canvassed Rockefeller loyalists for recommendations of possible writers. A number of names were mentioned, including Walter Lippmann, Stuart Chase, and other apparently unlikely candidates. Fosdick strongly recommended Frederick Lewis Allen. Abraham Flexner's first choice was Henry Steele Commager. Lee's own choices, strangely enough, were Charles Beard and James Truslow Adams.

His search took Lee far from American soil. He queried Emil Ludwig, who had just completed his mammoth work on Napoleon. Ludwig allowed the enterprising publicist to pay his fare to America, but after meeting the elder Rockefeller he decided that he wasn't interested. It didn't matter, for Lee had found his man. It was Winston Churchill, member of Parliament, who had recently finished his life of his noble ancestor, the Duke of Marlborough. Sensing that this was a man with a fate to match the Rockefellers, Lee sailed for England and had several discussions with Churchill, who finally agreed to put aside his history of the English-speaking peoples for two years to take on the project. In return, however, the Rockefellers would have to advance him fifty thousand pounds. Overriding Lee's enthusiasm, Junior refused to put up what amounted to a quarter of a million dollars in the middle of the Depression.

When Lee died in 1934, the matter was still unresolved. JDR3 was conscripted to help find the man who would write his grandfather's life. He talked to his old professors at Princeton and with other working historians. Their suggestions prominently featured a name that had been only an also-ran on other lists. It was Allan Nevins, a 44-year-old professor of history at Columbia whose recent biography of Grover Cleveland had won a Pulitzer Prize.

Nevins's primary liability, as Alfred Harcourt had told Junior, was that he was simply "too dull." However, as the flamboyant Churchill and other candidates fell by the wayside for various reasons, this came to seem a relatively mild disability.

In 1934, Nevins was formally offered the job. At first he turned it down because of the press of other commitments, but President Nicholas Murray Butler of Columbia saw the offer with a fund-raiser's keen eye for marriages of convenience. It could be a way of consolidating the relationship with the Rockefellers that had begun with the Rockefeller Center lease; he persuaded the reluctant historian to reconsider. By 1935, Nevins was hard at work on the project.

By the time his work appeared in its second edition, Nevins felt constrained to remind his audience of his "disinterestedness" regarding the Rockefellers: "I have kept myself free from financial obligations and have in fact accepted heavy penalties in devoting so much time and toil to a book whose royalties can hardly meet my personal costs of research." In these and other insistences that his work was value-free, done without obligation to the family, there was the anxious tone of one who protests too much. In point of fact, he was the beneficiary of Inglis's unique ten-year research project, which had cost Junior more than $100,000 and provided him with invaluable data that could never again be duplicated. Nevins was also able to demand that Junior pay for the services of an assistant. This was Frank Hill, who worked on the project for three years, intensively researching Senior's early life and eventually writing some 90,000 words on the period up to 1890.*

The first edition of the work appeared in 1940, titled *John D. Rockefeller: The Heroic Age of American Enterprise.* The title was the key to the work. The Gilded Age of economic warfare was recast as a golden age of economic consolidation. If not totally sympathetic in every particular, the view of John D. was extremely understanding throughout. Whatever the costs, his career was justified because of its cen-

---

*Hill later noted: "We had some material showing that Rockefeller's father had had an affair with a young woman and that one of the reasons the father was so little in evidence was that he was dodging in and out of the county where he lived to avoid being brought into court to answer charges brought by this young woman." Hill also intimated that Junior was not happy with this line of inquiry. The Vanderbeak episode was left purposely ambiguous in the final text.

tral importance in the grand design of America's industrial progress. Nevins's scholarship could not be faulted, and his unique monopoly of intimate detail about the family (and the company that underpinned its greatness) placed his book in a class by itself. Soon after its publication *The Heroic Age of American Enterprise* had swept other biographies, from Lloyd to Flynn, off the library shelves, exactly the task for which it had been intended.

If Nevins had done well by the Rockefellers, the connection with the family had hardly injured his career. The Rockefeller biography became his best-known book, and one of the most prominent works in the new school of business history sympathetic to the American economic system. In the postwar years his reputation continued to rise as he became head of the History Department at Columbia, founder of the Oral History Project there, and one of the most influential men in his profession. He was never one of Junior's inner circle, but he continued to feel a stake in the family's history. An example of his helpfulness came in 1948, when he wrote Junior to inform him that Standard of Indiana had just appointed historian Paul Giddens to prepare its official corporate history. Noting that Giddens would naturally be compelled to deal with the Stewart proxy fight, Nevins confidently advised cooperation: "My opinion is that all relevant materials ought to be handed over to him with the proviso that he show you and Mr. Debevoise whatever he writes on the subject. If his treatment is brief, room will remain for a separate monograph. I could at some future time, when the moment is ripe, interest one of my abler candidates for the doctorate in it, or the Harvard [Business] School could find a writer."

By 1950, Nevins was at work on another edition of the Rockefeller biography. His interest had been piqued by a new cache of Senior's correspondence "lost" since 1932. At that time, during the move of the family office from 26 Broadway to Room 5600, some letterbooks containing Senior's personal correspondence were placed in a storage room and accidentally walled in. After "rediscovering" the letterbooks during an inventory and realizing that the largely personal correspondence they contained showed his father in a sympathetic light, Junior took the initiative of alerting Nevins to the find.

The reworking probably would have been done sooner or later at any rate. Occupying a strategic place as a leading "revisionist" business historian, Nevins had been particularly sensitive to the new intellectual currents of the cold war. Unabashedly imperial in foreign policy, yet jittery with self-doubts reified in its fear of domestic Communism, America was ready for an affirmative reassessment of the capitalist system that would dispel all vestigial doubts left over from the red thirties. In effect Rockefeller and all the other titans of the Gilded Age became the beneficiaries of a patriotic syllogism. They had pioneered the development of the modern American economy; this economic system brought more freedom and happiness than any other system yet devised; therefore its founders must be men of vision and courage. Unfairly, unpatriotically criticized by a previous generation, these men were not really robber barons, but industrial statesmen. The view of Standard Oil and John D. advanced subtly in Nevins's first edition, while the New Deal was in progress, could now be proclaimed triumphantly.

Published in 1953 with the new title *John D. Rockefeller: A Study in Power*, the book was suffused with the spirit of the fifties. Even the form had changed. In its first edition it had taken Nevins 130 pages to cover Senior's first 18 years. In this one, the same material was condensed into 25 pages to save room for what became a detailed apologia regarding the first 40 years of Standard Oil.

In its prior incarnation, the biography had attempted to explain Rockefeller's character. Moreover, Nevins had been at least mildly critical of the more flagrant abuses of the company. But in *A Study in Power* he dropped even the guise of nonpartisanship. He described the transformation of the small, fragmented business world into one of agglomerates of power (which others had seen as cruel and immoral) in the hallowed tones being used elsewhere at this same time in discussions of the "national interest." He noted in the preface: "Had our pace been slower and our achievement weaker, had we not created so swiftly our powerful units in steel, oil, textiles, chemicals, electricity, and automotive vehicles, the free world might have lost the First World War and most certainly would have lost the Second." He might have been surprised to know that it was almost word for word the defense Stalin had used when criticized for his brutal policy of forced collectivization in the Soviet Union.

The McCarthy era was not a time when many voices would be raised against a posthumous celebration of the "Great Barbecue" of the Gilded Age. Generally Nevins's book was reviewed even more favorably in the second edition than in the first. An isolated note of dissent came from Oscar

Handlin, who charged in the *New England Quarterly* that *A Study in Power* was "essentially an apologetic." Handlin went on to say of Nevins:

> He feels himself deeply involved in the defense of his subject, so deeply that he flinches at every aspersion on Rockefeller or his family. Indeed, respect for the protagonist endows his very calling with preeminence; business was "the central field of usefulness" of the period drawing the most ambitious and most able men of the nation. Rockefeller thus acquires a special virtue by his vocation that seems to set him above such contemporaries as, say, O. W. Holmes, Jr., or Henry James or Willard Gibbs.

The basic flaw in the biography was clearly perceived: "How this truly religious and by his own lights honest man could for decades break the law of the land evades Professor Nevins. His full energies go rather to the elaboration of an intricate web of justification for Rockefeller's actions."

Such quibbles did not concern Junior. He was quite pleased with Nevins's work. It was the book he had always wanted—a work that not only exonerated the first Rockefeller from the more heinous charges laid against him, but also staked out a claim of greatness. Without such a book, the myth Junior had committed himself to propagating could not have thrived. The fountainhead from which all the Rockefellers flowed had to be pure: the money which buoyed them all in seas of power could not be tainted.

While he had overseen the long effort to write his father's life, Junior had been busy elsewhere. He had encouraged his friend Raymond Fosdick to set down the official story of the founding and work of both the General Education Board and the Foundation. He had been pleased and cooperative when Mary Ellen Chase, a member of the faculty of Smith College, had written a sympathetic account of the life of his late wife, Abby.

In 1949, with his keen sense that the Rockefellers not only had made history but in some sense *were* history, Junior began considering turning the family's voluminous files into an archive. The National Records Management Council was called in for advice. Historians themselves, the consultants saw the immense value of the Rockefeller papers, which were astonishingly complete by virtue of the compulsion Senior and Junior shared to keep every scrap of paper dealing with family affairs, both personal and financial.* The Council urged Junior to proceed with the establishment of an archive. He did not have to be forced. These files would be the final proof of an assertion his father had calmly made during one of his conversations with Inglis: "History will prove that we were right."

Junior conceived his life's work in modest terms. If someone had told him he was a myth-maker, he would have been puzzled and embarrassed. He saw himself as a detail man. If he had done anything, it was merely to create the conditions that would allow the truth to flourish. When, shortly after the appearance of the second edition of Nevins's work, Nelson approached him on behalf of the other Brothers to suggest that Fosdick do their father's biography, Junior's reaction was predictably self-effacing: "Whatever would you find to write about?" He was finally persuaded to sit for the portrait, as he later said, because he wanted his grandchildren "to know the sort of man I tried to be."

Fosdick never even bothered to assert his impartiality in treating Junior's life. It was not only that he was a friend, but who could think ill of a man who had devoted all his adult years to giving away millions of dollars in acting as a steward for the well-being of mankind? It probably never occurred to Fosdick that there was any alternative to seeing Junior as a gentle, bespectacled knight who had dedicated his life to slaying the dragon Wealth. Not surprisingly, his book bears a closer resemblance to medieval hagiography than modern biography. Setting the tone for what follows, the opening sentences of *John D. Rockefeller Jr.: A Portrait* ring with the solemnity of a Gregorian chant:

This is the story of a man who through adversity rose to eminence and even greatness. In the shaping of human

*There were 327,000 pieces of correspondence generated by Senior and Junior just up to 1916. This did not count outgoing mail, copies of which were kept in letterbooks averaging 500 pages in length. Junior filled 71 of these letterbooks between 1897 and 1916 just with letters pertaining to his children, his homes, and his charitable gifts. Senior filled 179 letterbooks from 1879 to 1916 on business matters exclusive of Standard Oil, and another 42 in the same period on personal matters. As the office swelled in size and function during Junior's rule as family patriarch, the files grew correspondingly. Junior decreed that the Family Archives should end with his death, with his sons having the option of including their papers later if they so desired. Up to 1960, therefore, the Archives comprise 1,750 cubic feet.

life handicaps take many forms. Sometimes the adversity is ill health or an unhappy environment. More often, perhaps, it is poverty and the narrow limitations it imposes. In the case of John D. Rockefeller, Jr., it was wealth—a stifling kind of wealth which might easily have sapped his energies and blighted his life. ... [Yet] Mr. Rockefeller emerged as a man of simplicity, modesty, intuitive courtesy, and democratic tastes. More than that, he became obsessed with the idea that the wealth which he had inherited must be employed to promote the well being of his fellow men; and in a long lifetime he devoted himself to this purpose with constructive imagination and undiscourageable patience.

Yet in his desire to provide his old friend with a proper canonization, Fosdick failed to appreciate his greatest labor: redeeming the Rockefeller family, diversifying the great fortune and firmly rooting its power in the developments of the modern state, and making the Rockefellers as much an institution as a family. Certain people and events that might have shown this process—the true Rockefeller epic—at work are sacrificed to Fosdick's notion of propriety. Ivy Lee, for instance, is mentioned just twice in the book, neither time as the subject of a sentence. The Chase Bank and the role it played in family affairs are mentioned not at all. Junior's gifts to restore Reims, Versailles, and other monuments after World War I are covered in exhaustive detail, but with the exception of the drama surrounding Colonel Stewart, nothing is said about his business relationship with the Standard Oil companies whose most important stockholder he continued to be. That part of Junior's life dedicated to the eleemosynary is admiringly chronicled; the rest, including his efforts as father and husband, is virtually ignored. The final effect is of a man known very well in profile, but never seen full-face.

Although beginning from a friend's vantage point rather than a biographer's, Fosdick's book ends up much like Nevins's. It is "correct," yet it manages to ignore vast areas of motive and character, finally grinding down the contours of an interesting—if terribly constricted—personality to such a degree that it is less a man that is described than the tribulations and triumphs of a figure from allegory. For Fosdick as for Junior himself, psychological complexity was threatening, an aspect of the human enterprise not easily controlled and therefore best avoided altogether.

The literature on the Rockefellers is basically Manichaean: the "official" works done from unlimited access to private sources are obsequious in appreciation of their subject; the "critical" books are either created in isolation, in the main from newspaper clippings and conjecture (as is the case of Myer Kutz's recent *Rockefeller Power*), or so motiveless in their malignancy (like William Hoffman's *David*, promoted by Lyle Stuart into one of the publishing successes of a few seasons ago) that they forfeit any claim to authenticity. Those who find it profitable to exaggerate the family's "hidden empire" are as firmly imprisoned in the Rockefeller myth as the kept biographers.

The serious student of this family is handicapped not only by tight control of primary sources, but also by the paucity of secondary material. The study of wealth and power has not yet become an acceptable discipline among academics. Consequently there are very few independent (yet knowledgeable and scholarly) works on the oil industry, on the great foundations the Rockefellers established, or on the family's membership in the elite groups guiding the development of America's foreign and domestic policy during this century. For that matter, there has been no study of the impact of the Rockefellers' millions in shaping the growth of the social sciences and other fields in higher education, fields that have so loyally ignored exactly these subjects.

We were fortunate, therefore, not to have to rely exclusively on books and printed sources. We jammed a foot inside the door guarding the Rockefellers' privacy, and were allowed at least a glimpse of their family life. This opportunity came about because certain of the Rockefeller Cousins who did not feel bound by the suspicion of their elders or by the bureaucratic rules of the braintrust in Room 5600 saw merit in our project. (To a degree it intersected with their own desire to unravel the dynastic process whose end product they were.) Because we interviewed many of the Cousins at great length, we could not be dismissed out of hand by the family elders. To a minor degree at least, we became beneficially entangled in the generational conflict, with Room 5600 granting us a restricted entrée to its operations as a way of proving to the Cousins that the Rockefeller family was not the monolithic holding operation it often seemed to be.

Our relationship with the Cousins also helped us gain permission to work in the Rockefeller Family Archives, a stunning resource of a kind only the Rockefellers, with their special sense of a manifest destiny, could possess. We did not have unlimited access to the records. We could see materials only up to 1960. With the exception of the letterbooks of Senior and Junior and a small selection of other letters, we could not see personal correspondence between family members. The living Rockefellers' affairs which were dealt with in files after the 1960 cutoff date were closed to us, as were other items that would be of great interest, such as Nelson's detailed oral history regarding his wartime service in Washington in the coordinator's office. Yet as the following notes and references show, we have benefited greatly from seeing even the tip of the iceberg of letters, records, and memorabilia occupying an immense number of cubic feet in an unmarked room on the bottom floor of the RCA building.*

This book is a sort of serendipity. Although caught in a squeeze that forced them to countenance us, Room 5600 always regarded us with suspicion. We were outsiders whose motives were not fully known and whose acts could not be either anticipated or controlled. Were our hearts pure of critical intent? Would we profane the sacred totems? Our anomalous status was summarized in the attitude of the current head of public relations for the family, a soft-spoken, former Associated Press reporter from Virginia named George Taylor, Jr. Mr. Taylor was unfailing in his courtesy to us. We enjoyed several lunches with him—at the family's expense—in the Rainbow Room. When he asked us what our "thrust" was, we told him that in our opinion the Rockefellers had suffered from being treated either as saints or demons, and that our book would be part of neither camp. But the question kept coming up. On one memorable occasion it was posed in surprisingly bald terms: "Will your book be favorable or unfavorable toward the Rockefellers?" Nothing better summarizes the family's attitude toward books and the people who write them than the fact that our answer—that we planned simply to draw a realistic and full-blooded portrait of the family—could never really satisfy him.

*The Family Archives will soon be moving to Tarrytown to join the records of the Rockefeller Foundation, the Rockefeller Brothers' Fund, and Rockefeller University in a mammoth archival center at Hillcrest, the estate of Martha Baird Rockefeller, which has been remodeled with a $5 million grant from the Brothers Fund so that its 31 rooms can be used as offices and study areas; the more than 20 million pieces of paper making up the collection will be stored in nearby underground vaults.

Notes

PAGE

3   "Is this clean money?": The "tainted money" incident is recounted in detail in Allan Nevins, *John D. Rockefeller: A Study in Power* (New York, 1953), II, 435 ff. (this work is hereafter referred to as Nevins). Detail on the background and circumstances of the gift can be found in Frederick T. Gates's unpublished *Autobiography*, which is housed along with letters and other Gates papers in the Archives of the Rockefeller Foundation. Allan Nevins edited a brief selection of this work and published it as "The Memoirs of Frederick T. Gates" in *American Heritage*, April 1955; see pp. 76–80 of this selection for Gates's description of the controversy. The Reverend Washington Gladden presented his version of the incident in his autobiographical *Recollections* (Boston, 1909).

4   His fortune amounted to: For this type of factual information we have relied on Nevins, the various works by Raymond B. Fosdick cited below, and other authorized or semiofficial books done with unlimited access to Rockefeller records, unless specifically stated otherwise.

5   When a New York journalist: The journalist was prominent Hearst editor Arthur Brisbane. See Joseph I. C. Clarke, *My Life and Memories* (New York, 1925), p. 353.

7   "The stories are": W. O. Inglis, "Notes of a Conversation with Mrs. Mary Ann Rudd," Rockefeller Family Archives.

7   His father: For biographical data on William Avery Rockefeller, see Allan Nevins, *John D. Rockefeller: The Heroic Age of American Enterprise* (New York, 1940), I, 7 ff. (the original version of his biography of Rockefeller). Also John T. Flynn, *God's Gold* (New York, 1932), pp. 54 ff. The first fully developed portrait of the elder Rockefeller was assembled by Ida Tarbell as part of her epoch-making *History of the Standard Oil Company* (New York, 1904), I, 220 ff., first serialized in *McClure's*, Vol. 25, 1902. In addition to reporting the Vanderbeak rape episode and showing that "Big Bill" was in and out of money troubles much of his life (including being the defendant in a suit by his father-in-law, John Davison, to recover a $1,500 loan), Tarbell also suggests that he may have been involved in a

miscellany of semicriminal activities, including "fencing" horses stolen by a gang of local rustlers. However ambivalent he might have been about his father, John D. bitterly resented the publication of this information, insisting—as he told Inglis in a 1920 conversation—that William Avery Rockefeller was actually a man of great probity and judgment. It is likely that the trauma produced by the revelations of the elder Rockefeller's escapades was an important factor contributing to the extraordinary sobriety of succeeding Rockefeller generations, and to their determination to maintain a veil of secrecy over their private lives.

8 "I've seen it": Dennis was one of many old family acquaintances in the Moravia and Oswego area interviewed by W. O. Inglis as part of the groundwork for his biography. The reminiscences are collected in Inglis, "Conversations in the Moravia Neighborhood, 1917," Rockefeller Family Archives.

8 "Dr. William A. Rockefeller, the Celebrated": The handbill is reprinted in John K. Winkler, *John D. Rockefeller: A Portrait in Oils* (New York, 1929), p. 12.

9 "I simply want": Letter from Rockefeller to D. L. Howatt, steward of his Forest Hill estate, November 18, 1905, Rockefeller Family Archives.

10 "Never mind": John D. Rockefeller. *Random Reminiscences of Men and Events* (New York, 1909), p. 34.

10 "He was a great storyteller": Quoted in Raymond B. Fosdick, *John D. Rockefeller Jr.: A Portrait* (New York, 1956), p. 27.

11 In a bigamous marriage: Flynn, p. 438. According to Dr. Joseph Ernst, director of the Rockefeller Family Archives, there may even have been a second bigamous marriage. Archive sources also confirm the assumed name "Levingston."

11 "John, what do you want?": This anecdote was published in the New York *World*, January 15, 1899.

12 Graduating in 1855: The best account of Rockefeller's coming of age in Cleveland is Grace Goulder, *John D. Rockefeller: The Cleveland Years* (Middletown, Conn., 1973).

12 "Look! Look": Flynn, p. 61.

12 "It is an opportunity": Nevins, I, 18.

12 Ledger A: This document is in the Rockefeller Family Archives and was inspected by the authors.

13 "I cheat my boys": Winkler, *John D.*, p. 14.

13 "I confess": *Random Reminiscences*, p. 47.

14 Younger brother Frank: Nevins, I, 27.

14 Chalked the number 18: Goulder, p. 57.

14 "I sent more than twenty": Inglis, "Conversations with Rockefeller," Rockefeller Family Archives.

15 "Be moderate": Flynn, p. 133.
15 An event that impressed: For further details on the great Pennsylvania oil rush, see Paul Giddens, *The Birth of the Oil Industry* (New York, 1938). Also Harold F. Williamson and Arnold Daum. *The American Petroleum Industry* (Evanston, Ill., 1959).
16 Four years after: For a discussion of the impact of the railroads on the development of the oil industry, see George R. Taylor and Irene D. Neir, *The American Railroad Network, 1861–1890* (Cambridge, Mass., 1956), and Rolland H. Maybee, *Railroad Competition and the Oil Trade 1855–1873* (Mt. Pleasant, Mich., 1940).
16 Engaged to Laura Spelman: For background on the Spelman family and details of the courtship and marriage, see Goulder, pp. 62 ff.
17 "She was full of mirth": Lucy's description of Cettie was given to W. O. Inglis and is cited by Nevins, p. 28.
17 "Her judgment was always better:" Winkler, *John D.*, p. 68.
18 "The only time": Quoted in Tarbell, I, 43.
19 "One of the most important": Inglis, "Conversations with Rockefeller."
19 "I'm bound to be rich!": Winkler, *John D.*, p. 67.
20 "None of us": Inglis, "Conversations with Rockefeller."
20 "It was a friendship": *Random Reminiscences*, p. 12.
21 "The ability to deal": Quoted in Albert Z. Carr, *John D. Rockefeller's Secret Weapon* (New York, 1962), front papers.
21 In this situation: Rockefeller's strategic use of transportation is the focus of Carr's *John D. Rockefeller's Secret Weapon*. A history of the Union Tank Car Company (one of the galaxy of firms making up the great Standard trust), Carr's book is based on access to Union Tank Car's corporate records. For another view of the Standard's use of the railroads, see Ralph Hidy and Muriel Hidy, *Pioneering in Oil* (New York, 1955), pp. 24–40, the first volume of the official history of Standard Oil. There is also the early but nonetheless valuable report of the Hepburn Committee, the first governmental agency to investigate the activities of the trust: New York Legislative Assembly, *Report of the Special Committee on Railroads, Appointed Under a Resolution of the Assembly*, February 1879, 5 vols. (Albany, 1880).
23 Oath: Flynn, p. 154.
23 They had two alternatives: Tarbell, I. 65: " . . . Mr. Alexander, of Alexander, Scofield and Company, gave his reason for the selling: 'There was a pressure brought to bear upon my mind, and upon almost all citizens of Cleveland engaged in the oil business, to the effect that unless we

went into the South Improvement Company we were virtually killed as refiners; that if we did not sell out we should be crushed out.... We sold at a sacrifice, and we were obliged to. There was only one buyer in the market, and we had to sell on their terms or be crushed out, as it was represented to us. It was stated that they had a contract with railroads by which they could run us into the ground if they pleased. After learning what the arrangements were I felt as if, rather than fight such a monopoly, I would withdraw from the business, even at a sacrifice. I think we received about forty or forty-five cents on the dollar on the valuation which we placed upon our refinery.' "

23   "I have ways": Testimony of former Rockefeller partner Isaac Hewitt before the New York State Senate investigating committee. Cited in Tarbell, I, 66.

24   "We have a combination": Flynn, P. 160.

24   Moving his two children's bodies: Winkler, *John D.*, p. 66, quotes Frank as saying, "No one of my blood will rest upon land controlled by that monster John D. Rockefeller."

24   "It was right": Inglis, "Conversations with Rockefeller."

25   "The procedure": Ibid.

26   "They could not hope": Ibid.

26   "You never saw": Tarbell, I, 105.

28   Sitting in the sun of Saratoga: Ibid., I, 146.

28   "You'd better not know": Flynn, p. 174, Tarbell, II, 129, also notes Rockefeller's fetish for secrecy: "Men who entered into running agreements with Mr. Rockefeller were cautioned 'not to tell their wives,' and correspondence between them and the Standard Oil Company was carried on under assumed names."

29   Henry Demarest Lloyd: Called by Lincoln Steffens "the father of muckraking," Lloyd was, successively, an attorney, a journalist, and then an important socialist theorist. After working as an assistant to Supreme Court Chief Justice Salmon P. Chase, he took a job as an editorial writer for the New York *Tribune.* In the mid-1870s he became fascinated with Rockefeller and the Standard. His 1881 article about the trust, "The Story of a Great Monopoly," was published in the *Atlantic*. It greatly influenced Charles Edward Russell, the celebrated muckraker, who would later say, "It was a turning point in our history." Lloyd spent several more years tracking the trust and gathering data for *Wealth Against Commonwealth*, which was published by Harper Brothers in 1894 after being turned down as too controversial by several other publishers. The book had an immense circulation and laid out the boundaries that would be fully explored by Tarbell. Edward Everett Hale called it "the most important book since *Uncle Tom's Cabin*." The Standard made no answer to Lloyd's charges, although he offered

to present documentary proof for his detailed discussion of the company's misdeeds before any board of disinterested scholars or clergymen who might be asked to inquire into the matter. Over the next few years, the trust would attempt to ruin his reputation by planting rumors that Lloyd had made much of the George Rice matter because he had a cabal with the aggrieved oil man to share in whatever damages he might be awarded from suits against Rockefeller. The debate about *Wealth Against Commonwealth* continues to the present day, with Allan Nevins serving as the trust's champion against Lloyd's charges. In *John D. Rockefeller: The Heroic Age of American Enterprise*, II, 336, Nevins attacked the book and called Lloyd's use of facts "one of the most dishonest pieces of so-called history I have ever read." In the second edition of his biography, *John D. Rockefeller: A Study in Power*, II, 330 ff., he returned to the attack, saying of *Wealth Against Commonwealth:* "As a piece of business history (which it purports to be) it is ludicrous; as a contribution to biographical data upon Rockefeller it is at best misleading, at worst maliciously false." Yet Lloyd's biographer, Chester McArthur Destler, checked 420 of the total of 648 references to source material in *Wealth Against Commonwealth* and found only 10 inaccuracies, which were in areas "not of great import." Destler concludes that "Lloyd's pioneering report on the methods by which the oil monopoly was established and maintained remains substantially unaltered" in what has become the standard view of the trust's first thirty years. See Chester McArthur Destler, *American Radicalism, 1865–1901* (New London, Conn., 1946), p. 144. For details of Lloyd's life and career, see Destler, *Henry Demarest Lloyd and the Empire of Economic Reform* (Philadelphia, 1963).

29 They saw him: See John D. Rockefeller, Jr., "Recollections of My Father," dictated 1920, Rockefeller Family Archives.

30 One Cleveland woman: Goulder, p. 26.

32 "Your March inventory": Nevins, I, 281.

32 "Have you ever tried thirty-eight?": Ibid.

32 "I can see him now": Fosdick, p. 109.

32 An independent named John Teagle: Tarbell, II, 38.

34 "How are you": Flynn, p. 342. For a thorough discussion of George Rice's long struggle against the Standard, including a facsimile of the famous "turn another screw" letter, see Flynn, pp. 257 ff. Also Henry D. Lloyd, *Wealth Against Commonwealth* (New York, 1894), Chapter 17.

34 "Pioneering don't pay": Long before the Tidewater pipeline was completed, Rockefeller was aware of its capacity for revolutionizing the transport of oil. He was also quite aware, as one independent oil man told the Hepburn Committee, that "transportation is the milk in the Stan-

dard's coconut of success." But he did not build a compete-
tive pipeline because the Standard already controlled the
railroads and could therefore dictate favorable freight policy
and rates for itself, while also receiving rebates on others'
shipments. On May 22, 1879, in fact, Rockefeller had replied to a Standard official in Cleveland who suggested constructing their own pipeline: "Note your suggestions in
regard to the Tide Water Pipe. We entertain no doubt of the
railroads' ability to compete for the transportation of oil
and we do not want to invest any money in the transportation enterprises in competition with the roads." After the
Tidewater had proved the innovation to be dangerous to the
Standard's status quo, Rockefeller decided that the innovation must be brought under control and he besieged the
company from within and without. (For details of the long,
complex, and unsuccessful fight waged by the Tidewater to
keep control of its own stock, see Tarbell, II, 16 ff.) The inability to defeat competitors like the Tidewater and George
Rice on purely economic grounds appears to have undermined
the arguments Nevins and other apologists (beginning with
Standard attorney S. C. T. Dodd) put forth that the trust's
monopoly was inevitable and in fact resulted in significant
gains in economic efficiency. Actually, the economies of scale
and the cost efficiencies that were attributable to the Standard's incredible expansion were not great enough to drive
the competition from the field. At the peak of Rockefeller's
control of the oil industry in 1882, the Standard had 95
percent of the market. But in the early 1900s, especially after the fabulous Spindletop gusher in Texas and the equally
rich discoveries in the Glenn Pool and elsewhere in the Indian Territory, the trust was no longer able to maintain its
hold, as refineries sprang up beyond its reach on the Gulf
Coast. In some sense, therefore, the monopoly was broken
even before the dissolution decree of 1911. For further details on the impact of new supplies of crude, see Hidy, pp.
393–403.

35 Samuel C. T. Dodd: Flynn (p. 48) writes of Dodd: "He
was an eccentric genius. He was a lover of classic literature,
had a weakness for exercising his literary powers, wrote occasional magazine articles and at intervals even broke into
verse. He wrote the first poem on petroleum to appear in
print:

>   The Land of Grease! The Land of Grease
>   Where burning oil is loved and sung;
>   Where flourish arts of sale and lease
>   Where Rouseville rose and Tarville sprung;
>   Eternal Summer gilds them not
>   But oil wells render dear each spot.

After Dodd hit upon this device [the concept of the trust] he became a man of one idea and busied his mind inventing fictions for Standard managers to hide behind. . . . He affords an instructive example of the curious phenomenon which advocacy works in an honest mind. For himself he always insisted on receiving a very modest retainer for his services to the company. . . . He insisted that ownership of the company's stock would deprive him of that perfect detachment essential to sound legal service to his client." For Dodd's own ideas on trusts, see his book *Combinations: Their Uses and Abuses* (New York, 1888). "To stop co-operation of individuals and aggregation of capital," Dodd wrote, "would be to arrest the wheels of progress—to stay the march of civilization—to decree immobility of intellect and degradation of humanity. You might as well endeavor to stay the formation of the clouds, the falling of the rains, or the flowing of the streams, as to attempt to any means or in any manner to prevent organization of industry, association of persons, and the aggregation of capital to any extent that the evergrowing trade of the world may demand."

35   "The type of a system": *Report of the Committee on General Laws on the Investigation Relative to Trusts.* Transmitted to the New York Legislature March 6, 1888 (Albany, 1888). See Introduction.

36   "Really your notion": Ibid., p. 398.

36   "A philanthropic institution": New York *World*, November 21, 1908.

36   "You could argue": Tarbell, II, 141.

36   Headquarters in New York: The move was in stages. Nevins specifies 1877 as the year when the Standard's business was actually centered more in New York than Cleveland. Beginning in the fall of 1882, Rockefeller moved his family to New York permanently, tired of bringing them back and forth between Manhattan and Cleveland. (According to William Manchester's *Rockefeller: A Family Portrait* [New York, 1959], p. 28, one family member who came on one of the trips to New York was old William Rockefeller, who was supposed to have said after seeing his famous son's huge skyscraper on Broadway, "Well, that do beat all I ever see," and then vanished back into his westward movements.) Even after the shift, however, Rockefeller returned to Forest Hill for summers and holidays. Messenger boys on bicycles would carry reports and papers to him there from the trust's Cleveland office. He had a telegraph operator on permanent duty to take messages from Archbold and other lieutenants in New York.

37   "I never knew anyone": George C. Rogers, "Recollections of John D.," *Saturday Evening Post*, July 30, 1921, p. 16.

37   Proconsuls of the great Standard: With the exception of
James Stillman (see Anna Burr, *The Portrait of a Banker*
[New York, 1927], and John K. Winkler, *The First Bil-
lion: The Stillmans and the National City Bank* [New
York, 1934]), there has been relatively little written in the
way of full-length studies about the "Standard Oil Gang."
The William Rockefeller–Stillman dynasty is described in
"The House of Rockefeller," *Fortune,* December 1931, and
also in Cleveland Amory's *Who Killed Society?* (New
York, 1960), pp. 380 ff. Even less attention has been paid
to Payne, Archbold, Flagler, and Rogers, although they
were not only among the most powerful men of their time,
but also among the most interesting. Flagler, for instance,
became one of the first of the modern real estate developers,
using his millions to help the railroads penetrate the state of
Florida, especially that part of the line which finally connected Jacksonville to Miami. Nevins (II, 282) says of him:
"He may well be called the creator of Miami." Flagler also
constructed a string of luxury hotels in the Saint Augustine
area and, in his most ambitious work, extended the railroad
into Key West. He always retained his loyalty to his old
friend Rockefeller, although his interests took him farther
and farther away from the trust in his later years. The same
was not true of Rogers. Moody, brilliant, more complex
than the others Rockefeller gathered around him, Rogers
had a taste for culture that was otherwise lacking in the
Standard organization. He had met Mark Twain after being
impressed with *Innocents Abroad* and helped the author
take care of the large debts that threatened to sap his
creative energies and bankrupt his pocketbook as well as his
career in the early 1890s. Twain later said of Rogers, "He
is not only the best friend I ever had, but is the best man I
have ever known." (See Albert Bigelow, *Mark Twain* [New
York, 1912], for an account of the friendship.) People on
Wall Street, however, saw a different side of Rogers, a side
that made them hate and fear him. Rogers was an ally of E.
H. Harriman in some of the economic wars of the day, and
his role in the notorious Amalgamated Copper scandal was
only one of several ruthless schemes in which he was involved. Nevins's estimate of Rogers (II, 283) is as follows:
"He was an astute organizer, a reckless plunger in finance, a
cruel and implacable fighter. His fits of anger were notorious." This unusually critical view taken by Nevins is possibly explained by the fact that relations with the Rockefellers
had chilled considerably in the early 1900s, especially after
Rogers allowed himself to be extensively interviewed by Ida
Tarbell when she was completing her book.

37   "There is no question": For Vanderbilt's entire testimony, see Hepburn Committee hearings, II, 1668 ff.

38   University revolution: It was, interestingly, at the Yale

Scientific School that Professor Benjamin Silliman developed the first commercial process for refining oil into gasoline. On the revolution in higher education, see Laurence R. Veysey, *The Emergence of the American University* (Chicago, 1965). On the industrial orientation of the emerging university science, see Charles F. Thwing. *A History of Higher Education in America* (New York, 1906), pp. 462 ff.

39 "Drink all the oil": Nevins, II, 97.

39 Rockefeller offered: Before, Rockefeller had scorned involvement in the ownership of crude, but seeing the Bradford fields of Pennsylvania dry up changed his mind. For a discussion of the importance of the Lima fields to the Standard's future, see Hidy, pp. 155–201.

39 Frasch process: For an enlightening summary of the work of Herman Frasch in removing the sulfur from the "skunk bearing oils" of the Lima field, see Paul Giddens's corporate history of Standard of Indiana, *Standard Oil Company: Oil Pioneer of the Middle West* (New York, 1955), pp. 6 ff.

39 Archbold abroad: In 1893 *Bradstreet's* reported that discussions had taken place between the Standard and the "Russian oil kings, the Nobels and Rothschilds" regarding "a scheme for parcelling out between them the whole of the refined oil markets of the world." Discussions broke down when the Russian Minister of Finance refused to support the Standard plan, which would have compelled all Russian refiners to join in one organization for the purpose of selling in the export market. See Williamson and Daum, pp. 646–653.

40 "Open Door" notes: See William Appleman Williams, *The Tragedy of American Diplomacy* (New York, 1962), for an interpretation of their significance in the shaping of American foreign policy.

40 By the 1890s: According to one of Libby's letters, petroleum had forced its way into "more nooks and corners of civilized and uncivilized countries than any other product in history emanating from a single source." In a letter to Henry Flagler, July 23, 1888, cited in Walter LaFeber, *The New Empire: An Interpretation of American Expansion 1860–1898* (Ithaca, N.Y., 1969), p. 23.

41 American Economic Supremacy: At the 1908 Republican national convention, Chauncey Depew summarized the spirit of the American Century: "The American people now produce $2 billion more than they can consume.... We have our market in Cuba, in Puerto Rico, in Hawaii ... and we stand in the presence of 800,000,000 people, with the Pacific as an American lake and the American artisans producing better and cheaper goods than any other country in the world. ... Let the production go on ... let factories do their best, let labor be employed at the highest wages,

because the world is ours!" For similar sentiments of the time see Lloyd C. Gardner, ed., *A Different Frontier* (Chicago, 1966).

42 "No, sir": New York Senate, *Report on Investigations Relative to Trusts* (Albany, 1888), p. 420.

42 "The art of": New York *World,* October 12, 1898.

42 "If our civilization": Henry D. Lloyd, *Wealth Against Commonwealth*, ed. Thomas C. Cochran (New York, 1963), p. 168.

43 Rockefeller himself had not participated: The Amalgamated Copper scheme was exposed by Thomas Lawson, a Wall Street speculator who was the broker on the deal. His *Frenzied Finance* (1906) is one of the classics of the muckraking era. For an account of this and other activities of the Standard Oil Gang, see Matthew Josephson's *The Robber Barons* (New York, 1962), pp. 394 ff.

44 "Viewed as a whole": John Moody, *The Truth About the Trusts* (Westport, Conn., 1968), p. 493.

44 Especially after 1902, when Ida Tarbell's: Tarbell's *Life of Lincoln* had already given her a following and dramatically increased the circulation of *McClure's*. The new assignment to muckrake the trust was tailor-made for her, since she had been born in the Oil Regions and remembered as a child hearing her father's friends talking of Rockefeller's depredations in the South Improvement scheme. While she was researching her book on the Standard, Mark Twain called on S. S. McClure and said that his friend Henry Rogers would like an opportunity to speak to the author. When Tarbell arrived at 26 Broadway and was shown to his office, Rogers asked, "Is there any way we can stop this?" She replied, "No, there is no way in the world in which you can prevent the publication of this story." Rogers then asked her to agree to allow him at least to answer the charges she was considering making against the Standard. In all, Tarbell had some twenty audiences with him and gradually formed an appreciation of his candor. (Later Rockefeller apologists like Nevins would imply that Rogers had been currying favor with Tarbell to make his own part in the story more palatable.) In 1902, after nearly three years of research, the first installment of Tarbell's monumental work was published in *McClure's*, where it ran for the next two years; it appeared in book form in 1904, acclaimed as the finest piece of writing of its kind yet to appear in America. (For details on the writing of *The History of the Standard Oil Company*, see Tarbell's autobiography, *All in the Day's Work* [New York, 1939].) After the muckraking classic had appeared, Tarbell's name became anathema to Rockefeller (although his son would become friendly with her before her death). Flynn (p. 389) says: "In the South a friend undertook to suggest he would reply

on some points to Miss Tarbell. 'Not a word,' Rockefeller interrupted. 'Not a word about that misguided woman.'"

44 Revolver beside his bed: "There was little suggestion then [in the 1890s] that he was even human, let alone virile. Yet ... Nelson's father remembers him sitting at a supper table in Cleveland one evening when the house burglar alarm rang and a frightened maid cried out that there was a burglar in one of the upstairs bedrooms. John D. called for his revolver and, without waiting for it, dashed to the back door to intercept the burglar, who escaped him by sliding down a pillar. Later in New York the dynast insisted on driving his son to the railroad station at a time when anarchists were threatening to kill him. Junior suggested they take a bodyguard, but John D. wouldn't hear of it. 'I can take care of myself,' he said. 'If any man were foolish enough to attack me, it would go hard with him.'" Manchester, p. 25.

44 "I was crucified": Inglis, "Conversations with Rockefeller."

45 "Standard oil will make me": Rogers, p. 16.

45 Diligently scripted notebooks: These are in the Rockefeller Family Archives and were examined by the authors.

47 "God gave": Nevins, II, 435.

48 "The problem of our age": This essay appears in Carnegie's *The Gospel of Wealth and Other Essays.* For insight into Carnegie's theory and practice of philanthropy, see Joseph F. Wall's authoritative biography, *Andrew Carnegie* (New York, 1970).

48 "I would that": Rockefeller's letter is quoted in Burton J. Hendrick, *The Life of Andrew Carnegie* (New York, 1933), II, 349.

48 A distant cooperation: The philanthropic box score is cited by Wall, p. 823.

48 "Never before": Ibid.

48 Some favored: The faction with the Baptist leadership supporting the construction of the Morgan Park Theological Seminary appealed strongly to Rockefeller's sense of thrift. He was wary of committing himself to constructing a university out of whole cloth, even though his daughter Bessie's father-in-law, Augustus H. Strong (then president of the Rochester Theological Seminary), lobbied strenuously for such a monument and argued that it would greatly ennoble both the donor and the entire Baptist communion. Even aside from financial considerations, however, the West was the logical place for an important Baptist institution, and Rockefeller knew it. The church had always been active on the frontier, controlling its unruly spirits and keeping the fluid social structure from hemorrhaging in chaos. ("The gospel is the most economic police on earth," one Baptist missionary leader had written in an article on its social mission years before the University of Chicago controversy.

See Clifford S. Griffin, "Religious Benevolence as Social Control, 1915–1960." *The Mississippi Valley Historical Review,* Vol. 44, June 1957 to March 1958.) A report of the American Baptist Educational Society (one of whose leading figures, a young man named Frederick T. Gates, would soon take on an important role in Rockefeller's life) argued persuasively that a western university would have more value for the church than an eastern competitor with the Ivy League schools because one-half of all Baptists in the country lived in the Plains states and the West. Prepared by temperament to commit himself to Chicago because the price tag was announced as $600,000 as opposed to the $20 million he was told the eastern school would cost to build, Rockefeller's decision was made easier by these ideological considerations.

Richard J. Storr's *Harper's University* (Chicago, 1966) is the only account of the origins of the university that draws on material in the Rockefeller Family Archives. For a critical view of Rockefeller influence in the institution's early years, see Upton Sinclair, *The Goose-step: A Study of American Education* (Pasadena, Calif., 1923), Chapter 51, "The University of Standard Oil."

49 Superior in creative genius: Flynn, p. 339.

49 "The best investment": Quoted in Thomas W. Goodspeed, *History of the University of Chicago* (Chicago, 1916), pp. 397–398.

49 "Neither in": Cited in Nevins, II, 199.

50 "One would": Raymond B. Fosdick. *The Story of the Rockefeller Foundation* (New York, 1952), p. 2.

51 "I am in trouble": Gates, MS *Autobiography.* Cited also in Nevins, II, 198. By taking the job of Rockefeller's chief aide, Gates precipitated the retirement of George D. Rogers, Rockefeller's long-time private secretary, who had himself hoped someday to fill such a role. The minister realized that his new position would open him to criticism, and that some of the odium attached to Rockefeller would inevitably rub off on him. Yet the power that he would have access to, he decided, would more than compensate. Gates was far from naïve. On the contrary, he had already developed a shrewd appraisal of the role other people might play in his plans. When he was still secretary of the American Baptist Educational Society, he wrote a memo to fund raisers which advised: "Let the victim talk freely, especially in the earlier part of the interview while you use the opportunity to study his peculiarities. . . . Appeal only to the nobler motive. His own mind will suggest to him the lower and selfish ones. But he will not wish you to suppose he has thought of them." (This memo is part of the *Gates Papers* in the Rockefeller Foundation Archives, which the authors were

able to inspect through the courtesy of Foundation archivist William Hess.)

51 "I found not a few": Gates, MS *Autobiography*. For a similar development in Carnegie's philanthropic career, see Wall, Chapter 22, "Philanthropy Becomes Big Business."

52 The $1 billion mark: The question of whether the Rockefeller fortune ever literally reached the $1 billion level has become almost a scholarly quibble. Based on records made available to him by John D. Rockefeller, Jr., Nevins (II, 404) asserts that "shortly after the dissolution, one of the year-end inventories of his fortune showed that it amounted to $815,647,596.89. Probably when the stock market was highest before the recession of 1913 it would have totalled about $900,000,000." But other writers, from Winkler and Flynn to the more recent *Rockefeller's Billions* (New York, 1965) by Jules Abels, have estimated that the fortune went well over the $1 billion mark. It is possible that Nevins failed fully to account for the immense appreciation of the Standard's stock in the wild buying spree that erupted following the Supreme Court dissolution decree. Arguments about the exact figure obscure the primary point. Rockefeller was surrounded by rich men, but none of them had anything like his wealth. According to Gustavus Myers's *History of the Great American Fortunes* (Chicago, 1910), the fabulous Astor, Vanderbilt, and Carnegie fortunes amounted to no more than $50 million, $100 million, and $450 million, respectively, at their peak. Throw in the accumulation of Harriman and Morgan, and the total is still less than Rockefeller's.

52 67 major investments: For a résumé of Rockefeller investments at this time, see Nevins, II, 197.

52 "Most of these properties": *Random Reminiscences*, p. 116.

52 "He is shrewd": Gates, MS *Autobiography*, cited by Nevins, II, 208.

53 Gates used the leverage: The Merritts' suit charged Rockefeller with fraud and misrepresentation. It was an assertion that found a wide and willing audience, so completely had the negative image of Rockefeller taken hold. Rockefeller's settlement for the nuisance value of the Merritt brothers' suit only seemed another proof of his guilt when it came to light, and when the matter continued to ferment in the popular culture, one more turbulent addition to the notoriety gathered around the Rockefeller name. But the reality in this case was far from the melodramatic stereotype of a large tycoon fleecing a small family business. Actually the Merritts were themselves patently guilty of stock watering and other sharp practices of the times. The controversy raged for years, with the Merritts airing their grievances in Pulitzer's New York *World* and in other pa-

pers, and Gates finally bursting with outrage and taking up the pen to defend himself and his employer in a thirty-page pamphlet, "The Truth About the Merritts." (The Mesabi story and the founding of U.S. Steel are recounted in *Random Reminiscences*, pp. 120 ff.; Nevins, II, 245–275; Wall, pp. 593 ff.; and the article "Iron Ore—Making and Remaking the Map of Steel," *Fortune*, May 1931.)

54 "I have never"; Inglis, "Conversations with Rockefeller."

54 His son "would undoubtedly": Flynn, p. 350.

54 "I am not anxious": Nevins, II, 271.

55 Morgan stood stunned: The incident is dramatized in Herbert L. Saterlee, *J. Pierpont Morgan: An Intimate Biography* (New York, 1939), p. 363. Rockefeller's reaction was quite different. Cyrus Eaton, then a Cleveland boy working for the summer doing odd jobs around Forest Hill, was dispatched to carry the news to Rockefeller by his secretary, Mrs. Patteson. He got on his bicycle and rode to the golf course, where Rockefeller was in the middle of the game. He later recalled: "I rode as fast as I could. Mr. Rockefeller took the slip of paper I handed him, read it without comment and said, 'Please tell Mrs. Patteson to cancel the arrangements for the private car and tell Mrs. Rockefeller we will not be going to Buffalo tomorrow.' With that he returned to his golf game. It was a typical performance. Mr. Rockefeller never allowed himself to become upset or overwrought." Quoted by Goulder, p. 212.

56 Archbold letters: For a brief discussion of the letters, see Louis Filler, ed., *Crusaders for American Liberalism* (New York, 1961), pp. 141–145. The circumstances of their publication are recounted in W. A. Swanberg, *Citizen Hearst* (New York: 1959), pp. 272 ff. An office boy in charge of cleaning Archbold's office came across some routine correspondence and took it to an editor of William Randolph Hearst's New York *American*. The editor, Fred Eldridge, told the office boy that he would be interested in other, more telling letters and hired him as a spy. For the next fourteen months (1904–1905), letterbooks were systematically removed from Archbold's files, photographed at the offices of the *American*, and then replaced the next morning. In 1908, at the presidential nominating convention of his new Independence League party, Hearst himself produced and read some of the letters in his keynote address, having kept them in his safe for three years awaiting the right occasion. When his speech and the letters were printed the next day, September 18, 1908, it began one of the most sensational exposés of the era. Senator Foraker (himself a contender for the Republican presidential nomination) claimed that he had merely acted in his capacity as counsel for the trust, but Hearst responded by producing another letter from his files, in which Archbold asked the Ohio law-

maker to oppose a bill pending before the Senate that was
intended to strengthen the Sherman Anti-Trust Act, thereafter rewarding him with a $50,000 deposit for his good offices.

56 Trusts were "inevitable": For a discussion of Roosevelt's
antitrust policies, see Richard Hofstadter, *The Age of Reform* (New York, 1955), and Gabriel Kolko, *The Triumph
of Conservatism* (Chicago, 1963). The Roosevelt statement
is cited in Holfstadter's *The American Political Tradition*
(New York, 1973), p. 226.

57 Harriman: For Roosevelt's vendetta against Harriman,
see George Kennan, *E. H. Harriman* (Boston, 1922), Chapter 25, "The Break with Roosevelt." Kennan was Harriman's authorized biographer, and his is a partisan account.

57 "Judge Landis will be dead": Quoted in Goulder, p. 204.

58 "No disinterested mind": For the White decision, see
United States Supreme Court, *Standard Oil Company of
New Jersey et al. vs. the United States* (decision of May
15, 1911), 31 Supreme Court Reporter 502; 221 U.S. I.

58 "Dearly beloved": Winkler, *John D.,* p. 157.

58 Trust's life after death: For details, see Nevins, II, 382.
The Standard's economic power was actually no more
diminished by the dissolution than its position in the stock
market. A dozen years later, on March 3, 1923, a U.S. Senate Committe on Manufactures delivered a blistering report
of some 1,500 pages regarding the Standard companies.
"The dominating fact in the oil industry today," it declared,
"is its complete control by the Standard companies. Standard Oil today fixes the price which the producer of crude
oil receives at the well, the price which the refiner receives
for the gasoline and kerosene, as well as the retail price
paid by the consumer.... In respect to the above matters
and others which led to the outlawing of the Standard Oil
monopoly the same conditions exist as existed when the
decree of the Supreme Court was entered, and ... in some
respect the industry as a whole, as well as the public, are
more completely at the mercy of the Standard Oil interests
now than they were when the decree of dissolution was
entered in 1911." Cited in Paul Giddens, *Standard Oil Company: Oil Pioneer of the Middle West,* p. 315.

58 "Oh Merciful": The Roosevelt statement appears in a
more complete version in Nevins, II, 383.

59 "Your fortune": Gates, MS *Autobiography*.

59 "I trembled": Ibid. See also Gates's *American Heritage*
selection, p. 80.

59 Rockefeller Institute for Medical Research: For a brief
summary of Gates's views on the creation of the institute,
see ibid., pp. 72 ff. For an official history of the origins, organization, and achivements of the institute, see *The Rockefeller Institute for Medical Research* (New York, 1955).

60	"In these sacred": Gates MS *Autobiography: American Heritage* selection, p. 70.

60n. "He has not kept up" (footnote): Letter, Gates to Rockefeller, January 17, 1911, Rockefeller Family Archives.

60n. "The doctor came": Fosdick, *John D. Rockefeller Jr.*, p. 116.

61	General Education Board: The official history of the GEB is Raymond Fosdick's *Adventure in Giving* (New York, 1962). See also the official report of its early years: *The General Education Board: An Account of Its Activities, 1902–1914* (New York, 1915).

61	"An orderly and comprehensive system": Memo to GEB files from Gates, cited by Fosdick, *Adventure in Giving*, p. 129.

61	Standards for the reorganization: See ibid., pp. 150–174, for details on this reform.

62	"Is there a disease": Victor Heiser, *An American Doctor's Odyssey* (New York, 1936), p. 268.

62	"Nobody had ever": Ibid.

63	"I have lived with this": This Gates letter, dated June 3, 1905, is cited in Nevins, II, 387.

63	Foundation charter: Details of the efforts to secure a charter for the Foundation are in Fosdick's *Story of the Rockefeller Foundation*. More recently the officers of the Foundation commissioned Robert Chaplen to write the text for a volume commemorating the institution's first fifty years, also making the Foundation archives and the personal files of many of its executives available to him. It was published in 1964 as *Toward the Well-Being of Mankind*.

63	President Taft opposed: Nevins, II, 388.

63	"The one thing that the world": The Gompers statement appears in *The Report of the Commission on Industrial Relations* (the Walsh Commission) (Washington, D.C., 1916), IX, 8814.

64	"Engaged together": Letter, Gates to Dr. Wallace Buttrick, October 23, 1923, Rockefeller Family Archives.

64	"When you die": Fosdick, *Story of the Rockefeller Foundation*, p. 1.

65	"Uncover no surface": Murphy's statement and the fact that it summarized the protective attitude toward family and business matters is verified by the director of the Rockefeller Family Archives, Dr. Joseph Ernst.

65	"I followed my plan": Clarke, p. 352.

66	Rockefeller himself benefited: In his later conversations, Rockefeller claimed to regret the Standard's commitment to secrecy. Yet as Flynn shows, the company had been trying all along to get good press without really responding to public criticism. Thousands of dollars in payoffs had been funneled by Archbold to small magazines like *Gunton's* and *Southern Farm Record*. In turn, they defended the trust and its officers against criticism and attacked the works of Lloyd and Tarbell. The efforts to buy a coterie of apparently impartial defenders intensified as the trust's legal problems deepened; finally it began to bear fruit. "In 1905, Archbold's handyman Sibley [Congressman Joseph Crocker Sibley] in one of his numerous letters writes him: 'An efficient library bureau is needed, not for a day or a crisis, but a permanent healthy control of Associated Press and kindred avenues. It will cost money but will be the cheapest in the end.' Apparently something like that was done. An old journalist named J. I. C. Clarke was installed as publicity man.... Papers begin to speak a little more kindly of Standard Oil and Mr. Rockefeller.... Mr. Archbold turns up in the *Saturday Evening Post* with a defensive article and confesses that the company has made the mistake of not stating its side of the case. Then in 1908 Mr. F. N. Doubleday of the *World's Work* falls in with Mr. Rockefeller and is charmed with his simplicity, his directness, his lack of secrecy and so on.... Mr. Doubleday writes a very fulsome account of Rockefeller, draws a most alluring portrait and then disposes of all the ugly charges made against him. Then Rockefeller's 'Random Reminiscences of Men and Events' begins to run serially in the *World's Work* in October, 1908. It is then published as a book and is, of course, not so much a collection of reminiscences as a defense of Mr. Rockefeller's life and deeds" (Flynn, pp. 441–442).

65 Ivy Lee: For a scholarly biography of Lee, containing an account of his relations with the Rockefellers, see Ray Eldon Heibert, *Courtier to the Crowd* (Ames, Iowa, 1966).

66 "In some of the papers": Letter from John D. Rockefeller, Sr., to John D., Jr., July 25, 1924, Rockefeller Family Archives.

67 "Cleveland was some distance": Clarke, p. 359.

67 William Rockefeller: Frank Rockefeller always claimed that his brother William was under John D.'s thumb. Of the "other Rockefeller" in Standard Oil, *Fortune* wrote: "Because he had not John D.'s singleness of purpose, he had not John D.'s unshakeable belief in Standard Oil's continuing and unabated success. The result was that on more than one occasion he parted with some of his shareholdings, sold them at a profit to his brother, who retained them to make a still greater profit. With the capital so obtained, William went into other enterprises, notably railroads.... When he died in 1922, his estate was assigned a gross value of only $102,584,438—but he also left behind him the second great branch of the Rockefeller family." See "The House of Rockefeller," *Fortune*. December 1931, p. 57.

68 Ownership of Standard companies: See "The Rockefellers,

A Financial Power and a Family," *Fortune*, December 1931, p. 51.

68   "Mad about money": The Hanna quote was widely disseminated in his lifetime, but after his death his widow said, "My husband was such an admirer of Mr. Rockefeller that I cannot believe he ever thought such a thing, much less said it." Flynn, p. 173.

68   "Instead of spending": Flynn, p. 459.

68   "No, Rogers": George D. Rogers, p. 70.

69   "The price you propose": Letter from Senior to Junior, April 7, 1915, Rockefeller Family Archives.

70   "Well, I guess I'll see": Nevins, II, 416.

70   "That would be": Jo Davidson, *Between Sittings* (New York, 1951), p. 186.

70   Itinerary: For a more complete account of Rockefeller's daily schedule, see Nevins, II, 413.

70   Golf: Golf became as much a part of Rockefeller's private life as Standard Oil had once been and as much a part of his public image as giving away dimes. He approached the game with the doggedness with which he had once obliterated business rivals, spending years calmly perfecting the game's essentials. When he noted that he was not keeping his eye on the ball, he hired a caddy to follow him over the course saying, "Keep your head down! Keep your head down!" as he made each shot. When he realized he was shifting his stance just before hitting the ball, he had a caddy pound croquet wickets over each foot. His Baptist conscience compelled him to make a strict accounting of his strokes. Flynn (p. 450) writes: " 'If his ball went into the woods,' said a well-known publisher who played with him often, 'he plays it out no matter how many strokes it takes and counts them all. I have played with Andy Carnegie, also. And I found that Andy would bear watching—he would cheat a little on the score.' Rockefeller himself complained to a friend 'that he was sorry to say he had met ministers who did not hesitate to cheat a bit on the link.' Then he gave a humorous imitation of a well-known minister kicking the ball surreptitiously from behind a stump. In golf Rockefeller followed a principle he adhered to in business. George Harvey once asked him to what one thing more than another he attributed the success of the Standard Oil Company. After pondering a while, Rockefeller replied, 'To the fact that we never deceived ourselves.' "

71   "God bless Standard Oil": These newsreels, along with other footage of Rockefeller and moving pictures taken by a private photographer of Junior, Abby, and their children at a young age, are kept in the Rockefeller Family Archives and occasionally shown at Christmas parties and other family occasions. The authors were able to view this unique record by the courtesy of archive director Joseph Ernst.

71 Margaret: Margaret Strong became estranged from her
    father after Bessie's death. When asked by newsmen about
    his daughter's elopement with the marquis, Charles Strong
    replied, "I'm not in close touch with her. She's able to take
    care of herself." The Parmalee Prentices eventually became
    recluses to avoid the constant notoriety of the Rockefeller
    name and riches. Forsaking New York, they moved to a
    1,500-acre estate near Williamstown, Massachusetts, where
    Prentice himself spent far less time practicing law than in
    experimenting wih "scientific agriculture" and in translating
    children's stories and fairy tales into Latin for the edifica-
    tion of his children. For details on the marriages and chil-
    dren of Bessie, Alta, and Edith, see *The New York Times*,
    May 24, 1937, special supplement commemorating John D.
    Rockefeller's death.

72 Edith: *Fortune*, December 1931, has some material on
    Edith, but the best source is Amory, pp. 385 ff.

II *The Son*

75 And on January 29: Unless otherwise specified, we have
    relied on Raymond Fosdick's *John D. Rockefeller Jr.: A
    Portrait* (New York, 1956), for the basic facts on Junior's
    life. (This work is hereafter referred to as Fosdick, *Jr.*)
    Based on extensive conversations with Junior and complete
    access to family records and papers, the Fosdick book is an
    "official" biography in the same sense as Nevins's work on
    Senior.

75 Edith Rockefeller would refer: Cited in Clarence Bar-
    ron, *More They Told Barron* (New York, 1931), p. 265.

75 "Lower middle class people": This statement is recorded
    in the copious notes Fosdick made of his conversations with
    Junior, much of which did not finally find its way into the
    book. The authors have inspected these notes in the Rocke-
    feller Family Archives. (Hereafter referred to as Fosdick
    Notes.)

76 "He was one of us": Fosdick Notes. Other data on
    Junior's childhood come from Junior's own "Recollections
    of My Father," dictated August 1920, and also in the
    Family Archives.

76 "The world is full of Sham": Cited in Grace Goulder,
    John D. Rockefeller: The Cleveland Years (Middletown,
    Conn., 1973), p. 117.

76 "She always sat next to Father": "Recollections of My
    Father," Rockefeller Family Archives. Eliza Rockefeller
    died on March 28, 1889. Flynn writes that she had long
    since decided that her errant husband was dead to her and
    ordered a tombstone reading: "Mrs. Eliza Rockefeller,
    Widow of William Rockefeller." See John T. Flynn, *God's*

Gold (New York, 1932), p. 296. But Dr. Joseph Ernst, director of the Rockefeller Family Archives, has shown the authors a photograph of the tombstone, which bears no such inscription.

77 "I had to wear hand-me-downs": Fosdick Notes.

77 "There was a persuasion in her touch": Fosdick, pp. 18–19.

77 "The boy's mother": Cited in Allan Nevins, *John D. Rockefeller: A Study in Power* (New York, 1953), II, 213.

77 "My precious jewels": Goulder, p. 140.

78 "Talked to us constantly about *duty*": Fosdick, *Jr.*, p. 43.

78 "Am I right?": "Recollections of My Father," Rockefeller Family Archives.

78 "Everything centered around the home": Fosdick, *Jr.*, p. 35.

79 "He who conquers self": Rockefeller's letterbooks are preserved in the Family Archives.

79 "It was there like air": Fosdick, *Jr.*, p. 189.

79 "Practicing the violin": Junior's mother rewarded diligence the same way his father did—with money. In a 1927 interview, Junior said, "The discipline of my early years was in the hands of my mother. She had a balanced system of rewards for good conduct. I was induced, for instance, to pursue violin studies by receiving five cents for each hour of conscientious practice." See John B. Kennedy, "My Father Never Said Don't: An Authorized Interview with John D. Rockefeller Junior," *Collier's*, March 5, 1927.

80 She marked a "C": Fosdick, *Jr.*, p. 24.

81 He spent much of the winter: See Goulder, pp. 152–153.

81 "Shy, ill-adjusted": Fosdick, *Jr.*, p. 139.

81 "Three colored men in the class": Letter from Junior to Grandmother Spelman, September 24, 1893, Rockefeller Family Archives.

82 "Largely given over to pleasure": See Fosdick, *Jr.*, p. 68.

82 "You can celebrate": Letter, Cettie Rockefeller to Junior, January 27, 1895, Rockefeller Family Archives.

82 "I cannot tell you": Letter, Senior to Junior, January 26, 1895, Rockefeller Family Archives.

83 The character of "Johnny Rock": For details on Junior's college years, see Fosdick, *Jr.*, pp. 45–82.

83 "Every man on his own feet": Letter, Junior to Cettie Rockefeller, June 13, 1896, Rockefeller Family Archives.

83 "It would give me the greatest pleasure": Letter, Junior to Cettie Rockefeller, February 23, 1897, Rockefeller Family Archives.

83 "Set a standard of enjoyment": Letter, Cettie Rockefeller to Senior, March 1, 1897, Cited in Fosdick, *Jr.*, p. 69.

84 "My ideas and opinions change": Letter, Junior to Grandmother Spelman, February 26, 1896, Rockefeller Family Archives.

84 "My one thought from the time I was a boy": Fosdick Notes.

84 It was a heady moment: In his history of the stock market, Robert Sobel writes, "It paid to be a bull during the 1897–1906 period, and most of the speculators and operators acted as such, making and spending fortunes. With the perspective of a half a century we now know that this was one of the two biggest bull markets in the nation's history. . . . In 1897 there were but eight industrial firms capitalized at over $50 million; six years later the number of these giants had reached forty." Robert Sobel, *The Big Board* A History of the New York Stock Market (New York, 1965), p. 155 ff.

85 "I never had the satisfaction": Fosdick, *Jr.*, p. 87.

85 "From the day I entered": John D. Rockefeller, Jr., speech before the New York Chamber of Commerce, April 6, 1950.

86 "I think it would do you good": The letter from Henry Cooper, whom Junior would eventually employ in the family office, is cited in Fosdick, p. 89.

86 "I had no difficulty": Fosdick Notes.

86 "I had no opportunity to shape": Quoted by A. W. Atwood, "The Rockefeller Fortune," *Saturday Evening Post*, June 30, 1921, p. 101.

87 All the U.S. Leather stock he could get: Junior was introduced to David Lamar by George Rogers, his father's longtime private secretary. The episode of the "fleecing" is recounted in Fosdick, *Jr.*, pp. 99 ff.

87 "All right, John": "Recollections of My Father," Rockefeller Family Archives.

87 "My one thought and purpose": Letter, Junior to Senior, November 11, 1899; Rockefeller Family Archives.

88 "With the hereditary grip": Cited in Fosdick, *Jr.*, p. 126.

88 "Young Rockefeller: *New York Times*, April 9, 1905.

88 "Men, we need fifteen dollars": John K. Winkler, *John D. Rockefeller: A Portrait in Oils* (New York, 1929), p. 196.

89 One widely circulated cartoon: It appeared in the New York *World* on February 2, 1901.

89 "A rose by any other name": Cited in Fosdick, *Jr.*, p. 131.

89 The coin was framed: Winkler, p. 184.

90 The Aldriches were a powerful family: For the Aldrich genealogy, see Herbert O. Brigham and Mary H. Brigham, *Ancestry of Nelson Wilmarth Aldrich and Abby Pearce Chapman* (Providence, 1938).

90 A moment in the country's evolution: For a portrait of the emergence of "society," see E. Digby Baltzell, *The Protestant Establishment* (New York, 1964). Also Dixon Wecter, *The Sage of American Society* (New York, 1970).

91 As commanding a name: The standard biography of

Senator Aldrich is Nathaniel Stephenson, *Nelson W. Aldrich: A Leader in American Politics* (New York, 1930).

91   "Bringing politics and business closer": Stephenson, p. 240.

91   Even if the match: But it was, in fact, widely assumed to be an economic partnership, building monopoly through marriage. David Graham Philips called it a case of "the chief exploiter of the American people [being] closely allied with the chief schemer in the service of their exploiters." Phillips, *Treason of the Senate* (Chicago, 1960), p. 82.

91   His name was penciled: For details of the courtship, see Mary Ellen Chase, *Abby Aldrich Rockefeller* (New York, 1950).

92   "I was very fond of her": Fosdick Notes.

92   "Of course you love": Cited in Fosdick, *Jr.*, p. 100.

92   Something of a prig: Authors' interview with Nelson Aldrich, Jr., nephew of Abby Aldrich Rockefeller.

93   "For several days past": *New York Times*, October 10, 1901.

93   A rhapsodic letter: It reads in part: "When I think that had you not reflected my own heart to me as you did, and had I waited even one or two weeks longer, this larger, fuller, happier life might have been forever lost to me, it makes me shudder, and thank God from the depths of my heart. I could bring you no daughter, Mother, whom you would love and yearn over and be more proud of than Abby. She will add new brightness and honor to the name which I am so proud, so very proud, to give her." Letter, Junior to Cettie Rockefeller, August 24, 1901, Rockefeller Family Archives.

93   "She seems a wife": Letter, Cettie to Junior, June 25, 1902, Rockefeller Family Archives. Cited in Fosdick, *Jr.*, p. 103.

93   Kept calling her "Mrs. Roosevelt": Chase, p. 33.

93   "Your father is afraid": Ibid.

93n. Junior would always: Chalmers Roberts, *First Rough Draft* (New York, 1973), p. 157.

94   They found a mansion: The details on the Eyrie come from Dr. Joseph Ernst, director of the Rockefeller Family Archives.

95   Discussing the matter with an associate: The associate was Dr. Ernst, who worked closely with John D. Rockefeller, Jr., in setting up the Family Archives.

96   "No little interest": *Cosmopolitan*, June 1905.

96   His father's struggle for control: For details on the struggle for the Mesabi iron ore properties, see Nevins, II, 245–272.

96   "Well, what's your price": Fosdick, *Jr.*, p. 105.

96   Cettie Rockefeller wrote: Letter, Cettie to Junior, March 5, 1901, Rockefeller Family Archives.

97   An effusive note: Letter, Junior to Senior, January 13, 1902, Rockefeller Family Archives.

97   "Gates was the brilliant dreamer": Fosdick, *Jr.*, p. 111.

98   The father would invest: The exact figure comes from the Rockefeller Family Archives.

98   Sought out Dr. William Welch: For Junior's role in the founding of the institute, see Fosdick, *Jr.*, pp. 112–116.

98   A historic train tour: The trip is described at length in the Robert C. Ogden papers in the Library of Congress. See also Fosdick, *Jr.*, pp. 117 ff.

98   The Atlanta Female Baptist Seminary: John D. Rockefeller, Sr.,'s support of what would become Spelman Seminary began in 1882 when he heard two New England women, Misses Sophia B. Packard and Harriet E. Gills speak at a Cleveland church about the school they had opened for Negro girls and women the previous year in Atlanta. He had put $250 into a collection plate and arranged for the two women to meet Cettie the next day. A warm friendship sprang up among the three of them. Two years later, in 1884, Senior chartered a private car so that his family, including the ten-year-old Junior, could go to Atlanta for the school's third anniversary celebration. The elder Rockefeller made one of his rare public speeches on the occasion, and over the next few years gave $316,000 to the project, including a $40,000 grant for a brick classroom building that was later named Rockefeller Hall. The founders of the school wanted to name the school after him, and when he begged off, selected the Spelman name to honor the abolitionist sympathies of Cettie's mother and father. See Goulder, pp. 175–177.

99   "The philanthropists acquiesced": Louis B. Harlan, *Separate and Unequal* (New York, 1968), p. 80. In 1908 Edwin A. Alderman, president of the University of Virginia and trustee of the General Education Board, told a Carnegie Hall audience that one of the most constructive acts of "Southern genius in reference to the Negro has been the limitation of the whole idea of manhood suffrage, thus removing blacks from politics and centering their thoughts on industrial life." See Alderman's book, *The Growing South* (New York, 1908), pp. 12 ff.

99   Dr. Wallace Buttrick: In his history of the GEB, Fosdick discusses Buttrick's central importance to the institution, noting that the team of Gates and Buttrick "dominated the G.E.B. in its first two decades." Raymond Fosdick, *Adventure in Giving* (New York, 1962), pp. 17 ff. The Rockefeller Foundation Archives contain Buttrick's papers and memorabilia.

99   Group that met at Junior's house: The meetings are described by Fosdick in *Adventure in Giving*, pp. 7–8. The initial trustees of the GEB included Ogden, who was named

president: J. L. M. Curry, former Confederate officer who had become chief agent for the Slater and Peabody funds, the only philanthropies operating on a significant scale in the antebellum South; and George Foster Peabody, a partner of Morgan and benefactor of the Peabody Fund. The dominant presence of northern industrialists on the GEB reflected the general interest of their class in southern development. Historian C. Vann Woodward writes: "As the old century drew to a close and the new century progressed through the first decade, the penetration of the South by Northeastern capital continued at an accelerated pace. The Morgans, Mellons and Rockefellers sent their agents to take charge of the region's railroads, mines, furnaces, and financial corporations, and eventually many of its distributive institutions." *Origins of the New South* (Baton Rouge, La., 1967), pp. 291–292.

99n. "Face the music": Cited in Harlan, p. 78. For Baldwin's career, see John G. Brooks, *An American Citizen: The Life of William H. Baldwin, Jr.* (Boston, 1910).

99 Rockefeller in magnitude: In *Adventure in Giving*, Fosdick calculates that by comparison, the endowments of the Peabody and Slater funds were between $1 and $2 million, and the Southern Education Board had spent only $400,000 in its entire 14-year existence.

100 "On the Robert Ogden trips: W. E. B. Du Bois, *Autobiography* (New York, 1968), p. 230. Du Bois had also criticized the Rockefellers' impact on the black South earlier in his career. In a 1925 issue of *Crisis*, he wrote: "It is a shame that our dependence on the rich for donations to absolutely necessary causes makes honest criticism increasingly difficult among us. If someone starts to tell the truth or disclose incompetency or rebel at injustice, a chorus of 'Sh! You're opposing the General Education Board!' or 'Hush, You're making enemies in the Rockefeller Foundation' will get you."

101 "A study of the map of the world": Letter, Gates to Senior, April 17, 1905. Gates later wrote: "This letter marks my denominational and religious emancipation, and it is . . one of the very few which Mr. Rockefeller singled out for words of approval." MS *Autobiography*, Rockefeller Foundation Archives.

102 Yellow Fever Commission: Gorgas had been chief sanitary officer of the U. S. Army during the occupation of Cuba, where he had conducted an anti-yellow-fever campaign, and had then gone to Panama to supervise the sanitation measures involved in the building of the canal. One of the doctors working under Gorgas in Panama was Victor Heiser, the "medical diplomat" who would later become commissioner of health for the U.S. colonial government in the Philippines and a director of the International Health

Board. As Heiser recalls, public health was seen to have significant strategic implications; see Victor Heiser, *An American Doctor's Odyssey* (New York, 1936), Chapter 5, "Little Brown Brother." When the U.S. Army took charge of Luzon, for instance, the threat of epidemic had been as dangerous as the threat of "anarchy." The dramatic success of subsequent public health programs neutralized both threats by creating an aura of benevolence around the occupation. Military historian John M. Gates writes: "The American policy of benevolence ... played a much more important role in the success of the pacification program than fear did." *Schoolbooks and Krags: The United States Army in The Philippines 1898–1902* (Westport, Conn., 1973), p. 277. But it was not only the military that was newly interested in the tropical zones and hence in diseases like malaria and yellow fever. Changing conditions in the oil industry beginning with the Spindletop gusher and the opening of the great Gulf fields in 1901 unleashed frantic competition for crude that soon took wildcatters below the equator. In 1918, when the Standard Oil Company of New Jersey established its first Medical Department, many of the techniques it employed had been developed by the Rockefeller Foundation's public health programs. "Jersey Standard's struggle against tropical disease," comments the official corporate history, "formed an integral segment of Latin American producing operations and constituted a dramatic phase of relations between private business and national interests there. In Latin America doctors soon came to be recognized as an integral part of the oil-producing organization." Without these doctors, the authors add, "the search for petroleum reserves might well have failed, and in certain areas the political brew, already seething, might have boiled over even sooner." George S. Gibbs and Evelyn K. Knowlton, *The Resurgent Years 1911–1927* [Vol. II of official Standard history] (New York, 1956), p. 394.

102   The China Medical Board: The Rockefeller Foundation Archives contain some forty cubic feet of material on this organization. For a semiofficial history, see Mary E. Ferguson, *China Medical Board and Peking Medical College* (New York, 1970). For an excellent academic study throwing considerable new light on Junior's administrative hold on the China Medical Board, see Mary Brown Bullock's unpublished doctoral dissertation, "The Rockefeller Foundation in China" (Stanford University, 1973). The authors are obliged to Ms. Bullock for the opportunity to see her work.

102   John R. Mott: Mott was general secretary of the International Committee of the YMCA and executive secretary of the World Student Christian Federation. In a letter to his Secretary of State, William Jennings Bryan, proposing that

Mott be appointed the first U.S. ambassador to the China republic, Woodrow Wilson wrote: "The thing most prominent in my mind is that the men now most active in establishing a new government and a new regime for China are many of them members of the YMCA, and many of them are also men trained in American universities. The Christian influence, direct or indirect, is very prominently at the front and I need not say ought to be kept there. Mr. John R. Mott, whom I know very well and who has as many of the qualities of statesman as any man of my acquaintance, is very familiar with the situation in China, not only that, but he enjoys the confidence of men of the finest influence all over the Christian world." (These men "of the finest influence" included such individuals as Wilson's own friend Cleveland Dodge, whose wealth came from Phelps, Dodge & Company, largest importers of metals and cotton in America in the nineteenth century. Dodge was a trustee of the Laura Spelman Rockefeller Memorial Fund, a director of the YMCA, and confidant of Mott, as well as being a director of the National City Bank, which, along with Standard Oil, had spearheaded the advance of U.S. businesses into China.) Mott was a lifetime associate of Junior's and a key influence on his missionary philanthropies over the next four decades. During Mott's lifetime, Junior gave $8 million to the YMCA and nearly $6 million to the YWCA, and at his friend's death he set aside $250,-000 to establish the John R. Mott Memorial Scholarship Fund. Basil Mathew's *John R. Mott, World Citizen* (New York, 1934), is the standard biography; the Wilson letter can be found on page 436. See also C. H. Hopkins, *History of the YMCA in North America* (New York, 1951), and Sherwood Eddy, *A Century with Youth* (New York, 1944).

103   "Investment in leadership": See Raymond B. Fosdick, *The Story of the Rockefeller Foundation* (New York, 1952), Chapter 21.

103   "It seemed like an impossible task": Fosdick Notes.

104   "I never worked harder": Ibid.

104   Attorney named Raymond B. Fosdick: In his autobiography, Fosdick recalled the meeting. "I had first met Mr. Rockefeller in 1910 when he was chairman of the Special Grand Jury in Manhattan investigating the so-called White Slave traffic. A trim, youthful-looking figure eight or nine years older than I, he had called at my office to discuss the problems growing out of his grand jury experience. The findings of the jury had profoundly disturbed him, and in his earnest way he was searching for some method by which what was then euphemistically known as 'the social evil'—as if there were no others—could be continuously and scientifically studied." Raymond Fosdick, *Chronicle of a Generation* (New York, 1958), pp. 124–125.

104 The bureau sent Abraham Flexner: The pioneering
study is *Prostitution in Europe* (New York, 1914); Flexner
recounts his work with Junior in his *Autobiography* (New
York, 1960), pp. 116 ff.

105 Police administration: Fosdick's book on the Europeans'
police techniques is *European Poilce Systems* (New York,
1919). In *Chronicle of a Generation,* he wrote: "The outstanding impression I received from my study in Europe
was that police administration there was a distinct career
which attracted the best brains obtainable. With few exceptions, it was divorced from politics. Its elaborate training
schools for recruits had no counterpart in the United States.
Its methods of crime detection were based on scientific procedures far beyond anything that was known in America at
the time" (p. 128). The work on American police (*American Police Systems* [New York, 1920]), which Fosdick
prepared by studying departments in every American city of
more than 100,000 people, was far less sympathetic. In it he
wrote: "In America the student of police travels from one
political squabble to another, too often from one scandal
to another. . . . There is little conception in policing as a profession or as a science to be matured and developed. It is a
job, held perhaps by the grace of some mysterious political
influence, and conducted in an atmosphere sordid and
unhealthy."

105 "So much was contributed": "Mr. Junior's Beneficences:
An Audit," *Fortune,* July 1936, p. 45.

105 The opium menace: According to the Bureau of Social
Hygiene (BSH) files in the Rockefeller Foundation Archives, in 1924, when Fosdick had become head of the
BSH, he got Junior to make a $10,000 grant to the fledgling
Foreign Policy Association's Committee on the International Traffic in Opium. For an interesting insight into the
impact of organizations like the BSH on the future of
American narcotics policy (the dual features of treatment of
addiction through substances like methadone and simultaneous criminalization), see David Musto, *The American Disease* (New Haven, Conn., 1973), especially pp. 97 ff.

106 "Young Mr. Rockefeller": A. H. Lewis, "What Rockefeller
Will Do," *Cosmopolitan,* July 1905.

106 Resigned as vice-president: Eight years earlier, he had
written his father after resigning his directorship in the National City Bank: "I intimated to Mr. Stillman that it was
with large banks as it was with other large corporations
nowadays, practically impossible for the directors to know
anything about the business or to have any voice in its
management, while at the same time they stood to the public as guarantors for the conduct of the business." Letter,
Junior to Senior, December 4, 1902, Rockefeller Family Archives. In the matter of the Standard, Junior gave the fol-

lowing reason for his resignation to Fosdick: "I gradually became aware of usages and actions for which as a member of the board I felt responsible, but which as a single individual I had little or no voice in determining. I made up my mind that I could not become responsible for the acts of other people" (Fosdick Notes). It is likely that the publicity received by the City Bank and the Standard, respectively, as a result of the Amalgamated Copper scandal and the Supreme Court case, had as much to do with the decision as the issues he mentioned. When the Colorado Fuel and Iron Company was called to account for the Ludlow Massacre, Junior would plead that as a director he was not in a position of real authority—as if that defense had just occurred to him for the first time.

107   Rockefeller increased his investment: for details on the family investment in CF&I, see the findings of the U.S. Commission on Industrial Relations, 1913–1915, whose *Final Report* was submitted to Congress in 11 volumes in 1916. Junior's testimony regarding the family's investment and influence in the company begins at VIII, 7763. For a detailed analysis of events before, during and after the strike, see Graham Adams, Jr., *The Age of Industrial Violence, 1910–1915* (New York, 1966), and especially George S. McGovern's doctoral dissertation, "The Colorado Coal Strike, 1913–1914" (University of Michigan, 1953). The dissertation is the basis for a later book, George S. McGovern and Leonard F. Guttridge, *The Great Coalfield War* (New York, 1972).

107   The miners' low wages: For a vivid description of conditions at the mines, see the IRC *Final Report*, IX, 8532 ff. See also U.S. House of Representatives, *Conditions in the Coal Mines of Colorado: Hearings Before a Subcommittee of the Committee on Mines and Mining,* 2 vols. (Washington, D. C., 1914).

107   "Even their mules": Letter, Bowers to Junior, May 13, 1913, Rockefeller Family Archives.

108   "When such men as these": Letter, Bowers to Junior, October 11, 1913, Rockefeller Family Archives.

108   "Standing between the country and chaos": Cited in Fosdick, *Jr.,* p. 144.

110   A telegram of support: Flynn, p. 458.

110   "I do not think I shall die": Frick's statement is cited in Joseph F. Wall's *Andrew Carnegie* (New York, 1970), p. 563.

111   "[The mediator] was told": The complete correspondence between Bowers and Junior regarding the strike appears in the IRC *Final Report*, IX, 8411–8449.

112   "I believe that you are concerned": The exchange between Congressman Foster and Junior can be found in *Conditions in the Coal Mines of Colorado,* II, pp. 2873 ff.

113 Upton Sinclair's pickets: The irrepressible Sinclair was largely responsible for making the Ludlow case a *cause célèbre* in New York. In his *Autobiography,* he later recalled how he had begun the picket lines in front of 26 Broadway along with four "militant ladies": "We walked for perhaps five minutes, and then policemen politely told us to walk somewhere else; when we politely refused, they told us we were under arrest.... We were put into a patrol wagon and taken to the police court, and again I told the story, this time to the judge ... [who] found me guilty of disorderly conduct and fined me three dollars. I declined to pay the fine, and so did the four ladies, so each of us got three days instead of three dollars. ... We kept the demonstration going a couple of weeks ... [and then] a group of students of the Ferrer School, an anarchist institution, came down to march, and later decided to carry the demonstration to the Rockefeller estate in Pocantico Hills." *The Autobiography of Upton Sinclair* (New York, 1962), pp. 200–201.

113 "If you were men": Cited in McGovern thesis, p. 419.

113 The Socialist periodical: See *Appeal to Reason,* May 30, 1914.

114 Criticism came from more than a handful: For this and other press reactions, see McGovern thesis, pp. 364–427. However, criticism was far from universal. The august *New York Times,* for instance, sympathized with the mine operators and seemed especially concerned to shield the young Rockefeller from attack. Following his testimony before the Subcommittee on Mines, the *Times* praised his understanding of social problems and deplored the fact that "so self-controlled and philosophical" an individual had to be "badgered and scolded" by government investigators. The article validated the prudence of Junior's course in identifying himself as a civic leader whose wealth stood behind the most advanced cultural and scientific institutions of New York and the country.

115 "Crowds are led by symbols": Ivy Lee, speech to American Railroad Guild, May 19, 1914, Ivy Lee Papers, Princeton University Library.

115 Son of a liberal Georgia preacher: For biographical data on Ivy Lee, see Ray Eldon Hiebert, *Courtier to the Crowd* (Ames, Iowa, 1966).

116 "My father and I are much misunderstood": IRC *Final Report,* VIII, 7899 ff.

117 "The level of the hired gunman": Carl Sandburg, "Ivy L. Lee, Paid Liar," New York *Call,* March 7, 1915.

117 "I believe this publicity policy": Letter, Lee to Junior, August 16, 1914, Rockefeller Family Archives.

117 Fifteen years earlier: Biographical data for Mackenzie King can be found in Bruce Hutchison, *The Incredible Canadian* (New York, 1953), and R. MacGregor Dawson,

William Lyon Mackenzie King: A Political Biography (Toronto, 1958).

117 "How terribly broken down": Cited in F. A. McGregor, *The Fall and Rise of Mackenzie King* (Toronto, 1962). During the period of the Ludlow strike and King's close association with the Rockefellers, McGregor was the Canadian's personal secretary, and also a peripheral participant in the events.

118 A man with Mackenzie King's background: It was Greene who invited King to meet with Junior. Eliot sent a wire urging him to accept the invitation. The telegram's peculiarly revealing wording showed how important the Harvard president thought the matter was: "Opportunity offered by request to you from Rockefeller group is immense. You might greatly serve all white race industries and show way to industrial concord in whole world" (McGregor, pp. 93–94).

118 "Seldom have I been so impressed": Fosdick, *Jr.*, p. 154.

119 "The keeper of the vineyards": See McGregor, pp. 132–133. King was of two minds about accepting the job, although he never admitted his ambivalence to his new employer. The Fabian in him was somewhat repelled by Junior's reactionary cast of mind. He wrote in a letter to a friend: "In accepting [Junior's offer of employment] I had to consider that I was prejudicing my political future for all time to come. . . . that I would not be harangued against as a Liberal politician, but as a 'Standard Oil man.' . . . I would have rejected it utterly had the offer come to enter the service of the Standard Oil industry and not to work under a foundation where money was held in trust" (cited by McGregor, p. 103). But the pragmatist in King asserted itself in his final acceptance of the job and in the advice he gave Rockefeller in a letter pointing out that "after hostilities [of World War I] close, thousands of men and their families in the Old World are going to seek further employment here in the New. In certain industries, it is going to be easy for employers to find all the labor they desire, and unions will be confronted with a new problem" (cited by McGovern and Guttridge, p. 297).

119 "Such a pseudo-union": The Gompers statement is cited by Fosdick, *Jr.*, p. 166.

120 The Industrial Relations Commission had been created: For an analysis of the work of this historic commission, see James Weinstein, *The Corporate Ideal in the Liberal State, 1900–1918* (Boston, 1968). Also, Selig Perlman, *A History of Trade Unionism in the United States* (New York, 1922).

120 When Junior first appeared: See IRC *Final Report*, VIII, 7763 ff.

121 "It is not their money": For John Lawson's testimony, see IRC *Final Report*, VIII, 8006.

121   "Here was a man": *New Republic,* January 30, 1915, pp. 12-13.

122   When Walsh recalled Junior: For the second round of Rockefeller's testimony, see IRC *Final Report,* IX, 8592 ff.

123   This passage between the two: IRC *Final Report,* IX, 8602.

124   Bowers had broken down: McGovern and Guttridge, p. 331.

125   Its final report: For a summary of findings, see IRC *Final Report,* I, 17–169. They went so far as to hold Junior responsible in legal as well as moral terms: ". . . We find that the final and full responsibility for . . . all the deplorable results, such refusal [to confer with miners' representatives] must be placed upon Mr. John D. Rockefeller and Mr. John D. Rockefeller Junior" (p. 266).

125   Walsh was hamstrung: The primary commission report, signed by Walsh and the three commission representatives from labor, was condemned as too partisan in a dissenting report filed by Mrs. Borden Harriman and the three business representatives on the commission. The commission had, in fact, been racked by such dissension since its beginning. Early in the proceedings, Walsh had come into conflict with his research director, Charles McCarthy, a renowned academic who had made a name for himself as a Progressive at the University of Wisconsin and architect of social reform legislation. McCarthy had been a classmate of Junior's at Brown; he was fired after the files of 26 Broadway were subpoenaed and Walsh discovered that he had surreptitiously written Rockefeller during the hearings urging him to "get some machinery for making consistent explanations" and other advice. (For details on the intrigue and politics in the IRC, see Weinstein, pp. 198 ff.) Walsh himself disappeared from public view after the commission delivered its final report. Yet he did not forget the issues raised by Ludlow, especially the question of the Rockefeller Foundation's involvement. Among his private papers is an essay entitled "The Great Foundations." In it he writes: "From the knowledge I have gained in my work as Chairman of the Federal Commission on Industrial Relations, I . . . challenge the wisdom of giving public sanction and approval to the spending of a huge fortune through such philanthropies as that of the Rockefeller Foundation. . . . Mr. Rockefeller is taking money obtained through the exploitation of thousands of poorly nourished, socially submerged men, women and children, and spending these sums, through a board of personal employees, in such fashion that his estate is in a fair way not only to exercise a dominating influence in industry, but, before many years, to exact a tribute of loyalty and subserviency to him and his interests from the whole profession of scientists, social workers and

economists. . . . Already there are thousands of eager young scholars and scientists who know that someday, for the sake of their work, they may be drawn into the retinue of the foundations. It will become increasingly bad form for a man engaged in social betterment work to speak ill of Rockefeller, Carnegie, and the other plunderers." The Frank Walsh Papers, New York Public Library.

125 The death of Cettie Rockefeller: It occurred on March 12. A few weeks later the tax case was dropped. On August 11 the remains were taken from the Archbold vault and transported to Cleveland for burial there.

126 Small caravan of automobiles: For details on Junior's trip to Colorado, see Fosdick, *Jr.*, pp. 160 ff.; McGregor, pp. 178 ff.; McGovern and Guttridge, pp. 333 ff.

126 "That incident, and the publicity": cited in Fosdick, *Jr.*, p. 162.

127 "I went into your washhouses": for a firsthand account of Junior's speech at Pueblo, see McGregor, pp. 181–182. The text of Junior's speech was printed later in a slightly altered form in Junior's *The Personal Relation in Industry* (New York, 1923), pp. 90–106. This book, composed of speeches written largely by Lee, was to be the enduring testament to Junior's transformation on the question of labor. Lee arranged for it to be published by Boni and Liveright. However, Junior was concerned about that house's reputation for publishing avant-garde modern fiction. He told Lee that he did not want to legitimate such works with his good name. On August 23, 1923, Lee replied: "I am enclosing herewith a copy of the many books which anyone would consider worth while. There is no question, however, that they are publishers of a number of novels representing what you and I would consider the less desirable tendencies in modern fiction, but I rather imagine we would find such books on the list of nearly every publisher. . . . I certainly don't believe the fact that Boni and Liveright publish a book by you will increase the sale of any books which they publish which, perhaps, you and I would think had just as well not be printed at all. . . . Mr. Liveright told me he would like to talk to you and believed he could satisfy your mind on all points at issue. He is writing a publisher's note which will say that the book was being published on their initiative as a valuable contribution to the betterment of industrial relations." Four years later, on December 21, 1927, Lee forwarded a royalty statement with an undertone of amusement at the Rockefeller punctilio: "You may want a little pin money for Christmas, so I have much pleasure in enclosing herewith Boni & Liveright's check for $591.90 as the royalties on your book." Both letters are in the Ivy Lee Papers, Princeton University Library.

128n. The Rockefeller return on the CF&I: After questioning Junior closely on the appreciation of the company's stock and getting him to admit that it meant a $9 million profit for his father, Walsh pointed out that in the 12 years the family had controlled the company the total wages paid were only $92 million. He then hammered away at the contrast: *"Mr. Walsh*—'My question is finally, would you consider it just and socially desirable that fifteen thousand employees who had worked for twelve years, and many of them have been crippled and sacrificed their lives, should, as a matter of justice, receive [only] ten times as great a return as one man who has not visited the property—as a matter of social justice?' *Mr. Rockefeller, Junior*—'I cannot make any comparative statement. I think the employees should receive fair wages, and I think they have. I think capital is entitled to a fair return. There has not been a fair return. I think as between the two, the employees have fared better than the capital.'" IRC *Final Report*, VIII, 7847 ff.

128   The Rockefeller Plan: A study of the Rockefeller Plan—or the King Plan, as it might have been more appropriately known—during the first eight years, concluded that the Colorado Fuel and Iron Company adjusted its wage scale to that of its unionized competitors. Every wage increase granted by CF&I in the decade after the strike came as the result of increases won by the United Mine Workers in their campaigns. The company continued to deny workers the right to hold independent meetings; the local YMCA, which Junior had endowed on his trip west (and on whose board sat several CF&I officials), refused to allow workers to meet there. (See Ben M. Selekman and Mary Van Kleeck, *A Study of the Industrial Representation Plan of the Colorado Fuel and Iron Company* (New York, 1924).

128   "I wish I had had you": Cited by McGregor, p. 195.
129   "I was merely King's mouthpiece": Fosdick, *Jr.*, p. 161.
129n. "I doubt if": Cited by McGregor, p. 276.
129   Mackenzie King "had influenced the thinking": But the association with Rockefeller had a corresponding effect on King. In January 1918, his connection with the Foundation came to an end when he completed the manuscript of *Industry and Humanity: A Study in the Principles Underlying Industrial Reconstruction*. Junior immediately offered to underwrite him as an industrial relations counselor, and King accepted. Soon he was advising several large corporations including International Harvester, Bethlehem Steel, and the Standard Oil companies. His doubts about the Rockefeller connection, expressed secretly in letters and diary entries four years earlier, had evaporated. The "practical" approach he took to labor problems was reassuring to the firms for

which he consulted, especially because he showed them ways of making concessions in form rather than fact. His private thoughts about the conditions in the companies he worked for, however, were much harsher than anything he allowed himself to say publicly. After viewing labor conditions at the Consolidation Coal Company properties (on whose board Raymond Fosdick and Colonel Arthur Woods represented the Rockefeller interest), he wrote in his diary: "As one goes about these camps, so numerous that one can scarcely remember them, and sees the enormous wealth controlled by a handful of capitalists, one cannot but feel that the system which permits this sort of control is absolutely wrong, unjust, and indefensible; and that there will not be an end to social unrest until the transition is made to joint control" (McGregor, p. 170). For an interesting analysis of the contradictions in King's thought, see the introduction by David Jay Bercusson in the reissued *Industry and Humanity* (Toronto, 1973).

130 Behind-the-scenes struggle: In 1920 a worried Fosdick wrote King: "It seems to me that Mr. Rockefeller should be in a mood not only where he will agree on this principle [collective bargaining] but where he will fight for it. . . . It is only through such a spirit of liberalism that revolution can be avoided—if indeed it can be avoided." King couldn't have agreed more. "The day has gone by when organized Labor forces can any longer be ignored by Capital," he lectured Junior. Rockefeller would usually agree with his mentor, but then his natural distrust of unionism would assert itself and he would vacillate. After one such episode of backsliding in 1921, King wrote in disgust: "To come out against [collective bargaining] is to put yourself and the industries with which your name is associated in the path of certain destruction. . . . To come out in favor of it . . . is to put you where you may help change what is at the moment a great militant force arrayed against capital to the detriment of society into a great cooperative force which will work with capital for the good of society." Junior was finally won over by the pragmatic appeal of this argument, although the employees of the Colorado Fuel and Iron Company would be denied an independent union until the Wagner Act of 1935 outlawed the company union concept that he and King had created. Letters, Raymond Fosdick to Mackenzie King, September 19, 1919; King to Junior, October 6, 1919, Rockefeller Family Archives.

130 War relief: For a résumé of Junior's war work, see Fosdick, *Jr.*, pp. 202 ff.

131 "Now realize what it means": Hiebert, p. 167.

132n. "The Standard Oil Company cannot hope": For complete text of memo, see Gibbs and Knowlton, p. 292.

132 Tea at the White House: "In April, after the Supreme

Court decision dissolving the Standard Oil, [Senator Nelson] Aldrich made an appointment to visit the White House with his daughter and her husband, John D. Rockefeller Jr., for lunch. Taft didn't want anyone to know of the visit. He had the usher telephone Senator Aldrich to drive to the East Entrance where the party was hustled by the side door into the White House. Taft directed that no entry or minute of the visit be made anywhere" (Flynn, p. 449).

133 Rockefeller started making his fortune over: For decades, the Rockefeller Family Office concealed the exact amount Junior had been given, fearing that if the figure were known, some enterprising statistician might stalk the fortune through the fluctuations of the stock market and figure out the current size of the estate. The veil was probably impenetrable by such means. It was finally drawn aside voluntarily on September 23, 1974, when Nelson Rockefeller began his Senate confirmation hearings with a statement revealing the exact figure. Speaking of his grandfather, the first John D., Nelson said: "During his lifetime. . . . he gave his only son, my father, a total of $465 million." Committee on Rules and Administration, U.S. Senate, *Hearings on the Nomination of Nelson A. Rockefeller to be Vice President of the United States* (Washington, D.C., 1974), p. 44.

134 "Years of effort and striving": Letter, Junior to Senior, July 7, 1933, Rockefeller Family Archives.

134 "Neither Father nor I": Fosdick, *Jr.*, p. 197.

134 It is difficult to imagine: Once Senior remarked to the journalist W. O. Inglis, "I may say that I have never had the time to become really acquainted with my son. He has been very busy always." Inglis passed the comment on to Junior, who wrote back a letter clearly intending to rationalize the remark but instead at least partially authenticating it: "I was quite touched by Father's statement. . . . Our relationship has always been a very close and beautiful one, but I suppose it is always difficult for parents to realize that their children have grown up and to give to their views and opinions the same weight which they would attach to similar expressions coming from outsiders. It is perhaps for this reason that Father has not felt that he knew me intimately. There is no subject that I have not always been happy to discuss with Father, but as you yourself have observed, he is inclined less and less to discuss subjects which he does not himself initiate; hence our serious interchange of view is perhaps more limited than might otherwise be the case." Inglis to Junior, January 31, 1918; Junior to Inglis, February 19, 1918, Ivy Lee Papers, Princeton University Library.

135 "For your Christmas check": Letter, Junior to Senior, December 26, 1920, Rockefeller Family Archives.

135 Fosdick later admitted: See Fosdick Personal File,
     Rockefeller Family Archives.
135 Senior had complained: Thomas M. Debevoise Personal
     File, Rockefeller Family archives.
136 "In all the years of my business association": Ibid.
137 "Anything to do with convenience": Fosdick Notes,
     Rockefeller Family Archives.
137 Charles of London: The details on the redecorated office
     were supplied by Dr. Joseph Ernst.
137 Gates, whose eclipse: Enraged by the way Junior turned
     the other cheek in testimony before the Industrial Relations
     Commission, Gates had fumed: "It may be urged that this
     policy is the Christian policy. I would have exposed this
     man Walsh. If necessary, I would have carried the matter
     so far as to invite arrest, and been carried struggling and
     shrieking from the courtroom for the purpose of getting my
     case vividly, powerfully, before the people of the United
     States." Gates Papers, Rockefeller Foundation Archives. But
     his departure was not only a matter of political principle;
     money was also involved. Since coming to the Rockefellers'
     service, Gates had never felt adequately compensated for his
     work. He felt that Junior undervalued his services "in order
     to pave the way for as low a compensation as possible," and
     was reluctant to name a fee for his work, which Junior in-
     sisted he do. By 1915 this matter had come to a head,
     when, on June 29, Gates gave in and wrote Junior a pained
     letter telling him that he felt his services in connection with
     the family's interests in the Western Maryland Railroad
     were worth $10,000, and in connection with Consolidation
     Coal Company, $50,000. He expected to be paid generously
     by the Rockefellers without having to name his own com-
     pensation. He felt humiliated by having to put the figures
     on paper, and soon stopped working for the family (al-
     though not the foundations) as an employee. Rockefeller
     Family Archives.
138 Gulliver's predicament: "You remember how Gulliver,
     thrown on the shores of a strange island, and falling into a
     deep sleep, awoke at last to find himself bound hand and
     foot with thousands of tiny ropes, and every individual hair
     of his head fastened to a stake. He could speak, breathe and
     wink, but move or act he could not. The vast man was en-
     slaved to the Lilliputians, a people six inches tall. If this
     vast Rockefeller fortune is so invested as to require a large
     force of experts and small subordinates to look after it, the
     end will be that its owners will at last, in spite of the most
     able and strenuous exertions, be the unwilling slaves of
     these very men." Letter, Gates to Junior, September 1,
     1908, Rockefeller Family Archives.
138 Aides Junior had inherited: For a view of the organiza-
     tion and operation of the family's office in the early 1900s,

see the testimony of Jerome Greene, Ivy Lee, and Charles O. Heydt in the IRC *Final Report*, VIII and IX.

139 Illustrating his points: The anecdote comes from the Warren Weaver Memoir in the Columbia Oral History Project.

139 Rewrite the obituary: See Hiebert, p. 127.

139 Police commissioner: The details about Woods's career come from Dr. Joseph Ernst of the Rockefeller Family Archives.

140 Raymond Fosdick: Allan Nevins later called Fosdick "one of the great body of young idealists trained in the doctrines and spirit of progressivism in the decade preceding World War I." Junior often asked him to come to work for the family, but Fosdick always refused. As Rockefeller family attorney John Lockwood says, "Ray realized that he had more value to himself and the Rockefellers if he maintained his independence. That's why he kept an office in his law firm, and stayed outside the Rockefeller Office." Authors' interview with John Lockwood.

140 It was Fosdick: Fosdick constantly brought new ideas and individuals to Junior's attention. He also helped him gain distance from the compelling personality and ideas of Gates. For instance, on January 11, 1927, Gates wrote Junior a memorandum on the General Education Board arguing that GEB money should be given as endowments to universities. Junior asked Fosdick for his reaction, and on February 15, got this response: "The amounts of money involved in college and university education are now so enormous that the sums which we have at our disposal are relatively insignificant, and on a *quantitative* basis could scarcely affect the situation one way or another. Our money can be used, however, to affect the situation on a *qualitative* basis. . . . [We must] raise standards in university work in a few selected centers—standards which will ultimately affect university teaching everywhere in the United States." This approach was the one the GEB ultimately followed. Even more important was Fosdick's impact on Junior's view of international affairs. On January 7, 1927, Gates had written a waspish memorandum on world philanthropy giving his views regarding nations deserving financial assistance. Of Japan, he said: "Above all nations she hates America, and intrigues against us, with our enemies. To serve her, even if she needed it, would be to do a disservice to ourselves." Of China: "She is anarchy, with no central authority, and the local factions of the dismembered empire fighting each other. . . . I regret our lavish expenditures there." On the Middle Eastern nations: "We may as well leave all Mohammedan countries to the slow processes of geologic time. Money spent on education has only made them abler for evil, and money spent on Missions has been wholly wasted." Of

the Latin and Mediterranean countries: "Ethnologists have not found the Latin races to be intrinsically valuable to the well-being of humanity." Gates's formula was to pay token attention to these parts of the world and concentrate aid on helping Britain gain its pre-World War I status: "I feel that the British Empire holds the secret of the progress of civilization and with the United States is the best hope for the well-being of the race. If we love God or man, let us work with and for England and her associated English-speaking states." Nothing could have summarized the difference in outlook between Gates and Fosdick more clearly, and in his February 15, 1927, memorandum, Fosdick wrote: "I am in complete and fundamental disagreement. It represents an expression of the exploded Nordic theory, which centers all the virtue in the world in the Anglo-Saxon race. I am equally unconvinced that our help should be centered on English-speaking states and dependencies. Mr. Gates' point of view on this whole matter has no support in scientific circles and can be attacked on too many grounds to justify extended discussion in this letter." Fosdick's own predilections in international affairs were indicated in a report by Abraham Flexner regarding permanent world government that he had sent Junior with his enthusiastic endorsement a few months earlier, December 6, 1926. It said in part: "The modern world may be likened to a great business of which every country is an essential and complex department. Hitherto each department (nation) has been pursuing its own will or fancy. When ultimately and inevitably this world business has become hopelessly entangled, when divergent interests have been created, when pride has been wounded and passions aroused—then the department heads have been hastily brought together to agree on concerted action for the purposes of avoiding bankruptcy." Rockefeller Family Archives.

141   Industrial Relations Counsellors: for a view of the organization and its work, see Clarence J. Hicks, *My Life in Industrial Relations* (New York, 1941). Hicks began his career at the YMCA, where his talents in personnel management brought him to Junior's attention. He was sent to Colorado to handle labor relations for CF&I after the strike and eventually became labor relations director of Jersey Standard.

142   Throwing the full weight of the Fund: There are some 100 cubic feet of records on the Laura Spelman Rockefeller Memorial Fund in the Rockefeller Foundation Archives. For a summary of Ruml's work in sharpening the focus of the Fund and aligning it with Merriam, see Barry D. Karl, *Charles Merriam* (Chicago, 1974).

142   Arthur Packard: According to information supplied by Dr. Joseph Ernst, it appears that Packard's role was the

result of Junior's attempt to formalize personal (as opposed to institutional) giving. In 1922 he set up an Advisory Committee made up of Debevoise, William Richardson (a personal friend), and Thomas Appleget (an office employee specializing in philanthropy). Initially this committee's function was to consult with Junior on his annual gifts, but as his career branched into national and international affairs, the committee acted more or less autonomously. Appleget became chiefly responsible for Junior's personal giving, having the power to give up to two thousand dollars without his principal's approval. He recruited Arthur Packard as an aide, and Packard soon succeeded him. Under Packard's influence, this function became an increasingly important one, with an independent philanthropic department developing inside the Office whose duty was not only to respond to requests for Rockefeller money, but also to take the initiative in uncovering new fields where a philanthropic investment might be wisely made. (Details on the evolution of the almoner's role come from Rockefeller Family Archives.)

142   Birth control: It was Fosdick who first alerted Junior to Margaret Sanger's Planned Parenthood movement and to the importance of birth control in general. He had discussed the matter with Beardsley Ruml, and in 1925, Ruml (then director of the Laura Spelman Rockefeller Memorial Fund) wrote Fosdick: "I agree that we should push the Birth Control Movement in all appropriate ways, even though, as you say, the cause will ultimately be won [anyhow]. It remains true, it seems to me, that any conceivable amount we could properly and conservatively put behind the movement would be infinitesimal as compared with the aggregate social benefits." In 1931, just before Junior gave $5,000 to Margaret Sanger for a birth control clinic, Fosdick wrote him a letter calling the population problem "one of the great perils of the future." Because of the publicity Sanger attracted, Arthur Packard was soon investigating other, less "senational," organizations in the field. (Details distilled from Birth Control file, Rockefeller Family Archives.)

142   "I never know where John is: Fosdick, *Jr.*, p. 403.

143   Little town of Williamsburg: For an account of the decision to undertake the restoration, see Fosdick, *Jr.*, pp. 272–301. See also John J. Walklet and Thomas K. Ford, *A Window on Williamsburg* (Williamsburg, Va., 1966). The authors visited the town and interviewed some of the current employees, including Ms. Bland Blackford, archivist of the Colonial Williamsburg Foundation.

144n.   "I am convinced": Fosdick, *Jr.*, p. 196. Although possibly for the wrong reasons, Senior was probably right about the Morgan collection. Calling it "late and semi-mass-produced Chinese art, including many identical sets of objects," English critic Gerald Reitlinger says of the Morgan collection: "It was a monopoly collection, made with all the meteoric conservatism of high finance according to a taste which was doubtless considered as firmly based as a rock, but which had been nothing more than a fad forty or fifty years ago, when it was new. By all the normal rules, this part of the Pierpont Morgan Collection was due for a drastic fall. But there were no normal rules, because three multi-millionaires who had failed to break Morgan's monopoly wanted the porcelain. . . . Eventually Morgan's porcelain . . . was brought by J. D. Rockefeller, Henry Clay Frick, and P. A. B. Widener. . . . The three shares totalled $3,350,000. . . . It should be added that the dearest porcelain in all collection history was sold when three quarters of the world were at war . . . and when, in any case, international taste was already two moves ahead of what might have been the latest thing in the days of the greenery-yallery Grosvenor Gallery, but was now merely Middle Western." Reitlinger, *The Economics of Taste* (New York, 1963), pp. 213–214.

145   The modern works which Abby ordered: For a good summary of Abby Aldrich Rockefeller's role in establishing the modern art movement in America, see Russell Lynes's history of the Museum of Modern Art, *Good Old Modern* (New York, 1973). She recognized the irony involved in the fact that Rockefeller should sponsor avant-garde art, especially when much of it was the work of painters with radical political affiliations. Matthew Josephson tells an amusing anecdote in his recent memoir of the thirties: "Ben Shahn—now so well fleshed in the ripeness of age and success, then a lean and hungry fellow—informed me cheerfully that Mrs. Rockefeller had purchased a number of his pictures and hung them up in her bedroom, together with some of William Gropper's canvases, remarking: 'Come the Revolution, they will find I have some Groppers and Ben Shahn's pictures of Sacco and Vanzetti in my house, and they will perhaps spare me." Josephson, *Infidel in the Temple* (New York, 1967), p. 123. In the Depression, Abby would give Shahn and other impoverished artists she admired work painting portraits of horses in the Rockefeller stable at $250 a head. See Lynes, p. 345.

145   "I am interested in beauty": Fosdick, Jr., p. 329.

145   "As much as I hate not to do anything": Letter, Junior to Nelson, April 18, 1953, Rockefeller Family Archives.

145   "One of the most romantic": James J. Rorimer, *Medieval Monuments at the Cloisters* (New York, 1941), p. 5.

145   The Barnard Cloisters: "Ever since his visit to George Grey Barnard's cloister museum . . . Rockefeller's interest in medieval art and architecture had been growing stronger. The art of the Middle Ages . . . was marked by superb

craftsmanship. . . . And the profoundly religious spirit of Gothic and Romanesque sculpture went straight to Rockefeller's Baptist soul. When Barnard offered in 1925 to sell his cloister museum to the Metropolitan for $700,000, Rockefeller . . . quietly turned over to the museum shares of stock worth slightly more than a million dollars. . . . By 1927, Rockefeller and the Metropolitan had come to feel that the Fort Washington Avenue site was inadequate. . . . It so happened that Rockefeller himself owned fifty-six acres of wooded land not far to the north, overlooking the Hudson. He had bought it in 1916 and offered it to New York City as a public park; the city had refused the gift because of the landscaping expenses involved. Now Rockefeller renewed his offer, saying he would pay for the landscaping himself, but requesting that four acres at the north end of the tract be set aside for a new museum building of medieval art." Calvin Tompkins, *Merchants and Masterpieces* (New York, 1970), pp. 253–254.

146   His vacation home: For the founding of Acadia National Park, see Fosdick, pp. 302–306. For the development of the area as an upper-class retreat, see Cleveland Amory, *The Last Resorts* (New York, 1952), pp. 260–326.

146   Horace Albright: The Rockefellers' trip west is described in Albright's memoir in the Columbia Oral History Project. He kindly arranged for the authors to see a copy of the memoir at the University of California's Bancroft Library and also discussed some of the material in it in a brief interview.

147   "*Ideal* projects": Albright memoir. For three decades, political controversy and pressure from Wyoming residents stalled the acceptance of the 30,000 acres of Jackson Hole land Junior had assembled at a cost of $1.5 million. Finally, in 1950, the Jackson Hole Monument was annexed, becoming the centerpiece of the Grand Teton National Park. By that time Junior had spent several million more building the JY Ranch for himself (eventually it would become the summer home of his son Laurance) and constructing the Grand Teton Lodge and other tourist facilities operated by his conservative foundation, the Jackson Hole Preserve, Inc. For a history of the area and of the pressures and controversies surrounding the creation of the National Monument, see David Saylor, *Jackson Hole, Wyoming* (Norman, Okla., 1970), pp. 175 ff., pp. 193-199.

148   "This is Mr. Rockefeller!": Authors' interview with Newton Drury, who also kindly made Save-the-Redwoods League files available for inspection.

148   Later Junior would give money: For a tribute to Junior's conservation career, see Nancy Newhall, *A Contribution to the Heritage of Every American* (New York, 1957).

149   The competing Protestant denominations: For back-

ground on Junior's ecumenism, see the Gates Papers, Rockefeller Foundation Archives; "Religion" files in Rockefeller Family Archives; also E. B. Sanford, *Origins and History of the Federal Council* (New York, 1916); C. H. Hopkins, *The Rise of the Social Gospel in American Protestantism, 1865–1915* (New Haven, 1967): and Mathews, *John R. Mott*. Dr. Joseph Ernst feels that Junior's attitude toward disharmony in the church was largely determined by the feuding he encountered among the small Protestant churches around Seal Harbor after buying his summer home there.

149   "Would that I had the power": Speech at Baptist Social Union, December 13, 1917, Rockefeller Family Archives.

150   "I have done so": Letter, Junior to Layman's Inquiry, August 17, 1932, Rockefeller Family Archives.

150   These strands came together: For further details, see Fosdick, *Jr.*, pp. 220 ff.

151   The fundamentalists: See Norman F. Furniss, *The Fundamentalist Controversy, 1918–1931* (New Haven, Conn., 1954). Also, Harry Emerson Fosdick, *The Living of These Days* (New York, 1956), pp. 144–176.

151   "No unusual result": H. E. Fosdick, *The Living of These Days*, p. 146.

151   Lee promptly printed the sermon: Hiebert, pp. 225–228. Lee urged Junior to allow the pamphlet to be distributed under his name, but Junior refused to become involved in the controversy.

151   "An explosion of ill-will": John R. Straton, pastor of the Calvary Baptist Church in New York, said: "We are driven to the conclusion that Dr. Fosdick is not only a Baptist bootlegger, but that he is also a Presbyterian outlaw.... Dr. Fosdick is ... the Jesse James of the theological world." H. E. Fosdick, *The Living of These Days*, p. 153.

151n. The confrontation was continued: For an interesting account, including Dulles's participation, see Townsend Hoopes, *The Devil and John Foster Dulles* (New York, 1973), pp. 9–10.

151   The two men already knew each other: The meeting is described in H. E. Fosdick, *The Living of These Days*, pp. 177 ff.

152   "As you know": Letter, Junior to H.E. Fosdick, December 19, 1927, Rockefeller Family Archives.

152   "I took it for granted": Letter, H. E. Fosdick to Junior, December 22, 1927, Rockefeller Family Archives.

153   Riverside Church: For details on the founding of the church, see Fosdick, pp. 220 ff. The authors also interviewed John C. Bennett, former head of Union Theological Seminary.

153   $23 million: This figure comes from the records of the Rockefeller Family Archives.

154 Terrified of sickness: Back on June 1, 1909, Junior had
     written an interesting letter to Gates, who himself was just
     recovering from an illness: "It seems to me clear that was
     my own case four or five years ago when I had a nervous
     breakdown, it will take a number of months to bring about
     the result [rehabilitation]." Rockefeller Family Archives.

154 Michigan sanatorium: See *Abby Aldrich Rockefeller's
     Letters to Her Sister Lucy* (New York, 1957), p. 85. This
     volume of correspondence (hereafter referred to as *Abby
     Letters*) was personally selected and privately printed after
     his wife's death by Junior. A copy is in the authors' pos-
     session.

155 "At this large dinner": Ickes, *The Secret Diary of
     Harold Ickes* (New York, 1954), II, 208.

155 Billed his brother-in-law: Winthrop Aldrich personal file,
     Rockefeller Family Archives.

155 "What do I want with more money": New York
     Tribune, March 19, 1919.

156 "This estate is going to require": Memo, Gates to
     Junior, March 8, 1911, Rockefeller Family Archives.

156 Equitable Trust: For a company history, see R. Carlyle
     Bailey, *The Equitable Life Assurance Society of the United
     States* (New York, 1967). For the sequence of events lead-
     ing to the Rockefellers' purchase, see Arthur M. Johnson,
     Winthrop W. Aldrich (Boston, 1968), pp. 81 ff.

157 "Many of the fine qualities": Letter, Junior to Charles
     Evans Hughes, December 9, 1918, Rockefeller Family Ar-
     chives.

158 Albert H. Wiggin: The history of the Chase under Wig-
     gin is summarized by Johnson, pp. 100 ff. See also "Biggest
     Banker—Portrait of Wiggin of the Chase," *Fortune*, June
     1930. For a biography written by his daughter, see Marjorie
     Wiggin Prescott, *New England Son* (New York, 1949).

158 Particularly Cuba: In addition to heading a banking syn-
     dicate that financed more than $80 million in loans to the
     Machado dictatorship in Havana, the Chase had granted the
     President himself a personal loan of $130,000 with little
     prospect of repayment, an unsecured $45,000 loan to his
     construction company, and $89,000 to his shoe factory. In
     1931, while most of the Cuban government's employees re-
     mained unpaid because of the Depression, the Chase re-
     ceived payment on its debt. One of its officials noted, "It is
     only due to our close contact and friendship with General
     Machado . . . that we are receiving the payment at so early
     a date." (These facts came to light in the 1934 Senate hear-
     ings into stock exchange policies and are summarized in
     Robert F. Smith, *The United States and Cuba* [New Haven,
     Conn., 1960], pp. 122 ff.)

158 American Express: at the same time this merger was
     taking place, the law firm of Murray and Aldrich was un-

dergoing changes that would make it almost as important in
the legal world as the Chase was in banking. In May 1929,
it had merged with the firm of Webb, Patterson and Hadley.
(Vanderbilt Webb, a specialist in real estate, eventually
took on the legal affairs of Colonial Williamsburg and other
Rockefeller projects; Robert Patterson left the firm in 1930
to become a federal judge and, eventually, Secretary of War
in the Truman administration.) In 1931, as Aldrich was becoming more and more involved in the Chase merger,
Junior got the firm to bring in an old college friend, Albert
Milbank, and the firm of Milbank, Tweed, Hope and Webb
was formed. (For details on the history and evolution of the
firm, see the work by two of its later partners, Timothy
Pfeiffer and Georges W. Jacques, *Law Practice in a Turbulent World* [New York 1965]; also Paul Hoffman, *Lions in
the Street* [New York, 1973].) One of the partners, Harrison Tweed, alter discussed the negotiations that brought
Milbank (until 1931 a member of the law firm of Masten
and Nichols) into the expanded Murray, Aldrich firm:
"Frankly we did not like the idea of a merger with the
whole Masten and Nichols outfit. The original idea had
been that we could bring into our firm the lawyer who was
at that time the head of Masten and Nichols, Albert Milbank ... [who] had John D. Rockefeller [Junior's] confidence.... However, Mr. Milbank wasn't willing to leave his
whole firm in the lurch, so the problem was to merge the
whole kit and kaboodle." Tweed goes on to say that several
partners in the Murray, Aldrich firm wanted to say, "To hell
with the whole thing! Let's go ahead and see where we end
up without Milbank, or Masten and Nichols, or perhaps
without Rockefeller!" But Junior and the Chase were too important as clients, and the merger was consummated. (See
the Harrison Tweed Memoir in the Columbia Oral History
Project.)

158 "In no small measure a monument": Johnson, p. 36.
159 A step farther: For details on Aldrich's career as
banking reformer, see Johnson, pp. 149 ff. Also, "Bank Reform by Bankers," *Business Week,* April 26, 1933.
159 A stalking horse: This thesis was later put forward by
Ferdinand Lundberg, *America's Sixty Families* (New York,
1938), p. 461.
160 Under grueling review: See Senate Committee on
Banking and Currency, *Hearings on the Securities Act*
(Washington, D.C., 1933), and Senate Committee on
Banking and Currency, *Hearings on Stock Exchange Practices* (Washington, D.C., 1934). Also, Ferdinand Pecora,
Wall Street Under Oath (New York, 1939).
160 Cut adrift: See Johnson, pp. 167 ff.
160 President Roosevelt told Aldrich: Johnson, p. 181.

160   "It should be recognized": Johnson, p. 182. Although Aldrich realized that it was expedient to occupy the role momentarily, as the banking crisis cooled, he reverted to a more comfortable conservative stance. The differences between him and Wiggin, Pecora wrote five years later, "were of sensational interest to the country in 1933, for in the minds of the general public, Mr. Aldrich meant the Rockefellers, and his placatory attitude was taken by the public to indicate a willingness on the part of the vast Rockefeller interests to cooperate with the still emerging New Deal. More recent pronouncements would seem to indicate that Mr. Aldrich's enthusiasm for reform has perhaps undergone a certain cooling process with the passage of the years and the change in circumstances. But at that time, at any rate, he fairly out-Heroded Herod" (Pecora, p. 137).

161   Robert W. Stewart: For an account of Stewart's career, see Paul H. Giddens, *Standard Oil Company (Indiana): Oil Pioneer of the Middle West* (New York, 1955), pp. 210 ff.

161   A ditty he himself had composed: Giddens, p. 333.

162   "If petroleum is to have another Rockefeller": *New York Times,* April 12, 1925.

162   The trust had been broken: For the shuffle to reorganize the trust after the Supreme Court decision, see Gibbs and Knowlton, especially, pp. 15–43.

163   Refused to do business: The thesis that the fight between Stewart and the Rockefellers was at least partially precipitated by Stewart's defiance of the Standard system is argued by Albert Z. Carr, *John D. Rockefeller's Secret Weapon* (New York, 1962), pp. 202 ff.

163   A merger: For details on Stewart's struggle to secure an independent supply of crude for Indiana, see Giddens, pp. 238–249.

164   Stewart's own involvement: For details, see Giddens, pp. 361 ff. Also, Senate Committee on Public Lands and Surveys, *Hearings on Leases upon Naval Oil Reserves* (Washington, D.C., 1929).

165   "Yourself, your company": Telegram, Junior to William M. Burton, March 22, 1925.

166   Ralph Pulitzer: Giddens, p. 369.

166   "I have personally": Junior's testimony is cited by Fosdick, *Jr.,* p. 237.

166n. Rodgers then wrote an editorial: The anecdote comes from Cleveland Rodgers's memoir in the Columbia Oral History Project.

167   The field marshal: For Aldrich's role in the Stewart ouster, see Johnson, pp. 61–66.

167   Coded telegrams: The authors have inspected them in the Rockefeller Family Archives.

167 He invoked his record: For Stewart's strategy in the struggle, see Giddens, pp. 403–435.

169 "In all the discouraging mess": Chicago *Evening Post*, February 13, 1928.

169 "Conscience and courage": This is also Fosdick's view of the matter. He says, of the Indiana proxy fight, "Nor did anything that the younger Rockefeller ever undertook prove so conclusively his courage and integrity" (*Jr.*, p. 229).

169 Indiana's new directors decided to sell: For circumstances of the sale of Pan American Petroleum, see Giddens, pp. 489 ff.

169n. "The more I hear": Letter, Debevoise to Seubert, April 5, 1929, Rockefeller Family Archives.

170 "These are days": Senior's statement on the Depression was reprinted in Ivy Lee's pamphlet, *History Repeats and Depressions Do Pass* (New York, 1933). John Kenneth Galbraith says of this statement: "So far as the record shows, it was spontaneous. However, someone in Wall Street—perhaps someone who knew that another appeal to President Hoover to say something specifically encouraging about stocks would be useless—may have realized that a statement from Rockefeller would, if anything, be better." Galbraith, *The Great Crash* (New York, 1961), p. 124.

171 To peg Standard Oil: Junior and his aides were extremely upset by the Hoover administration's inaction on the economic situation. In 1930 the President attempted to placate them by appointing Colonel Arthur Woods to head a task force on unemployment. Woods went to Washington convinced that a billion-dollar public works project was immediately needed. When Hoover vetoed a bill providing for a federal employment agency, Woods resigned in annoyance and returned to New York. Rockefeller Family Archive sources.

171 An epic sign of faith: For a semiofficial history of Rockefeller Center based on material in the Rockefeller Family Archives and interviews with many of the principals, see David Loth, *The City Within a City* (New York, 1966).

171 "A man gets into a situation": Fosdick, *Jr.*, p. 266.

171 $45 million of which: Loth, p. 59.

172 Forced to sell some Standard of New York: Wallace Harrison, authors' interview.

172 Grandfather's ruler: Ann Rockefeller Pierson, authors' interview.

172 The decision showed spunk: Fosdick (*Jr.*, p. 265) sees the decision to proceed as just another element in Junior's complex fate that "required a high degree of courage." Such a view was not shared by a contemporary article in *Fortune*: "To Mr. Rockefeller came a simple, clear idea, an idea that measured up to the stature of his fortune. Then to

Mr. Rockefeller came man after man, hurtling, each with something to do with the idea. Almost from his acceptance of it, the Junior Rockefeller was on the defensive. More personalities, more ideas, pressed in on him. His back was to the wall; he was submerged. Rockefeller Center will be an accomplished fact. Rockefeller's marks are upon it—one can feel in its lines his cautiousness, his thoughtfulness, his forethoughtfulness, his careful weighing of this plan and that—but they are all the marks of negation. Nowhere is the bold stroking of the creator, the firm, hard lines of the man who conceives. In it there is everything John D. Rockefeller might want—a monument, an investment (whether he makes 6 percent or 2). Everything he might want but the freedom of greatness." "The Rockefellers in Finance," *Fortune*, December 1931, p. 132.

172 "I envy you": Ibid., p. 130.

172 The old Cleveland estate: See "Mr. Rockefeller Returns to Cleveland," *Fortune*, July 1931, pp. 30 ff.

173 Modern housing: Details on the Bayonne housing, the Bronx apartments, and the Paul Laurence Dunbar apartments (including the statement by Charles O. Heydt) are in the respective files for these enterprises in the Rockefeller Family Archives.

174 "From now on": Loth, p. 42.

174 Lewis Mumford: In December 1933 *New Yorker,* Mumford wrote about the Center: "It lacks the distinction, the strength, the confidence of good architecture, just because it lacks any solidity of purpose and sincerity of intention. On the one hand the projectors have eaten into a colossal fortune with a series of bad guesses, blind stabs, and grandiose inanities; on the other, they have trimmed and played for a decent mediocrity. And the whole effect of the Center is mediocrity—seen through a magnifying glass."

174 "Through all the publicity": Letter. Debevoise to Lee, January 23, 1933. Ivy Lee Papers, Princeton University Library.

175 "The family name plastered all over": Fosdick, *Jr.*, p. 269.

175 The name of the project: "John R. Todd . . . asked Lee to come up with a name for it and he 'cudgelled' his brain. He turned down 'Radio City' as 'catchy', valuable only from the standpoint of amusement, not renting.... Rockefeller did not want to have his name connected with the project, but Lee finally said, 'It is unquestionable that the natural name for the district would be something like Rockefeller Center' " (Hiebert, p. 140). "John Todd argued for the name 'Rockefeller' on the ground that it was a good drawing card. 'It's your money,' Raymond Fosdick remembered him saying in the course of one meeting. 'Why not use the name?' " (Loth, p. 70).

175 "I'm like your bike": Cited in Joe Alex Morris, *Those Rockefeller Brothers* (New York, 1953), p. 13.

175 "I think you might say": *Abby Letters*, p. 238.

175 Funeral services: For details see Nevins, II, 424–425; also *New York Times*, May 25, 1937.

III *The Brothers*

PAGE

179 "No child of mine": Cleveland Amory, *Who Killed Society?* (New York, 1960), p. 370.

180 Their spending money: Joe Alex Morris, *Those Rockefeller Brothers* (New York, 1953), p. 26.

180 "I was always so afraid": Fosdick Notes (on conversations with Junior), Rockefeller Family Archives.

181 John 3rd was most often rewarded: Morris, *Those Rockefeller Brothers*, p. 16.

181 "Who do you think we are": The ancedote appears in a slightly different form in Morris, *Those Rockefeller Brothers*, p. 21. It was told by the brothers during the CBS documentary on the family telecast in the fall of 1973. See also Cleveland Amory, *The Last Resorts* (New York, 1952), p. 316. Wealth was a subject much on the minds of the Rockefeller elders. In 1909, Senior wrote Junior, "I know that you and Abby will be careful to educate the children in financial matters as we sought to educate you, that they may understand the value of money and make the very best of it." Cited in Allan Nevins, *John D. Rockefeller: A Study in Power* (New York, 1953), II, 410. Junior hardly needed reminding. He told a *Saturday Evening Post* interviewer: "Wealth will go only to those of them who show fitness and the ability to handle it wisely; neither their father, nor grandfather, will leave them money unless they give evidence that they know how to lead decent, useful lives." A. W. Atwood, "The Rockefeller Fortune," *Saturday Evening Post*, June 11, 1921.

181 Even Winthrop: The recollection comes from "A Letter to My Son," an unpublished typescript memoir Winthrop dictated of his experiences up to the end of World War II. A copy of the memoir is in the Rockefeller Family Archives. The authors were given permission to see it by Winthrop's son, Winthrop Paul Rockefeller.

182 3,500-acre estate: For an interesting "inside" view of Pocantico, see Tom Pyle, *Pocantico* (New York, 1964). (For thirty-five years, Pyle worked as the Rockefellers' head groundskeeper.) While the daily life Pyle describes was taking place, Junior was working hard to consolidate the estate. His efforts came on a variety of fronts, and on March 23, 1929, his ten-year effort was climaxed by the announcement that he had paid $900,000 to the New York Central to get the railroad to relocate its tracks, which cut through the es-

tate, to the old colonial village of East View, on the outskirts of Tarrytown. Junior had bought East View (consisting of the homes of 46 families, a post office, and some dance halls) for $825,000 and had ordered that the houses, many of them built during the historic Dutch period, be razed. After this was completed, he turned his attention to the nearby town of Pocantico Hills, making it the personal equivalent of a company town. On July 17, 1929, the *New York Times* wrote, "Pocantico Hills seemed destined today to go the way the hamlet of East View went—into the ever-growing Rockefeller estate. John D. Rockefeller, Jr., purchased two more parcels of land in the community today. Now there are only 12 parcels of land in the neighborhood which the Rockefellers do not own. Thirty-five years ago, Pocantico Hills was a thriving village of nearly 1,500 persons. Today the population is under one hundred, and there are only about a dozen families left." (For details on the New York Central's tracks, the purchase of East View, and the evolution of Pocantico Hills into a satellite of the Rockefeller estate, see the *New York Times*, March 22, 23; May 29; and July 17, 1929.)

183   The boys got "red bugs": "A Letter to My Son."

183   "We never leave any litter": Pyle, p. 85.

184   Grandfather had been sick: "A Letter to My Son."

184   "Even in the machine age": Cited in Morris, *Those Rockefeller Brothers*, p. 17.

184   The role of teacher: See John C. Fistere, "The Rockefeller Boys," *Saturday Evening Post*, August 16, 1938, p. 34.

185   Help the porter: For a description of the Rockefeller brothers on the trip west, see the Horace Albright memoir in the Columbia Oral History Project.

186   He left that to his wife: "She always seems to understand them," Junior said of Abby. "She has the intuition, the sympathy, and the patience" (Fosdick, p. 426).

186   "Your father": Mary Ellen Chase, *Abby Aldrich Rockefeller* (New York, 1950), p. 44.

186   She was kidnapped: Lucy Aldrich wrote a firsthand account of this experience, "A Week-End with Chinese Bandits," in the *Atlantic Monthly*, November 1923.

187   "We sang hymns": Joe Alex Morris, *Nelson Rockefeller* (New York, 1960), p. 21. (Hereafter, to distinguish between the two Morris books, *Those Rockefeller Brothers* will be cited as *TRB* and *Nelson Rockefeller* as *NR*.)

187   Abstinence: Morris, *TRB*, p. 29.

187   "Can I beat my brothers?": Pyle, p. 122.

188   "Two cousins": "A Letter to My Son."

189   "When you boys come home": Chase, p. 43.

188   Winthrop on a seesaw: The incident is related at length in "A Letter to My Son."

189 Babs: The details about her youth are distilled from authors' interviews with family members.

189 He was tall, blond, athletic: Pyle, p. 82.

189 "Cerebral nunnery": Authors' interview with David
Rockefeller, Jr.

189 "As so many sticks": Pyle, p. 82.

189 "Discouraging letter": Chase, p. 61.

190 Brainchild of Abraham Flexner: For further details on
the evolution of Lincoln, see Raymond Fosdick, *Adventure
in Giving* (New York, 1962), pp. 215–225; also, Abraham
Flexner, *An Autobiography* (New York, 1960), and Laurance A. Cremin. *The Transformation of the School* (New
York, 1961), especially pp. 281–291. The following is also
based on authors' interviews with Mrs. Linda Storrow and
Mrs. Louise Marr.

191 "I never in my life": Morris, *NR*, p. 16.

191 "Prince of Wales": See *The Outlook*, December 18,
1929, pp. 617–618.

192 Princeton: JDR3's years in college and directly afterward are discussed in Morris, *TRB*, pp. 43 ff.

192 "I don't think": Fistere, "The Rockefeller Boys," p. 36.

193 "A cool, pale beauty": The writer is Aline Saarinen. The
statement is cited by Russell Lynes, *Good Old Modern*
(New York, 1973), p. 279.

193 Institute for Pacific Relations: The Rockefeller family
was involved in this organization since its beginnings, when
Ray Lyman Wilbur (Stanford president, trustee of the
Rockefeller Foundation, and Secretary of the Interior under
Hoover) wrote to Junior to tell him that the institute was
being formed: "The necessity for a better understanding and
a closer cooperation between the Pacific peoples concerning
their common interests and problems ... has inspired the
proposal by citizens of Hawaii of an unofficial international
institute to be held in Honolulu in July, 1925." Letter, Wilbur to Junior, March 10, 1925, Rockefeller Family Archives. This advice fit in perfectly with the internationalist
agenda Fosdick and other close advisers were already
pressing on Rockefeller. By 1930, when JDR3 attended the
institute's Kyoto conference, Junior was a major sponsor of
the organization.

193 Juvenile delinquency: See Leonard Harrison, *Youth in
the Toils* (New York, 1938), preface by John D. Rockefeller 3rd.

193 Junior did expect his sons: Junior always thought of
himself primarily as a transition between the first Rockefeller generation and the third; he venerated his father and
had an epic future in mind for his children. In 1917, following America's entry into World War I, his friend and
Associate Walter Hines Page, recently named ambassador to
the Court of St. James's, urged Junior to visit England and

make the friends and connections that were vital to the accumulation of social power. ("If we manage wisely the opportunity that these great tragic events have given us," Page wrote, "we will put ourselves distinctly in the lead of the English-speaking world and therefore in the lead of the whole world.") Junior was not unmindful of the yield, but didn't want to take the risks of an Atlantic crossing. He replied, "Being my father's only son, he now being 78 years old, there have fallen on my shoulders and will increasingly, responsibilities that are unique and obligations equally unique. . . . Perhaps the greatest contribution I can make to the world will be the rearing of these six children in such a manner as will make them useful citizens." Rockefeller Family Archives.

194 "My father": Authors' interview with JDR3.

194 "John was": Authors' interview with Howard Knowles.

195 Left-handedness: Morris, NR, p. 13.

195 "The example of my grandfathers": Geoffrey T. Hellman, "Best Neighbor," New Yorker, April 18, 1942, p. 24.

196 "Very high I.Q.": Ibid., p. 22.

197 "A warped and erroneous view": Ray Eldon Hiebert, Courtier to the Crowd (Ames, Iowa, 1966), p. 128.

197 "I don't know when": Morris, NR, p. 44. In his thesis (for which he received an "A") Nelson breezily dismissed charges against the Standard trust and its founder, as this sample indicates: "It might be well to mention a very important point and one that has never been understood by the public—namely the reason for Mr. Rockefeller's silence all through the history of the Standard Oil Company in the face of bitterest attack and slander. There are two main reasons: 1. That the accusations were false and therefore would fall of their own weight when time had revealed the truth. 2. That if any public explanation of the real reasons for the great and quick successes of the company were attempted, it might have been made so full and explicit that it would necessarily invite other capitalists to come into the business and do likewise." Cited by Morris, NR, pp. 45 ff.

197 "It seems funny": Morris, NR, p. 68.

197 "Just to work my way": Ibid., p. 50.

198 "In love with Tod": Ibid., p. 50.

198 Mary Clark: See Frank Gervasi, The Real Rockefeller (New York, 1964), pp. 61 ff.; also Morris, NR, pp. 81 ff.

199 Gandhi: "At New Delhi, they called on the Viceroy of India. . . . Rockefeller also had a letter to Gandhi and was rather put out, upon arriving in New Delhi, to find that the Mahatma was in jail and not receiving. The Rockefellers went to Bombay and later returned to New Delhi to call on Gandhi, who was by then out of jail and available in a restricted way, for social life. 'The first day we went to his house it was his day of silence because he didn't say a

word. He wrote me a note saying, "Come back tomorrow. I'll talk to you." We got there at five in the morning, and then piled in his car and went to the fort in the old part of the city.... He told us his whole background, his relations with the British. It gave me the Indian point of view. I have a great interest in the other person's point of view. He showed no interest in me whatever' " (Hellman, p. 24).

200 "My justification": Letter, Nelson to Junior, July 3, 1933, Rockefeller Family Archives.

200 He wrote his father: Letter, Nelson to Junior, July 3, 1933, Rockefeller Family Archives. Morris quotes the letter too (*NR*, p. 98), but in a way that illustrates how a strategically elided sentence can alter the character of documentary evidence. "My plan is to become more familiar with all phases of your real estate interests and to avail myself of every opportunity to get acquainted with your oil, coal, and banking interests" becomes "My plan is to become more familiar with all phases of your . . . interests." The result is to negate the fact that Nelson was fascinated by the immensity of the economic power invested in the Rockefeller name and anxious to use it to further his own interests: it allows for a more flattering interpretation of his character as one whose most profound desire is to promote the general good, for the image—to use Morris's term—of "the good knight."

201 "For many years": Memo, Debevoise to Nelson, October 18, 1935, Rockefeller Family Archives.

203 "I have today": Letter, Junior to Laurance, December 18, 1934, Rockefeller Family Archives. His sons were well into their twenties, but Junior had not given up his pedagogic duties, as the formidable tone of the concluding sentences of this letter suggests: "The trust fund set up for you will add somewhat to your present surplus income. It has the same machinery for its care and distribution as those for the older children. This has been done in the hope and confident belief that I can safely add thereto from time to time as your experience grows and you demonstrate your ability to carry easily larger responsibilities. As that happens, I should hope that you would be disposed to continue to devote any surplus over and above what may be reasonably necessary for your current living expenses and to enable you to meet the obligations, social, civic, and philanthropic, properly falling upon one in your walk of life, to building up for yourself a principal fund adequate to meet the larger responsibilities of life that will come to you as the years go by."

203 Inheritance tax: See Ferdinand Lundberg, *America's Sixty Families* (New York, 1937), pp. 464–465.

204 Young George Meany: The arrangement between Meany

and Nelson is referred to in Nelson Cruickshank's memoir in the Columbia Oral History Project.

205 "Graceful little speeches": Hellman, p. 26.

205 Junior Advisory Committee: For a summary of Nelson's early career in the Museum of Modern Art, see Lynes, pp. 75 ff.

205 "I learned my politics": Lynes. p. 151.

206n. "From time to time": Letter, Junior to his sons, July 25, 1945, Rockefeller Family Archives.

207 Nelson went to London: There was never any doubt about what the trip was for. Shortly after Nelson had returned to the United States, he wrote to his father asking for reimbursement for the trip, whose purpose had been (he said) "to make possible the continuation of the study of banking which I had been carrying on for many months in the Chase Bank here in New York and also to enable me to have some contact with foreign bankers, as well as the foreign representatives of oil companies in which we have substantial stock interests." Letter, Nelson to Junior, February 9, 1937, Rockefeller Family Archives.

207 "I have talked with him": Letter, Nelson to Fred Gehle, June 18, 1935, Rockefeller Family Archives.

207 Venezuelan crude: For a history of the fields of Lake Maracaibo and the growth of Venezuela's oil economy, see Edwin Lieuwen, "A History of Petroleum in Venezuela" (Ph.D. dissertation, University of California, 1952).

208 Gómez: For details on the dictatorship, see Herbert Wendt, *The Red, White and Black Continent* (New York, 1964).

208 Up Venezuela's Orinoco: See Morris, *NR*, pp. 111 ff.

208 "Unless something unforeseen": Ibid.

209 "Much of a reader": Authors' interview with Carl Spaeth.

209 Arthur Proudfit: For a history of Creole's early experiences in Venezuela, see "Creole Petroleum," *Fortune*, February 1949.

210 *Compania:* The following is distilled from files on the Venezuelan venture in the Rockefeller Family Archives.

210 Nelson had gone to Jersey: Authors' interview with Carl Spaeth.

210 The summer of 1940: Letter, Robert Bottome to Nelson, August 15, 1940, Rockefeller Family Archives.

210n. "The idea rather appeals": Letter, Robert Bottome to Nelson, March 16, 1940, Rockefeller Family Archives.

211 "To postpone such programs": Letter, Carl Spaeth to Nelson, September 19, 1940, Rockefeller Family Archives.

211 A war council: Discussed by Morris, *NR*, pp. 125 ff.

211 "The sort of men": Attributed to Rovensky as a characteristic statement by Wallace Harrison during authors' interview. Carl Spaeth adds: "Joe Rovensky was the 'check-it-

out' man. 'If it looks all right with Joe,' Nelson used to say, 'then it's all right.' There were two types of meetings: those Rovensky had with Nelson alone and those involving the rest of us. I don't know what went on when they were alone, but when I was there, Rovensky said little. He played his cards close to his vest. He was the wise man among us" (authors' interview).

212 "Big, round, rumbling": Robert Moses, *Public Works* (New York, 1970), p. 629. Wallace Harrison says, "Bee Ruml was a genius. He had been pals with Robert Hutchins at the University of Chicago and was brilliant in the way that others in that crowd were. He was the intellectual of The Group" (authors' interview).

212 "Regardless of whether the outcome": Cited in Morris, *NR*, p. 129.

212 James Forrestal: For details on his life and government service, see Arnold A. Rogow, *James Forrestal* (New York, 1963).

213 Come to Washington: For details on the Forrestal offer, see Morris, *NR*, pp. 130–131. William Clayton, who later worked with Rockefeller in the OIAA, states that Paul Nitze told him that Forrestal did not think Nelson was the best man for the job, and had placed him third on a list of ten names which were taken to Roosevelt for his choice. He told Nitze, "Nelson doesn't have the kind of ability needed for the job." But the President selected him over the other candidates. Clayton memoir in the Columbia Oral History Project.

213 Willkie: "Before he could finish explaining his reservations about going to Washington, Willkie's rich, gravelly baritone broke in. 'If I were President in a time of international crisis, such as today, and I asked someone to come to Washington to help in the field of foreign affairs, and he turned me down for political reasons, I don't need to tell you what I would think of him. Of course you should go'" (Gervasi, p. 74).

214 Socially adept: Details of Laurance's early adulthood are distilled from the authors' interviews with various family members.

214 Princeton: For Laurance's college experiences, see Morris, *TRB*, pp. 100 ff.; also, Richard A. Smith, "The Rockefeller Brothers," *Fortune*, March 1955, p. 166.

215 Passing his finals: On March 23, 1934, Abby Aldrich Rockefeller wrote her sister Lucy of Laurance: "He has found a brilliant Boston lawyer, who is tutoring him. As you perhaps know, Laurance did very well at the law school when it was a question of using his own initiative, but he allowed his work to get very much behind when the question of just pure grind and learning the fundamentals of the law had to be solved. Suddenly he seems to have awakened

to the fact of just where he stood and that unless he did something he would not pass his examinations." *Abby Aldrich Rockefeller's Letters to Her Sister Lucy* (New York, 1957), pp. 213–214. (This work is hereafter referred to as *Abby Letters*.)

215 Cholly Knickerbocker: See Fistere, p. 38.

216 James S. McDonnell: Details come from authors' interview with Gordon Le Bert, archivist for the McDonnell-Douglas corporation. Also, McDonnell files in Rockefeller Family Archives.

216 So deeply involved: Laurance was anxious to weld his own early investment efforts to the family's financial base. On July 8, 1938, R. C. Oertel, a representative of Jersey Standard, met with Laurance to ask him to use his influence to get Eastern Airlines to use Esso aviation fuel. On August 19, Laurance responded, "As you know, the company [Eastern] is now exclusively using Gulf products and I am naturally anxious that a way can be found to justify a change." Eastern Airlines files, Rockefeller Family Archives.

216 "As you know": Letter, Laurance to Junior, November 27, 1940. Rockefeller Family Archives.

217 Children of JDR3 and Babs: See Part IV of text.

217 Winthrop's vulnerability: See "A Letter to My Son": *Abby Letters*. For a more antiseptic view of Winthrop's youth and adolescence, see Morris, *TRB*, pp. 107 ff.

218 Childhood impression: Authors' interview with confidential source.

218 At Lincoln: Authors' interview with Mrs. Linda Storrow.

218 "Thank fortune": *Abby Letters*, p. 169.

218 Winthrop's accounts: See "A Letter to My Son."

219 "Unfortunately, I got over that": Ibid.

219 Roughneck: Winthrop relates his oil field experiences in detail in "A Letter to My Son." On July 25, 1935, Abby wrote her sister Lucy, "[Winthrop] simply adores what he is doing and everybody says that he is making many friends and doing awfully well. Nelson says that he is much impressed with the seriousness with which Winthrop has entered into the work and the grasp he has of the whole situation" (*Abby Letters*, p. 203). "[Texas offered] a way of life that suited him far better than Pocantico ever had. From his first long visit out there, the West caught and held Winnie. . . . He loved the great expanses of land, the breezy comradeship he found in Texas. Men's names weren't too important out here —a fellow was still judged, in ranch country, by how well he could ride and shoot. In a man's world, Winnie could win his spurs anytime" (Pyle, p. 123).

219 A revolver: When newspaper accounts suggested that Winthrop carried a revolver, family sources denied it. How-

ever, Tom Pyle writes: "He showed me, with great pride, a wicked-looking, .45 nickel-plated revolver that he'd brought back to Pocantico from Texas. When I examined it, I found the serial number had been filed off.

" 'Where did you get this, Win—' I asked him.

" 'From a drifter—a fellow who just blew into the ranch one day looking for a day's work.'

" 'Well, you better get rid of it,' I warned him. 'It's hot.' "Winnie's face fell with disappointment. But he reported it, and orders came through from the office to dispose of the gun, which we did" (pp. 123–125).

220 "Wissy-Wissy": In an oral history taped at Winrock, Arkansas, October 18, 1973, Mrs. Margaret Black, Winthrop's housekeeper, confidante, and sometime hostess, told Dr. Joseph Ernst that "Winthrop hated it when Nelson would introduce him as, 'This is my little brother, Wissy Wissy.' It was the name he'd taunted him with when they were children."

220 "Give him the army": Authors' interview with confidential source.

220 "Uncle John": Authors' interview with Peggy Rockefeller.

221 Horace Albright: See Albright memoir.

221 Private collection: In 1948, David gave $2,500 to the museum to go toward the salary of a coleopterist. Between 1941 and 1949, he gave over $15,000 for the purchase of beetle specimens. When he sent his own collection to the museum in the late fifties to be catalogued, there were some 110 unidentified species in it. Museum of Natural History file, Rockefeller Family Archives.

221 "Fat and lazy": Pyle, p. 78.

222 "David was younger": Authors' interview with Mrs. Marr.

222 "He has a fine mind": Letter, Junior to King, March 9, 1936, Rockefeller Family Archives.

222 David went to London: For a summary of David's early adulthood, see Morris, *TRB*, pp. 125 ff.

222 "Winny is coming along": Letter, Nelson to David, January 20, 1938, Rockefeller Family Archives.

223 "David Rockefeller was in": Ickes, *The Secret Diary of Harold Ickes* (New York, 1954), II, 655.

223 "City Hall": Cited by William Hoffman in *David* (New York, 1971), p. 99.

223 "The danger": Morris, *TRB*, p. 130.

224 I. G. Farben: See Richard Sasuly, *I. G. Farben* (New York, 1947), also, Senate Subcommittee on War Mobilization, *Report on I. G. Farben* (Washingcon, D.C., 1946). Ivy Lee found that working with Hitler's image was different from manipulating the public relations of American businessmen. In a memo to German Foreign Minister von

Ribbentrop, he sought to indicate the interpretation Germany should try to put on its rearmament activities: "The National Socialist government has repeatedly proclaimed its sincere desire for international peace. . . . It should be clearly understood that the German people are not asking for arms but for equality of rights." He urged that the 2.5 million man army be described only as a group "between the ages of 18 and 60, physically well trained and disciplined, but not armed, not prepared for war, and organized only for the purpose of preventing for all time the return of the Communist peril" (Hiebert, pp. 290–291).

224 Truman Committee: See *Newsweek*, June 8, 1942, for an account of the committee, including the statement by Truman; also Merle Miller, *Plain Speaking* (New York, 1973), pp. 173 ff., for Truman's own account of the committee's work.

224 "It is only another": William E. Dodd, *Ambassador Dodd's Diary* (New York, 1941), p. 155.

224 Disturbed after six: Hiebert, p. 311.

224 "The country has lost": Telegram, Nelson to Mrs. Ivy Lee, November 9, 1934, Rockefeller Family Archives.

225 Elegant letter: "From the early days of my contact with your husband it became clear to me that his point of view was the same as ours, that complete sincerity, honesty and integrity were the fundamental principles which regulated his daily life. . . . What he did for us in the Colorado situation and in the general relation of our family and business interest to the public thereafter was of the greatest value." Letter, Junior to Mrs. Ivy Lee, August 26, 1935, Ivy Lee Papers.

225 Rockefellers were mobilized: Some saw the family as class heroes. Walter Hope, a partner in the Milbank, Tweed firm, wrote Junior a letter at the onset of the war commending his success as a parent. After noting that each of the five brothers was serving his country, Hope said: "We have been going through a period when the possession of wealth has been under scrutiny, if not suspicion. Furthermore, the impact of war has furnished more powerful weapons to those who, behind the scenes, are working for a general levelling process, regardless of the human and spiritual values lost hereby. The public has not as yet wholly made·up its mind, and under these circumstances, a visual demonstration of a sense of individual responsibility and a stewardship of wealth in the public interest is exceedingly helpful." Letter, Walter Hope to Junior, January 20, 1942, Rockefeller Family Archives. Junior sent a copy of the letter to each of his sons.

225 USO: One of Junior's aides from this period says, "He put a lot of time and money into the USO. There's no doubt that he was the driving force behind the organization

and personally held it together." Authors' interview with Lindsley Kimball.

226 A series of benches: Chase p. 95.

226 War news: Ibid., p. 91.

226 "The Eager Beaver": David Lillienthal, *The Journals of David Lillienthal* (New York, 1966), III, 134.

226 Experts: "Bee Ruml was a kind of genius. He would come to Washington after a couple of weeks with a whole new set of ideas. He wasn't a counsellor like Rovensky. He was more an idea man, a moving resource. Ruml was only unlike Harrison, who was there primarily because he was loyal. Nelson liked Wally, and he never had to worry about him coming out with dangerous or controversial ideas. Lockwood was very sharp, usually on the bearish side of things, which Nelson's enthusiastic nature needed." Authors' interview with Carl Spaeth.

226 "Yes-man": Stewart Alsop, *Nixon and Rockefeller* (New York, 1960), p. 87.

227 One woman: Authors' interview wih Mrs. Linda Storrow.

227 Plunged ahead: For details on the early days of OIAA, see Morris, *NR*, pp. 133 ff.

227 "Nelson was addicted": Authors' interview, confidential source.

228 Hemispheric ties: For a study of the United States' Latin American policy before and during Nelson's tenure at OIAA, see David Green, *The Containment of Latin America* (Chicago, 1971); also, Lloyd Gardner, *Economic Aspects of New Deal Diplomacy* (Madison, Wis., 1964).

228 "A major objective": See Nelson Rockefeller, "Hemispheric Solidarity," *Survey Graphic*, March 1941.

228 Rovensky plan: Green, p. 139.

228n. OIAA memo: Ibid., p. 140.

229 Totalitarian propaganda": Rockefeller, Hemispheric Solidarity."

229 Tours and exchanges: For an insider's view of the work of the Coordinator's Office, see the Francis Jamieson memoir in the Columbia Oral History Project. The authors are grateful to Mrs. Linda Storrow for supplying her personal copy and the permission to quote from it.

229 Conservative critics: See Morris, *NR*, pp. 147 ff.

230 Henry Wallace: See Blum, ed., *The Price of Vision: The Diary of Henry A. Wallace* (New York, 1973), p. 146.

230 Most glamorous: When *Life* magazine discussed Nelson's job, for instance, the story was headlined "Celebrated Young Heir Runs a Much Discussed and Increasingly Important Washington Bureau."

230 Jamieson: Details of his early career come from the memoir in the Columbia Oral History Project; facts regarding his work with the OIAA and later career are drawn

both from the memoir and from interviews with Carl
Spaeth, John Lockwood, Wallace Harrison, and Jamieson's
widow, Mrs. Linda Storrow.

230n. "Incidental to his job":   *New Republic*, July 2, 1945, pp.
9–11.

231   Long-term economic development: In 1942, Nelson recruited J. D. LeCron to direct the Food and Supply Division of the Institute of Inter-American Affairs (a satellite
organization of OIAA). LeCron's job was increasing production of food in Latin America through cooperative funding
and manpower. His projects had to be cleared by the Division of Economic Operations of the State Department,
headed by Emile G. Collado (later a vice-president and
director of Jersey Standard). Collado so frustrated LeCron,
and he got so little support from Rockefeller, that he ultimately concluded that economic development was not taken
seriously in the coordinator's office and resigned in disgust.
See the J. D. LeCron memoir in the Columbia Oral History
Project.

231   "Very definite ideas": Letter, Laurance Duggan to Summer Welles, December 29, 1942, cited in Green, p. 135.

231   "In Latin America": Sanchez statement cited in Green,
p. 111.

232   "With a full heart": Letter, Junior to Nelson, May 18,
1944, Rockefeller Family Archives.

232   The *President* who wanted him: See Morris, *NR*, p. 184.
In fact, Nelson had been angling unsuccessfully for the Assistant Secretary's job for some time. Describing "the parade
of ambitious men" at Shangri-la (as Roosevelt's mountain
retreat was called), William O. Douglas writes of the period
a year before Rockefeller actually got the post: "I particularly remember a weekend with Nelson Rockefeller. . . . He
wanted at that time to be the Assistant Secretary of State in
charge of Latin American Affairs. He talked about it as we
hiked the countryside and I expressed my support of his
ambition.

" 'Will the Boss offer me the job?' he kept asking me.

"I was not in on the secret, but I did know FDR. So
when, on our return to quarters late that afternoon, Nelson
asked me what I thought his chances were, I replied, 'Nelson, if FDR was going to make you Assistant Secretary of
State he would not bring you down here for a weekend,
keeping you full of suspense.'

" 'Then why was I invited?'

" 'I'm not sure, but I think it's a consolation prize.' "
Douglas, *Go East, Young Man* (New York, 1974), pp.
364–365.

233   Defense Board meeting: Nelson recalled the scene seven
years later when testifying before the House Committee on
Foreign Affairs in support of President Truman's Mutual

Security program. The testimony was reprinted as "A New Approach to International Security," *Department of State Bulletin*, August 27, 1951, pp. 328 ff.

233 Inter-American Conference: For events leading up to the conference, see Morris, *NR*, p. 189.

234 Carried by Rockefeller: A. A. Berle, Jr., noted in his diary at the time, "Leo Pasvolsky and others objected on the grounds that it committed the United States to use of force, whereas at the Dumbarton Oaks conference they had agreed that no one should be allowed to use force without consent of the World Council [U.N.]. . . . At this point, Generals Embick, Strong, Walsh and Hertford blew up, pointing out . . . that by breaking up the unity of the hemisphere . . . we sacrificed a military entity capable of defense. . . . In point of fact, the Act of Chapultepec . . . was finally accepted by the American government owing to strenuous efforts by Mr. Nelson Rockefeller and Senator Warren Austin, [and] the American naval and military delegates." Berle, *Navigating the Rapids, 1918–1971* (New York, 1973), pp. 471–475.

234 "My bureau": Authors' interview with Nicolo Tucci. Tucci adds, "I was a very innocent person in those days. I became aware rather slowly that these people [in the coordinator's office] were only after their own interests and that they were sort of sorry that they had to fight the Nazis."

235 Avra Warren: Even the loyal Jamieson was skeptical about Warren, noting that his "only difference of opinion with Mr. Rockefeller on Argentina was the reliance he was compelled to place on such advisers as Avra Warren." (Jamieson memoir).

235 San Francisco: For a summary of Nelson's relations with Stettinius and Vandenberg, and his activities at the founding U.N. conference, see Morris, *NR*, pp. 234 ff.

235 "He jumped energetically": Authors' interview with Alger Hiss.

235 "A solid group": Cited in Green, p. 234.

236 "Nobody seemed to know": Ibid., p. 210.

236 Admiral Harold C. Train: The incident is recounted in detail in the Harold Train memoir, Columbia Oral History Project.

237 "Continually worried": Charles E. Bohlen, *Witness to History* (New York, 1974), pp. 206–207.

237 Showdown with the Russians: For an excellent account of the conflict, see Green, pp. 209–250.

238n. "The regime": Post editorial cited in Morris, *NR*, p. 212.

238 Dinner with Senator Vandenberg: The meeting is described in Arthur Vandenberg, *The Private Papers of Senator Vandenberg* (Boston, 1952), p. 187.

239 "Continuous inter-American policy": Rockefeller's letter to Stettinius is cited by Green, p. 226.

239 Outraged: Dulles's reaction is noted by Morris, *NR*, p. 218.

239 "I served notice": The senator had a curious way of justifying his support of the world organization. In a diary entry omitted from the published *Private Papers*, he wrote: "[Hamilton Fish] Armstrong said that no matter how bad the League [proposed U.N.] might be, it is better than nothing; that if we are headed for trouble with Russia, it is better to have a mechanism that can utilize the world against her." Cited by Green, p. 233.

240 "Taking the position": The full text of the exchange is reprinted by Gabriel Kolko in *The Politics of War, 1943–1945* (New York, 1968), pp. 470–473.

240 "Regionalism": Green, p. 231.

241n. Rio Pact: For details, see Edwin Lieuwen, *Arms and Politics in Latin America* (New York, 1961), pp. 196–197.

241n. Dulles apologized: Morris, *NR*, p. 230.

241 "No use talking": Ibid.

241 "I didn't want to resign": James Desmond, *Nelson Rockefeller* (New York, 1964), p. 132.

242 "We, the undersigned": Rockefeller Brothers Fund file, Rockefeller Family Archives.

243 "Fresh period": Authors' interview with JDR3.

244 "Mr. Rockefeller, Jr.": Authors' interview with John Lockwood.

244 He was not pleased: Ibid.

244 Locating the U.N.: See the Jamieson memoir; also, William Zeckendorf, *The Autobiography of William Zeckendorf* (New York, 1970), pp. 63–78.

244 Annoyed and embarrassed: Jamieson says, "It became a source of personal embarrassment to Nelson because he found he could not deliver on his offer.... I think perhaps Nelson, in his enthusiasm, was slightly resentful of his father's inability to do so [break the lease].... It was inability on his father's part, with perhaps some unwillingness or slight resentment that there'd been no consultation in advance of the offer." Jamieson memoir.

245 "Just give money": Ibid.

245 Potentially serious: Zeckendorf, pp. 76–77.

245 "Why Pa": Jamieson memoir.

246 "The brothers felt": Authors' interview with Lindsley Kimball.

246 "The Rockefeller family": Nelson's memorandum and the consultant's study are on file in the Rockefeller Family Archives.

246n. "No one in this family": Authors' interview with confidential source.

246 Debevoise: Authors' interview with John Lockwood.

247 Struggle for power: Ibid.

247 "Nelson got me in": Ibid.

248   Rockefeller Center: See Rockefeller Center file in Rocke-
       feller Family Archives.

249   Expanded the estate's borders: Details on new buildings
       come from Pyle; also, communications from Dr. Joseph
       Ernst.

250   Junior caused a scene: Author's interview with Marion
       Rockefeller Weber.

250   She spent the days: For Abby's last years, see Chase,
       pp. 155 ff.

250   "I don't think": Author's interview with Steven Rocke-
       feller.

250   Hills Realty: The following details come from Hills Re-
       alty file, Rockefeller Family Archives.

250   "Sale of the stock": Memorandum, Nelson to Junior,
       January 22, 1952, Rockefeller Family Archives. Junior's re-
       sponse was, characteristically, to restate the proposal in its
       most precise terms: "In other words, the sale of my stock is
       made with the understanding that during my life, under the
       terms of my life estate, I am to continue to maintain, oper-
       ate, handle and enjoy the property *exactly* as at present *and*
       just as though the sale of stock had not been made." Nel-
       son's response was in the affirmative.

250   "I presume": Hills Realty file, Rockefeller Family Ar-
       chives.

251   Brothers' respective interests: The percentages come
       from Hills Realty file, ibid.

252    $58 million: Junior's gift is discussed in the Rockefeller
       Brothers Fund file in the Rockefeller Family Archives.

253   Veterans' problems: Winthrop discusses his study at length
       in "A Letter to My Son."

253   Socony-Vacuum: Ibid.

254   "I think Winthrop": *Abby Letters*, p. 284.

254   Winthrop often felt humiliated: The apartment incident
       is mentioned by Mrs. Margaret Black in the detailed oral
       history taped by Dr. Joseph Ernst at Winrock shortly after
       Winthrop's death. She was present during Winthrop's tele-
       phone call to his father and discussed it with him afterward.

254   "Awfully nice guy": Authors' interview with George Gil-
       der.

254   The marriage: For an account, see the *New York
       Times*, February 14, 1948.

255   "I was surprised": Cited in Cleveland Amory, *Who
       Killed Society?*, p. 380.

255   The birth: See *New York Times*, September 14, 1948.

255   Temporarily taking title: Hills Realty file, Rockefeller
       Family Archives.

256   Gone south: The following details come from authors'

interviews with various family members. See also R. A. Smith, pp. 130–131.

257 "My show": Cited in Arkansas *Gazette*, February 23, 1973.

257 Nelson dominated: Authors' interview with John Lockwood.

257 "Public relations": Ibid.

258 " 'Chart man' ": Ibid.

258 Friele: Details on Friele and his background come from the Rockefeller Family Archives.

258 AIA: For a history of this organization, see Martha Dalrymple, *The AIA Story*, published by the American International Association for Economic and Social Development (New York, 1968). Dalrymple is a former AP journalist recruited by Jamieson during the war to serve as a press section head for the OIAA; she returned with Nelson to private life and the AIA and IBEC.

258 "You more than anyone": Letter, Nelson to Junior, September 6, 1946, Rockefeller Family Archives.

259 Betancourt: The fact that Betancourt invited Nelson to come to Caracas in 1947 to discuss investing in the country was itself something of a vindication. In 1939, as the editor of *Ahora* and leader of the Democratic Action party, Betancourt had attacked Rockefeller when he toured Venezuela in his capacity as director of Creole Petroleum. "After looking over his vast oil properties," Betancourt had written, ". . . he will return to his office atop Rockefeller Center. . . . Behind him will remain Venezuela producing 180 million barrels for the Rockefellers" (Morris, *NR*, p. 118).

259 Middle Eastern oil: On March 12, 1947, President Truman had addressed Congress in a speech that marked the formal beginning of postwar ideological conflict. "The loud talk was all of Greece and Turkey," commented *Time's* report, "but the whispers behind the talk were all of the ocean of oil to the south." The deserts of Arabia, Iran, Iraq, and the sheikhdoms of the Persian Gulf covered an estimated 150 billion barrels of oil. *Time* noted, "As the U.S. prepared to make its historic move, a potent group of oil companies also came to a historic decision. With the tacit approval of the U.S. and British governments, the companies concluded a series of deals—the biggest ever made in the blue-chip game—to develop and put to full use this ocean of oil. Standard Oil Company (New Jersey) . . . was the natural leader of the group, as Standard's internationalminded president, Eugene Holman, was the one who had a big hand in drafting the breathtaking plans. Jersey Standard and its partners were going to spend upwards of $300,000,-000 in the stormy Middle East to bring out the oil" (*Time*, March 24, 1947). The climactic move in this process came eight years later, in 1953, when the United States overthrew

the nationalist regime of Mossadegh in a coup engineered
by Secretary of State John Foster Dulles and his brother
Allen, head of the CIA. Dulles then sent his aide Herbert
Hoover, Jr., to the major U.S. oil companies to work out an
agreement between them consistent with the U.S. "national
interest." The negotiations resulted in a new consortium for
Iranian oil, with five U.S. majors (Jersey Standard, Cal
Standard, Socony-Vacuum, Gulf, and Texaco) getting a 40
percent cut of what had formerly been a British operation.
Details of this agreement were outlined in official telegram
4241 (March 30, 1954) to Dulles from the new ambassador
in London, Winthrop Aldrich. Less than a year earlier, the
Department of Justice had filed a suit naming the five consortium participants as co-conspirators in a worldwide oil
cartel, operating under principles of the Red Line Agreement which monopolized foreign oil production and fixed
world prices. The cartel's control of world oil allowed it to
make the relatively high price of Texas Gulf oil into an "in-
flexible world base price." (Thus, if the cost of producing
this oil was $3.00 a barrel, but only 25 cents a barrel in,
say, Kuwait, the oil companies could charge $3.00 a barrel
on Kuwait oil and pocket the $2.75 difference.) The price-
fixing arrangement was a source of fabulous profit to the oil
companies, and in the face of the Justice Department suit,
their representatives went directly to the State Department
and National Security Council asking for immunity. They
could point out that by consenting to—indeed, motivat-
ing—the formation of the Iranian consortium after the
1953 coup, the U.S. Government had in fact officially sanctioned the monopoly that its Justice Department lawyers
were threatening to break up. The argument was persuasive;
the suit was dropped. Thus, nearly one hundred years after
the South Improvement scheme, the vitality of John D.
Rockefeller's early principles of oil organization were once
again validated. And in its decision that the Middle East oil
consortium was acting in "the national interest," the National Security Council reestablished at the highest priority
the ghost of the oil monopoly the U.S. Supreme Court had
tried to strike down forty-two years earlier. See the U.S.
Senate Subcommittee on Multinational Corporations, *The
International Petroleum Cartel, the Iranian Consortium, and
U.S. National Security* (Washington, D.C., 1974).

260   "One of these": Dalrymple, p. 9.

260   IBEC: For a case study of this corporation, see Wayne
      G. Broehl, *The International Basic Economy Corporation*
      (New York, 1968).

260n. Coca-Cola: The anecdote is told by Robert W. Hudgens
      in his memoir in the Columbia Oral History Project.
      Hudgens was a former investment banker who had run a
      program of supervised farm credit for the New Deal's Farm

Security Administration similar to the one Nelson had him oversee in Brazil for AIA.

260 "Economic development": Dalrymple, p. 10. According to Broehl, the Deputy Secretary of State of New York objected that the statement might mislead investors and make them think that IBEC was not being run for profit. IBEC attorneys overcame the objection by arguing that Latin Americans "tended to fear Yankee imperialism" and the preamble would help allay this fear (Broehl, p. 9).

260 Lincoln School: "Publicly, Columbia Teachers College had announced its decision to merge Lincoln with Horace Mann, another experimental school. But privately Columbia felt Lincoln had been infiltrated by a lot of Communist teachers, and wanted to close it down. Along with some other Lincoln alumni, Nelson got involved in the defense of Lincoln. There was a lot of intrigue and he got in over his head." Authors' interview with John Lockwood.

260 Others say: Authors' interview with Carl Spaeth.

261 *Das Kapital*: See Morris, *NR*, p. 340.

261n. Romualdi: Serafino Romualdi, *Presidents and Peons* (New York, 1967), p. 20. See also Joseph C. Goulden, *Meany* (New York, 1972), pp. 224–225, 329–334.

262 $4.5 million: Morris, *NR*, p. 253.

262 VBEC: Ibid., pp. 140 ff.

262 VBEC ran into difficulties: Speaking in 1952, Frank Jamieson already admitted the failure. "If we made any propaganda mistakes in Venezuela—and I'm convinced we did—our chief mistake was that we oversold the program to the public. . . . So, very much in spite of ourselves, we found ourselves in a situation where we were being regarded as a kind of panacea for the ills of the whole food and agriculture problems of the country. Under the pressure for action we overexpanded, we didn't properly inform ourselves about the problem, and we relied too heavily on North American experts and gave too little consideration to our lack of knowledge of the country in which we were going to operate. We operated large farms, a modern fishing business, milk pasteurization plants, wholesale food businesses, and retail supermarkets. The farms were largely failures. . . . Our fishing operation has not been successful. . . . An offshoot of our farming operation was a chicken business, which has not been successful and has been abandoned" (Jamieson memoir).

262 CADA: For this program, see Broehl, pp. 35 ff.

262 "This talk": Rockefeller's IBEC," *Fortune*, February 1955.

262 "Rockefeller seems": Ibid.

263 "Father": Authors' interview with Tom Braden. Braden's wife, Joan, was an employee of Nelson at AIA, and he was told this story personally by Nelson.

263   CADA: Initially 80 percent of the stock on CADA's shelves came from the United States and only 20 percent from domestic producers. Over the years, the reversal of this ration would be cited as a measure of IBEC's success. But what had actually happened was that in the intervening period, U.S. firms formerly exporting goods to Venezuela had established plants there. "As a result, the same brand names were still available to the customer, though the products now displayed the words *Hecho en Venezuela*, made in Venezuela" (Broehl, p. 123).

264   Half its income: IBEC *Annual Report*, 1968.

264   IBEC's turnabout: Nelson rationalized the disappearance of IBEC's "conscience" by pointing out that the more idealistic AIA was still in business. Yet in fact its programs received only minimal attention after IBEC was born. Moreover, the symbiosis between the two institutions was often more complex than indicated by the division which made one of them philanthropic and the other profit-making. Shortly after it had been established, for instance, AIA conducted a market survey of the hybrid corn industry in Brazil. It discovered that a Brazilian company (Agroceres Limitada) was just getting ready to begin commercial production of the only developed hybrid in the country. This information was turned over to IBEC, which then went to the Brazilian owners of Agroceres and proposed that a new company be formed between them. As the new enterprise (called SASA) grew, it required more and more capital. The original provisions of the agreement, under which the Brazilian partners would have been able to purchase up to 51 percent of the stock after ten years, were declared unworkable, and the Brazilians had to settle for a much smaller percentage than they originally anticipated. Over the years, SASA became one of the half-dozen largest hybrid seed corn companies in the world, and a star in IBEC's corporate constellation. (See Broehl, pp. 50 ff.; Dalrymple, pp. 17–18.) Another example of the effects of IBEC's changed personality came in Venezuela. When Rockefeller's corporation entered the milk-producing field there, there was one indigenous competitor, INLACA. IBEC was able to undercut INLACA's efforts by mixing powdered milk obtained as part of a U.S. government surplus food program with water and fresh milk. When it had cornered the market, it drove up milk prices to 32 cents a liter, about 50 percent higher than prevailing U.S. prices.

264   Ben Hardy: Morris, *NR*, p. 275.

265   He was delighted: Ibid.

265   "Put together":   Ibid.

266   *Partners in Progress*:   In his foreword, Nelson set the tone for the report: "As the last war drew to a close, there was a stirring of the people the world over—an awakening

that found expression in the formation of the United Nations. . . . Today, after five years of frustration and disillusionment, where are we? One-third of the people of the world have lost their freedom and are herded together under Soviet imperialism. The remaining two-thirds of the world's population is coming to see that the relentless pressure of military aggression from without and political subversion from within cannot be ignored or appeased. . . . Clearly nothing can be done now that diverts our energies from the important task of military mobilization for defense. Is that enough? Can it alone win a war today?" *Partners in Progress: A Report to President Truman by the International Development Advisory Board* (New York, 1951).

267 In measured tones: See Morris, *NR*, p. 278.

267 *A New Approach:* For an analysis of these concerns and the development of postwar American foreign policy, see Gabriel Kolko and Joyce Kolko, *The Limits of Power: The World and United States Foreign Policy, 1945–1954* (New York, 1972), pp. 624 ff.

267 "As a nation": See Hearings Before the Committee on Foreign Affairs of the U.S. House of Representatives on the Mutual Security Program, 1951, p. 354.

268 "I'm just going": The exchange is cited by Morris, *NR*, p. 280.

269 A. A. Berle, Jr., noted: Berle, p. 599.

269 Aldrich, Eisenhower, financial community: Aldrich had frequent contacts with Eisenhower from the time he accepted the post of president of Columbia. In 1951 he sounded Eisenhower out for U.S. presidential aspirations during a trip to Paris. The Washington *Herald Tribune* (December 1, 1952) wrote that Aldrich "went all out to land the nomination for Eisenhower, applying financial pressure on industrial enterprises throughout the nation to this end." (For further details, see Arthur M. Johnson, *Winthrop W. Aldrich* [Boston, 1968], pp. 372 ff.) But while Aldrich, as president of the Chase and known emissary of the Rockefellers, was an important figure, he was just one of many financial leaders courting the former general. On November 28, 1950, Clarence Dillon, the aged founder of Dillon, Read, invited Eisenhower to one of a series of meetings where the pillars of American finance and industry wooed him for the Republican party. Among those present were Russell Leffingwell, senior partner of J. P. Morgan & Company; John Schiff, senior partner of Kuhn, Loeb; Jeremiah Milbank; and John D. Rockefeller, Jr. See Peter Lyon, *Eisenhower* (New York, 1974), p. 414.

270n. Dulles and McCloy: See Townsend Hoopes, *The Devil and John Foster Dulles* (Boston, 1973), pp. 135 ff.

270n. "Every Republican": See James T. Patterson, *Mr. Republican* (Boston, 1972), p. 571.

270 Rockefeller's proposals: See Morris, *NR*, pp. 286–287.

270 Walter Smith: The general's feud with Nelson was related by Tom Braden in the course of authors' interview.

271 "Never impressed me": William Mitchell memoir, Columbia Oral History Project.

271 Special Assistant: See Dwight D. Eisenhower, *Mandate for Change* (New York, 1963), p. 511.

271 Nature of the post: For a discussion, see Dillon Anderson memoir, Columbia Oral History Project.

272 Dulles was still a roadblock: "The President would pick up a phone," Rockefeller later noted, "and say, 'Foster, Nelson has an idea,' and that would be enough to get Dulles' back up." Cited by Desmond, p. 144.

272 Eisenhower and Dulles: For a detailed discussion of Dulles's cold war theories and differences of opinion with the President, see Hoopes, especially pp. 193 ff.

272 May 10, 1955: The momentousness of this brief space in history is described by Nobel Peace Prize winner Philip Noel-Baker in *The Arms Race* (London, 1958).

273 Quantico: For details on the seminar and its relevance to the "Open Skies" proposal, see Morris, *NR*, pp. 299 ff.

274 "The time has come": Cited in Gervasi, p. 178.

274 Withdraw all the disarmament proposals: "The United States (declared Stassen) does now place a reservation upon all of its pre-Geneva substantive positions taken in this sub-committee or in the Disarmament Commission or in the U.N. on these questions in relationship to levels of armament." Noel-Baker, p. 22.

274 Rovere: See Richard Rovere, *Affairs of State* (New York, 1956), p. 290.

274 Dulles himself remained skeptical: See Lyon, pp. 664–665.

275 Humphrey: See Desmond, p. 144; also Gervasi, p. 186.

275n. $18 billion: Gervasi, p. 185.

275 December 31, 1955: Morris, *NR*, pp. 303 ff.

276 Like John J. McCloy: For a study of the role such figures have played in American policy, see Gabriel Kolko, *The Roots of American Foreign Policy* (Boston, 1969). David Halberstam's description of Lovett might well stand for the whole genus that shuttled between private industry and government service, and maintained an orbit around the Rockefeller family and its institutions. [He] understood power, where it resided, how to exercise it. He had exercised it all his life, yet he was curiously little known to the general public. The anonymity was not entirely by chance, for he was the embodiment of the public servant-financier who is so secure in his job ... that he does not need to seek publicity.... He lived in a world where young men made their way up the ladder by virtue not just of their own brilliance and ability but also of who their parents

were, which phone calls from which old friends had preceded their appearance in an office.... He was a twentieth century man who did not hold press conferences, who never ran for anything. The classic insider's man." Halberstam, *The Best and the Brightest* (New York, 1972), p. 5.

277 Accepted all the responsibilities: The confining intellectual boundaries within which JDR3 moved are suggested by a letter he wrote to his father just before the end of the war thanking him for adding to his trust fund and for indicating approval of his "philanthropic efforts." In phrasing and innuendo it bore an almost uncanny similarity to letters Junior had written Senior when he too was over forty years old but still emotionally dependent on the relationship: "While it is awfully good of you to say what you do about my example to the rest of the family, whatever I have done in this connection has been made very easy by standards set by you and Grandfather over the years. ... While the financial contributions made by you and Grandfather over the years have in many respects been unique in this country, if not in the world, in my judgement what the family has come to stand for in the minds of the public is based on more than that. The family has become a symbol of a 'way of life' which the American public admires and respects. This on the one hand makes our responsibilities even greater than those of stewardship, and on the other opens many doors leading to untold opportunities for usefulness." Letter, JDR3 to Junior, January 5, 1945, Rockefeller Family Archives.

277 "Padded cell": Authors' interview with Donald McLean.

277 "Natural aristocracy": Cited in Lynes, p. 379.

277 Privately she was sensitive: Authors' interview with confidential source.

278 "John's development": Authors' interview with Donald McLean.

278 "John got ahold of me": Ibid.

279 Navy Bureau: Details on JDR3's military service come from Rockefeller Family Archives.

279 Three-man committee: See Halberstam, pp. 334 ff.

279 Roundtable: See U.S. Department of State, *Transcript of Roundtable Discussion on American Policy Toward China,* October 6, 7, & 8, 1949, Washington, D.C. Confidential. (Subsequently de-classified.)

280 "On U.S. trade": A copy of the agenda of the meeting bearing JDR3's underlining and marginalia exists in the Rockefeller Family Archives.

280 "Much of the discussion": Letter, JDR3 to Philip Jessup, October 13, 1949, Rockefeller Family Archives.

281n. Dulles: For details on Dulles's efforts to revitalize his career following the loss of the Senate seat, see Hoopes, pp. 88 ff.

281 Dulles and JDR3: Details come from John D. Rockefeller

3rd's memoir in the Dulles Oral History Project at Princeton, which the authors were allowed to inspect by Mr. Rockefeller.

282   "Little to do": Ibid.

282   88-page document: The authors have seen this document on microfilm courtesy of JDR3 and the Dulles Oral History Project, Princeton University.

282   "Want to be a part": Letter, John Foster Dulles to Paul Hoffman, September 10, 1951, Rockefeller Family Archives.

282   "A major step": Authors' interview with JDR3.

283   "Big bully": Authors' interview with Donald McLean.

283   Japan Society: Details from files in Rockefeller Family Archives.

283n. "My own decision": Letter, JDR3 to John J. McCloy, June 8, 1953, Rockefeller Family Archives.

284   *Sayonara:* JDR3's reaction to Logan was that the film was a moving experience and would be good for U.S.–Japanese relations on the whole, but he suggested that the "anti-American aspects" of the portrayal of some U.S. servicemen be "toned down." See Japan Society files, Rockefeller Family Archives.

284   "I take the liberty": The letter is in the Birth Control files of the Rockefeller Family Archives.

285   The logical place: In its 1948 *Annual Report,* the Foundation had noted, "Population experts are deeply concerned with problems in the Far East, where social innovations in areas of dense population pressure and limited resources present an ominous prospect."

285n. Cardinal Spellman: Authors' interview with Frank Notestein.

285   Could not get backing: Hugh Romney, vice-president of the Foundation, says, "JDR3 never really defined himself as head of the Foundation. When JDR3 proposed it, population stabilization was discussed. But it was felt that the Foundation had no business getting in this field. JDR3 never pushed anything down anyone's throat when he was there. He also had to go outside to create the Agricultural Development Council." Authors' interview.

285   "Well, I pushed": Authors' interview with JDR3. Asked if he felt it was his hereditary right to expect the Foundation to support his programs, he replied, "No, I believed that the strength of the Foundation was in the president and trustees and the most important function I could serve was helping create an able leadership, and a strong Foundation board and management." Ibid.

286   Men's room: The meeting was described by Donald McLean in an authors' interview.

286   "It could be": Ibid.

286 "The hard-liners": Authors' interview with Frank Notestein.

286 Arthur Packard: Authors' interview with Lindsley Kimball.

287 "Even though": Authors' interview with Donald McLean.

287 Population Council: For a brief overview of the
council's funding, activities, and policies, see *The Population
Council, 1952–1964: A Report to the Council* (New York,
1965).

287n. Frederick Osborn: Authors' interview with Frank Notestein.

287 State Department digest: For this document, Draper's
committee, and the evolution of the population movement
generally, see Phyllis T. Piotrow, *World Population Crisis:
The United States Response* (New York, 1973).

289n. Ambassadorship to Indonesia: Authors' interview with
Donald McLean.

289 Trip to the Orient: The commercial possibilities he saw
during these sojourns made JDR3 succumb to an entrepreneurial itch for one of the few times in his life. In the
early 1950s, he founded Products of Asia, an importing firm
dedicated to making high-quality Oriental merchandise
available to Americans. JDR3 found himself writing notes
that sounded like those of any wholesaler, as in this letter
to Douglas Overton, an Orientalist he had installed as executive director of the Japan Society: "As to Products of
Asia, we have been having some interesting negotiations in
connection with the acquisition of sales rights for Dynasty
Products, which, as you know, are manufactured by Man-
darin Textiles, Limited, in Hong Kong. If the deal goes
through, I think we will add a quality product which would
be more in line with my original concept than our sweater
effort, although I do appreciate the importance of volume
sales if the operation is to be financially successful." Rockefeller Family Archives.

289 "We'd be up": Authors' interview with Lewis Lapham.

290 "I wrote Foster": Authors' interview with JDR3.

290 Howard Hughes: Authors' interview with William Zeckendorf. See also Zeckendorf, pp. 155 ff.

292 He prided himself: The details about Laurance and his
life style are distilled from authors' interviews with his children, Laura Rockefeller Chasin, Lucy Rockefeller Waletzky,
and Marion Rockefeller Weber. Also, Mary Dadd, former
governess in Laurance's household.

292 "His continuity": Cited by Richard A. Smith, "The
Rockefeller Brothers," *Fortune*, March 1955.

292 The war: Details on Laurance's wartime work came
from the Rockefeller Family Archives.

293n. McDonnell: These details come from authors' interview

with Gordon LeBert, head of external relations for the McDonnell-Douglas corporation.

293 "Our company": Letter, J. S. McDonnell to Laurance, June 4, 1941, Rockefeller Family Archives. This is not the only case when Laurance was concerned with his prewar investments. In 1938 he had purchased $5,000 worth of stock in Vitarama, an experimental cinematic process that would eventually evolve into Cinerama. Just before the war, Vitarama made training mechanisms which used the 3-D process to simulate combat conditions for mock-gunnery practice. The Navy brought thirty-one of them. After he enlisted, Laurance arranged further contact between the Navy brass and Vitarama executives for a preview of the company's streamlined version of this process, which eventually resulted in a $5 million contract to Vitarama. Vitarama files, Rockefeller Family Archives.

293n. McDonnell stock: See McDonnell file in Rockefeller Family Archives; communication from Gordon LeBert.

294 "Never really demobilized": *Time*, August 24, 1959, p. 70.

294 Piasecki: Authors' interview with Frank Piasecki.

294 Reaction Motors: See Morris, *TRB*, pp. 168 ff. or a listing of many of Laurance's postwar investments.

294 "Ten-year risk cycle": "In my enterprises," Laurance told Richard Smith, "you need a calendar, not a stop watch. They're geared to a ten-year cycle." *Fortune*, March 1955.

295 Associates were different: Authors' interview with Frank Piasecki.

295 Peaceful use: Perhaps because it was a source of energy more potent even than the petroleum whose marketing their grandfather had pioneered, the Rockefeller Brothers were enthusiastic early supporters of the movement to apply nuclear power to the solution of domestic energy needs. While Laurance was investing in Nuclear Development Associates, Nelson was dealing with the issue from his vantage point in the Eisenhower administration. Upon becoming the President's Special Assistant, he found the "Atoms for Peace" program languishing and managed to persuade Eisenhower to revive it and offer research reactors to those under-developed nations willing to train nuclear physicists, and to assist the technically advanced countries in developing more sophisticated nuclear power capabilities. (See Gervasi, pp. 183–184.) Meanwhile, David was involved in the decision of the Chase to form one of the first atomic energy divisions in American banking, and in 1954 had become a director of the Fund for Peaceful Atomic Development, a blue-ribbon lobbying effort dedicated to "prompting the dissemination throughout the world (to the extent consistent with national security) of knowledge and understanding relating to the peaceful uses of atomic energy." See

Fund for Peaceful Atomic Development, *Statement of Purpose,* July 1955.

296   "We just don't have money":   Morris, *TRB,* p. 35.
296   Rockefeller Brothers, Inc: For details on this organization up to 1961, see Rockefeller Brothers, Inc., file, Rockefeller Family Archives.
296   "This is just to give":   Letter, Randolph Marston to Chase Bank, November 12, 1946, Rockefeller Family Archives.
296   "To make a study":   See *Filatures et Tissages Africains* file, Rockefeller Family Archives.
296   Labor was cheap: Ibid.
297   "It was interesting":   Cited in Morris, *TRB,* p. 174.
297   Other personal investments: See also Stephen R. Weissman, *American Foreign Policy: The Congo* (Ithaca, N.Y., 1974), especially pp. 36–37; also, Kwame Nkrumah, *Neo-Colonialism: The Last Stage of Imperialism* (London, 1965), pp. 212–213.
297   JDR3 disapproved: Authors' interview with John Hodgkin, former chief accountant to the Rockefeller family.
298   Laurance in charge: Ibid.
298   Lewis Strauss: For a summary of his life, see Lewis L. Strauss, *Men and Decisions* (New York, 1962).
299   Office Management Committee: Details on Strauss's tenure in Room 5600 come from Rockefeller Family Archives.
299   Renewal of the Center's lease: Ibid.
299   Dilworth: John Lockwood says, "When Cutler died, there was a vacuum in the financial aspect of the Office. Debevoise and the other old guard advisers of Mr. Rockefeller, Jr., tried to bring in Richard Mansfield from the Chase, where he'd been a vice-president. They were able to get him in for a time, primarily because Nelson was otherwise occupied at that moment and didn't have a candidate of his own for the job. But Mansfield didn't work out, mainly because the Brothers hadn't had a hand in his selection. After him came Strauss, then there was a lengthy interviewing process—mainly by Laurance and David—and Dilworth was selected."
299   Paying off: See Richard A. Smith, *Fortune,* March 1955; also, authors' interviews with Frank Piasecki and John Menke, head of United Nuclear.
300n. "Rockefeller and his associates":   Authors' interview with John Menke.
300   Itek: Details based primarily on authors' interview with Duncan E. MacDonald. See also Itek *Annual Reports,* 1958–1961.
301   First decade and a half: See "Venture Capitalist," *Barron's,* August 14, 1961.
302   Tell his children: Authors' interview with Marion Rockefeller Weber. Of course, Laurance had, to some degree,

been "destined" to assume the family's conservation interests. On May 29, 1945, Kenneth Chorley, head of Jackson
Hole Preserve, Inc., had written Junior about the snafu regarding the gift of Grand Teton lands to the National Park
Service. Suggesting that Junior transfer the lands from his
own private ownership to that of Jackson Hole Preserve,
Inc., until the government made up its mind what to do, he
noted that making JHPI into an important institution would
"give Laurance a definite experimental basis to further explore his interest in the West and in conservation. . . ."
Chorley added: "I gather Laurance is looking for something
outside the office on which he might center his interest.
This program might be the means of focusing that interest
on not only a very worthwhile project, but also on one of
national significance." Jackson Hole Preserve, Inc., file,
Rockefeller Family Archives.

303 "Critical and strategic": See Department of State *Bulletin*, August 27, 1951.

303 Presidential Commission: See Presidential Commission
on Materials Policy, *Resources for Freedom* (Washington,
D.C., 1952).

303 Conclusions of *Resources for Freedom:* There was nothing
new in the business community's advocacy of "efficiency" in
the use of natural resources. In fact, this term had become
something of a code word in the period following the Red
Line Agreement of 1928, when the oil majors had set out to
raise the price of petroleum. Realizing that antitrust laws
prohibited a direct price-fixing agreement, they turned to the
Ivy Lee-inspired American Petroleum Institute as the center
of a lobbying effort to convince federal and state governments that permitting crude to be produced in unlimited
amounts would be "wasteful." To restrict unlimited output,
they urged the enforcement of a fixed price minimum in the
name of conservation. By the mid-1930s, almost all states
had accepted the argument and were enforcing laws that
equated selling oil at a low price with economic waste,
which they ruled illegal. As a result, the conservation program (as a 1974 congressional report would charge) "has
become merely a price-fixing mechanism." For the historical
development of the efficiency-conservation issue, see Samuel
P. Hays, *Conservation and the Gospel of Efficiency* (New
York, 1969); also, U.S. Senate Subcommittee on Multinational Corporations, *The International Petroleum Cartel.*

303 "We Americans": A copy of the Osborn speech is in the
Rockefeller Family Archives.

304 Brookings paper: See Resources for the Future, *Annual
Report,* 1953 and 1954.

304n. "Yeast is to bread": Cited in Frank J. Taylor, "His Millions for the Big Outdoors," *Saturday Evening Post,* December 16, 1961.

305 He went to Laurance: See Moses, pp. 819–820.

305 Dorado Beach Hotel: See Dorado Beach file, Rockefeller
     Family Archives.

305 Caneel Bay Plantation: See Caneel Bay file, Rockefeller
     Family Archives.

306 Nearly 6,000 acres: See Virgin Island National Park file,
     Rockefeller Family Archives.

306 "Close to nature": Cited in "Laurance Rockefeller—
     Economic Development with a Conservationist's Touch,"
     Hotel Business, December 1972. Ed Crafts, former head of
     the Interior Department's Bureau of Outdoor Recreation
     (who worked closely with Laurance for several years), says,
     "His concept of recreation is different from a lot of people's.
     At the cookouts and late suppers he holds at the resorts, in
     the middle of servants, tablecloths and all that, he will look
     off at the distance and see the mountains and say, 'Well, isn't
     this a wonderful outdoor experience!' It is, but it isn't the
     typical outdoor experience." Authors' interview.

306 "The trend": Jackson Hole Preserve, Inc., files, Rocke-
     feller Family Archives.

307 American Conservation Association: See ACA file in
     Rockefeller Family Archives.

307 "Harpo": Cited by Richard A. Smith, *Fortune,* March
     1955, p. 116.

308 Same morning ritual: The following details about
     David's personal life are distilled from conversations with
     his children.

308 Latin America: This was one area where the con-
     vergence of family and bank matters was particularly neat.
     Soon after assuming his new post, David made a trip to
     Brazil with Nelson, touring AIA facilities and observing the
     beginnings of IBEC. In 1948 he joined Nelson in founding
     the IBEC Research Institute, a nonprofit organization con-
     ducting agricultural research which was later merged with
     AIA. In 1949, as a result of David's efforts, the Chase
     Bank's International Investment Corporation teamed with
     IBEC to create the Inter-American Finance and Investment
     Corporation in Brazil. See Morris, *TRB,* p. 130: Dalrymple,
     pp. 40–41.

308 Executive vice-president: For a summary of David's rise
     at the Chase and the revision of banking policy in the post-
     war era, see "David Rockefeller, Banker's Banker,"
     Newsweek, April 3, 1967.

309n. The Manhattan Company: For this bank's background,
     see "History of the Chase Manhattan," New York *Daily
     News,* Special Supplement (printed by the Chase Manhat-
     tan), July 1969.

310 "Among the top men": "The New No. 1 Bank,"
     Business Week, February 12, 1955.

310 " 'Rocky' ": Interview with a Chase vice-president who requests his name not be used.

310 "I'm appalled that anyone": Ibid.

310 Peggy: Interview with Richard Rockefeller.

310 David's art interests: For David's involvement in the Museum of Modern Art, see Lynes, pp. 400 ff.

311 Detlev Bronk: Son of a well-known Baptist minister and scion of an old New York family which had given its name to the Bronx, Detlev Bronk had been instrumental in founding the discipline of biophysics while at the University of Pennsylvania. He first became an adviser to the Rockefeller Institute in 1946 and not long after became an official science adviser to President Truman, a post he continued to fill under Eisenhower and Kennedy. When Bronk was elected president of the National Academy of Sciences in 1950, his primary support came from physicists who felt that the Soviet threat mandated immediate development of hydrogen weaponry. Bronk's opponent for the presidency, James B. Conant, by contrast, was identified with arms controls and international supervision of atomic energy. See Daniel S. Greenberg, *The Politics of Pure Science* (New York, 1967), p. 14, 127n.

311 Morningside Heights: See Gertrude Samuels, "Community at Work," *New York Times Magazine*, August 6, 1950. Also, Morris, *TRB*, p. 254: Harry Emerson Fosdick, *The Living of These Days* (New York, 1956), pp. 315 ff.

312 Contributed $104,000: Morningside Heights files, Rockefeller Family Archives.

312n. Columbia University students: For a summary of their views, see *Who Rules Columbia*, a pamphlet growing out of the strike and published by the North American Conference on Latin America (NACLA) (New York, 1969). The pamphlet charges that "the information of Morningside Heights in 1947 was the major factor in Columbia's decision to remain [at its present location] and to resist the encroachment of surrounding slums" (p. 28).

313 "The province": Morris, *TRB*, p. 255.

313 "The heart pump": Cited by E. J. Kahn, Jr., in "Resources and Responsibilities," *New Yorker*, January 9, 1965.

314 "Wall Street Maneuver": See Zeckendorf, pp. 264 ff.

314 "Occupied by commercial slums": Cited in "David Rockefeller," *New Yorker*, July 23, 1960, p. 16.

314 "Trade Center seems logical": Ibid.

314n. Safe bet: See David Leinsdorf and Donald Etra, *Citibank: Ralph Nader Study Group Report on First National City Bank* (New York, 1974), pp. 141–153, for an analysis of the large New York banks and the World Trade Center, Port Authority, and Downtown Lower Manhattan Association. For a study of the history and operation of the Public

Authorities, see Robert A. Caro, *The Power Broker* (New York, 1974).

315 Resources of the Chase: In the files the authors have inspected in the Rockefeller Family Archives, there are repeated instances in which bank personnel have been conscripted in family business as consultants and analysts. Laurance's venture capital companies (Marquardt Aircraft, for instance, received a $300,000 Chase loan after Laurance's investment) also profited from the relationship.

316n. Eastern and American: For details on the proposed merger, see U.S. House of Representatives, Committee on the Judiciary, *Proposed Merger of Eastern Airlines and American Airlines* (Washington, D.C., 1962).

316 "Unquestionably": Chase Bank files, Rockefeller Family Archives.

317n. Aldrich patriotism: For details, see Johnson, *Winthrop Aldrich*, pp. 338–348.

317 Council on Foreign Relations: For background, see Joseph Kraft, "School for Statesmen," *Harper's*, July 1958; Anthony Lukas, "The Council on Foreign Relations," *New York Times Magazine*, November 21, 1971; also, G. William Domhoff, *The Higher Circles* (New York, 1970).

317 Junior's donation: Between 1927 and 1951, the Laura Spelman Rockefeller Memorial Fund and the Rockefeller Foundation had combined to give $1,032,000 to the council. Junior, meanwhile, had given a total of $239,375 personally, including $75,000 toward the purchase of the Pratt Mansion as a headquarters. Council on Foreign Relations file, Rockefeller Family Archives.

317 David's most important activity: Authors' interview with George Gilder.

317 $23,000: Council on Foreign Relations file, Rockefeller Family Archives.

318 "Informed consensus": Authors' interview with George Gilder.

318 David and Hochschild group: See Council on Foreign Relations *Annual Reports*, 1958–1959.

318 Insistence of Nelson: The decision to open a Lagos branch office is documented in the Rockefeller Brothers Fund file, Rockefeller Family Archives.

319 Robert Fleming: His background is contained in a written communication sent to the authors.

319n. "One element": Fleming's report is in the Rockefeller Brothers Fund file, Rockefeller Family Archives.

319 $10,000: The gift was a sop to the Aga Khan, funneled through the African-American Institute. Rockefeller Brothers Fund head Dana Creel (himself a member and later chairman of the institute board) had advised David against lending his name to the cancer center in a savvy memorandum of November 20, 1959: "A disturbing rumor, and it

can't be said to be more than a rumor, keeps popping up that the real backing in Kenya for Wood's plan [Dr. Michael Wood, director of the foundation] rests with a small white settler group.... My fear is that the nationalists do now to some extent and may later to a much greater extent, view it as a self serving move by some of the white settlers." Rockefeller Brothers Fund file, Rockefeller Family Archives.

319 "I forgot": Ibid.

320n. Nigeria's Independence Day: "Its significance must necessarily exceed that of other West African countries, if only for Nigeria's greater size. However, I suspect that in a more subtle way, the event may provide the West with a greater opportunity than all other celebrations combined. In the first place, Nigeria is for the moment more wedded to the West than any of the other countries with the possible exception of Liberia. Economically it is the most conservative; that is, it is the most committed to free enterprise.... And it has the greatest cadre of trained government people and administrators to take over responsibility should the necessity be forced upon them." Letter, Robert Fleming to Rockefeller Brothers Fund headquarters, March 7, 1960, Rockefeller Family Archives.

320 "I am very pleased": Letter, David to Sir Ernest Vesey, March 4, 1960, Rockefeller Family Archives.

320n. AAI and CIA funding: Authors' interviews with William R. Cotter, president of African-American Institute. Also letter from previous president, Waldemar Neilson, to AAI board of trustees, February 28, 1967, copy provided to the authors by Mr. Cotter.

322 "With Nelson": Berle, p. 667.

322n. Museum of Primitive Art: "After a brief flirtation with pre-Columbian and other primitive objects in its earliest years, the Metropolitan decided that it had no use for them, and accordingly farmed them out on long-term loan to the Brooklyn Museum, the American Museum of Natural History, and other institutions. [Dudley T.] Easby, who had once served with Nelson Rockefeller in the government's Office of Inter American Affairs, was painfully aware that in 1939, Rockefeller had offered funds to finance a Metropolitan archaeological expedition to Mexico, and the offer had been turned down ... [because the museum] thought that Mexican art did not warrant digging up. . . . Interest in the art of African, pre-Columbian, and other 'primitive' cultures has risen notably since the 1930s, and Easby never wholly gave up hope that the Metropolitan might one day recall its loaned specimens and restore them to favor. Now they are all back—together with the four thousand treasures from the Rockefeller Collection. With the diplomatic assistance of Mrs. Vincent Astor, one of his most useful trustees, [museum director Thomas] Hoving overcame the effects of the [1939] rejection and the Metropolitan swallowed in one great gulp the Museum of Primitive Art Rockefeller had founded in 1957 to house his growing collection." Calvin Tompkins, *Merchants and Masterpieces* (New York, 1970), p. 350.

322 One hundred employees: Figure supplied by Rockefeller Family Archives.

323 No Strong Identity: In its first decade, the Brothers Fund had spent an average of $200,000 a year in grants to civic organizations and other traditional recipients of charitable gifts, including the YMCA, Boy Scouts, and Red Cross. After Junior's endowment of $58 million in 1957, making the Fund the fourth-largest foundation in the nation, its program became far more ambitious. In the future it would underwrite large gifts to the Population Council, Conservation Foundation, and other causes and institutions with which the Brothers—singly and together—had become identified. See Brothers Fund *Annual Reports*; also, Rockefeller Brothers Fund file, Rockefeller Family Archives.

323 Mayor: Morris, *NR*, p. 310. Interestingly, some seventeen years earlier, Charles Hilles, Republican national committeeman, had suggested Junior's name as a possibility for mayor of New York. But the rehabilitation of the Rockefeller name had not yet progressed far enough for an appeal to be made to the electorate, or, as Ivy Lee suggested more delicately in a letter to Junior: "Great as my admiration for you is, I do not believe the time has yet come when you could be regarded as popular in the political sense." Letter, Ivy Lee to Junior, July 13, 1929, Rockefeller Family Archives.

323 Irving Ives: Morris, *NR*, p. 310.

323n. Rayburn: The origins of the Rayburn Library and the decision to make a $300,000 grant to it despite expert opinions about its worth are documented in the Rockefeller Brothers Fund file, Rockefeller Family Archives.

324 *Prospect: See Prospect for Tomorrow: The Rockefeller Panel Reports* (Garden City: 1961). In addition to research in the Family Archives, the authors have conducted interviews touching on the Panel Studies with Emmet J. Hughes, Dana Creel, and John Lockwood, all of whom served on the Planning Committee, and Townsend Hoopes, executive director of Panel II.

324 Illustrious and influential names: "Many who joined the Overall Panel of the Special Studies Project were aware that they were in the presence of someone who might be President of the United States in the 1960s or 1970s. Their decision to join the group was not unaffected by that awareness. ... They were flattered to be asked and enjoyed the attention paid to them by a man [Nelson] who believed

absolutely in the critical importance of the enterprise." Stephen Graubard, *Kissinger, Portrait of a Mind* (New York, 1973), pp. 108–109. (Graubard is a friend and former colleague of Kissinger who interviewed Rockefeller in preparing his book.)

324 Six panels: For a November 20, 1956, meeting of the overall panel, Nelson provided what amounted to a keynote address for the entire project. "There can be little doubt that we are living through a revolutionary period.... On the economic and social plane, there has occurred what has been called the revolution of rising expectations, which cause the peoples of the world to rebel against standards of living, as well as social and racial barriers: which have remained virtually unchanged for centuries. This ferment is fed by newly awakened hopes for freedom and human dignity and by the rapidity with which the aspirations of hitherto inarticulate peoples can be communicated. And these factors, of themselves explosive enough, are manipulated by the Sino-Soviet bloc, organized to exploit all hopes and dissatisfaction for its own ends." Rockefeller Brothers Fund file, Rockefeller Family Archives.

324 Dean Rusk: The thrust of the International Security Panel is captured in a letter Kissinger wrote Rusk telling him that his panel should be directed toward a long-range view of American policy. He used the Mideast situation as an example: "It seems to me that when a situation reaches a crisis like the present [1956] Middle East situation, the only routes that are open are on the level of maneuver or military force. On the other hand, if we had been clear, say five years ago, about the relation of the Middle East to American interests in general, about our possibilities of affecting events in that region, and about the nature of the revolution that was preparing itself, either the crisis would not have occurred or we could have dealt with it with greater sureness." Letter, Kissinger to Rusk, November 27, 1956, Rockefeller Family Archives.

324n. Kissinger and CFR: For the importance of the CFR panel to Kissinger's career, see Marvin Kalb and Bernard Kalb, *Kissinger* (New York, 1974), pp. 52 ff.

325n. "Nelson Rockefeller became": Graubard, p. 110.

325 Teller, Strauss, Dean: Within the panel, these men formed a powerful lobby in behalf of nuclear testing. In 1955, Strauss [as head of AEC] had moved to counter reports of the dangers of radioactive fallout from nuclear testing. He turned to his friend Detlev Bronk, then president of the National Academy of Sciences and head of the Rockefeller Institute. "Dr. Bronk agreed that ... a study [of the biological effects of radiation] was within the proper area of concern of the Academy. Accordingly, with funds provided by the Rockefeller Foundation so that both the men

and the means were independent of government, the study was undertaken.... The National Academy of Sciences issued its report in two sections, one titled 'A Report to the Public' ... [which] states: 'Except for some tragic accidents affecting small numbers of people, the biological damages from peacetime activities (including the testing of atomic weapons) has been essentially negligible.'" Strauss, *Men and Decisions*, p. 415.

325   "At issue":   See Preface, *Prospect for America*.

325   His keenest interest: Authors' interview with Townsend Hoopes.

325   "When the Security":   *Prospect for America*, p. 155.

325   Internal dissension: Authors' interview with Townsend Hoopes.

326   "Wondrous sentence":   I. F. Stone, *Polemics and Prophecies, 1967–1970* (New York, 1972), p. 40.

326   "Our security":   *Prospect for America*, p. 113.

326   Nelson rushed: See Special Studies Project files, Rockefeller Family Archives.

327   Prepared by Kissinger: Ibid.

327   "Ever since World War II":   Cited by Gervasi, p. 195.

327n.   "Hey, Pierre":   Authors' interview with Tom Braden.

327   Leaving Laurance: Laurance had also been a member of Panel II. He would work almost as hard to ensure the distribution of the published Panel Studies as Nelson had to bring them together. In 1961, when *Prospect for America* was to be published, he hosted a luncheon for leading "opinion makers." Henry Luce, Hedley Donovan, Dorothy Schiff, and others were there. Beside the name of each individual on Laurance's copy of the invitation list, Emmet Hughes—then working in Room 5600 as head of public relations—noted their importance in the world of media. (Beside Malcolm Muir's name, for instance, he penciled, "Will one day probably have complete editorial control of *Newsweek*.") In addition to hosting luncheons, Laurance also paid careful attention to sales of the book, including scrutiny of monthly sales figures supplied by Doubleday. See Special Studies Project file, Rockefeller Family Archives.

327   Resistance: Authors' interview with Emmet Hughes. Cf. Gervasi, p. 203.

328   Tom Dewey: Desmond, p. 161.

328   A long shot: Gervasi, p. 207.

328   Malcolm Wilson: "Wilson's political posture in 1958 was rather paradoxical. At forty-four, he was rounding out twenty years as Assemblyman from Yonkers.... He was quite possibly the most powerful individual in the Assembly with the exception of the Speaker.... On the other hand, Wilson's personal advancement appeared to be stymied.... He was at the age when the logic of politics almost required upward movement. But his field of action was circum-

scribed. For, great though his influence was, he had no wide popular following as he was realist enough to know" (Desmond, p. 159).

328   "What we need":   See Morris, *NR*, p. 319.

328   State tour: Authors' interview with Steven Rockefeller.

329   "That's it":   Cited in Desmond, p. 176.

329   Undermine confidence in Harriman: See Morris, *NR*, p. 324.

330   Campaign style: Authors' interview with Steven Rockefeller.

330   "What's he ever done":   Cited in Desmond, p. 184.

330   "Crowds quiver":   Essay reprinted (and updated) in Thomas B. Morgan, *Self Creations: 13 Impersonalities* (New York, 1965), p. 115.

331   "What you are doing":   Letter, Junior to sons, February 26, 1955, Rockefeller Family Archives.

332   If his sons wanted ready money: It was not entirely a happy arrangement as far as they were concerned. Laurance once noted to family attorney Donal O'Brien, "For years we had to pick up crumbs from father's table." Authors' interview with Abby Rockefeller.

333   Cover of *Time:*   See "The Good Man," *Time*, September 24, 1956.

333   "He sat down":   David Lillienthal, *The Journals of David Lillienthal* (New York, 1966), II, 303.

333   After the funeral: Authors' interviews with various members of the Rockefeller family.

334   Relations became strained: Authors' interview with Abby Rockefeller.

334   "Mr. Rockefeller":   Authors' interview with confidential source.

334   Sunday dinners: These affairs are described at length in Part IV.

335   Rise at seven: Details on Junior's personal habits have been distilled from letters from the Rockefeller Family Archives.

335   Increasingly feeble: Ibid.

336   "Quite powerful":   Authors' interview with John D. Rockefeller IV.

336   Mourned discreetly: The stained glass window Nelson commissioned Henri Matisse to do in memory of Abby Aldrich Rockefeller at the Union Hills Church at Pocantico Hills purposely avoided symbolism. The companion piece David commissioned Chagall to do a decade after Junior's death in his memory takes as its theme the story of the Good Samaritan.

336   "Grandfather's death":   Authors' interview with Steven Rockefeller.

336   Frank Jamieson: Authors' interview with Mrs. Linda Storrow.

337   Inaugural: See *New York Times*, January 2, 1960.

337   Picassos: Gervasi, p. 225.

337   "Montana roadshow":   T. H. White, *The Making of the President 1960* (New York, 1961), p. 69.

337   "I hate the idea":   Ibid., p. 71. Yet it was Rockefeller's sense of the portentous links between his own destiny and the nation's, rather than a vendetta, that motivated his campaign. Oren Root, who opened an office in Washington and became Nelson's special assistant for federal and interstate relations during the short-lived campaign, recalls Rockefeller telling him, "The country's in real danger, Oren, confronted with vast perils both foreign and domestic. We do not have much time. We can, of course, do many worthwhile things here in New York, but the great issues will be decided in Washington." Oren Root, *Persons and Persuasions* (New York, 1974), p. 155.

338   "Almost a dependency":   T. H. White, *The Making of the President 1968* (New York, 1969), p. 263.

339   "Taking soundings":   For a summary of Nelson's maneuvering in 1959, see Desmond, pp. 215 ff.; also White, *Making 1960*, pp. 66–77.

339   Withdrawal: For text of speech and interview with Nelson, see *New York Times*, December 27, 1959.

339   Met Nikita Khrushchev: Chalmers Roberts, *First Rough Draft* (New York, 1973), p. 161. Not long after the meeting with the Soviet Premier, Nelson was interviewed on a television news show. When a questioner asked how long the United States and the USSR could go on "not trusting each other," Nelson erupted, "Oh, I think you can trust them all right. I think you can trust them to try to carry out their stated objective of the domination of the world" (Morris, *NR*, pp. 353–354).

340   "Deeply concerned":   Desmond, p. 260.

340   Avoid any disunity: For events leading to the Compact of Fifth Avenue, see White, *Making 1960*, pp. 196 ff.

341   "Richard E. Nixon":   Desmond, p. 282.

341   "A good hand":   Berle, p. 715.

342n. $4 million bunker: *New York Times*, February 22, 1960.

342n. Nelson's Pocantico shelter: *New York Times*, March 5, 1960.

342n. Laurance's Pocantico shelter: Authors' interviews with Laurance's children.

342n. Jack Bronston: quoted by Jack Newfield in "The Case Against Nelson Rockefeller," *New York*, March 9, 1970.

342n. Nehru: The meeting between Nelson and Nehru took place in John K. Galbraith's presence and was later recounted by Anthony Lewis during Nelson's confirmation hearings. *New York Times*, November 21, 1974.

343   Woo the Republican right: See Robert D. Novak, *The Agony of the GOP 1964* (New York, 1965), pp. 46 ff.,

67ff. See also George Gilder and Bruce Chapman, *The Party That Lost Its Head* (New York, 1906), pp. 121 ff.

343   "Rocky's really not such a bad fellow": Novak, p. 74.

343   "Political fakery": Ibid., p. 69.

343   "It is very hard for me": *New York Times*, April, 11, 1963.

344   Fact-finding junket: Authors' interview with confidential source.

344   "Tod was smart": Authors' interview with George Gilder.

344   "Frank felt": Authors' interview with Mrs. Linda Storrow.

345   Fire: See Gervasi, p. 243.

345   Louis Lefkowitz: See Desmond, pp. 291 ff.

345   Separation: See *New York Times*, November 19, 1961.

345   Loss of Michael: See Milt Machlin, *The Search for Michael Rockefeller* (New York, 1972).

346   "Ever since": Cited in Desmond, p. 303.

346   At Tod's apartment: The scene is described by Anne-Marie Rasmussen, *There Was Once a Time* (New York, 1975), pp. 147–149.

346   Robert Morgenthau: For details on the 1962 campaign, see Desmond, pp. 307 ff.

346   Walter Lippmann: See *Newsweek*, April 1, 1963, p. 15.

347   "The remarriage": Authors' interview with Abby Rockefeller.

347   Wedding: See *New York Times*, May 5, 1963.

347   Happy and Robin: Authors' interviews with members of the fourth Rockefeller generation. See also T. H. White, *The Making of the President 1964* (New York, 1965), pp. 98 ff.

348   "Robin was the chief force": Authors' interview with confidential source.

348   "I'm not sure": Ibid.

348   "Nelson was really deeply in love": Authors' interview with Mrs. Linda Storrow.

348   "She was just dazzling": Authors' interview with George Gilder.

349   Gallup Poll: Novak, p. 148.

349   Considerate release for his family: "The new Mrs. Rockefeller did not want him to run for the Presidency; no one in fact wanted him to run except himself." White, *Making 1964*, p. 105.

349   July 14, 1963, he unveiled: See Novak, pp. 208–209.

350   "Nothing wrong": Gilder and Chapman, p. 126.

350   Political apparatus: Ibid., p. 120.

350   Contributions: U.S. Senate, *Hearings into the Nomination of Nelson Rockefeller to be Vice President*, pp. 657–658. Commenting on the $100,000 donation from Babs and the $25,000 from David, Nelson told the senators: "It

happened that I was divorced. It happened that I was re-married. It happened that some members of the family were upset.... It happened that these two were.... This was a gesture of friendship and love and affection from two members of my family who had been upset."

350n. "Hiring him": Authors' interview with John Lockwood.

350n. Eisenhower would never forgive: Lyon, p. 838. See also White, *Making 1964*, p. 93n.

351 Cruel campaign: Authors' interview with Tom Braden. For details on the California primary, see Novak, pp. 383 ff.; White, *Making 1964*, pp. 150 ff.

353 "Being President?": See Richard Reeves, "The Nation-wide Search for Nelson Rockefeller," *New York*, September 4, 1974, p. 8.

353 "A strong, decent face": Norman Mailer, *"Cannibals and Christians* (New York, 1966), p. 32.

353 Withdrawal: See *New York Times*, July 26, 1965.

353 Lindsay campaign: Authors' interview with Congressman Ogden Reid, Jr.

354 "No-knock" law: For a polemical summary of Rockefeller's record on crime and civil liberties issues from 1959 to 1968, see Sidney Zion, "Rocky The Cop," *Ramparts*, June 15, 1968. (Zion was *New York Times* legal correspondent and a former assistant U.S. attorney.)

354 Campaign against O'Connor: See Neal R. Peirce, *The Megastates of America* (New York, 1972), pp. 49 ff.

355 "I believe Rocky": Cited by Reeves. p. 9.

355 "You shoot at him": Cited by Nick Thimmesch, *The Condition of Republicanism* (New York, 1968), p. 113.

355 Romney: For an interesting account of Nelson's support of Romney, see White, *Making 1968*, pp. 43 ff.

355 Morrow, Gilder, Kissinger: Authors' interview with George Gilder.

356 He came to Nelson: "Three times on board [shipboard 1967 National Governors' Conference], closeted with Rockefeller in Rockefeller's cabin on the sun deck, he pleaded with New York's governor to let him off the hook. He was through, Romney insisted: Nelson must run for President. But Rockefeller would not—the plan was for Romney to run as the governors' candidate. He must go on with it." White, *Making 1968*, p. 69.

356 Withdrawal: See *New York Times*, March 22, 1968.

356 Reentry: See *New York Times*, May 1, 1968.

356 Hughes and Kissinger: Authors' interview with George Gilder.

357n. "Go see Henry": Kalb and Kalb, p. 16.

357 "Black Book": Authors' interview with Linda Edgerly, former assistant archivist for the Family Archives.

357 "He wanted:" Authors' interview with Steven Rockefeller.

358 Kissinger's insistence: Authors' interview with George Gilder.

358 $8 million: George Thayer, *Who Shakes the Money Tree* (New York, 1973), p. 162.

360 A pamphlet: Phyllis Schlafly, *A Choice—Not an Echo* (Alton, Ill., 1964), p. 6.

360 Rockefellers and Communists: The "international conspiracy" of which the Rockefellers have traditionally been presumed guilty by the right wing (see Morris Beale, *The House of Rockefeller* [Washington, D.C., 1959], and Emanuel Josephson, *Rockefeller Internationalist* [New York, 1952]) is the subject of a recent, widely circulated tract by Gary Allen, *None Dare Call It Conspiracy* (Seal Beach, Calif., 1972); see especially Chapter 6, "Rockefeller and Reds."

361 Ingenious diagrams: See, for example, *The Rockefeller Empire in Latin America,* published by the North American

361 Right's fear of conspiracy: A prime bugaboo has been Congress on Latin America, 1969.
   the Bilderberg organization of businessmen and politicians from all the Western nations (it was founded by Prince Bernhard of the Netherlands as an adjunct to NATO) which meets periodically to discuss common problems. Because David is a member of the organization and has hosted its annual meetings at Colonial Williamsburg, conspiracy theorists have always assumed that it was the modern equivalent of the Bavarian Illuminati. However, while the group may have the form of conspiracy—elite membership and behind-the-scenes meetings—there is no evidence to support the claim that that is its function.

361 $60 billion: See Victor Perlo, *The Empire of High Finance* (New York, 1957), p. 327.

361 $5 billion: See Ferdinand Lundberg, *The Rich and the Super-Rich* (New York, 1969), p. 191.

363 $25,000: See Geoffrey T. Hellman, "Out of the Cocoon on the Fifty Sixth Floor," *New Yorker,* November 4, 1972.

363 JDR3 paused: Authors' interview with Jerry Swift, former JDR3 aide.

364 Tod as house guest: Authors' interview with Steven Rockefeller.

364 "One who loved": Authors' interview wih Hope Rockefeller Spencer.

365 "A peaceful China": Address to Asia Society, Rockefeller Family Archives.

365 "For the past twenty years": Cited in Hellman article.

366 "My principal reservation": Asia Foundation file, Rockefeller Family Archives.

366 Creation of Magsaysay Foundation: See Magsaysay Foundation file, Rockefeller Family Archives.

367n. Landsdale: For his career in the CIA, see Victor Marchetti and John Marks, *The Cult of Intelligence* (New York, 1973), pp. 50–51.

367 "Any organized means": Ibid.

367 Founding members: See Council on Foreign Relations file, Rockefeller Family Archives.

368 JDR3 and Diem: Communication from Dr. Joseph Ernst, director of Rockefeller Family Archives. See also Peter Dale Scott, "The Vietnam War and the CIA-Financial Establishment," in Mark Selden, ed., *Re-Making Asia* (New York, 1974), p. 128.

368 William Henderson: Ibid., p. 127.

368 Young's letter: See Russell Fifield, *The American Commitment in Southeast Asia* (New York, 1973), p. 259.

368 SEADAG: Authors' interview with Jerry Bass, program coordinator of SEADAG.

368 "Part of its expanding effort": Authors' interview with Joseph Fischer.

369 Samuel P. Huntington: See Noam Chomsky, *American Power and the New Mandarins* (New York, 1969), p. 42.

369 Demonstration: Authors' interview with Jon Livingston, managing editor of *Bulletin of Concerned Asian Scholars*.

369 "Rockefeller's style": Authors' interview with Joseph Fischer.

369 Japan Society: For further details, see Hellman article.

369 "I had been": Authors' interview with JDR3.

370 Charles Spofford: Authors' interview with Donald McLean.

371 "Frankly": Authors' interview with William Zeckendorf.

371 "John . . . has a veneer": See Hellman article.

371 Raising the deficit: Lincoln Center files, Rockefeller Family Archives.

371 Hubbard estate: *New York Times*, November 2, 1959.

371 "I was exploring": Authors' interview with JDR3.

372 J. Paul Getty: The exchange of letters on Lincoln Center is in the Rockefeller Family Archives.

372 Upset with Brothers Fund: Authors' interview with Jerry Swift.

372 "The Fund had gotten": Authors' interview wih Emmet Hughes.

372 Sincere pursuit: Authors' interview with Jerry Swift.

373 Population: The interest in population had always been a natural complement to JDR3's involvement in Asian affairs. However, occasionally, when he tried to force the connection, the result was amusing. On February 27, 1959, his cousin Richard Aldrich, whom Nelson had put in charge of IBEC's operations in Brazil, wrote JDR3: "As you may or may not know, Nelson, David and Laurance own 40% of a large tract of land in Mato Grosso. The remaining 60% is owned by Walther Moreira Salles, prominent Brazilian banker and diplomat, together with Maurico Verdier. Dur-

ing the past three years they have been negotiating with the Japanese embassy to acquire about 100 families (for settlement and farming on the land). At the outset the embassy was extremely enthusiastic and promised 100 families. Subsequent to this, numbers of families promised have been reduced . . . and to this date the farm area has not received any. . . . Thinking of your interest in Japan . . . Verdier approached me the other day asking for your assistance. . . . I realize that any direct interest on your part, given Nelson's ownership of the farm, could involve certain public relations problems . . . but I hope that in some way you can be helpful to us." JDR3 replied, "It would hardly seem to me that this was the type of thing in which either the Japan Society or myself personally should get involved. On the other hand, Japan does have a population problem . . . and this looks like a good opportunity for 100 families." Japan Society file, Rockefeller Family Archives.

373 Pop Council: For an official summary of its growth and activities over its first twelve years, see *The Population Council, 1952–1964: A Report,* July 1965.

373 "John had dropped": Authors' interview with Fred Jaffe, vice president of Planned Parenthood.

373 Dean Rusk: For a detailed view of JDR3's lobbying activities on the population front during the Johnson administration, see Piotrow, pp. 88–89.

373 Nixon's inauguration: Ibid., pp. 194 ff.

374 The final report: *Population and the American Future* (New York, 1972).

374 He took pride: Authors' interview with Hope Rockefeller Spencer.

375 "I consider abortion": *New York Times,* May 6, 1972.

375n. Nixon snub: Authors' interview with Hope Rockefeller Spencer and Fred Jaffe.

375n. Nelson vetoed it: For the complete text of his veto message, see *New York Times,* May 14, 1972.

375 "He thought it": Authors' interview with Hope Rockefeller Spencer.

376n. "Approaching taxes": Authors' interview with John Hodgkin, former chief accountant in Room 5600.

377 "He tried to get us": Authors' interview with Hugh Romney.

377 Youth Task Force: See JDR3 Fund *Annual Report,* 1971.

377 "The problem was": Authors' interview with confidential sources.

378 "He went over": Authors' interview with Jerry Swift.

378 Alida: Authors' interview with Alida Rockefeller.

378 "To try the new": Authors' interview with JDR3.

379 "Toughest assignments": John D. Rockefeller 3rd, *The Second American Revolution* (New York, 1973), p. xi.

379 "My thesis": Ibid., p. 7.

380 "The idea was": Authors' interview with John Harr. (Formerly an employee of the State Department, Harr joined JDR3 as chief aide shortly after the departure of Donald McLean.)

381 All but Laurance: Laurance's attitude toward the documentary was described by one of his associates who wishes to remain anonymous.

382 ORRRC's findings: Published as *Outdoor Recreation for America* (Washington, D.C., January 1962).

382 $800,000: American Conservation Association files, Rockefeller Family Archives.

383 "Quality of life": See John Kenneth Galbraith, *The Affluent Society* (New York, 1958).

383 "Business can take": Laurance's speech reprinted in *Vital Speeches,* January 1, 1966.

384 Lady Bird: "Laurance Rockefeller and Johnson worked pretty closely together. Laurance courted Lady Bird on the beautification issue and got far better access to the presidency as a result of it than he managed to get to Nixon. LBJ stood in awe of the Rockefellers. They represented the established Eastern aristocracy to him, and he liked the association. Laurance can pretty much see Nixon whenever he wants, get an audience, that is, but he doesn't have the same kind of clout as he did with LBJ." Authors' interview with Mike Feldman, former counsel to JFK and, more briefly, Lyndon Johnson.

384 "Great stone house": Lady Bird Johnson, *A White House Diary* (New York, 1970), p. 674.

385 "Number-one conservationist": Ibid., p. 241.

386 Nelson recruited: Allan Talbot, *Power Along the Hudson* (New York, 1972), p. 88.

386 "Imaginative long-term solution": Nelson A. Rockefeller, *Our Environment Can Be Saved* (New York, 1970), p. 79.

386 Laurance followed suit: Talbot, p. 85.

386 Robert Moses: For details on Nelson's efforts to force Moses out of the State Council job so he could replace him with Laurance, see Caro, pp. 1070 ff.

386 Scenic Hudson: For details on this organization, see Talbot, pp. 96–115.

386 Palisades: For a summary of Junior's efforts to preserve the Palisades, see Fosdick, *John D. Rockefeller, Jr.: A Portrait* (New York, 1956), pp. 321–324.

387 Federal Power Commission: See William Rodgers, *Rockefeller's Follies* (New York, 1966), pp. 109–111. "Perhaps most significant from the FPC point of view was Laurance Rockefeller's public support of Con Ed in 1964" (Talbot, p. 120).

387 "Governor Rockefeller": See the *Cornwall Local,* March 25, 1965.

387   $10 million: For the calculation based on the TNEC, see Lundberg, *The Rich and the Super-Rich,* p. 187.

387   "The people who own Con Ed": Robert H. Boyle, *The Hudson River: A Natural and Unnatural History* (New York, 1966), p. 163.

387   Richard Ottinger: Authors' interview with William ("Mike") Kitzmiller, former legislative assistant to Congressman Ottinger and a principal of events discussed below.

388   Hudson River Valley Commission: Talbot, pp. 140 ff.

388   In 1957: The history of Interstate 87 and the Rockefeller estate is summarized by Talbot, pp. 165 ff. See also Alan Mowbray, *Road to Ruin* (New York, 1969), pp. 167 ff.

389   Confidential Interior Department memo: Reprinted in U.S. House of Representatives, Subcommittee on Fisheries and Wildlife Conservation, *Hearings on the Impact of the Hudson River Expressway Proposal* (Washington, D.C., 1969), p. 114.

389   Pocantico's potential: For discussion and documentation, see Part IV, below.

390   "That's odd": Rodgers, p. 179.

390   "People were begging": Authors' interview with Charles Stoddard.

390   Compelling case: See U.S. House Subcommittee on Fisheries and Wildlife, *Hearings,* pp. 11–25.

390   Udall on record: Ibid. p. 110.

390   "It seemed to me": Authors' interview with Stewart C. Udall.

391   "Mr. Rockefeller said": For the complete text of the memo, see U.S. House Subcommittee on Fisheries and Wildlife, *Hearings,* p. 113.

391n. "Dead Issue": Cited by Myer Kutz, *Rockefeller Power* (New York, 1974), p. 189.

392   Udall stood back: The following account comes largely from authors' interview with Michael McCloskey, executive director of the Sierra Club.

392   Byzantine political situation: See William V. Shannon, "Mr. Reagan, Mr. Rockefeller, and the Redwoods," *New York Times,* August 27, 1967.

393n. Save-the-Redwoods League: Authors' interview with Newton Drury, director of the league.

393   Laurance shuttled: Authors' interview with Michael McCloskey.

394   "This park": Authors' interview with Stewart Udall.

395   "Purpose": The complete public relations plan for the opening is in the Caneel Bay Plantation file, Rockefeller Family Archives. Laurance returned to the relation between tourism and parks in a speech during the dedication ceremonies for the Virgin Islands National Park: "The Virgin Is-

lands are on the threshold of a new era when more and
more people are becoming aware of their uniquely pleasant
climate, their magnificent beaches, their scenic splendor. . . .
We have seen the revolutionary impact that air transport
has had on travel habits. We know that jet transports with
their cruising speeds of five and six hundred miles an hour,
are bringing these once distant islands within a morning's
journey of the great metropolitan cities of the eastern seaboard. Indeed the travel and recreation potential of the Virgin Islands—their foremost industry—will mean continued
economic growth in the years ahead, and this means new
opportunities for everyone" (Ibid.).

395   Saint Croix: "In 1965 [Leon] Hess [of Amerada-Hess]
      . . . was looking for broader fields of operation. . . . He toyed
      with the idea of building a refinery in the Bahamas but was
      persuaded by David Rockefeller, president of the Chase
      Manhattan Bank and one of Hess Oil's principal bankers, to
      look into the possibilities of the Virgins, where the Rocke-
      feller family owned a lot of real estate, including four thou-
      sand acres on St. Croix." Edward A. O'Neill, *Rape of the
      American Virgins* (New York, 1972), p. 127.

395   $20 million Mauna Kea: For a good account of Lau-
      rance's decision to build the Mauna Kea and develop the
      surrounding area, see "Laurance Rockefeller—Economic
      Development with a Conservationist's Touch," *Hotel
      Business*, December 1972.

396   "This is an uplifting": Ibid.

396   "Mr. Rockefeller insists": Ibid.

397   Eastern Airlines trade: See *Wall Street Journal*, Septem-
      ber 28, 1967.

397   Dilrock-Eastern: See *Wall Street Journal*, May 29, 1968.

397n. "It was well known": Authors' interview with Robert
      Beckman.

397   Haleakala: *New York Times*, January 11, 1969.

397   The price tag: The Family Office will not reveal the ex-
      act figure of Laurance's conservation philanthropies. The
      figure of less than $10 million is based on the authors' esti-
      mates from available data.

398   "A curious study": Authors' interview with Stewart Udall.

398   "If anybody but a Rockefeller": Authors' interview with
      Charles Stoddard.

398   A special Commission: See *Joint House-Senate Collo-
      quium to Discuss a National Policy for the Environment*,
      July 17, 1968 (Washington, D.C., 1968), pp. 4–12.

399   Unsigned memorandum: See Talbot, p. 143.

399   $50,000 a year: See Conservation Foundation *Annual
      Reports*, 1948–1970.

400   "Rabid conservationists": Cited by Boyle, p. 163n.

400 Friends of the Earth: Authors' interview with David Brower.

400n. New England Nuclear reprimanded: Authors' interview with Leo Goodman, nuclear power consultant; see also AEC documents file on New England Nuclear.

400 An emeritus: Out of the center of events, Laurance has devoted himself to playing a modest role on the periphery of the dialogue on urban growth. Two of his recent endeavors have involved the underwriting of a study on new towns (*Man and His Urban Environment: A Manual of Specific Considerations For the 70s and Beyond* [New York, 1972]) and chairmanship of a Task Force on Land Use and Urban Growth sponsored by Rockefeller Brothers Fund (*The Use of Land: A Citizens Policy Guide to Urban Growth* [New York, 1973]).

400 "Just because": Authors' interview with Gene Setzer.

401 Theodore Roszak: Authors' interview with Marion Rockefeller Weber.

402 "Well, no politician": Authors' interview with Lucy Rockefeller Waletzky.

402 "I feel sad": Authors' interview with Laura Rockefeller Chasin.

402 "He depends": Authors' interview with Marion Rockefeller Weber.

402 "Zen-like": Rockefeller Family Archives.

403 Telephone call: Authors' interviews with the children of David Rockefeller and with George Gilder.

403 "Hell, I don't know": Cited by Roland Evans and Robert Novak, *Nixon in the White House* (New York, 1971), p. 23.

404 "The equivalent": See *Finance*, January 1969.

405 Growing dominance: For a probing look at this trend, see U.S. House of Representatives Committee on Banking and Currency, *Commercial Banks and Their Trust Activities: Emerging Influence on the American Economy*, 2 vols. (Washington, D.C., 1968).

405n. Transportation industry: For the Chase's stockholding position in this sector, see U.S. House of Representatives, *Commercial Banks and their Trust Activities*. Also, U.S. Senate Committee on Government Operations, *Disclosure of Corporate Ownership* (Washington, D.C., 1974).

405 President of the Chase: For a summary of the Rockefeller-Champion regime, see *Newsweek*, April 3, 1967, pp. 72 ff.

406 David's contribution: See religion files, Rockefeller Family Archives.

406 Art acquisition: "To date, the Chase has invested nearly five hundred thousand dollars in art. . . . Champion, whose tastes are more conservative than Rockefeller's, could sit in on the purchasing sessions if he cared to, but he doesn't. . . .

The sessions are spirited. Alfred Barr [member of the Chase Art Acquisition Committee and former director of MOMA] is constantly trying to prod Rockefeller, whose vote counts heavily, and whose veto does too, into accepting more and more outré paintings. Rockefeller, who also believes in balance and respects the views of Champion and the other traditionalists he has to work with, tries to placate them by buying a few representative pieces. Not long ago, he approved of one thoroughly naturalistic landscape, priced at eighteen hundred dollars, even though he could scarcely bear to look at it without grimacing." Kahn, *New Yorker*, January 9, 1965.

407 "I'd go down": Authors' interview with Richard Reeves.

407 "He holds": Authors' interview with George Gilder.

408 "To our loss": Authors' interview with Richard Rockefeller.

408 Kennedy administration: For relations between JFK and the business community, see Hobart Rowen, *The Free Enterprisers, Kennedy, Johnson and the Business Establishment* (New York, 1964).

408 "Economic growth": David Rockefeller, "International Financial Challenges: A Question of Priorities," speech delivered at the Far East Financial Forum, 1971, distributed by the CMB.

410 3,000-word letter: See *Life*, July 6, 1962.

410 "Concern and dismay": Ibid.

410 "I am not sure": Cited by Arthur M. Schlesinger, Jr., *A Thousand Days* (Boston, 1965), p. 649.

411 "There's nothing on earth": cited by Kahn, *New Yorker*, January 9, 1965.

411 "Helluva nice guy": Authors' interview with Walter Heller. JFK had appointed him as a balance on the left to the conservative economic advice he knew he would get from Secretary of the Treasury Dillon. (Heller says, "Kennedy put it to me this way: 'I'm going to have Dillon over on the right and I want you to be a balance wheel on the left of center.' ")

411 Tax cut: See Leon Keyserling, *Progress on Poverty* (Washington, D.C., 1964). Also Leo Huberman and Paul Sweezy, "The Kennedy-Johnson Boom," in David Mermelstein and Marvin Gettleman, eds., *The Great Society Reader* (New York, 1967).

412 Alliance had been generated: See Jerome Levinson and Juan de Onis, *The Alliance That Lost Its Way* (New York, 1970).

412 Punta del Este: Ibid., pp. 50 ff.

413 Richard Aldrich: Ibid., p. 52.

413 "Firm commitment": See *New York Times*, April 24, 1963.

413n. David merged: Levinson and de Onis, p. 159.

413 Paunch Corps: *New York Times*, September 17, 1963.

414   "From conservative Latin American groups":   New York Times, April 14, 1963.

414   Thomas Mann: Ibid., pp. 87 ff.

414   "Move to ensure":   Rusk quoted in New York Times, April 4, 1965.

414   "Overly ambitious concepts":   David Rockefeller, "What Private Enterprise Means to Latin America," Foreign Affairs, April 1, 1966, p. 408.

415   "This is your country":   Authors' interview with Richard Goodwin.

416   "In the past":   Cited by Harry Magdoff, The Age of Imperialism (New York, 1969), p. 176.

416   Full-page ad: See New York Times, September 9, 1965.

416   Conference with Ky: Authors' interview with Peggy Rockefeller. See also New York Times, July 19, 1966.

417   "At least $10 billion":   New York Times, April 25, 1968.

417   Sharpeville: See Jim Hoagland, South Africa: Civilizations in Conflict (Boston, 1972), pp. 338–344; also, John Hatch, A History of Postwar Africa (New York, 1965), pp. 222 ff.

417   To restore confidence: For the activities of the consortium, see Hoagland, pp. 342 ff. Also, "Partners in Apartheid—United States Policy on South Africa," Africa Today, March 1964, p. 4.; and "A Special Report on American Involvement in the South African Economy," Africa Today, January 1966, pp. 12 ff.

418   "Make South Africa White":   See "Partners in Apartheid," Africa Today.

418   Standard Bank: For more on merger, see "World Links, Standard Bank," Financial Mail [London], February 11, 1972.

418   Protest: Authors' interviews with the Reverend George Houser, executive director of the American Committee on Africa, and Jim Smith of the Corporate Information Center of the National Council of Churches. See also Summary Report on the Bank Campaign, The American Committee on Africa (n.d.), 164 Madison Avenue, New York.

419   Stockholders' meeting: H. E. Heinemann, "Chase Bank Defends South African Loans," New York Times, March 29, 1967.

419   "None of us holds":   David's remarks were distributed in printed form by the CMB.

420   Argument was already familiar: Authors' interview with Peggy Rockefeller and Richard Rockefeller.

420   We who care: Authors' interview with Marion Rockefeller Weber.

420n.   "No way":   Hoagland, p. 349.

420n.   "More economic progress":   Ibid., p. 210.

420   $200,000:   Rockefeller Brothers Fund file, Rockefeller Family Archives.

420 "The moment has arrived": David Rockefeller, "The Social Responsibilities of Business to Urban America," address to Conference of Financial Executives Institute, 1968.

421 Urban Development Bank: See "What Will It Take to Bring Cities Back to Life—An Interview with David Rockefeller," *U.S. News and World Report*, June 7, 1971, pp. 50–56.

421 Failed to sustain: The same charge was leveled by Congressman Wright Patman, David's perennial antagonist. After David had expressed his concern to provide low-cost housing loans during their television debate "Banks and the Poor" in November 1970, Patman retorted, "How deep is this concern? I have had the staff of the Banking and Currency Committee look behind these claims and we have discovered that nationwide the commercial banks have devoted only slightly more than 8% of their loans to housing. And much of this 8% is in high priced housing." Later the Texas lawmaker added, "In the Chase Manhattan Bank . . . they are only putting an insignificant amount into housing, but . . . they have plenty of money to go into Resorts International [owner of a string of gambling casinos in the Caribbean] which operates for a profit. . . . They have had plenty of money for speculation. They have had plenty of money for everything, except one of the essentials of family life—adequate shelter. They didn't have any money for that." (See transcript of "Banks and the Poor," National Educational Television.)

421 Midtown expressway: Authors' interview with Paul Du-Brul, assistant to Bronx Borough Chief Robert Abrams.

421 Manhattan Landing: See Robert Abrams, "Manhattan Landing is an Ill Conceived Plan," *New York Times*, July 2, 1972.

422 Whitney Young: Junior had maintained the contact with black organizations begun with his involvement in Tuskegee, Hampton, Spelman, and other black Southern colleges at the turn of the century. For a time he had made token donations of some $500 a year to the NAACP. However, in 1938, his philanthropy adviser, Arthur Packard, wrote a letter to Rockefeller questioning the future of this relationship because he was upset by the NAACP's insistence on trying to push an antilynching bill through the Senate. Packard regarded this as a radical act, too radical for the Rockefellers to be involved in, but recommended a continuation of the annual donation nonetheless because "abrupt termination of the $500 gift might be regarded as a rebuke and would carry with it the possibility of some kind of controversy." (NAACP file, Rockefeller Family Archives.) At the same time that he was concerned about the "radical" program of the NAACP, however, Packard was enthusiastically behind the program of the Urban League. Beginning their support

of the organization in the 1920s, the Rockefellers were contributing nearly 35 percent of the league's budget by 1940 and were deeply involved in its internal affairs and management. After returning from the Army, Winthrop went on the league's board of trustees and in 1952 contributed $100,000 toward a permanent headquarters. When Winthrop left for Arkansas and the league began to drift, Brothers Fund head Dana Creel searched for someone to take over a leadership role, finally deciding on Fund employee and troubleshooter Lindsley Kimball. On July 22, 1958, Creel wrote Winthrop: "I have now had several talks with Lindsley Kimball about the Urban League situation and the possibility of his going on the board to see what he could do from inside to (1) strengthen the board, (2) sharpen and possibly redirect the program, (3) help in the selection of Granger's [Lester Granger, aging white director of the league] successor." (Urban League files, Rockefeller Family Archives.) Kimball, who became chairman of the league board, had heard Whitney Young speak at a 1957 sociology convention. Then a professor at a southern Negro college, Young had reached the top of his profession. He had little or no hope of being hired by a Northern school. He was receptive to Kimball's suggestion that he belonged in the "action arena." Kimball then arranged for both Young and his wife to receive a two-year General Education Board fellowship for postgraduate work at Harvard. Meanwhile he persuaded Granger to step down, softening the blow by the grant of a two-year traveling fellowship from the Rockefeller Foundation (of which Kimball was vice-president). With Granger out of the picture, Kimball installed Young as the Urban League's executive director. (Authors' interview with Lindsley Kimball.) In the next decade Young—who had joined King, Wilkins, and Farmer as the movement's "Big Four"—would raise the league's budget from $325,000 to $6,100,000, making it the country's blue-chip civil rights organization. Much of the expanded support came from the Ford Foundation and from individuals (like Henry Ford II, whom Winthrop had helped to interest in the Urban League in 1948) with whom Young now associated in the National Alliance of Businessmen and the Urban Coalition, and whose generosity increased after the Watts riot of 1965. But more than $1 million would come from contributions of the Rockefeller Brothers Fund and the Foundation, of which Young became a trustee in 1968. This background of generosity must necessarily have been on Young's mind when it came time for him to help save David Rockefeller from having to hear the story about the Emperor's new clothes. (For a history of the first thirty years of the league, see Nancy Weiss, *The National Urban League 1910–1940* [Oxford, 1974].)

422 Young succeeded: See *New York Times*, July 23, 1970.

423 New towns: See David Rockefeller, "New Towns and Urban Rehabilitation," reprinted in *Vital Speeches*, April 1, 1971, pp. 354–357.

423 Columbia, Maryland: "The Chase Manhattan Bank, the Connecticut General Life Insurance Company and the Teachers Insurance and Annuity Association have invested $80 million in this five-by-nine-mile city which has office buildings, stores, a community college and a hospital in a downtown section surrounded by seven villages, each with a maximum population of 15,000. . . . Scattered around the perimeter of the city are industrial parks, including General Electric's $350 million appliance park, which can employ 12,000 people in a plant half again as big as the Pentagon" (Kutz, p. 111).

423 David's real estate: These real estate investments are summarized annually in the confidential Report to the Board of Managers of Rockefeller Family and Associates, which is distributed to family members. The authors have obtained copies of the reports for the years 1968–1974.

423 L'Enfant Plaza: See Zeckendorf, pp. 205 ff.

423 "Well, I'm the guy": Ibid., pp. 224.

423 Embarcadero Center: Details of the investment are in the Report to the Board of Managers cited above.

424 David pointed out: Authors' interview with James Bronkema, manager of Embarcadero Center.

424 Stavros Niarchos: Details of the Atlanta investment are shown in the Report to the Board of Managers.

424 "When I worked": Authors' interview with Richard Reeves.

425 Wright Patman: The Texas populist had been a gadfly buzzing annoyingly around the heads of the large metropolitan banks for years, challenging their explanation of policies and asserting that their increasing accumulation of power was dangerous. David's statements seemed especially to raise Patman's hackles, and the two men clashed repeatedly. (In their television debate of November 1970 on the NET—"Banks and the Poor"—Patman's nettlesome charges drew a rare sarcasm from Rockefeller: "I understand that when he was a young man, he was once turned down for some loan that he tried to make in his local Texas bank, and he seems to have taken a rather dim view of bankers ever since.") The banks' responsibility to provide low-cost housing loans was one issue over which the two men had quarreled. Another involved the Penn Central's bankruptcy in June 1970. The Chase had lent the railroad considerable sums, and its trust department held large blocs of its stock. Stuart Saunders, chairman of the Penn Central, was also a director of the Chase. Because of these close ties, the bank had been privy to the impending bankruptcy

three weeks before it was made public. During that time it had taken steps to unload quietly a quarter of a million shares of Penn Central stock, soon to be practically worthless. When David appeared before Patman's Banking and Currency Committee in April 1971 to testify on a bill to make such director interlocks illegal, he demurred. "In the final analysis," he said, "major reliance must be placed on the uncompromising integrity and good sense of corporate officers and directors." It was just such an assumption of altruism that elicited Patman's special irony. "The Chase's pietistic utterances," he said, "are limited only by the speed of its mimeograph machines." (For the Chase involvement in the Penn Central, see Christopher Elias, *The Dollar Barons* [New York, 1973], p. 232.)

425   The Chase was an oil bank: Ironically, Standard of New Jersey would always remain tied into the National City Bank. It had gotten the account because of William Rockefeller's ties to James Stillman; the ties were too solid to be broken later when Junior gained control of the Chase, although it often occurred ·to the bank's executives that they deserved these large accounts. On December 16, 1930, for instance, Chase vice-president Henry Cooper wrote Thomas Debevoise: "At different times in the past, I have discussed with you or Bert [Cutler] the possibility of getting a bigger share of this company's [Socony] business. . . . I am a rather prejudiced and ignorant person, but I cannot quite understand why the City Bank should get the great bulk of the business and we get the fringe end. It seems to me that it ought to be the other way around." Junior was chary of disturbing the status quo and raising the question of the family's relationship to the oil companies, yet as it became clear that the ability to parlay the power inherent in the family institutions would be crucial to the Brothers' bid for power, accommodations were made that benefited the Chase. On June 18, 1935, Nelson wrote to Fred Gehle, another Chase vice-president, who had asked if there was any way of getting the accounts of Standard of Kentucky. After noting that the Rockefeller Family had no stock in this company, Nelson added, "I talked with him [Mr. Resor, treasurer of Standard of New Jersey] at some length yesterday and he is arranging to transfer, gradually, some twenty accounts of their subsidiaries to the Chase National Bank. . . . Upon my return from Europe I will take up with Socony Vacuum the question of a closer relationship." Chase National Bank file, Rockefeller Family Archives. The Chase is a lender to the oil companies. It is also a trustee for many of the private fortunes—not just the Rockefellers—whose wealth is in oil stocks. The Chase is also a recognized leader in oil banking through its prestigious Petroleum Department. "Even before the war, the Chase had

developed a Petroleum Department and was widely regarded as the New York bank most knowledgeable concerning loans on proven oil and gas properties in connection with their development, purchase and merger. Since the war, such loans by the Chase have exceeded a total of one billion dollars." Timothy Pfeiffer and George W. Jacques, *Law Practice in a Turbulent World* (New York, 1965), p. 218.

426n. "David goes through Russia": Authors' interview with George Gilder.

426   Nicolae Ceausescu: See *New York Times*, October 15, 1970.

426   Nasser: See Jack Anderson column for January 20, 1970.

426   Anwar Sadat: See *New York Times*, March 11, 1971.

427   "Plate glass curtain": See *New York Times*, March 6, 1971.

427   "800 million people": See *New York Times*, March 10, 1971. In his Singapore speech, David had reminded listeners that before the decade was over, U.S. oil companies were planning to spend $35 million in capital investments along the western rim of the Pacific, including the waters off China and Vietnam. (The Provisional Revolutionary Government of South Vietnam, equally pragmatic, would renegotiate the agreement with Gulf and other U.S. oil majors not long after the fall of Saigon.) The Communist countries had raw materials to develop and growing consumer needs to be met. As Rockefeller would tell a select Swedish audience a few weeks later (see *New York Times*, May 15, 1971), if the U.S. did not supply the Chinese with advanced goods and equipment, other countries would. He remained confident, however, that Western technologies penetrating Communist societies would be an avant-garde winning acceptance for Western ideas. In his "plate glass curtain" speech of March 6, 1971, he ended by saying of Communist governments: "A disenchantment with controlled government planning can be seen in countries like Poland and Yugoslavia. . . . One wonders how long it will be before the people of Cuba grow disillusioned with the bleak economic outlook Communism has brought them."

427   Payoff: See "What Does David Rockefeller Want for Christmas?," *Forbes*, December 15, 1973, pp. 24–32.

427   Arab nations: For a summary of the CMB's Mideast intentions for 1974, see *American Banker*, February 11, 1974.

427   Impressed Kissinger: Authors' interview with George Gilder.

427   "I think I have": This comment was made during a taped interview with writer Jim Gollin for a story on the Rockefeller family that was never completed. Mr. Gollin kindly allowed the authors to listen to this tape.

428   "The first member": Ibid.

428   October 12, 1972: See "Why There is a New Face at

the Chase Manhattan," *Business Week*, November 4, 1972. In addition to published sources, the authors have interviewed the following individuals in an effort to understand the policies of the CMB and David's responsibility for them: David Cates, of David Cates and Co., bank analysts; Michael Hudson, former Chase analyst and now free-lance banking consultant; Ed Foldessy, *Wall Street Journal* correspondent; Stanley Brown, financial writer; Sanford Rose of *Fortune;* T. A. Wise of Lazard Frères.

428 First six months: Ibid.

428 "The Chase at Ebb Tide—": See *New York Times*, June 4, 1972.

429 "A stunning move": "Why There is a New Face," *Business Week*.

429 "Take the rap": Ibid.

429 "Best name": Cited in Elias, p. 93.

429 Chase's assets: See *Forbes*, December 15, 1973.

429 "At the Chase": *Newsweek*, October 23, 1972.

430 "These offers": "The Chase at Ebb Tide?" *New York Times*, June 4, 1972.

430 "The Chase of late": *Business Week*, November 4, 1972.

430 Credit-card system: See *Forbes*, December 15, 1973.

430 Foreign branches: *Business Week*, November 4, 1972.

431 "Rockefeller is viewed": Ibid.

431 "David Rockefeller": Authors' interview with Sanford Rose.

431 "At no time": *New York Times*, June 4, 1972.

431 "Unflappable": Authors' interview with Sanford Rose.

432 Despised Nelson: Authors' interview with David's children.

432 Enterprising publisher: The book Lyle Stuart promoted onto the best-seller lists was William Hoffman's *David* (New York, 1971).

432 "People will believe": Authors' interview with Richard Rockefeller.

433 Ceremonial meeting: Authors' interview with Abby Rockefeller.

434 Farewell address: The address was printed and distributed by Winthrop. The authors have a copy.

435 "Winthrop got us to come": Authors' interview with Mrs. Linda Storrow.

436 AIDC: See Joe Alex Morris, "Hillbilly Rockefeller," *Saturday Evening Post*, September 29, 1956.

437 "I don't know": Cited in *Arkansas Gazette*, February 23, 1973.

437 "Pin-striped suit syndrome": Authors' interview with John Ward, former aide to Winthrop.

437 "Because he broke": Authors' interview with George Gilder.

438 Rebuilding party: For a summary of Winthrop's political

career in Arkansas, see *Arkansas Gazette* edition memorializing his death, February 23, 1973.

438   "Effort to rebuild": Ibid.

439   AIDC: Ibid.

439   43 percent: See *New York Times*, November 5, 1964.

439   57 percent: See *New York Times*, November 10, 1966.

440   Legislative plan: Winthrop's career as governor is summarized in *Arkansas Gazette*, February 23, 1973.

440n. Case histories: Ibid., pp. 6 ff.

440   "Our prisons stink": Cited by Tom Murton and Joe Hyams, *Accomplices to Crime* (New York, 1969), p. 17.

441   Unmarked graves: Ibid., pp. 188 ff.

441   Reelected in 1968: New York Times, November 7, 1968.

442   "Legislators were paying": Pine Bluff Commercial, June 2, 1968.

442   Vortex of failure: Mrs. Margaret Black, Winthrop's friend and confidante for fifteen years and a close witness of his deterioration, discusses the changes that came into his personal life after 1968 on the taped interview conducted by Dr. Joseph Ernst (Rockefeller Family Archives). The following details draw on her insights.

443n. "I don't care": Margaret Black, taped interview.

443   Third term: For results of the election, see *New York Times*, November 5, 1970.

443   Confucian gems: Authors' interview with Lee Robins, a journalist who covered Governor Rockefeller in 1967.

444    $20 million: *Arkansas Gazette*, February 23, 1973.

444   Winrock Enterprises: See *Annual Reports*, 1973, 1974.

444   A vehicle: Authors' interview with Richard Moore, now chief aide to Winthrop Paul Rockefeller.

444   Coalition: Authors' interview with Robert Scriven of Rockefeller Brothers Fund. Mr. Scriven was assisting Winthrop in this project.

445   Affairs in order: Mrs. Margaret Black, taped interview.

445   Remade his will: Authors' interview with confidential source.

445   Ritual lottery: It was a way of handling the problem of distributing mementos and personal effects within the family. It had been used after the deaths of Abby, Lucy Aldrich, and "Aunt Martha" Baird. Margaret Black was Winthrop's "representative" at the distribution of Martha Baird's effects (some of which were actually Junior's). The items were catalogued and then evaluated by experts for estate tax purposes. Then the members of the family each made their selections, with some later making trades to get items they had especially wanted. In the case of Martha Baird's estate, for instance, Winthrop got a Chinese vase which David particularly wanted and later persuaded him to trade in exchange for three paintings, one of them a Botticelli. Those items no one wanted were sold, as in Martha Baird's estate

when nobody in the family claimed a red lacquered table
that had once belonged to Marie Antoinette and it was later
auctioned off for $425,000. In the case of Winthrop's ef-
fects, he had stipulated that his son would have first choice.
Win Paul passed up the Botticelli and instead took an
Ingres landscape of which his father had been particularly
fond. Mrs. Margaret Black, taped interview.

446 Funeral: See *Arkansas Gazette*, March 5, 1973.

446 "He was always": Authors' interview with Marion
     Rockefeller Weber.

447 Lacking any felt sense of loss: Ibid.

448 "Brother apart": Authors' interview with Emmet
     Hughes.

448 "I think this generation": Authors' interview with JDR3.

448 JDR3, Laurance, David: Authors' interviews with their
     children.

448 Nelson and children: Authors' interviews with Joan
     Braden.

449 "Nothing stands in Rockefeller's way": Reeves, p. 8.

449 "I remember bidding": Ibid.

450n. "What does he get": Authors' interview with Paul Weiss-
     man, former aide to Arthur Goldberg.

451 "At least Rockefeller": Authors' interview with George
     Gilder.

451 Flash point came in 1968: Authors' interview with
     Richard A. Brown, former Mayor Lindsay's legislative li-
     aison with Albany.

451 "Cowardice": The Lindsay statement is cited in *Time*,
     September 2, 1974, p. 20.

452 "The Nelson I once knew": Authors' interview with
     Congressman Ogden Reid.

452n. Expenditures: For Thayer's, see his *Who Shakes the
     Money Tree*, p. 163. Nelson's detailed list of contributions
     was submitted to the Senate Rules Committee during his
     confirmation hearings. (See *Hearings into the Nomination
     of Nelson A. Rockefeller to Be Vice President*, Appendix
     VIII, pp. 43–57.) CBS's estimates were made in the course
     of a television commentary about the family first broadcast
     in December 1973.

452 Half the proceeds: Authors' interview with William
     ("Mike") Kitzmiller, legislative aide to Congressman Reid.

452 Reid's office estimates: Ibid.

452 Pharaoh: See Richard Reeves, "Carey vs. Wilson, and in
     Each Corner Nelson Rockefeller," *New York Times Maga-
     zine*, October 27, 1974.

453 Robert Moses: See Caro, Chapters 46 and 47.
     Rose.

453 Nelson and banks: Authors' interview with Sanford
453 World Trade Center: See statement by Congresswoman
     Bella Abzug, "The Disqualifications of Nelson Rockefeller,"

in U.S. House of Representatives, Committee on the Judiciary, *Hearings into the Nomination of Nelson Rockefeller to be Vice President of the United States* (Washington, D.C., 1975).

454 "Nelson is a true democrat": Authors' interview with William Farrell.

454n. Honeymoon trip: UPI dispatch, October 6, 1974.

454 Nelson called on him: See *The Rockefeller Report on the Americas* (Quadrangle edition, New York, 1969), p. 5.

455 Robert W. Porter: The entourage is listed in *Rockefeller Report on the Americas,* pp. 11–13.

455 $750,000: See *New York Times,* October 19, 1974.

455 Latin American trip: Described in Levinson and de Onis, pp. 331–318. See also *New York Times* accounts, May 12, 20, 28; June 3, 17, 23, 30; July 7, 1969.

456 "Forces of anarchy: *Rockefeller Report on the Americas,* p. 60.

457 "Failure to maintain": Ibid., p. 39.

457 Nixon: The response came indirectly, in a speech made late in 1969: "We recognize that enormous, sometimes explosive forces for change are operating in Latin America. These create instabilities and bring changes in governments. On the diplomatic level, we must deal realistically with governments in the inter-American system as they are." See Levinson and de Onis, pp. 317 ff. Nelson would, of course, keep a hand in Latin American policy as a member of the President's Foreign Intelligence Advisory Board and would no doubt be aware of his friend Kissinger's role, as head of the "40 Committee," in orchestrating the downfall of Chile's Allende government.

457 He *was* order: In submitting his *Report on the Americas* to President Nixon, Rockefeller defended his decision not to cancel the remainder of the Latin America trips after it was clear that the violence that had marked his first visits would continue: "Had we canceled the visits, it would have been seen as weakness and fear on the part of the United States government. That would have done much to discredit the United States and the other Americas" (p. 9).

458 "Second rate mind": Cited by Kalb and Kalb, p. 25.

458n. L. Judson Morhouse: See Senate *Hearings into the Nomination,* especially pp. 600–601, 650–653.

459 "I frankly think": Authors' interview with Paul Weissman, Goldberg aide during the election.

459 State AFL-CIO: The endorsement (the unions had remained neutral, itself a kind of victory for a Republican, in 1966) represented the culmination of Nelson's long relationship with George Meany and the other state labor leaders. It was about this time that Meany, asked by a writer why he got on so well with Rockefeller, replied, "Nelson is satisfied with his own share, and he don't try to keep the

other feller from getting his. He doesn't have that mean streak you find in some of these Republican businessmen." Joseph Goulden, *Meany* (New York, 1972), p. 404.

459 "To 'lower' himself": Authors' interview with Victor Gotbaum.

460 Record on civil liberties: See Sidney Zion, *Ramparts* article; Newfield, *New York* article.

460 "It can only undermine": *New York Times,* August 26, 1970.

460 "Welfare cheats": Writing of Rockefeller's address to Goldwater Republicans the previous week, reporter Francis X. Clines notes, "His prepared speech included the line, 'I decided in New York State that we were going to get the cheats and chiselers off the taxpayer's back,' but deleted it when he spoke, although the tone of his talk was in line with the dropped matter." *New York Times,* October 31, 1973.

461 "Hard-liner": Authors' interview with Congressman Ogden Reid.

461 "Vacillation and indecision": Russell G. Oswald, *Attica—My Story* (New York, 1972), p. 94.

461 Team of observers: For a moving account of the role these observers played in the Attica tragedy, see Tom Wicker, *A Time to Die* (New York, 1975).

461 "The committee of observers": Herman Badillo and Milton Haynes, *A Bill of No Rights: Attica and the American Prison System* (New York, 1972), p. 85.

462 "Governor": Wicker, p. 214.

462 "In life": See the McKay Commission's *Official Report of the New York Special Commission on Attica* (New York, 1972), p. 323.

462 Oswald called Nelson once more: Ibid.

462 "With the exception": Ibid., p. xi.

462 "Time to die": *New York Times,* September 14, 1971.

463 "Our hearts go out": *New York Times,* September 15, 1971.

463 "What it tells": *New York Times,* October 4, 1971.

463 "First": See Wicker, pp. 215 ff.

463 "Should have gone to Attica": McKay Commission, p. 325.

464 "The assault on Attica": Safire quoted in Reeves, "The Nationwide Search for Nelson Rockefeller," p. 8.

464 "Attica is the symbolic Rockefeller act": Authors' interview with Tom Morgan.

464n. Robert E. Fischer: See House *Hearings into the Nomination,* pp. 577 ff.

466 Featured speaker: *New York Times,* October 27, 1973.

466 "I don't think": Cited by Richard Reeves in "Old Faces of '73 Lying in Wait for '76," *New York,* December 24, 1973, p. 6.

466   Resigning the governorship: See *New York Times*, December 12, 1973.

466   One of his first acts: See Robert H. Connery and Gerald Benjamin, *Governing New York State—The Rockefeller Years* (New York, 1974), pp. 133 ff. This book is a generally favorable review of Nelson's governorship and the only such work yet completed. It was done with the cooperation of Albany and of the Rockefeller Family Office. However, during the vice-presidential confirmation hearings, it was revealed that Nelson had given $81,000 to the Academy of Political Sciences, which underwrote the book, at the time that it was being completed. See Senate *Hearings into the Nomination of Nelson Rockefeller*, pp. 565–566.

467   Construction Fund: Ibid., p. 138.

467   "The greatest system": Cited in *New York Times*, December 12, 1973.

467   Transportation program: Caro, pp. 1134 ff.

468   Housing Finance Agency: Connery and Benjamin, pp. 188 ff.

468   Pure Waters Act: Discussed at length in Rockefeller, *Our Environment Can Be Saved*, pp. 51–73.

468   "All of these financing schemes": See "Debt-Like Commitments of the State of New York: A Report on the State's Use of Public Corporations to Finance Capital Improvements Without Voter Approval," published by the Office of the State Comptroller, January 1973. Comptroller Arthur Levitt's objections to Rockefeller's plans are outlined at length in a series of reports (of which this is one) called "New York State Comptroller's Studies on Issues in Public Finance" (Albany, 1972–1974).

469   "The most spectacularly": Cited by Eleanor Carruth, "What Price Glory on the Albany Mall," *Fortune*, June 1971, p. 92.

469   "The greatest thing": Ibid.

469   "Like a trout": Ibid., p. 94.

470   Cost $263 per usable foot: Ibid., p. 95.

471   *Final* Cost: See "Audit of New York State, New York City, and Public Authorities," published by the State Comptroller's Office, Albany, April 25, 1973.

471   "I'll never forget": Authors' interview with Wallace Harrison.

471   "Mean structures": *New York Times*, November 22, 1973.

472   1970 Report: Connery and Benjamin, p. 153.

472   Welfare policies: Ibid.

473   Narcotic Addiction Control Commission: See "Audit of New York State, New York City and Public Authorities," p. 13.

473 Rockefeller acknowledged: See *New York Times*, January 4, 1973.

473 New drug program: Ibid.

474 Taxes: For a summary, see *New York Times*, December 12, 1973.

474n. "Archie Bunker law": Charge originally made by Deputy Police Chief Bonacurn. See *New York Times*, January 15, 1973.

474n. "Rockefeller's simplistic": *New York Times*, January 4, 1973.

474n. "The strange alliance": *New York Times*, May 9, 1973.

474 "On a scale so massive": See "Statewide Public Authorities; A Fourth Branch of Government?" published by the Office of the State Comptroller, Albany, November, 1972, p. 1.

474 "The problem of financing": *New York Times*, November 8, 1961.

476 "OK, wise guy": See William Kennedy, "Rocky is 64 going on 35," *New York Times Magazine*, April 29, 1973.

476 Hans Haake: Sophy Burnham, *The Art Crowd* (New York, 1973), p. 165.

476 Financing Critical Choices: See "Selected Issues and the Positions of Nelson A. Rockefeller, Nominee for Vice President," Committee on the Judiciary, U.S. House of Representatives, November 1974, p. 129.

475 Encyclopedic technique: Authors' interview with Peter Wallison, treasurer of the commission; see also "Our Democracy Has Decisions to Make," pamphlet published by the Third Century Corporation, 1973.

477 139 aides: *New York Times*, October 21, 1974.

477 "A review": "Our Democracy Has Decisions to Make."

478 "Harass and drive a President": See *New York Times*, February 11, 1974.

478 Telling reporters how pleased: See *New York Times*, August 22, 1974.

480 "Hiya, Pete!": "Rocky's Road to No. 2," *Newsweek*, September 2, 1974, p. 18.

480 Family members: Authors' interviews with members of the fourth Rockefeller generation.

480 "There is a strong feeling": New York *Post*, October 21, 1974.

480 "Not since Lady Godiva": *New York Times*, August 25, 1974.

481 "If you gave": See *New York Times*, September 24, 1974.

481 Opening statement: Senate *Hearings into the Nomination*, pp. 41–79.

482 "This myth": Ibid., p. 23.

482 Financial data: Ibid., pp. 49 ff.

482 Dropped $20 million: Dan Dorfman, "Inside Chase

Manhattan: First Look at Rocky's Net Worth," *New York,* September 30, 1974. Appearing before Nelson's Senate testimony, this article was based on a copy of Nelson's two trust accounts at the Chase, which the authors had been given an opportunity to inspect. The document showed that the '34 Trust had been worth $126,776,331 as of June 28, 1974, and had dropped in value to $106,272,184 by August 23. Later Dorfman secured a copy of David Rockefeller's trust, worth $155,238,523, and printed a copy of his entire portfolio in *New York,* October 12, 1974.

482 $33 million: For Nelson's explanation of the origins of this figure, see Senate *Hearings into the Nomination,* p. 48.

482 Byrd calculated: Senate *Hearings into the Nomination,* p. 80.

482 David was often heard: Authors' interviews with David Rockefeller's children.

483 TNEC: Its findings are summarized in Ferdinand Lundberg, *The Rich and the Super-Rich,* p. 159.

483 "The total holdings": Senate *Hearings into the Nomination,* p. 57.

484 "Big Seven" banks: See U.S. Senate Committee on Government Operations, *Disclosure of Corporate Ownership* (Washington, D.C., 1974), p. 30. For the general growth of institutional investments, see U.S. Securities and Exchange Commission, *Institutional Investor Study Report,* U.S. House Document, no. 92–64, Part 8, p. ix. From 1962 to 1970, institutional holdings of securities listed on the New York Stock Exchange increased from 31.1 percent to 39.4 percent. See also U.S. House of Representatives Committee on Banking and Currency, *Commercial Banks and Their Trust Activities,* pp. 1–5.

484 "If you go": *New York Times,* September 26, 1974.

485 "The greatest nation": Senate *Hearings into the Nomination,* pp. 81–82.

486 "It was great": *New York Times,* September 24, 1974.

486 Mark Hatfield: Senate *Hearings into the Nomination,* pp. 97–98.

487 "Better Shape": *New York Times,* October 6, 1974.

487 $50,000 to Henry Kissinger: In the Senate hearings, it was revealed that Kissinger asked for an opinion from the White House on the propriety of accepting the gift. It was Egil Krogh, Jr., who wrote back on January 15, 1969: "Based on the philanthropic nature of the Rockefellers [*sic*], and expressly upon the fact that the contemplated gift of money to you is based only upon your close friendship . . . we find that such a gift would not violate either the statutes, Executive Order, or regulations involving conflict of interests." Senate *Hearings into the Nomination,* p. 883.

487 Logue and Ronan gifts: Senate *Hearings into the Nomination,* pp. 529 ff., 639–640.

487 Philanthropies: See "Summary of the Gifts to Nelson A. Rockefeller," House *Hearings into the Nomination*, pp. 40–43.

488 "The unbought voice": Senate *Hearings into the Nomination*, p. 510.

489 Taxes: Ibid., pp. 507–508.

489 "In dollar terms": *New York Times*, October 20, 1974.

490 "Evidently what happened": Senate *Hearings into the Nomination*, p. 514.

490 "Extremely downcast": Authors' interview with Lucy Rockefeller Waletzky.

490 "Clarifying" statement: Senate *Hearings into the Nomination*, pp. 514–515.

491 Political contributions: Ibid., pp. 480 ff.

491 "Rockefeller benefactions": *New York Times*, October 13, 1974.

491 "My sole intent": Senate *Hearings into the Nomination*, p. 472.

492 "I would like to just": Ibid., p. 620.

493 "Rockefeller and his gifts": *New York*, October 28, 1974.

494 "This is a family": Cited in New York *Post*, October 21, 1974.

494 "Radical shakeup": Authors' interview with Steven Rockefeller.

495 "A serious mistake": House *Hearings into the Nomination*, p. 164.

495 "I have a feeling": Ibid., p. 237.

495 Dilworth had been on phone: Authors' interviews with members of the fourth Rockefeller generation.

496 $1.3 billion: House *Hearings into the Nomination*, pp. 848–849.

496 "It may be of interest": Ibid., p. 777.

496 Rockefeller family holdings: Ibid., 848–849.

497n. "Let me put it": Authors' interview with Malcolm MacIntyre; former president of Eastern Airlines.

497 George Hinman: House *Hearings into the Nomination*, p. 787.

IV *The Cousins*

PAGE
501 The Cousins: In preparing this part of the book, the authors spent more than two hundred hours interviewing members of the fourth Rockefeller generation. The interviews, formal and informal, were conducted over a two-year period with the following Cousins: From the JDR3 family, Alida, Hope and Jay; from the Nelson family, Steven, Mary, Ann, and Rodman; from the Laurance family, Lucy, Marion, and Laura; from the David family, Abby, David,

Jr., Richard, Peggy, and Neva. Within each family, at least one member (and in some cases more than one) was interviewed for at least ten hours. Because the format of this part of the book is somewhat different from the first three parts, relying far more on interviews than on archival or print sources, it would be cumbersome to note in the following pages each statement attributed to one of the Cousins in the text. Unless otherwise specified, therefore, statements cited in the text are from authors' interviews. As far as details about the family and its life-style are concerned, we have noted only those details given by only one cousin, not when it is part of the general recollection of the entire group.

509 Farming at Pocantico: Interview with Abby Rockefeller. See also Tom Pyle, *Pocantico* (New York, 1964), pp. 208–210.

509 Michael was attacked: Authors' interview with Laura Rockefeller Chasin.

510 "Murder in the Dark": Authors' interview with Abby Rockefeller.

510 "Raiding" the gardeners: Authors' interview with Marion Rockefeller Weber.

510 Contraband comic books: Author's interview with Laura Rockefeller Chasin.

511 Outdoor pool: Authors' interview with Steven Rockefeller.
Rockefeller (New York, 1950), p. 84.

511 "I don't know why": Mary Ellen Chase, *Abby Aldrich*

511 He frequently annoyed their fathers: See Anne-Marie Rasmussen, *There Was Once a Time* (New York, 1975), p. 48.

513 Sunday lunch: All of the Cousins attended these occasions, and the details are distilled from their joint recollections.

514 "Tomorrow is your birthday": Letter, Junior to Steven, April 18, 1945, Rockefeller Family Archives.

515 Trust funds: The authors have inspected some Cousins' trust instruments and portfolios.

515 "On my twenty-first birthday": Letter, Michael to Junior, July 10, 1959. Rockefeller Family Archives.

517 Laurance's children: The details come from authors' interview with Lucy Rockefeller Waletzky.

518 Nelson's children: The details come from authors' interview wih Marion Rockefeller Weber.

520 Peggy: The details come from authors' interviews with her children.

524 "We have reluctantly": Letter, JDR3 to Henry Luce, February 5, 1968, Rockefeller Family Archives.

524n. "Nowhere else": See "Miss Chapin's," *Fortune*, August 1931, p. 41.

527 "Despite what would appear": Authors' interview with Bill Greenbaum.

530 Michael: All of the Cousins who were approximately his age and knew him talk of Michael; however, the authors have relied most heavily on interviews with Steven Rockefeller.

530 "When you first": Cited in "A great American Family," *Life,* July 11, 1960, p. 84.

530 "I want to do": Frank Gervasi, *The Real Rockefeller* (New York, 1964), p. 244.

531 Michael knew he had now become: Authors' interview with Steven Rockefeller.

531 "He suffered": Milton Machlin, *The Search for Michael Rockefeller* (New York, 1971), p. 165.

532 "The Asmat is filled": Cited in *The Asmat of New Guinea, The Journal of Michael Clark Rockefeller* (New York, 1967), p. 43.

533 "He listened to me": Machlin, p. 216.

533 One that gained some acceptance: Ibid., pp. 225 ff.

533 "Primary purpose": See "Michael C. Rockefeller Memorial Fellowship, Statement of Intent by the Founders." The statement continues: "It is intended that the holder of the Fellowship will use it to heighten his awareness of and sensitivity to the people of such a culture and will thereby broaden and deepen the reach of his mind and further discover and clarify the purpose of his life. . . . The main portion of the individual's time should be spent in more intensive and more personal involvement with the people of the culture in which he is traveling or residing than normal tourist travel would entail. . . . The year should be planned with the idea of exploration, challenge and new discovery." Copies of this document were kindly supplied to the authors by Steven Rockefeller.

534 "Public Attitudes": The authors have a copy of this report.

535 "My father": Authors' interview with Michael Ansara.

540 Larry gave $10,000: Authors' interview with Michael McCloskey.

540 "I really couldn't tell you": Rasmussen, p. 27.

541 Long cashmere scarf: Authors' interview with Bob Rafelson.

542 "Great-Grandfather tipped ten percent": Authors' interview with Mrs. Linda Storrow.

549 Article for *Life:* See *Life,* June 20, 1960, pp. 28–29.

551 Charlie Peters: Authors' interview with Charlie Peters.

552 Wedding: See *New York Times,* April 2, 1967.

555 "Dilworth was brought into": Authors' interview with Malcolm MacIntyre.

555 "I'm a quondam lawyer": Authors' interview with J. Richardson Dilworth.

556 Change in directory: Details supplied by Dr. Joseph Ernst of Rockefeller Family Archives.

556 Donal O'Brien: Authors' interview with his predecessor, John Lockwood.

556 "The Brothers Fund": Authors' interview with Dana Creel.

556n. Fund contributions: Communication from Dr. Joseph Ernst.

558 "Fidelity Trust": The trusts consisted of 20,000 shares for each family, split evenly among the children in it. In David's family of six children, for instance, each one got proportionately less than in JDR3's family of four or Babs's of two. As of 1974 each of the families' shares would have amounted to $30 to $35 million; a member of the Laurance family, therefore, with four fourth-generation members, would have had about $8 million in his or her Fidelity Trust Account, at least in the familes of David, Nelson, and Laurance, the Cousins' Fidelity Trust account has been augmented by gifts of approximately $1 million from their fathers. Also, Junior had created for each Cousin a series of smaller trusts in December 1943, with the Chase as trustee. The financial holdings of one cousin (whose trust instruments and sample portfolio the authors were allowed to copy) showed the following as of 1971: $9,509,889 for the Fidelity Trust; $458,000 for the '43 Chase Trust; $960,000 in stocks from the father.

558 "What's all this talk": Authors' interview with Abby Rockefeller.

559 "Severe lecture": Ibid.

559 Cache of letters: Authors' interview with Linda Edgerly, former assistant archivist, Rockefeller Family Archives.

561 Plans for Pocantico: The plans discussed below were Attachment B ("Review by Harmon Goldstone of several studies and recommendations made over the last decade for future use of the Pocantico property and the status of present plans") in a memorandum sent to the Cousins by Peter O. Crisp of Room 5600 on February 5, 1973. The authors have a copy of this document.

562 Giving Pocantico: For additional details, see Robert D. McFadden, "Pocantico Hills to be saved for Public," *New York Times*, September 21, 1970.

563 Letter to Dana Creel: Copy supplied the authors by Marion Rockefeller Weber.

565 "You don't know": Authors' interview wih Lucy Rockefeller Waletzky.

567 "Chase Manhattan Bank": Letter, Catherine Tracy to Marion Rockefeller Weber, May 3, 1974. Copy supplied the authors by Mrs. Weber.

567 Family directory: The authors have a copy of this document.

568 $6 million: Authors' interview with confidential source.

568 Family Fund: "The Rockefellers are involved with power, prestige, the collection of information, and doing good as they see it. They create institutions that enhance the potential for all these things. The Family Fund is such an institution." Authors' interview with Harold Snedcof, employee of the Family Fund. The authors have inspected copies of correspondence between individuals in the fourth generation and the Family Fund, and have discussed the activities and decision-making structure of the Fund with several of the Cousins. See also Family Fund *Annual Reports*, 1972–1974.

568 Martha Baird's will: For an accounting of her estate, see *New York Times*, February 4, 1971.

569 Three issues: Memorandum, Catherine Tracy to Cousins, May 3, 1973.

570 David, Jr., speech: "Speech Delivered Before Council on Foundations, New England Conference on Foundations and Philanthropy," October 6, 1972.

571 "We then turned": Minutes, Peggy Rockefeller to Cousins, January 14, 1974. A copy is in the possession of the authors.

573 "There's really": Authors' interview with J. Richardson Dilworth.

575 Disposition of his estate: Authors' interview with Richard Moore, aide to Winthrop Paul Rockefeller.

575 Win Paul: The following details are distilled from conversations with various Cousins.

575 Conflict with old associates: Authors' interview with confidential source.

576 "Like the State Department": Ibid.

576 Winthrop's will: Ibid.

583 "The vision of 'empire'": U.S. House of Representatives, Committee on the Judiciary, *Hearings into the Nomination of Nelson Rockefeller to Be Vice President of the United States* (Washington, D.C., 1975), p. 874.

584 "The one way for Peggy": Authors' interview with Bill Greenbaum.

586 Private competition: "There's a lot of tension there. The marriage with Senator Percy's daughter was not the sort of thing to warm the cockles of Nelson's heart." Author's interview with Emmet Hughes.

586 "John D. Smith IV": Richard Reeves, "One Rockefeller Who May Make It," *New York Times Magazine*, October 4, 1970, p. 74.

587 Jay's expenditures: See Anthony Wolff, "I Love the Name," *Saturday Review*, August 26, 1972, p. 28; also, Nor-

man C. Miller, "Scion of the Times," *Wall Street Journal*, August 16, 1972.

587 Losing gubernatorial campaign: Jay would later claim that he had been beaten by strip miners and other "vested interests" in West Virginia. However, Phil Tracy ("A Schlocky Rocky," *Village Voice*, November 16, 1972) disputes this notion. "Jay's two-year term as a legislator proved somewhat underwhelming. The only major issue to come before the legislature, increased benefits for victims of black lung disease, turned out to be one which, in Jay's own words, 'I really missed the boat on.' ... His most memorable action as Secretary of State was the decision to come out for the total abolition of strip mining. According to his staff, the decision was made after a long and careful study of the question. However, it might be noted that Jay's announcement came almost exactly one month after several incumbents in the state legislature were defeated by relatively unknown opponents running on an anti-strip mining platform."

599 "It was a really bad article": Authors' interview with Roxanne Dunbar.

609 Anne-Marie Rasmussen: The romance, marriage, and eventual divorce are the subjects of Rasmussen's *There Was Once a Time*.

615 "If I were in Vietnam": *New York Times*, June 8, 1967.

616 "It's a free country": *New York Times*, June 9, 1967.

The Family

John Davison Rockefeller

John Davison Rockefeller (1839-1937)
  m. 1864 Laura Celestia ("Cettie") Spelman (1839-1915)

  Bessie Rockefeller Strong (1866-1906)
    m. 1889 Charles Augustus Strong (1862-1940)

  Alice Rockefeller (1869-70)

  Alta Rockefeller Prentice (1871-1962)
    m. 1901 Ezra Parmalee Prentice (1863-1955)

  Edith Rockefeller McCormick (1872-1932)
    m. 1895 Harold Fowler McCormick (1872-1941)
    d. 1921

  John Davison Rockefeller, Jr. (1874-1960)
    m. 1901 Abby Greene Aldrich (1874-1948)
    m. 1951 Mrs. Martha Baird Allen (1895-1971) ·

John Davison Rockefeller, Jr.

John Davison Rockefeller, Jr. (1874-1960)
  m. 1901 Abby Greene Aldrich (1874-1948)
  m. 1951 Mrs. Martha Baird Allen (1895-1971)

  Abby ("Babs") Rockefeller Mauzé (1903-   )
    m. 1925 David M. Milton (1900-   )
    d. 1943

Abby Rockefeller Mauzé

Abby ("Babs") Rockefeller Mauzé (1903-   )
  m. 1925 David M. Milton (1900-   )

750

d. 1943
m. 1946 Dr. Irving H. Pardee (1892-1949)
m. 1953 Jean Mauzé (1903-74)

Abby ("Mitzi") Milton O'Neill (1928-   )
  m. 1949 George Dorr O'Neill (1926-   )

Marilyn Milton Simpson (1931-   )
  m. 1953 William Kelly Simpson (1928-   )

John Davison Rockefeller 3rd

John Davison Rockefeller 3rd (1906-   )
  m. 1932 Blanchette Ferry Hooker (1909-   )

Sandra Ferry Rockefeller (1935-

John ("Jay") Davison Rockefeller IV (1937-   )
  m. 1967 Sharon Lee Percy (1944-   )

Hope Aldrich Rockefeller Spencer (1938-   )
  m. 1959 John Spencer (1930-   )
  d. 1969

Alida Davison Rockefeller (1949-   )
  m. 1946 Dr. Irving H. Pardee (1892-1949)
  m. 1953 Jean Mauzé (1903-74)

John Davison Rockefeller 3rd (1906-   )
  m. 1932 Blanchette Ferry Hooker (1909-

Nelson Aldrich Rockefeller (1908-   )
  m. 1930 Mary ("Tod") Todhunter Clark (1907-   )
  d. 1962
  m. 1963 Mrs. Margaretta ("Happy") Fitler Murphy
    (1926-   )

Laurance Spelman Rockefeller (1910-   )
  m. 1934 Mary French (1910-   )

Winthrop Rockefeller (1912-73)
  m. 1948 Mrs. Barbara ("Bobo") Sears (nd)
  d. 1954
  m. 1956 Mrs. Jeannette Edris (1918-   )
  d. 1971

David Rockefeller (1915-   )
  m. 1940 Margaret ("Peggy") McGrath (1915-   )

Nelson Aldrich Rockefeller

Nelson Aldrich Rockefeller (1908-   )
    m. 1930 Mary ("Tod") Todhunter Clark (1907-   )
    d. 1962
    m. 1963 Mrs. Margaretta ("Happy") Fitler Murphy
        (1926-   )

    Rodman ("Roddy") Clark Rockefeller (1932-   )
        m. 1953 Barbara Ann Olsen (1930-   )

    Ann Clark Rockefeller Coste (1934-   )
        m. 1955 Robert Laughlin Pierson (1926-   )
        d. 1966
        m. 1970 Lionel R. Coste (1933-   )

    Steven Clark Rockefeller (1936-   )
        m. 1959 Anne-Marie Rasmussen (1938-   )
        d. 1970

    Michael Clark Rockefeller (1938-61)

    Mary Clark Rockefeller Morgan (1938-   )
        m. 1961 William Justice Strawbridge, Jr. (1936-   )
        d. 1974
        m. 1974 Thomas Morgan (1926-   )

    Nelson Aldrich Rockefeller, Jr. (1964-   )

    Mark Fitler Rockefeller (1967-   )

Laurance Spelman Rockefeller

Laurance Spelman Rockefeller (1910-   )
    m. 1934 Mary French (1910-   )

    Laura Spelman Rockefeller Chasin (1936-   )
        m. 1956 James Herbert Case III (1935-   )
        d. 1970
        m. 1971 Dr. Richard M. Chasin (1936-   )

    Marion French Rockefeller Weber (1938-   )
        m. 1965 Warren Titus Weber (1941-   )

    Dr. Lucy Aldrich Rockefeller Waletzky (1941-   )
        m. 1964 Dr. Charles Hamlin (1939-   )
        d. 1969

  m. 1970 Dr. Jeremy Peter Waletzky (1943-   )

Laurance ("Larry") Rockefeller, Jr. (1944-   )

Winthrop Rockefeller

Winthrop Rockefeller (1912-73)
  m. 1948 Mrs. Barbara ("Bobo") Sears (nd)
  d. 1954
  m. 1956 Mrs. Jeannette Edris (1918-   )
  d. 1971

Winthrop Paul ("Win Paul") Rockefeller (1948-   )
  m. 1971 Deborah Cluett Sage (1951-   )

David Rockefeller

David Rockefeller (1915-   )
  m. 1940 Margaret ("Peggy") McGrath (1915-   )

David Rockefeller, Jr. (1941-   )
  m. 1968 Sydney Roberts (1943-   )

Abby Aldrich Rockefeller (1943-   )

Neva Goodwin Rockefeller Kaiser (1944-   )
  m. 1966 Walter Jacob Kaiser (1931-   )

Margaret ("Peggy") Dulany Rockefeller (1947-   )

Richard Gilder Rockefeller (1949-   )

Eileen McGrath Rockefeller (1952-   )

Acknowledgements

Our families gave us aid and comfort during the nearly three years it took to complete this book. A number of other people also helped, perhaps in ways and to degrees they may not have realized: Phil and Blanche Horowitz, Moss and Florence Roberts, and the Cunningham and Ceresa families in New York; Peter Stone, Bob Kaldenbach, David and Jackie Allswang, Jim Johnson and Robert Peterson, William Kornhauser, Doris Collier, and the Giachinos in California.

Mehrene Larudee, Rick Brown, Warren Bishop, Peter Dale Scott, Rick Edwards, and Charles Schwartz provided useful research materials. Dr. Joseph Ernst answered interminable queries with scholarly equanimity, and made the Archives hospitable to us. Walter Morrison helped during a crisis, as he always has.

Georges Borchardt helped get the project moving. And Marian Wood, our editor at Holt, believed in the book from the very beginning, worked to improve it, and made sure that its karma was good at every step of the way. We were lucky to be able to work with her.

P.C. and D.H.
Oakland/Berkeley,
January 13, 1975

Index